# Professional Stage

# Module E

# Tax Planning
# (Finance Act 1999)

# Revision Series

1757/F00

**British Library Cataloguing-in-Publication Data**

A catalogue record for this book is available from the British Library.

Published by AT Foulks Lynch Ltd
Number 4
The Griffin Centre
Staines Road
Feltham
Middlesex
TW14 0HS

ISBN 0 7483 4175 7

© AT Foulks Lynch Ltd, 2000

**Acknowledgements**

The past ACCA examination questions are the copyright of the Association of Chartered Certified Accountants. The answers to the questions from June 1994 onwards are the answers produced by the examiners themselves and are the copyright of the Association of Chartered Certified Accountants. The answers to the questions prior to June 1994 have been produced by AT Foulks Lynch Ltd.

We are grateful to the Chartered Institute of Management Accountants and the Institute of Chartered Accountants in England and Wales for permission to reproduce past examination questions. The answers have been prepared by AT Foulks Lynch Ltd.

# CONTENTS

| | | Page |
|---|---|---|
| **Preface** | | x |
| **How to use the answer plans** | | xi |
| **Section 1** | Syllabus and examination format | xiii |
| **Section 2** | Analysis of past papers | xv |
| **Section 3** | General revision guidance | xviii |
| **Section 4** | Examination techniques | xxiii |
| **Section 5** | Key revision topics | xxvii |
| **Section 6** | Updates | xxxiv |
| **Section 7** | Practice questions (detailed below) | 1 |
| **Section 8** | Answers to practice questions (detailed below) | 21 |
| **Section 9** | New Syllabus Examinations | |
| | **June 94**     Questions, Answers and Examiner's comments | 61 |
| | **December 94**     Questions, Answers and Examiner's comments | 90 |
| | **June 95**     Questions, Answers and Examiner's comments | 118 |
| | **December 95**     Questions, Answers and Examiner's comments | 152 |
| | **June 96**     Questions, Answers and Examiner's comments | 184 |
| | **December 96**     Questions, Answers and Examiner's comments | 212 |
| | **June 97**     Questions, Answers and Examiner's comments | 243 |
| | **December 97**     Questions, Answers and Examiner's comments | 276 |
| | **June 98**     Questions, Answers and Examiner's comments | 306 |
| | **December 98**     Questions, Answers and Examiner's comments | 334 |
| | **June 99**     Questions, Answers and Examiner's comments | 363 |
| | **December 99**     Questions and Answers | 391 |
| **Tax Rates and Allowances** | | 415 |
| **Topic Index** | | 421 |

| Question number | | Questions Page | Answers Page |
|---|---|---|---|
| | **INCOME TAX** | | |
| | **Schedule E** | | |
| 1 | Binary plc *(D93)* | 1 | 21 |

**Examiner plus - the examiner's official answers**
*Further questions on this topic from the real exams with the examiner's official answers.*

| | | | |
|---|---|---|---|
| 23 | Down and out trust *(J94)* | 65 | 82 |
| 35 | Venus plc *(J95)* | 121 | 142 |
| 45 | Techno plc *(J96)* | 186 | 198 |
| 55 | Charles Choice *(J97)* | 243 | 250 |
| 66 | Usine Ltd *(D97)* | 281 | 301 |
| 78 | Duncan McByte *(D98)* | 338 | 358 |
| 88 | Landscape Ltd *(D99)* | 394 | 404 |

| Question number | | Questions Page | Answers Page |
|---|---|---|---|

**Schedule A**

| 2 | Vernon *(D89)* | 2 | 23 |

---

**Examiner plus - the examiner's official answers**
*Further questions on this topic from the real exams with the examiner's official answers.*

| 48 | Muriel Grand *(J96)* | 189 | 207 |
| 56 | William Wiles *(J97)* | 244 | 253 |

---

**Capital allowances**

| 3 | Margaret *(J88)* | 3 | 26 |

**Schedule D Cases I and II**

| 4 | Lex Hubbard *(D91)* | 4 | 28 |

---

**Examiner plus - the examiner's official answers**
*Further questions on this topic from the real exams with the examiner's official answers.*

| 27 | Stirling Hill *(D94)* | 92 | 104 |
| 31 | Li and Ken Wong *(J95)* | 118 | 124 |
| 42 | Basil Nadir *(D95)* | 157 | 179 |
| 47 | Harry Chan *(J96)* | 187 | 204 |
| 63 | Alex Zong *(D97)* | 278 | 291 |
| 74 | Tony Tort *(D98)* | 335 | 344 |
| 80 | Delia Jones *(J99)* | 364 | 373 |
| 89 | Fiona Fung *(D99)* | 395 | 406 |

---

**Partnerships**

| 5 | Boris, Steffi and Ivan *(J91)* | 5 | 30 |

---

**Examiner plus - the examiner's official answers**
*Further questions on this topic from the real exams with the examiner's official answers.*

| 43 | Smart and Sharp *(J96)* | 184 | 190 |
| 53 | Alphabet Engineering *(D96)* | 215 | 234 |
| 59 | Ming and Nina *(J97)* | 247 | 266 |
| 76 | Sally and Trevor Acre *(D98)* | 336 | 350 |
| 87 | Basil and Sybil Perfect *(D99)* | 393 | 403 |

---

**CAPITAL GAINS TAX**

| 6 | Victoria and Evelyn *(J91)* | 6 | 33 |

---

**Examiner plus - the examiner's official answers**
*A further question on this topic from the real exams with the examiner's official answer.*

| 49 | ABC Ltd *(D96)* | 212 | 218 |

iv

| Question number | | Questions Page | Answers Page |
|---|---|---|---|
| | **INHERITANCE TAX** | | |
| 7 | Richard *(D90)* | 7 | 35 |
| 8 | Edith Day *(D93)* | 8 | 37 |

| **Examiner plus - the examiner's official answers** | | | |
|---|---|---|---|
| *Further questions on this topic from the real exams with the examiner's official answers.* | | | |
| 33 | Maud Smith *(J95)* | 120 | 133 |
| 41 | Michael Earl *(D95)* | 156 | 175 |
| 44 | Albert Bone *(J96)* | 185 | 194 |
| 58 | Dorothy Lake *(J97)* | 246 | 261 |
| 62 | Monty Noble *(D97)* | 277 | 287 |
| 81 | Arthur Rich *(J99)* | 365 | 377 |
| 86 | Jane Macbeth *(D99)* | 392 | 401 |

| | **TRUSTS** | | |
|---|---|---|---|
| 9 | George Rowe *(D90)* | 9 | 40 |

| | **VAT** | | |
|---|---|---|---|

| **Examiner plus - the examiner's official answers** | | | |
|---|---|---|---|
| *A question on this topic from the real exams with the examiner's official answer.* | | | |
| 70 | Yaz Pica *(J98)* | 309 | 322 |
| 83 | Gewgaw Ltd *(J99)* | 367 | 383 |

| | **CORPORATION TAX** | | |
|---|---|---|---|
| | **Calculation** | | |
| 10 | Steamdriven Computer Company Ltd *(J90)* | 10 | 42 |

| **Examiner plus - the examiner's official answers** | | | |
|---|---|---|---|
| *Further questions on this topic from the real exams with the examiner's official answers.* | | | |
| 19 | White Stallion Ltd *(J94)* | 61 | 70 |
| 37 | Highrise Ltd *(D95)* | 152 | 159 |
| 54 | Ongoing Ltd *(D96)* | 217 | 239 |
| 67 | Velo Ltd *(J98)* | 306 | 313 |
| 75 | Star Ltd *(D98)* | 336 | 347 |
| 84 | Easy Speak Ltd *(J99)* | 368 | 387 |

| | **Purchase of own shares** | | |
|---|---|---|---|
| 11 | Sally Jones | 12 | 44 |

| **Examiner plus - the examiner's official answers** | | | |
|---|---|---|---|
| *Further questions on this topic from the real exams with the examiner's official answers.* | | | |
| 29 | Abdul Khan *(D94)* | 93 | 110 |
| 72 | Bluetone Ltd *(J98)* | 311 | 328 |

| Question number | | Questions Page | Answers Page |
|---|---|---|---|

**Groups**

| 12 | H Ltd *(J91)* | 13 | 46 |

---

**Examiner plus - the examiner's official answers**
*Further questions on this topic from the real exams with the examiner's official answers.*

| 26 | Zoo plc *(D94)* | 91 | 102 |
| 34 | Ocean plc *(J95)* | 121 | 138 |
| 46 | Hydra Ltd *(J96)* | 187 | 201 |
| 57 | Expansion Ltd *(J97)* | 245 | 257 |
| 90 | Apple Ltd *(D99)* | 397 | 408 |

---

**Close companies**

| 13 | Grudge Ltd *(D90)* | 13 | 48 |

**OVERSEAS ACTIVITIES**

**Income tax**

| 14 | Eric Fasthand *(D93)* | 15 | 50 |

---

**Examiner plus - the examiner's official answers**
*Further question on this topic from the real exams with the examiner's official answers.*

| 30 | Ken Sing *(D94)* | 95 | 113 |
| 40 | Angus Ash *(D95)* | 155 | 171 |
| 51 | Walter Smith *(D96)* | 214 | 225 |
| 68 | Barney Hall *(J98)* | 307 | 316 |
| 85 | Oliver Seas *(D99)* | 391 | 399 |

---

**Corporation tax**

| 15 | Magee Inc *(D91)* | 15 | 52 |

---

**Examiner plus - the examiner's official answers**
*Further questions on this topic from the real exams with the examiner's official answers.*

| 22 | Mountain Ltd *(J94)* | 64 | 80 |
| 32 | Ukul Ltd *(J95)* | 119 | 130 |
| 60 | Eyetaki Inc *(J97)* | 248 | 271 |
| 64 | Paddington Ltd *(D97)* | 279 | 295 |
| 79 | Global plc *(J99)* | 363 | 370 |

---

**GENERAL–TAX PLANNING**

| 16 | Mr Gog *(J91)* | 17 | 54 |
| 17 | Martin Lennox *(J90)* | 18 | 56 |
| 18 | Mr Ray *(J90)* | 19 | 58 |

| Question number | | Questions Page | Answers Page |
|---|---|---|---|

**Examiner plus - the examiner's official answers**
*Further questions on this topic from the real exams with the examiner's official answers.*

| | | | |
|---|---|---|---|
| 21 | Clark Kent *(J94)* | 63 | 76 |
| 24 | Desmond and Myrtle Cook *(J94)* | 66 | 85 |
| 25 | Grey Ltd *(D94)* | 90 | 99 |
| 28 | Clifford Jones and Dinah Smith *(D94)* | 92 | 107 |
| 36 | Garden Ltd*(J95)* | 122 | 146 |
| 38 | Sonya Rich *(D95)* | 153 | 163 |
| 39 | Fred Barley *(D95)* | 154 | 167 |
| 50 | Lucy Lee *(D96)* | 213 | 222 |
| 61 | Cecile Grand *(D97)* | 276 | 283 |
| 65 | Chow Tong *(D97)* | 280 | 298 |
| 77 | Schooner Ltd *(D98)* | 337 | 355 |
| 82 | Harold and Wilma Chan *(J99)* | 366 | 380 |

**PERSONAL FINANCE**

**Examiner plus - the examiner's official answers**
*Questions on this topic from the real exams with the examiner's official answers.*

| | | | |
|---|---|---|---|
| 20 | Ming Lee *(J94)* | 62 | 73 |
| 52 | Jock and Maggie McHaggis *(D96)* | 214 | 229 |
| 71 | Mary Mole *(J98)* | 310 | 326 |

**NEW SYLLABUS EXAMINATIONS WITH THE EXAMINER'S OFFICIAL ANSWERS**

### JUNE 1994 EXAMINATION

| | | | |
|---|---|---|---|
| 19 | White Stallion Ltd (Corporation tax calculation) | 61 | 70 |
| 20 | Ming Lee (Personal finance) | 62 | 73 |
| 21 | Clark Kent (General - tax planning) | 63 | 76 |
| 22 | Mountain Ltd (Overseas activities) | 64 | 80 |
| 23 | Down and Out trust (Schedule E) | 65 | 82 |
| 24 | Desmond and Myrtle Cook (General - tax planning) | 66 | 85 |

### DECEMBER 1994 EXAMINATION

| | | | |
|---|---|---|---|
| 25 | Grey Ltd (General – tax planning) | 90 | 99 |
| 26 | Zoo plc (Groups) | 91 | 102 |
| 27 | Stirling Hill (Schedule D Case I and II) | 92 | 104 |
| 28 | Clifford Jones and Dinah Smith (General - tax planning) | 92 | 107 |
| 29 | Abdul Khan (Purchase of own shares) | 93 | 110 |
| 30 | Ken Sing (Overseas income) | 95 | 113 |

### JUNE 1995 EXAMINATION

| | | | |
|---|---|---|---|
| 31 | Li and Ken Wong (Schedule D Case I and II) | 118 | 124 |
| 32 | Ukul Ltd (Overseas activities) | 119 | 130 |
| 33 | Maud Smith (Inheritance tax) | 120 | 133 |

| Question number | | Questions Page | Answers Page |
|---|---|---|---|
| 34 | Ocean plc (Groups) | 121 | 138 |
| 35 | Venus plc (Schedule E) | 121 | 142 |
| 36 | Garden Ltd (General - tax planning) | 122 | 146 |

**DECEMBER 1995 EXAMINATION**

| 37 | Highrise Ltd (Corporation tax - calculation) | 152 | 159 |
| 38 | Sonya Rich (General - tax planning) | 153 | 163 |
| 39 | Fred Barley (General - tax planning) | 154 | 167 |
| 40 | Angus Ash (Overseas income) | 155 | 171 |
| 41 | Michael Earl (Inheritance tax) | 156 | 175 |
| 42 | Basil Nadir (Schedule D Cases I and II) | 157 | 179 |

**JUNE 1996 EXAMINATION**

| 43 | Smart and Sharp (Partnerships) | 184 | 190 |
| 44 | Albert Bone (Inheritance tax) | 185 | 194 |
| 45 | Techno plc (Schedule E) | 186 | 198 |
| 46 | Hydra Ltd (Groups) | 187 | 201 |
| 47 | Harry Chan (Schedule D Cases I and II) | 187 | 204 |
| 48 | Muriel Grand (Schedule A) | 189 | 207 |

**DECEMBER 1996 EXAMINATION**

| 49 | ABC Ltd (Capital Gains tax) | 212 | 218 |
| 50 | Lucy Lee (General - tax planning) | 213 | 222 |
| 51 | Walter Smith (Overseas income) | 214 | 225 |
| 52 | Jock and Maggie McHaggis (Personal Finance) | 214 | 229 |
| 53 | Alphabet Engineering (Partnerships) | 215 | 234 |
| 54 | Ongoing Ltd (Calculation) | 217 | 239 |

**JUNE 1997 EXAMINATION**

| 55 | Charles Choice (Schedule E) | 243 | 250 |
| 56 | William Wiles (Schedule A) | 244 | 253 |
| 57 | Expansion Ltd (Groups) | 245 | 257 |
| 58 | Dorothy Lake (Inheritance tax) | 246 | 261 |
| 59 | Ming and Nina (Partnerships) | 247 | 266 |
| 60 | Eyetaki Inc (Overseas activities - CT) | 248 | 271 |

**DECEMBER 1997 EXAMINATION**

| 61 | Cecile Grand (General - tax planning) | 276 | 283 |
| 62 | Monty Noble (Inheritance tax) | 277 | 287 |
| 63 | Alex Zong (Schedule D Case I and II) | 278 | 291 |
| 64 | Paddington Ltd (Overseas activities - corporation tax) | 279 | 295 |
| 65 | Chow Tong (General - tax planning) | 280 | 298 |
| 66 | Usine Ltd (Schedule E) | 281 | 301 |

| Question number | | Questions Page | Answers Page |
|---|---|---|---|

**JUNE 1998 EXAMINATION**

| | | | |
|---|---|---|---|
| 67 | Velo Ltd (Corporation tax – calculation) | 306 | 313 |
| 68 | Barney Hall (Overseas activities – income tax) | 307 | 316 |
| 69 | Moon Ltd (Corporation tax – groups) | 308 | 320 |
| 70 | Yaz Pica (VAT) | 309 | 322 |
| 71 | Mary Mole (Personal finance) | 310 | 326 |
| 72 | Bluetone Ltd (Corporation tax – purchase of own shares) | 311 | 328 |

**DECEMBER 1998 EXAMINATION**

| | | | |
|---|---|---|---|
| 73 | Ming Wong (Overseas activities - income tax) | 334 | 340 |
| 74 | Tony Tort (Schedule D Case I and II) | 335 | 344 |
| 75 | Star Ltd (Corporation tax - calculation) | 336 | 347 |
| 76 | Sally and Trevor Acre (Partnerships) | 336 | 350 |
| 77 | Schooner Ltd (General - tax planning) | 337 | 355 |
| 78 | Duncan McByte (Schedule E) | 338 | 358 |

**JUNE 1999 EXAMINATION**

| | | | |
|---|---|---|---|
| 79 | Global plc (Overseas activities - corporation tax) | 363 | 370 |
| 80 | Delia Jones (Schedule D Cases I and II) | 364 | 373 |
| 81 | Arthur Rich (Inheritance tax) | 365 | 377 |
| 82 | Harold and Wilma Chan (General - tax planning) | 366 | 380 |
| 83 | Gewgaw Ltd (VAT) | 367 | 383 |
| 84 | Easy-Speak Ltd (Corporation tax - calculation) | 368 | 387 |

**DECEMBER 1999 EXAMINATION**

| | | | |
|---|---|---|---|
| 85 | Oliver Seas (Overseas activities – income tax) | 391 | 399 |
| 86 | Jane Macbeth (Inheritance tax) | 392 | 401 |
| 87 | Basil and Sybil Perfect (Partnerships) | 393 | 403 |
| 88 | Landscape Ltd (Schedule E) | 394 | 404 |
| 89 | Fiona Fung (Schedule D Cases I and II) | 395 | 406 |
| 90 | Apple Ltd (Corporation tax – groups) | 397 | 408 |

# PREFACE

The new edition of the ACCA Revision Series, published for the June and December 2000 examinations, contains a wealth of features to make your prospects of passing the exams even brighter.

## Examiner Plus

This book contains all the new syllabus examinations from June 1994 up to and including December 1999 plus the examiner's official answers. All the exams from June 1994 to December 1999 are set out in chronological order at the back of the book.

We have cross referenced all these questions to their topic headings in the contents pages so you can see at a glance what questions have been set on each syllabus area to date, topic by topic.

The inclusion of these questions and answers really does give students an unparalleled view of the way the new syllabus examinations are set and, even more importantly, a tremendous insight into the mind of the Examiner. The Examiner's answers are in some cases fairly lengthy and whilst the Examiner would not necessarily expect you to include all the points that his answers include, they do nevertheless give you an excellent insight into the sorts of things that the Examiner is looking for and will help you produce answers in line with the Examiner's thinking.

## Features

*Step by Step Answer Plans* and *'Did you answer the question?'* checkpoints are fully explained on the following two pages.

*Tutorial Notes*

The answers to the new syllabus examinations are the answers written by the examiner but we have of course updated them for the Finance Act 1999. This sometimes changes the nature of a question as changes in legislation since the question was originally set alter the way the question works. We have therefore included tutorial notes at various points in the answers to indicate any such changes or to highlight significant technical points that will help you understand the answer. The tutorial notes are clearly identified with the heading *Tutorial note*, the note being enclosed in brackets.

*Topic Index*

The topics covered in all the answers have been indexed. This means that you can easily access an answer relating to any topic which you want to consider by use of the index as well as by reference to the contents page at the front of the book.

The Revision Series also contains the following features:

- Practice questions and answers - a total bank of around 90 questions and answers
- An analysis of the new syllabus exams from June 1994 to December 1999
- Update notes to bring you up to date for new examinable documents and any changes to legislation as at 1 December 1999.
- The syllabus and format of the examination
- General Revision Guidance
- Examination Technique - an essential guide to ensure that you approach the examinations correctly
- Key Revision Topics
- Formulae and tables where appropriate

# HOW TO USE THE ANSWER PLANS AND 'DID YOU ANSWER THE QUESTION?' CHECKPOINTS

## STEP BY STEP ANSWER PLANS

**A key feature in this Revision Series is the Step by Step Answer Plans,** produced for all new syllabus exam questions from June 1995 to June 1999.

Students are always being told to plan their answers and this feature gives you positive assistance by showing you how you should plan your answer and the type of plan that you should produce before you attempt the question.

Of course, in the exam, your answer Plan can be less fully written than ours because you are writing it for yourself. We are producing an answer plan which communicates the details to you the student and therefore is of necessity much fuller. However, all the detail is there, written in a way which shows you the lines along which you should be thinking in order to produce the answer plan.

You will notice that the Answer Plans often start and finish with the exhortation that you must make sure that you have read the question and that you are answering it correctly. Each time you write down the next step in the Answer Plan, you must ask yourself - 'Why am I including this step?' 'Is it relevant?' 'Is this what the Examiner has asked me to do and expected me to do?'

### Help with the answer

In addition, if you really do get stuck with the question and cannot see how to approach it, you may find it helpful to turn to the answer page, **cover up the answer itself!,** and start to read the Answer Plan. This may trigger your memory such that you can then return to the question itself and gain all the benefit of doing the question properly without reference to the answer itself.

### Practice makes perfect

Like all elements of examination technique the time to learn how to plan your answers is not in the examination itself. You have to practise them now - every time you produce an answer - so that when you come to the examination itself these answer plans will be second nature.

It is probably a good idea to sketch out your answer plans in the way we have produced them here (but remember they can be briefer) and then compare them swiftly to our Answer Plan at the back of the book (don't look at the answer itself at this stage!).

This may indicate that you have completely missed the point of the question or it might indicate one or two other areas that you might wish to explore.

Then, without having yet looked at the answer itself, start writing your answer proper and then compare that with the examiner's own answer.

## 'DID YOU ANSWER THE QUESTION?' CHECKPOINTS

**This is another feature included in the Revision Series**. They are included in the new syllabus exam answers from June 1995 to June 1999.

At various points of the answers, you will come across a box headed **'Did you answer the question'**, followed by a brief note which shows you how the printed answer is answering the question and encourages you to make sure that your own answer has not wandered off the point or missed the point of the question completely.

This is an invaluable feature and it is a discipline you must develop as you practise answering questions. It is an area of examination technique that you must practise and practise again and again until it becomes second nature. How often do we read in an Examiner's report that candidates did not answer the question the Examiner had set but had simply answered the question that they wanted him to set or simply wandered off the point altogether? You must make sure that your answers do not fall into that particular trap and that they do rigorously follow the questions set.

A good way of practising this aspect of examination technique is to imagine an empty box headed up 'Did you answer the question?' at the end of the paragraph or paragraphs you are about to write on a particular topic. Try and imagine what you are going to write in that box; what are you going to say in that box which justifies the two or three paragraphs that you are about to write. If you can't imagine what you are going to put in that box, or when you imagine it you find that you are struggling to relate the next few paragraphs to the question, then think very hard before you start writing those paragraphs. Are they completely relevant? Why are you writing them? How are they relevant to the question?

You will find this 'imagining the box' a very useful way of focusing your mind on what you are writing and its relevance to the question.

**SUMMARY**

Use the two techniques together. They will help you to produce planned answers and they will help you make sure that your answers are focused very fully and carefully on the question the Examiner has actually set.

# 1 SYLLABUS AND EXAMINATION FORMAT

## FORMAT OF THE EXAMINATION

The examination will have the following format:

|  | *Number of marks* |
|---|---|
| Four (out of six) questions of 25 marks each | 100 |

Time allowed: 3 hours

## *Introduction*

The syllabus includes everything examinable in Paper 7, the Tax Framework, but extends and deepens the coverage. It also includes some new areas. Topics will be examined so that emphasis is given to simple planning to minimise or defer tax; the application of the tax knowledge to problems encountered in practice; and the inter-relationship of taxes.

**(1)    OVERVIEW OF PERSONAL BUSINESS TAXATION**

      (a)     Interactions between different taxes in a range of situations or transactions.

      (b)     Tax planning; the application of tax planning measures appropriate to the particular situation.

**(2)    CAPITAL GAINS TAX**

Application of Capital Gains Tax to individuals and corporate taxpayers, with emphasis on business situations.

**(3)    INHERITANCE TAX**

      (a)     Principles and scope.

      (b)     Rules basis and application.

      (c)     Calculating the tax due by clients.

      (d)     Minimising/deferring tax liabilities by identifying/applying relevant exemptions, reliefs and allowances.

**(4)    TRUSTS**

Application to trusts of Income Tax, Capital Gains Tax and Inheritance Tax.

**(5)    VALUE ADDED TAX**

The application of Value Added Tax to transactions and other activities of corporate taxpayers.

**(6)    CORPORATE TAXATION**

      (a)     Groups and consortia.

(b)     The provisions covering liquidations and areas such as disincorporations, purchases of own shares, sales and acquisitions of subsidiaries, and share for share amalgamations.

(c)     Implications of a company being classed as an investment or close company.

**(7)     OVERSEAS ACTIVITIES GIVING RISE TO TAXATION LIABILITIES**

(a)     Definition of residence, ordinary residence and domicile.

(b)     The taxation of UK income and gains of non-domicile individuals.

(c)     Overseas income and gains: the UK tax treatment of overseas income and gains of UK resident individuals and companies, including relief for double taxation.

(d)     Overseas persons, the UK tax treatment of income and gains arising within the UK to non-resident individuals and companies.

(e)     The Inheritance Tax position regarding overseas assets of UK individuals and UK assets of non-resident individuals.

(f)     Business structures, including a UK branch/subsidiary of a foreign company/group and a foreign branch/subsidiary of a UK company/group.

(g)     Anti-avoidance legislation relating to overseas activities, income or persons.

**(8)     GENERAL**

(a)     Inter-relationship of taxes: the effect of any of the taxes in a given situation or on a particular transaction.

(b)     Anti-avoidance: appreciation of the main areas of anti-avoidance legislation and of the enquiry and investigation procedures of the Inland Revenue and Customs and Excise.

**(9)     PERSONAL FINANCE**

(a)     Assisting clients in the determination of personal financial objectives, taking into account such factors as individual circumstances, expectations and the economic environment.

(b)     Determining financial needs of clients (how much, when, for how long, and for what purpose?).

(c)     Regulations affecting investment advisers, and ethical considerations, including the definition of investment business.

(d)     Advising on sources and costs of different forms of finance and their applicability to different circumstances including

    (i)      bank borrowing
    (ii)     finance houses
    (iii)    mortgages
    (iv)     money and capital markets.

(e)     Advising on investment of clients' personal funds

    (i)      insurance policies
    (ii)     pension funds
    (iii)    unit trusts, investment trusts and open ended investment companies (OEICs)
    (iv)     Individual Savings Accounts (ISAs)
    (v)      equity shares
    (vi)     gilt edged securities and other bonds
    (vii)    real property
    (viii)   banks and building societies
    (ix)     National Savings.
    (x)      Enterprise investment scheme
    (xi)     Venture capital trusts

# 2 ANALYSIS OF PAST PAPERS

| Topics | J94 | | D94 | | J95 | | D95 | | J96 | | D96 | | J97 | | D97 | | J98 | | D98 | | J99 | | D99 | |
|---|---|---|---|---|---|---|---|---|---|---|---|---|---|---|---|---|---|---|---|---|---|---|---|---|
| **Income Tax** | | | | | | | | | | | | | | | | | | | | | | | | |
| Trading aspects/ Badges of trade | | | 3 | ○ | | | | | | | | | | | 5 | ○ | 4 | | | | 6 | ○ | | |
| Basis periods | 2 | ● | | | 1 | ○ | 3/6 | /● | | | 5 | ○ | 5 | ● | 3 | ● | | | | | 2 | ● | 3 5 | ● ● |
| Capital allowances | 1/3 | ●/● | 3 | ● | /2/4 /6 | ●/● ●/○ | 1/3 | /● | | | 5 | ● | 5 6 | ●/● ● | 3 | ● | 1 | ○ | 5 | ● | 2 | ● | 5 | ● |
| Loss relief | 3 | ○ | | | | | 3 | ○ | | | | | 5 | ○ | | | 4 | ● | 4 | ● | | | 5 | ○ |
| Partnerships | | | 4 | ● | 1 | ● | | | 1 | ○ | 5 | ○ | 5 | ○ | | | | | | | | | 3 | ○ |
| Profit adjustment | 1 | ● | 3 | ● | 1/6 | ●/● | 6 | ○ | | | | | 5 | ● | 5 | ● | | | | | | | 5 | ● |
| **Employment** Benefits in kind | 3/5 | ●/○ | 6 | ○ | 5 | ○ | | | | | | | 1 | ○ | 6 | ○ | 2 | ● | 6 | ○ | 5 | ● | 4 | ○ |
| Employed v self-employed | | | | | 5 | ○ | 6 | ○ | | | | | | | | | 4 | ● | | | 5 | ● | 4 | ● |
| **General matters** EIS relief | | | 5 | ○ | 6 | ○ | | | | | 6 | ● | 2 | ○ | 5 | ● | 5 | ● | | | | | | |
| Foreign element | | | 6 | ● | 2 | ● | 4 | ○ | | | 3 | ○ | 6 | ● | | | 2 | ○ | 1 | ○ | 4 | ● | 1 | ○ |
| Investment advice | 2/5 | ○/● | | | 3 | ○ | 2 | ○ | 2 | ● | | | | | | | 5 | ○ | | | 4 | ○ | | |
| Payable/ repayable computations | 2/6 | ●/● | 4 | ● | 3 | ○ | 6 | ○ | 5 | ○ | | | | | 1 | ○ | 4 | ○ | 2 | ○ | | | | |
| Planning | 2/6 | ○/● | 1/4 | /○ | | | | | | | 2/4 | /○ | | | | | 2 | ● | 5 | ● | 4 | ○ | 1 5 | ● ● |
| Rental income | 6 | ● | 4 | ● | | | 4 | ● | 6 | ○ | | | | | 2 | ○ | | | 6 | ● | 4 | ● | 1 | ● |
| Trusts | | | 4 | ○ | | | | | | | | | | | | | | | | | | | | |
| Pensions | | | | | | | | | | | 5 | ○ | 1 | ○ | 6 | ● | | | 2 | ● | 4 | ● | | |

## Key

The number refers to the number of the question where this topic was examined in the exam.

Topics forming the whole or a substantial part of a question:

□     Compulsory     ○     Optional

Topics forming a non-substantial part of a question

■     Compulsory     ●     Optional

# Tax Planning

| Topics | J94 | | D94 | | J95 | | D95 | | J96 | | D96 | | J97 | | D97 | | J98 | | D98 | | J99 | | D99 | |
|---|---|---|---|---|---|---|---|---|---|---|---|---|---|---|---|---|---|---|---|---|---|---|---|---|
| **CGT** Basic computations | 1 | ● | | | 6 | ● | 3/5 | ●/● | | | | | 4 | ● | 3 | ● | 1 | ● | 4 | ● | 2 | ● | 1 | ● |
| Foreign aspects | | | 6 | ○ | 2 | ○ | | | | | | | | | | | 2 | ● | | | | | 1 | ● |
| Holdover relief for gifts | 6 | ● | | | 1 | ● | 3/5 | ○/○ | | | | | 4 | ● | | | | | 6 | ● | | | | |
| Retirement relief | 2/6 | ●/○ | 5 | ● | 6 | ● | 3 | ○ | | | 1 | ○ | | | | | 6 | ○ | 4 | ● | 3 | ● | 5 | ● |
| Rollover/Incorporation/Reinvestment relief | 1 | ● | 5 | ○ | 4/6 | ●/● | | | 1/6 | ●/● | 5 | ● | 3 | ● | 3 | ● | 1 | ○ | 3 | ● | 2 | ● | | |
| Trusts | | | 4 | ● | | | | | | | | | | | | | | | | | | | | |
| **IHT** BPR/APR | 6 | ● | 4/6 | ●/● | 3/6 | ●/● | 3/5 | ●/○ | 1 | ● | 1 | ○ | 4 | ● | 2 | ● | 6 | ● | | | 3 | ● | 2 | ● |
| Death estate | 6 | ● | 4/6 | ○/● | 3 | ○ | 5 | ● | 2 | ○ | | | 4 | ● | 2 | ○ | 6 | ○ | | | 3 | ● | 2 | ○ |
| Foreign aspects | | | 6 | ● | | | 5 | ● | | | 3 | ● | | | | | | | 1 | ○ | | | | |
| General planning | 6 | ● | 4 | ○ | 3 | ● | 2/3 | ○/● | 2 | ● | | | 4 | ● | 2 | ● | | | | | 3 | ● | 2 | ● |
| Lifetime transfers | 3/6 | ○/● | | | 3 | ● | 3/5 | ●/● | 2 | ● | 2 | ○ | 4 | ● | 2 | ● | 6 | ● | | | 3 | ● | 2 | ○ |
| QSR | | | 6 | ● | | | | | | | | | | | | | | | | | 2 | ● | | |
| Trusts | | | 4 | ● | 3 | ● | | | 2 | ● | | | | | 2 | ● | | | | | 3 | ● | | |
| **Corporation Tax** Dividends v remuneration | | | 1 | ○ | | | 2/4 | ○/○ | | | | | | | | | | | | | | | | |
| Administration | | | | | | | | | | | | | | | | | | | | | 1 | ● | | |
| Foreign element | 4 | ○ | | | 2 | ○ | 4 | ○ | | | | | 6 | ○ | 4 | ○ | | | | | 1 | ○ | | |
| General MCT computation | 4 | ● | 1 | ● | 2 | ● | 1 | ○ | | | | | 3 | ● | | | | | 3 | ● | 6 | ○ | | |
| Groups & consortia | | | 2 | ○ | 4 | ○ | 1 | ● | 4 | ○ | 6 | ○ | 3 | ○ | | | 3 | ○ | 3 | ● | 1 | ● | 6 | ○ |
| Purchase of own shares | | | 5 | ○ | | | | | | | 1 | ● | | | | | 6 | ● | | | | | | |
| Trading loss reliefs | 1 | ○ | 1/2 | ●/● | 4 | ● | 1 | ● | 4 | ● | 6 | ● | | | | | 3 | ● | | | | | 6 | ● |
| Rewarding employees | | | | | | | | | 3 | ○ | | | 1 | ● | | | | | | | 5 | ● | | |

## Key

The number refers to the number of the question where this topic was examined in the exam.

Topics forming the whole or a substantial part of a question:

☐    Compulsory        ○    Optional

Topics forming a non-substantial part of a question

■    Compulsory        ●    Optional

| Topics | J94 | | D94 | | J95 | | D95 | | J96 | | D96 | | J97 | | D97 | | J98 | | D98 | | J99 | | D99 | |
|---|---|---|---|---|---|---|---|---|---|---|---|---|---|---|---|---|---|---|---|---|---|---|---|---|
| **NI**<br>NI Classes 1; 1A etc | 2 | ● | 1/4 | ●/● | 1/5 | ●/● | 2/6 | ●/● | | | | | 1 | ● | | | | | | | 2/5 | ●/● | 3 | ● |
| **VAT**<br>Benefit-in-kind aspects | | | | | 5 | ○ | | | | | | | | | | | | | | | | | | |
| Groups | 5 | ○ | | | 4 | ● | | | | | | | | | | | | | | | | | | |
| Input/output tax | 5 | ○ | 3 | ○ | 5/6 | ●/○ | | | | | | | 5/6 | ●/● | 3 | ● | | | 5 | ● | 2/5 | ●/● | 3 | ● |
| Partial exemption | 5 | ○ | | | | | | | | | | | | | | | | | | | | | 3 | ● |
| Registration | | | 3 | ○ | 1 | ● | 6 | ○ | | | 2 | ○ | | | | | 4 | ○ | | | | | 3 | ● |
| Penalties | | | | | | | | | | | | | | | | | 4 | ● | | | 5 | ● | | |

## Key

The number refers to the number of the question where this topic was examined in the exam.

Topics forming the whole or a substantial part of a question:

| □ | Compulsory | ○ | Optional |
|---|---|---|---|

Topics forming a non-substantial part of a question

| ■ | Compulsory | ● | Optional |
|---|---|---|---|

# 3 GENERAL REVISION GUIDANCE

## PLANNING YOUR REVISION

### What is revision?

Revision is the process by which you remind yourself of the material you have studied during your course, clarify any problem areas and bring your knowledge to a state where you can retrieve it and present it in a way that will satisfy the Examiners.

Revision is not a substitute for hard work earlier in the course. The syllabus for this paper is too large to be hastily 'crammed' a week or so before the examination. You should think of your revision as the final stage in your study of any topic. It can only be effective if you have already completed earlier stages.

Ideally, you should begin your revision shortly after you begin an examination course. At the end of every week and at the end of every month, you should review the topics you have covered. If you constantly consolidate your work and integrate revision into your normal pattern of study, you should find that the final period of revision - and the examination itself - are much less daunting.

If you are reading this revision text while you are still working through your course, we strongly suggest that you begin now to review the earlier work you did for this paper. Remember, the more times you return to a topic, the more confident you will become with it.

The main purpose of this book, however, is to help you to make the best use of the last few weeks before the examination. In this section we offer some suggestions for effective planning of your final revision and discuss some revision techniques which you may find helpful.

### Planning your time

Most candidates find themselves in the position where they have less time than they would like to revise, particularly if they are taking several papers at one diet. The majority of people must balance their study with conflicting demands from work, family or other commitments.

It is impossible to give hard and fast rules about the amount of revision you should do. You should aim to start your final revision at least four weeks before your examination. If you finish your course work earlier than this, you would be well advised to take full advantage of the extra time available to you. The number of hours you spend revising each week will depend on many factors, including the number of papers you are sitting. You should probably aim to do a minimum of about six to eight hours a week for each paper.

In order to make best use of the revision time that you have, it is worth spending a little of it at the planning stage. We suggest that you begin by asking yourself two questions:

- How much time do I have available for revision?
- What do I need to cover during my revision?

Once you have answered these questions, you should be able to draw up a detailed timetable. We will now consider these questions in more detail.

## How much time do I have available for revision?

Many people find it helpful to work out a regular weekly pattern for their revision. We suggest you use the time planning chart provided to do this. Your aim should be to construct a timetable that is sustainable over a period of several weeks.

### Time planning chart

|        | Monday | Tuesday | Wednesday | Thursday | Friday | Saturday | Sunday |
|--------|--------|---------|-----------|----------|--------|----------|--------|
| 00.00  |        |         |           |          |        |          |        |
| 01.00  |        |         |           |          |        |          |        |
| 02.00  |        |         |           |          |        |          |        |
| 03.00  |        |         |           |          |        |          |        |
| 04.00  |        |         |           |          |        |          |        |
| 05.00  |        |         |           |          |        |          |        |
| 06.00  |        |         |           |          |        |          |        |
| 07.00  |        |         |           |          |        |          |        |
| 08.00  |        |         |           |          |        |          |        |
| 09.00  |        |         |           |          |        |          |        |
| 10.00  |        |         |           |          |        |          |        |
| 11.00  |        |         |           |          |        |          |        |
| 12.00  |        |         |           |          |        |          |        |
| 13.00  |        |         |           |          |        |          |        |
| 14.00  |        |         |           |          |        |          |        |
| 15.00  |        |         |           |          |        |          |        |
| 16.00  |        |         |           |          |        |          |        |
| 17.00  |        |         |           |          |        |          |        |
| 18.00  |        |         |           |          |        |          |        |
| 19.00  |        |         |           |          |        |          |        |
| 20.00  |        |         |           |          |        |          |        |
| 21.00  |        |         |           |          |        |          |        |
| 22.00  |        |         |           |          |        |          |        |
| 23.00  |        |         |           |          |        |          |        |

1    First, block out all the time that is **definitely unavailable** for revision. This will include the hours when you normally sleep, the time you are at work and any other regular and clear commitments.

2    Think about **other people's claims on your time**. If you have a family, or friends whom you see regularly, you may want to discuss your plans with them. People are likely to be flexible in the demands they make on you in the run-up to your examinations, especially if they are aware that you have considered their needs as well as your own. If you consult the individuals who are affected by your plans, you may find that they are surprisingly supportive, instead of being resentful of the extra time you are spending studying.

3    Next, give some thought to the times of day when you **work most effectively**. This differs very much from individual to individual. Some people can concentrate first thing in the morning. Others work best in the early evening, or last thing at night. Some people find their day-to-day work so demanding that they are unable to do anything extra during the week, but must concentrate their study time at weekends. Mark the times when you feel you could do your best work on the

timetable. It is extremely important to acknowledge your personal preferences here. If you ignore them, you may devise a timetable that is completely unrealistic and which you will not be able to adhere to.

4      Consider your **other commitments**. Everybody has certain tasks, from doing the washing to walking the dog, that must be performed on a regular basis. These tasks may not have to be done at a particular time, but you should take them into consideration when planning your schedule. You may be able to find more convenient times to get these jobs done, or be able to persuade other people to help you with them.

5      Now mark some time for **relaxation**. If your timetable is to be sustainable, it must include some time for you to build up your reserves. If your normal week does not include any regular physical activity, make sure that you include some in your revision timetable. A couple of hours spent in a sports centre or swimming pool each week will probably enhance your ability to concentrate.

6      Your timetable should now be taking shape. You can probably see obvious study sessions emerging. It is not advisable to work for too long at any one session. Most people find that they can only really concentrate for one or two hours at a time. If your study sessions are longer than this, you should split them up.

### What do I need to cover during my revision?

Most candidates are more confident about some parts of the syllabus than others. Before you begin your revision, it is important to have an overview of where your strengths and weaknesses lie.

One way to do this is to take a sheet of paper and divide it into three columns. Mark the columns:

**OK     Marginal     Not OK**

or use similar headings to indicate how confident you are with a topic. Then go through the syllabus (reprinted in Section 1) and list the topics under the appropriate headings. Alternatively, you could use the list of key topics in Section 5 of this book to compile your overview. You might also find it useful to skim through the introductions or summaries to the textbook or workbooks you have used in your course. These should remind you of parts of the course that you found particularly easy or difficult at the time. You could also use some of the exercises and questions in the workbooks or textbooks, or some of the questions in this book, as a diagnostic aid to discover the areas where you need to work hardest.

It is also important to be aware which areas of the syllabus are so central to the subject that they are likely to be examined in every diet, and which are more obscure, and not likely to come up so frequently. Your textbooks, workbooks and lecture notes will help you here. Remember, the Examiner will be looking for broad coverage of the syllabus. There is no point in knowing one or two topics in exhaustive detail if you do so at the expense of the rest of the course.

### Writing your revision timetable

You now have the information you need to write your timetable. You know how many weeks you have available, and the approximate amount of time that is available in each week.

You should stop all serious revision 48 hours before your examination. After this point, you may want to look back at your notes to refresh your memory, but you should not attempt to revise any new topics. A clear and rested brain is worth more than any extra facts you could memorise in this period.

Make one copy of this chart for each week you have available for revision.

Using your time planning chart, write in the times of your various study sessions during the week.

In the lower part of the chart, write in the topics that you will cover in each of these sessions.

**Example of a revision timetable**

| **Revision timetable**<br>Week beginning: | Monday | Tuesday | Wednesday | Thursday | Friday | Saturday | Sunday |
|---|---|---|---|---|---|---|---|
| Study sessions | | | | | | | |
| Topics | | | | | | | |

**Some revision techniques**

There should be two elements in your revision. You must **look back** to the work you have covered in the course and **look forward** to the examination. The techniques you use should reflect these two aspects of revision.

Revision should not be boring. It is useful to try a variety of techniques. You probably already have some revision techniques of your own and you may also like to try some of the techniques suggested here, if they are new to you. However, don't waste time with methods of revision which are not effective for you.

- Go through your lecture notes, textbook or workbooks and use a highlighter pen to mark important points.

- Produce a new set of summarised notes. This can be a useful way of re-absorbing information, but you must be careful to keep your notes concise, or you may find that you are simply reproducing work you have done before. It is helpful to use a different format for your notes.

- Make a collection of key words which remind you of the essential concepts of a topic.

- Reduce your notes to a set of key facts and definitions which you must memorise. Write them on cards which you can keep with you all the time.

- When you come across areas which you were unsure about first time around, rework relevant questions in your course materials, then study the answers in great detail.

- If there are isolated topics which you feel are completely beyond you, identify exactly what it is that you cannot understand and find someone (such as a lecturer or recent graduate) who can explain these points to you.

- Practise as many exam standard questions as you can. The best way to do this is to work to time, under exam conditions. You should always resist looking at the answer until you have finished.

- If you have come to rely on a word processor in your day-to-day work, you may have got out of the habit of writing at speed. It is well worth reviving this skill before you sit down in the examination hall: it is something you will need.

- If you have a plentiful supply of relevant questions, you could use them to practise planning answers, and then compare your notes with the answers provided. This is not a substitute for writing full answers, but can be helpful additional practice.

- Go back to questions you have already worked on during the course. This time, complete them under exam conditions, paying special attention to the layout and organisation of your answers. Then compare them in detail with the suggested answers and think about the ways in which your answer differs. This is a useful way of 'fine tuning' your technique.

- During your revision period, do make a conscious effort to identify situations which illustrate concepts and ideas that may arise in the examination. These situations could come from your own work, or from reading the business pages of the quality press. This technique will give you a new perspective on your studies and could also provide material which you can use in the examination.

# 4 EXAMINATION TECHNIQUES

## THE EXAMINATION

This section is divided into two parts. The first part considers the practicalities of sitting the examination. If you have taken other ACCA examinations recently, you may find that everything here is familiar to you. The second part discusses some examination techniques which you may find useful.

### The practicalities

### What to take with you

You should make sure that you have:

- your ACCA registration card
- your ACCA registration docket.

You may also take to your desk:

- pens and pencils
- a ruler and slide rule
- a calculator
- charting template and geometrical instruments
- eraser and correction fluid.

You are not allowed to take rough paper into the examination.

If you take any last-minute notes with you to the examination hall, make sure these are not on your person. You should keep notes or books in your bag or briefcase, which you will be asked to leave at the side of the examination hall.

Although most examination halls will have a clock, it is advisable to wear a watch, just in case your view is obscured.

If your calculator is solar-powered, make sure it works in artificial light. Some examination halls are not particularly well-lit. If you use a battery-powered calculator, take some spare batteries with you. For obvious reasons, you may not use a calculator which has a graphic/word display memory. Calculators with printout facilities are not allowed because they could disturb other candidates.

### Getting there

You should arrange to arrive at the examination hall at least half an hour before the examination is due to start. If the hall is a large one, the invigilator will start filling the hall half an hour before the starting time.

Make absolutely sure that you know how to get to the examination hall and how long it will take you. Check on parking or public transport. Leave yourself enough time so that you will not be anxious if the journey takes a little longer than you anticipated. Many people like to make a practice trip the day before their first examination.

## At the examination hall

Examination halls differ greatly in size. Some only hold about ten candidates. Others can sit many hundreds of people. You may find that more than one examination is being taken at the hall at the same time, so don't panic if you hear people discussing a completely different subject from the one you have revised.

While you are waiting to go in, don't be put off by other people talking about how well, or badly, they have prepared for the examination.

You will be told when to come in to the examination hall. The desks are numbered. (Your number will be on your examination docket.) You will be asked to leave any bags at the side of the hall.

Inside the hall, the atmosphere will be extremely formal. The invigilator has certain things which he or she must tell candidates, often using a particular form of words. Listen carefully, in case there are any unexpected changes to the arrangements.

On your desk you will see a question paper and an answer booklet in which to write your answers. You will be told when to turn over the paper.

## During the examination

You will have to leave your examination paper and answer booklet in the hall at the end of the examination. It is quite acceptable to write on your examination paper if it helps you to think about the questions. However, all workings should be in your answers. You may write any plans and notes in your answer booklet, as long as you cross them out afterwards.

If you require a new answer booklet, put your hand up and a supervisor will come and bring you one.

At various times during the examination, you will be told how much time you have left.

You should not need to leave the examination hall until the examination is finished. Put up your hand if you need to go to the toilet, and a supervisor will accompany you. If you feel unwell, put up your hand, and someone will come to your assistance. If you simply get up and walk out of the hall, you will not be allowed to re-enter.

Before you finish, you must fill in the required information on the front of your answer booklet.

## Examination techniques

## Tackling Paper 11

You must answer four out of six questions. One of the aims of this paper is to consider the interrelationship of the various taxes. You should therefore expect most questions to deal with more than one tax.

The Examiner will be looking for broadly based knowledge of the taxation system, rather than minutely detailed knowledge of specific topics or taxes.

Some questions may ask you to restrict your answer to certain taxes. This will be done either to make it possible for you to answer the question in the time available or to avoid repetition within the paper. It is essential that you follow these instructions, as you will be given no marks for consideration of taxes which are specifically outside the scope of the question and will waste valuable time.

You will be given some tax rates and allowances on the paper. These are shown at the back of this book. You should be aware of what information you will, and will not, be provided with.

## Your general strategy

You should spend the first ten minutes of the examination reading the paper. If you have a choice of question, decide which questions you will do. You must divide the time you spend on questions in proportion to the marks on offer. Don't be tempted to spend more time on a question you know a lot about, or one which you find particularly difficult. If a question has more than one part, you must complete each part.

On every question, the first marks are the easiest to gain. Even if things go wrong with your timing and you don't have time to complete a question properly, you will probably gain some marks by making a start.

Spend the last five minutes reading through your answers and making any additions or corrections.

You may answer written questions in any order you like. Some people start with their best question, to help them relax. Another strategy is to begin with your second best question, so that you are working even more effectively when you reach the question you are most confident about.

Once you have embarked on a question, you should try to stay with it, and not let your mind stray to other questions on the paper. You can only concentrate on one thing at once. However, if you get completely stuck with a question, leave space in your answer book and return to it later.

## Answering the question

All Examiners say that the most frequent reason for failure in examinations, apart from basic lack of knowledge, is candidates' unwillingness to answer the question that the Examiner has asked. A great many people include every scrap of knowledge they have on a topic, just in case it is relevant. Stick to the question and tailor your answer to what you are asked. Pay particular attention to the verbs in the question.

You should be particularly wary if you come across a question which appears to be almost identical to one which you have practised during your revision. It probably isn't! Wishful thinking makes many people see the question they would like to see on the paper, not the one that is actually there. Read a question at least twice before you begin your answer. Underline key words on the question paper, if it helps focus your mind on what is required.

If you don't understand what a question is asking, state your assumptions. Even if you do not answer in precisely the way the Examiner hoped, you may be given some credit, if your assumptions are reasonable.

## Presentation

You should do everything you can to make things easy for the marker. Although you will not be marked on your handwriting, the marker will find it easier to identify the points you have made if your answers are legible. The same applies to spelling and grammar. Use blue or black ink. The marker will be using red or green.

Use the margin to clearly identify which question, or part of a question, you are answering.

Start each answer on a new page. The order in which you answer the questions does not matter, but if a question has several parts, these parts should appear in the correct order in your answer book.

If there is the slightest doubt when an answer continues on another page, indicate to the marker that he or she must turn over. It is irritating for a marker to think he or she has reached the end of an answer, only to turn the page and find that the answer continues.

Use columnar layouts for computations. This will help you to avoid mistakes, and is easier to follow.

Use headings and numbered sentences if they help to show the structure of your answer. However, don't write your answers in one-word note form.

It is a good idea to make a rough plan of an answer before you begin to write. Do this in your answer booklet, but make sure you cross it out neatly afterwards. The marker needs to be clear whether he or she is looking at your rough notes, or the answer itself.

## Computations

Before you begin a computation, you may find it helpful to jot down the stages you will go through. Cross out these notes afterwards.

It is essential to include all your workings and to indicate where they fit in to your answer. It is important that the marker can see where you got the figures in your answer from. Even if you make mistakes in your computations, you will be given credit for using a principle correctly, if it is clear from your workings and the structure of your answer.

If you spot an arithmetical error which has implications for figures later in your answer, it may not be worth spending a lot of time reworking your computation.

If you are asked to comment or make recommendations on a computation, you must do so. There are important marks to be gained here. Even if your computation contains mistakes, you may still gain marks if your reasoning is correct.

Use the layouts which you see in the answers given in this booklet and in model answers. A clear layout will help you avoid errors and will impress the marker.

## Essay questions

You must plan an essay before you start writing. One technique is to quickly jot down any ideas which you think are relevant. Re-read the question and cross out any points in your notes which are not relevant. Then number your points. Remember to cross out your plan afterwards.

Your essay should have a clear structure. It should contain a brief introduction, a main section and a conclusion. Don't waste time by restating the question at the start of your essay.

Break your essay up into paragraphs. Use sub-headings and numbered sentences if they help show the structure of your answer.

Be concise. It is better to write a little about a lot of different points than a great deal about one or two points.

The Examiner will be looking for evidence that you have understood the syllabus and can apply your knowledge in new situations. You will also be expected to give opinions and make judgements. These should be based on reasoned and logical arguments.

### Reports, memos and other documents

Some questions ask you to present your answer in the form of a report or a memo or other document. It is important that you use the correct format - there are easy marks to be gained here. Adopt the format used in sample questions, or use the format you are familiar with in your day-to-day work, as long as it contains all the essential elements.

You should also consider the audience for any document you are writing. How much do they know about the subject? What kind of information and recommendations are required? The Examiner will be looking for evidence that you can present your ideas in an appropriate form.

# 5 KEY REVISION TOPICS

The aim of this section is to provide you with a checklist of key information relating to this Paper. You should use it as a reminder of topics to be revised rather than as a summary of all you need to know. Aim to revise as many topics as possible because many of the questions in the exam draw on material from more than one section of the syllabus. You will get more out of this section if you read through Section 3, *General Revision Guidance*, first.

Paper 11 is very much concerned with identifying elections and reliefs that will minimise a taxpayer's liability. In this Section you should be looking briefly at some of the most important claims that can be made, revising any conditions that must be met, and identifying the relevant time limits. All sections refer to ICTA 1988, unless otherwise stated.

At the end of each of the following revision sections we recommend that you attempt the questions listed under that heading in the contents pages. Virtually all of these questions are actual past exam questions and are therefore usually on more than one topic. They are invariably under a particular heading because that best describes the content of the question but there will often be other parts to the question on topics falling later in the order of revision. If you need to, therefore, leave questions to practice after you have revised these other topics. Just keep a note of what remains to be done.

Remember, if you practice all the past questions set since June 1994 under the new syllabus - and the old syllabus questions selected for this book - you will be revising most of the topics likely to be set in future papers.

## 1    SCHEDULE E

You should have a clear understanding of:

- The factors used to distinguish employed from self-employed status.
- The date emoluments are 'received'.
- The rules and reliefs on termination payments.
- The approved incentive schemes - ie, the three share based schemes.

On benefits you should be familiar with all the rules on all the common forms - eg, cars and loans - and be able to discuss tax efficient remuneration packages to include such exempt items as canteen facilities.

For National Insurance you should know the basic rules on

- Employment earnings - Classes 1 and 1A.
- Self-employed profits - Classes 2 and 4.

Think about planning aspects. For example, avoid Class 1 by paying a director/shareholder a dividend instead of a bonus. Also, steps taken to reduce other forms of taxation can result in a higher NI liability. For example, the potential extra Class 2/4 exposure of bringing a spouse in as a partner.

Refer to chapters 6 to 8 of the Lynchpin and attempt all the questions shown under the heading of Schedule E on the contents page of this book.

## 2    SCHEDULE A

For income tax purposes you should know:

- The 'single business' treatment of income from property
- Rent a room relief
- The 'other single business' treatment of income from furnished holiday lettings
- The taxation/relief for lease premiums.

Refer to chapter 2 of the Lynchpin and attempt all the questions shown under the heading of Schedule A on the contents page of this book.

## 3    CAPITAL ALLOWANCES

You should know what assets qualify for the following different categories of capital allowances and how the allowances are calculated:

- Plant and machinery
- Industrial buildings and hotels
- ABAs
- Patents and know-how
- Scientific research allowances.

As well as knowing the basic rules  you must learn the non-standard situations such as IBA balancing charges following some periods of non-industrial use and tax planning aspects such as the need to disclaim FYA to reduce a potential balancing charge on the main pool.

Refer to chapters 10 and 11 of the Lynchpin and attempt the question shown under the heading of Capital Allowances on the contents page of this book.

## 4    SCHEDULE D CASES I AND II

Concentrate on:

- Badges of trade - you are more likely to have to apply them than just list them
- Profit adjustment - a lengthy computation is more of a paper 7 topic but adjustments are still likely in paper 11
- Basis periods - all aspects of CYB are important, including change of accounting date
- Relief for trading losses.

Not only must you know the rules but you must be able to discuss planning matters such as the relative merits of different accounting dates or options for the use of a trading loss.

Refer to chapters 9 and 12 of the Lynchpin and attempt all the questions shown under the heading of Schedule D Cases I and II on the contents page of this book.

## 5    PENSION PROVISION

We assume that you do not need to revise the basic Taxable Income/Income Tax layouts and general tax administration as they are heavily examined at paper 7.  However, if you choose to do so, here would be a good place to refresh your memory on these topics using chapters  1, 4 and 22 of the Lynchpin.

At this stage we consider the taxation of investments (other than property - see section 2 above) with emphasis on tax favoured 'vehicles'.  Pension contributions is a good example - relatively safe, but long term; tax relief on the way in, but with complex rules limiting relief, and tax on the pension generated.

Not only should you learn the rules for ISAs, pensions, EISs, VCTs and National Savings but you should think about their comparative suitability. For example, National Savings may not be appropriate for a taxpayer needing to spend the capital in the near future.

Refer to chapter 3 of the Lynchpin and attempt the question shown under the heading of Pension Provision on the contents page of this book.

## 6 PARTNERSHIPS

You may not have covered this topic for paper 7 as it was excluded from the syllabus until recently. For Paper 11 you need to know:

- The income tax rules whereby a partner is treated as a soletrader in respect of his share of the adjusted partnership profits. This means knowing:
  - How profits/losses are allocated
  - How a change in PSA is dealt with
  - How a partner coming in or leaving is assessed
- The NIC rules - again each partner is separate
- The CGT treatment of partnership assets - calculate gains/losses and allocate share to each partner.

Refer to chapter 13 of the Lynchpin and attempt all the questions shown under the heading of Partnerships on the contents page of this book.

## 7 CAPITAL GAINS TAX

You must revise the rules learnt for paper 7 with particular emphasis on the opportunities to mitigate the tax - retirement relief, gift relief, incorporation relief, rollover relief for replacing business assets, EIS deferral relief and taper relief.

Instead of just producing basic gain calculations you will be more likely to have to comment on such tax planning matters as using annual exemptions, losses, and the exemption for intra-spouse or intra-group transfers.

Refer to chapters 14 to 21 of the Lynchpin and attempt all the questions shown under the heading of Capital Gains Tax on the contents page of this book.

## 8 INHERITANCE TAX

Revise the main topics:

- The general layout of the chargeable estate on death
- The basis of the charge on death
- The role of trusts
- How the IHT impact on an estate is allocated between beneficiaries - eg, IHT on specific legacies is paid out of residue
- The valuation rules including the rules for 'related' property.
- Valuation reliefs - BPR, APR and relief for pre-death fall in value.
- Tax credit reliefs - QSR and DTR
- Post-death reliefs
  - Quoted shares sold at a loss within 12 months.
  - Land sold at a loss within 4 years of death.
  - Related property sold below RP valuation in the 3 years post-death.
  - Deeds of variation within 2 years of death.

- Treatment of lifetime gifts
  - PETs v CLTs
  - The 4 lifetime exemptions
    - Normal expenditure out of income
    - Annual exemption
    - Marriage exemption
    - Small gifts exemption
  - Taper relief
- Overseas aspects
- Gifts with reservation
- Associated operations
- Due dates and instalment option
- Planning opportunities.

As IHT is not tested at Paper 7, there is a tendency for the Paper 11 examiner to take a mainly "Framework" approach to IHT. However, the planning side is also tested and you should have this in your mind. For example, if the question says a potential donor might live a further 6 years at a pinch, his gift of a PET will probably become chargeable but it is still worthwhile because:

- Annual exemptions are utilised
- For death after 3 years any tax charged on the gift attracts taper relief
- Value chargeable is "frozen" but there would be relief for fall in value.

On the other hand if the property attracts 100% BPR it might be advisable not to make the gift to avoid the risk of the donee selling the property before the donor dies and thereby losing the BPR entitlement. Another factor favouring this course is the tax free uplift of the CGT base cost on death. By doing nothing the potential donor avoids both IHT and CGT.

Refer to chapters 29 to 33 of the Lynchpin and attempt all the questions shown under the heading of Inheritance Tax on the contents page of this book.

## 9    TRUSTS

This is a very unpopular part of the syllabus but is not a particularly difficult topic. Legally a trust arises where a settlor - (the person with the assets) - transfers the assets to trustees with instructions (the trust deed) on such matters as who is (or will be or may be) entitled to the income and capital of the trust - ie, the beneficiaries.

Historically, trusts were a means of separating the ownership and control of assets from the right to the income. The trustees are the 'legal owners' of the assets but the income from or use of the assets can either be accumulated (ie, rolled up in the trust as part of the trust capital) or enjoyed by a beneficiary either as of right (a 'life interest') or at the discretion of the trustees ie, a discretionary trust. A wealthy father could ensure an income for his profligate son but, by putting the income generating assets in the hands of trustees, he prevents him from dissipating his share of wealth .

Revise:

- The types of trust
- The income tax treatment of trusts
- The CGT treatment of trusts
- The IHT treatment of trusts.

You can probably see that the taxation of trusts was developed over many years in a piecemeal fashion. There was an attempt several years ago to replace the IT and CGT rules with an integrated framework but this was largely abandoned. You have to keep the rules for the three taxes quite separate. For example, for most purposes of IHT a life tenant is treated as if he actually owned the trust assets - in law he does not - and the same hypothesis is irrelevant for considering IT and CGT.

Refer to chapter 34 of the Lynchpin and attempt the question shown under the heading of Trusts on the contents page of this book.

**10      VAT**

The main VAT topics to revise are:

- Registration/deregistration requirements
- Administration basics such as tax points and tax invoices
- Exempt/Zero rated categories
- Foreign/EU aspects
- Categories of irrecoverable input tax
- Partial exemption treatment
- Cash accounting and annual accounting
- Group registration
- Rules against business splitting
- The main elements in the penalty regime - eg, default surcharge.

Refer to chapters 35 and 36 of the Lynchpin and attempt the questions shown under the heading of VAT on the contents page of this book. Note that this is a case in point of the key topic being only part of the question. Unfortunately we have to do this for VAT as it is seldom the main topic of a question. The examiner has stated that for June 1999 onwards VAT is likely to be given more weight and the second VAT question (Gewgaw Ltd) shows the examiner is as good as his word on this statement.

**11      CORPORATION TAX - CALCULATION**

Revise the following basic areas:

- The Self Assessment administration requirements including quarterly instalment paydays
- The basic PCTCT layout including the modifications needed to fit in loss reliefs
- The basic GCT - IT = MCT components especially for 'long' periods of account and FY straddle.
- Quarterly accounting for IT
- The loss relief rules with emphasis on all aspects of S.393A(l) including cessation of trade.

Refer to chapters 21 to 25 of the Lynchpin and attempt all the questions shown under the heading of Corporation Tax - Calculation on the contents page of this book.

**12      CORPORATION TAX - PURCHASE OF OWN SHARES**

Refer to chapter 28 of the Lynchpin and attempt both of the questions shown under the heading of Corporation Tax - Purchase of Own Shares on the contents page of this book.

**13      CORPORATION TAX - GROUPS**

You should have a clear understanding of the following topics and be able to apply the rules and identify planning opportunities.

- Groups and consortia:
    - 51% definition
        - Group interest and charges
        - Impact of associates on CT rates

- 75% definitions
  - Group relief for losses etc.
  - Capital gains group reliefs.

Refer to chapter 26 of the Lynchpin and attempt all the questions shown under the heading of Corporation tax - Groups on the contents page of this book.

## 14     CORPORATION TAX - CLOSE COMPANIES

Although the following are not mainstream topics they can be tested and should be understood:

- Investment companies
- Close companies
- Benefits
- Loans

Refer to chapter 27 of the Lynchpin and attempt the question shown under the heading of Corporation Tax - Close Companies on the contents page of this book.

## 15     OVERSEAS ACTIVITIES - INCOME TAX

Overseas tax matters for individuals usually hinge around one or more of their residence, ordinary residence and domicile status. Revise the definitions of these terms and the Revenue's concession on residence status. You should also be prepared for questions on:

- The basic Sch E exposure for overseas earnings
- The liability on overseas income including the remittance basis
- Relief for overseas travel costs
- The operation of double tax relief
- The CGT rules on foreign gains and losses.

Refer to chapter 37 (paras 1 - 12) of the Lynchpin and attempt all the questions shown under the heading of Overseas Activities - Income Tax on the contents page of this book.

## 16     OVERSEAS ACTIVITIES - CORPORATION TAX

A knowledge of this area is frequently tested. Concentrate on:

- The rules for determining company residence
- The implication of a company being UK resident
- The DTR computational techniques
- The alternative of treating foreign tax as an expense
- The anti-avoidance rules on CFCs and transfer pricing
- The options for a UK company trading abroad
- The options for an overseas company trading in the UK.

Refer to chapter 37 (paras 13 to 21) of the Lynchpin and attempt all the questions shown under the heading of Overseas Activities - Corporation Tax on the contents page of this book.

## 17    GENERAL - TAX PLANNING

Essentially you have been encouraged throughout your studies to consider the tax planning opportunities available. Generally you are given a situation or proposed transaction and you have to suggest ways of mitigating the tax exposure. Some typical situations are:

- Choice of investments
- Maximising husband and wife reliefs
- Maximising reliefs for groups
- Timing of events for a business
- Designing remuneration packages
- Extracting profits tax efficiently from a family company.

Refer to chapter 40 of the Lynchpin and attempt all the questions shown under the heading of General - Tax Planning on the contents page of this book.

## 18    PERSONAL FINANCE

Refer to chapters 38 and 39 of the Lynchpin and attempt all the questions shown under the heading of Personal Finance on the contents page of this book.

# 6 UPDATES

**Examinable documents**

The ACCA Official Textbook (published in July 1999) and Revision Series for Paper 11 are fully up-to-date for the Finance Act 1999, which was enacted in July 1999. This is examinable in both June and December 2000.

The September 1999 issue of the ACCA Students' Newsletter carries a detailed article on the impact of the FA 1999 on the tax papers for June and December 2000. You are strongly recommended to read it as a useful summary of topical issues. However, all the guidance on syllabus exclusions, had been made available when the AT Foulks Lynch study material was updated for FA 1999, so the article's contents have been fully taken into account in your FA 1999 study material.

**Extension of starting rate band to savings income (apart from dividends)**

The FA1999 introduced the starting rate band, whereby the first £1,500 of taxable income is taxed at the starting rate of 10%. The starting rate band was not to apply to savings income. This led to the anomalous position that an individual whose taxable income comprised bank interest would be taxed at 20% on the first £1,500 of taxable income, whereas an individual whose taxable income comprised, say, pensions would only be taxed at 10% on the first £1,500 of taxable income.

It was announced in the pre-budget statement in November 1999 that the starting rate band would for 1999/00 be extended to savings income other than dividend income (which is taxed at the Schedule F rate). This change does not affect the rate of CGT payable by an individual.

This change was announced after the study manuals were published and so is not reflected in the study material. It will not be legislated for until the Finance Act 2000. You should read the ACCA Students' Newsletter in case the examiner indicates whether the revised treatment will be examined in June or December 2000.

Example.

Bill, a single man aged 50, receives building society interest of £4,800 during 1999/00.

Prior to the extension of the starting rate band to savings income (other than dividends) Bill's income tax computation would be:

|  | £ |
|---|---|
| Building society interest £4,800 × $\frac{100}{80}$ | 6,000 |
| Less personal allowance | 4,335 |
| Taxable income | 1,665 |
| £1,665 @ 20% | 333 |
| Less tax deducted at source £6,000 × 20% | (1,200) |
| Income tax repayable | (867) |

Following the extension of the starting rate band to savings income (other than dividends), Bill's income tax computation is:

|  | £ |
|---|---|
| Building society interest £4,800 × $^{100}/_{80}$ | 6,000 |
| Less personal allowance | 4,335 |
| Taxable income | 1,665 |
| £1,500 @ 10% | 150 |
| 165 @ 20% | 33 |
|  | 183 |
| Less tax deducted at source £6,000 × 20% | (1,200) |
| Income tax repayable | (1,017) |

# 7 PRACTICE QUESTIONS

| 1 | **BINARY PLC** |

Binary plc runs a nationwide chain of health clubs, with each club being run by a manager who oversees a number of full-time staff. As from 6 April 1999, the company has provided an additional benefits package to each of its managers, who are paid a basic salary of £32,000 pa. The package, which applies only to the managers and not the staff, is as follows:

(1)     Each manager was provided with a new 1800cc diesel powered motor car at a cost of £19,035 each. Subsequent to their purchase, each car was fitted with a mobile telephone costing £140, and this was invoiced for separately to the purchase of the motor car. Both figures are inclusive of VAT. None of the managers drives more than 2,500 business miles a year, and private fuel and telephone calls are paid for by Binary plc.

(2)     2,000 £1 ordinary shares in Binary plc were issued to each manager. Managers paid the par value for their shares, although the value of each share at 6 April 1999 was £5.50. Each manager was also given an option to buy a further 4,000 shares at their value as at 6 April 1999, less a discount of 40%. The options were provided free, and must be exercised within three years of their issue. The ordinary shares of Binary plc are forecast to be worth £12.00 by 5 April 2002.

(3)     A profit sharing scheme was set up whereby each manager will be paid an annual bonus based on the increase in profit made by their respective club compared to the previous year. The scheme ensures a minimum annual payment to each manager of £2,000, which will be paid three months after Binary plc's year end of 31 March.

(4)     Free membership to the health clubs was provided to each manager. Membership normally costs £400 pa, and Binary plc calculates that this figure is made up as follows:

|  | £ |
|---|---|
| Direct cost | 20 |
| Variable overhead cost | 80 |
| Fixed overhead cost | 200 |
| Profit | 100 |
|  |  |
| Membership fee | 400 |

Each of the health clubs currently has surplus capacity, although the budgeted membership has been exceeded.

(5)     Each manager was provided with a round sum entertainment allowance of £1,200 pa to be used on entertaining present and prospective club members.

**You are required:**

(a)     to explain the income tax and National Insurance contribution implications for the managers arising from the provision of their additional benefits package;                                      **(14 marks)**

(b)     to explain the corporation tax, National Insurance contribution and VAT implications for Binary plc arising from the provision of the additional benefits package.                    **(11 marks)**

You should assume that the tax rates for 1999/00 apply throughout.

**(Total:  25 marks)**
*(ACCA Dec 93)*

---

## 2      VERNON

(a)     Vernon, a married man, has owned three unfurnished investment properties, number 1, 2 and 3 Shercock Avenue for many years.  Numbers 1 and 2 have been let out under tenant's repairing leases while Number 3 has been let out under a landlord's repairing lease.  All leases are at a full commercial rent, the rent on Numbers 1 and 3 being payable quarterly in advance, on the normal quarter days.  The rent on Number 2 is payable monthly in advance, on the first day of the month. The receipts and expenditure statements in respect of each property for the two years ended 5 April 2001 were as follows:

|                  | Number 1 | | Number 2 | | Number 3 | |
| --- | --- | --- | --- | --- | --- | --- |
| Year ended       | 5.4.00 | 5.4.01 | 5.4.00 | 5.4.01 | 5.4.00 | 5.4.01 |
|                  | £ | £ | £ | £ | £ | £ |
| Rents received   | 2,300 | 2,900 | - | 8,400 | 3,800 | 4,200 |
| Expenditure:     |  |  |  |  |  |  |
|    Maintenance | 2,810 | 730 | 1,020 | 1,210 | 940 | 870 |
|    Repairs     | - | - | 1,600 | - | 1,700 | - |
|    Legal fees  | - | - | 200 | - | - | - |
|                  | (2,810) | (730) | (2,820) | (1,210) | (2,640) | (870) |
| Net receipts     | (510) | 2,170 | (2,820) | 7,190 | 1,160 | 3,330 |

The following facts also apply:

(i)     The tenant of Number 1 did not pay all the rent due for the year ended 5 April 2000 and owed £100 at the end of the year.  This was paid in June 2000 and has been included in the figure of £2,900 above.

The quarterly rental was £600, increasing to £700 from the quarter commencing 24 June 2000.

In July 1999 the property was decorated at a cost of £2,000.  This is included in the maintenance costs of £2,810.

(ii)    The tenant of Number 2 left the property on 30 April 1999, owing rent of £600.  Despite taking the tenant to court and incurring legal fees of £200 as a result, Vernon was unable to recover the unpaid rent.  The repair expenditure of £1,600 was for repairing damage to the premises caused by the defaulting tenant.  Once the repairs had been completed, Number 2 remained empty until eventually Vernon found a new tenant.  The premises were re-let on 1 May 2000, again under a tenant's repairing lease, at the rate of £700 per month.

(iii)   The repairs carried out at Number 3 consisted of replacing three old fireplaces with a central heating system.

The quarterly rental was £950, increasing to £1,050 from the quarter commencing 24 June 2000.

---

Vernon's only other source of income apart from his rents was net interest of £5,000 pa on a debenture from Rupert Ltd, a company resident in the Republic of Ruritania. Ruritania does not have a double tax agreement with the United Kingdom and imposes a 30% withholding tax on gross interest.

Vernon's wife has no taxable income.

**You are required:**

(i)     to explain clearly which items in the receipts and expenditure statements will require adjustments and which will not require adjustment. Show the finally adjusted income figures for each property;       **(4 marks)**

(ii)     to compute Vernon's income tax liabilities for 1999/00 and 2000/01, showing how losses are relieved. Except for the abolition of MCA from April 2000, assume 1999/00 income tax rates and allowances apply also to 2000/01.

           **(6 marks)**

(b)     Joe Kerr, a married man, has traded as a fashion retailer since 1 May 1995. His tax adjusted profits/(losses) before capital allowances in recent years have been as follows:

|  | £ |
|---|---|
| Year ended 28.2.99 | 10,138 |
| Year ended 29.2.00 | (6,400) |
| Year ended 28.2.01 | 4,200 (estimated) |

The written-down value of pooled plant and machinery was £12,750 at 1 March 1998. In June 1998 he had acquired a small computer with an expected useful life of four years for £750, which he sold for £700 in January 2000. A short life asset election has been submitted. Joe claimed the maximum permitted writing-down and first year allowances for the period ended 28 February 1999, but the position is still open for the subsequent years. Joe also received furnished rental income of £4,200 in the year ended 5 April 1999, which rose to £7,000 pa thereafter.

Joe wishes to claim any loss relief available in the earliest years of assessment possible. He would like, if possible, to avoid wasting any of his personal allowances. His wife works as a supermarket manageress with a salary of £15,000 pa over the years concerned.

He has no other income to set the loss against in the years prior to 1998/99.

**You are required** to compute Joe's taxable income for the years of assessment 1998/99 to 2000/01 inclusive, explaining briefly the loss relief strategy which you have adopted. Assume that 1999/00 rates and allowances apply also to 2000/01.       **(15 marks)**

           **(Total: 25 marks)**

           *(ACCA Dec 89)*

## 3     MARGARET

Margaret, a fashion designer, and Janet a colleague of hers, plan to set up in partnership making clothes designed by Margaret.

Their intended commencement date is 1 January 2000 and accounts will be made up to 30 June each year, their first accounts covering the period ended 30 June 2001. They expect profits in the early years of business to rise rapidly.

They expect to incur substantial capital expenditure on:

(i)     a new freehold factory, complete with lighting, plumbing, heating and fittings;
(ii)    a second-hand storage warehouse;
(iii)   miscellaneous plant;
(iv)    patents.

**You are required** to prepare a concise report for Margaret and Janet dealing with:

(a)     The matters to be considered in deciding whether fittings comprised in the new factory are likely to be regarded as part of the building or as plant.                                              **(6 marks)**

(b)     The allowances available on each of the above four types of expenditure.          **(4 marks)**

(c)     The relief available for any 'short life' assets assuming the required election is made.     **(5 marks)**

(d)     The basis of assessment of profit for the first five years of the partnership, and the manner in which capital allowances are calculated.                                                     **(4 marks)**

(e)     The options open to Margaret and Janet if in the first accounting period the available capital allowances exceeded the assessable profit.                                            **(6 marks)**

**(Total: 25 marks)**

*(ACCA June 88)*

---

## 4    LEX HUBBARD

You have been asked to provide advice at today's date (which you should assume is 6 April 1999) to Mr Lex Hubbard. Mr Hubbard is due to commence self-employment as a dentist on 1 July 1999. Mr Hubbard's wife may possibly work for him as a part-time receptionist. Mr Hubbard is unsure whether, if she does so, he should pay her for her services, and how much he should pay her. Mr Hubbard understands that the current market rate for a part-time dental receptionist is £3,700 pa. Projected profits (before charging depreciation and any wages for Mrs Hubbard) are as follows:

|                         |        £ |
| ----------------------- | -------: |
| Period ended 30.4.00    | 55,000   |
| Period ended 30.4.01    | 69,000   |
| Period ended 30.4.02    | 52,000   |

No adjustments to these figures for tax purposes are anticipated.

Mr Hubbard will acquire second-hand equipment costing £24,000 on 1 July 1999, and new equipment costing £15,000 on 1 December 2000. Second-hand equipment with an original cost of £14,000 is expected to be sold for £16,000 on 1 December 2000 and further new equipment with an expected useful life of four years and an expected nil scrap value will be acquired for £24,000 on the same day.

Mr Hubbard also has the following sources of income and outgoings:

(1)     Cash held in National Savings Bank investment account; interest credited to 5 April 1999: £7,000; anticipated interest to be credited to 5 April 2000; £8,000. The account was opened on 1 June 1995.

(2)     Mr Hubbard owns three furnished properties, numbers 4, 5 and 6 Cyanide Park. These are let out to tourists during the year at an average rental of £12 per day. Letting expenses are negligible. Number 4 is available for letting for 120 days in the year, while numbers 5 and 6 are available

---

through the year. It is anticipated that during 1999/00 number 4 will be let for 75 days, number 5 will be let for 60 days and number 6 will be let for 90 days. A disposal of number 4 would give rise to a substantial capital gain, while disposals of numbers 5 and 6 would give rise to nil gain/nil loss outcomes. The total value of the properties is £130,000.

(3)     Interest payable on a mortgage loan of £56,000 on Mr Hubbard's principal private residence is expected to be £7,000 (gross) for the year to 5 April 2000. The mortgage is in the MIRAS scheme and is in the joint names of Mr and Mrs Hubbard.

Mr Hubbard has heard that it may be advisable to transfer his non-business assets to Mrs Hubbard and also to make a special claim in respect of his mortgage interest, in order to maximise the benefits of independent taxation. He wonders whether it would be possible to ensure that Mrs Hubbard would be obliged to return any assets gifted to her if Mr Hubbard required them at a later date. Mrs Hubbard currently has no income or assets in her own right.

**You are required:**

(a)     to calculate Mr Hubbard's projected Schedule D Case I profits and capital allowances for 1999/00 to 2002/03 inclusive, assuming that he wishes to maximise his claims for capital allowances. Ignore any possible payment of wages to Mrs Hubbard;                                                                    **(8 marks)**

(b)     to explain how much of Mr Hubbard's rental income qualifies as income from furnished holiday lettings. Would your answer differ if the letting of Number 6 included a 5 week let to one family?
                                                                                                                         **(4 marks)**

(c)     to discuss Mr Hubbard's best strategy for maximising the tax benefits of independent taxation. As part of your discussion, you should consider whether Mr Hubbard should pay any wages to Mrs Hubbard and, if so, how much. You should also bear in mind any relevant IHT, CGT or NIC considerations. Use tax rates for 1999/00 in your illustrations.                                   **(13 marks)**
                                                                                                                **(Total: 25 marks)**
                                                                                                            *(ACCA December 1991)*

---

### 5      BORIS, STEFFI AND IVAN

---

(a)     Boris, Steffi and Ivan are partners in a leisurewear business which commenced on 1 November 1998. Up until 30 June 2000, the partners shared profits in the ratio 3:3:1, after charging a salary of £2,000 to Ivan. After that date, the partners shared profits in the ratio 4:3:2, after charging a salary of £10,000 to Ivan. Recent partnership profits/(losses) after making all necessary tax adjustments are as follows:

| | |
|---|---|
| Year to 31.10.99 | £28,000 |
| Year to 31.10.00 | (£30,000) |

You should assume that the partners' individual assessable shares of profits in 2001/02 will be £30,000, £35,000 and £40,000 respectively. You should also assume that 1999/00 tax rates and allowances apply for all relevant years of assessment.

Ivan, who is single, has no other income apart from his partnership profits, and had none in earlier years. He is anxious to know how to make best use of his share of the loss incurred in the year to 31 October 2000. He understands that he has a choice between a claim against total income under S380 ICTA 1988, or alternatively against future trading profits under S385 ICTA 1988.

**You are required:**

(i)    to compute the partnership profits assessable in respect of each of the partners for 1998/99 and 1999/00 and the overlap profits for each partner;    **(6 marks)**

(ii)   to compute the loss relief available to each of the partners;    **(6 marks)**

(iii)  to advise Ivan whether he should claim relief under S380 or S385 taking both income tax and NIC considerations into account. Show all supporting calculations.    **(4 marks)**

(b)   Boris (who is aged 30) and his wife Martina enjoy the following income in addition to his partnership profits:

|  | Year ended | |
|---|---|---|
|  | *5.4.99* | *5.4.00* |
| *Self* | £ | £ |
| Interest received on National Savings Bank ordinary account (opened June 1995) | 220 | 200 |
| Interest received on building society account | 9,700 | 11,456 |
| Interest on National Savings Certificates | 100 | 120 |
| *Wife* | | |
| Unfurnished rental income | 200 | 300 |

Boris intends to claim relief under S380 in respect of the earliest year possible.

**You are required** to compute Boris's income tax and Class 4 NIC liabilities for 1999/00, indicating clearly any items on which he is not taxable.    **(6 marks)**

(c)   Boris has paid pension contributions so as to obtain the maximum amount of relief for all years of assessment up to 1996/97. He paid no contributions in respect of 1997/98, when his earnings from non-pensionable employment were £9,643.

**You are required** to advise Boris as to the maximum relief he can claim in respect of the payment of personal pension contributions for the years 1998/99 to 2001/02 inclusive.    **(3 marks)**

**(Total: 25 marks)**
*(ACCA June 1991)*

---

## 6    VICTORIA AND EVELYN

(a)   Victoria held 20,000 shares in Forum Follies plc which she purchased in May 1989 for £50,000. In January 2000, Exciting Enterprises plc acquired all the share capital of Forum Follies plc. Under the terms of the take-over shareholders in Forum Follies received 3 ordinary shares and 1 preference share in Exciting Enterprises plc plus £1 cash for every 2 shares previously held in Forum Follies plc. Immediately after the take-over the ordinary shares in Exciting Enterprises are quoted at £3 each and the preference shares at £1.50 each.

**You are required** to calculate any gain assessable on Victoria (before annual exemption) for 1999/00.    **(7 marks)**

(b)     Evelyn purchased shares in Dassau plc, a quoted company, as follows:

|  | No. of shares | Cost £ |
|---|---|---|
| December 1974 | 2,000 | 3,000 |
| December 1984 | 1,000 | 2,000 |
| April 1987 1 for 2 rights issue | | £2 per share |

In November 1999 Evelyn sold 4,000 shares for £16,000.

The market value of the shares on 31 March 1982 was £1.75 each.

No election has been, or will be made, under S35(5), TCGA 1992, to have all pre-31 March 1982 acquisitions re-based to 31 March 1982.

**You are required** to calculate Evelyn's capital gain for 1999/00 (before annual exemption).

**(12 marks)**

**(Total: 19 marks)**

*(ACCA June 91)*

---

# 7     RICHARD

You have been asked to provide tax advice at today's date (which you should assume to be 1 February 2000) to the personal representatives of Richard.  Richard was aged 65 and died on 2 November 1999, leaving the following assets:

|  | Probate Value £ | Current Value £ |
|---|---|---|
| 1,000 shares in Bluechip plc (a quoted company with a share capital of 2,000,000 shares) | 22,000 | 17,000 |
| 2,500 shares in Giltedge plc (a quoted company with a share capital of 3,000,000 shares) | 15,000 | 20,000 |
| 6,000 shares in Nobody Ltd (a private investment company with a share capital of 100,000 shares) | 39,000 | 30,000 |
| Private residence | 190,000 | 230,000 |
| Holiday home | 55,000 | 40,000 |
|  | 321,000 | 337,000 |

Potential selling costs are estimated at 2% of sale price in respect of each asset.

Richard had made the following transfers prior to his death:

(1)     Annual gifts of £3,000 made out of capital to his nephew, Oscar on 6 April of each year.

(2)     A gift of £144,000 cash to a discretionary trust on 3 September 1991.  All taxes on the gift were borne by the trustees.

(3)     A gift of £147,000 cash to his son Boris on his marriage on 1 September 1996.

(4)     A gift of 10 acres of farmland to his son, Christian on 1 July 1997.  The land was valued at £150,000 and was subject to a mortgage of £55,000.  Richard had occupied the land and farmed it since January 1988.  Christian sold the land to an unconnected third party on 11 October 1999 for £120,000.  He used the proceeds to pay off the mortgage and also to buy himself a yacht.

In his will Richard left all his assets to his sons Boris and Christian. He appointed his brother Nigel as his executor. He was confident that his sons would look after his widow, Maria, who is aged 73 and owns no assets in her own right. Maria is in very poor health and is not expected to live much longer.

**You are required:**

(a)     to calculate the IHT arising as a result of Richard's death;                                          **(8 marks)**

(b)     to explain whether the IHT arising could be reduced by disposing of all or any of Richard's assets before winding up his estate. Indicate any possible disadvantage in such a course of action;

**(6 marks)**

(c)     to explain whether it would be advisable from an IHT viewpoint to alter the terms of Richard's will. Outline the conditions which must be satisfied for such an alteration to be valid for IHT purposes;

**(5 marks)**

(d)     to describe briefly Nigel's responsibilities as executor for making returns in respect of IHT on his brother's estate. State when any IHT due should be paid in order to avoid interest charges, bearing in mind the availability of instalment relief. Explain who becomes liable if Nigel fails to account for the IHT due to the Inland Revenue.                                          **(6 marks)**

**(Total: 25 marks)**

*(ACCA December 1990)*

## 8     EDITH DAY

Edith Day is a wealthy 78 year old widow. She has asked for your advice in respect of a number of gifts that she is planning to make in the near future. Her only previous gift was one of £246,000 into a discretionary trust on 15 August 1993. The proposed gifts are as follows:

(1)     A gift of a holiday cottage worth £70,000 to her grandson Michael. The cottage was bought in June 1987 for £18,000. As a condition of the gift, Edith would have the free use of the cottage for six months each year.

(2)     A gift of an antique casket worth £8,000 to her granddaughter Susan in respect of her forthcoming wedding. Edith had inherited the casket from her uncle in October 1988 when it was valued at £1,500.

(3)     A gift of 10,000 £1 ordinary shares in Daylight Ltd into a discretionary trust for the benefit of her nieces and nephews, who are all aged under 16. Daylight Ltd is an unquoted trading company with a share capital of 20,000 £1 ordinary shares. Edith currently holds 15,000 shares in the company, with the remainder being held by her children. A 25% holding is worth £9 per share, whilst 50% and 75% holdings are worth £11 and £12 per share respectively. Edith acquired her shares at par upon the company's incorporation in June 1987, and was a director for the first five years of its existence. She has not been involved with the running of the company since then.

25% of Daylight Ltd's assets are in the form of investments in supplier companies.

(4)     A gift of agricultural land and buildings with an agricultural value of £150,000 to her son John. Edith purchased the land in October 1988 for £65,000, and has always let it out to tenants. The most recent tenancy agreement comes to an end in six months time, and Edith has obtained planning permission to build residential accommodation on the land. The value of the land with planning permission is £250,000. John already owns the neighbouring land, and the value of this land will increase from £180,000 to £220,000 as a result of the gift.

Any capital gains tax arising from the above gifts will be paid for by Edith, and she will also pay any inheritance tax arising from the gift into the discretionary trust [gift (3)]. Any inheritance tax arising on the other gifts will be paid for by the respective donee.

**You are required** to advise Edith of the inheritance tax and capital gains tax implications arising from the above gifts, assuming that all of the gifts are made on 10 March 2000. Your answer should include any tax planning points that you consider relevant.

You should ignore the effect of annual exemptions both for inheritance tax and for capital gains tax.

In respect of the gift into the discretionary trust [gift (3)], you are not expected to advise on the possible future tax liabilities of the trust itself. **(Total: 25 marks)**
*(ACCA Dec 93)*

---

## 9 GEORGE ROWE

At today's date (which you should assume is 1 July 1999), George Rowe, a single man aged 42, is expected to earn £65,000 from his employment as an oil company executive for the year ended 5 April 2000 (subject to PAYE of £18,942). During the year George expects to receive net dividends of £27,000 from his shareholdings.

On 6 April 1999, George had sold quoted shares in a multinational company Gong plc, which realised a capital gain of £90,000. He also intends to transfer further shares in Gong plc, with a value of £263,000 into a trust for his brother Bob, on 5 April 2000. This transfer will realise a further capital gain of £35,000. Bob is aged 12 and lives with George who has maintained him since the death of their parents in 1994. George is unsure whether the trust for Bob should be an accumulation and maintenance trust or a discretionary trust (of which George would not be a beneficiary). George has made no previous transfers of any assets. He will pay any taxes or costs associated with setting up the trust. George is in excellent health.

George had acquired a house in Derby, together with grounds of just under half a hectare on 1 August 1981 for £280,000. The house is subject to a mortgage from a building society of £100,000, bearing a fixed rate of interest of 10% pa. There was no change in the value of the house up to 31 March 1982. Unfortunately it has recently been decided that a motorway is to be built close to the house and as a result it is currently worth only £200,000. George's history of occupation of the house is as follows:

| | |
|---|---|
| 1.8.81 - 30.6.82 | Occupied |
| 1.7.82 - 31.12.83 | Sent by employer to Saudi Arabia |
| 1.1.84 - 30.9.90 | Occupied |
| 1.10.90 - date | Working in various parts of the UK on a nine year tour of duty |

George intends to sell the house on 31 December 1999 but is unsure whether or not he should reoccupy the house between 1 October 1999 (when his UK tour of duty ends) and 31 December 1999. He will rent a flat in Brighton from 1 January 2000 at a rent of £400 per month payable in advance from a friend of his who lives in the USA.

**You are required:**

(a) to discuss the current and potential CGT and IHT implications for George of setting up (i) an accumulation and maintenance trust for Bob; (ii) a discretionary trust for Bob; **(10 marks)**

(b) to compute George's income tax payable for 1999/00; **(8 marks)**

(c) to discuss whether George should occupy the house in Derby between 1 October 1999 and 31 December 1999. Show all supporting calculations. **(7 marks)**
**(Total: 25 marks)**
*(ACCA December 1990)*

---

## 10    STEAMDRIVEN COMPUTER COMPANY LTD

The Steamdriven Computer Company Ltd has faced a declining market in recent years.  As at today's date (which you should assume is 1 November 1999) it is expected to make a net **unadjusted** trading loss of £11,750 in the six months ending on 31 March 2000.  Results for the previous three years (**before** any adjustments for tax purposes) have been as follows:

|  | Trading profits £ | Bank interest £ |
|---|---|---|
| Year ended 30 September 1997 | 10,000 | - |
| Year ended 30 September 1998 | 3,000 | - |
| Year ended 30 September 1999 | 4,000 | 400 |

The projected balance sheet at 31 March 2000 on a going concern basis is as follows:

|  | £ | £ |
|---|---|---|
| Fixed assets |  |  |
| Office (at valuation) |  | 120,000 |
| Fixed plant and machinery | 50,000 |  |
| Less:  Depreciation | (30,000) | 20,000 |
|  |  | 140,000 |
| Current assets |  |  |
| Trading stock | 34,000 |  |
| Cash | 500 |  |
|  | 34,500 |  |
| Less:  Creditors (including 1999 corporation tax) | (29,000) |  |
| Net current assets |  | 5,500 |
| Total assets |  | 145,500 |
| Financed by: |  |  |
| Share capital |  | 50,000 |
| Retained profits |  | 95,500 |
|  |  | 145,500 |

The projected profit and loss account for the 6 months to 31 March 2000, again on a going concern basis, is as follows:

|  | £ | £ |
|---|---|---|
| Sales |  | 97,000 |
| Opening stock | 37,000 |  |
| Purchases | 60,000 |  |
| Less:  Closing stock | (34,000) | (63,000) |
| Gross profit |  | 34,000 |
| Less:    Staff and administrative costs | 42,050 |  |
| Depreciation | 2,500 |  |

|                  |        |          |
|------------------|--------|----------|
| Patent royalties | 1,250  |          |
| Bank interest    | (50)   | (45,750) |

| Net loss | (11,750) |
|----------|----------|

Mr Ludd, who owns 99.9% of the company's issued share capital, proposes that the company should sell all of its assets on 31 March 2000 for cash to an unconnected third party for a total amount of £131,000, attributable as follows:

|                     | £       |
|---------------------|---------|
|                     |         |
| Goodwill            | -       |
| Office              | 100,000 |
| Plant and machinery | 2,000   |
| Trading stock       | 29,000  |
|                     | 131,000 |

Immediately after the assets are sold the company would cease trading and the liquidation of the company would commence. The company would pay all of its current liabilities and distribute the balance of cash to its shareholders shortly afterwards. Mr Ludd is unsure which of three alternative methods the company should adopt:

(1)     to distribute all of the cash *before* 6 April 2000,
(2)     to distribute all of the cash *after* 6 April 2000,
(3)     to make distributions both before and after 6 April 2000.

The company is expected to agree and receive any repayments of corporation tax, including any arising out of its trading loss, by 7 June 2000. It is estimated that these amounts will just be sufficient to cover the liquidator's fees so that no further cash will be distributed to the company's shareholders.

The following information is also available:

(1)     Patent royalties of £1,250 were payable on each of 31 March and 30 September each year.

(2)     All of the plant and machinery was acquired on 1 April 1994. The company has claimed maximum writing-down allowances (but no other allowances) in respect of this expenditure.

(3)     In computing depreciation for accounts purposes the company uses a straight-line basis and applies the same depreciation rate to all of the plant and machinery.

(4)     The company has no associated companies and has not paid dividends for several years.

(5)     In February 1992 the company had disposed of an asset acquired in May 1985, giving rise to a chargeable gain of £150. The company elected that the gain should be held over by reference to the expenditure on plant and machinery noted in (2) above. The company has made no chargeable disposal since February 1992.

(6)     The disposal of the office will give rise to a nil gain/nil loss position for CGT purposes.

(7)     Mr Ludd inherited his shares in the company in March 1987, when they had a probate value of £50,000.

(8)     Mr Ludd who is single, in good health, and aged 40, will have total income of £30,000 in 1998/99 and total income of £10,000 in 2000/01. He plans to retain all of his existing capital assets (except his shares in the company) for the foreseeable future.

(9)      You should assume that all staff and administrative expenses are fully allowable.

Assume that the rate of interest on overpaid corporation tax is 3.5%.

**You are required:**

(a)      to compute the final corporation tax liabilities of the company in respect of the periods commencing 1 October 1996 and ending 31 March 2000.                                    **(17 marks)**

(b)      to compute the total amount which should be repaid to the company by the Inland Revenue on 7 June 2000.                                                                                         **(3 marks)**

(c)      to advise Mr Ludd as to which alternative method of distibuting cash by the company is preferable.
**(5 marks)**
**(Total:  25 marks)**
*(ACCA June 90)*

---

## 11      SALLY JONES

Sally Jones has been a shareholder and the managing director of Zen Ltd since its incorporation on 1 January 1994.  Zen Ltd is a UK resident company manufacturing computer equipment.  Sally is 58 years old and has been a widow since her husband died on 12 May 1999.  Following her husband's death she has decided to retire as managing director of Zen Ltd on 31 December 1999 and plans to dispose of most of her shareholding on the same date.

Zen Ltd has a share capital of 60,000 £1 ordinary shares of which Sally holds 31,000.  The remaining shares are held by the other directors who are not related to Sally.  She would like to dispose of 20,000 of her shares but none of the other directors are in a position to purchase them.  However, Zen Ltd currently has surplus funds and is prepared to purchase 20,000 of Sally's shares at their market value of £280,000.  This will result in a chargeable gain for her, after indexation but before any reliefs, of £245,000.

Sally is paid director's remuneration of £24,000 pa, and she also receives an annual bonus based on Zen Ltd's annual results.  For the year ended 31 March 1999 the bonus was £4,200, and for year ended 31 March 2000 it is expected to be £5,700.  The bonuses are agreed by the directors prior to the relevant year end, and then paid on the following 30 April.  Zen Ltd is also to give Sally an ex gratia lump sum upon her retirement of £40,000, which she is not contractually entitled to.  This is to be paid on 31 March 2000.

Sally has no other income or outgoings apart from a pension of £950 per month that will commence upon her retirement.  She has an adopted child aged 17 who is currently studying full-time at college.

**You are required:**

(a)      to outline the conditions to be met for the purchase of Sally's shares by Zen Ltd to qualify for the special treatment applying to a company's purchase of its own shares.  Your answer should indicate whether or not these conditions are met;                                                              **(7 marks)**

(b)      Assuming that the purchase of Sally's shares qualifies for the special treatment,

(i)      to calculate her taxable income for 1999/00, and
(ii)     to calculate her capital gains tax liability for 1999/00;

Your answer should include an explanation of the treatment of Sally's annual bonuses and ex gratia payment.                                                                                           **(10 marks)**

---

(c)     What deductions will Zen Ltd be entitled to when calculating its corporation tax liability for the year ended 31 March 2000 in respect of the payments and emoluments provided to Sally.  Your answer should include a consideration of NIC.     **(8 marks)**

**(Total: 25 marks)**

---

## 12     H LTD

H Ltd owns 76% of the ordinary share capital of A Ltd and 40% of the ordinary share capital of D Ltd.  The remaining ordinary shares in A Ltd are owned by individual members of the general public.  The remaining ordinary shares in D Ltd are owned equally by P Ltd and Q Ltd, both of which are unconnected with H Ltd or with each other.  A Ltd owns 80% of the ordinary share capital of B Ltd which in turn owns 75% of the ordinary share capital of C Ltd.  H Ltd owns 5% of the ordinary shares in B Ltd and 0.1% of the ordinary shares in C Ltd.  The remaining ordinary shares in B Ltd and C Ltd are owned by individual members of the general public.  All of the companies concerned are trading companies resident in the UK.  The issued share capital of each company consists of ordinary shares only.

**You are required:**

(a)     (i)     to state, giving reasons, which set (or sets) of the above companies form a group (or groups) for capital gains purposes;

        (ii)    to describe the general tax treatment of a transfer of an asset from one group company to another where the asset was a fixed asset of the first company but forms part of the trading stock of the second company;

        (iii)   to describe the second company's right of election in these circumstances and indicate when such an election would be likely to be favourable;     **(9 marks)**

(b)     (i)     to state, giving reasons, which of the above companies can surrender trading losses to other companies, in each case identifying those other companies concerned;

        (ii)    to explain the rules regulating the amount of the loss which can be surrendered in each case;

        (iii)   Would your answer to (b) (i) have been different if firstly Q Ltd was not resident in the UK or secondly A Ltd was not resident in the UK;     **(9 marks)**

(c)     (i)     to state, giving reasons, which of the above companies can elect to pay debenture interest or charges on income to other companies without accounting for income tax;

        (ii)    to explain the benefit of such an election.     **(7 marks)**

**(Total:  25 marks)**

*(ACCA June 1991)*

---

## 13     GRUDGE LTD

(a)     Grudge Ltd is the parent company of a group which includes its three wholly owned manufacturing subsidiaries, Envy Ltd, Ire Ltd and Poison Ltd.  The shares in Grudge Ltd are owned equally by Dr Choler (the managing director of Grudge Ltd), Mr Borgia and Miss Nightshade.  Envy Ltd has made trading losses in recent years as a result of excessive staffing levels.  The group has had insufficient funds to finance the necessary redundancies in Envy Ltd which are estimated to cost £210,000.  At today's date (which you should assume is 1 April 2000) Dr Choler is considering personally purchasing Envy Ltd on 6 April 2000. The following additional information is available:

(1)     Dr Choler would acquire the shares in Envy Ltd for £200,000. Their current market value is estimated to be £250,000.

(2)     Dr Choler would subsequently subscribe £210,000 for a further issue of shares in Envy Ltd. This would provide the company with sufficient funds to finance the redundancy programme.

(3)     Dr Choler would borrow £100,000 from a UK bank to assist him in acquiring his shares in Envy Ltd. The balance of £310,000 would come from his own resources.

(4)     Dr Choler intends to finance his loan repayments and associated interest costs out of personal loans made to him by Envy Ltd.

(5)     Dr Choler would not be actively engaged in the management of Envy Ltd, although he would continue to act as managing director of Grudge Ltd at a salary of £95,000 pa. He has no other income apart from this salary.

(6)     Dr Choler wishes to know if he can obtain income tax relief for his interest costs.

(7)     Grudge Ltd had acquired the shares in Envy Ltd for £10,000 on 6 April 1974. The value of the shares on 31 March 1982 was £100,000. Grudge Ltd held no other assets at 31 March 1982.

(8)     After Envy Ltd had been acquired by Dr Choler, it would immediately implement the redundancy programme. Dr Choler wishes to know if the expenditure would be allowable for corporation tax purposes.

(9)     Envy Ltd currently has unused trading losses of £300,000. Dr Choler wishes to know if these will be available to set against future trading profits of the company.

(10)    In August 1994 Envy Ltd had transferred buildings to Ire Ltd at their then market value of £80,000. The buildings had cost Envy Ltd £60,000 in November 1989.

**You are required** to explain the potential tax implications arising on the proposed sale of Envy Ltd for:

(i)     Dr Choler;
(ii)    Envy Ltd; and
(iii)   the other companies in the Grudge Ltd group.                                    **(21 marks)**

(b)     Grudge Ltd and its subsidiaries have been registered as a group for VAT purposes. None of the group companies make exempt supplies but Envy Ltd exports 90% of its production outside the European Union, with the remaining 10% being sold to other group members.

**You are required** to describe the VAT implications for Envy Ltd of leaving the Grudge Ltd group.
**(4 marks)**
**(Total: 25 marks)**
*(ACCA December 1990)*

## 14    ERIC FASTHAND

You are the tax adviser to Eric Fasthand, a self employed guitar player who is resident, ordinarily resident and domiciled in the UK. Eric has recently accepted a contract to play guitar for the Rolling Rocks band on their forthcoming world tour. The tour will commence on 1 June 1999, and end on 30 September 2000. The first three months will be spent in the United Kingdom, where 40 concerts will be played. The remainder of the tour will be overseas, when 10 concerts will be played per month. During November 1999 and also during March 2000, the band will not play any concerts because they will be recording their new album. Eric will be paid a fee of £750 per concert, with a bonus of £20,000 at the end of the tour for satisfactory completion. He will not be involved in the recording of the new album, and will probably return to the UK during these two months. All costs of travelling and accommodation will be paid for by the band, although Eric will have to provide his own instruments and equipment. The contract states that Eric will not be allowed to undertake any other work whilst on tour, apart from during the two months the band is recording. Eric started his guitar playing on 1 June 1998 and makes up his accounts to 31 May, and makes profits of £60,000 pa. He is single, and has no other income or outgoings. The Rolling Rocks band operates via a limited company that is resident in the UK.

**You are required:**

(a)    to outline the criteria which would be used to decide as to whether Eric will be classified as employed or self-employed;                                                                   **(7 marks)**

(b)    to outline the income tax implications arising from Eric's contract with the Rolling Rocks band if he is treated as:

    (i)     self-employed; and

    (ii)    employed,

during the period of the contract.

Your answer should concentrate on the basis that Eric will be assessed to tax, and include advice as to whether or not it would be beneficial for him to remain outside the UK during the two months that the Rolling Rocks band are recording. Calculations of his tax liabilities arising from the contract should be included as appropriate.

You are not expected to discuss National Insurance contribution, VAT or pension contributions, and you should assume that the tax rates and allowances for 1999/00 apply throughout.                **(18 marks)**

**(Total:  25 marks)**

*(ACCA Dec 93)*

## 15    MAGEE INC

(a)    Magee Inc is a non-resident holding company which currently owns directly all of the issued share capital of a number of companies. It intends to form a new 100% subsidiary, Gavin Ltd, at today's date, which you should assume is 1 July 1999.

Gavin Ltd will carry out all its trading operations through a permanent establishment in Ruritania, a country which does not have a double tax treaty with the UK. Magee Inc is considering three possible structures for Gavin Ltd, as follows:

    (i)     Incorporation in the UK, with directors' meetings being held in Ruritania.

    (ii)    Incorporation in Ruritania, with directors' meetings being held in the UK.

    (iii)   Incorporation in Ruritania, with directors' meetings being held in Ruritania.

**You are required** to state the residence position of Gavin Ltd under each of the above structures, giving reasons for your conclusions in each case.                                           **(4 marks)**

(b)    Assume that Gavin Ltd will be formed as a non-resident company on 1 July 1999 but will become resident on 1 September 1999. The first set of accounts will be for the 15 months to 30 September 2000, the year end of all the other subsidiaries of Magee Inc. Accounts will be prepared on a yearly basis thereafter.

**You are required** to set out the accounting periods of Gavin Ltd, up to and including 30 September 2001, explaining the basis for your calculations.                                          **(4 marks)**

(c)    Gavin Ltd is likely to incur heavy trading losses in its first three years of operation. Magee Inc's objective is that these losses should be offset against the profits of its other UK resident subsidiaries. Once it has become resident, Gavin Ltd's annual Schedule D Case I losses are likely to be slightly less than the combined annual trading profits of those subsidiaries.

**You are required** to explain briefly how Magee Inc should reorganise its shareholdings in order to achieve its objective, and indicate whether it would incur any CGT liabilities on the reorganisation.
**(4 marks)**

(d)    Assume that Magee Inc will in fact reorganise its shareholdings so that Gavin Ltd's trading losses can be offset against the trading profits of its other UK subsidiaries. One of these subsidiaries, Casey Ltd, is due to dispose of a warehouse in six month's time (ie, December 1999).

Details are as follows:

|  | £ |
|---|---|
| Cost, June 1981 (net of grant of £10,000) | 100,000 |
| Market value, 31.3.82 | 80,000 |
| Enhancement expenditure, December 1992 | 12,000 |
| Estimated sale proceeds | 300,000 |

Incidental expenses are estimated as follows:

|  | £ |
|---|---|
| Estate agent's fees | 3,000 |
| Legal fees | 2,000 |
| Valuer's fee for valuing building at 31.3.82 | 250 |

Approximately ten months after the building is sold, Casey Ltd intends to acquire computer equipment costing £250,000 with an expected useful life of four years. The equipment will be fixed to the company's premises. The managing director of Casey Ltd understands that the gain on the sale of the building may be eligible for 'rollover relief'.

Neither Casey Ltd nor any of the other UK resident subsidiaries of Magee Inc has disposed of any capital assets since 6 April 1993.

Some other UK resident subsidiaries of Magee Inc own chargeable assets in respect of which an election for March 1982 valuations to apply without reference to original cost would be favourable. No assets owned on 31 March 1982 had previously been disposed of by any of the group companies.

**You are required:**

(i)     to calculate the capital gain arising on the sale of the office building;

(ii)    to state (giving reasons) whether Casey Ltd is entitled to any 'rollover relief' and, if so, how the relief is granted, and for what length of time;

(iii)    to explain the factors which would need to be considered before deciding whether or not the election for the March 1982 valuation to apply without reference to original cost should be made in respect of the disposal by Casey Ltd;

(iv)    to state the time limits for making the election mentioned in (iii) and by whom it must be made.    **(13 marks)**

**(Total: 25 marks)**

*(ACCA December 1991)*

---

## 16    MR GOG

Mr Gog, who was born in Ruritania in 1939, came to live and work in Scotland in May 1984. Mr Gog, whose wife has died, hopes to return to Ruritania when he is seventy. Mr Gog is in good health.

Details of Mr Gog's assets and liabilities at today's date (which you should assume is 5 April 2000), together with their current market values, are as follows:

| | £ |
|---|---|
| Deposit account with National Bank of Ruritania (held with branch in Glob, the capital of Ruritania and opened May 1997) | 60,000 |
| Current account with UK bank held in Glasgow | 23,000 |
| Private residence (located in Scotland) | 127,000 |
| 10,000 shares in Bah plc, an investment company quoted on the UK Stock Exchange with a total issued share capital of 5,000,000 shares | 150,000 |
| 3.5% War Loan Government Stock, Nominal value £80,000 | 27,000 |
| Ruritanian antique kept in private residence | 6,000 |
| Scottish farm acquired in January 1984 and occupied since that date by farming tenants. The current tenancy commenced in January 1997 and Mr Gog has the right to obtain vacant possession within two years if he so wishes | 116,000 |
| | 509,000 |
| Less: Building society mortgage loan on private residence (8% fixed rate) | (40,000) |
| | 469,000 |

Further information is available as follows:

(1)    On 1 June 1999 Mr Gog disposed of an investment property located in Ruritania. The disposal gave rise to a nil gain/nil loss position for CGT purposes.

(2)    Mr Gog had let out the property since its acquisition in July 1997 at a rent of £300 per month (gross) payable at the end of each month. The rents were subject to Ruritanian tax at a rate of 20%. Ruritania does not have a double tax treaty with the UK. Mr Gog transferred £200 of his rental income each month to Scotland, any balance remaining being lodged to his Ruritanian bank account.

(3)    Mr Gog acquired his shares in Bah plc for £20,000 in August 1991. Mr Gog has not received any dividends from Bah plc since he acquired the shares.

(4)    Mr Gog acquired the 3.5% War Loan Stock for £25,400 in January 1997;

(5)    Mr Gog acquired the antique for £5,000 in April 1997.

---

(6)     Due to the availability of previous years' losses, no taxable income has arisen from the farmland for several years. The farmland was acquired in January 1983 at a cost of £65,000.

(7)     Interest credited to the Ruritanian bank deposit account has been as follows:

|  |  |
|---|---|
| Year ended 5.4.99 | £2,000 |
| Year ended 5.4.00 | £1,500 |

These amounts are net of Ruritanian tax of 10%. No amounts of this interest were brought back into the UK.

(8)     Mr Gog's gross salary for the year ended 5 April 2000 was £31,500, which was subject to PAYE of £6,700.

(9)     Mr Gog is anxious to transfer some assets, other than his private residence, to his son Enrico. Enrico, who is 23, was born in Scotland and intends to remain there for the rest of his life. Enrico is keen to manage the farm in Scotland. Mr Gog would like to transfer assets to Enrico as quickly as possible. Mr Gog is however not prepared to make transfers which could give rise to IHT liabilities if he were to die within the next seven years. He understands that he may be able to avoid such liabilities by making transfers of 'excluded property' as well as using his 'nil rate band'. Mr Gog is also not prepared to make transfers of assets which would give rise to CGT liabilities. He intends to leave the balance of assets retained by him to a charity under his will.

(10)    Mr Gog has made no previous transfers of assets.

**You are required:**

(a)     to compute Mr Gog's income tax payable for 1999/00;                                   **(7 marks)**

(b)     to explain to Mr Gog his likely present domicile status for IHT purposes, and why this may alter in future years;                                                                                  **(4 marks)**

(c)     to advise Mr Gog as to which of his assets he should transfer on 5 April 2000. Show all supporting calculations. You should assume that Mr Gog is non-UK domiciled for IHT purposes at 5 April 2000;                                                                              **(12 marks)**

(d)     Assuming that Mr Gog follows your advice under (c) to describe the IHT consequences of his dying before 6 April 2007.                                                                        **(2 marks)**

**(Total:  25 marks)**
*(ACCA June 1991)*

---

## 17     MARTIN LENNOX

Mr Lennox, a civil servant, inherited a site consisting of a hectare of land from his mother in June 1998, when it had a probate value of £30,000. At that time he was advised that there was a prospect of land in the area being developed for residential use at some time in the future. In the same month, Mr Lennox signed a contract to acquire a further ⅖ of a hectare of land adjoining the site which he had inherited. The second site cost £26,000 plus legal fees of £2,000, and in order to pay for it Mr Lennox had to take out a loan of £15,000 on 1 August 1998. The loan carried a fixed interest rate of 8% pa and was repayable in five years time or on earlier sale of the property. No use was made of the land apart from occasional lettings to weekend campers.

In July 1999 Mr Lennox obtained planning permission to build houses on both sites, subject to improvements being made to their drainage. In December 1999 he entered into a contract with a builder to carry out the necessary improvements for a price of £15,000. The work was completed and paid for in January 2000. All the land was sold to a property developer for £125,000 on 31 March 2000, and the loan was immediately repaid.

Mr Lennox completed his return of income for the year to 5 April 2000 on the basis that the disposal of the land was a capital transaction. After making enquiries the Inspector of Taxes wrote to Mr Lennox stating that the profit was assessable under Schedule D Case I. As Mr Lennox did not amend his self-assessment accordingly, the Inspector amended the self assessment. Mr Lennox appealed against the amendment, and the case was brought before the General Commissioners, who determined the appeal in favour of the Inspector.

Mr Lennox's marginal rate of tax is 40%.

**You are required:**

(a)    to explain briefly the criteria employed by the courts to determine whether or not an isolated sale transaction constitutes an adventure in the nature of trade;                                              **(8 marks)**

(b)    on the basis of (a) above, to explain whether or not you would agree with the decision of the General Commissioners;                                                                                         **(5 marks)**

(c)    to calculate Mr Lennox's tax liability on the disposal of the land (i) assuming that it is treated as a trading transaction, and (ii) assuming that it is treated as a capital transaction. Ignore any NIC implications.                                                                                          **(6 marks)**

**(Total: 19 marks)**
*(ACCA June 90)*
*(as amended)*

---

## 18    MR RAY

You act as tax adviser to Mr Ray who is a widower aged 63 and who has been in business for thirty years retailing ladies' fashions under the name of 'Fabwear'. Leonard, his only child, is aged 23 and is anxious to take part in managing the business. Mr Ray is considering two possible proposals as to how this might be achieved. You should assume that today's date is 6 April 2000.

The first proposal would be to appoint Leonard as a salaried manager on 1 July 2000 earning £25,000 pa. If he was still alive at that time, Mr Ray would retire on 30 June 2007 and make a gift of the entire business to Leonard. The second proposal would be to make an immediate gift of the entire business to Leonard on 1 July 2000. Mr Ray would stay on as a partner sharing 50% of the profits, which would reflect the fair value of his contribution to the running of the business. He would however no longer have any interest in the assets of the business. Mr Ray would again intend to retire on 30 June 2007.

The following information is also available:

(1)    Mr Ray has been informed by his doctor that, in view of the condition of his heart, he is relatively unlikely to survive six years, and is virtually certain to die within the next nine years.

(2)    Mr Ray does not own any non-business assets, apart from his private residence which is valued at £262,000. This is not expected to increase greatly in value. Mr Ray has left all his assets in his will to Leonard.

(3)    Apart from net current assets of £58,000, the main asset of Mr Ray's business is his shop which is currently valued at £240,000. One fifth of the shop has been let out for many years to a firm of accountants at a commercial rent. It is estimated that a sale of the entire shop would give rise to a chargeable gain of £40,000. However, further appreciation beyond the rate of inflation is most

---

unlikely. The value of goodwill is currently negligible and even with the projected trend of rising profits is unlikely to exceed £30,000 in the future.

(4)     The accounts of Fabwear are made up to 30 June each year. Trading profits have been steady at £50,000 pa in recent years but would be expected to increase progressively by 10% pa (after charging Leonard's salary) if Leonard were to join the business.

(5)     The tax written-down values and market values of plant and machinery are both insignficant.

**You are required** to advise Mr Ray on the income tax, National insurance, VAT, inheritance tax and capital gains tax implications for him and for his estate of the two alternative proposals. Outline briefly the main conditions which must be met before any relevant claims for relief can be made.      **(25 marks)**
*(ACCA June 90)*

**ANSWERS TO PRACTICE QUESTIONS**

---

| 1 | **BINARY PLC** |
|---|---|

(a) **Motor cars**

Company car

The managers are all employees earning over £8,500 pa, and they will therefore be assessed under Schedule E on the benefit of the motor cars and fuel by reference to the original cost and fuel benefit tables. Because business use is insubstantial, that is not over 2,500 miles pa, the cash equivalent for the car will be based on 35% and not a lower percentage. The car charge will be based on the list price which is assumed to be equal to the cost of £19,035. The provision of a mobile telephone is a separate benefit and exempt. The benefits assessable will be:

|  | £ |
|---|---|
| Car (19,035 × 35%) | 6,662 |
| Fuel - diesel | 1,540 |
| Total benefits | 8,202 |

There are no National Insurance contribution implications for the managers in respect of the direct provision of either a motor car or a mobile telephone.

**Shares and share options**

The managers will be assessed under Schedule E on the difference between the market value of the shares issued to them, and the amount that they paid for them. Each manager will therefore be assessed on £9,000 [2,000 × (5.50 − 1.00)]. There is no possibility of the issue of shares being approved as a profit sharing scheme, and thereby avoiding the assessment, since only the managers are entitled to participate.

There will be no Schedule E charge in respect of the options given to purchase further shares, until the options are exercised. The assessment will then be based on the market value of the shares at that date, less the amount paid for the shares. Each manager would then be assessed on £34,800 {4,000 × [12.00 - (5.50 × 60%)]}. To have qualified as an approved share option scheme, and thus avoiding the Schedule E assessment, the options would have had to have been exercisable not earlier than three years after their grant, and the price paid would have had to have been not manifestly less than their market value at the date of grant. The managers are already earning in excess of the upper limit for the purposes of employees Class 1 National Insurance contribution, and so no further National Insurance contribution liability will arise.

**Bonus payments**

The bonus payments will be regarded as additional salary payments, and will be assessable as normal under Schedule E on the receipts basis. The managers are already earning in excess of the upper limit for the purposes of employees Class 1 National Insurance contribution, and so no further National Insurance contribution liability will arise.

**Free membership**

The cost of the provision of free membership to the health clubs will be assessed on the managers as a benefit under Schedule E. Following the case of **Pepper v Hart** (1992), 'cost' for this purpose is the marginal cost of providing the benefit, rather than the average cost. It should be noted that the situation here is similar to the **Pepper v Hart** case in that the budgeted number of members has been exceeded (and hence fixed costs have been fully recovered) and the managers are utilising surplus capacity. The benefit for each manager would therefore appear to be £100 (20 + 80), being the extra costs incurred by Binary plc as a result of the provision of free membership.  There are no National Insurance contribution implications for the managers in respect of the provision of free membership to the health clubs.

### Entertainment allowance

The round sum entertainment allowances will be assessed on the managers as an expense payment under Schedule E.  However, a claim under S198 ICTA 1988 will be available in respect of expenditure actually incurred on entertaining.  Although any element of the round sum payments not used in meeting business expenditure would be subject to employees Class 1 National Insurance contribution, there will again be no further liability since the maximum amount is already being paid.

*(Tutorial note:*

Expenditure on entertaining is not deductible for Schedule D Case I purposes.  However, when an individual claims under S198, expenditure must be 'wholly, exclusively and necessarily for the purpose of the duties of employment' and can include entertainment expenditure.*)*

(b)    **Motor cars**

Binary plc will be able to claim capital allowances on the cost of the cars and mobile telephones.  The allowances for the cars will be 25% on a reducing balance basis, but subject to a maximum allowance of £3,000 in respect of each car, as they cost in excess of £12,000.    First year allowances may be available at 40% on the mobile phones if the expenditure is incurred by 1 July 2000 and Binary plc is not a large company for Companies Act purposes.

The VAT element of the mobile telephones can be reclaimed, provided there is business use, as they were supplied and invoiced separately to the cars.  This amounts to £21 $\left(140 \times \frac{7}{47}\right)$ per mobile telephone, and capital allowances will therefore be based on the net figure of £119 (140 – 21).  The VAT element of the motor cars is not reclaimable, so capital allowances will be based on the full cost of £19,035, subject to the £3,000 restriction as above.

The cost of diesel will be deductible in full for corporation tax purposes, and input tax will also be reclaimable in full.  However, because fuel is being provided for private use, Binary plc will have to account for output VAT based on specific VAT fuel scales.  The annual charge will be £116.91 $\left(785 \times \frac{7}{47}\right)$ per car.  Alternatively, the output charge could be avoided by not reclaiming any input tax in respect of fuel.  The cost of telephone charges will be deductible in full for corporation tax purposes.  VAT input tax will be reclaimable in respect of business usage.

Binary plc will have to pay employers' Class 1A National Insurance contribution of £1,000.64 (8,202 × 12.2%) in respect of the car and fuel benefits provided to each manager.  This figure will be deductible for corporation tax purposes.

### Shares and share options

Binary plc will not be entitled to any deduction in respect of the issue of either the shares or the share options, since it has not incurred any expenses as a result.

Unless the shares are neither quoted nor marketable, employer's Class 1 National Insurance contributions will be payable on the issue of shares at an undervalue.  It will also be payable on the grant of the options, based on the discount on the exercise price over the current market value.  The National Insurance contributions are deductible for corporation tax purposes.

### Bonus payments

The bonus payments, and the related employers' Class 1 National Insurance contribution at the rate of 12.2%, will be deductible as normal for corporation tax purposes.  Since payment is to be made within nine months of the relevant year end, the deduction will be in the year to which the bonus relates.

**Free membership**

The additional costs of £100 incurred in providing membership to the health clubs for the managers will be deductible in full for the purposes of corporation tax. Any input VAT included in this figure will also be reclaimable in full.

**Entertainment allowance**

The round sum entertainment allowance will not be deductible for the purposes of corporation tax. Employers' Class 1 National Insurance contribution at the rate of 12.2% will be due on any element of the round sum payments not used in meeting business expenditure, although this will be deductible for corporation tax purposes. Input VAT incurred on actual entertainment will not be reclaimable.

---

## 2    VERNON

(a)    (i)    Rental income is assessed under Schedule A as if the letting were a business, referred to as a 'Schedule A business'. The rents must be assessed on an accruals basis ie, by reference to the period to which they relate, rather than the date on which they were due (or paid). The lost rent on Number 2 would be assessable in 1999/00 under these rules, but Vernon will obtain a deduction for the bad debt as an expense.

The rules for the deduction of expenses, such as maintenance, repairs and legal fees, follow the normal rules for deductions allowable in taxing a trade. The maintenance and legal fees will be allowable in full, but the repairs to Number 3 will be disallowed, being in the nature of improvements. The repairs on Number 2 will be allowable.

|  | Number 1 | | Number 2 | | Number 3 | |
|---|---|---|---|---|---|---|
| Year ended | *5.4.00* | *5.4.01* | *5.4.00* | *5.4.01* | *5.4.00* | *5.4.01* |
|  | £ | £ | £ | £ | £ | £ |
| Rent for year (W1) | 2,400 | 2,700 | 600 | 7,700 | 3,800 | 4,100 |
| Expenditure |  |  |  |  |  |  |
| Maintenance | 2,810 | 730 | 1,020 | 1,210 | 940 | 870 |
| Repairs |  |  | 1,600 |  |  |  |
| Legal fees |  |  | 200 |  |  |  |
| Bad debt |  |  | 600 |  |  |  |
|  | 2,810 | 730 | 3,420 | 1,210 | 940 | 870 |
| Net receipts | (410) | 1,970 | (2,820) | 6,490 | 2,860 | 3,230 |

(ii)

|  | *1999/00* | *2000/01* |
|---|---|---|
|  | £ | £ |
| Schedule D Case IV | | |
| £5,000 × 100/70 = | 7,143 | 7,143 |
| Schedule A (W2) | - | 11,320 |
|  | 7,143 | 18,463 |
| Less: PA | (4,335) | (4,335) |
| Taxable income | 2,808 | 14,128 |
| Tax payable | | |
| -/1,500 at 10% | - | 150 |
| 2,808/7,143 at 20% | 562 | 1,429 |
| 14,128 − 1,500 − 7,143 at 23% | | 1,261 |

| | | |
|---|---:|---:|
| Less: Tax credit on MCA | (197) | - |
| | 365 | 2,840 |
| Less: Double tax relief (W3) | (365) | (1,429) |
| Tax payable | - | 1,411 |

## WORKINGS

**(W1)**

| | Number 1 | | Number 2 | | Number 3 | |
|---|---:|---:|---:|---:|---:|---:|
| *Year ended* | *5.4.00* | *5.4.01* | *5.4.00* | *5.4.01* | *5.4.00* | *5.4.01* |
| Rent for quarter beginning | | | | | | |
| 25 March | 600 | 600 | | | 950 | 950 |
| 24 June | 600 | 700 | | | 950 | 1,050 |
| 29 September | 600 | 700 | | | 950 | 1,050 |
| 25 December | 600 | 700 | | | 950 | 1,050 |
| Rent for April 1999 | | | 600 | | | |
| Rent for May 2000 – March 2001 | | | | | | |
| 11 × £700 | | | | 7,700 | | |
| Total | 2,400 | 2,700 | 600 | 7,700 | 3,800 | 4,100 |

**(W2)** **Schedule A**

| | 1999/00 £ | 2000/01 £ |
|---|---:|---:|
| No 1 | (410) | 1,970 |
| No 2 | (2,820) | 6,490 |
| No 3 | 2,860 | 3,230 |
| | (370) | 11,690 |
| Less: Loss b/f | | (370) |
| Sch A assessment | | 11,320 |

Loss relief is given first by aggregating the profits and losses from all the three properties, so that the losses on Numbers 1 and 2 are partly relieved against the profit on Number 3. The unrelieved balance is then carried forward, and deducted from the Schedule A assessment for the next year.

**(W3)** **Double tax relief**

| | 1999/00 £ | 2000/01 £ |
|---|---:|---:|
| Taxable income including Sch D Case IV | 2,808 | 14,128 |
| A Tax thereon (see above) | 365 | 2,840 |
| Taxable income excluding Sch D Case IV | - | 6,985 |
| B Tax thereon at 10/23% | - | 1,411 |
| Tax attributable to Schedule D Case IV (A – B) = | 365 | 1,429 |

In both cases the UK tax attributable to the Case IV income is less than the Ruritanian tax of £(7,143 – 5,000) = £2,143, so that the former becomes the measure of the double tax relief available.

*(Tutorial notes:* If double tax relief is claimed, the foreign income is included in the UK tax computation inclusive of the foreign tax deducted. The tax relief is then the lower of:

(a)     the UK tax; and

(b)     the foreign tax.

To maximise the double tax relief, the foreign income is regarded as the most highly taxed slice of income. Thus in working 2, the calculation at B treats the taxable income excluding Schedule D Case IV as taxed at 10% on the first £1,500 and 23% thereafter.

The tax credit for the MCA would be given in priority to double tax relief though, of course, for 2000/01 it is no longer available.

If Vernon's wife had taxable income, and she and Vernon had elected that the MCA should be transferred by her, it would be beneficial not to claim DTR in 1999/00. Instead the net interest of £5,000 would be taxable, giving a liability of £(5,000 − 4,335) at 20% = £133. Vernon's wife would have a tax reduction from the MCA of £197, a net saving of £64.)

(b)

|  | *1998/99* | *1999/00* | *2000/01* |
|---|---|---|---|
|  | £ | £ | £ |
| Schedule D Case I (W2) | 6,575 | - | 1,936 |
| Schedule A | 4,200 | 7,000 | 7,000 |
| Total income | 10,775 | 7,000 | 8,936 |
| Less: Section 380 loss (W3) | (6,580) | - | - |
|  | 4,195 | 7,000 | 8,936 |
| Less: Personal allowances | (4,195) | (4,335) | (4,335) |
| Taxable income | Nil | 2,665 | 4,601 |

The MCA tax credit will be surrendered to the wife for 1998/99 to avoid wastage.

**WORKINGS**

**(W1)     Capital allowances**

|  | *Pool* | *Short life asset* | *Total* |
|---|---|---|---|
| y/e 28.2.99 | £ | £ | £ |
| WDV b/f | 12,750 |  |  |
| Additions |  | 750 |  |
| WDA 25%/FYA 50% | (3,188) | (375) | 3,563 |
|  | 9,562 | 375 |  |
| y/e 29.2.00 |  |  |  |
| Disposal Jan 00 |  | (700) |  |
| WDA (restricted) | (505) |  | 505 |
|  | 9,057 | BC (325) | (325) |
| y/e 28.2.01 |  |  |  |
| WDA 25% | (2,264) |  | 2,264 |
| WDV c/f | 6,793 |  |  |

(W2)    **Schedule D Case I assessment**

|  |  | £ |
|---|---|---:|
| **y/e 28.2.99** | | |
| Adjusted profit | | 10,138 |
| Less: Capital allowances | | (3,563) |
| | | 6,575 |
| **y/e 28.2.01** | | |
| Adjusted profit | | 4,200 |
| Less: Capital allowances | | (2,264) |
| | | 1,936 |

| Assessments | £ |
|---|---:|
| **1998/99** | |
| y/e 28.2.99 | 6,575 |
| **1999/00** | |
| y/e 29.2.00  Loss | Nil |
| **2000/01** | |
| y/e 28.2.01 | 1,936 |

(W3)    **Section 380 Loss Relief**

|  | £ | £ |
|---|---:|---:|
| Loss 29.2.00 | | (6,400) |
| WDA | 505 | |
| Less: Balancing charge | (325) | (180) |
| Total loss available | | (6,580) |
| 1998/99 S380 | | (6,580) |
| Balance | | Nil |

The strategy adopted has been to ensure no wastage of personal allowances, while at the same time ensuring relief is obtained as rapidly as possible. This has been achieved as follows:

The net capital allowances for y/e 29.2.00 should be restricted so that the loss off set in 1998/99 leaves sufficient income available to absorb Joe's personal allowance. Because a lower amount of capital allowances have been claimed for y/e 29.2.00 this leaves a higher written-down value in the pool as the basis for capital allowance claims in future years.

---

## 3    MARGARET

(a)    There is no statutory definition of plant. The everyday meaning of the words was interpreted by the courts in Yarmouth v France 1887 as follows:

Plant '. . . in its ordinary sense includes whatever apparatus is used by a business man for carrying on his business - not his stock in trade which he buys or makes for sale; but all goods and chattels fixed or movable, live or dead, which he keeps for permanent employment in his business.'

The place in which the business is carried on is excluded. When this test is applied to fittings in a building, whether a fitting qualifies as plant depends on the nature of the business in which it is used, and on all other particular circumstances of each case. If an item fulfils a function in the carrying on of the trade it is generally treated as plant, if an item is merely part of the setting in which the trade is carried on it will not qualify as plant. Decided cases suggest that:

(i)      Normal light fittings are likely to be considered as part of the cost of the building, whereas special lighting providing atmosphere or ambience is likely to qualify as plant.

(ii)     General plumbing will usually be treated as building expenditure, whereas heating equipment and its installation will probably qualify as plant.

(iii)    False ceilings will be treated as part of the cost of the building, but moveable partitions, or decorative window screens will probably qualify as plant.

*Note:* the writing down allowance is 4% on buildings but 25% on plant.

(b)      Expenditure on industrial buildings qualifies for a writing down allowance of 4% on the original cost of the building. No initial allowance can be claimed. If the building is second-hand, the writing down allowance available is the residue of expenditure after sale spread over the remaining life of the building. Its life is deemed to be 25 years.

Expenditure on plant qualifies for a writing down allowance of 25% of the unrelieved expenditure at the end of the accounting year (including any additions during the year). Expenditure incurred before 2 July 2000 qualifies for first year allowances of 40%.

Expenditure on the purchase of patents qualifies for writing down allowances, calculated in the same way as for plant but kept in a separate patent pool.

Expenditure on the grant or registration of a patent is an allowable expense in computing trading profits.

(c)      A short-life asset is one which is expected to have a working life of no longer than four years after the end of the period in which the expenditure was incurred. Expenditure on a short-life asset is 'de-pooled' and treated as a separate pool by itself with first year allowances of 40% or writing down allowances of 25% calculated in the normal way.

On disposal of the asset within the above time limit there will be an appropriate balancing adjustment.

If the asset has not been disposed of by the end of those four years, the written down value is transferred to the general pool and treated as normal plant.

(d)      The business starts in the tax year 1999/00 and the first accounts cover the 18 months period ended 30 June 2001.

The assessment for the first five years will be as follows:

| | |
|---|---|
| 1999/00 | 1.1.00 to 5.4.00 |
| 2000/01 | 6.4.00 - 5.4.01 |
| 2001/02 | 12 months ended 30.6.01 |
| 2002/03 | Year ended 30.6.2002 |
| 2003/04 | Year ended 30.6.2003 |

Capital allowances are given for periods of account ie, capital allowances will given for the 18 month period ended 30 June 2001, and then for the years ending 30 June 2002, 30 June 2003 and so on. Capital allowances are given by treating the allowance as a trading expense of that period. Note that for the 18 month period, any writing down allowances must be increased proportionately, so that the 25% allowance available for plant and machinery become $25\% \times {}^{18}\!/_{12}$ ie, 37.5%. However, expenditure qualifying for first year allowances receives an FYA of 40% regardless of the length of profit period.

(*Tutorial note:* the basis of assessment for businesses that start trading is as follows:

Year 1                 actual profit from commencement to 5 April

Year 2                 either:

        (a)        12 month ending with the accounting date in the year, or

        (b)        12 months from commencement date **unless** no account period ends in the year, in which case the fiscal year basis applies

Year 3                 12 months ending with the account date in the year)

(e)      The options would include:

    (i)       Not claiming full capital allowances - possibly to give an assessable DI figure which, when deducted from income, leaves an amount assessable on Margaret and Janet equal to their personal allowances. This would ensure that relief for personal allowances is not lost.

    (ii)      Claiming full capital allowances so as to produce a Schedule DI loss. Such a loss would be allocated between Margaret and Janet and each would then decide how to claim for their share. The options open to each would be:

        -         to claim the loss against any other income of the tax year or the preceding year (S380 TA 1988)

        -         to claim the loss against any income of the three years preceding the year of the loss, starting with the earliest year (S381 TA 1988).

---

## 4      LEX HUBBARD

(a)      (i)       Profit assessments

        

| Profits: | | | |
|---|---|---|---|
| Period ended 30.4.00 | £(55,000 – 9,600) | 45,400 |
| Year ended 30.4.01 | £(69,000 – 9,850) | 59,150 |
| Year ended 30.4.02 | £(52,000 – 7,387) | 44,613 |

Assessments

| | | |
|---|---|---|
| 1999/00 | (1.7.99 – 5.4.00) | |
| $\%_{10}$ × £45,400 | | 40,860 |
| | | |
| 2000/01 | (1.7.99 – 30.6.00) | |
| £45,400 + $\%_{12}$ × £59,150 | | 55,258 |
| | | |
| 2001/02 | (1.5.00 - 30.4.01) | 59,150 |
| | | |
| 2002/03 | (1.5.01 - 30.4.02) | 44,613 |

(*Note:*  overlap profits (1.7.99 - 5.4.00) and (1.5.00 - 30.6.00)
        $\%_{10}$ × £45,400 + $\%_{12}$ × £59,150 = £50,718)

    (ii)      Capital allowances

| | Pooled assets £ | Depooled assets £ | Total allowances £ |
|---|---|---|---|
| 1.7.99 - 30.4.00 | 24,000 | | |
| FYA @ 40% | (9,600) | | 9,600 |
| | 14,400 | | |
| 1.5.00 - 30.4.01 | | | |
| Acquisitions | 15,000 | 24,000 | |

|  |  |  |  |
|---|---|---|---|
| Sale proceeds (limited to cost) | (14,000) |  |  |
|  | 15,400 |  |  |
| WDA at 25% = | (3,850) | (6,000) | 9,850 |
|  | 11,550 | 18,000 |  |
| 1.5.01 - 30.4.02 |  |  |  |
| WDA at 25% = | (2,887) | (4,500) | 7,387 |
| WDVs c/f | 8,663 | 13,500 |  |

(b)   The income from number 4 cannot qualify because it will not be available for letting for at least 140 days in the year of assessment. Number 5 does not meet the condition that it should be let for at least 70 days in the year of assessment, but the letting periods of numbers 5 and 6 can be aggregated, so that each is regarded as exceeding 70 days (ie, $(60 + 90)/2 = 75$). Lettings in excess of 31 days to the same tenant cannot count towards the let period. The number of qualifying days for which number 6 was let is reduced to $90 - 35 = 55$, so that none of the rental income qualifies as income from furnished holiday lettings if number 6 is let to one family for 5 weeks.

(c)   It seems desirable from an income tax perspective that Mrs Hubbard should work for Mr Hubbard. Mr Hubbard may have difficulties in justifying a payment of wages to Mrs Hubbard in excess of £3,700 pa as being wholly and exclusively incurred for the purposes of his profession: cf Copeman v Flood.

The payment of wages of up to £3,700 to Mrs Hubbard will result in a corresponding saving of tax at Mr Hubbard's marginal rate, which will clearly be 40%. The payment will represent taxable income in Mrs Hubbard's hands and she will be subject on it to tax at 10%/23% (assuming that her personal allowances will be utilised in any event against income from the assets transferred to her by Mr Hubbard: see below).

Wages of £3,700 pa ie, £71.15 per week will attract employee's class 1 NI contributions of $£(71 - 66) = £5 \times 10\% = £0.50$ per week ie, £26 per annum. Mr Hubbard will not be liable for employer's NI contributions as the earnings threshold of £83 pw is not exceeded.

On the other hand, wages of just under £66 pw ie, £3,432 pa would be free of employee's (as well as employer's) NI contributions. The question therefore is whether Mr Hubbard should pay the maximum tax deductible wage of £3,700 pa or only £3,432 pa to Mrs Hubbard. The difference in wages of £268 (ie, £5.15 per week) would produce a net income tax saving of £268 at $(40 - 23)\% = £45.46$. However, the additional NI contribution costs would be £26. It would certainly be advantageous for Mrs Hubbard to pay Class 1 for the benefits she would then become entitled, such as retirement pension, statutory maternity pay etc.

It would also seem advisable for Mr Hubbard to make an outright gift of his cash and of the rental properties to Mrs Hubbard (subject to possibly retaining a small share in number 4 - see below). The income tax advantage would arise from the fact that Mrs Hubbard's personal allowance of £4,335 can be used to cover the income otherwise taxable at 40% in Mr Hubbard's hands. The excess of the income over £4,335 will be taxable at a rate of only 10/23% in Mrs Hubbard's hands as compared to a rate of 40% if no transfer was made. If such a gift were made, it should be noted that Mrs Hubbard is under no obligation to ever return them. If the gift were not an outright gift, the income would still be taxed as if it were Mr Hubbard's.

No capital gains tax will arise in respect of the transfer of Cyanide Park from Mr Hubbard to Mrs Hubbard, as such disposals are deemed to take place at a consideration which gives rise to a nil gain/nil loss position. In effect, Mrs Hubbard will inherit her husband's base cost and entitlement to indexation relief from his acquisition date (up to April 1998) on any future disposal of the property by her. Furthermore some or all of the gain arising on a future disposal of the property by Mrs Hubbard will be liable at a rate of 20% whereas it would all be liable at a rate of 40% if it arose in the hands of Mr Hubbard. It may be worth while for Mr Hubbard to retain a small interest in number 4 sufficient that £7,100 out of any future gain net of taper relief will be attributed to him and will therefore utilise his annual exemption. The couple must declare their proportionate share in the income (which must correspond to their share in the capital), or else the income will be split equally for tax purposes. From an IHT viewpoint the transfer of assets to Mrs Hubbard would normally ensure that her nil rate band will be fully utilised on her death. However, if Mrs Hubbard was under a legal obligation to return the assets, this would appear to give rise to a gift with reservation, so that the assets would effectively remain in Mr Hubbard's estate. It is important that the gift is outright to be effective for both IHT and income tax purposes.

As far as mortgage interest is concerned, as the loan is in joint names the allowable interest will be split 50 : 50 between the couple. It is possible to jointly elect to share the relief in any proportion they wish, but as relief is given at source and at only 10% regardless of the payer's marginal tax rate, there is no tax advantage to be gained in the Hubbard's current position. The relief is abolished from 6 April 2000 in any case.

*(Tutorial notes:*

(1)     **Capital allowances**

(i)     The basis periods for capital allowances under the Schedule D rules follow the periods of account. The allowances are then deducted from the profit to give the Schedule DI assessment (with the net profits being time apportioned in the opening years if necessary).

(ii)    Capital allowances are available as usual on second-hand equipment.

(iii)   A taxpayer may elect to have the asset 'de-pooled' and the capital allowances calculated separately. This is beneficial where he expects to dispose of an item of machinery or plant within four years from the end of the accounting period in which the expenditure was incurred. On the disposal of the asset within that period a balancing charge or allowance will arise. The effect of the election is to accelerate the capital allowances.

(2)     **Furnished holiday lettings**

In order for holiday accommodation to qualify as furnished holiday lettings for a year, the accommodation must:

-       be available for letting to the general public as holiday accommodation for at least 140 days; and

-       be actually let for at least 70 days; and

-       not normally be in the same occupation for a continuous period of more than 31 days in a period of seven months in the tax year, including the period of at least 70 days during which it is actually let.

(3)     **Mortgage interest relief**

Interest payments made through MIRAS are no longer a deduction from income, therefore no tax advantages can be gained by electing to share the interest in different proportions.*)

## 5     BORIS, STEFFI AND IVAN

(a)     (i)                                     **Assessable profits 1998/99**

|  | | Boris £ | Steffi £ | Ivan £ |
|---|---|---|---|---|
| 1.11.98-5.4.99 | | | | |
| $\frac{5}{12} \times 28,000 =$ | 11,667 | | | |
| Salary - Ivan $\frac{5}{12} \times 2,000$ | (833) | | | 833 |
| Shared 3:3:1 | 10,834 | 4,643 | 4,643 | 1,548 |
| | 11,667 | 4,643 | 4,643 | 2,381 |

### Assessable profits 1999/00

|  | | Boris £ | Steffi £ | Ivan £ |
|---|---|---|---|---|
| 1.11.98 - 31.10.99 | 28,000 | | | |
| Salary - Ivan | (2,000) | | | 2,000 |
| Shared 3:3:1 | 26,000 | 11,143 | 11,143 | 3,714 |
| | 28,000 | 11,143 | 11,143 | 5,714 |

### Overlap profits

|  | Boris £ | Steffi £ | Ivan £ |
|---|---|---|---|
| Overlap period 1.11.98 - 5.4.99 | | | |
| Overlap profits (as above) 11,667 | 4,643 | 4,643 | 2,381 |

(ii)

### Loss relief available

|  | | Boris £ | Steffi £ | Ivan £ |
|---|---|---|---|---|
| (a) 1.11.99 - 30.6.00 | | | | |
| $\frac{8}{12} \times (30,000) =$ | (20,000) | | | |
| Salary - Ivan | | | | |
| $\frac{8}{12} \times 2,000$ | (1,333) | | | 1,333 |
| Shared 3:3:1 | (21,333) | (9,143) | (9,143) | (3,047) |
| | (20,000) | (9,143) | (9,143) | (1,714) |
| (b) 1.7.00 - 31.10.00 | | | | |
| $\frac{4}{12} \times (30,000) =$ | (10,000) | | | |
| Salary - Ivan | | | | |
| $\frac{4}{12} \times 10,000$ | (3,333) | | | 3,333 |
| Shared 4:3:2 | (13,333) | (5,926) | (4,444) | (2,963) |
| | (10,000) | (5,926) | (4,444) | 370 |
| (a) + (b) | (30,000) | (15,069) | (13,587) | (1,344) |

*Note:* if one partner makes a profit, and two make a loss, the notional profit is reallocated to the loss making partners. In this instance, although Ivan has a profit for the period 1.7.00 - 31.10.00, his overall result is a loss so the adjustment is not needed.

(iii) Ivan's assessable profits, and thus his total income, for 1998/99 to 2001/02 inclusive will be as follows:

|  | 1998/99 £ | 1999/00 £ | 2000/01 £ | 2001/02 £ |
|---|---|---|---|---|
| Schedule D Case I | 2,381 | 5,714 | Nil | 40,000 |

A claim for relief under S380 can be only made for 1999/00 (as there is nil income in 2000/01). This would result in a saving of income tax of £1,344 × 10% = £134. There would be no saving of Class 4 NIC for 1999/00 as his share of profits is below the lower threshold at £7,530. A claim under S385 could alternatively be made for 2001/02, resulting in an income tax saving of £1,344 at 40% = £538

(Ivan would of course be subject to the higher rate of income tax in 2001/02). There would be no Class 4 NIC consequences in view of the low ceiling on liability (currently £26,000). Despite the delay in claiming under S385, this option is clearly preferable.

S381 loss relief (carry back in the opening years of a trade) is not at issue here, since Ivan had no income prior to commencing the partnership.

*(Tutorial note:* in this sort of question, it is essential to remember that both profits and losses are divided between the partners in the profit sharing ratio of the period of account.*)*

(b)      Boris: Income tax 1999/00

|  | £ | Non savings income £ | Savings income £ |
|---|---|---|---|
| NSB (200 – 70) | 130 | - | 130 |
| BSI 11,456 × 100/80 | 14,320 | - | 14,320 |
| National Savings Certificates - exempt | - |  |  |
| Wife's income - assessable on her | - |  |  |
| Schedule D Case I | 11,143 | 11,143 | - |
|  | 25,593 | 11,143 | 14,450 |
| Less:  S380 | (15,069) | (9,643) | (5,426) |
| Less:  Personal allowance | (4,325) | - | (4,335) |
| Taxable | 6,189 | 1,500 | 4,689 |
| Income tax at 10%/20% | 1,088 |  |  |
| Less:  tax credit on MCA 1,970 @ 10% | (197) |  |  |
| Less:  Tax suffered at source (14,320 × 20%) | (2,864) |  |  |
| Tax payable | Nil |  |  |
| *Note:* Repayment due | £1,973 |  |  |

The S380 claim will reduce Class 4 NIC profits to nil, so that there will be no liability.

(c)      Boris's net relevant earnings for 1998/99 to 2001/02 inclusive will be calculated as follows:

|  | 1998/99 £ | 1999/00 £ | 2000/01 £ | 2001/02 £ |
|---|---|---|---|---|
| Schedule D Case I | 4,643 | 11,143 | Nil | 30,000 |
| Section 380 covered by Schedule D Case I |  | (11,143) |  |  |
| Excess loss c/f (15,069 – 11,143) = |  |  |  | (3,926) |
|  | 4,643 | Nil | Nil | 26,074 |

|  | £ |
|---|---|
| Unused relief for 1997/98: £9,643 × 17.5% = | 1,687 |
| Relief available for 1998/99: £4,643 × 17.5% = | 813 |
| Relief available for 2001/02: £26,074 × 17.5% = | 4,563 |
| Total relief available for 2001/02: | 7,063 |

No relief is available for 1999/00 or 2000/01.

| 6 | VICTORIA AND EVELYN |
|---|---|

(a)     **Victoria**

The consideration due to Victoria is:

|  | £ |
|---|---|
| 30,000 ordinary shares at £3 | 90,000 |
| 10,000 preference shares at £1.50 | 15,000 |
| 10,000 × £1 cash | 10,000 |
|  | 115,000 |

Since the cash element (£10,000) exceeds 5% of £115,000 (£5,750) it cannot be deducted from Victoria's acquisition cost.

The original cost of £50,000 will be apportioned:

|  | £ |
|---|---|
| 30,000 ordinary shares in Exciting Enterprises plc $50,000 \times \dfrac{90,000}{115,000} =$ | 39,130 |
| 10,000 preference shares in Exciting Enterprises plc $50,000 \times \dfrac{15,000}{115,000} =$ | 6,522 |
| Cash $50,000 \times \dfrac{10,000}{115,000} =$ | 4,348 |
|  | 50,000 |

Calculation of gain:

|  | £ |
|---|---|
| Cash element | 10,000 |
| Attributable cost | (4,348) |
| Unindexed gain | 5,652 |
| Indexation allowance $4,348 \times \dfrac{162.6 - 115.0}{115.0}$ | (1,800) |
| Indexed gain | 3,852 |

(b)     **Evelyn**

(i)     FA 1985 pool

|  | Number of shares | Unindexed cost £ | Indexed cost £ |
|---|---|---|---|
| December 1984 | 1,000 | 2,000 | 2,000 |
| Indexation allowance: (to April 1985) $\dfrac{94.78 - 90.87}{90.87} = .043$ |  |  | 86 |
|  | 1,000 | 2,000 | 2,086 |
| Indexed rise: (to April 1987) $\dfrac{101.8 - 94.78}{94.78} \times 2,086$ |  |  | 155 |
|  | 1,000 | 2,000 | 2,241 |

| | | | |
|---|---|---|---|
| April 1987 (1 for 2 rights) | 500 | 1,000 | 1,000 |
| | 1,500 | 3,000 | 3,241 |

Indexed rise: (to April 1998)

$$\frac{162.6 - 101.8}{101.8} \times 3,241 \qquad\qquad 1,936$$

| | | | |
|---|---|---|---|
| | 1,500 | 3,000 | 5,177 |

Calculation of gain:

| | £ |
|---|---|
| Sale proceeds $16,000 \times \dfrac{1,500}{4,000}$ | 6,000 |
| Less: Cost | (3,000) |
| Less: Indexation allowance (5,177 − 3,000) | (2,177) |
| Gain | 823 |

(ii)    1982 holding - Calculation of pool

| | Number of shares | Cost £ |
|---|---|---|
| December 1974 | 2,000 | 3,000 |
| April 1987 (1 for 2 rights) | 1,000 | 2,000 |
| | 3,000 | 5,000 |

| Calculation of gain | | Cost £ | 31.3.82 value £ |
|---|---|---|---|
| $16,000 \times \dfrac{2,500}{4,000}$ | | 10,000 | 10,000 |
| Cost $\dfrac{2,500}{3,000} \times 5,000$ | | (4,167) | |

| | | | |
|---|---|---|---|
| 31.3.82 Market value 2,000 at £1.75 | 3,500 | | |
| Rights issue 1,000 at £2 | 2,000 | | |
| | 5,500 | | |
| $5,500 \times \dfrac{2,500}{3,000}$ | | | (4,583) |

| | | | |
|---|---|---|---|
| Unindexed gain | | 5,833 | 5,417 |

Indexation allowance:

Original shares (March 1982 to April 1998)

$$\frac{162.6 - 79.44}{79.44} = (1.047)$$

$$3,500 \times \frac{2,500}{3,000} = 2,917 \times 1.047 \qquad\qquad (3,054) \qquad (3,054)$$

Rights shares (April 1987 to April 1998)

$$\frac{162.6 - 101.8}{101.8} = (0.597)$$

$$2,000 \times \frac{2,500}{3,000} = 1,666 \times 0.597 \qquad\qquad (995) \qquad (995)$$

| | | | |
|---|---|---|---|
| Gain | | 1,784 | 1,368 |

Lower gain is £1,368

| Summary | | £ |
|---|---|---|
| (i) | Gain | 823 |
| (ii) | Gain | 1,368 |
| | | ———— |
| Gain for year | | 2,191 |
| | | ———— |

*(Tutorial notes:*

(1)     In a take-over situation, the following rules apply:

  (i)     Determine the market value of the take-over consideration.

  (ii)    The cost of the original holding is allocated to the different elements of the take-over consideration pro rata to the market values of those elements.

  (iii)   At the time of the take-over the only gain that arises is in respect of cash consideration.

(2)     A disposal of shares after 5 April 1998 is matched with previous acquisitions as follows:

  (i)     acquisitions in the following 30 days
  (ii)    acquisitions since 5 April 1998 (LIFO basis)
  (iii)   the 1985 pool
  (iv)    the frozen 1982 pool

(3)     Rights issues

  (i)     For matching purposes, rights shares are treated as acquired on the same date as the shares on which they are offered as rights.

  (ii)    For indexation purposes, the IA is based on when the consideration is actually paid for the rights shares.

(4)     Taper relief

  A quoted company is unlikely to be a 'qualifying company' for individual shareholders and therefore the non-business asset rate of taper relief can be assumed to apply–ie, 100% of gain chargeable.*)

---

## 7     RICHARD

(a)     The gift on 1 September 1996 now becomes a chargeable transfer, as follows:

| | £ |
|---|---|
| Transfer of value | 147,000 |
| Less: Marriage exemption | (5,000) |
| | ———— |
| Chargeable transfer | 142,000 |
| | ———— |

For the purposes of calculating the tax applicable to this transfer, the chargeable transfer on 3 September 1991 (being made within the previous seven years) must also be taken into account ie,

| | £ | £ |
|---|---|---|
| Chargeable (as above) | | 142,000 |
| Less: Nil rate band | 231,000 | |
| Less: Previous CLT | (144,000) | (87,000) |
| | ———— | ———— |
| | | 55,000 |
| | | ———— |

---

|  |  |
|---|---:|
| IHT at 40% | 22,000 |
| Less: Taper relief £22,000 × 20% | 4,400 |
| | ———— |
| IHT payable | 17,600 |
| | ———— |

The gift on 1 July 1997 also becomes a chargeable transfer as follows:

|  | £ |
|---|---:|
| Sale price (lower than transfer value) | 120,000 |
| Less: Mortgage | (55,000) |
| | ———— |
| | 65,000 |
| | ———— |
| IHT at 40% | 26,000 |
| | ———— |

*(Note:* agricultural property relief is not available since Christian disposed of the property prior to Richard's death.*)*

Richard's estate is liable to IHT of £321,000 × 40% = £128,400.

*(Note:* The £231,000 nil band has been fully used by the £142,000 and £95,000 gross gifts in the previous 7 years. The reduction in the land value only affects the calculation of IHT on that particular transfer.)

(b)     (i)     If the executors sell the shares in Bluechip plc within 12 months of Richard's death then the selling price (before deducting the selling costs) can be substituted for the probate value. This would currently result in an IHT saving of £(22,000 – 17,000) = £5,000 × 40% = £2,000. If the executors were to sell any of the shares in Giltedge plc within the same period then any gain arising on that sale would have to be deducted from the loss on the sale of the Bluechip shares. No relief would be available on a disposal of the shares in Nobody Ltd as this relief is restricted to quoted shares and securities.

     (ii)     If the executors disposed of Richard's holiday home within four years of the date of Richard's death, probate value could again be reduced by the loss on disposal, before deducting selling costs. This would currently generate an IHT saving of £(55,000 – 40,000) = £15,000 × 40% = £6,000. Once again, if the executors were to sell Richard's private residence within three years of the date of death any gain arising on that sale would have to be deducted from the loss on the holiday home. (Only losses, not gains, on sales of land in the fourth year following death are taken into account.)

The saving in IHT must be weighed against the possible commercial inadvisability of selling assets whose price may be temporarily depressed. Further, the CGT losses incurred by the executors (ie, the difference between probate value and net sale proceeds) will probably go to waste, whereas if the assets were passed directly on to the beneficiaries they could realise the capital losses in their own right, possibly saving CGT at a rate of up to 40%.

(c)     (i)     It would seem advisable for Boris and Christian to agree to vary Richard's will so that £231,000 of Richard's estate passes to Maria. This will effectively enable her to use her exempt threshold which would otherwise be wasted on her subsequent death.

         The IHT on Richard's taxable estate will be reduced by £231,000 × 40% = £92,400 as transfers between spouses are exempt. On the basis that Maria leaves the assets thus redirected to Boris and Christian, no tax will be payable on her death as her death transfer will be covered by her exempt threshold.

     (ii)     The main conditions for the variation to be effective for IHT purposes are as follows:

         (a)     The variation must be executed within two years of death.

         (b)     The variation must be signed by those beneficiaries who are surrendering benefits under the will.

(c)    A written election that the variation will apply for IHT purposes must be submitted to the Inland Revenue within six months of its execution.

(d)    No consideration must be received in respect of the variation by any of the beneficiaries concerned (other than a variation in respect of the same will).

(d)    Nigel is responsible for delivering an account to the Inland Revenue within 12 months of the end of the month of death ie, by 30 November 2000. The account must detail all the property comprised in Richard's estate at the date of death. Probate will not be granted until the account has been delivered and all IHT due (other than that eligible for instalment relief) has been paid. Interest will run on IHT paid after the end of the sixth month following the end of the month of death (ie, 31 May 2000). While instalment relief may be claimed on land and certain holdings in unquoted companies, interest still runs on unpaid IHT in the case of land not used in a business and shares in investment companies.

If Nigel fails to pay the IHT due, then the following persons may be assessed:

(i)    Beneficiaries under the will to the extent that they receive assets under the will.

(ii)    Purchasers of land where the Inland Revenue have registered a charge against the land for the IHT due, up to the amount of the charge.

(iii)    Executors *de son tort* ie, persons who meddle in the administration of the estate with the result that they are deemed to be executors.

*(Tutorial notes:*

(1)    Gift of farmland to Christian.

Christian may claim relief for the fall in value of the lifetime transfer, so that the IHT payable by him on Richard's death is computed by reference to the lower value of £120,000.

This relief operates where property has been transferred in the 7 years before the transferor's death and either

(i)    the property has been sold by the transferee before the transferor's death and the sale proceeds were less than the value at the time of the original transfer. It must be a bona fide sale to an unconnected person; or

(ii)    the open market value is less on the transferor's death than it was at the time of the transfer, if the transferee or his spouse still own the property.

(2)    There is no business property relief on the shares in Nobody Ltd, as the company is an investment company.*)

---

## 8    EDITH DAY

**Inheritance tax implications**

Edith's previous chargeable lifetime transfer of £246,000 on 15 August 1993 is within seven years of 10 March 2000. This means that none of her nil rate band of £231,000 is available in respect of the gifts made on 10 March 2000. This will be relevant in respect of both chargeable lifetime transfers, and potentially exempt transfers (PETs) that become chargeable as a result of Edith's death within seven years. As a general planning point, consideration should be given to postponing gifts (1), (3) and (4) until after 15 August 2000 in order to benefit from the nil rate band (gift (2) is too small to worry about, and is, in any case, in respect of marriage).

(1)    Where an individual makes a gift of property but reserves a benefit for his or her self, it will be a gift with reservation. The aim of this legislation is to prevent a person 'freezing' the value of an asset by making a gift, yet still enjoying the use of the asset. Short holiday visits to the cottage would not be caught by the provisions, but six months free use is clearly in excess of this. The gift of the cottage by Edith will be a PET for £70,000 as normal on 10 March 2000, but she will still be treated as beneficially entitled to the cottage. It

would then be included in her estate upon her death, at its value at that date. Since this could give rise to a double charge, being both a PET and part of Edith's estate, there is a relief that effectively only includes the higher IHT charge under each alternative. Edith could avoid these provisions by paying full consideration for the use of the cottage. If the value of the cottage is expected to materially increase before her death, it would be beneficial for her to do so.

(2)     The gift of the casket is in consideration of marriage, and will therefore qualify for an exemption of £2,500. The balance of the gift, £5,500 (8,000 – 2,500), will be a PET made on 10 March 2000.

(3)     The gift of 10,000 shares in Daylight Ltd will be a chargeable lifetime transfer on 10 March 2000 as follows:

|  | £ |
| --- | --- |
| Value of estate before the gift: 15,000 shares valued at £12 each | 180,000 |
| Value of estate after the gift: 5,000 shares valued at £9 each | 45,000 |
| Diminution in value | 135,000 |
| Business property relief - 100% × 75% × £135,000 | 101,250 |
| (No BPR on excepted assets) | |
|  | 33,750 |

Since Edith is to pay the IHT liability, the gift must be grossed up. The value of the transfer is therefore £42,188 ($33,750 \times \frac{100}{80}$). IHT of £8,438 (42,188 × 20%) will be due by 30 September 2000. Business property relief will only be available in respect of any additional IHT liability arising from Edith's death within seven years if the shares are still owned by the trust at that date, and are still relevant business property.

Since all of Edith's nieces and nephews are under the age of 25, it would probably be beneficial to instead set the trust up as an accumulation and maintenance trust. The gift would then be a PET.

(4)     The gift of agricultural land will be a PET for £250,000 on 10 March 2000. The increase in the value of John's property is irrelevant. If the PET becomes chargeable as a result of Edith dying within seven years, agricultural property relief may be available since she has owned the land for seven years, and it has been occupied for the purpose of agriculture. Relief will be based on the agricultural value of £150,000, and will be at the rate of 100% since Edith would appear to be entitled to vacant possession within 12 months of the date of the gift. However, relief will only be available if John still owns the land, and the land is still agricultural property, at the date of Edith's death. Since Edith has not run the farm as a business, business property relief would not appear to be available in respect of the value of the transfer not covered by agricultural property relief.

**Capital gains tax implications**

(1)     The time of disposal in respect of gifts for capital gains tax purposes is when the ownership of the asset passes to the donee. The reservation of benefit is therefore not relevant, and the gift of the holiday cottage will be a disposal as at 10 March 2000. The chargeable gain will be:

|  | £ |
| --- | --- |
| Deemed consideration | 70,000 |
| Cost | 18,000 |
|  | 52,000 |
| Indexation $18,000 \times \frac{162.6-101.9}{101.9}$ (0.596) | 10,728 |
| Chargeable gain | 41,272 |

---

(2)  The gift of the antique casket will be a disposal of a non-wasting chattel as at 10 March 2000, and will be subject to marginal relief as follows:

|  | £ |
|---|---|
| Deemed consideration | 8,000 |
| Cost | 1,500 |
|  | 6,500 |
| Indexation $1,500 \times \dfrac{162.6 - 109.5}{109.5}$ (0.485) | (727) |
| Chargeable gain | 5,773 |
| Limited to: $(8,000 - 6,000) \times \frac{5}{3}$ | 3,333 |

(3)  The gift of shares in Daylight Ltd will be valued at £110,000 (10,000 × 11) for the purpose of capital gains tax, being based upon the value of the 50% holding actually given away. Retirement relief will not be available, as Edith has not been a director or involved in running the company since 1992. However, the transfer will qualify for gift relief since there is an immediate charge to inheritance tax. Since the transfer is to a trust, Edith alone can elect for holdover relief to apply. The gain held over will be:

|  | £ |
|---|---|
| Deemed consideration | 110,000 |
| Cost | 10,000 |
|  | 100,000 |
| Indexation $10,000 \times \dfrac{162.6 - 101.9}{101.9}$ | 5,957 |
| Gain held over | 94,043 |

The base cost of the discretionary trust's shares will be £15,957 (110,000 – 94,043). Taper relief which would otherwise be based on ownership up to 10 March 2000 will be entirely wasted.

If the gift were to an accumulation and maintenance settlement rather than to a discretionary trust, gift relief would still be available as the shares are unquoted. There would, however, be a restriction in the amount of relief available relating to the investments. The proportion that could be held over is given by the fraction $\dfrac{\text{Chargeable business assets}}{\text{Chargeable assets}}$. The proportion remaining chargeable would be tapered to 85%.

(4)  The gift of agricultural land to John will be valued at its open market value of £250,000. Since Edith does not appear to have been running a business in respect of the land retirement relief will not be available. The farm land is eligible for agricultural property relief, and so the transfer will qualify for gift relief. The gain held over will be:

|  | £ |
|---|---|
| Deemed consideration | 250,000 |
| Cost | 65,000 |
|  | 185,000 |
| Indexation $65,000 \times \dfrac{162.6 - 109.5}{109.5}$ (0.485) | 31,525 |
| Gain held over | 153,475 |

The base cost of John's land will be £96,525 (250,000 – 153,475).

---

| 9 | GEORGE ROWE |
|---|---|

(a)     (i)     **Accumulation and maintenance trust**

For IHT purposes, the transfer of £263,000 will be a potentially exempt transfer (PET). Assuming that George survives for seven years following the transfer (which seems likely as he is relatively young and in good health), then no IHT liability will arise. Further, the transfer will be disregarded when calculating IHT on any subsequent transfers or on George's ultimate death. If George does die within the seven year period, IHT will be payable as follows:

|  | £ |
|---|---|
| Transfer | 263,000 |
| Less:   Annual exemption 1999/00 | (3,000) |
|         Annual exemption 1998/99 | (3,000) |
| Net transfer | 257,000 |
|  |  |
| IHT£231,000 × 0% | - |
|       £26,000 × 40% | 10,400 |
| £257,000 | 10,400 |

The tax calculation above will be reduced if the nil band has been increased by the date of death. A taper relief also applies where death occurs within three to seven years following the transfer, rising from 20% of the tax (after three years) to 80% (after six years).

Full liability to CGT will arise on the gain of £35,000 at George's marginal income tax rate of 40% ie, £14,000. This is because the transfer is neither chargeable to IHT when made (it is a PET) nor referable to a business asset, and is thus ineligible for holdover relief.

(ii)     **Discretionary trust**

For IHT purposes this is a chargeable transfer, which would be grossed up at the lifetime rate of 20% to reflect the fact that George is bearing the tax, as follows:

|  | £ |
|---|---|
| Net transfer (see (ii) above): | 257,000 |
| Less:  Nil rate band | (231,000) |
|  | 26,000 |
|  |  |
| IHT payable 31.10.00    26,000 × $\frac{20}{80}$ | 6,500 |
| Gross transfer 257,000 + 6,500 | £263,500 |

On George's death within seven years, the IHT on the gross transfer of £263,500 will be recalculated using the rates applicable at the date of death. The death tax is tapered for death occurring between three and seven years after the gift and credit is given for the life tax of £6,500 already paid Currently, a death rate of 40% applies. No refund of any part of the IHT already paid can be made, however.

Because the transfer is chargeable to IHT, George can elect that the gain arising can be 'held over' ie, deducted from the trustees' base cost rather than assessed on him.

(b)     **George's income tax 1999/00**

|  | £ | £ |
|---|---|---|
| Schedule E |  | 65,000 |
| Schedule F |  |  |
| Net | 27,000 |  |
| Add tax credit 27,000 × 10/90 | 3,000 |  |
|  |  | 30,000 |
| Total income |  | 95,000 |
| Statutory total income |  |  |
| Less:    PA |  | (4,335) |
| Taxable income |  | 90,665 |

| Tax: | 1,500 × 10% | 150 |
|---|---|---|
|  | 26,500 × 23% | 6,095 |
|  | 32,665 × 40% | 13,066 |
|  | 30,000 × 32½% | 9,750 |
|  | 90,665 | 29,061 |

| Less: | Tax credit on ACA (1,970 × 10%) | (197) |
|---|---|---|
|  | Tax credits on dividends | (3,000) |
|  | PAYE | (18,942) |
| Tax payable |  | 6,922 |

George will also be liable to deduct and account for income tax at 23% from payments of rent to his non-resident landlord (ie, £400 × 4 × 23% = £368). The tax must be paid over to the Revenue quarterly. Such payments are not deductible as a charge against total income.

(c)     **Occupation of house in Derby**

If George does not occupy the house before selling it he will incur a capital loss as follows:

|  | £ |
|---|---|
| Sale proceeds | 200,000 |
| Less: Cost | (280,000) |
| Unindexed loss | (80,000) |
| Less: Exempt proportion 138/213 (see workings below) = | 51,831 |
| Allowable loss | (28,169) |

*(Note:* George could not avail himself of extra statutory concession D4, as his duties have not prevented him from reoccupying his residence. Even if he could, he would not wish to do so for reasons discussed below.)

If George occupies the house before selling it, then he will be deemed to have occupied the house for the period between 1 October 1990 and 31 December 1996. This is because he will have been required to live elsewhere in the UK for work reasons over a period of four years coupled with periods of up to three years for any motive and those periods will have been preceded and followed by a period of actual occupation.

Accordingly the disposal of his residence will be entirely exempt and he will lose the benefit of the loss of £28,169. It follows that George should not reoccupy the house, in order to preserve his loss of £28,169 which can then be offset against his gain of £90,000.

**WORKING**

| | | (Deemed) Occupation: Months | Absence: Months | Total |
|---|---|---|---|---|
| 1.4.82 - 30.6.82 | Occupied | 3 | - | |
| 1.7.82 - 31.12.83 | Deemed occupied (overseas duties) | 18 | | |
| 1.1.84 - 30.9.90 | Occupied | 81 | - | |
| 1.10.90 - 31.12.96 | Absent | - | 75 | |
| 1.1.97 - 31.12.99 | Last three years | 36 | - | |
| | | 138 | 75 | 213 |

---

## 10    STEAMDRIVEN COMPUTER COMPANY LTD

(a)    Computation of chargeable profits:

| AP ended | 30.9.97 £ | 30.9.98 £ | 30.9.99 £ | 31.3.00 £ |
|---|---|---|---|---|
| Per accounts | 10,000 | 3,000 | 4,000 | |
| Add:    Depreciation | 5,000 | 5,000 | 5,000 | |
| Patent royalties | 2,500 | 2,500 | 2,500 | |
| | 17,500 | 10,500 | 11,500 | |
| Less:  Capital allowances (W2) | (5,274) | (3,955) | (2,966) | |
| Schedule D Case I | 12,226 | 6,545 | 8,534 | Nil |
| Chargeable gain | - | - | - | 150 |
| Schedule D Case III | - | - | 400 | 50 |
| | 12,226 | 6,545 | 8,934 | 200 |
| Less:    Section 393A loss relief | (9,726) | (4,045) | (6,434) | (200) |
| | 2,500 | 2,500 | 2,500 | - |
| Less:    Charges | (2,500) | (2,500) | (2,500) | (1,250) |
| Chargeable profits | - | - | - | - |

*Note:* S393A relief in earlier years is restricted to ensure that sufficient total profits remain to cover charges.

**WORKINGS**

(W1)    Adjusted trading loss:  AP to 31.3.00.

| | £ | £ | £ |
|---|---|---|---|
| Net loss per accounts | | | (11,750) |
| Add:    Depreciation | | | 2,500 |
| Patent royalties | | | 1,250 |
| | | | (8,000) |
| Less:  Loss on stock | | 5,000 | |
| Bank interest receivable | | 50 | |
| Capital allowances | | | |
| WDV 30.9.99 (W2) = | 8,899 | | |
| Less:  Proceeds | (2,000) | | |
| Balancing allowance | | 6,899 | (11,949) |

---

|  |  |
|---|---:|
| Adjusted loss | (19,949) |
| Add unrelieved trade charge | (1,250) |
|  | 21,199 |

(W2)   Capital allowances:

|  | £ |
|---|---:|
| WDV 30.9.96 50,000 × (0.75)$^3$ = | 21,094 |
| WDA 30.9.97 | (5,274) |
|  | 15,820 |
| WDA 30.9.98 | (3,955) |
|  | 11,865 |
| WDA 30.9.99 | (2,966) |
| WDV 30.9.99 | 8,899 |

(W3)   Loss relief utilisation:

|  | £ |
|---|---:|
| Loss - 6 months to 31.3.00 (W1) | (21,199) |
| Less:  Section 393A relief - AP 31.3.00 | 200 |
|  | (20,999) |
| Less:  S393A - AP 30.9.99 | 6,434 |
| Less:  S393A - AP 30.9.98 | 4,045 |
| Less:  S393A - AP 30.9.97 | 9,726 |
| Unused balance | £794 |

(W4)   Chargeable gains:

The 'held over' gain is brought back into charge following the sale of the plant and machinery.

(b)   Repayments for corporation tax will be due to the company as follows:

|  | Loss relief £ |  | SCR % |  | Repayment £ |
|---|---:|:--:|---:|:--:|---:|
| AP ended 30.9.99 | 6,434 | at | 20.5 | = | 1,319 |
| AP ended 30.9.98 | 4,045 | at | 21 | = | 849 |
| AP ended 30.9.97 | 9,726 | at | 22.5 | = | 2,188 |
|  |  |  |  |  | 4,356 |

(c)   Total cash to be distributed by the company is as follows:

|  | £ | £ |
|---|---:|---:|
| Per balance sheet |  | 145,500 |
| Less:   Loss on stock | 5,000 |  |
| Loss on office | 20,000 |  |
| Loss on plant | 18,000 | (43,000) |
| Proceeds = |  | 102,500 |
| Cost | 50,000 |  |
| Indexation $50,000 \times \dfrac{162.6 - 100.6}{100.6}$ | 30,815 | (80,815) |
| Gain |  | 21,685 |

Mr Ludd should ensure that his annual exemption of £7,100 for 1999/00 as grossed up to £8,353 to take account of 85% taper relief, is not wasted. Thus the company should distribute:

$$\frac{8,353}{21,685} \times £102,500 = £39,483$$

on or before 5 April 2000. The balance should be distributed on or after 6 April 2000 for the following reasons:

(i)     This makes use of the 2000/01 annual exemption.

(ii)    Gains on business assets after 5 April 2000 (on assets held on 17.3.98) are tapered to 77.5%.

(iii)   The balance of Mr Ludd's basic rate income tax band for 2000/01 can be used (at 20%).

(iv)    Any CGT arising will be due a year later.

***(Tutorial notes:***

(1)     All the plant and machinery was acquired on 1.4.94. In order to arrive at the written down value at 30.9.99 in working 2 note the short cut method of using $£50,000 \times (0.75)^6$ rather than calculating the capital allowances for each of the six years involved could have been used.

(3)     The rules for loss relief under S393A are modified for losses arising in the 12 months before a company ceases trading. Any unrelieved trade charges of that period can be added to a loss, or indeed can convert a profit into a loss (given that such charges could not be carried forward under S393(9) ICTA 1988) - see workings 1 and 3 and the loss can be carried back 36 months, not just 12 months.*)

# 11     SALLY JONES

(a)     The conditions to be met for the purchase of a company's own shares to qualify for the special treatment are as follows:

(i)     The company buying its own shares must be an unquoted company, which Zen Ltd is.

(ii)    The company must be a trading company, which Zen Ltd is.

(iii)   The vendor of the shares must be resident and ordinarily resident in the UK in the year of assessment that the purchase takes place. Sally would appear to be UK resident.

(iv)    The vendor must have held the shares for the five years prior to the purchase, which Sally has.

(v)     The vendor's shareholding must be substantially reduced or eliminated by the purchase. This condition is considered as being met if the shareholding is reduced by at least 25%. Sally has a 51.67% holding at present, and will hold 27.5% (11,000 of the remaining 40,000 shares) after the purchase. Her holding will therefore be reduced by 46.78% ((51.67 − 27.5)/51.67) and so the condition is met.

(vi)    The vendor must not immediately after the purchase be 'connected' with the company. Connection is considered as controlling more than 30% of the company's voting power or issued share capital. After the purchase Sally only has a 27.5% shareholding so the condition is met.

(vii)   The final condition that must be met is that the purchase of the shares must be wholly or mainly for the benefit of the trade carried on by the company, and not to benefit the vendor. The Inland Revenue has indicated four circumstances which satisfy this test, of which the retirement of a proprietor of a company to make way for new management is one. However, the Inland Revenue require the vending shareholder to dispose of his or her entire shareholding, apart from a minimal holding kept for sentimental reasons. Since Sally is only 'substantially reducing' her shareholding, this test is not met unless Zen Ltd is to purchase her remaining shareholding at a later date.

Zen Ltd may apply in writing to the Inland Revenue for clearance as to whether or not the proposed purchase meets the above conditions.

(b)    (i)    Taxable income 1999/00

|  | £ |
|---|---|
| Schedule E |  |
| Director's remuneration (nine months) | 18,000 |
| Bonus *(Note 1)* | 5,700 |
| Ex gratia payment *(Note 2)* | 40,000 |
| Pension | 2,850 |
|  | 66,550 |
| Less:   PA | (4,335) |
| Taxable income | 62,215 |

*Notes:*

(1)    Earnings are taxed in the year of receipt.

The time of receipt for directors' earnings is the earliest of:

(a)    the earlier of

(i)    the time payment is made;
(ii)    the time entitlement to payment arises;

(b)    when the amount is credited in the company's accounting records;

(c)    the end of the company's period of account (if the amount has been determined by then);

(d)    when the amount is determined (if this is after the end of the company's period of account).

Sally's annual bonus for the year ended 31 March 1999 will be assessed in 1998/99. As the bonus was determined by 31 March 1999, Zen Ltd's year end, the time of receipt for the bonus is taken as 31 March 1999.

Sally's bonus for the year ended 31 March 2000 will be assessed in 1999/00 as this is the final year of assessment that she was a director of Zen Ltd.

(2)    Sally's ex-gratia payment paid by Zen Ltd on her retirement is assessable in full under Schedule E in 1999/00. Termination payments are either exempt, partially exempt or entirely chargeable.

Payments on termination for compensation for loss of office are partially exempt; the first £30,000 is free of income tax but any excess is taxable. The Inland Revenue will take the view that this is not a compensation payment, but a payment made on retirement. They consider such payments to be lump sum payments under unapproved pension schemes, and so taxable in full.

Provided that Sally is not already a member of an approved pension scheme and the payment is within the statutory limits on lump sum payments from approved schemes (3/80 of final salary for each year of service) it may be possible to obtain approval for such a deemed pension scheme, so that the whole payment in exempt. Unfortunately, the limit for Sally is $3/80 \times 24,000 \times 6 = £5,400$ and so the ex gratia payment is too large to qualify and will be taxable in full.

(3)  Sally is also entitled to WBA and APA but these are given as a tax credit against tax liability and not as a deduction in calculating taxable income

(ii)  Capital gains tax liability 1999/00

|  | £ | £ |
|---|---|---|
| Capital gain | | 245,000 |
| Retirement relief  200,000 × 60% | 120,000 | |
| (245,000 − 120,000) × 50% | 62,500 | |
| | | 182,500 |
| Chargeable gain | | 62,500 |
| Tapered to 85% | | 53,125 |
| Annual exemption | | 7,100 |
| | | 46,025 |
| Capital gains tax at 40% | | 18,410 |

(c)  Zen Ltd will be entitled to the following deductions for corporation tax purposes in respect of the year ended 31 March 2000.

(i)  Directors remuneration of £18,000 plus employers' class 1 NIC of £2,196 (18,000 at 12.2%).

(ii)  Bonus payment of £5,700 plus employers class 1 NIC of £695 (5,700 at 12.2%).

(iii)  It is debatable whether the ex gratia payment will be deductible. This is because the payment may not be considered to be wholly and exclusively for the purpose of Zen Ltd's trade as a result of Sally's voluntary retirement. Should the payment be allowed (or part thereof) it will be deductible in the current year. NIC is only due on ex gratia payments where there is contractual entitlement. Due to Sally's controlling shareholding this may also be a matter of debate.

No deduction is available to Zen Ltd in respect of the purchase of its own shares.

## 12    H LTD

(a)  (i)  A capital gains group broadly consists of a principal company, its 75% subsidiaries (the minimum required 75% relationship being based primarily on ordinary share capital, as defined) and also the 75% subsidiaries of those subsidiaries and so on, but excluding a company in which the principal company has an interest in its ordinary share capital (direct or indirect) of 50% or less.

Thus H Ltd (the principal company), A Ltd (H's 75% subsidiary) and B Ltd (A's 75% subsidiary and a [(76% × 80%) + (5%)] = 65.8% subsidiary of H Ltd) form a capital gains group. C Ltd, although a 75% subsidiary of B Ltd, is only a [(65.8% × 75%) + .1%] = 49.5% subsidiary of H Ltd and thus is outside the group.

There cannot be additional capital gains groups with either A Ltd or B Ltd as the principal member, since a company cannot be the overall holding company of such a group if it is a 75% subsidiary of another company.

(ii)  The transfer of the fixed asset will be regarded as taking place for a consideration which gives rise to a nil gain/nil loss position for capital gains purposes (ie, the asset will normally be deemed to be sold and acquired for a consideration equal to its cost plus indexation allowance to date). Thus, no chargeable gain or loss accrues to the transferor company. Where the fixed asset is immediately taken into its trading stock by the transferee company, it is treated as having disposed of the asset for a consideration equal to its current market value. This will give rise to a chargeable gain or loss depending on the deemed acquisition cost (see above). The asset will be included in the company's cost of sales at market value for Schedule D Case I purposes.

(iii)    The transferee company may elect that the chargeable gain or loss on the deemed disposal should be ignored and instead be effectively used to reduce or increase its cost of sales respectively for Schedule D Case I purposes. One situation where the election will be favourable is where the deemed disposal gives rise to a capital loss which cannot be offset against chargeable gains; by making the election, the capital loss will be in effect transformed into a Schedule D Case I expense, thus providing immediate tax relief.

(b)    (i)    A 'loss group' broadly consists of a company and all of its 75% subsidiaries (the minimum required 75% relationship is based primarily on ordinary share capital, as defined). The 75% relationship may be direct or indirect. Thus H Ltd and A Ltd form a loss group but H Ltd, A Ltd and B Ltd do not, as B Ltd is only an indirect 65.8% subsidiary of H Ltd (see (a) above). Similarly A Ltd and B Ltd form a group, as do B Ltd and C Ltd. There is no rule preventing a company belonging to more than one loss group. H Ltd and A Ltd can surrender losses to each other, as can A Ltd and B Ltd, and B Ltd and C Ltd.

A 'consortium' exists where, inter alia, at least 75% of the ordinary share capital of a UK resident company (the 'consortium company') is owned directly by other UK resident companies (the 'consortium members'). Each company must own at least 5%, but less than 75%, of the ordinary share capital of the consortium company. Thus, D Ltd is a consortium company, with H Ltd, P Ltd and Q Ltd comprising the consortium members. D Ltd can surrender its trading losses to H Ltd, P Ltd and Q Ltd and vice versa.

(ii)    In the case of group relief, losses may be surrendered in whole or in such lesser proportion as is desired, up to the amount of the chargeable profits of the claimant company. The surrendering company need not claim against its own profits before surrendering the loss. The position regarding consortium relief is more complicated. Where the consortium company, ie, D Ltd surrenders a loss, the maximum share available for each of the consortium members is equal to the proportion of ordinary shares which it owns in the consortium company (ie, 40%, 30% and 30% for H Ltd, P Ltd and Q Ltd respectively). Where one of the consortium members surrenders a loss to D Ltd, the maximum proportion of D Ltd's chargeable profits available to absorb the loss is equal to the proportion of the ordinary shares which the consortium member holds in D Ltd. Thus eg, if H Ltd surrenders a loss to D Ltd, the relief claimed can not exceed 40% of D Ltd's profits. Where the consortium company makes a loss it is deemed to have used this primarily to make the maximum claim possible under S393A (relief against chargeable profits of any description). Subject to this restriction, the amount of the loss surrendered can be any amount up to the maximum permitted.

(iii)    If Q Ltd had been a non-resident company, then only 70% of the ordinary share capital of D Ltd would be owned by UK resident companies. As a result, no consortium relief would be available. If A Ltd was non-resident then it would not be included in a 'loss' group; thus the only 'loss' group in existence would be that comprising B Ltd and C Ltd.

(c)    (i)    Interest and charges on income may be paid without accounting for income tax where the paying and recipient companies are members of the same 51% group. Broadly, a 51% group consists of a company and its 51% subsidiaries, (the minimum required 51% relationship is based primarily on ordinary share capital, as defined, and may be direct or indirect). Thus, A Ltd may pay interest to H Ltd without deducting income tax. B Ltd can similarly pay interest gross to A Ltd and also to H Ltd as it is an 80% and 65.8% subsidiary of these companies respectively. Again, C Ltd can pay interest gross to B Ltd, a company of which it is a 51% subsidiary, but not to H Ltd, which only owns 49.5% of C Ltd (see above).

Although the term '51% group' is used, the qualifying effective holding is in fact >50% (eg, 50.5% would qualify).

In addition, a consortium company may pay interest and charges to a consortium member without deducting income tax. Thus, D Ltd can elect to pay any interest or charges on income gross to H Ltd, P Ltd and Q Ltd.

(ii)    The benefit in making the election to pay interest and charges gross is one of cash flow. Income tax deductions must normally be accounted for under the quarterly accounting system by the payer, at the latest 3½ months after the interest or charge is paid. While any income tax suffered can generally be offset against the payer's corporation tax liability, this will not take place until nine months after the end of the company's accounting period.

*(Tutorial notes:* The first thing to do in a question like this is draw a diagram of the various shareholdings as follows:

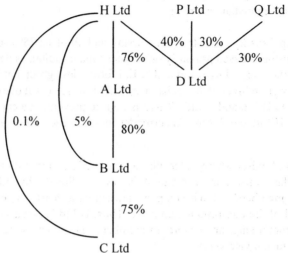

This sort of question shows how essential it is to learn what constitutes a group for each of the special group reliefs.*)*

---

## 13    GRUDGE LTD

(a)    **Dr Choler**

(i)     Dr Choler will be able to claim full relief for interest on the loan to acquire shares in Envy Ltd as

-       Envy Ltd will be a close trading company; and

-       Dr Choler will have a material interest (ie, more than 5%) in the ordinary share capital of the company.

(ii)    If Dr Choler borrows money from the company at less than the official rate of interest to finance his loan repayments and associated interest costs he is receiving a benefit in kind from the company, and these borrowings will be treated as a distribution. The amount of any benefit in kind to be taken into account as a distribution is the cash equivalent which would have been assessed on the participator if he had been a director or employee earning at least £8,500 p.a. The amount of the benefit is the official rate of interest × the average balance of the beneficial loan outstanding during the relevant tax year. However, if part of the beneficial loan is used to replace the original bank loan, to that extent, tax relief will be available, as the original loan will have qualified for relief. As the original loan is repaid, there will of course be a reduction in the allowable interest costs associated with it. *Note:* The loan from the company may not be legal under the Companies Acts.

(iii)   As Dr Choler is a director of Grudge Ltd, and the shares he is acquiring in Envy Ltd are at an undervalue of £50,000 it is likely that he will be taxable on this amount under Schedule E principles (Weight v Salmon). The Schedule E liability takes priority over any potential deemed distribution rules (close company providing benefits to participators).

**Envy Ltd**

(i)     As the redundancy payments appear to be associated with a rationalising of its workforce, as opposed to a cessation of its trade, Envy Ltd should be able to claim a deduction for the payments under

---

general Schedule D principles. The Revenue will not, in any event, challenge redundancy payments of up to three times the statutory redundancy entitlements over and above the statutory amount, even where an identifiable part of the trade is discontinued. The redundancy payments will therefore increase the amount of Envy Ltd's trading losses by £210,000.

(ii)    The losses should be available for carry forward against future trading profits despite the change in ownership of Envy Ltd providing: (a) a major change in the nature or conduct of the trade does not occur within the following three years, and (b) the activities undertaken by Envy Ltd had not become small or negligible and there is subsequently a major revival of its trade (this does not seem to be applicable).

(iii)   A loan to Dr Choler will constitute a loan to a participator. This produces a consequent liability on the company to account for 'penalty tax' at a rate of 25% of the loan. The exclusion for loans of up to £15,000 is not available as Dr Choler holds a material interest in the company (nor indeed is he a full-time employee). The penalty tax is due for payment 9 months from the end of the accounting period in which the loan is made or written off. It is repayable to the company proportionately, as the loan is repaid.

(iv)    No tax consequences arise for Envy Ltd on leaving the Grudge Ltd capital gains group within six years of the inter-group disposal of the building to Ire Ltd, since Envy Ltd was the **transferor** company.

**Grudge Ltd group**

**Grudge Ltd**

A capital gain of £40,700 arises on the disposal of the shares in Envy Ltd, calculated as set out below:

|  | | *31.3.82 MV* | *Cost* |
|---|---|---|---|
|  | | £ | £ |
| Consideration (MV) | | 250,000 | 250,000 |
| Less: | 31.3.82 MV | (100,000) | |
|  | Original cost | | (10,000) |
|  | | 150,000 | 240,000 |
| Less: | Indexation allowance | | |
|  | £100,000 × $\dfrac{166.3 - 79.44}{79.44}$ = (1.093) | (109,300) | (109,300) |
|  | | 40,700 | 130,700 |

Lower gain of £40,700 applies.

**All group companies**

Once Envy Ltd is sold, the group will have one less associated company for future accounting periods. This may or may not be relevant, depending on the profitability of each company.

(b)    While Envy Ltd remained in the Grudge Ltd VAT group, all supplies of goods from it to other group members were disregarded for VAT purposes. Envy Ltd was also jointly and severally liable for the VAT liability of the group as a whole. On leaving the group Envy Ltd must account for VAT on all supplies to group members. Because 90% of its sales are zero-rated, it is likely that Envy Ltd will be in a permanent repayment situation. The company may elect to make returns on a monthly rather than a quarterly basis in order to improve its cash flow.

## 14    ERIC FASTHAND

(a)    The distinction between employment and self-employment is essentially whether the contract is one for a contract of service assessable under Schedule E, or a contract for services assessable under Schedule D. The distinction is often hard to draw, however, and a number of tests need to be considered:

### The control test

Does one party, the employer, have control over the other party, the employee? For example, can the employer tell the employee when, where and how to perform the services. If the answer is 'no', then the other tests will have to be considered, since the absence of control is unlikely by itself to indicate self-employment. If the answer is 'yes', then this is a strong indication that a contract of service exists, although the test may not be conclusive by itself. As far as Eric is concerned, he has been engaged to play guitar when and where the contract stipulates, and this is an indication of a contract of service. However, even though he is not going to be involved in the recording of the new album, he is likely to have some artistic input into the performance of the songs already written by the Rolling Rocks band, and this would indicate a contract for services.

### The mutual obligations test

Has one party an obligation to provide work, and has the other party an obligation to do the work provided? If the answer is yes, this is an indication of a contract of service. In **Davies v Braithwaite** (1933), an actress who entered into a series of separate engagements to appear on film, stage and radio was held to be self-employed. The number of her engagements was a deciding factor. This should be compared with the case of **Fall v Hitchen** (1973), where a ballet dancer, who was employed under a contract which allowed him to take other work with the consent of his employer, was held to be employed. A deciding factor here was that there was only one contract which provided for a first call on his time. Eric is contracted to play for a set number of dates, and cannot undertake any other work during all but two months of the tour. This indicates a contract of service.

### The economic reality test

Do the activities of the person providing the services form a trade or profession in their own right? The case of **Market Investigations Ltd v Minister of Social Security** (1969) listed a number of factors that must be considered in respect of the person performing the service:

(i)    Does that person provide his or her own equipment?

(ii)    Does that person hire his or her own helpers?

(iii)    What degree of financial risk does that person take?

(iv)    What degree of responsibility for investment and management has that person got?

(v)    Does that person have an opportunity of profiting from sound management in the performance of his or her task?

Eric is providing his own instruments and equipment, and will be paid a bonus based on a satisfactory performance. These are both indications of self-employment, but the other factors indicate that he is employed as, for example, his fees do not appear to be dependent on the financial success of the tour.

### The integration test

Does the party providing the services do so as an integral part of the other party's business? If the answer is 'yes', this is an indication of a contract of service. For example, the position of a chauffeur, who is normally integrated into a business, can be compared to that of a taxi driver, who is not. Eric is only on a short-term contract, and there are no indications of integration, such as the entitlement to sick pay or holiday pay. This is therefore an indication of self-employment.

Other factors that would have to be considered are:

(i)     Eric must execute the work personally, which indicates a contract of service;

(ii)    the fact that Eric is currently self-employed, although there is no reason why a person cannot be both employed and self-employed at the same time.

On the evidence available. Eric would appear to be performing a contract of service, and will be assessed under Schedule E as an employee. However, the decision is not clear-cut. The case of **Hall v Lorimer** (1994) held that the fact that only personal services are provided is no bar to being regarded as self-employed.

(b)     **Self-employed**

If Eric is treated as self-employed, his earnings from the tour will be included as part of his normal Schedule D Case II profits, since it would be unlikely that the contract would be considered as a new trade. Eric will play 110 dates (40 UK plus 70 overseas) during the year ended 31 May 2000, and 40 dates (all overseas) during the year ended 31 May 2001. His fees for the year ended 31 May 2000 will therefore be £82,500 (110 × 750), and this will be assessed under the current year basis in 2000/01. For the year ended 31 May 2001 he will receive fees of £30,000 (40 × 750) plus the bonus of £20,000, and these will be assessed in 2001/02. For both years, tax will be due in two equal instalments on 31 January in the tax year, and 31 July following the tax year with any adjustments to the tax liability being made on the following 31 January. Eric's present self-employed activities will presumably amount to £40,000 $\left(60,000 \times \frac{8}{12}\right)$ during the year ended 31 May 2001.

Whether a proportion of the bonus should be accrued in the year ended 31 May 2000 is debatable. Although the majority of the dates are played during this year, the bonus is only due upon satisfactory completion of the tour. Under generally accepted accounting principles, the profit would not be recognised until payment was assured. The costs of travelling and accommodation that are to be paid for by the Rolling Rocks band will not result in additional assessable profits, since these expenses will all be deductible. The only exception might be if Eric were to stay overseas on holiday during the two months that the Rolling Rocks band are recording. The accommodation during this period, and possibly a proportion of the travelling expenses would then be treated as additional receipts for the relevant year.

Eric will not be outside the UK for a complete tax year, and will therefore remain resident in the UK throughout the period of the contract. All of his profits will therefore be subject to income tax in the UK. The case of **Ogilvie v Kitton** (1908) decided that it is almost impossible for a UK resident sole trader to have overseas trading profits assessable under Schedule D Case V. Whether Eric returns to the UK or not during the two months that the Rolling Rocks band are recording, is therefore irrelevant. Capital allowances will be available in respect of his instruments and equipment. Eric's income tax liabilities for 2000/01 and 2001/02 on the income from the new contract are likely to be as follows:

|  |  | 2000/01 £ | 2001/02 £ |
|---|---|---|---|
| New contract - fees | | 82,500 | 30,000 |
| - bonus | | – | 20,000 |
| Schedule D Case II | | 82,500 | 50,000 |
| Personal allowance* | | (4,335) | (-) |
| Taxable income | | 78,165 | 50,000 |
| Income tax: 1,500 at 10% | | 150 | - |
| 26,500 at 23% | | 6,095 | - |
| 50,165/50,000 at 40% | | 20,066 | 20,000 |
| | | 26,311 | 20,000 |

*  It is assumed that personal allowances and starting and basic rate tax bands are set against income from other self employment in 2001/02.

**Employed**

If Eric is treated as employed, his earnings from the tour will be assessed under Schedule E on the current year basis, with income tax due being collected under the PAYE system. During 1999/00 Eric will play 40 dates in the UK, and 50 dates overseas (ignoring dates played during the first five days of April), with a further 60 dates being played overseas during 2000/01. Schedule E earnings are assessed on a receipts basis, so the bonus of £20,000 will fall to be taxed in 2000/01. His income will therefore be:

|         |                       | £      |
|---------|-----------------------|--------|
| 1999/00 | UK (40 × 750)         | 30,000 |
|         | Overseas (50 × 750)   | 37,500 |
| 2000/01 | Overseas (60 × 750)   | 45,000 |
|         | Bonus                 | 20,000 |

As already discussed, Eric will remain resident in the UK throughout the period of the contract, and therefore liable to UK income tax on his worldwide income including his overseas earnings. The costs of travelling and accommodation paid for by the Rolling Rocks band will be assessable on Eric as he is a 'higher paid employee'. However, he should be able to claim deductions against this as follows:

(i)     All travelling incurred necessarily in the performance of his duties.

(ii)    The costs of travelling overseas and returning to the UK. This will cover the journeys during the two months that the Rolling Rocks band are recording.

(iii)   Board and lodgings whilst overseas.

Capital allowances will be available in respect of Eric's instruments and equipment as under Schedule D.

Whether Eric's previous self-employment is treated as ceasing on 31 May 1999, or whether it will be treated as continuing, will be a matter of fact. The deciding factor would probably be whether Eric continued the business upon the completion of the contract. Assuming that the business is treated as continuing, his Schedule E earnings will be taxed at 40% in 1999/00 (since Schedule D earnings are £60,000). Assuming he makes no business profits in the year to 31 May 2000 (ie, taking holiday in November 1999 and March 2000) he will only have Schedule E income for 2000/01. The Schedule E income tax payable will be as follows:

|                              | 1999/00 £ | 2000/01 £ |
|------------------------------|-----------|-----------|
| New contract  -  fees        | 67,500    | 45,000    |
|           -  bonus           |           | 20,000    |
| Schedule E                   | 67,500    | 65,000    |
| Less:  Personal allowance    | (4,335)   | (4,335)   |
| Taxable income               | 63,165    | 60,665    |
| Income tax at; 10%, 23%, 40% | 25,266    | 19,311    |

Classification does not alter the amount of income assessed but does influence the years in which the income is assessable. There is a significant delay if the income is assessed under Schedule D I.

## 15    MAGEE INC

(a)     (i)    Gavin Ltd will be resident in the UK as it is incorporated there. The location of the directors' meetings is irrelevant in this case.

(ii)    Gavin Ltd will probably be resident in the UK if the directors' meetings are held there. This is because a company will be UK resident if its central management and control abides in the UK, regardless of where it is incorporated. Normally, central management and control will abide wherever the directors meet. However, if, for example, the major policy decisions affecting Gavin Ltd were in fact made by Magee Inc then this would not be the case, and Gavin Ltd would be non-UK resident.

(iii)    Gavin Ltd will probably be resident in Ruritania and not the UK as it is not incorporated in the UK and central management and control would normally be exercised in Ruritania, as this is where the directors hold their meetings. If, despite this, central management and control in reality was exercised in the UK Gavin Ltd would be resident there.

(b)    From 1 July 1999 to 31 August 1999 Gavin Ltd will be outside the scope of corporation tax, as it will be a non-resident company trading outside the UK. On 1 September 1999 it will come within the charge to corporation tax as a UK resident company and this will trigger off the commencement of its first accounting period. Its first accounting period will end on 31 August 2000 ie, 12 months after it commences, since the company's period of account does not end prior to that date. Gavin Ltd's second accounting period will run from 1 September 2000 to 30 September 2000, which marks the end of the company's period of account. Gavin Ltd's third accounting period will run from 1 October 2000 to 30 September 2001 (12 months from the commencement of the second accounting period and also the end of the company's period of account).

(c)    Magee Inc should ensure that Gavin Ltd and all of its other UK resident subsidiaries form a loss group. At the moment, they fail to do so because they are all subsidiaries of a non-resident company. One solution would be for Magee Inc to transfer all of its shares in its UK subsidiaries, including Gavin Ltd, to a new UK resident company which would act as a holding company for the UK resident companies. Disposal of assets by a non-resident company which is not trading in the UK are outside the scope of corporation tax, so that no liabilities will arise.

(d)    (i)

|  | Cost £ | 31.3.82 MV £ | Rebasing election £ |
|---|---|---|---|
| Consideration | 300,000 | 300,000 | 300,000 |
| Less: Expenses | (5,250) | (5,250) | (5,250) |
|  | 294,750 | 294,750 | 294,750 |
| Less: Cost/rebased cost | (100,000) | (80,000) | (80,000) |
| Enhancement | (12,000) | (12,000) | (12,000) |
| Indexation - cost | | | |
| $£100,000 \times \dfrac{165.6 - 79.44}{79.44}(1.085)$ | (108,500) | (108,500) | |
| $£80,000 \times \dfrac{165.6 - 79.44}{79.44}(1.085)$ | | | (86,800) |
| Indexation - enhancement | | | |
| $£12,000 \times \dfrac{165.6 - 139.2}{139.2}(0.190)$ | (2,280) | (2,280) | (2,280) |
| Gain | 71,970 | 91,970 | 113,670 |

Original cost applies, assuming
  rebasing election does not apply          71,970

*(Tutorial note:* Election under S35(5) TCGA 1992 (General rebasing election)

A once-and-for-all election may be made that gains and losses arising on all assets held at 31 March 1982 should be computed by reference to their 31 March 1982 values. This also extends to the calculation of the indexation allowance.

In the case of a group of companies, the election must be made by the parent company on behalf of the whole group.*)*

(ii)    Casey Ltd will be eligible to make a claim for rollover relief to the extent that the proceeds from the disposal of the warehouse are reinvested in a 'qualifying asset' within three years of the disposal. A 'qualifying asset' includes fixed plant and machinery which does not form part of a building. It would appear that the computer falls within this description. The relief available will be equal to the gain of £71,970 (assuming that the general rebasing election is not applicable) less the £44,750 not reinvested (ie, £294,750 less £250,000; in practice the incidental sale expenses are taken into account for these purposes). This leaves a chargeable gain of £44,750 and a gain eligible for relief of £(71,970 – 44,750) = £27,220. Because the computer is a 'depreciating asset' (ie, it has an expected useful life of less than 60 years) the 'rolled over' element of the gain is not deducted from its base cost, but instead the gain is held in suspense until the earliest of the following events occurs:

–    the computer is disposed of
–    the computer ceases to be used for the purposes of the trade
–    ten years have expired (this is irrelevant in the present case).

It would appear therefore that the 'rolled over' gain will be treated as arising on or about the fourth anniversary of the acquisition of the computer. However, if prior to that date, Casey Ltd (or any other companies in the same 'capital gains' group) acquire a qualifying, non-depreciating asset the 'rolled-over' gain can be deducted from the base cost of that asset instead.

(iii)    All of the companies in the loss group will also be members of an identical 'capital gains' group. Accordingly a decision as to whether or not to elect for March 1982 valuation to apply without reference to original cost (ie, under S35(5) TCGA 1992) will be binding in respect of disposals by all of the group companies, including Casey Ltd. The election will have retrospective effect and will lead to Casey Ltd's gain being recomputed at £113,670 (see (i) above), but may reduce potential corporation tax liabilities in respect of other assets owned by group members on 31 March 1982. It will be necessary therefore to weigh up the potential future corporation tax savings as a result of making the election against the potential additional corporation tax incurred on the disposal by Casey Ltd. This will involve taking into account the amounts of corporation tax involved as well as the timing of the potential liabilities.

(iv)    A decision to elect under S35(5) will need to be made by the 'principal member' of the group (ie, the newly formed UK resident holding company, if the structure proposed in (c) is adopted). The election must be made within two years of the end of the accounting period in which the disposal by Casey Ltd takes place (ie, by 30 September 2002).

## 16    MR GOG

(a)                                   **Income tax 1999/00**

|  |  | £ |
|---|---|---:|
| Schedule D Case V |  |  |
| Rents remitted to 5.4.00   £400/0.80 |  | 500 |
| Bank interest - none remitted |  | - |
| Schedule D Case III - War Loan £80,000 × 3.5% |  | 2,800 |
| Schedule E |  | 31,500 |
|  |  | 34,800 |
| Statutory total income |  | 34,800 |
| Less:  Personal allowance |  | (4,335) |
| Taxable income |  | 30,465 |
| Income tax | 1,500 at 10% = | 150 |
|  | 26,500 at 23% = | 6,095 |
|  | 2,465 at 40% = | 986 |
|  | 30,465 | 7,231 |

| | | |
|---|---|---:|
| Less: | Double tax relief £(500 – 400) = | (100) |
| | PAYE | (6,700) |
| | | |
| Tax payable | | 431 |

(b)   Because Mr Gog was born in Ruritania and eventually intends to return there permanently, it is likely that he will retain his Ruritanian domicile of origin. The fact that he has lived in the UK for many years will not result in the loss of his Ruritanian domicile unless his presence in the UK is accompanied by an intention to remain there indefinitely. However, under the IHT rules, where an individual has been resident in the UK for at least 17 out of the 20 tax years ending with the tax year in question, he will be regarded as UK domiciled in that year. Mr Gog became a UK resident in the tax year 1984/85 and will have been resident for 17 consecutive tax years in the tax year 2000/01 (ie, the tax year commencing 6 April 2000).

(c)   From an IHT viewpoint, the preferred strategy for Mr Gog is firstly to dispose of his overseas assets while he is still regarded as non-UK domiciled. This is because such assets will be excluded property for IHT purposes and are in effect completely exempt. Because Mr Gog is ordinarily resident in the UK his investment in Government Stocks cannot rank as excluded property, despite his non-domiciled status. The antique, because it is located in the UK, is regarded as a UK asset. This strategy presents no CGT problems as far as the Ruritanian bank account is concerned, and therefore these funds should be transferred immediately.

If Mr Gog wishes to avoid any potential IHT on lifetime transfers, the maximum value which he can transfer on 5 April 2000 to his son is £237,000 (ie, nil rate band of £231,000 plus the 1998/99 and 1999/00 annual exemptions of £3,000 each). Even if he dies within seven years, no IHT will be payable.

All of Mr Gog's assets are available for immediate disposal to Enrico other than his private residence (which he wishes to retain). His strategy should be to give away an IHT value of up to £237,000, without incurring any CGT problems. This involves giving away exempt assets, any assets which produce nil gain/nil loss disposals and, finally, any other assets producing net gains of up to £7,100, since these will be covered by the CGT annual exemption.

The UK deposit account, being cash, the Government stocks and the antique (exempt under the chattels rules) are all exempt CGT. The farm produces nil gain (W2). In addition to these assets, Bah plc shares may be gifted, to the extent that the gain arising does not exceed £7,100.

The gain on the shares in Bah plc cannot be 'held over'. This is because the shares do not constitute a qualifying asset for gift relief. They are also clearly not business assets for taper relief purposes.

On this basis, the following transfers of non-excluded assets should be made by Mr Gog:

| | £ | £ |
|---|---:|---:|
| Farm | 116,000 | |
| Less:   Agricultural property relief (100%) | (116,000) | |
| | | |
| | | - |
| Antique | | 6,000 |
| Government Stock | | 27,000 |
| UK deposit account | | 23,000 |
| Shares in Bah plc (W1) | | 8,469 |
| | | |
| | | 64,469 |

*Note:*

(1)    No BPR available.

(2)    It is assumed that Enrico would retain the farm, so that the Agricultural Property Relief would remain available if Mr Gog were to die before 6 April 2007.

---

**WORKINGS**

(W1)    Disposal of all Bah plc shares

|  | £ |
|---|---|
| Consideration | 150,000 |
| Less:  Cost | (20,000) |
| Indexation, $£20,000 \times \dfrac{162.6-134.1}{134.1} =$ | (4,250) |
| Chargeable gain | 125,750 |

Therefore a gift of $\dfrac{150,000 \times 7,100}{125,750} = £8,469$ worth of shares produces a gain of £7,100.

(W2)    Disposal of farmland

|  | *Cost* £ |
|---|---|
| Consideration | 116,000 |
| Cost/31.3.82 MV | (65,000) |
| Indexation $65,000 \times \dfrac{162.6-86.84}{86.84}$ (0.872)  (restricted) | (51,000) |
|  | Nil |

(d)    On Mr Gog's death within seven years no IHT would arise, as the deemed disposition of his assets to the charity would be exempt.  The PETs made on 5.4.2000 would become chargeable lifetime transfers but would be covered by the nil rate band (the value of the PETs would not be recalculated upwards on death).

*(Tutorial note:*

(1)    As Mr Gog is domiciled in Ruritania, the remittance basis applies to his Schedule D Case V income.

(2)    Schedule D Case V income is included in the tax computation at its gross equivalent.  The double tax relief is then the lower of

(i)      UK tax; and
(ii)     the foreign tax.

In this case the relief is the foreign tax of £100.

(3)    Relief of 10% is given at source on interest payments made through MIRAS.

(4)    For IHT purposes, property situated outside the UK owned by an individual domiciled outside the UK is excluded property.  However, certain government securities are only excluded property if they are owned by a person neither domiciled nor ordinarily resident in the UK.

(5)    Business property relief is only available on shares in a quoted trading company when transferred out of a controlling holding.*)

---

## 17    MARTIN LENNOX

(a)    The main distinction which has been made by the courts in this area is that between an asset held as an investment, and one which is held only with the intention of resale at a profit, ie, which is merely the subject of a 'deal'.  A profit on the latter will be assessed under Schedule D Case I as arising as a result of an 'adventure in the nature of trade'.  An asset must fall into either one or the other category at any one time

**(Simmons v IRC)**. However, a trader may switch an asset from one category to another by appropriating one of his capital assets into his trading stock. Usually an investment is held for a period of time, whereas 'dealing' stock is bought and sold as quickly as possible. However, some 'dealing' assets such as land are long term in nature and may be held for a considerable time before being resold and may even be rented out during the period of ownership. Also, assets acquired for investment may have to be sold off after only a brief period of ownership in case of an emergency **(West v Phillips)**, or to take advantage of an opportunity for a windfall gain **(IRC v Reinhold)**.

Where the asset does not provide any income, or the owner does not obtain personal enjoyment from his ownership, this reduces the likelihood of it being held as an investment. This is especially so if it is a commodity which is normally traded in and is not usually the subject of investment (eg, volumes of aircraft linen bought and resold in **Martin v Lowry**). However, an asset held with the only purpose being to enjoy capital appreciation may still be an investment **(Marson v Martin)**. In **Wisdom v Chamberlain** the purchase and resale of silver bullion was held to be an adventure in the nature of trade but an influential factor was the fact that the bullion had been purchased by borrowed money, and was therefore obviously not a part of the taxpayer's 'investment portfolio'.

The occupation and interests of the taxpayer may be relevant, thus, for example, it is often difficult for a builder to argue that he is holding land as an investment. The use of one's commercial knowledge is symptomatic of a 'deal'. A history of similar, previous transactions is also suggestive of a 'course of dealing' **(Pickford v Quirke)**.

Where work is done to make the property more marketable then this will clearly amount to a trading operation **(CIR v Livingston)**. However, simply making an asset more attractive to potential purchasers will not be so regarded **(Hudson's Bay v Stevens)**. The distinction is fine; thus from **CIR v Iswera** it appears that buying land and selling it shortly afterwards in small plots is in itself indicative of a trading operation. The existence of a highly developed marketing and selling organisation is again likely to suggest that a commercial 'deal' is involved.

If it is obvious from the facts that trading has occurred, then the motive of the taxpayer is irrelevant. If, however, the facts on their own do not clearly point to trading, then the taxpayer's account of his motives for buying and selling, if accepted by the courts, may be the deciding factor. Thus, in **Taylor v Good** a purchase followed by a sale shortly afterwards of a house was held to be a capital transaction because it was accepted that the taxpayer had originally meant to occupy it as his residence but later changed his mind.

*(Note:* students may also appropriately cite the so-called 'badges of trade', which cover most, but not all, of the points noted above. A much briefer answer could score full marks.*)*

(b)     The disposal of the land which Mr Lennox inherited from his mother would not usually be considered as constituting an adventure in the nature of trade, as he had not acquired it with a view to reselling it at a profit. Further, it would not appear that Mr Lennox has any other experience in land-dealing. However the purchase of the second site is closer to trading, as the land produced only minimal income and Mr Lennox actually incurred interest costs in holding it. It would appear that Mr Lennox had intended to repay his loan out of the sale proceeds of the land, which is again not suggestive of an investment transaction. The fact that planning permission was obtained is probably not an influential factor, but the improvements made to the land is perhaps suggestive of a trade in land development, although clearly it amounted to considerably less than full-scale development. The short time-scale involved would also point towards trading.

On balance it seems likely that Mr Lennox embarked on an 'adventure' in July 1999, and at that time brought the land which he had inherited from his mother into his trading stock. It would follow that the decision of the General Commissioners was correct, although it is likely that in a borderline case like this, that if they had reached the opposite conclusion the courts would not have overturned their verdict (see **Edwards v Bairstow**).

*(Note:* Students who reached a different conclusion, if based on sensible reasoning, could also have obtained up to full marks.)

(c)     (i)     **'Trading' profit**

|  | £ | £ |
| --- | --- | --- |
| Sale proceeds |  | 125,000 |
| Less: Cost of land and legal fees | 28,000 |  |

|  |  |  |
|---|---:|---:|
| Land appropriated at market value | 30,000 |  |
|  | 58,000 |  |
| Improvements | 15,000 |  |
| Interest £15,000 × 8% × $\frac{20}{12}$ | 2,000 |  |
|  |  | (75,000) |
| Profit |  | 50,000 |
| Income tax at 40% = |  | 20,000 |

(ii)    **Capital profit**

|  | £ | £ |
|---|---:|---:|
| Consideration |  | 125,000 |
| Less:  Acquisition costs (as above) | 58,000 |  |
| Indexation allowance - Nil, acquired post April 1998 | - |  |
| Enhancement | 15,000 |  |
|  |  | (73,000) |
|  |  | 52,000 |
| Less:  Annual exemption |  | (7,100) |
|  |  | 44,900 |
| CGT at 40% |  | 17,960 |

---

## 18    MR RAY

(a)    **Leonard as employee**

Mr Ray would have to account for employer's National Insurance on Leonard's wages, ie, £25,000 at 12.2% = £3,050.  He would also have to account to the Revenue for PAYE and employee's National Insurance deducted from Leonard's wages (although this would not constitute an extra cost for Mr Ray).  The total cost, ie, £28,050 would be deductible in computing his trading profits.  No VAT implications would arise.

Mr Ray would not make a gift of the business to Leonard for a further seven years; we are told that he will probably die in the meanwhile.  If he dies before making the gift, the business will form part of Mr Ray's death estate.  At current values, this would incur an IHT liability of £31,600 as follows.

|  | £ | £ |
|---|---:|---:|
| Net current assets | 58,000 |  |
| Shop (4/5 × £240,000) = | 192,000 |  |
|  | 250,000 |  |
| Less:  BPR at 100% | (250,000) | - |
| Shop (1/5 × £240,000) |  | 48,000 |
| Private residence |  | 262,000 |
|  |  | 310,000 |
| Less:  Exempt band |  | (231,000) |
|  |  | 79,000 |
| IHT at 40% = |  | 31,600 |

---

It appears that in the meanwhile the shop and house may have appreciated in value to some extent. Goodwill may also have acquired a value of up to £30,000 but this would be covered by 100% BPR. Thus (ignoring any uplifts in the IHT exempt band) additional IHT exposure may be incurred at a rate of 40% on this capital appreciation.

All latent capital gains would be automatically eliminated on death, as death transfers are exempt CGT.

If Mr Ray survives to 30 June 2007 then the transfer of the business he makes at that date will be a PET, and thus not liable to IHT at the date of transfer. However, as it appears that Mr Ray would die within the following two years the transfer will become chargeable on his death so that a similar IHT exposure to that outlined above will arise, without the benefit of tapering relief. However, the lifetime transfer would attract two annual exemptions, amounting to £6,000 in total. Business property relief would be lost if Leonard had disposed of the business prior to the date of Mr Ray's death. The value of the business will be taken as at the date of the original transfer, rather than at the date of Mr Ray's death.

Mr Ray will almost certainly incur chargeable capital gains on the lifetime disposal of his assets. However, given that he is aged over 50 and will have owned the business for more than 10 years any business gains are liable to be comfortably covered by retirement relief of £200,000. This would almost certainly leave no gain in charge eligible for a claim for 'holdover relief' in respect of a gift of business assets.

The gain on the non-business proportion of the shop would not be eligible for retirement relief or gift relief or taper relief at the business rate. The gain of £40,000 × 1/5 = £8,000 would be covered in part by Mr Ray's annual exemption of £7,100; the balance of £900 would be liable at 40% at current rates ie, £360. No credit for this would be given against any IHT levied on the same transfer.

The income tax cessation rules will apply to Mr Ray on his retirement or earlier death. The assessment for the final tax year will be actual profits from the end of the basis period of the preceding year until cessation.

(b)    **Leonard as partner**

The admission of Leonard into partnership on 1 July 2000 does not cause a cessation of Mr Ray's trade. The profits arising after 1 July 2000 will be allocated equally between Mr Ray and Leonard. The income tax cessation rules will apply to Mr Ray on his retirement or earlier death exactly as if he were a sole trader.

Leonard will be treated as if he had commenced trading on 1 July 2000, and the commencement rules will accordingly apply. He will be allocated with 50% of the profits arising after 1 July 2000 and assuming an accounting date of 30 June, his taxable profits would be calculated as follows:

2000/01
     50% of profits arising between 1.7.00 and 5.4.01
     ie, 50% × 9/12 × y/e 30.6.01
2001/02
     50% of profits of y/e 30.6.01

On Leonard's eventual cessation overlap relief will be given for the overlap profits (ie, those of the overlap period 1.7.00 − 5.4.01).

Mr Ray and Leonard would each be responsible for paying his own income tax and NI contributions.

For VAT purposes, the partnership is a separate entity and thus Mr Ray should deregister his sole tradership and ensure that the partnership re-registers in its own name. The partnership could take over the existing registration number but this entails it also assuming any of Mr Ray's prior VAT liabilities. No VAT arises on the transfer of the business assets from sole trader to partnership, as these form part of a going concern and the partnership is itself liable to register. On Mr Ray's retirement or death it would be necessary to ensure that Leonard was registered as a sole trader for VAT purposes; again, no adverse VAT implications should arise on the switch from partnership to sole tradership.

As noted in (a) above, a lifetime transfer would generate an immediate CGT liability of £360. Retirement relief would still be available notwithstanding Mr Ray's continuing involvement in the business.

Again, the transfer of the assets would be a PET and would be free of IHT if Mr Ray survived for the following seven years. 100% BPR will be available on the business assets transferred providing Leonard still owns them at the date of Mr Ray's death, should Mr Ray die within seven years and the PET became chargeable. BPR is not available on the shop, but two years of annual exemptions are available.

Because the profit sharing arrangements are of a bona fide commercial nature no question of a gift with reservation having been made should arise. The bequest of the house to Leonard would incur an IHT liability of £12,400 if death was more than 7 years later, as follows:

|  | £ |
|---|---|
| Private residence | 262,000 |
| Less:   Exempt band | (231,000) |
|  | 31,000 |

IHT at 40% = 12,400

This is using the current exempt band; by the time of Mr Ray's death it may have increased, thereby reducing the IHT liability. If Mr Ray died within 7 years of the gift, £42,000 (£48,000 - £6,000) of the nil band would have been used on the transfer of the shop. The IHT on death would become £(31,000 + 42,000) @ 40% = £29,200.

While it is probable that in fact Mr Ray will die within the seven year period, there is a chance that he may not. Further, even if he does so, the largest part of his wealth subject to IHT will be valued at today's values, before the effects of any capital appreciation (however modest) are felt. The benefit of two years' annual exemptions will again be obtained.

## JUNE 1994 QUESTIONS

## 19 (Question 1 of examination)

White Stallion Ltd runs a nationwide chain of estate agencies, making up its accounts to 31 July. The company has suffered declining results in recent years, and is therefore planning to restructure its business operations during July 2000 (you should assume that today's date is 15 April 2000). The company's plans are as follows:

(1) Three branches of the business are to be closed, with the respective premises being sold. Details of the premises to be sold are as follows:

| Branch | Purchased | Original cost £ | Current market value £ |
|--------|-----------|-----------------|------------------------|
| Apton | May 1990 | 75,000 | 120,000 |
| Bindle | October 1991 | 90,000 | 90,000 |
| Cotter | May 1994 | 88,000 | 75,000 |

The premises at Apton and Cotter are owned freehold, whilst the premises at Bindle are owned leasehold. The lease had 40 years to run at the date of purchase. Surplus land adjoining the premises at Cotter was sold for £27,000 in June 1994, at which date the market value of the property retained was £70,000.

(2) The employees from each branch to be closed will be made redundant, resulting in statutory and non-statutory redundancy payments totalling £45,800.

(3) Ten motor cars, which were all purchased in December 1998, are to be sold. Six of the motor cars, which cost £7,500 each, are to be sold for £4,000 each, whilst the other four motor cars, which cost £14,000 each, are to be sold for £9,000 each. The tax written-down value of White Stallion Ltd's motor car pool at 1 August 1999 was £11,500.

(4) The company is to sell its head office building, which cost £140,000 (including land of £50,000) in June 1988, for £285,000 (including land of £90,000). White Stallion Ltd is to relocate its head office to the Isle of Goats enterprise zone, where it is to purchase new premises for £115,000 (including land of £40,000).

(5) A review of White Stallion Ltd's trade debtors, which presently total £945,000, has identified specific doubtful debts of £56,500, of which £32,000 are overdue by more than six months. It has always been the company's policy to provide for a general bad debt provision of 5% on trade debtors.

Before taking into account the effect of the restructuring, White Stallion Ltd forecasts a substantial tax adjusted Schedule D Case I trading loss for the current year to 31 July 2000. A small trading profit is forecast for the following year to 31 July 2001, with steadily increasing profits thereafter. White Stallion Ltd's tax adjusted Schedule D Case I trading profits for recent years have been as follows:

|  | £ |
|--|---|
| Year ended 31 July 1997 | 2,450,000 |
| Year ended 31 July 1998 | 1,680,000 |
| Year ended 31 July 1999 | 1,400,000 |

The company has no other income or outgoings, has paid no dividends in recent years, and does not have any subsidiary companies.

**Required:**

(a) Advise White Stallion Ltd of the tax implications arising from each aspect of its restructuring, and the effect that each will have on its forecast Schedule D Case I trading loss for the year ended 31 July 2000. **(12 marks)**

(b) (i) Advise White Stallion Ltd of the possible ways of relieving its forecast Schedule D Case I trading loss for the year ended 31 July 2000;

(ii) Advise White Stallion Ltd as to which loss relief claims would be the most beneficial;

(iii) Advise White Stallion Ltd as to whether or not it would be beneficial to delay some aspects of its restructuring until after 31 July 2000. Your answer should indicate which aspects, if any, it would be beneficial to delay. **(9 marks)**

(c) Outline the principle differences between tax avoidance and tax evasion. Assuming that it is beneficial for White Stallion Ltd to delay certain aspects of its restructuring until after 31 July 2000, and does so, discuss how this strategy is likely to be viewed by the Inland Revenue.

Assume

(i) an RPI value for July 1999 of 166.8.
(ii) FY 1999 rates etc continue to apply for FY 2000. **(4 marks)**
**(Total 25 marks)**

## 20 (Question 2 of examination)

Ming Lee, a UK resident who was born on 9 June 1947, is a self-employed management consultant. For 1999/00 she will be assessable on Schedule D Case II profits of £102,000, and this level of profits is expected to remain the same for the foreseeable future. Ming has been assessed to the following Schedule D Case II profits since she commenced self-employment during 1992/93.

| Year of assessment | Schedule D Case II profits £ |
|---|---|
| 1992/93 | 26,000 |
| 1993/94 | 34,500 |
| 1994/95 | 47,000 |
| 1995/96 | 53,000 |
| 1996/97 | 63,500 |
| 1997/98 | 70,000 |
| 1998/99 | 89,500 |

Because she operates from rented office accommodation, Ming's only chargeable business asset is the goodwill of the business which is currently valued at £180,000. She plans to sell her business and retire in four or five years time. However, due to the high level of her profits, Ming is considering the incorporation of her business in the near future.

Ming has funds surplus to her requirements of £140,000, which are presently invested in an ordinary deposit account at a building society. She would like to invest these funds in a way that will reduce her overall liability to income tax. Apart from building society interest of £9,280 (net) pa, Ming, who is single, has no other income. Her only outgoing is interest of £12,000 pa (gross) on her mortgage of £120,000. Ming's only previous payment of a personal pension premium was one of £20,000 during 1996/97.

**Required:**

(a) Calculate the maximum amount of tax deductible contributions that Ming could make into a personal pension scheme for 1999/00. Advise Ming of whether or not it would be beneficial for her to actually contribute this maximum amount, and whether or not this is a suitable investment for her.

**(7 marks)**

(b) As an alternative to investing in a personal pension scheme, Ming is considering utilising her surplus funds as follows:

(i) Repaying some, or all, of her mortgage.

(ii)    Purchasing National Savings Certificates.

(iii)   Investing in an enterprise zone trust which will itself invest in commercial properties situated in enterprise zones.

Advise Ming of the suitability of each of these alternatives to her particular circumstances. Your answer should include an outline of the tax implications of each alternative.

**(8 marks)**

(c)    Outline the taxation factors that would have to be considered when deciding whether or not Ming should incorporate her business. You are not expected to include calculations in your answer, and you should ignore the implications arising from capital allowances and the private use of assets.

**(10 marks)**

You should assume that the tax rates and allowances for 1999/00 apply throughout.

**(Total 25 marks)**

---

| **21** | **(Question 3 of examination)** |
|---|---|

(a)    Clark Kent, aged 43, is to commence self-employment on 1 July 2000 running a business importing goods from the country of Guyani. Previously, Clark had worked in Guyani for five years, earning a salary of £26,000 pa, returning to the UK on 31 January 1999. During his period of employment in Guyani he was classed as non-resident in the UK. After returning to the UK, Clark immediately commenced employment with Krypton plc at a salary of £30,000 pa on a three year contract. Unfortunately the company ran into financial difficulties and terminated his contract on 31 May 2000.

Under the terms of his contract, Clark was paid compensation of £10,500 in respect of its premature termination, and was also allowed to purchase his 1800cc company motor car for £5,000, despite its actual market value being £7,000. The car had been purchased new on 1 June 1999 for £9,700, and Clark will use the car in his new business. From 1 June 1999 to 31 May 2000, Clark drove 24,000 miles of which 80% were for business purposes, and was not required to reimburse Krypton plc for the use of private petrol. The proportion of business to private usage is likely to remain the same when he becomes self-employed.

Clark has forecast that for his first year of trading to 30 June 2001 he will make a tax adjusted Schedule D Case I trading loss of £11,250 before taking account of capital allowances. For the following year to 30 June 2002 he forecasts a profit of £30,000, with steadily increasing profits thereafter. On 1 July 2000 he is to purchase two delivery vans costing £13,750 each. Clark is single, and has no other income or outgoings.

**Required:**

(i)    Calculate Clark's taxable income for the years of assessment 1997/98 to 2000/01, before taking into account relief for his forecast Schedule D Case I trading loss for the year ended 30 June 2001. Your answer should include an explanation of your treatment of Clark's compensation package from Krypton plc.

(ii)    Advise Clark of the possible ways of relieving his forecast Schedule D Case I trading loss for the year ended 30 June 2001. Your answer should state by what date each of the alternative loss relief claims should be made.

(iii)   Advise Clark as to which loss relief claims would be the most beneficial for him. Your answer should include calculations of the tax refunds that will be due to Clark. You should ignore the possibility of any repayment supplement being due.

You should assume that the tax rates and allowances for 1999/00 apply throughout.

**(19 marks)**

(b)    Clark is to raise the necessary finance for his new business by borrowing £85,000 from a wealthy grandparent. The interest on this loan will be at a commercial rate, but no date has been agreed for the repayment of the loan. The grandparent has stated that she is prepared to write off £25,000 of the loan upon the date of Clark's marriage, which is planned to take place in 18 months time, and to make a gift of the balance of the loan under the terms of her will. The grandparent is 75 years old, and due to ill health is unlikely to survive beyond the age of 80. She has made substantial gifts of assets in recent years.

**Required:**

Advise Clark and his grandparent of the taxation implications arising from the loan, and from its subsequent write off both at the date of Clark's marriage and upon the grandparent's death.

**(6 marks)**

**(Total 25 marks)**

---

## 22    (Question 4 of examination)

(a)    Mountain Ltd, a UK resident company, has two 100% owned overseas subsidiaries, Ararat Ltd and Logan Ltd, which it has owned for a number of years. Ararat Ltd is situated in the country of Arman, whilst Logan Ltd is situated in the country of Legus. Neither of the two companies are classed as controlled foreign companies. The majority of the group's profits are made in these two countries, so it is the group's policy that the two subsidiaries remit 50% of their distributable profits to the UK in order to fund Mountain Ltd's interest and dividend payments. For the year ended 31 March 2000 Mountain Ltd made a tax adjusted UK trading profit of £90,000. During the year it paid patent royalties of £140,000 (gross) and dividends of £310,000 (net), and received dividends of £15,500 (net) from UK companies. The results of the two overseas subsidiaries for the year ended 31 March 2000 are as follows:

|  | Ararat Ltd | | Logan Ltd | |
|---|---|---|---|---|
|  | £ | £ | £ | £ |
| Trading profit |  | 720,000 |  | 820,000 |
| Taxation |  |  |  |  |
| Corporation tax | 288,000 + 14000 |  | 98,400 |  |
| Deferred tax | – |  | 24,600 |  |
|  |  | 288,000 |  | 123,000 |
| Distributable profits |  | 432,000 – 14 |  | 697,000 |
| Dividends paid | 209000 | = 48000 |  |  |
| Net | 205,200 |  | 348,500 |  |
| Withholding tax | 10,800 |  | – |  |
|  |  | 216,000 |  | 348,500 |
| Retained profits |  | 216,000 |  | 348,500 |

The subsidiaries' dividends were all paid during, and are in respect of, the year ended 31 March 2000. Due to the disallowance of some expenses by the tax authorities in Arman, Ararat Ltd's actual tax liability was £14,000 higher than the figure provided for in its accounts. All of the above figures are in pounds sterling.

**Required:**

Calculate Mountain Ltd's final corporation tax liability for the year ended 31 March 2000. Your answer should include an explanation of your treatment of the patent royalties paid by Mountain Ltd.

**(16 marks)**

(b)    Mountain Ltd is concerned about the level of its worldwide tax charge, and is therefore considering the following alternative proposals:

(1)     Setting up an intermediate 100% holding company in the country of Utopia. The holding company would receive the dividends paid by Ararat Ltd and Logan Ltd, and then pay a corresponding dividend to Mountain Ltd. Utopia is a tax haven which does not levy tax of any kind.

(2)     Mountain Ltd providing some management services to either, or both, of the subsidiaries. A management charge of £60,000 would be raised on each subsidiary in respect of these services, being equivalent to what an unconnected third party would have been charged. For both subsidiaries, the management charge would be a deductible expense against trading profits.

(3)     Increasing or decreasing by £100,000 the dividend payments made by either, or both, of the subsidiaries.

**Required:**

Outline the tax implications arising from each of the three alternative proposals. Your answer should include calculations as appropriate, and you should indicate whether or not each of the proposals would be beneficial to the group as a whole.                                                                   **(9 marks)**
                                                                                                        **(Total 25 marks)**

(This question and the examiner's comments have been modified to exclude topics no longer examinable).

---

## 23     (Question 5 of examination)

(a)     You are the tax adviser to the Down and Out Trust, a charity based in London that has recently been set up to help orphans in England. The trust is recognised as a charity by the Inland Revenue. The trustees of the charity have raised the following queries:

(1)     Most of the trust's income will come from donations and from the investment of surplus funds, but it is also to run some trading activities such as the sale of greetings cards. The trustees want to know the trust's tax position, both for the purposes of income and for capital gains.

(2)     The trustees have a choice of investing surplus funds in either the shares of quoted 'blue chip' UK limited companies, producing dividend income of £700 pa (net) per £10,000 invested, or in gilt-edged UK government stocks, producing income of £900 pa (gross) per £10,000 invested. They want to know the tax implications for each of the alternative investments.

(3)     The trustees would like advice as to the alternative ways by which both limited companies and individuals could make donations to the charity. You should only consider those alternatives that attract tax relief, and you should set out any qualifying conditions that apply to each alternative.

(4)     The trust plans to recruit a number of part-time employees to whom it will pay a generous mileage allowance of £1.00 per mile for the use of their private motor cars. The trustees would like to know the tax implications of this arrangement.

(5)     The trust has just offered a senior management position at an annual salary of £25,000 to Joyce Black, who presently lives in Scotland. The trust will require Joyce to relocate to London, and to assist her in this move have offered her two alternative arrangements:

(i)     The trust will provide Joyce with accommodation for the first 18 months of her employment. The accommodation would consist of a flat in London which has recently been left to the trust under the terms of a benefactor's will. The flat has an annual rateable value of £6,500, and was valued at £85,000 at the date of the gift. The trust has furnished the flat at a cost of £5,400, and will continue to pay for the running costs of £1,300 pa.

(ii)    The trust will pay Joyce £12,750 towards the cost of her relocation. This figure is made up of the £2,200 costs of selling her property in Scotland, removal costs of £550, plus a contribution of £10,000 towards the cost of purchasing a property in London.

The trustees want to know the tax implications arising from each of these two alternative arrangements.

**Required:**

Draft a report to the trustees of the Down and Out Trust answering their queries. You should ignore the implications of National Insurance contribution throughout. **(14 marks)**

(b)     Skunk Ltd owns 70% of the ordinary share capital of both Zebra Ltd and Emu Ltd. All three companies are involved in the construction industry. Skunk Ltd's sales are all standard rated, whilst Zebra Ltd's and Emu Ltd's are zero-rated and exempt respectively. The companies' sales and purchases for the year ended 31 March 2000 are as follows:

|  | Sales<br>£ | Purchases<br>£ |
|---|---|---|
| Skunk Ltd | 1,170,000 | 480,000 |
| Zebra Ltd | 540,000 | 270,000 |
| Emu Ltd | 390,000 | 150,000 |

The purchases for all three companies are standard rated. In addition, Skunk Ltd incurred standard rated overhead expenditure of £300,000 which cannot be directly attributed to any of the three companies' sales. Skunk Ltd charges both of its subsidiary companies a management charge of £40,000 pa each in respect of the services of its accountancy department. All of the above figures are exclusive of VAT where applicable. Skunk Ltd and its two subsidiaries are not registered as a group for VAT purposes.

**Required:**

(i)      Calculate the VAT position of Skunk Ltd, Zebra Ltd and Emu Ltd for the year ended 31 March 2000;

(ii)     Advise Skunk Ltd of the conditions that must be met for itself and its two subsidiaries to register as a group for VAT purposes, and the consequences of being so registered;

(iii)    Advise Skunk Ltd of whether or not it would have been beneficial for itself and both its subsidiaries to have been registered as a group for VAT purposes throughout the year ended 31 March 2000. Your answer should be supported by appropriate calculations.

**(11 marks)**
**(Total 25 marks)**

---

## 24      (Question 6 of examination)

---

Desmond and Myrtle Cook, aged 62 and 67 respectively, are a wealthy couple who are each planning to make a gift to their only child, Judy aged 33. The gifts are to be made on 31 March 2000 (you should assume that today's date is 10 March 2000), and are as follows:

Desmond is to gift his furnished holiday cottage worth £161,000. During 1999/00 rental income of £16,200 was received in respect of the cottage, whilst the running costs amounted to £1,340. In addition, the roof of the cottage had to be replaced during May 1999 at a cost of £1,400 due to storm damage. The cottage was bought on 1 October 1986 for £23,000, and from that date until 31 March 1998, it was rented out as unfurnished accommodation. On 1 April 1998 the cottage was furnished, and from that date onwards has been rented out as furnished holiday accommodation, meeting the conditions for treatment as a 'trade' under Schedule A throughout the whole of this period.

Myrtle is to gift 8,000 of her 20,000 £1 ordinary shares in Artic Ltd, an unquoted trading company. She has been a full-time working director of this company, for the past eight years, earning a salary of £40,000 pa. Her 20,000 shares represent a shareholding of exactly 8%. The remainder of the company's share capital is held by unconnected persons. Artic Ltd's shares are worth £15.00 each for a holding of less than 5%, and £16.50 each for a holding of between 5% and 10%. All the assets of Artic Ltd are in use for the purpose of its trade. Myrtle inherited the shares on 1 April 1997 when they were valued at £48,000.

Both Desmond and Myrtle have made previous lifetime transfers of assets. Desmond made a gift of £98,000 in May 1994 to his brother. Myrtle made a gift of £160,000 in July 1993 to a discretionary trust for the benefit of her nephews. The couple's other assets consist of their jointly owned main residence which is worth £172,000, and investments held by Myrtle worth £250,000. These investments produce taxable income of £14,000 pa (gross). Apart from Desmond's pension of £3,600 pa, the couple have no other income or outgoings. Under the terms of their wills, both Desmond and Myrtle have left all of their assets to Judy.

**Required:**

(a)    (i)    Calculate their taxable income and chargeable gains for 1999/00;    **(11 marks)**

       (ii)   Calculate the inheritance tax liabilities that would arise if they were both to die during June 2002. You should assume that the holiday cottage and the 8,000 shares in Artic Ltd are still owned by Judy at that date.    **(7 marks)**

              Assume that Desmond and Myrtle make their gifts to Judy on 31 March 2000.

(b)    Outline tax planning measures that Desmond and Myrtle could take in order to reduce their overall liability to income tax, capital gains tax, and potential liability to inheritance tax. The couple do not wish to change their overall portfolio of investments.    **(7 marks)**

       You should assume that the tax rates and allowances for 1999/00 apply throughout.

                                                                              **(Total 25 marks)**

## JUNE 1994 EXAMINER'S COMMENTS

### General comments

The first examination session of this paper was sat by a high number of candidates. However, a substantial proportion of these were not adequately prepared. Too many candidates are failing due to a lack of basic knowledge and poor presentation. The poor presentation was particularly relevant for question 4(a). Candidates attempted to answer this question using a single column layout, but this approach made the correct treatment of the charge on income and ACT virtually impossible, unless time was wasted reproducing the same information in the form of workings.

**Question 1: part (a) tested candidates' ability to explain the tax implications arising from a company's restructuring of its business. Part (b) tested candidates' ability to explain the possible ways of the company relieving a trading loss; and advise on whether or not it would be beneficial to delay certain aspects of the restructuring. Part (c) tested candidates' knowledge of the difference between tax avoidance and tax evasion.**

This was a popular question and was reasonably well answered. In part (a), many candidates pooled all the motor cars, despite the fact that four of them cost over £12,000. Another common mistake was to state that a balancing adjustment would arise as a result of industrial buildings allowances having been given in respect of the head office building. Part (b) was quite well answered, although many candidates did not answer in the depth appropriate to a 9 mark section. A disappointing number of candidates are still confusing the taxation of limited companies and unincorporated businesses, and wrote about loss relief under S72 FA 1991 being given against capital gains. Part (c) was well answered.

**Question 2: part (a) tested candidates' ability to calculate the maximum amount of tax deductible personal pension contributions that a tax payer could pay. Part (b) tested candidates' ability to advise on the investment of surplus funds as regards either the repayment of a mortgage; purchasing National Savings Certificates; or investing in an enterprise zone trust. Part (c) tested candidates' ability to explain the tax factors that must be considered when deciding upon the incorporation of a business.**

This was another popular question, but was generally poorly answered. In part (a), very few candidates managed to correctly calculate the personal pension contribution that could be paid, with failure to restrict net relevant earnings to the earnings cap being the most common mistake. Other mistakes of a more serious nature included the use of building society interest as net relevant earnings, and failure to include unused relief brought forward from the previous six years. Part (b) was reasonably well answered, with the exception of enterprise zone trusts. Although this type of investment is not one that many candidates would have encountered before, those candidates who drew sensible conclusions (based on the fact that industrial buildings allowances at the rate of 100% are available in respect of commercial buildings purchased in enterprise zones) gained reasonable marks. Part (c) was reasonably well answered, but many candidates did not go into sufficient depth to gain high marks. Those candidates who wrote at length about the commencement rules applicable to limited companies, cannot expect to pass this examination.

**Question 3: Part (a) tested candidates' ability to calculate taxable income for an individual; advise on the possible ways of relieving a trading loss; and advise as to the most beneficial way of relieving the loss. Part (b) tested candidates' knowledge of the tax implications arising from the raising of finance by way of a loan from a relative, and from its subsequent write off.**

This was also a popular question, which was generally well answered. Some candidates wasted time by calculating tax payable, rather than taxable income. In respect of the loss relief aspects, many candidates, although answering correctly, did not go into sufficient depth to gain high marks. The inclusion of capital allowances in the loss claims was often poorly understood. Very few candidates attempted to calculate the tax refunds that were due. Again, time was wasted by a discussion of relieving the loss against capital gains under S72 FA 1991 when no mention of capital gains was made in the question. Part (b) was generally answered very well.

**Question 4: Part (a) tested candidates' ability to calculate the corporation tax liabilities of a limited company with two overseas subsidiaries. Part (b) tested candidates' ability to explain the tax implications arising from the setting up of an intermediate overseas holding company; the provision of management services to the subsidiaries; and the increase or decrease of the dividends paid by the subsidiaries.**

This question was very poorly answered. Those candidates that were well prepared had no problem in gaining full marks for part (a). Unfortunately, the remaining candidates had little idea on how to calculate the Schedule D case I income or on what basis to apportion the charge on income. As noted above, many candidates need to give more thought to the presentation of their answers. Part (b) was the most difficult section on the paper, and was very badly answered. Any sensible conclusion gained reasonable marks, but as regards the setting up of an intermediate holding company, for example, most candidates discussed the controlled foreign company legislation, without appreciating that the company was going to pay a dividend equal to its income, and therefore could not be a controlled foreign company.

**Question 5: part (a) tested candidates' ability to provide advice on the tax implications in respect of a number of queries raised by a charity. Part (b) tested candidates' ability to calculate the VAT position of a group of companies; to explain the conditions to be met in order to register as a group for VAT purposes; and the implications of registering.**

This was not a popular question, and was generally answered very poorly. Part (b) should have provided easy marks, but candidates displayed a limited knowledge of charitable donations, mileage allowances, and relocation costs. A number of candidates simply misread the question, and wrote at length about discretionary trusts. In part (b), it was disappointing that a large number of candidates could not correctly calculate the VAT payable or recoverable by the three group companies. A number of candidates even stated that an exempt company was entitled to recover VAT. Few candidates appreciated that a group VAT registration would lead to the group becoming partially exempt, and fewer still could then calculate the VAT position.

**Question 6: part (a) tested candidates' ability to calculate the taxable income, chargeable gains, and IHT liabilities arising in respect of a married couple who were both to make lifetime gifts to their daughter. Part (b) tested candidates' ability to provide tax planning advice to the couple in respect of their income tax, CGT and IHT liabilities.**

This was the most popular question on the paper, being attempted by nearly every candidate. On part (a), the income tax and the CGT aspects were answered quite well, although most candidates missed the wear and tear allowance available against the rental income. The IHT calculations presented more problems. Too many candidates did not appreciate that the shares in the unquoted company were valued differently for CGT and for IHT purposes, and the seven year cumulation period resulted in a number of confused answers. Some candidates calculated a joint IHT liability for the husband and the wife, whilst others did not split the liability between that arising in respect of lifetime gifts, and that arising on the estate at death. Candidates should note that business property relief is given before annual exemptions, and not after. In part (b) the tax planning advice was quite poor, especially as regards CGT.

# JUNE 1994 ANSWERS

## 19    (Answer 1 of examination)

(a)    **Closure of branches**

The disposal of the premises of the three branches to be closed will result in the following capital gains/losses:

|  | | Apton £ | Bindle £ | Cotter £ |
|---|---|---|---|---|
| Proceeds | | 120,000 | 90,000 | 75,000 |
| Cost | | 75,000 | | |
| $90,000 \times \dfrac{88.617}{95.457}$ (W) | | | 83,551 | |
| $88,000 \times \dfrac{70,000}{97,000}$ | | | | 63,505 |
| | | 45,000 | 6,449 | 11,495 |
| Indexation | $75,000 \times \dfrac{166.8 - 126.2}{126.2}$ (0.322) | 24,150 | | |
| | $83,551 \times \dfrac{166.8 - 135.1}{135.1}$ (0.235) | | 19,634 | |
| | $63,505 \times \dfrac{166.8 - 144.7}{144.7}$ (0.153) | | | 9,716 |
| Capital gains | | 20,850 | – | 1,779 |

Capital gains for the year ended 31 July 2000 will be £22,629 (20,850 + 1,779). (Indexation allowance cannot create a loss.)

WORKING

The lease has 31 years 3 months left to run at July 2000. The appropriate lease percentage is therefore:

$$88.371 + \tfrac{3}{12} (89.354 - 88.371) = 88.617$$

**Redundancy payments**

Statutory redundancy payments are a deductible expense where they are made in respect of employment wholly in a trade, profession or vocation carried on by the employer. Non-statutory redundancy payments are also allowable, unless made on the cessation of trading. Since White Stallion Ltd would appear to be discontinuing an identifiable part of its trade, the deduction of non-statutory redundancy payments may therefore be restricted to three times the statutory payment. White Stallion Ltd's Schedule D Case I trading loss for the year ended 31 July 2000 will therefore be increased by most, if not all, of the redundancy payments of £45,800.

**Motor cars**

The proceeds from the sale of the six motor cars originally costing £7,500 each will be deducted from the tax written-down value of the motor car pool for cars costing less than £12,000 as follows:

|  | Motor car pool £ |
|---|---|
| WDV brought forward | 11,500 |
| Disposal proceeds (6 × 4,000) | 24,000 |
|  | 12,500 |
| Balancing charge | 12,500 |
| WDV carried forward | – |

The balancing charge will reduce the Schedule D Case I trading loss for the year ended 31 July 2000.  The four motor cars originally costing £14,000 each, being 'expensive cars', will not have been pooled.  There will be a balancing allowance in respect of each car as follows:

|  | £ |
|---|---|
| Original cost | 14,000 |
| WDA – year ended 31 July 1999 | 3,000 |
|  |  |
| WDV carried forward | 11,000 |
| Disposal proceeds | 9,000 |
|  |  |
| Balancing allowance | 2,000 |

Balancing allowances of £8,000 (4 × 2,000) will increase White Stallion Ltd's Schedule D Case I trading loss for the year ended 31 July 2000.

**Sale of head office**

The sale of the head office building will result in a capital gain as follows:

|  | £ |
|---|---|
| Proceeds | 285,000 |
| Cost | 140,000 |
|  |  |
|  | 145,000 |
| Indexation $140,000 \times \dfrac{166.8 - 106.6}{106.6}$ (0.565) | 79,100 |
|  |  |
|  | 65,900 |

**Rollover relief**

It will not be possible to rollover the gain arising on the sale of the head office building against the cost of the new premises, since £170,000 (285,000 – 115,000) of the proceeds are not to be re-invested, and this figure exceeds the capital gain.

It will, however, be possible to rollover £15,850 of the gain arising on the premises sold at Apton as follows:

|  | £ |
|---|---|
| Proceeds | 120,000 |
| Re-investment | (115,000) |
|  |  |
| Proceeds not re-invested | 5,000 |
|  |  |
| Capital gain | 20,850 |
| Proceeds not re-invested | (5,000) |
|  |  |
| Gain rolled over | 15,850 |

This leaves a capital gain of £5,000 and is preferable to rolling over the gain arising on the premises at Cotter, as the gain involved in this case is only £1,779 (there would be no restriction on the amount of gain that could be rolled over as proceeds do not exceed the re-investment). The net chargeable gains for the year ended 31 July 2000 are £72,679 (65,900 + 5,000 + 1,779).

**Purchase of new head office**

The new head office is to be located in an enterprise zone, and will therefore qualify for a 100% initial allowance based on the cost of the building of £75,000 (115,000 – 40,000). This will increase the Schedule D Case I trading loss for the year ended 31 July 2000.

**Bad debts**

The annual increase or decrease in a general bad debt provision is non-deductible, and will therefore have been ignored in calculating the Schedule D Case I trading loss for the year ended 31 July 2000. If either a specific provision is set up, or the debts are actually written off, the bad debts of £56,500 will be deductible. If the debts are written off, a refund of VAT of £4,766 $\left(32,000 \times \frac{7}{47}\right)$ will be due in respect of those debts over six months old from the date payment was due. This refund will reduce the deductible bad debt figure to £51,734 (56,500 – 4,766).

(b)      (i)      White Stallion Ltd has three alternative ways of relieving its Schedule D Case I trading loss for the year ended 31 July 2000, as follows:

– Carrying the loss forward against future trading profits under S393(1) ICTA 1988. This does not appear to be beneficial, since the Schedule D Case I trading profits for the year ended 31 July 2001 are forecast to be small, with only steadily increasing profits thereafter. Relief for the loss would therefore be delayed, and would almost certainly only be at the small company rate.

– Claim under S393A(1) ICTA 1988 against total profits of the year ended 31 July 2000. This claim would only attract tax relief at the rate of 20%, since the only other income for this year is the capital gains of £72,679 arising on the sale of the head office building and the branches. However, this claim is necessary in order to make the following claim to carry back losses against total profits of the previous 12 months.

– Claim under S393A(1) ICTA 1988 against total profits of the year ended 31 July 1999. Relief will be obtained against profits at the rate of just over 32.5% on the excess over £300,000, with relief at just above 20% thereafter.

(ii)      Relieving the loss against total profits of the year ended 31 July 1999 under S393A(1) ICTA 1988 obtains relief at up to 32.5%, compared to 20% if the loss relief claim is restricted to total profits of the current year, or if the loss is carried forward against future trading profits. The most beneficial loss relief claim is therefore to claim under S393A(1) ICTA 1988 against total profits of the year ended 31 July 2000, and then against the total profits of the year ended 31 July 1999.

(iii)      It would be beneficial for White Stallion Ltd to delay until after 31 July 2000 any aspect of the restructuring that reduces the amount of its Schedule D Case I trading loss available for carry back to the year ended 31 July 1999. This will result in increased loss relief at up to just over 32.5%, with a corresponding increase in profits for the year ended 31 July 2001 assessable at 20%.

The aspects of the restructuring that should be delayed until after 31 July 2000 are as follows:

– The disposal of the six motor cars costing £7,500 each. Additional capital allowances of £2,875 (11,500 × 25%) will increase the Schedule D Case I trading loss for the year ended 31 July 2000, whilst the balancing charge of £15,375 (12,500 + 2,875) will then fall into the year ended 31 July 2001.

–      The disposal of the head office building and the Apton and Cotter premises. This will avoid the need for a loss claim against the total profits of the year ended 31 July 2000, thus increasing the loss to be carried back by £72,679

All other aspects of the reorganisation should be carried out during July 2000, with maximum allowances being claimed eg, the 100% initial allowances on the new head office building in the enterprise zone.

(c)      Tax avoidance involves the reduction of tax liabilities by the use of lawful means. In the case of the *Duke of Westminster v CIR* (1935) it was stated that 'every man is entitled if he can to order his affairs so that the tax attaching . . . . is less than it otherwise would be'. In more recent cases such as *WT Ramsey Ltd v CIR* (1981) and *Furniss v Dawson* (1984), the courts have set limits to the ambit within which this principle can be applied in relation to artificial arrangements to avoid tax. By contrast, tax evasion involves the reduction of tax liabilities by illegal means, eg, suppressing information or making false representation to the Inland Revenue.

White Stallion Ltd's strategy in maximising its trading loss available for carry back under S393A(1) ICTA 1988 would appear to be within the ambit of tax avoidance, since it involves the careful timing of transactions in order to optimise the company's tax position. However, if the reality of the situation was misrepresented, for example the motor cars were actually sold in July 2000 but the sales invoice was dated August 2000, then this comes within the scope of tax evasion.

*(Tutorial notes:*

(1)      When a short lease is disposed of the cost is calculated as:

$$\text{original cost} \times \frac{\text{lease percentage for duration of lease at time of disposal}}{\text{lease percentage for duration of lease at time of acquisition}}$$

(2)      Disposal of the premises at Cotter.

A part disposal took place in June 1994 when the land was sold, the cost using the $\frac{A}{A+B}$ formula would have been:

$$88,000 \times \frac{27,000}{27,000 + 70,000}$$

When the premises are sold in July 2000, the remainder of the original cost is used, ie:

$$88,000 \times \frac{70,000}{27,000 + 70,000}$$

(3)      Expensive cars

Remember that expensive cars are not pooled and a separate column is needed for each of them for capital allowance calculations.*)

---

## 20      (Answer 2 of examination)

(a)      Ming's maximum tax deductible personal pension is £98,300 calculated as follows:

|  | Net relevant earnings £ | Relevant percentage | Maximum premium £ |
|---|---|---|---|
| 1993/94 | 34,500 | 20 | 6,900 |
| 1994/95 | 47,000 | 25 | 11,750 |
| 1995/96 | 53,000 | 25 | 13,250 |
| 1996/97 | 63,500 | 25 | Nil (see below) |
| 1997/98 | 70,000 | 25 | 17,500 |

|        |        |     |        |
|--------|--------|-----|--------|
| 1998/99 | 87,600 | 25 | 21,900 |
| 1999/00 | 90,600 | 30 | 27,180 |
|        |        |     | 98,480 |

Unused relief is carried forward for six years, and utilised on a FIFO basis. Therefore, the excess premium of £4,125 [20,000 – (63,500 × 25%)] paid during 1996/97 would have utilised most of Ming's unused relief for 1992/93 (26,000 × 20% = £5,200). Her net relevant earnings for 1998/99 and 1999/00 are restricted to the earnings cap of £87,600 and £90,600.

Although Ming has sufficient Schedule D Case II profits for 1999/00 to utilise a personal pension premium of £98,480, it would be beneficial to limit the premium for this year to her earnings that are taxable at the rate of 40%. These are £81,265 as follows:

|                                |   £     |
|--------------------------------|---------|
|                                |         |
| Schedule D Case II             | 102,000 |
| BSI $(9,280 \times {}^{100}\!/_{80})$ | 11,600  |
|                                |         |
|                                | 113,600 |
| Personal allowance             | (4,335) |
|                                |         |
| Taxable income                 | 109,265 |
| 10/23% tax band                | 28,000  |
|                                |         |
| Taxable at 40%                 | 81,265  |

This premium can either be paid during 1999/00 or, alternatively, could be paid by 5 April 2001 with Ming electing before 31 January 2002 to have it related back to 1999/00. Ming's remaining unused relief of £17,215 (98,480 – 81,265) could be utilised by either:

(i)    Paying a premium before 5 April 2000 (assuming that it is not yet that date), and electing by 31 January 2001 to have it related back to 1998/99. This would also allow Ming's unused relief from 1992/93 of £1,075 (5,200 – 4,125) to be utilised.

(ii)   Carrying it forward and paying a premium in respect of 2000/01.

       Both of these options should attract tax relief at 40%.

Because Ming's personal pension scheme premiums should attract tax relief at 40%, this represents an attractive investment for her. When she retires, she will be entitled to receive up to 25% of the available benefit as a tax-free lump sum, and the pension that she receives may well only be taxed at 23% depending on her level of income at that date. The drawback to Ming paying into a personal pension scheme is that since she is already 52 years old, and plans to retire in four or five years time, the investment return in the form of a pension may be poor.

(b)    (i)    **Repayment of mortgage**

              Ming has a mortgage of £120,000, of which only the interest on the first £30,000 qualifies for tax relief, and this is limited to 10% and abolished altogether from 6 April 2000). By contrast, her building society interest is taxed at 40%. Taking into account the additional factor that mortgage interest rates are generally higher than rates on building society deposit accounts (Ming receives interest of £11,600 pa for her deposits which are presumably in excess of £140,000, yet pays mortgage interest of £12,000 on a £120,000 loan), Ming would benefit from paying off at least £90,000 (120,000 – 30,000) of her mortgage compared to leaving her money invested in the building society deposit account. Whether or not she should actually do this depends on the investment returns that she could make on alternative investments, but this option does have the attraction of being relatively risk-free.

(ii)     **National Savings Certificates**

The interest from National Savings Certificates is free of income tax, and this would therefore be an attractive investment when compared to Ming's building society deposit account. For the best yield, the certificates must be held for five years, but this should not be a problem given Ming's present level of income. The disadvantage is that there is a maximum investment of £10,000 per issue of certificates, and so would only utilise a proportion of Ming's surplus funds.

(iii)    **Enterprise zone trust**

An enterprise zone trust purchases commercial property in enterprise zones, and then rents it out. Provided certain conditions are met, the investor, Ming, is then able to claim 100% Industrial Buildings Allowances which are initially set against the rental income received, and then against other income. This investment therefore has the attraction of tax relief at 40% with the possibility of future capital gains. Also, there is no maximum amount that can be invested. The disadvantages are that there is an element of risk involved, and the investment must be considered as long-term, ie, for a minimum of at least five years. Provided the level of risk is acceptable, this represents an attractive investment for some of Ming's surplus funds.

(c)     The taxation factors that would have to be considered in deciding whether or not Ming should incorporate her business are as follows:

**Tax rates and payments**

On profits up to £300,000 companies only pay corporation tax at the rate of 20%. It will therefore be possible for Ming to reduce her overall tax liability (herself and the company) by restricting the amount of her director's remuneration. She could, for example, restrict her tax liability to 23% tax by limiting her director's remuneration to £20,735 (28,000 + 4,335 − 11,600). Profits would be rolled-up in the company, and could be withdrawn as a capital gain when the company is disposed of (or it could be liquidated). The availability of retirement relief would limit the tax charge on this gain although retirement relief is being phased out and will be completely abolished for disposals after 5 April 2003.

The due date of corporation tax is nine months after the end of the company's accounting period unless the company is 'large'. Income tax on profits from a trade is payable by reference to the accounts ending in the fiscal year, so that the time between earning the profits and paying the tax depends on the accounting year end. If Ming draws remuneration, PAYE must be deducted and paid to the Revenue monthly.

**National Insurance contributions**

As a director, Ming's NIC liability will almost certainly increase compared to her liability whilst self-employed, with the maximum contributions probably being due in both cases. The main additional cost will arise as a result of there being no maximum limit to employers' secondary Class 1 National Insurance contribution on Ming's director's remuneration. It would be possible to avoid this additional National Insurance contribution liability by withdrawing profits by way of dividends rather than director's remuneration. Dividends are not subject to National Insurance contribution and are neutral from an income tax point of view when compared to director's remuneration.

**Pension**

There is no reason why Ming should not continue with her personal pension scheme contributions following incorporation. It should be noted, however, that restricting director's remuneration in order to facilitate the income tax and National Insurance contribution planning outlined above, will also limit the amount of tax deductible premiums that could be paid into a personal pension scheme. Dividends do not count as net relevant earnings.

Alternatively, a company pension scheme could be set up. Contributions made by the company would be deductible against Schedule D profits, and would not be subject to a maximum limit. Contributions made by Ming would also be tax deductible against her director's remuneration, although her contributions would be restricted to 15% of those earnings. This is considerably less than Ming's present personal pension scheme limit of 30% of net relevant earnings. Other factors to consider are that the permissible benefits upon retirement under an occupational scheme are restricted according to the number of years service and the level of final remuneration, and that the earliest retirement age is 60 (compared to 50 for a personal pension scheme).  Inland Revenue approval is required for a scheme where these factors are improved upon.

### Cessation of sole tradership

Under the current year basis when Ming ceases trading, the assessment for the final year will be based on the profits earned since the end of the accounting period ending in the previous year, with relief being given for the transitional overlap profits.  The date of cessation can then be chosen so that the assessable profits in any one tax year are limited, so as not to exceed Ming's basic rate tax band.

### Capital gains

Ming's only chargeable business asset is goodwill, which will presumably result in a capital gain of £180,000 upon the cessation of the sole tradership.  Provided that the consideration from the company for the transfer of her business is wholly or mainly in the form of shares, this gain will automatically be heldover against the base cost of those shares.   However, it would be preferable to crystallise the gain by incorporating before 6 April 2000 when the retirement relief when limits are further reduced.  If Ming has traded between 7 and 8 years (since 1992/93) full exemption is available on between £140,000 and £160,000 of gain.  Once past 5 April 2000 the full exempt amount drops to £105,000 and £120,000.  It would be possible to disapply incorporation relief so as to utilise retirement relief at its highest value and not reduce the base cost of the shares.

Ming's entitlement to any unused retirement relief will not be affected by the incorporation of her business, since it is possible to add together the qualifying periods from the sole tradership and from the limited company.  She should therefore qualify for the maximum retirement relief in two or three years' time albeit at much reduced phased out values.

It will also be possible for Ming to defer any gains arising on the disposal of the shares in her company if re-investment is made by subscribing for (EIS) shares in another qualifying unquoted trading company.

### Value added tax

Ming is almost certainly registered for VAT due to the level of her business activities, and the company will be in a similar position.  There will be no VAT charge on the transfer of Ming's trade to the company since it will be disposed of as going concern.  It will also be possible for Ming to transfer her existing VAT registration number to the company.  As a consequence of this the company will take over any of her outstanding VAT liabilities.

*(Tutorial notes:*

(1)     When calculating the relief for personal pension premiums, note that the relevant percentage depends on the individual's age at the **beginning** of the tax year.

(2)     Part (b)  of the question, which asks for investment advice, is a typical question, and you must be familiar with the main investment opportunities and be able to comment on return, risk and accessibility.

(3)     This is a typical question from the current syllabus, in the way that it requires the ability to assess a situation and comment covering the impact on the various taxes.*)

---

## 21    (Answer 3 of examination)

(a)     (i)     **Clark Kent - taxable income 1997/98 to 2000/01**

Clark's income from employment in Guyani will not be assessable to UK income tax, since he was classed as non-resident in the UK during his five years in that country.  He therefore has no income assessable to UK taxation for 1997/98 and so this year is not shown in the calculations.

|  |  | *1998/99* | *1999/00* | *2000/01* |
|---|---|---|---|---|
|  |  | £ | £ | £ |
| Schedule E | – salary | 5,000 | 30,000 | 5,000 |
|  | – car benefit |  | 1,212 | 242 |

| | | | |
|---|---|---|---|
| – fuel benefit | | 1,283 | 257 |
| – compensation | | | 10,500 |
| – motor car | | | 2,000 |
| | 5,000 | 32,495 | 17,999 |
| Personal allowance | 4,335 | 4,335 | 4,335 |
| Taxable income | 665 | 28,160 | 13,664 |

Clark has driven 19,200 (24,000 × 80%) business miles during the 12 months that he had use of this company car, and therefore appears to qualify for the 15% rate of company car benefit, assuming that mileage is spread evenly throughout the 12 months.

His car benefit is £1,212 $(9,700 \times 15\% \times {}^{10}\!/_{12})$ for 1999/00 and £242 $(9,700 \times 15\% \times {}^{2}\!/_{12})$ for 2000/01. His fuel benefit is £1,283 $(1,540 \times {}^{10}\!/_{12})$ for 1999/00 and £257 $(1,540 \times {}^{2}\!/_{12})$ for 2000/01.

The compensation received by Clark for the loss of office is fully taxable, as it is received under the terms of his contract. His acquisition of the motor car would appear to form part of his compensation package, and will therefore also be taxable in full based on the market value of the car (£7,000) less the amount paid by him (£5,000), which amounts to £2,000. If the sale of the motor car at a reduced value was instead made as an exgratia payment rather than as a contractual entitlement, it would be exempt since it is within the £30,000 limit.

(ii) Clark's Schedule D Case I loss for the year ended 30 June 2001 is £23,250 made up as follows:

| | £ |
|---|---|
| Trading loss year ended 30 June 2001 | 11,250 |
| Add: Capital allowances (see below) | 12,000 |
| | 23,250 |

Capital allowances – year ended 30 June 2001

| | Pool £ | Motor car £ | Allowances £ |
|---|---|---|---|
| Additions | 27,500 | 5,000 | |
| FYA - 40% | 11,000 | | 11,000 |
| WDA – 25% | | (1,250) (80%) | 1,000 |
| WDV c/f | 16,500 | 3,750 | 12,000 |

The loss for a year of assessment is calculated on the same basis as profit (ie, applying opening year rules), except that if a loss-making period is part of the basis period for two years of assessment, the loss is allocated to the first year only. The loss is therefore:

| | £ | £ |
|---|---|---|
| 2000/01 (1 July 2000 to 5 April 2001) | | |
| 9/12 × 23,250 | | 17,437 |
| 2001/02 (y/e 30 June 2001) | 23,250 | |
| Less: Allocated to 2000/01 | (17,437) | 5,813 |

The losses may be utilised as follows:

(1) By carry forward under S385 ICTA 1988 against future trading profits. A claim must be made to establish the amount of loss within five years after 31 January following the end of the year of assessment of the loss, ie, by:

31 January 2007 for the loss of 2000/01

31 January 2008 for the loss of 2001/02

(2)　By set off under S380 ICTA 1988 against total income of the year of the loss or the previous year. Thus the 2000/01 loss of £17,437 may be set against other income in 2000/01 or 1999/00, provided a claim is made by 31 January 2003.

The 2000/01 loss of £5,813 may be set against the other income of 2001/02 or 2000/01, and the claim must be made by 31 January 2004.

(3)　Since the loss is incurred in the first four years of trading, Clark could claim loss relief under S381 ICTA 1988 against his total income of the three years preceding the year of assessment of the loss. Thus the loss of 2000/01 could be relieved against his total income of 1997/98 to 1999/00, earliest year first, and the loss of 2001/02 against his total income of 1998/99 to 2000/01, earliest year first. The claims must be made by 31 January 2003 and 31 January 2004 respectively.

(iii)　Clark has a loss of £17,437 for 2000/01, Clark's Schedule D Case I assessments for the first three years of trading will be:

|  | £ |
|---|---|
| 2000/01 (1 July 2000 to 5 April 2001) | Nil |
| 2001/02 (1 July 2000 to 30 June 2001) | Nil |
| 2002/03 (year ended 30 June 2002) (30,000 – 4,875) | 25,125 |

Capital allowances – year ended 30 June 2002

|  | Pool £ | Motor car £ | Allowances £ |
|---|---|---|---|
| WDV b/f | 16,500 | 3,750 | |
| WDA – 25% | (4,125) | (938) (80%) | 4,875 |
| WDV c/f | 12,375 | 2,812 | |

Carrying the loss forward under S385 ICTA 1988 against future trading profits would therefore not be beneficial due to the long delay in obtaining relief.

A claim under S380 ICTA 1988 for the 2000/01 loss is against total income for 2000/01 and/or 1999/00. As the loss is £17,437 a claim against total income of 2000/01 is not advised as this would result in the loss of almost all the personal allowance.

However, a claim against the income of 1998/99 would not waste the personal allowance, and results in saving some tax at 40% - though mainly at 23%.

Clark will receive a tax refund of £4,030 in respect of this loss relief claim as follows:

|  |  | £ |
|---|---|---|
| 28,160 – 28,000 | 160 @ 40% | 64 |
|  | 17,277 @ 23% | 3,974 |
|  | 17,437 | 4,038 |

A claim under S380 ICTA 1988 for the 2001/02 loss is against total income for 2001/02 and/or 2000/01. As there is no other income in 2001/02 a S380 claim is not available and therefore the loss can only be relieved in 2000/01. Clark will receive a tax refund of £1,337 in respect of this loss relief claim as follows:

£5,813 @ 23% = £1,337,

making a total refund of £5,375 (4,038 + 1,337)

Alternatively, Clark could claim under S381 ICTA 1988 for the losses of 2000/01 and 2001/02. As Clark has no income in 1997/98 this results in the loss being off set against his total income of £5,000 for 1998/99, with the balance of the loss of £18,250 (17,437 − 5,000 + 5,813) being set against his income of £32,495 for 1999/00. Clark's personal allowance for 1998/99 is wasted and £160 (28,160 − 28,000) of the loss will be relieved at the rate of 40% in 1999/00. Tax refunds totalling £4,291 (66 + 4,217) will be received in respect of this loss relief claim as follows:

|  |  | £ |
|---|---|---|
| 1998/99 | 665 × 10% | 66 |
| 1999/00 | 160 × 40% | 64 |
|  | 18,250 − 160 = 18,090 × 23% | 4,161 |
|  |  | 4,225 |

The claim under S380 ICTA 1988 results in a higher tax refund of £1,084 (5,375 − 4,291) compared to a claim under S381 ICTA 1988. The claim under S380 ICTA 1988 would appear to be the most beneficial. However, it should be noted that a claim under S381 ICTA 1988 utilises the income for earlier years rather than later years. This could be important if Clark should incur a subsequent trading loss in the first four years of assessment.

(b)    The loan from Clark's grandparent is unlikely to be treated as a transfer of value for the purposes of IHT at the date of the loan, since it carries a commercial rate of interest. If £25,000 of the loan is written off upon the date of Clark's marriage, this will therefore be a potentially exempt transfer at that date. No IHT will be due unless the grandparent dies within seven years of the loan being written off. Should that happen, the IHT liability will be as follows:

|  | £ | £ |
|---|---|---|
| Value transferred |  | 25,000 |
| Marriage exemption | 2,500 |  |
| Annual exemptions (2 at 3,000) | 6,000 |  |
|  |  | 8,500 |
| Chargeable transfer |  | 16,500 |
| IHT liability 16,500 at 40% |  | 6,600 |

This assumes that the grandparent's annual exemptions for the year of the gift and the preceding year are available, which will depend on the timing of other gifts made by her. It is also assumed that the rate of 40% is applicable, since the grandparent has made substantial gifts of assets within recent years. If the period between the date of the gift and the date of death is over three years, then tapering relief will be available. This reduces the amount of the IHT liability by a given percentage, commencing at 20%, and rising to 80% for gifts made more than six years prior to the date of death. The IHT liability will fall on Clark, and will be due within six months from the end of the month of the grandparent's death.

The balance of the loan of £60,000 will form part of the grandparent's estate, and will again be chargeable in full at 40%, assuming that the grandparent has made chargeable transfers of £231,000 or more within seven years of the date of her death. Since the write off of the loan is a specific gift, the IHT liability will fall on the residue of the grandparent's estate, and Clark will receive the net gift of £60,000. This assumes that the terms of the grandparent's will do not state that the gift bears its own tax.

Provided that the loan is used wholly and exclusively for the purposes of his business, Clark will be able to deduct the interest paid on the loan in calculating his Schedule D Case I trading profits.

---

## 22    (Answer 4 of examination)

---

(a)    **Mountain Ltd    mainstream corporation tax liability for the year ended 31 March 2000**

| | Total £ | UK £ | Overseas-Ararat Ltd dividend £ | Overseas Logan Ltd dividend £ |
|---|---|---|---|---|
| Schedule D Case I | 90,000 | 90,000 | | |
| Schedule D Case V (W1) | 367,000 | | 367,000 | |
| Schedule D Case V (W2) | 397,700 | | | 397,700 |
| | 854,700 | 90,000 | 367,000 | 397,700 |
| Less:  Charge on income | 140,000 | 90,000 | | 50,000 |
| PCTCT | 714,700 | – | 367,000 | 347,700 |
| Corporation tax at 30% | 214,410 | – | 110,100 | 104,310 |
| Less:    Double taxation relief (W1/2) | 159,300 | – | 110,100 | 49,200 |
| Find corporation tax liability | 55,110 | – | – | 55,110 |

The patent royalties, being a charge on income, have been allocated initially to UK income, and then against the overseas dividend from Logan Ltd.  This preserves the maximum amount of double taxation relief in respect of the overseas dividend from Ararat Ltd, which has the highest effective rate of overseas tax.  The full rate of corporation tax is applicable since there are three associated companies in the group:

$$\left( \frac{1,500,000}{3} = 500,000 \right)$$

WORKINGS

(W1)    Dividend from Ararat Ltd

Since Mountain Ltd owns over 10% of the share capital of Ararat Ltd, relief for the underlying tax paid in Arman is available as well as for the withholding tax.  The underlying relief is based on the amount of Arman tax actually paid (288,000 + 14,000 = £302,000), rather than the figure provided for in the accounts – *Bowater Paper Corporation v Murgatroyd* (1969).

| | £ |
|---|---|
| Dividend received | 205,200 |
| Withholding tax | 10,800 |
| | 216,000 |
| Underlying tax 216,000 × $\dfrac{302,000}{432,000}$ | 151,000 |
| Schedule D Case V income | 367,000 |

Total overseas tax (10,800 + 151,000) = 161,800

Double taxation relief is restricted to the amount of UK corporation tax on the dividend from Ararat Ltd (110,100), since this is less than the total overseas tax.  The effective rate of overseas tax is:

---

$$44.09\% \left( \frac{161,800}{367,000} \times 100 \right)$$

(W2)  Dividend from Logan Ltd

Since Mountain Ltd owns over 10% of the share capital of Logan Ltd, relief for the underlying tax paid in Legus is available. The underlying relief is based on the distributable profits per the accounts, after deducting deferred taxation.

|  | £ |
|---|---|
| Dividend received | 348,500 |
| Underlying tax $348,500 \times \dfrac{98,400}{697,000}$ | 49,200 |
| Schedule D Case V income | 397,700 |

Total overseas tax = £49,200

The total overseas tax is less than the amount of UK corporation tax on the dividend from Logan Ltd (104,310), and so can be relieved in full. The effective rate of overseas tax is:

$$12.37\% \left( \frac{49,200}{397,700} \times 100 \right)$$

(b)  (1)  Relief for underlying overseas tax paid is available even if the required 10% shareholding is held indirectly. The insertion of an intermediate holding company in the country of Utopia would not, therefore, preclude underlying tax relief. What it will do, however, is 'average' out the effective rate of overseas tax paid. Since the dividend from Ararat Ltd presently suffers a high effective rate of overseas tax of 44.09%, this should be beneficial since it will increase the amount of double taxation relief available. The UK corporation tax on the dividend received from the Utopian holding company will be £214,410 (367,000 + 397,700 − 50,000 = 714,700 × 30%). Since this is higher than the total overseas tax of £211,000 (161,800 + 49,200), the overseas tax can be relieved in full.

(2)  If Mountain Ltd raises a management charge of £60,000 on either, or both of, its subsidiaries, this will have the effect of increasing profits chargeable to UK corporation tax. Raising a management charge on Ararat Ltd would definitely be beneficial since it would presumably be deductible against profits subject to tax at the rate of 40% $\left( ^{288,000}\!/_{720,000} \times 100 \right)$ in Arman. A management charge raised on Logan Ltd would only attract tax relief at the rate of 12% $\left( ^{98,400}\!/_{820,000} \times 100 \right)$ in Legus, and would therefore not be beneficial.

It is possible that the management charge could be zero-rated as an international service, depending on its nature, but it is more likely to be standard rated. Since only subsidiaries that are resident in the UK can form part of a VAT group, this would be an additional cost. Although standard rating the charge to Ararat Ltd would still appear beneficial, the charge to Logan Ltd would make it even less tax efficient.

(3)  Increasing or decreasing the amount of the dividend paid by Ararat Ltd would have no tax implications, apart from the slightly increased or decreased amount of withholding tax that would be paid in Arman. This is because there is no additional UK corporation tax liability on the dividend received from this subsidiary. However, increasing Logan Ltd's dividend by £100,000 would increase the UK corporation tax charge by £20,117 as follows:

|  | £ |
|---|---|
| Dividend received (348,500 + 100,000) | 448,500 |
| Underlying tax $448,500 \times \dfrac{98,400}{697,000}$ | 63,318 |
|  | 511,818 |
| Less: Charge on income | 50,000 |
|  | 461,818 |
| Corporation tax at 30% | 138,545 |
| Less: Double taxation relief | 63,318 |
|  | 75,227 |
| Previous UK CT charge | 55,110 |
| Additional UK CT charge | 20,117 |

Mountain Ltd receives the additional dividend of £100,000 and has to pay a further £20,117 in corporation tax.

*(Tutorial note:* notice the effect of setting up an intermediate company in Utopia, this allows the overseas tax paid in the two companies to be averaged out.*)*

---

## 23     (Answer 5 of examination)

(a)     **The trust's tax position**

Registered charities are exempt from tax on investment income used solely for charitable purposes, and this will include income from donations and covenants. Profits from trading activities are not automatically exempt, but will be so where the trading is either in the course of carrying out the charity's primary purpose, or the trade is carried on mainly by beneficiaries of the charity. For example, if greeting cards were made by the orphans, the profits from trading would be exempt. In other cases, the profits from trading would be assessable as normal. A charity is not liable to capital gains tax in respect of gains arising on the disposal of assets where the gains are applied for charitable purposes.

**Investment alternatives**

Being exempt from tax, the trust will be able to reclaim the tax credit that is attached to the dividends that it receives from UK limited companies, although this is being phased out for charities from 6 April 2000. This credit is restricted to 21% of the net distribution (for 1999/00), and so the trust's gross income will be £847 $\left(700 \times \frac{121}{100}\right)$ per £10,000 invested but will decline up to and including 2003/04 as the recoverable rate of credit is phased out. Provided evidence is provided of charitable status, the interest from gilt-edged UK government stocks will be similarly exempt. Since the gross income from gilt-edged UK government stocks will be £900 per £10,000 invested, they would appear to produce the better rate of return. However, this ignores other factors such as the possibility of capital appreciation (or depreciation) and the comparative risk of the two alternatives.

**Donations**

There are a number of ways in which both limited companies and individuals can give to charity and receive tax relief on their donations, as follows:

(1)     Both limited companies and individuals can make covenants to charity. A covenant is a legally binding agreement signifying an enforceable obligation to make the payment. For individuals, the payer makes the payment net of basic rate income tax, and obtains tax relief on the payment as an

annual charge at his or her marginal rate of tax.  The charity can reclaim the tax deducted upon making a claim to the Inland Revenue.  The deed of covenant must be capable of exceeding three years, must be irrevocable during its first three years, and must not be for valuable consideration. For limited companies, charitable deeds of covenant are treated as a charge on income and will attract relief at their marginal rate of corporation tax.  The income tax deducted will be accounted for to the Inland Revenue under the quarterly accounting system, with payment being due 14 days after the relevant quarter.

(2)     Both limited companies and individuals can make one-off qualifying donations to charity under the gift aid scheme.  For individuals and close companies the minimum donation is £250 (net), with the payment being treated in the same way as a covenanted payment.  The gift must not be subject to any condition for repayment, and the total benefits received by the donee from the charity must not exceed the lower of:

(i)     2.5% of the net gift; and

(ii)    £250 per tax year.

The above conditions do not apply to gifts made by non-close companies.

(3)     Employees can authorise participating employers to deduct up to £1,200 pa from their earnings before tax, for passing on to charities of their choice.  The employee thus receives full tax relief on the donations made.

(4)     Limited companies, sole traders and partnerships can obtain a deduction against Schedule D Case I profits for donations to charity that are incurred wholly and exclusively for the purposes of their trade.  The donation must be small, and be to a charity that is local to the donor's business activities. This alternative is therefore unlikely to apply to the Down and Out Trust.

**Mileage allowances**

The employees will be assessed under Schedule E on the mileage allowances that they receive.  Against this they can claim the business proportion of car tax, insurance, repairs, maintenance and fuel.  They can also claim capital allowances on the cost of their cars, again restricted to the business proportion.  Alternatively, the employees could claim the mileage rates as allowed under the fixed profit car scheme.  The rates are based on a car's cylinder capacity, and replace the claim for expenses and capital allowances.  Any amount paid in excess of the mileage rates are taxable on the employee.

**Accommodation**

Joyce will be assessed under Schedule E on the benefit of the living accommodation provided to her.  The basic annual benefit will be £6,500 being the rateable value of the flat.  This benefit will be proportionally reduced where she does not have the use of the accommodation for the whole of the year of assessment. Although the value of the flat exceeds the expensive living accommodation limit of £75,000, the flat actually 'cost' nothing, and there is therefore no additional benefit.  Since Joyce will be earning £8,500 pa or more (and will therefore be classed as a higher paid employee), she will also be assessed on the benefit of the running costs of the flat of £1,300, and on the provision of furniture £1,080 (5,400 × 20%).  Again, both these benefits will be proportionally reduced where the accommodation is not available for the whole of the year of assessment.

**Relocation costs**

There is no taxable benefit in respect of eligible removal expenses up to £8,000 paid for by an employer provided the employee does not live within a reasonable daily travelling distance of the new place of employment, and the expenses are incurred by the end of the tax year following the one in which the employee commences employment at the new location.  This will cover Joyce's £2,200 costs of selling her property in Scotland, and her removal costs of £550.  Up to £5,250 (8,000 – 2,200 – 550) of the contribution of £10,000 towards the costs of purchasing a property in London will also be exempt if it represents eligible expenses of acquisition such as legal fees and stamp duty, or the cost of new domestic goods, such as carpets, where such existing goods are not suitable for the new residence.  That part of the contribution of £10,000 that is not exempt will be a taxable benefit assessable under Schedule E.

*(Tutorial note:* many students will have avoided this question because it deals with a charitable trust. Note, however, that only a very small part of the question deals with trusts, the rest covers straight forward topics such as donations and benefits in kind.*)*

(b)    (i)    The VAT position of Skunk Ltd, Zebra Ltd and Emu Ltd for the year ended 31 March 2000 is as follows:

|  | Skunk Ltd £ | Zebra Ltd £ | Emu Ltd £ |
|---|---|---|---|
| Sales | 1,170,000 | 540,000 | 390,000 |
| Management charge | 80,000 | – | – |
| Outputs | 1,250,000 | 540,000 | 390,000 |
| Output tax at 17.5% | 218,750 | – | – |
| Purchases | 480,000 | 270,000 | 150,000 |
| Overheads | 300,000 | – | – |
| Management charge | – | 40,000 | 40,000 |
| Inputs | 780,000 | 310,000 | 190,000 |
| Input tax at 17.5% | 136,500 | 54,250 | – |
| Net liability/(recovery) | 82,250 | (54,250) | – |

Emu Ltd cannot register for VAT, and therefore is not able to recover any of the input tax on its purchases or the management charge from Skunk Ltd. The group's overall liability to VAT is £28,000 (82,250 – 54,250).

(ii)    Two or more companies are eligible to register as a group for VAT purposes if:

–    one of them controls each of the others, or one person (whether a holding company, an individual or a business partnership) controls all of them; and

–    each of them is resident in the UK, or has an established place of business in the UK.

The consequences of being registered as a group for VAT purposes are that:

–    each VAT group must appoint a representative member which accounts for the group's output tax and input tax;

–    all members of the VAT group are jointly and severally liable for any tax due from the representative member;

–    any supply of goods or services by a member of the group to another member of the group is disregarded for VAT purposes;

–    any other supply of goods or services by or to a group member is treated as a supply by or to the representative member.

An application for group VAT registration must be made by one of the companies and takes effect from the date of receipt although Customs then have 90 days in which to refuse the application.

(iii)    If group VAT registration had applied throughout the year ended 31 March 2000, the group would have had to have charged output tax of £204,750 (1,170,000 × 17.5%). The management charges, being intra-group are disregarded.

The inclusion of Emu Ltd in the group registration will cause the group to be partially exempt due to that company's exempt outputs. That input tax which relates to supplies that are wholly used in making taxable supplies will be fully recoverable. It would therefore appear that the group could fully recover the input tax on the purchases made by Skunk Ltd and Zebra Ltd, which amounts to £131,250 (480,000 + 270,000 × 17.5%). The input tax of £26,250 (150,000 × 17.5%) on the purchases made by Emu Ltd will not be recoverable. The deductible proportion of the input tax of £52,500 (300,000 × 17.5%) suffered on the group's overhead expenditure will be found by the use of the 'standard method'. This is the ratio of taxable outputs to total outputs, with the fraction being rounded up to the next whole number. The relevant fraction is 82% as follows:

$$\frac{1,170,000 + 540,000}{1,170,000 + 540,000 + 390,000} = 81.43\% = 82\%$$

The recovery of the residual input tax, or 'pot', is therefore £43,050 (52,500 × 82%). The input tax attributable to exempt supplies of £35,700 (26,250 + 52,500 – 43,050) is greater than the *de minimis* limit of £625 per month on average, and is therefore disallowed.

The group's overall liability to VAT is thus £30,450 (204,750 – 131,250 – 43,050), which is £2,450 (30,450 – 28,000) more than the actual figure for the year. A group VAT registration would have therefore not been beneficial from a purely financial point of view. The figure of £2,450 can be reconciled by comparing the cost of the non-deductible input tax of £9,450 (52,500 – 43,050) to the saving of the output VAT of £7,000 (40,000 × 17.5%) on the management charge to Emu Ltd.

Other factors that would have to be considered when deciding on whether to apply for group registration or not are:

–    the saving in administration costs in only having to prepare one VAT return;

–    the fact that the refunds of VAT received by Zebra Ltd, due to it being zero-rated, will be received at an earlier date due to setting off the refunds against the group's overall VAT liability;

–    future changes to the group's financial position. For example, an increase in management charges could alter the decision.

---

## 24    (Answer 6 of examination)

(a)    (i)    **Desmond Cook – taxable income 1999/00**

|  | £ | £ |
|---|---:|---:|
| Schedule A |  |  |
| Rental income |  | 16,200 |
| Less: Expenses | 1,340 |  |
| Repairs | 1,400 |  |
| Wear and tear allowance (16,200 × 10%) | 1,620 |  |
|  |  | 4,360 |
|  |  | 11,840 |
| Pension |  | 3,600 |
| Statutory total income |  | 15,440 |
| Personal allowance |  | (4,335) |
| Taxable income |  | 11,105 |

The replacement of the cottage roof is an allowable expense, since it is a repair rather than an improvement.

## Myrtle Cook – taxable income 1999/00

|  | £ |
|---|---|
| Schedule E - Director's remuneration | 40,000 |
| Investment income | 14,000 |
| | |
| Statutory total income | 54,000 |
| Personal allowance | (4,335) |
| | |
| Taxable income | 49,665 |

As the result of the level of her statutory total income, Myrtle loses her entitlement to age allowance.

## Desmond Cook – chargeable gain 1999/00

|  | £ |
|---|---|
| Deemed consideration | 161,000 |
| Cost | 23,000 |
| | |
| | 138,000 |
| Indexation $23,000 \times \dfrac{162.6 - 98.45}{98.45}$ (0.652) | 14,996 |
| | |
| | 123,004 |
| Retirement relief (see note) | 18,223 |
| | |
| | 104,781 |
| | |
| Tapered to 85% | 89,064 |
| Annual exemption | 7,100 |
| | |
| Chargeable gain | 81,964 |

The cottage has been owned for 12.5 years, and has been let as furnished holiday accommodation for two years of that period. Therefore, £19,736 $\left(123,004 \times \frac{2}{13.5}\right)$ of the gain qualifies as a business asset, and since Desmond is over 50 years old, retirement relief will be available. Retirement relief at the rate of 100% is available on gains up to £40,000 (200,000 × 20%), so the whole of the £18,223 is exempt.

The business rate of taper relief is available in full because the cottage has been used for furnished holiday accommodaiton throughout the period since 6 April 1998.

## Myrtle Cook – chargeable gain 1999/00

|  | £ | £ |
|---|---|---|
| Deemed consideration (8,000 × 15.00) | | 120,000 |
| Cost $\left(48,000 \times \dfrac{8,000}{20,000}\right)$ | | 19,200 |
| | | |
| | | 100,800 |
| Indexation $19,200 \times \dfrac{162.6 - 156.3}{156.3}$ | | 774 |
| | | |
| | | 100,026 |
| Retirement relief     200,000 × 30% | 60,000 | |

$$100{,}026 - 60{,}000 \times 50\% \qquad\qquad 20{,}013$$

|  |  |
|---|---:|
|  | 80,013 |
|  | 20,013 |
| Gift relief | 20,013 |
| Chargeable gain | – |

Myrtle qualifies for retirement relief because she is over 50 years old and holds over 5% of the share capital of Artic Ltd. The relief is restricted to three years, being the period that she has owned the shares, since this is less than the eight year period that she has been a full-time working director. Provided that Myrtle and Judy jointly elect, the balance of the gain of £20,013 can be held over as a gift of business assets (Artic Ltd being an unquoted company). Taper relief cannot apply as none of the gain remains chargeable.

(ii)    **Desmond Cook – inheritance tax liability**

Desmond's gift of the holiday cottage on 31 March 2000 will be a potentially exempt transfer (PET). No IHT liability will therefore arise until his death during June 2002, which is within seven years of the date of the gift. Business property relief is not available in respect of the holiday cottage since this relief does not apply to land which is let.

|  |  | £ | £ |
|---|---|---:|---:|
| Value transferred |  |  | 161,000 |
| Annual exemptions | 1999/00 | 3,000 |  |
|  | 1998/99 | 3,000 |  |
|  |  |  | 6,000 |
| Chargeable transfer |  |  | 155,000 |
| IHT liability 155,000 at 0%. |  |  | Nil |

Desmond's previous gift of £98,000 during May 1994 is also a PET, and, since this is made more than seven years before the date of his death, is exempt from IHT. The IHT due on Desmond's estate will be as follows:

|  |  | £ |
|---|---|---:|
| Main residence $\left(^{172{,}000}\!/_{2}\right)$ |  | 86,000 |
| IHT liability | 231,000 – 155,000 = 76,000 at nil | Nil |
|  | 86,000 – 76,000 = 10,000 at 40% | 4,000 |
|  |  | 4,000 |

**Myrtle Cook – inheritance tax liability**

Myrtle's gift of the 8,000 shares in Artic Ltd on 31 March 2000 is also a PET, and so again no IHT liability will arise until her death during June 2002. Business property relief will be available at the rate of 100%, since the gift is of an unquoted shareholding and the shares are still held by Judy at the date of Myrtle's death. This assumes that the shares still qualify as business property at that date. Myrtle's previous gift of £160,000 during July 1993 is a chargeable lifetime transfer, being to a discretionary trust. Since it was made more than seven years before the date of her death, no further IHT liability will arise in respect of it. However, it is within seven years of the gift on 31 March 2000, and will reduce the £231,000 nil rate band available at that date by £154,000 (160,000 – 3,000 – 3,000).

|  |  | £ | £ |
|---|---|---|---|
| Value of shares held before the transfer | 20,000 × £16.50 |  | 330,000 |
| Value of shares held after the transfer | 12,000 × £15.00 |  | 180,000 |
| Value transferred |  |  | 150,000 |
| Business property relief – 100% |  |  | 150,000 |
|  |  |  | Nil |

The IHT due on Myrtle's estate will be as follows:

|  | £ | £ |
|---|---|---|
| Main residence $\left(^{172,000}/_2\right)$ |  | 86,000 |
| Investments |  | 250,000 |
| Shares in Artic Ltd (12,000 × 15.00) | 180,000 |  |
| Less:  Business property relief – 100% | (180,000) |  |
|  |  | - |
|  |  | 336,000 |

| IHT liability | 231,000 at 0% | Nil |
|---|---|---|
|  | 336,000 – 231,000 = 105,000 at 40% | 42,000 |
|  |  | 42,000 |

*(Tutorial note:* notice how often business property relief occurs in an IHT question.  Make sure that you learn the categories of assets to which BPR applies, and the relevant rate.  Note that when a PET becomes chargeable BPR is only available if the donee still owns the asset at the date of the donor's death.)

(b)   **Income tax**

Following the gift of his holiday cottage, Desmond's only income will be his pension of £3,600 pa.  It would therefore be beneficial to transfer the investments into his name so that the investment income is taxed at his marginal rate of 10% or 20% (on savings income) rather than Myrtle's 40%.  This also ensures that all of Desmond's personal allowances are utilised.  Although transferring the full £14,000 of investment income to Desmond would restrict his entitlement to the married couple's age allowance (his income of £17,600 exceeds the limit of £16,800 by £800), this is still beneficial because the additional tax liability of £240 (400 × 20% + 800 × 20%) resulting from the reduced allowance of £400 $\left(^{800}/_2\right)$ and the investment income of £400 is less than the saving of £320 (800 × 40%).

**Capital gains tax**

Desmond should postpone his gift of the holiday cottage until after 5 April 2000 so that it falls into 2000/01. This will not result in any significant tax saving (since he will have virtually the same amount of his basic rate band available if the income tax advice is followed), but will delay the CGT liability by 12 months.

Myrtle should reduce her gift to 7,500 shares so that she is left with a 5% holding $\left(8\% \times ^{12,500}/_{20,000} = 5\%\right)$ rather than the proposed 4.8% holding $\left(8\% \times ^{12,000}/_{20,000} = 4.8\%\right)$.  A subsequent gift of her shares would then qualify for retirement relief.  The base cost per share for Judy would therefore be increased because of the reduction in the gain held over.  It should be noted that a reduction in the number of shares gifted will also have IHT implications, as the value per share both before and after the gift will be £16.50.  However, provided Judy retains the shares, 100% BPR remains available.

If Myrtle further reduced her gift to 5,900 shares, the gains (after retirement relief) would be covered by her annual capital gains exemption, and there would be no need to make a hold over election.

**Inheritance tax**

After the gift of his holiday cottage, Desmond's estate is only worth £70,000. Myrtle should transfer assets to him to equalise their estates so that they are both in a position to benefit from the nil rate band of £231,000. However, this will only be relevant should he live for seven years after making the gift to Judy, since his nil rate band is utilised if the gift becomes chargeable. The income tax advice of transferring the investments worth £250,000 to Desmond will not achieve this aim, as it leaves Myrtle with a chargeable estate worth only £70,000. Some compromise between saving income tax and saving IHT would have to be decided.

Myrtle should postpone her gift of the shares in Artic Ltd until after July 2000 so that the previous gift of £160,000 to the discretionary trust during July 1993 drops out of her cumulative total. This would reduce the IHT liability to nil should the gift to Judy become chargeable ie, if Myrtle died within seven years, but after Judy had sold the shares.

# DECEMBER 1994 QUESTIONS

## 25    (Question 1 of examination)

Grey Ltd is an unquoted UK resident company involved in the advertising industry. The company has two directors, June White and Julie Black, who each own 50% of its ordinary share capital. Following the disposal of an investment on 20 January 2000, Grey Ltd has surplus funds of £160,000. The disposal resulted in a chargeable gain of £42,000. The directors would like to invest the surplus funds of £160,000 so as to provide for an entitlement to pension for themselves.

June is aged 43 and Julie is aged 44, and neither they nor Grey Ltd have made any previous payments in respect of an entitlement to a pension. Grey Ltd's forecast adjusted Schedule D Case I trading profit for the year ended 31 March 2000 is £85,000, which is after deducting directors' remuneration of £110,000 (£55,000 per director). The company's tax adjusted Schedule D Case I trading profits since its incorporation on 1 April 1993, together with details of directors' remuneration paid, are as follows:

| Year ended | Adjusted Schedule D Case I profit £ | Directors' remuneration paid £ |
|---|---|---|
| 31 March 1995 | 65,000 | 100,000 |
| 31 March 1996 | 56,000 | 110,000 |
| 31 March 1997 | 68,000 | 120,000 |
| 31 March 1998 | 77,000 | 130,000 |
| 31 March 1999 | 112,000 | 135,000 |

The adjusted Schedule D Case I profits are after the deduction of directors' remuneration. Grey Ltd has no other income or outgoings. June and Julie have always been remunerated equally, they are both single, and have no other income or outgoings. They are considering the following alternative ways of using the £160,000 to provide for their pensions:

(1)    Additional directors' remuneration will be paid equally to June and Julie, which they would then use to pay a premium into their own personal pension schemes. The amount of the additional directors' remuneration will be the balance of the £160,000 remaining after accounting for employers' Class 1 National Insurance contribution.

(2)    A dividend of £160,000 (net) will be paid, which June and Julie would again use to pay a premium into their own personal pension schemes.

(3)    Grey Ltd will set up its own self-administered occupational pension scheme, and invest the surplus funds of £160,000 directly into this scheme. The Inland Revenue have stated that such a scheme would qualify for their approval.

**Required:**

Advise both Grey Ltd and the directors of the corporation tax, income tax and National Insurance contribution implications arising from each of the alternative ways of providing for the directors' entitlement to a pension. Your answer should also include a brief appraisal of the advantages and disadvantages of each of the alternatives. You should ignore the possibility of any repayment supplement being due.

**(25 marks)**

## 26 (Question 2 of examination)

Zoo plc is the holding company for a group of companies. The group structure is as follows:

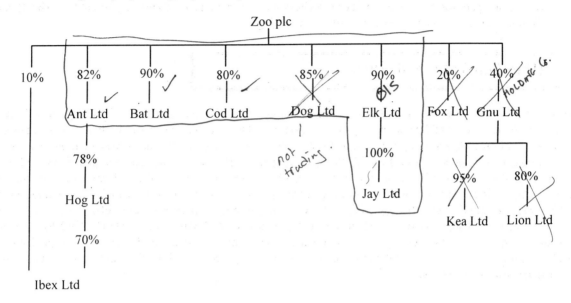

Each percentage shareholding represents a holding of ordinary share capital. The remaining share capital of Fox Ltd is held by Unit plc. The remaining share capital of Gnu Ltd is held equally by Volt plc and Watt plc. Unit plc, Volt plc and Watt plc are not otherwise connected with the Zoo plc group of companies. The remaining share capital of all the other companies is held by individual members of the general public. The shareholdings will all be held throughout the year ended 31 March 2000, with the exception of Zoo plc's 90% shareholding in Bat Ltd, which was acquired on 1 December 1999, and its 80% shareholding in Cod Ltd which was sold on 30 November 1999.

All of the Zoo plc group of companies have an accounting date of 31 March, with the exception of Bat Ltd which has an accounting date of 30 November. Bat Ltd is to produce accounts for the four month period to 31 March 2000 so as to make its accounting date coterminous with the other group companies.

The companies are all resident in the UK except for Elk Ltd, which is resident in the country of Overseabia. The companies are all trading companies except for Zoo plc and Gnu Ltd, which are holding companies, and Dog Ltd which has not yet commenced trading. For the year ended 31 March 2000, the trading companies are all forecast to be profitable, although some of them have made trading losses in the past.

For the year ended 31 March 2000, Zoo plc is forecast to have excess management expenses of £750,000. It paid a dividend of £1,200,000 on 15 July 1999, and will pay a further dividend of £2,800,000 on 14 January 1999.

**Required:**

(a) (i) To which companies will Zoo plc be able to surrender its excess management expenses for the year ended 31 March 2000? Your answer should be supported by appropriate reasons, and should also state any restrictions as to the amount of excess management expenses that can be surrendered in each case.

(ii) What factors should Zoo plc take into account when deciding as to which companies it should surrender its excess management expenses? Your answer should include a calculation of the corporation tax lower and upper limits that will be applicable to the Zoo plc group of companies for the year ended 31 March 2000. **(9 marks)**

(b) (i) Which companies could have transferred chargeable assets to Zoo plc during the year ended 31 March 2000 without incurring a chargeable gain or an allowable loss? Your answer should be supported by appropriate reasons.

(ii)    Why would it probably be beneficial for all of the eligible companies to transfer chargeable assets to Zoo plc prior to the chargeable assets being disposed of outside the group?

**(6 marks)**
**(Total 15 marks)**

(A further part for 10 marks has been omitted as it is a topic no longer examinable. The Examiner's Comments (see beyond) have been modified accordingly.

---

## 27    (Question 3 of examination)

Stirling Hill is a vintage motor car enthusiast. On 1 January 1999 he took out a loan of £40,000 at a fixed rate of interest of 10%, and spent £30,000 on having a workshop built. This was completed on 31 March 1999, when a further £8,000 was spent on tools and equipment. On 6 April 1999 Stirling bought a dilapidated vintage motor car for £3,000, and proceeded to restore it at a cost of £7,000 in spare parts. The restoration was completed on 30 June 1999. Unfortunately, Stirling was made redundant on 15 September 1999, and was forced to sell the motor car for £25,000. Not being able to find further employment, Stirling proceeded to buy three more dilapidated vintage motor cars on 15 October 1999 for £4,000 each. The restoration of these was completed on 28 February 2000 at a cost of £7,000 per motor car, and two of them were immediately sold for a total of £52,000. On 31 March 2000 Stirling obtained employment elsewhere in the country, so he immediately sold the workshop for £25,000, and repaid the loan of £40,000. Stirling personally retained the tools and equipment, which were worth £4,500, and the unsold vintage motor car which was valued at £25,000.

**Required:**

(a)    Briefly discuss the criteria which would be used by the courts in deciding whether or not Stirling will be treated as carrying on an adventure in the nature of a trade in respect of his vintage motor car activities.

**(8 marks)**

(b)    Explain whether or not you would consider Stirling to be carrying on an adventure in the nature of a trade.

**(5 marks)**

(c)    Calculate Stirling's tax liability arising from his vintage motor car activities during the period from 6 April 1999 to 31 March 2000 if he is treated as:

(i)     trading; and
(ii)    not trading.

You should assume that Stirling is a 40% taxpayer, and should ignore the implications of VAT and National Insurance contribution.

**(7 marks)**

(d)    Assuming that Stirling is treated as trading during the period from 6 April 1999 to 31 March 2000, advise him of the VAT implications arising from being so treated.

**(5 marks)**
**(Total 25 marks)**

---

## 28    (Question 4 of examination)

Clifford Jones and Dinah Smith, both of whom are divorced, are to marry on 30 April 1999. You should assume that today's date is 15 April 1999. Clifford is aged 48, whilst Dinah is aged 42. They have asked for your advice, and the following information is available:

(1)    Clifford and Dinah both commenced as self-employed practitioners in alternative medicine during late 1997. Clifford's practice is in London, and he makes tax adjusted profits of £60,000 pa. Dinah's practice is in Glasgow, and she makes tax adjusted profits of £15,000 pa. Clifford's business is valued at £125,000, whilst Dinah's is valued at £40,000. They will continue to run both practices once they are married, although they are unsure as to whether or not it would be beneficial to do so in partnership with each other.

Each year, Clifford and Dinah both contribute the maximum possible amounts qualifying for tax relief into personal pension schemes.

(2)    Clifford has a son, aged 22, from his previous marriage, who is presently studying full-time at university but lives with Clifford during the university holidays. Dinah has two daughters, aged 10 and 13, from her previous marriage, who both live with her.

(3)    Clifford has a house in London worth £220,000 with an outstanding endowment mortgage of £90,000, which was bought in 1994. Dinah has a house in Glasgow worth £85,000 with an outstanding endowment mortgage of £35,000, which was bought in 1996. Clifford and Dinah are paying gross mortgage interest under MIRAS of £7,200 pa and £3,500 pa respectively. Although they will continue to live in their separate houses after marrying, they will spend weekends and holidays together.

(4)    Clifford and Dinah jointly own a holiday cottage in Scotland worth £40,000, which produces taxable income of £5,000 pa. The cottage is 75% owned by Clifford and 25% by Dinah.

(5)    Clifford plans to sell a number of investments during June 1999, and this will result in chargeable gains of £7,500, £4,000 and £9,000, and an allowable loss of £400. Clifford will invest the proceeds of £50,000 in a building society deposit account, which will produce interest of £2,160 (net) during 1999/00. Neither Clifford nor Dinah will dispose of any other chargeable assets during 1999/00.

(6)    Clifford and Dinah have other assets worth £95,000 and £10,000 respectively.

(7)    Clifford and Dinah will both draw up new wills when they get married. Clifford is to leave one half of his London house to his son, with all of his remaining assets passing to Dinah, or his son if Dinah predeceases him. Dinah is to leave all of her assets to her daughters.

Clifford and Dinah do not feel that they are wealthy enough in order for either of them to make any substantial lifetime gifts of assets to their children. They are both concerned that their own children ultimately inherit the majority of their respective assets.

**Required:**

(a)    Advise Clifford and Dinah of the income tax implications arising from their forthcoming marriage on 30 April 1999.                                                                                     **(5 marks)**

(b)    Advise Clifford and Dinah of tax planning measures that they could take following their marriage on 30 April 1999. Your answer should be confined to the implications of income tax, capital gains tax and National Insurance contribution, and should include a calculation of their taxable income for 1999/00 prior to your advice. You are not expected to advise on tax-free investments such as ISAs.
                                                                                                       **(8 marks)**

(c)    Briefly discuss the inheritance tax implications arising from Clifford and Dinah's proposed new wills. Your answer should outline tax planning measures that they could take in order to reduce their potential IHT liability.                                                                              **(5 marks)**

(d)    Clifford is concerned that should Dinah outlive him, his son should inherit upon her death any assets that Clifford has bequeathed to Dinah under the terms of his will. Explain how this could be achieved by the use of an interest in possession trust. Your answer should include a brief description of how such a trust would be subject to income tax, capital gains tax and IHT up to, and including, the time that its assets are distributed to Clifford's son.
                                                                                                       **(7 marks)**
                                                                                                  **(Total 25 marks)**

---

**29    (Question 5 of examination)**

---

Abdul Khan, aged 56, has been a 20% shareholder in, and a full-time working director of, Slowdown Ltd, an unquoted trading company involved in the manufacture of electrical goods, since its incorporation six years ago. However, for the past two years Abdul has disagreed with the other directors of Slowdown Ltd over the company's business policies, and is therefore to resign as a director and dispose of his shareholding. Abdul is not 'associated' with any of the other shareholders of Slowdown Ltd. It has been agreed that Slowdown Ltd, which currently has surplus funds, will purchase Abdul's 20% shareholding on 31 January 2000 for £800,000, at which date he will also resign as a director. The shareholding consists of 100,000 £1 ordinary shares, and was subscribed for at par on 1 February 1994. As at 31 January 2000, Slowdown Ltd is forecast to have chargeable assets of £5,500,000, of which £750,000 are non-business assets. For the year ended 31 March 2000 Slowdown Ltd is expected to have profits chargeable to corporation tax of £1,200,000.

Abdul plans to use the proceeds from the sale of his shareholding in Slowdown Ltd to set up a new unquoted trading company on 30 June 2000. The company, called Fast-Track Ltd, will also be involved in the manufacture of electrical goods, with Abdul becoming its managing director from the date of incorporation. Fast-Track Ltd will have an issued ordinary share capital of £1,400,000, of which £1,190,000 will be subscribed for by Abdul. He will finance this subscription as follows:

(1)     Investing the proceeds of £800,000 from the sale of his shareholding in Slowdown Ltd.

(2)     Investing surplus funds of £160,000 that he has available. These funds represent the proceeds from the disposal of investments on 20 February 1999. The disposal resulted in chargeable gains of £48,000.

(3)     Abdul is to personally raise a bank loan of £230,000. The loan will be secured on his private residence, and will carry an interest rate of 9% pa.

The other £210,000 of Fast-Track Ltd's ordinary share capital will be subscribed for by Abdul's cousin Sheena, who inherited this money two years ago. Sheena is presently in employment, but plans to resign from this position during 2001 and become a director of Fast-Track Ltd.

Although Fast-Track Ltd is expected to be a profitable company, Abdul intends to withdraw most of these profits by way of remuneration and dividends. The company's shares are therefore unlikely to experience significant capital growth before Abdul's intended retirement in six or seven years time.

Abdul and Sheena are both 40% taxpayers, and both they, Slowdown Ltd, and Fast-Track Ltd are resident in the UK.

**Required:**

(a)     (i)     Advise Abdul of whether or not Slowdown Ltd's purchase of his 20% shareholding in that company is likely to qualify for the special treatment applying to a company's purchase of its own shares, and to therefore be treated as a capital gain;

        (ii)    Advise Abdul of whether it would be beneficial to have the purchase of his 20% shareholding treated as a distribution by Slowdown Ltd or as a capital gain under the special treatment. In advising Abdul, you should ignore the tax implications arising from his proposed subscription for ordinary shares in Fast-Track Ltd.     **(11 marks)**

(b)     Assuming that his disposal of his 20% shareholding in Slowdown Ltd is treated as a capital gain under the special treatment, advise him of the tax implications arising from his subscription for ordinary share capital in Fast-Track Ltd. In respect of any reliefs that might be available, your answer should briefly state any qualifying conditions that must be met.     **(9 marks)**

(c)     What income tax relief might Sheena be entitled to in respect of her subscription for ordinary share capital in Fast-Track Ltd? Your answer should briefly state the qualifying conditions that must be met for relief to be available.     **(5 marks)**

The tax rates and allowances for 1999/00 should be used throughout.     **(Total 25 marks)**

---

**30 (Question 6 of examination)**

Ken Sing, aged 59, has been living in the UK since July 1993, working for the London branch of the Pajan National Bank. Ken was born in the country of Pajan, where he is domiciled, and he plans to return there when he retires in June 2000. You should assume that today's date is 5 April 2000.

*[handwritten: -7 yrs.]*

Ken is paid a salary of £75,000 pa by the Pajan National Bank, and is provided with an 1800cc motor car which cost £38,000 in 1998. During 1999/00 Ken drove 15,000 miles of which 20% were for business purposes. All running costs, including petrol, are paid for by the bank. The Pajan National Bank also pays for Ken's private medical insurance premiums of £1,200 pa, and for his £1,500 pa membership of a golf club which is used to meet clients of the bank. Ken has an interest free loan of £90,000 from the bank, which was used to purchase his private residence in London. This cost £115,000 in July 1993, and is currently worth £275,000. PAYE of £33,500 was deducted from Ken's salary during 1999/00.

Ken also owned the following assets as at 5 April 2000:

(1) A house situated in Pajan worth £120,000, which is rented out for £10,000 pa. Pajanese tax at the rate of 30% is payable on the rental income. Ken remits £3,500 of the income to the UK each year, and invests the remainder in Pajan. In December 1999 Ken sold a plot of land attached to the house for £40,000. All of the proceeds from the disposal were remitted to the UK. The house and land were purchased in May 1996 for £100,000.

(2) 100,000 £1 ordinary shares in High-Growth plc, an investment trust quoted on the UK Stock Exchange at 102 –110. High-Growth plc has an issued share capital of 10,000,000 shares, and paid a dividend of nine pence per share during 1999/00. Ken inherited the shares as a specific gift on the death of an uncle in September 1996 when they were worth £45,000. The uncle was domiciled in the UK, and paid IHT of £80,000 on an estate valued at £350,000.

*[handwritten: — NO BPR; — 1/4 up; — QSR]*

(3) 20,000 £1 ordinary shares in Small-Time Ltd, an unquoted UK resident trading company with an issued share capital of 250,000 shares. Ken has sat on the board of the company as a non-executive director since June 1997. This post is unpaid, and Small-Time Ltd has not paid a dividend in recent years. Ken's shareholding is worth £65,000 and was subscribed for at par in December 1993. Small-Time Ltd has assets worth £1,050,000, of which £50,000 are investments in quoted shares.

*[handwritten: —BPR. ; no R Relief]*

(4) Bank deposits of £65,000 with the Pajan National Bank opened in June 1997, of which £45,000 is held at the London branch, and £20,000 at the main branch in Pajan. Interest has been credited to these accounts as follows:

|  | London branch £ | Pajan branch £ |
|---|---|---|
| Year ended 5 April 1999 | 2,500 | 1,020 |
| Year ended 5 April 2000 | 2,240 | 850 |

*[handwritten: — IRRELEVANT; 1000.]*

Interest is stated net of tax, which in the case of the Pajanese branch is at the rate of 15%. All of the interest arising in respect of the Pajanese branch has been remitted to the UK.

In December 1999 Ken sold a set of paintings situated in his Pajan residence for £8,000. The paintings were purchased in March 1985 for £2,800. Ken deposited the proceeds from the disposal in his bank account in Pajan.

*[handwritten: — IRRELEVANT. wasting chattles]*

Under the Pajanese tax system, capital gains are not subject to taxation. There is no double taxation treaty between the United Kingdom and Pajan.

Ken has been a widower for a number of years, and has left all of his assets to his children under the terms of his will.

**Required:**

*[handwritten: ONLY AVAILABLE FOR WOMEN.]*

(a) Calculate Ken's income tax and CGT liabilities for 1999/00. **(9 marks)**

---

(b)     Advise Ken of his liability to IHT were he to die before returning to Pajan in June 2000. Your answer should include an explanation of why Ken's assets are or are not subject to IHT.

**(9 marks)**

(c)     When he returns to Pajan, Ken plans to dispose of all of this assets situated in the UK. Advise him of his liability to CGT if he were to dispose of these assets:

      (i)       before returning to Pajan; and
      (ii)      after returning to Pajan.

You should assume that all disposals are made in June 2000, and that Ken will be liable to CGT at the rate of 40% during 2000/01.     **(7 marks)**

You should use the tax rates and allowances for 1999/00 throughout, and should assume that the value of Ken's assets will not materially alter in the foreseeable future. Assume that the official rate of interest is 10%.

**(Total 25 marks)**

# DECEMBER 1994 EXAMINER'S COMMENTS

## General comments

As with the June 1994 diet, there was again a high number of candidates sitting this paper.  Unfortunately, poor examination technique was again in evidence.  Taking question 2 as an example, those candidates who scored badly did so because they missed many of the easier marks available.  Typically, such a candidate would say which of the companies in the group qualified, but would not state why they qualified, or why the other companies did not qualify.  Although this was quite a long paper, many candidates wasted time by, for example, calculating the income tax liability in question 4(b) when this was not required.

**Question 1: this question tested candidates' ability to explain the tax implications arising from three alternative ways of providing for directors' entitlement to a pension.  The alternatives consisted of the directors either making contributions to a personal pension scheme, funded by additional directors' remuneration or a dividend, or the company setting up its own self-administered occupational pension scheme.**

This was not a popular question, and was poorly answered by most of those candidates who attempted it.  The calculation of NIC was poorly done.  From the company's viewpoint, two of the alternatives resulted in a trading loss.  Although many candidates correctly identified these consequences, they then made little attempt to show how the trading loss could be relieved.  From the directors' viewpoint, very few candidates correctly calculated the maximum tax deductible personal pension premium that the directors could pay, since they ignored the net relevant earnings from previous years.  This is particularly disappointing as this topic was also examined at the previous diet, and the calculation was quite straightforward. (These comments have been modified to exclude references to topics no longer examinable).

**Question 2: part (a) tested candidates' knowledge as to which companies in a group qualified for the surrender of excess management expenses from the holding company, and the factors that should be taken into account when making such a surrender.  Part (b) tested candidates' knowledge as to which companies in a group qualified to transfer chargeable assets to the holding company without incurring a chargeable gain or an allowable loss, and why such a transfer would be beneficial.**

This was a popular question, and was generally answered very well.  Many candidates scored high marks, with an unprecedented number achieving a maximum mark of (originally) 25.  The aspect of the question that gave candidates the most difficulty was identifying that the holding company was a member of a consortium, and the reliefs that were then available.  The problem for those candidates who did not score high marks was often one of poor examination technique.  A sensible approach for each part of the question would have been to have listed all the companies in the group, and then to have stated whether or not each company qualified, along with appropriate reasons and details of any restrictions.

**Question 3: part (a) tested candidates' knowledge of the criteria used by the courts in deciding whether or not a tax-payer person is trading.  Part (b) tested candidates' ability to explain whether or not the tax-payer would be treated as trading in respect of the purchase and disposal of four motor cars.  Part (c) tested candidates' ability to calculate the tax liability if the tax-payer was (i) treated as trading, and (ii) treated as not trading.  Part (d) tested candidates' ability to advise on the VAT implications if the tax-payer was treated as trading.**

This was also a popular question, which was again generally well answered.  In part (a), most candidates correctly identified the badges of trade, but some lost marks by not adequately explaining each badge.  Most candidates came to the correct conclusion in part (b), that the tax-payer would not be treated as trading in respect of the first disposal, but would be treated as trading in respect of the second.  However, hardly any candidates appreciated that the treatment of the second disposal might have an impact upon the treatment of the first disposal.  Those candidates who discussed whether the tax-payer was employed or self-employed scored low marks.  In part (c), it was disappointing that many candidates could not calculate the correct capital allowances available, and demonstrated little knowledge of the treatment  of pre-trading expenditure and own consumption.  Many candidates did not appreciate that motor cars are exempt from CGT.  In part (d), most candidates appreciated that the tax-payer must register for VAT, although many were confused as to the precise application of the VAT registration rules.

**Question 4: part (a) tested candidates' ability to advise on the income tax implications arising from a couple's forthcoming marriage. Part (b) tested candidates' ability to advise on tax planning measures that could be taken by the couple following their marriage. Part (c) tested candidates' ability to advise on the IHT implications of the couple's proposed new wills. Part (d) tested candidates' knowledge of the use and taxation of an interest in possession trust.**

This was the most popular question on the paper, and was well answered by many candidates. In part (a), a number of candidates were confused about the relationship of the MCA with the APA. Many candidates did not appreciate that the MCA would not be restricted in the year of marriage, and ignored the fact that relief for mortgage interest would be restricted to one residence following marriage. By their treatment of mortgage interest, and their advice that transferring some or all of the MCA to the spouse would be beneficial, it was apparent that some candidates were not up to date with tax legislation. Part (b) was quite well answered, although a number of candidates wasted time by calculating the couple's income tax liability which was not required by the question. Part (c) was generally poorly answered, with too many candidates discussing lifetime gifts, despite the question stating that this was not an option. Part (d) was again poorly answered, with many candidates not appreciating that the trust would be set up under the terms of the taxpayer's will, and discussing PETs at length. Other candidates confused the taxation of an interest in possession trust with that of a discretionary trust.

**Question 5: part (a) tested candidates' knowledge of a company purchasing its own shares, and ability to advise on whether or not it would be beneficial for the special treatment to apply. Part (b) tested candidates' knowledge of rollover relief on the re-investment of the proceeds of a disposal. Part (c) tested candidates' knowledge of the income tax relief available under the enterprise investment scheme.**

This was the least popular question on the paper, although there were some good answers from some of those candidates attempting it. However, for many candidates this was a fourth choice question, in which case it was poorly answered. Part (a) was generally well answered, with a number of candidates correctly calculating the CGT liability. In part (b), most candidates appreciated that re-investment relief was available, and were aware of most of the qualifying conditions. However, the interaction of reinvestment relief with retirement relief presented a problem. In part (c), many candidates demonstrated that they were not up to date with tax legislation, by not showing awareness of the enterprise investment scheme.

**Question 6: part (a) tested candidates' ability to calculate the income tax and CGT liabilities of a taxpayer who is resident in the UK but domiciled overseas. Part (b) tested candidates' ability to calculate the IHT liability of a tax payer who is domiciled overseas, and to advise on the location of assets for IHT purposes. Part (c) tested candidates' ability to advise on a taxpayer's liability to CGT before and after leaving the UK.**

Again a popular question, with many candidates scoring high marks. This was despite the fact that in part (a), many candidates were unaware of the application of the remittance basis when calculating the income tax and CGT liabilities of a taxpayer resident in the UK but who is domiciled overseas. The Schedule E aspects were well answered. In part (b), many candidates were aware of the deemed domicile rule, and the location of assets for the purposes of IHT. Most problems were caused by the calculation of business property relief and quick succession relief. A number of candidates lost marks by not including a calculation of the IHT liability in their answer. Part (c) was reasonably well answered, although several candidates granted retirement relief when it was not due.

## DECEMBER 1994 ANSWERS

## 25    (Answer 1 of examination)

(a)    **Additional directors' remuneration**

**Implications for Grey Ltd**

Employers' Class 1 National Insurance contribution of £17,397 $\left(160,000 \times {}^{12.2}/_{112.2}\right)$ will be due in respect of the additional directors' remuneration.

The additional directors' remuneration of £142,603 (160,000 − 17,397) plus the employer's Class 1 National Insurance contribution of £17,397 will be deductible for corporation tax purposes against the profits for the year ended 31 March 2000.

This will result in an adjusted Schedule D Case I trading loss of £75,000 (85,000 − 142,603 − 17,397). The loss can be relieved by claiming under S393A(1) ICTA 1988 to set it against total profits of the year ended 31 March 2000, and then setting it against the total profits of the year ended 31 March 1999 as follows:

|  | £ | *Year ended* | |
| --- | --- | --- | --- |
|  |  | *31 March 1999* £ | *31 March 2000* £ |
| Schedule D Case I profits |  | 112,000 | – |
| Capital gain |  | – | 42,000 |
|  |  | 112,000 | 42,000 |
| Less:  Section 393A(1) |  | 33,000 | 42,000 |
| PCTCT |  | 79,000 | – |
| Corporation tax at 21% |  | 16,590 | – |

The payment of additional directors' remuneration of £160,000 will therefore reduce Grey Ltd's corporation tax liabilities for the years ended 31 March 1999 and 2000 by a total of £32,330 ((127,000 × 20%) + (33,000 × 21%)).

**Implications for the directors**

June and Julie will each receive additional directors' remuneration of £71,301 $\left({}^{142,603}/_{2}\right)$. No additional employee's Class 1 National Insurance contribution will be due, as they are already earning in excess of the upper limit of £26,000.

The maximum tax deductible personal pension that each director can pay in 1999/00 is £77,620 calculated as follows:

|  | £ |
| --- | --- |
| 1994/95 | 50,000 |
| 1995/96 | 55,000 |
| 1996/97 | 60,000 |
| 1997/98 | 65,000 |
| 1998/99 | 67,500 |
| 1999/00 | 55,000 |
| Additional (restricted) | 35,600 |
| Net relevant earnings | 388,100 |

Maximum premium at 20% = £77,620

Only £35,600 of the additional directors' remuneration qualifies as net relevant earnings due to the earnings cap of £90,600 (55,000 + 35,600).

The full amount of the additional directors' remuneration can therefore be used to pay a premium into a personal pension scheme in 1999/00. This being the case, there will be no income tax liability in respect of the additional directors' remuneration. The payment of the personal pension premium will effectively obtain relief at the rate of 40%. The directors will pay the premiums net of basic rate tax, and will obtain higher rate relief by way of their PAYE codings or as a refund on submission of a tax return. The premiums must either be paid before 5 April 2000, or by 5 April 2001 provided a claim is made by 31 January 2002 to relate them back to 1999/00.

*(Tutorial note:* the 20% rate applies as both directors were between age 36 and 45 at the start of all the tax years concerned.*)*

(b)     **Payment of a dividend**

        **Implications for Grey Ltd**

        There are no National Insurance contribution implications in respect of the payment of a dividend.

        **Implications for the directors**

        Since dividend income does not qualify as net relevant earnings, the maximum tax deductible personal pension that can be paid is £70,500 calculated as follows:

|  | £ |
|---|---:|
| Net relevant earnings as per (a) | 388,100 |
| Less: Additional directors' remuneration | 35,600 |
| Net relevant earnings | 352,500 |

Maximum premium at 20% = 70,500

June and Julie will both be assessed to tax on a gross dividend of £88,889 $\left(^{160,000}/_2 \times ^{100}/_{90}\right)$. Although the additional income available for the payment of a personal pension premium appears to be £60,000 (88,889 less tax at 32.5%), the payment of such a premium would result in sufficient tax saving to enable the maximum tax deductible premium of £70,500 to be paid. However, a personal pension premium cannot be off-set against dividend income, and June and Julie are only to receive directors' remuneration of £55,000 for 1999/00. Also, for 1999/00 onwards if dividend income is reduced by personal allowances etc the 10% tax credit is cancelled so enough remuneration should remain to cover the personal allowance. They should therefore consider claiming before 31 January 2001, to have at least £19,835 (70,500 – 55,000 + 4,335) of the premium related back to 1998/99.

This will result in an overall tax saving of £9,545 as follows:

| | | £ | £ |
|---|---|---:|---:|
| Tax savings | | | |
| 1998/99: | 19,835 × 40% | | 7,934 |
| 1999/00: | 28,000 × 32½% | | 9,100 |
| | 22,665 × 40% | | 9,066 |
| | 50,665 | | |
| | 26,500 × (23% – 10%) | | 3,445 |
| | | | 29,545 |

Extra tax payable on the dividend:

|  |  |  |
|---|---|---|
| 88,889 at 32½% | 28,889 |  |
| Less: 88,889 at 10% | (8,889) | 20,000 |
|  |  | 9,545 |

The tax saving re the 23% band is as a result of dividend income being taxed at the rate of 10% when it falls in the basic rate tax band of £1,500 to £28,000, rather than at the rate of 23%.

*(Tutorial note:* It may be easier to see how the tax savings in 1999/00 came about using the following computations:

|  | *Without PPS*<br>£ | *With PPS*<br>£ |
|---|---|---|
| Sch E | 55,000 | 55,000 |
| Less: PPS |  | (50,665) |
| Dividend | 88,889 | 88,889 |
| PA | (4,335) | (4,335) |
| Taxable income | 139,554 | 88,889 |

| Tax: |  |  |  |
|---|---|---|---|
| 1,500 × 10% / | 28,000 × 10% | 150 | 2,800 |
| 26,500 × 23% / |  | 6,095 |  |
| 22,665 × 40% / |  | 9,066 |  |
| 50,665 |  |  |  |
| 88,889 × 32½% | 60,889 × 32½% | 28,889 | 19,789 |
| 139,554 | 88,889 | 44,200 | 22,589 |

In both situations the dividend tax credit of £8,889 is available to set against the 1999/00 tax liability.*)*

June and Julie will also have dividend income not invested of £9,500 each (80,000 – 70,500). There are no National Insurance contribution implications in respect of the payment of a dividend.

(c)     **Occupational pension scheme**

**Implications for Grey Ltd**

The payment of a premium of £160,000 into an occupational pension scheme will be deductible for corporation tax purposes. If the deduction is allowed for the year ended 31 March 2000, the situation will be exactly the same as for the payment of additional directors' remuneration, in that there will be a tax adjusted loss of £75,000 for this year leading to a reduction of £32,330 in corporation tax liabilities. Employers Class 1 National Insurance contribution is not payable in respect of pension contributions. The full £160,000 can therefore be invested.

**Implications for the directors**

There are no implications for the directors, as an employer's contributions into an approved occupational pension scheme do not represent benefits in kind.

**Summary**

The three alternative ways of using the £160,000 of surplus funds to provide for the directors' entitlement to a pension result in net investment as follows:

|  | Directors' remuneration £ | Dividend £ | Occupational scheme £ |
|---|---|---|---|
| Amount invested in pension scheme | 142,603 | 141,000 | 160,000 |
| Funds retained | – | 19,000 | – |
| Income tax refunds | – | 19,090 | – |
| Corporation tax refunds | 32,330 | – | 32,330 |
|  | 174,933 | 179,090 | 192,330 |

The investment in the self-administered occupational pension scheme results in a substantially greater sum being invested. Other points that should be taken into account include:

(i)     Both June and Julie are relatively young, and a personal pension would probably be more flexible than an occupational scheme should either of them cease to be directors of Grey Ltd.

(ii)    The conditions to be met to gain approval for an occupational pension scheme will be more restrictive than normal, as the scheme will include directors controlling more than 20% of the company's share capital.

(iii)   If June and Julie are appointed as trustees of a self-administered occupational pension scheme, they will have wide investment powers. For example, they could use the pension funds to invest in or make loans to Grey Ltd.

(iv)    There is no limit to the ultimate pension payable under a personal pension scheme. Under an occupational scheme, the ultimate pension payable will be limited by reference to a director's final remuneration and number of years' service. This would probably only be a problem for June and Julie if substantial further pension contributions are to be made.

On balance, the self-administered occupational pension scheme appears to be the most favourable option.

*(Tutorial note:* During June 1996 the Pension Schemes Office announced a relaxation in the requirement to spread pension contributions of less than £500,000. Students were unlikely to be penalised if they were unaware of this change, and discussed spreading the payment over several years.)

---

## 26    (Answer 2 of examination)

(a)     (i)     Zoo plc will be able to group relieve its excess management expenses under S402 ICTA 1988 to 75% subsidiaries that are resident in the UK. To qualify as a 75% subsidiary, Zoo plc must hold not less than 75% of the subsidiary's ordinary share capital, have the right to receive not less than 75% of the subsidiary's distributable profits, and have the right to receive not less than 75% of the subsidiary's net assets were it to be wound up. It is assumed that Zoo plc's ordinary share holdings give an equivalent entitlement to distributable profits and to net assets in the event of a winding up. The 75% holding must be an effective interest which is held either directly or indirectly.

Zoo plc will therefore be able to group relieve its excess management expenses to Ant Ltd (82% holding), Bat Ltd (90% holding) and Cod Ltd (80% holding). Bat Ltd was only acquired as a subsidiary on 1 December 1999. Group relief will therefore be limited to $^4/_{12}$ of Zoo plc's excess management expenses for the year ended 31 March 2000. The set-off will be against Bat Ltd's profits chargeable to corporation tax (PCTCT) for the four month period to 31 March 2000. Cod Ltd ceased to be a subsidiary on 30 November 1999. Group relief will therefore be limited to the lower of $^8/_{12}$ of Zoo plc's excess management expenses and $^8/_{12}$ of Cod Ltd's PCTCT. Group relief will be further limited if arrangements existed prior to 30 November 1999 for Cod Ltd to leave the group. Although Dog Ltd is a 75% subsidiary, it has not yet commenced trading, and is therefore unlikely to have any profits against which a group relief claim can be made. Group relief cannot exceed the available PCTCT of the claimant company. The claimant company is deemed to utilise any of its own losses brought forward in calculating the PCTCT available for group relief.

Zoo plc does not have the requisite 75% shareholding in Hog Ltd (82% × 78% = 63.96%) or Ibex Ltd (82% × 78% × 70% = 44.77% + 10% = 54.77%). It is not possible for Zoo plc to surrender excess management expenses to Ant Ltd, with that company then surrendering them to Hog Ltd. Elk Ltd is not resident in the UK, and therefore does not qualify. Its subsidiary, Jay Ltd, also does not qualify despite being resident in the UK itself.

Zoo plc will also be able to group relieve its excess management expenses where it is a member of a consortium. A consortium exists where 75% of the ordinary share capital of a company (the consortium company) is owned by UK resident companies, none of which have a holding of less than 5% (the members of the consortium). However, the group relief provisions override the consortium relief provisions, so Fox Ltd which is a 75% subsidiary of Unit plc, cannot also be a consortium company. Gnu Ltd qualifies as a consortium company as at least 75% of its share capital is owned by a consortium of Zoo plc (40%), Volt plc (30%) and Watt plc (30%). Gnu Ltd itself is unlikely to have any PCTCT, but consortium relief is extended to 90% trading subsidiaries of a consortium holding company. Zoo plc can therefore surrender its excess management expenses to Kea Ltd (95% held by Gnu Ltd). The surrender will be limited to 40% of Kea Ltd's profits, being Zoo plc's interest in the share capital of Gnu Ltd. Lion Ltd is not a 90% subsidiary of Gnu Ltd.

*(Tutorial note:* in order to group relieve management expenses, the claimant company and also any intermediary companies must be UK resident. The fact that Elk Ltd is not resident in the UK prevents management expenses being surrendered to Jay Ltd.*)*

(ii)    The most important factor to be taken into account by Zoo plc when deciding as to which companies it should surrender its excess management expenses to, is the rate of corporation tax applicable to those companies. Surrender should be made initially to companies subject to corporation tax at the marginal rate of 32.5%. The amount surrendered should be sufficient to bring the claimant company's PCTCT down to the lower limit. Surrender should then be to those companies subject to full rate of corporation tax of 30%, and lastly to companies subject to corporation tax at the small companies rate of 20%. This planning is facilitated by the fact that Zoo plc can specify the amount of excess management expenses to be surrendered in each case.

For the Zoo plc group of companies, the relevant lower and upper limits are £37,500 $\left(^{300,000}/_8\right)$ and £187,500 $\left(^{1,500,000}/_8\right)$ respectively. Both limits are divided by eight, as this is the number of associated companies in the group. The definition of an associated company includes non-UK resident companies (Elk Ltd), companies that are only associated for part of an accounting period (Bat Ltd and Cod Ltd), but excludes dormant companies (Dog Ltd). Fox Ltd and Gnu Ltd are also excluded as they are not controlled by Zoo plc. Gnu Ltd, Kea Ltd and Lion Ltd form a separate group, for which the lower and upper limits will be £100,000 $\left(^{300,000}/_3\right)$ and £500,000 $\left(^{1,500,000}/_3\right)$ respectively.

Another factor to consider is the interaction with double taxation relief. Zoo plc's surplus management expenses should not be surrendered to a company where this results in that company being unable to utilise double taxation relief.

(b)    (i)    It would have been possible for 75% subsidiaries to have transferred chargeable assets to Zoo plc during the year ended 31 March 2000 without incurring a chargeable gain or an allowable loss. The definition of a 75% subsidiary is looser than for group relief, in that the required 75% holding must only be met at each level in the group structure. This will include Hog Ltd (78% held by Ant Ltd), but not Ibex Ltd as it is not a 75% subsidiary of either Hog Ltd directly (70% holding) or Zoo plc indirectly (54.77% holding). A further requirement is that Zoo plc should have an effective holding of more than 50%, and this test is met in the case of Hog Ltd (63.96% holding). Bat Ltd (90% holding) and Cod Ltd (80% holding) will be included in respect of assets transferred whilst they were members of the group, as will Ant Ltd (82% holding) and Dog Ltd (85% holding). Elk Ltd (90% holding) is excluded, being a non-UK resident company, but Jay Ltd (100% held by Elk Ltd) is included despite having a non-UK resident parent company. Gnu Ltd (40% holding) is not a 75%

subsidiary, and the relief does not extend to consortium companies. Kea Ltd and Lion Ltd are therefore both excluded, as is Fox Ltd (20% holding) which is also not a 75% subsidiary.

*(Tutorial note:* Elk Ltd being non resident does not exclude Jay Ltd from the group for the purpose of transferring chargeable assets.*)*

(ii)    It would probably be beneficial for all of the eligible 75% subsidiaries to transfer chargeable assets to Zoo plc prior to their disposal outside the group, because unlike trading losses, capital losses cannot be group relieved. Arranging that wherever possible, chargeable gains and allowable losses arise in the same company (Zoo plc), will result in the optimum use being made of capital losses. These can either be off-set against chargeable gains of the same period, or carried forward against future chargeable gains.

Also, Zoo plc will be able to utilise its excess management expenses against any chargeable gains. This would be particularly relevant where the company making the transfer is a 75% subsidiary for the purposes of chargeable assets, but not for the purposes of group relief. Zoo plc is also likely to have a lower rate of corporation tax than most other group companies, should chargeable gains be subject to corporation tax.

---

## 27    (Answer 3 of examination)

(a)    The Final Report of the Royal Commission on the Taxation of Profits and Income (1955) concluded that there could be no single test as to what constitutes trading, but suggested certain tests, the badges of trade, designed to determine whether or not the purchase and resale of property is a trading transaction. The tests are as follows:

### The subject matter of the transaction

Property which does not yield an income nor gives personal enjoyment to its owner is likely to form the subject matter of a trading transaction. Other property such as land, works of art and investments are more likely to be acquired for the income and/or personal enjoyment that they provide. The disposal of such items will more often give rise to a gain or loss of a capital nature, rather than a trading profit. In **Rutledge v IRC** (1929), the taxpayer purchased one million rolls of toilet paper for £1,000, which was resold at a profit of £11,000. This was held to be an adventure in the nature of a trade, since it was inconceivable that the rolls of toilet paper were acquired for any purpose other than realising a profit. A similar view was taken in the case of **Martin v Lowry** (1927), where the subject matter of the transaction was 44 million yards of government surplus aeroplane linen. It is possible for any asset bought as an investment to be subsequently reclassified as trading stock.

### The length of ownership

The sale of property within a short time of its acquisition is an indication of trading. By itself, however, this is not a 'strong' badge as, for example, stocks and shares will often be bought and sold on an active basis without giving rise to an adventure in the nature of a trade.

### Frequency of similar transactions

Repeated transactions in the same subject matter will be an indication of trading. This badge is of particular importance when an isolated transaction would not otherwise be treated as an adventure in the nature of a trade. In the case of **Pickford v Quirke** (1927), it was held that although the single purchase and resale of a cotton mill was capital in nature, a series of four such transactions amounted to trading. Hence, subsequent transactions may trigger a Schedule D Case I liability in respect of earlier transactions.

### Work done on the property

Carrying out work to the property in order to make it more marketable, or taking steps to find purchasers, will indicate a trading motive. In the case of **Cape Brandy Syndicate v IRC** (1921), the syndicate was held to be trading when it purchased a quantity of brandy which was then blended, recasked, and sold in lots over an 18 month period. However, a taxpayer is entitled to make an asset more attractive to potential purchasers, without this being an indication of trading.

### Circumstances responsible for the realisation

A forced sale to raise cash for an emergency will by presumption indicate that the transaction is not an adventure in the nature of a trade.

### Motive

If a transaction is undertaken with the motive of realising a profit, this will be a strong indication of trading. However, the absence of a profit motive does not prevent a person from being treated as trading. In the case of Wisdom v Chamberlain (1968), the taxpayer was held to be trading when he bought £200,000 of silver as a hedge against devaluation, and later resold it at a profit of £50,000.

There are a number of other 'badges' which also need to be considered. For example, is the subject matter of the transaction in some way related to the trade otherwise carried on by the taxpayer? What was the source of finance for the transaction? Was the asset acquired deliberately, or unintentionally such as by gift or inheritance?

No single badge will usually be decisive, and it will be necessary to consider the facts surrounding the transaction.

(b)  **Disposal of first motor car**

Taken by itself, the purchase and resale of the first motor car by Stirling would probably not be treated as a trading transaction. Vintage motor cars are commonly owned both for the personal enjoyment that they provide and for their investment potential. It is not unusual for the owners of such cars to spend both time and money restoring them. In the case of Stirling, this conclusion is re-enforced by the length of ownership after restoration from 30 June 1999 to 15 September 1999, and by what would appear to be a forced sale upon him being made redundant. A factor against this conclusion is that Stirling has taken out a loan in order to build a workshop, equip it, and also, it would appear, to partly finance the purchase of the first motor car. For a definitive decision to be reached, more information would be needed regarding Stirling's financial position at the time that he was made redundant (was this a genuine forced sale?), and also as to his motive in restoring the car. Did he plan to keep it for his personal enjoyment or investment potential, or was its disposal always envisaged?

The purchase and resale of the other three motor cars would appear to be an adventure in the nature of a trade. This conclusion is supported by the fact that Stirling would appear to be devoting substantially the whole of his time to the enterprise, by the number of transactions, and by the immediate sale of two of the motor cars upon their restoration being completed. It would be difficult to argue that this was a forced sale.

The most difficult consideration in the case of Stirling, is whether, as in the case of **Pickford v Quirke** (1927), his subsequent trading transactions result in the purchase and resale of the first motor car also being treated as a trading transaction. In the case of **Leach v Pogson** (1962), the taxpayer established 30 driving schools which were then sold. He contended that the sale of the first driving school was capital in nature, but it was held that the subsequent 29 transactions (which were trading transactions) could be taken into account when considering the first transaction. This can be contrasted with the case of **Taylor v Good** (1974), where it was held that because there was no intention of trading at the time an asset was purchased, the disposal of the asset was not an adventure in the nature of a trade but instead subject to capital gains tax. **Taylor v Good** concerned a single transaction however, and it would appear on balance that Stirling may be treated as trading in respect of all of the motor cars purchased and resold.

(c)  **Treated as trading**

If Stirling is treated as trading during the period from 6 April 1999 to 31 March 2000, he will be liable under Schedule D Case I. The following must be taken into account:

(i)  Loan interest paid prior to 6 April 1999, which will be deductible as pre-trading expenditure as it was incurred within seven years of the start of trade.

(ii) The capital allowances that will be available in respect of tools and equipment, and the Industrial Buildings Allowance that will be available in respect of the workshop. In both cases, balancing allowances will be due in respect of the fall in value between 6 April 1999 and 31 March 2000.

(iii) Following the case of **Sharkey v Wernher** (1956), the motor car retained by Stirling at 31 March 2000 must be included at its market value of £25,000, rather than at its cost of £11,000 (4,000 + 7,000).

Stirling's liability to income tax will be as follows:

|  | £ | £ |
|---|---:|---:|
| Sale proceeds (2 × 25,000 + 52,000) |  | 102,000 |
| Cost of motor cars [3,000 + (3 × 4,000)] | 15,000 |  |
| Cost of spare parts (4 × 7,000) | 28,000 |  |
| Loan interest $\left(40,000 \times 10\% \times {}^{15}\!/_{12}\right)$ | 5,000 |  |
| Capital allowances: |  |  |
| Plant and machinery (8,000 − 4,500) | 3,500 |  |
| Industrial building (30,000 − 25,000) | 5,000 |  |
|  |  | 56,500 |
| Taxable profit |  | 45,500 |
| Income tax at 40% |  | 18,200 |

**Treated as not trading**

If Stirling is treated as not trading during the period from 6 April 1999 to 31 March 2000, he will instead be subject to capital gains tax. Since motor cars, including vintage motor cars, are exempt from capital gains tax, he will not have any tax liability.

*(Tutorial note:* any motor car (including those with business use) is exempt from capital gains tax if it is suitable for private use. Included in this category are vintage and veteran cars.*)*

(d) If Stirling is treated as trading during the period from 6 April 1999 to 31 March 2000, he will be making taxable supplies for the purposes of VAT. A person making such supplies becomes liable to compulsory registration if during any 12 month period the value of his or her taxable supplies exceeds £51,000. However, registration is avoided if taxable supplies during the following 12 month period can be shown to be less than £49,000. This would apply to Stirling, assuming that he will not have any taxable supplies during the year ended 31 March 2001.

However, a person must also register if there are reasonable grounds for believing that taxable supplies will exceed £51,000 in the following 30 days. Stirling would not have been under an obligation to register for VAT in respect of the sale of his first motor car as the taxable supply was only £25,000. He will, however, be liable to be registered in respect of, and account for output tax on, the sale of the two motor cars on 29 February 2000, as the taxable supply amounted to £52,000.

Output tax will also be due on the motor car retained by Stirling on 31 March 2000. For VAT purposes, goods taken for private purposes are valued at market value. Stirling's output tax therefore amounts to £11,468 $\left(77,000 \times {}^{7}\!/_{47}\right)$.

Against this Stirling could set any pre-registration input tax paid in respect of the cost of spare parts, which will probably amount to £3,128 $\left(3 \times 7,000 \times {}^{7}\!/_{47}\right)$. The purchase of the motor cars was unlikely to have been a taxable supply, and therefore no input tax is recoverable. However, input tax can be reclaimed in respect of tools and equipment amounting to £1,191 $\left(8,000 \times {}^{4}\!/_{47}\right)$, and £4,468 $\left(30,000 \times {}^{7}\!/_{47}\right)$ in respect of the workshop, since these were still owned by Stirling at the date of VAT registration. There will be a corresponding liability to output tax when the business ceases of £670 $\left(4,500 \times {}^{7}\!/_{47}\right)$ and £3,723 $\left(25,000 \times {}^{7}\!/_{47}\right)$ respectively.

Stirling's overall VAT liability is therefore likely to be £7,074 (11,468 + 670 + 3,723 − 3,128 − 1,191 − 4,468). This would reduce his income tax liability in (c) by £2,830 (7,074 × 40%). Stirling could have reduced his VAT liability by operating a second-hand goods scheme. Output VAT would then only be due on the margin between the selling and purchase prices of the motor cars, and therefore input tax would have effectively been obtained in respect of the cost of the motor cars.

Stirling should have notified HM Customs & Excise of his liability to register by 30 March 2000, being the end of the 30 day period that his supplies exceeded £51,000. He would then have been registered from 29 February 2000. If Stirling did not notify HM Customs & Excise by 30 March 2000, he would be liable to a late notification penalty of 5% of the net tax due. This amounts to £354 (7,074 × 5%), unless he can show a reasonable excuse for the failure to notify. Late payment interest may also be due.

---

## 28 (Answer 4 of examination)

(a) The income tax implications arising from Clifford and Dinah's forthcoming marriage on 30 April 1999 are as follows:

(i) At present, both Clifford and Dinah are entitled to the additional personal allowance (APA) of £1,970, since they each have a qualifying child living with them at some time during the tax year. Clifford's son is aged 16 or more, but is attending a full-time course of education at an educational establishment, whilst Dinah can claim in respect of either of her daughters as they are both under 16. The APA only obtains tax relief at 10%. Once married, they will only be entitled to the married couple's allowance (MCA) of £1,970, which again only attracts tax relief at 10%. MCA would appear to be available despite Clifford and Dinah living in separate houses after marrying, because they will almost certainly be living together for part of the tax year. The MCA will not be reduced in the year of marriage, since the marriage is to take place prior to 5 May 1999. Dinah will be entitled to the APA for 1999/00, but not thereafter, as she will be a single woman at some time during the year. Therefore Clifford and Dinah will be entitled to the same allowances for 1999/00 as a result of their marrying. Although Dinah can elect to receive half of the MCA, or Clifford and Dinah can jointly elect to have all of the MCA, transferred to her, this will not result in any tax saving. (The MCA and APA have been abolished for 2000/01 onwards.)

*(**Tutorial note:** the MCA is reduced in the year of marriage by $\frac{1}{12}$ for each complete tax month (ie, 6th to 5th in the following month) that has elapsed before the marriage takes place.)*

(ii) At present, both Clifford and Dinah are obtaining tax relief at the rate of 10% for a proportion of their mortgage interest as follows:

$$\text{Clifford} \quad 7,200 \times \frac{30,000}{90,000} = 2,400 \text{ at } 10\% = £240$$

$$\text{Dinah} \quad 3,500 \times \frac{30,000}{35,000} = 3,000 \text{ at } 10\% = £300$$

Once married, Clifford and Dinah will only be entitled to relief in respect of mortgage interest arising from the mortgage on the residence that was purchased first. This is Clifford's so relief of £300 will be lost. The statutory concession for the first 12 months do not apply in this situation, as neither spouse is to vacate their respective property. Although Clifford and Dinah can elect to have the qualifying interest allocated between them in whatever proportion they choose, this again will not result in any tax saving. In any case, mortgage interest relief is abolished for interest paid after 5 April 2000.

The overall increase in Clifford's and Dinah's annual income tax liability as a result of marriage will therefore be £300 in 1999/00 and nil hereafter.

---

(b)    **Income tax and NIC**

At present, Clifford and Dinah's taxable income is as follows:

|  |  | Clifford £ | Dinah £ |
|---|---|---|---|
| Schedule D Case II |  | 60,000 | 15,000 |
| Personal pension contributions | 60,000 at 25% | 15,000 | |
|  | 15,000 at 20% | | 3,000 |
|  |  | 45,000 | 12,000 |
| Schedule A $\left(^{75}/_{25}\right)$ |  | 3,750 | 1,250 |
| BSI $\left(2,160 \times ^{100}/_{80}\right)$ |  | 2,700 | |
|  |  | 51,450 | 13,250 |
| Personal allowances |  | 4,335 | 4,335 |
| Taxable income |  | 47,115 | 8,915 |

*(Tutorial note:* it is assumed that Clifford and Dinah make a joint declaration regarding the true split of the rental income.*)*

The mortgage interest and the MCA are irrelevant for the purposes of tax planning, as relief is given by way of tax credits at the rate of 10%.

Clifford therefore falls into the 40% tax bracket. Clifford and Dinah should aim to reduce Clifford's income, without Dinah, herself, becoming liable to 40% tax. The potential annual income tax saving if Dinah's 23% tax band can be fully utilised is £3,244 (28,000 – 8,915 × 17%). This can be achieved by transferring income from Clifford to Dinah as follows:

(i)    Clifford and Dinah could form a partnership of their two separate practices, and, for example, share profits equally. However, this will result in an additional Class 4 National Insurance contribution liability each year since Dinah is currently paying less than the maximum annual contribution. Her additional annual National Insurance contributions would be £660 (26,000 – 15,000 at 6%). It will also result in a reduction in qualifying personal pension scheme contributions, since Clifford can contribute a maximum of 25% of his profits (he is aged between 46 and 50), whilst Dinah can only contribute 20% (she is aged between 36 and 45).

      *(Tutorial note:* this part of the question demonstrates the need to consider all aspects when planning to reduce tax. By forming a partnership, Clifford and Dinah may reduce their income tax liability, but this will affect National Insurance contribution and personal pension scheme contributions, as well as the capital gains tax position on future disposals.*)*

(ii)    The income arising from the jointly owned furnished holiday cottage will be assessed on Clifford and Dinah equally, provided no joint declaration is made to the Inland Revenue. Alternatively, a joint declaration could be made specifying that Dinah is entitled to, say, 100% of the income from the cottage, but this would require her to be beneficially entitled to a corresponding interest in the property.

(iii)    The building society deposit account could be put into their joint names. The interest arising from the account would then be assessed on Clifford and Dinah equally. It is not possible to make a joint election in respect of a jointly held bank or building society account. Note that this would increase the potential tax saving as the interest would be taxed at 20% in Dinah's hands, compared to 40% in Clifford's.

      Another option would be for Clifford to use the proceeds of £50,000 to repay part of his mortgage. This should be beneficial as he is not receiving tax relief in respect of the interest on £60,000 of his mortgage, and also because mortgage interest rates are generally higher than the rates on building society deposit accounts. Also, it would not involve the gift of any assets to Dinah, which is relevant as Clifford is concerned that his son ultimately inherits the majority of his assets.

**Capital gains tax**

The following CGT planning measures could be taken by Clifford and Dinah following their marriage:

(i)     Clifford should transfer the investments that result in the chargeable gain of £7,500 and the capital loss of £400 to Dinah prior to their disposal. The transfer will be at no gain/no loss, and will utilise Dinah's 1999/00 annual exemption of £7,100. There is no benefit in transferring chargeable gains in excess of this amount to Dinah unless her 23% tax band will not be fully utilised for 1999/00.

(ii)    Forming a partnership and possibly transferring a greater proportion of the holiday cottage into Dinah's ownership will maximise any CGT reliefs that might be available upon future disposals, such as the annual exemption and retirement relief.

A final point is that when considering tax planning of this nature, it is important that the 'risk' of transferring assets to a spouse is compared to the relatively small tax saving.

(c)     At present, Clifford has an estate valued at £395,000, whilst Dinah has an estate valued at £105,000, as follows:

|  | *Clifford* £ | *Dinah* £ |
|---|---|---|
| Businesses | 125,000 | 40,000 |
| Business property relief at 100% | 125,000 | 40,000 |
|  | – | – |
| Property | 220,000 | 85,000 |
| Holiday cottage $(^{75}/_{25})$ | 30,000 | 10,000 |
| Building society deposit | 50,000 | |
| Other assets | 95,000 | 10,000 |
|  | 395,000 | 105,000 |

An endowment mortgage is repaid upon death by the related life assurance contract, and is not therefore deductible as a debt.

If Clifford dies first, only £110,000 of his estate, being one half of the value of his London house $(^{220,000}/_2)$, will be chargeable to IHT. The balance of his estate bequeathed to Dinah will be exempt, and Clifford is not therefore fully utilising his nil rate band of £231,000. He would be advised to either leave a higher proportion of his London house to his son (for example, 95% × 220,000 = £209,000), or to leave him some other chargeable assets (any assets except for his business) to the value of £121,000 (231,000 – 110,000). This will ultimately save IHT of £48,400 (121,000 at 40%). When Dinah subsequently dies, she would then have an estate valued at £269,000 (395,000 – 231,000 + 105,000), which will utilise her nil rate band of £231,000 and result in an IHT liability of £15,200 (269,000 – 231,000 at 40%).

If Dinah dies first, all of her estate of £105,000 will be chargeable to IHT. Her nil rate band of £231,000 is therefore not being fully utilised, and Clifford would be advised to transfer chargeable assets (again any assets except for his business) worth £126,000 (231,000 – 105,000) into her name. When Clifford subsequently dies, he would then have an estate valued at £269,000 (395,000 – 126,000), which will again result in an IHT liability of £15,200. There is no reason why the lifetime gift of £126,000 to Dinah should not be bequeathed to Clifford's son under the terms of her will. Also this transfer of assets is in line with the income tax planning measure already outlined.

In both circumstances, the IHT liability is postponed until the death of the second spouse.

(d)     The use of an interest in possession trust would allow Clifford, the settlor, to bequeath assets to trustees under the terms of his will, to hold for the benefit of Dinah during her lifetime, and upon her death to pay the capital of the trust to his son. The use of such a trust will ensure that Clifford's son ultimately inherits his assets upon the death of Dinah. The trust would be subject to tax as follows:

### Income tax

From the date of Clifford's death, the income of the trust assets will belong to the trust. The trustees will have to account for income tax on the trust income at the basic rate of 23%, other than savings income which will be at the rate of 20% (or 10% for dividend income). Trustees expenses will not be deductible.

The trust will not receive any personal allowances to set against its income. The payments of income to Dinah will be made net of lower or basic rate tax (or 10% tax on dividends), and she will be assessed to income tax on the gross income of the trust as it arises in the trust. If she is a basic rate taxpayer, there will be no further liability, but if she is a 40% taxpayer there will be an additional liability of 17% (40 − 23), or 20% (40 − 20) in respect of savings income (or 22½% (32½ − 10) in respect of dividends).

The trustees will be required to send a certificate to her showing the grossed up amount of the payments together with the tax deducted.

### Capital gains tax

Since the trust is to be set up under the terms of Clifford's will upon his death, there will be no CGT liability at that date. The trustees will take over the assets with a deemed base cost equivalent to their market value at the date of Clifford's death.

During its lifetime, the trust will attract CGT in respect of any disposals resulting in a chargeable gain. This should only arise where it sells investments or assets in order to buy other investments or assets. The trustees will be entitled to one half of the annual exemption, amounting to £3,550 $\left(\frac{7,100}{2}\right)$, and will have a CGT rate of 34% regardless of Dinah's marginal rate of tax.

Upon Dinah's death, the trust assets will be paid to Clifford's son. This is again a transfer on death, and so there will be no CGT liability at that date. Clifford's son will take over the assets with a deemed base cost equivalent to their market value at the date of Dinah's death.

### Inheritance tax

For IHT purposes, the assets of the trust will be treated exactly the same as if Clifford had bequeathed them absolutely to Dinah under the terms of his will, and she in turn bequeathed them absolutely to Clifford's son. The assets will therefore form part of Clifford's estate as in (c), and in turn will form part of Dinah's estate when she dies. The IHT liability will thus be nil upon Clifford's death, and £15,200 (assuming the IHT planning advice is followed) upon Dinah's death. The one difference will be that the trustees will be responsible for paying the IHT in respect of the trust assets.

---

## 29    (Answer 5 of examination)

(a)    (i)    Slowdown Ltd's purchase of Abdul's 20% shareholding is likely to qualify for the special treatment because the following conditions are met:

–    The purchasing company, Slowdown Ltd, is unquoted.

–    Slowdown Ltd is a trading company.

–    Abdul, the vendor, is resident, and presumably ordinarily resident, in the UK in the year of assessment that the purchase is to take place.

–    Abdul had held the shares for six years prior to the purchase, and so the five year ownership test is met.

–    Abdul is disposing of all of his shares in Slowdown Ltd. The 'substantial reduction' test is not therefore relevant.

–  Abdul will not be 'connected' with Slowdown Ltd immediately after the purchase of his shares. The 'continuing connection' test is therefore not relevant.

–  The purchase of shares appears to be wholly or mainly for the benefit of the trade carried on by Slowdown Ltd, and not for the benefit of Abdul. The Inland Revenue has indicated four circumstances which satisfy this test, of which the disagreement over the management of the company would appear to be met. This test will only be satisfied, however, if the disagreement is having an adverse effect on the running of Slowdown Ltd's trade.

Slowdown Ltd may apply in writing to the Inland Revenue for clearance as to whether or not the proposed purchase will meet the above conditions.

(ii)  If the special treatment does not apply, then Abdul will be assessed on the grossed up distribution of £777,778 $(700,000 \times {}^{100}\!/_{90})$. This will result in an additional income tax liability of £175,000 for 1999/00, being £777,778 at 32½% less the tax credit of £77,778.

If the special treatment does apply, then Abdul's disposal of his shares in Slowdown Ltd will be treated as a capital gain. Because Abdul is over 50 years old, has been a full-time working director of Slowdown Ltd, which is a trading company, and has owned not less than 5% of its ordinary share capital, he will be entitled to retirement relief in respect of the disposal. This will be restricted:

–  by a factor of 60% since he has only been a full-time working director and a shareholder for six years;

–  to the proportion of the gain represented by the ratio of Slowdown Ltd's chargeable business assets to its total chargeable assets.

Abdul's CGT liability will be £128,255 as follows:

|  | £ | £ |
|---|---|---|
| Sale proceeds |  | 800,000 |
| Cost |  | 100,000 |
|  |  | 700,000 |
| Indexation $100,000 \times \dfrac{162.6 - 142.1}{142.1}$ |  | 14,426 |
| Capital gain |  | 685,574 |

Proportion relating to chargeable business assets

| | | |
|---|---|---|
| $685,574 \times \dfrac{4,750,000 \, (5,500,000 - 750,000)}{5,500,000}$ |  | 592,087 |
| Retirement relief |  |  |
| $200,000 \times 60\%$ | 120,000 |  |
| $480,000^* - 120,000 = 360,000 \times 50\%$ | 180,000 |  |
|  |  | 300,000 |
|  |  | 292,087 |
| Proportion relating to chargeable non-business assets |  |  |
| $685,574 - 592,087$ |  | 93,487 |
|  |  | 385,574 |
| Tapered to 85% |  | 327,738 |

| | |
|---|---|
| Annual exemption | 7,100 |
| | 320,638 |
| Capital gains tax at 40% | 128,255 |

*£800,000 × 60% = £480,000 (which is less than £592,087)

If the special treatment applies, Abdul's tax liability is £128,255 compared to £175,000 if it does not apply, which is a saving of £46,745 (175,000 – 128,255) and is clearly beneficial. In any case, if the conditions for the special treatment are met, the relief is compulsory.

Although not required by the question, it should also be noted that deferral relief on the re-investment of the sale proceeds from the sale of the shares in Slowdown Ltd (see part (b)) will only be available if the special treatment is applicable.

*(Tutorial note:* notice that neither the company nor Abdul can chose as to whether the special treatment applies. If the conditions for the special treatment are met, there is no choice, the special treatment must apply.*)*

(b)    **Re-investment of the proceeds of £800,000**

Abdul will be entitled to EIS deferral relief on the re-investment of the proceeds from the disposal of his shares in Slowdown Ltd in the ordinary share capital of Fast-Track Ltd. Relief is available since Fast-Track Ltd is an unquoted trading company, and the re-investment is within the period beginning one year before and ending three years after the date of the disposal. Relief will be withdrawn if within five years of acquiring the shares Abdul emigrates, or Fast-Track Ltd ceases to be a qualifying company.

The amount of the relief will be the lower of:

(i)      the gain of £685,574 arising on the disposal of the shares in Slowdown Ltd;
(ii)     the cost of shares in Fast-Track Ltd, being £1,190,000;
(iii)    the amount specified in the claim for the relief.

Abdul is not expecting his shareholding in Fast-Track Ltd to experience significant capital growth. There is therefore the possibility that when the shareholding is disposed of, the retirement relief that should be available will not be fully utilised. Since deferral relief is applied before retirement relief, it would appear sensible to limit the relief claimed to £377,221 as follows:

| | £ |
|---|---|
| Proportion relating to business assets not covered by retirement relief | 292,087 |
| Proportion relating to non-business assets | 93,487 |
| | 385,574 |
| Annual exemption (grossed up at 100/85 for taper relief) | 8,353 |
| Claim for EIS deferral relief | 377,221 |

The full amount of retirement relief presently available, the appropriate amount of taper relief and the annual exemption for 1999/00 are therefore utilised.

**Re-investment of the proceeds of £160,000**

Abdul will also be entitled to EIS deferral relief on the re-investment of the proceeds from the disposal of his investments on 20 February 1999 in the ordinary share capital of Fast-Track Ltd. The conditions to be met are as above, so the potential relief will be limited to £48,000, being the chargeable gains resulting from the disposal. Assuming that Abdul did not otherwise utilise his CGT annual exemption for 1998/99, it would be beneficial to limit the claim to £41,200 (48,000 – 6,800) so that it is not wasted.

Total EIS deferral relief claimed is therefore £418,421 (377,221 + 41,200). This does not, however, reduce the base cost of Abdul's shares in Fast-Track Ltd which remains at £1,190,000.

**Bank loan of £230,000**

Abdul will obtain tax relief in respect of the interest paid on the bank loan of £230,000. The loan will be for a qualifying purpose since it is to be used to purchase ordinary shares in a close company (Fast-Track Ltd will be controlled by five or fewer shareholders), in which Abdul will have a material interest (in excess of 5%). Tax relief will amount to £8,280 pa (230,000 × 9% × 40%).

(c)     Sheena's subscription for ordinary share capital in Fast-Track Ltd should qualify for income tax relief under the enterprise investment scheme (EIS). The following conditions must be met for relief to be available:

(i)     The shares subscribed for must be new ordinary shares.

(ii)    The company issuing the shares must be an unquoted trading company.

(iii)   The gross assets of a company must not exceed £15 million before EIS shares are subscribed for, nor £16 million immediately after the subscription

(iv)    The maximum income tax relief for an investor in any one tax year is a subscription of £150,000.

(v)     Relief will be withdrawn if shares are not held by the investor for at least five years.

(vi)    The investor must not be connected with the issuing company. An investor is connected with a company if he or she is an employee of the company, although the investor is allowed to become a paid director of the company at a later date without affecting his or her entitlement to the relief. An investor is also connected with the company if he or she is a shareholder with over 30% of the company's share capital. For this purpose, shareholdings of 'associates' must be taken into account, but this is not relevant in this case since a cousin is not an associate.

(vii)   The issuing company must be trading in the UK, whether or not it is incorporated in the UK. The investor must be liable to UK income tax, whether or not he or she is resident in the UK.

Sheena is only subscribing for 15% of Fast-Track Ltd's ordinary share capital $\left( ^{210,000}\!/_{1,400,000} \times 100 \right)$, and so condition (vi) will be met. However, she will only obtain tax relief on £150,000 of her subscription, and this will be at the lower rate of 20%. Her tax relief for 2000/01 will therefore be £30,000 (150,000 × 20%), although this will be reduced to the amount of her income tax liability for this year if this is less than £30,000. If Fast-Track Ltd does not require the full amount of the subscription money immediately, consideration should be given to Sheena delaying £60,000 of her subscription until 6 April 2001, so that additional tax relief is obtained. There will be no CGT on Sheena's disposal of the shares, provided she holds them for at least five years.

---

## 30     (Answer 6 of examination)

---

(a)     Since he has been employed in the UK since July 1993, Ken will be both resident and ordinarily resident in the UK for 1999/00. However, he is domiciled in Pajan, and will therefore only be assessed on his overseas income under Schedule D Cases IV and V on the remittance basis.

**Ken Sing – Income tax liability 1999/00**

|  | £ | £ |
|---|---:|---:|
| Schedule E |  |  |
| Salary |  | 75,000 |
| Car benefit (38,000 × 25%) |  | 9,500 |
| Fuel benefit |  | 1,540 |
| Beneficial loan (90,000 × 10%) |  | 9,000 |
| Private medical insurance |  | 1,200 |

| | |
|---|---:|
| Golf club subscription | 1,500 |

Schedule D Case V

| | |
|---|---:|
| Rents remitted $\left(3,500 \times \frac{100}{70}\right)$ | 5,000 |
| Bank interest remitted $\left(850 \times \frac{100}{85}\right)$ | 1,000 |
| Dividends $\left(100,000 \times 9p = 9,000 \times \frac{100}{90}\right)$ | 10,000 |
| Bank interest $\left(2,240 \times \frac{100}{80}\right)$ | 2,800 |
| | 116,540 |
| Personal allowance | 4,335 |
| Taxable income | 112,205 |

| Income tax: | | |
|---|---|---:|
| | 1,500 at 20% | 150 |
| | 26,500 at 23% | 6,095 |
| | 74,205 at 40% | 29,682 |
| | 10,000 at 32½% | 3,250 |
| | | 39,177 |

| | | |
|---|---:|---:|
| Mortgage interest $\left(9,000 \times \dfrac{30,000}{90,000} \times 10\%\right)$ | | (300) |

Double taxation relief

| | | |
|---|---:|---:|
| Rents (5,000 × 30%) | 1,500 | |
| Bank interest (1,000 × 15%) | 150 | |
| | | (1,650) |

Tax suffered at source

| | | |
|---|---:|---:|
| PAYE | 33,500 | |
| Dividends (10,000 × 10%) | 1,000 | |
| Bank interest (2,800 × 20%) | 560 | |
| | | (35,060) |
| Tax payable | | 2,167 |

### Ken Sing – Capital gains tax liability 1999/00

**Sale of land in Pajan**

| | £ |
|---|---:|
| Sale proceeds | 40,000 |
| Cost $100,000 \times \dfrac{40,000}{120,000 + 40,000}$ | 25,000 |
| | 15,000 |
| Indexation $25,000 \times \dfrac{162.6 - 152.9}{152.9}$ (0.063) | 1,575 |
| | 13,425 |
| Annual exemption | 7,100 |
| Chargeable gain | 6,325 |
| Capital gains tax 6,325 at 40% | 2,530 |

As for income tax, Ken will only be assessed to CGT in respect of remitted gains from overseas assets. His set of paintings are therefore not subject to CGT as they were situated in Pajan at the date of disposal, and the proceeds have not been remitted to the UK.

(b)    Ken is domiciled in Pajan, and has only been resident in the UK for the past seven years of assessment. He will therefore only be liable to IHT in respect of his assets situated in the UK if he were to die. Whether he dies before or after returning to Pajan is in fact irrelevant for the purposes of IHT. Ken's IHT liability would be as follows:

**Ken Sing – Inheritance tax computation**

|  | £ | £ |
|---|---:|---:|
| *Personalty* | | |
| Shares in High-Growth plc (100,000 at 104p) | | 104,000 |
| Shares in Small-Time Ltd | 65,000 | |
| Business property relief: $65,000 \times \dfrac{1,000,000}{1,050,000} \times 100\%$ | 61,905 | |
| | | 3,095 |
| Bank account – UK branch | | 45,000 |
| | | 152,095 |
| *Realty* | | |
| Freehold property – London residence | 275,000 | |
| Bank loan | 90,000 | |
| | | 185,000 |
| Chargeable estate | | 337,095 |

|  |  | £ |
|---|---|---:|
| Inheritance tax payable: | 231,000 at Nil | – |
| | 106,095 at 40% | 42,438 |
| Quick succession relief: | $45,000 \times \dfrac{80,000}{350,000} \times 40\%$ | 4,114 |
| | | 38,324 |

Quick succession relief will be available in respect of Ken's inheritance of 100,000 £1 ordinary shares in High-Growth plc from his uncle in September 1996. If Ken were to die before returning to Pajan in June 2000, this would be between three and four years from the date of the inheritance, and so the relevant percentage is 40%.

It has been assumed that Ken's beneficial loan is repayable on his death, and that it is secured against the London residence.

Land and buildings are situated where they are physically located, so Ken's property in London is chargeable, whilst his property in Pajan is not. Registered shares and securities are situated where they are registered, or where they would normally be dealt with in the ordinary course of business. The shares in both High-Growth plc and Small-Time Ltd are therefore chargeable. Bank accounts are situated at the branch which maintains the account, so the deposit at the London branch is chargeable, whilst the deposit at the Pajanese branch is not.

*(Tutorial notes:*

(1)    High Growth plc shares are valued using the $\frac{1}{4}$ up principle $102 + \frac{1}{4}(110 - 102) = 104p$.

(2)    The London residence is Ken's principal private residence. This is exempt from CGT, but fully chargeable to IHT.*)*

(c)   **Disposal prior to returning to Pajan**

If Ken disposes of his UK assets prior to returning to Pajan, he will be subject to CGT on their disposal as follows:

**London residence**

Ken's London residence would appear to be his principal private residence. So any gain arising on its disposal would be completely exempt from CGT.

### Shares in High-Growth plc

| | £ |
|---|---:|
| Sale proceeds (100,000 at 102p) | 102,000 |
| Cost | 45,000 |
| | 57,000 |
| Indexation $45,000 \times \dfrac{162.6-153.8}{153.8}$ | 2,575 |
| | 54,425 |

### Shares in Small-Time Ltd

| | £ |
|---|---:|
| Sale proceeds | 65,000 |
| Cost | 20,000 |
| | 45,000 |
| Indexation $20,000 \times \dfrac{162.6-141.9}{141.9}$ | 2,918 |
| | 42,082 |

Although Ken has been a director of Small-Time Ltd since June 1997, he has not been a full-time working director, and so retirement relief is not available.

**Bank deposit account**

The closure of a bank deposit account is not subject to CGT.

**Summary**

| | £ |
|---|---:|
| Shares in High-Growth plc | 54,425 |
| Shares in Small-Time Ltd | 42,082 |
| | 96,507 |
| Annual exemption | 7,100 |
| Chargeable gains | 89,407 |
| Capital gains tax  89,407 at 40% | 35,763 |

**Disposal after returning to Pajan**

A person who is neither resident nor ordinarily resident in the UK is not normally liable to CGT, although special rules apply to temporary non-residents. As Ken has been UK resident since July 1993 he will not be able to use the split year treatment for capital gains tax. Ken will therefore be liable to CGT on any gains made between the date of departure and the year end.

Ken should therefore defer the disposals of the two shareholdings until after 5 April 2001 to avoid a charge to CGT. (A charge would be incurred if he were to become UK resident again before 5 April 2006). The disposal of the London residence is exempt, and need not be postponed.

## JUNE 1995 QUESTIONS

## 31    (Question 1 of examination)

You are the tax adviser to Li and Ken Wong. Li (Ken's wife) has been a self-employed solicitor for a number of years, whilst Ken has recently commenced self-employment as a hairdresser. They are both aged 42, and have no other sources of income. They have a son aged 22 who is presently studying to be a solicitor. They have asked for your advice on the following matters:

(a)    Li's fee income is £45,000 pa, all of which relates to work done for the general public in a highly competitive market. At present, she is not registered for VAT. Li's standard rated expenses amount to £2,600 pa, and her zero rated expenses amount to £1,800 pa. She has been offered a new contract from a VAT registered company worth £15,000 pa. In order to take on this contract, Li will have to employ a full-time secretary at a salary of £9,000 pa. Although the value of the contract may grow in the future, she wants to know if it will be profitable in the short term for her to accept it. All of the above figures are net of VAT.

(b)    Assuming that the contract is accepted, Li wants to know whether the following alternatives to employing a full-time secretary would be beneficial. The alternatives are:

　　(i)    employing two part-time secretaries on salaries of £4,650 pa each; or
　　(ii)    paying a self-employed secretary £9,350 pa.

(c)    Li plans to bring her son into partnership as an equal partner as soon as he qualifies as a solicitor, which should be during late 2000. The business has a number of assets, although the only chargeable asset is goodwill. The son will not introduce any capital or make any payment upon his admittance as a partner. Li would like to know the tax implications of bringing her son into partnership.

(d)    Ken commenced trading on 6 April 2000, and estimates that his tax adjusted Schedule D Case I profits (before capital allowances) will be £1,600 per month for the first 12 months of trading, £2,000 per month for the following 12 months, and £2,500 per month thereafter. On 6 April 2000 he purchased fixtures and fittings at a cost of £6,000. Ken wants to know the tax implications of making up his accounts to either 31 March or to 30 April, and the taxable profits of each relevant year of assessment deriving from his first three accounting periods in each case.

(e)    Li has provided legal services to Ken's business. She dealt with the legal aspects of Ken obtaining his business premises on a short lease during April 2000, and also acted for Ken during June 2000 when he was sued for compensation by a customer who lost all of her hair after having it cut at his shop. Li has made no charge as yet for the work done. The couple want to know:

　　(i)    if a charge must be made for the work done; and
　　(ii)    if a charge is not necessary, whether it would in any case be beneficial to make a charge.

**Required:**

Advise Ken and Li in respect of the matters that they have raised.

**Marks for this question will be allocated on the basis of:**

**5 marks to (a)**
**3 marks to (b)**
**6 marks to (c)**
**7 marks to (d)**
**4 marks to (e)**

**(25 marks)**

---

### 32    (Question 2 of examination)

---

(a)    Ukul Ltd is a UK resident company involved in management consultancy. The company has a branch in the country of Ulandi, which is controlled from that country. This branch has experienced substantial growth in recent years, and now accounts for 75% of Ukul Ltd's business. Ukul Ltd's results for the year ended 31 March 2000, split between the UK and Ulandi, are as follows:

|  | Total £ | UK £ | Ulandi £ |
|---|---|---|---|
| Profit per accounts (before taxation) | 116,000 | 29,000 | 87,000 |
| Tax-adjusted profits |  |  |  |
| Under UK legislation | 120,000 | 30,000 | 90,000 |
| Under Ulandian legislation | n/a | n/a | 87,000 |

The branch in Ulandi is subject to Ulandian corporation tax at the rate of 18%. The Ulandian branch remits 50% of its profits after tax to the UK in order to fund Ukul Ltd's dividend payments. Ulandi does not impose any type of withholding tax on remittances out of the country. There is no double taxation treaty between the UK and Ulandi, and Ulandi is not a member of the European Union. All of the above figures are in pounds sterling.

**Required:**

Calculate Ukul Ltd's corporation tax liability for the year ended 31 March 2000.          **(4 marks)**

(b)    Ukul Ltd is planning to incorporate its branch in Ulandi. It will achieve this by transferring the branch's trade to a newly formed 100% subsidiary that will be resident in Ulandi. As far as the Ulandian tax system is concerned, the subsidiary would be taxed in exactly the same way as the branch. The subsidiary would remit 50% of its distributable profits (ie, accounting profits after tax) as dividends to the UK.

Ukul Ltd is planning to replace its computer systems in the near future. A substantial proportion of this expenditure will be in respect of computers that are to be used in Ulandi. The Ulandian tax system does not give any relief for capital expenditure.

**Required:**

Advise Ukul Ltd of the tax implications arising from the incorporation of its branch in Ulandi. Your answer should include a calculation of what Ukul Ltd's corporation tax liability for the year ended 31 March 2000 would have been, if the branch had been incorporated as a 100% subsidiary at the beginning of that year.

**(9 marks)**

(c)    Sasha Khan, who is employed by Ukul Ltd's Ulandian branch in Ulandi, is to be assigned to the UK for a period of 15 months. During this period, she will be employed and paid by Ukul Ltd in the UK. For the 15 month period, Sasha will stay in rented accommodation, and will rent out her main residence situated in Ulandi. Sasha is resident and domiciled in Ulandi.

**Required:**

Advise Sasha of the UK tax implications arising from her 15 months period of employment in the UK. You are not expected to discuss personal allowances, expense claims or double taxation relief claims.

**(4 marks)**
**(Total 17 marks)**
**(as amended)**

---

---

### 33    (Question 3 of examination)

---

WBA

Maud Smith is a <u>71 year old pensioner</u> who has been made a <u>widow as a result of the death of her husband,</u> aged 77, on <u>7 April 1999</u> (you should assume that today's date is 6 April 2000). Maud inherited all of her husband's estate upon his death, and now owns the following assets:

(1)    Her main residence which is currently valued at £130,000.

(2)    20,000 50p ordinary shares in Sparks & Mincer plc, a 'blue chip' UK company currently quoted at 410–426. Sparks & Mincer plc regularly pays a dividend of 12 pence per share each year.

(3)    45,000 £1 ordinary shares in Bit-Part Ltd, an unquoted trading company with a share capital of 200,000 ordinary shares. The other shares in the company are held equally by Maud's three children. Bit-Part Ltd paid a dividend of 9 pence per share during 1999/00. Maud inherited all of these shares from her husband, who had originally acquired them at their par value in March 1984. The shares were valued at £160,000 on 7 April 1999, and are currently worth £205,000. Maud is planning to make a gift of these shares to her children.

(4)    UK government stocks with an interest rate of 4%, and a nominal value of £100,000. These are currently quoted at 90–94, and are due for redemption in 2001.

(5)    25,000 units in Global Trust, a unit trust quoted in the UK at 210–218. The trust is aimed at capital growth, and therefore only paid a dividend of £450 (net) during 1999/00.

(6)    Deposits of £96,000 in an 'instant access' account with the Sprat & Minnow Building Society. This is a small building society, but is paying a high rate of interest of 6.45% pa (net).

(7)    £10,000 in the National Savings Pensioners Guaranteed Income Bond, which pays a gross interest rate of 7%.

During 1999/00 Maud received income of <u>£2,560</u> (net) as the life tenant of an interest in possession trust set up by her brother. The trust holds assets consisting of UK government stocks worth £65,200. Maud's only other income is the UK state pension of £3,471 pa, and a private pension of £1,200 pa (gross). Her husband did not have any taxable income for 1999/00.

Under the terms of her will, Maud has left all of her estate to her family. Her only previous lifetime gift of assets was a gift of £116,000 to a discretionary trust for the benefit of her children in June 1993.

Maud considers herself to be a risk adverse investor. She wishes to maximise her income, whilst not risking the capital value of her assets.

**Required:**

(a)    (i)    Calculate the income tax <u>refund</u> that Maud will be entitled to for 1999/00; and

(ii)    Calculate the IHT liability that would arise if Maud were to die during April 2000. Your answer should indicate who is liable for the tax, and by what date.

**(12 marks)**

(b)    Advise Maud of the tax implications that would arise from a gift of her 45,000 ordinary shares in Bit-Part Ltd to her children if the gift is made:

(i)    as a lifetime gift during April 2000; or
(ii)    by varying the terms of her husband's will.

Your answer should include advice as to whether or not it might be beneficial for Maud to instead make the gift to her grandchildren. **(7 marks)**

(c)    Advise Maud as to the suitability of her present portfolio of investments as regards her stated investment criteria. Your answer should include brief suggestions as to how Maud's portfolio of investments might be improved upon in terms of making it more tax efficient or reducing risk. **(6 marks)**

---

You should assume that the tax rates and allowances for 1999/00 apply throughout.

**(Total 25 marks)**

## 34 (Question 4 of examination)

You are the tax adviser to Ocean plc, the holding company for a group of companies involved in the retail jewellery trade. For some time, Ocean plc has been trying to dispose of three loss making subsidiary companies. These subsidiaries are Tarn Ltd, Loch Ltd and Pool Ltd, all of which are 100% owned. Ocean plc has received an offer from Sea plc, an unconnected company also involved in the retail jewellery trade, who wishes to purchase the following:

(1)     80% of the ordinary share capital of Tarn Ltd.
(2)     40% of the ordinary share capital of Loch Ltd.
(3)     All of the net assets of Pool Ltd.

In each case, the consideration paid by Sea plc will be in the form of cash. Each of these subsidiary companies owns a number of freehold shops whose value is substantially in excess of their original cost. In the case of Tarn Ltd, these shops were acquired from Ocean plc. All three subsidiary companies have unutilised trading losses. However, it is likely that Sea plc's marketing expertise will result in them becoming profitable within two or three years. All of the above companies are registered for VAT.

**Required:**

Draft a report covering the tax implications arising from the disposal as they affect:

(a)     Ocean plc;
(b)     Tarn Ltd, Loch Ltd and Pool Ltd; and
(c)     Sea plc.

You should include tax planning advice as appropriate.

Your answer should be structured under the following headings as appropriate: 'capital gains tax', 'group status', 'VAT', 'trading losses' and 'capital allowances'.

**(25 marks)**

## 35 (Question 5 of examination)

Venus plc is a manufacturer of confectionery. The company provides its directors and its salesmen with company motor cars, but also offers a cash alternative. The company motor cars of a director and a salesman are due to be replaced.

The director will be entitled to a new 3000cc petrol powered motor car with a list price of £30,000. The salesman will be entitled to a new 1300cc diesel powered motor car with a list price of £11,000. Venus plc purchases its company motor cars outright from a UK supplier. As a result of the volume of its business, the company receives a discount of 5% on the list price of all motor cars purchased. The director's motor car will be replaced after two years' use, at which time it will be sold for £19,000. The salesman's motor car will be replaced after three years' use, at which time it will be sold for £6,000. The director drives 18,000 miles per year, of which 2,000 are for business purposes. The salesman drives 30,000 miles per year, of which 20,000 are for business purposes. Venus plc will pay for all the annual running costs of the two motor cars as follows:

|  | Director's car £ | Salesman's car £ |
|---|---|---|
| Petrol/diesel | 1,645 | 2,115 |
| Servicing/repairs | 705 | 470 |
| Insurance/road tax | 1,000 | 450 |

The salesman, but not the director, will be required to reimburse Venus plc for the cost of private fuel.

The cash alternative offered by Venus plc is a one-off cash payment of £13,500 in the case of the director, or £5,250 in the case of the salesman. If either the director or the salesman opts for this alternative, they would then be expected to use their own private motor car for business mileage. Venus plc pays a business mileage allowance of 55 pence per mile to directors, and 10 pence per mile to salesmen. Both of these rates are within the limits set by the fixed profit car scheme. The director and the salesman would both purchase private cars of the same make and model as the company car that they would have been provided with, and will incur the same running expenses as would have been incurred by the company.

The director is paid £40,000 pa, and the salesman is paid £18,000 pa. Venus plc pays corporation tax at the rate of 30%, and is registered for VAT.

All of the above figures are inclusive of VAT where applicable.

**Required:**

(a)     Advise Venus plc as to whether the provision of a company motor car or the payment of the cash alternative is the most beneficial from its point of view.

(12 marks)

(b)     Advise the director and the salesman as to whether the acceptance of a company motor car or the receipt of the cash alternative is the most beneficial from their point of view. Your answer should include advice as to whether or not it would be beneficial for the director and the salesman to claim for business running costs and capital allowances as an alternative to the fixed profit car scheme.

(13 marks)

You are not expected to take the time value of money into account when answering this question.

(Total: 25 marks)

---

## 36     (Question 6 of examination)

(a)     Garden Ltd is an unquoted company involved in the manufacture of gardening equipment. Due to a rapid expansion of its trade, the company requires an additional factory. Two alternative options have been identified as follows:

(i)     A new factory can be constructed by a building company. This will take six months to complete, and will cost £470,000 as follows:

|  | £ |
|---|---:|
| Land | 80,000 |
| Levelling the land | 10,300 |
| Architects and legal fees | 24,300 |
| Ventilation and heating systems | 12,500 |
| Fire alarm and sprinkler system | 6,400 |
| Strengthened concrete floor to support machinery | 16,500 |
| General offices | 62,500 |
| Factory | 187,500 |
| VAT | 70,000 |
|  | 470,000 |

(ii)     A suitable factory is available for rent. The owners of the factory are prepared to grant a 40 year lease for a premium of £470,000. The annual rent payable will be £35,250. The owners will exercise their option to tax the grant of the lease, and it will therefore be standard rated. Both figures are inclusive of VAT where applicable.

Whichever alternative is chosen, it will be financed as follows:

(i)     A loan of £200,000 will be raised by an issue of 12% debentures. If the alternative of building the new factory is chosen, the debenture interest relating to the period of construction will be capitalised.

(ii)    A warehouse will be sold for £270,000 (including land of £90,000). The warehouse cost £120,000 (including land of £50,000) when it was acquired seven years ago. The warehouse was originally built 10 years ago at a cost of £102,000 (including land of £42,000). It has always been used to store raw materials. The relevant RPI factor in respect of this disposal is 0.360.

Garden Ltd is registered for VAT. None of the above buildings are situated in Enterprise Zones.

**Required:**

Advise Garden Ltd of the tax implications arising from the two alternatives, and from the financing of whichever alternative is chosen. **(13 marks)**

(b)    During August 1999 Garden Ltd increased its share capital to 1,000,000 ordinary shares, by issuing 500,000 new ordinary shares at £1 per share. These were subscribed for as follows:

|  | *Shares* |
| --- | --- |
| Alex Bush | 50,000 |
| Carol Daisy | 200,000 |
| Edward Fern | 200,000 |
| Gary Hedge | 50,000 |
|  | 500,000 |

Garden Ltd's original share capital of 500,000 ordinary shares has been held by Alex Bush since 1985.

Alex and Gary have been directors of Garden Ltd since 1985, whilst Carol and Edward are going to be appointed as directors during 2000. Carol and Edward have not previously been employed by the company.

Alex is 57 years old, Gary is 51, whilst Carol and Edward are both 40. None of the shareholders are connected to each other. They are all 40% taxpayers. Carol financed the cost of her shareholding by selling a property for £350,000, which resulted in a chargeable gain of £225,000.

Due to its rapid expansion, Garden Ltd is planning to obtain a Stock Exchange listing within the next two or three years. This will be achieved by the company issuing 500,000 new ordinary shares on the Stock Exchange.

**Required:**

Advise each of the shareholders of Garden Ltd of the tax implications arising from:

(i)    their subscription for new ordinary share capital in Garden Ltd during August 1999.

(ii)    Garden Ltd's proposed listing on the Stock Exchange in two or three years time.

**(12 marks)**
**(Total 25 marks)**

# ANSWERS TO JUNE 1995 EXAMINATION

## 31    (Answer 1 of examination)

### Examiner's comments and marking guide

**Part (a) tested candidates' ability to advise on the VAT implications of exceeding the VAT registration limit. Part (b) tested candidates' knowledge of the NIC implications of taking on an employee. Part (c) tested candidates' knowledge of the tax implications of a sole trader admitting a partner so as to become a partnership. Part (d) tested candidates' ability to calculate the tax assessments that would arise upon commencement under the current year basis. Part (e) tested candidates' knowledge of the tax implications arising from the provision of services at below market value.**

This was a popular question, being attempted by the majority of candidates. There were some very good answers to this question, but too many candidates missed a lot of the relatively easy marks that were available. In part (a), it was often not appreciated that voluntary registration for VAT would not be beneficial as regards the current position. In part (b), several candidates confused employers' NIC with employees' NIC, and as a result turned a simple one line calculation into a page of workings. The majority of candidates answered this part correctly. (Comments on part (c) deleted as no longer relevant to updated version.) Part (d) was very well answered as regards an accounting date of 31 March, but few candidates were able to correctly calculate the assessments with an accounting date of 30 April. Too many candidates simply tried to adapt the figures in the first part of their answer. Part (e) was badly answered, with most candidates ignoring the respective tax rates of the two taxpayers, and the fact that one of the legal services provided was not a deductible expense.

|  |  | *Marks* |
|---|---|---|
| (a) | Offer of new contract | |
| | Pre-contract net profit | 1 |
| | VAT registration | ½ |
| | Absorb VAT on general public supplies | ½ |
| | Highly competitive market | ½ |
| | Could add VAT to new contract | ½ |
| | Recover input tax | ½ |
| | Employer's Class 1 | ½ |
| | Post-contract net profit | 1 |
| | Decrease in net profit | ½ |
| | Not attractive in short term | ½ |
| | | |
| | Available | 6 |
| | | |
| | Maximum | 5 |
| | | |
| (b) | Secretarial | |
| | Cost of full-timer | ½ |
| | Class 1 employer's | ½ |
| | Cost of part-timers | ½ |
| | Class 1 employer's | ½ |
| | Saving | ½ |
| | Post tax saving | ½ |
| | Practical problem of two | ½ |
| | NIC saving if self-employed | ½ |
| | Post tax saving | ½ |
| | Admin advantages | ½ |
| | | |
| | Available | 5 |
| | | |
| | Maximum | 3 |

(c)    Future partnership
       (Income tax aspects have been updated for CYB)

| | |
|---|---:|
| IT effect on Li | 1 |
| IT effect on partner commencing | 2 |
| Option for different capital sharing | 1 |
| CG effect of admission if capital sharing equal | 1 |
| With revaluation | 1 |
| Without revaluation | 1 |
| Holdover relief N/A | ½ |
| Revenue's attitude to valuation | 1 |
| IHT effect as connected | ½ |
| BPR at 100% | ½ |
| IHT effect of Li dying within 7 years | 1 |
| Available | 10½ |
| Maximum | 6 |

(d)    Commencement of trading

| | |
|---|---:|
| CAs | 2 |
| Adjusted profit under each option | 2½ |
| Assessment under 31 March y/e | 1½ |
| Assessment under 30 April y/e | 1½ |
| Overlap profits | 1 |
| Discussion | 2½ |
| Available | 11 |
| Maximum | 7 |

(e)    Work done

| | |
|---|---:|
| General discussion | 3 |
| Charge on lease | 1½ |
| Charge on compensation | 3½ |
| Available | 8 |
| Maximum | 4 |
| Available | 40½ |
| Maximum | 25 |

## ( Step by step answer plan )

**Overview**

There is quite a lot to do here for 25 marks even though the question has been made easier by being divided into 5 virtually independent parts. The main context is of business with income tax, NIC and VAT considerations for a number of tax planning proposals. One proposal (c) also has a CGT/IHT aspect.

**Step 1**    Read through the question carefully and note that after the scene setting in the first paragraph you can concentrate on each part separately.

**Step 2**    For part (a) start by computing Li's annual net profit before accepting the new contract.

**Step 3**    Discuss briefly the effect of accepting the contract - ie, the need to register for VAT and to pay a secretary and Class 1 employer's NIC.

**Step 4**    Compute the annual net profit assuming the contract is accepted and conclude whether, on this basis, she should accept.

**Step 5**    Identify the three alternatives in part (b) and evaluate them - remember the first option was calculated in part (a). Then discuss which would be the best option bringing in any practical non-tax points which would be relevant. There are only three marks for part (b) so a lengthy answer would not be appropriate.

**Step 6**    Attend now to part (c) noting that there are 6 marks so you should cover several points. Apart from the general tax effects of introducing a new partner it is clear from the question that the capital aspects of the partner being a relative and not introducing capital should be mentioned. The following topics should feature in your rough answer plan:

- Income tax effect on Li
- Profit assessment rules for the son commencing
- Capital gain position where Li is effectively disposing of a 50% share for nil consideration
- IHT treatment of the gifted share.

**Step 7**    Read part (d) carefully and note that it offers 7 marks.

**Step 8**    Compute the capital allowances and then the adjusted profit for the first three periods of account under the two alternative accounting dates.

**Step 9**    Schedule out the assessments based on these profits identifying any overlap profits generated.

**Step 10**    Discuss carefully the advantage of one date over the other. You can usually assume for paper 11 that more marks will be given in this situation for intelligent analysis of results than for correct number crunching.

**Step 11**    Don't disregard part (e) even if, as is likely, you are running out of time. A few brief comments to the point could earn most of the 4 marks.

**Step 12**    For part (e), identify clearly the questions and start your answer with an explanation of the principles arising in the first question including any relevant case law.

**Step 13**    Answer the second part of part (e), remembering that there are two provisions of service for which a charge could be made. Keep them separate in your answer.

### The examiner's answer

(a)    **Offer of new contract**

At present, Li is making a net profit of £40,145 pa as follows:

|  |  | £ | £ |
|---|---|---|---|
| Fee income |  |  | 45,000 |
| Expenses: | Standard rate $(2,600 \times {}^{47}\!/_{40})$ | 3,055 |  |
|  | Zero rated | 1,800 |  |
|  |  |  | 4,855 |
| Net profit |  |  | 40,145 |

If Li accepts the new contract, then she will exceed the annual VAT registration limit of £51,000, and will have to register for VAT. It would appear that Li will have to absorb the output tax in respect of the work done for the general public herself, due to the market being highly competitive. She should be able to charge

VAT on top of the value of the new contract, since the company is VAT registered. Li will be able to recover the input tax in respect of her standard rated expenses. She will have to pay employers' Class I National Insurance contribution at the rate of 12.2% on the excess of the secretary's salary of £9,000 pa over £4,335. If she accepts the new contract her net profit therefore becomes £39,329 as follows:

|  |  | £ | £ |
|---|---|---|---|
| Fee income [(45,000 × $^{40}/_{47}$) + 15,000] |  |  | 53,298 |
| Expenses: | Standard rated | 2,600 |  |
|  | Zero rated | 1,800 |  |
|  | Secretarial salary | 9,000 |  |
|  | NIC (9,000 − 4,335) = £4,665 × 12.2% | 569 |  |
|  |  |  | 13,969 |
| Net profit |  |  | 39,329 |

This is a decrease in net profit of £816 (40,145 − 39,329), which represents reduced post tax income of £490 (816 less 40%). In the short term, the contract is not therefore profitable.

(b)    **Secretarial**

A full-time secretary on a salary of £9,000 represents a total cost of £9,569 due to employers' Class I National Insurance contribution being due as in (a) above. If Li instead employs two part-time secretaries on salaries of £4,650 pa, then only £76 (4,650 − 4,335 = 315 × 12.2% = 38 × 2) of employers' Class I National Insurance contribution will be due. The total cost is therefore £9,376 [76 + (4,650 × 2)], The small post tax saving of £116 [(9,569 − 9,376) less 40%] is unlikely to compensate for the problems arising as a result of employing two secretaries. If Li uses a self-employed secretary, then there will be no additional National Insurance contribution cost. The total cost is therefore £9,350, which is a post tax saving of £131 [(9,569 − 9,350) less 40%]. Since there should also be administrative savings in using a self-employed secretary, this would appear to represent the most beneficial option. However, if the secretary works full-time then Revenue may successfully contest that she is an employee and not self-employed.

(c)    **Future partnership**

For income tax purposes, the admission of Li's son into partnership in late 2000 is not treated as a cessation of Li's business. The profits will be allocated between Li and her son in accordance with their profit sharing ratios during the underlying period of account, and each will be treated as trading in her or his own right.

Li will therefore be assessed on the current year basis as normal.

Li's son will also be assessed on the current year basis, but the commencement rules will apply as he starts trading during 2000. The assessment for 2000/01 is based on the profits arising between his becoming a partner and 5 April 2001. The 2001/02 assessment is based on the profits of the accounting year ending in 2001/02 or, if Li's son had not been a partner throughout the year, on the profits of Li's son's first 12 months of trading. Where profit periods overlap, overlap profits are generated for relief on Li's son leaving the partnership.

There is no reason why the new partnership cannot have a capital profit sharing basis whereby Li retains a 100% share of the assets of the business, with her son only sharing revenue profits. Assuming that this is not the case, Li will be treated as disposing of a 50% share of the goodwill to her son upon his admittance into partnership. The son will be treated as acquiring a corresponding 50% share. The calculation is normally based on the current balance sheet value of the goodwill plus the indexation allowance (if any). Provided that the goodwill is not revalued in the balance sheet prior to the son's admission, the disposal by Li will therefore be at no gain/no loss. If goodwill is revalued in the balance sheet, then Li will have a capital gain based on 50% of this figure. Because the transaction is between connected persons, the Inland Revenue may require that the market value of the goodwill be used rather than its current balance sheet value. This will only be the case if the transaction is not at arm's length. Holdover relief for a gift of business assets would be available in this situation.

As the transaction is between connected persons, the transfer of 50% of the business from Li to her son is likely to be treated for IHT purposes as a potentially exempt transfer (PET). However, business property relief at the rate of 100% should be available if the PET were to become chargeable as a result of Li dying within seven years of the transfer.

*(Tutorial note:* When this question was first set changes in the composition of old partnerships were dealt with under the old rules. This topic is no longer examinable, and the question has been updated to cover the admission of a new partner under the new rules, which is examinable.)

(d)    **Commencement of trading**

Ken will be assessed on the current year basis. His capital allowances under each accounting date will be as follows:

| | £ | | | £ |
|---|---|---|---|---|
| Year ended 31 March 2001 | | Period ended 30 April 2001 | | |
| Addition | 6,000 | | | 6,000 |
| FYA – 40% | 2,400 | 40% | | 2,400 |
| WDV c/f | 3,600 | | | 3,600 |
| Year ended 31 March 2002 | | Year ended 30 April 2002 | | |
| WDA – 25% | 900 | 25% | | 900 |
| WDV c/f | 2,700 | | | 2,700 |
| Year ended 31 March 2003 | | Year ended 30 April 2003 | | |
| WDA – 25% | 675 | 25% | | 675 |
| WDV c/f | 2,025 | | | 2,025 |

Ken's taxable profits for the first three accounting periods under each accounting date will be:

| | £ |
|---|---|
| Accounting date of 31 March | |
| Year ended 31 March 2001 (12 × 1,600) 19,200 – 2,400 | 16,800 |
| Year ended 31 March 2002 (12 × 2,000) 24,000 – 900 | 23,100 |
| Year ended 31 March 2003 (12 × 2,500) 30,000 – 675 | 29,325 |
| Accounting date of 30 April | |
| Period ended 30 April 2001 [(12 × 1,600) + 2,000] 21,200 – 2,400 | 18,800 |
| Year ended 30 April 2002 (11 × 2,000) + 2,500] 24,500 – 900 | 23,600 |
| Year ended 30 April 2003 (12 × 2,500) 30,000 – 675 | 29,325 |

The taxable profits for the relevant years of assessment in respect of these profits will be as follows:

| Accounting date of 31 March | £ |
|---|---|
| 2000/01 (year ended 31 March 2001) | 16,800 |
| 2001/02 (year ended 31 March 2002) | 23,100 |
| 2002/03 (year ended 31 March 2003) | 29,325 |
| Total assessments | 69,225 |

There are no overlap profits

| Accounting date of 30 April | £ |
|---|---|
| 2000/01 (6 April 2000 – 5 April 2001) 18,800 × $12/13$ | 17,354 |
| 2001/02 (1 May 2000 – 30 April 2001) 18,800 × $12/13$ | 17,354 |
| 2002/03 (year ended 30 April 2002) | 23,600 |

|  | 58,308 |
| --- | --- |
| 2003/04 (year ended 30 April 2003) | 29,325 |
| Total assessments | 87,633 |

There are overlap profits for the period 1 May 2000 to 5 April 2001 of £15,908 (18,800 × $^{11}/_{13}$).

An accounting date of 30 April results in the delay between earning profits and having to pay the related tax liability being 11 months longer compared to an accounting date of 31 March. However, an accounting date of 30 April results in increased total assessments of £18,408 (87,633 − 69,225). Although relief of £15,908 will be allowed for overlap profits, this will not normally be given until the cessation of trading.

Although the assessments based on the first three years of trading are higher if a 30 April year end is chosen, they form the basis of four years of assessments. In fact with a 30 April year end the assessments for 2000/01 to 2002/03 are £58,308, compared to £69,225 with a 31 March year end.

The 2003/04 assessment with a 31 March year end is based on the profits of the year to 31 March 2004. Whilst profits continue to rise, the assessment will always be lower if a 30 April year end is chosen, until the cessation of trade. In the final year higher assessable profits will arise under a 30 April year end, as an extra 11 months of profit will be assessed. The benefit of the brought forward overlap relief may be significantly reduced by inflation by that time.

*(Tutorial notes:* under CYB, capital allowances are given for periods of account. Where the period of account is other than for 12 months, the capital allowances must be adjusted accordingly. For the 13 month period ending 30 April 2001, any WDA is 25% × $^{13}/_{12}$. As the expenditure is incurred by 1 July 2000, 40% FYA is available. The length of the period of account of expenditure has no effect on the FYA.

It is the adjusted profit figure less capital allowances that is used in calculating the assessments (ie. capital allowances are treated as an expense).*)*

(e) **Work done**

The rule in *Sharkey v Wernher* (1955) that own consumption (including consumption by friends and relatives) must be valued at market value, does not apply to professional persons. This was established in the case of *Mason v Innes* (1967) where an author was not assessed on the market value of a copyright gifted to his father. Therefore, there is no requirement for Li to raise a charge on Ken for the legal work that she has performed for him. She will, however, be disallowed any related costs.

If a charge for either of the items of work done is raised, then Li will be assessed on the income at the rate of 40% due to the level of her profits. Since Ken's costs of obtaining a short lease on his business premises will not be a deductible expense against his Schedule D Case I profits, it would not be beneficial to raise a charge for this work.

If a charge is raised in respect of the work done re the compensation claim, then the cost will be a deductible expense for Ken. If he makes his accounts up to 31 March, then it would not be beneficial to raise a charge as tax relief will only be obtained at the rate of 23%. If, however, Ken makes up his accounts to 30 April then it may be beneficial to raise a charge. He will obtain tax relief of effectively 42% (23% × 2 × $^{12}/_{13}$), since the profits for the first period of trading form the basis of the assessments for both 2000/01 and 2001/02. Although relief for overlap profits will be correspondingly reduced, this may not be available until the business ceases.

---

## 32    (Answer 2 of examination)

---

### Examiner's comments

Part (a) tested candidates' ability to calculate the corporation tax liability of a company with an overseas branch. Part (b) tested candidates' ability to calculate the corporation tax liability of a company with an overseas subsidiary. Part (c) tested candidates' ability to explain the tax implications of a person resident and domiciled overseas coming to the UK for a period of employment.

This was not a popular question, although it was answered quite well by many candidates. Part (a) was generally well answered. There were a number of very good answers to part (b). In part (c), too many candidates confused the rules for a person coming to the UK, with the rules for a person leaving the UK. Very few candidates considered whether the person would be resident for one or for two years of assessment.
(The comments have been substantially edited to exclude reference to topics no longer examinable).

### Step by step answer plan

#### Overview

This is the 'foreign element' question. It mainly concerns corporation tax and DTR but it also covers other overseas aspects such as CFCs and the IT treatment of an individual coming to work in the UK.

**Step 1**    Read through the question carefully. It is clear that part (a) can be answered without reference to any later part so concentrate on that part first.

**Step 2**    Explain the basis of taxing the overseas source profits and compute PCTCT.

**Step 3**    Compute GCT on PCTCT and deduct DTR. This item will require a separate working.

**Step 4**    Read part (b) noting that there are 9 marks available.

**Step 5**    Compute Ukul's PCTCT on the basis described and compute CT using a separate working for DTR. Explain briefly any less obvious point such as relief for the underlying tax.

**Step 6**    Discuss the difference between the branch and the subsidiary options based on your computations.

**Step 7**    Re-read part (b) to identify any other matters to cover. A separate paragraph on each of the following seems appropriate:
- whether or not the sub would be a CFC
- Relief for the planned capital expenditure
- Effect on tax rates of creating an associate
- Timing advantage of tax payable on overseas profits if subsidiary
- Capital gains relief on incorporating foreign branch.

**Step 8**    Read part (c). There are only 4 marks on offer but they are fairly easy to earn as long as you cover the following
- Discuss R/OR status
- Discuss treatment of UK earnings
- Explain taxation of overseas rents for a non-domiciliary.

---

## The examiner's answer and marking guide

(a)   **Ukul Ltd – Corporation tax liability for the year ended 31 March 2000**

As the Ulandian branch is controlled from that country, its profits will be assessed under Schedule D Case V. Ukul Ltd will be assessed to UK corporation tax on the full amount of the branch profits, regardless of the amount remitted to the UK. *(1½m)*

|  | £ | Marks |
|---|---|---|
| Schedule D Case I | 30,000 | |
| Schedule D Case V | 90,000 | |
| Profits chargeable to corporation tax | 120,000 | |
| Corporation tax at 20% | 24,000 | 1 |
| Less: Double taxation relief (W1) | 15,660 | |
| | 8,340 | |

WORKING

(W1)   Double taxation relief

Ulandian corporation tax of £15,660 (87,000 at 18%) will be paid in respect of the branch profits. Since this is less than the amount of UK corporation tax on the branch profits (90,000 at 20% = £18,000), it can be relieved in full. *(1½m)*

(b)   If Ukul Ltd's Ulandian branch had been incorporated as a 100% subsidiary at the beginning of the year ended 31 March 2000, its corporation tax liability would have been as follows: *(1½m)*

|  | £ |
|---|---|
| Schedule D Case I | 30,000 |
| Schedule D Case V (W1) | 43,500 |
| Profits chargeable to corporation tax | 73,500 |

|  | £ | Marks |
|---|---|---|
| Corporation tax at 20% | 14,700 | 1 |
| Less: Double taxation relief (W1) | 7,830 | |
| Corporation tax liability | 6,870 | |

WORKING

(1)   Dividend from subsidiary and double taxation relief

Since Ukul Ltd will own over 10% of the share capital of the Ulandian subsidiary, relief for the underlying tax paid in Ulandi would be available. The distributable profits of the subsidiary would be £71,340 (87,000 less 18% tax), so a dividend of £35,670 (71,340 × 50%) would be received by Ukul Ltd. *(1½m)*

|  | £ | Marks |
|---|---|---|
| Dividend received | 35,670 | |
| Underlying tax $35,670 \times \dfrac{15,660}{71,340}$ | 7,830 | |
| Schedule D Case V income | 43,500 | 1 |

*Official* ACCA *Revision Series, published by AT Foulks Lynch*

The Ulandian tax is less than the amount of UK corporation tax on the dividend that would be received from the subsidiary ($43,500 \times 20\% = £8,700$), and so can be relieved in full. *(1m)*

*(Tutorial note:* the underlying tax is calculated as:

$$\text{Dividend received (plus tax credit, if applicable)} \times \frac{\text{tax actually paid}}{\text{profits available for distribution}})$$

The other tax implications arising from the incorporation of the Ulandian branch are as follows:

**Controlled foreign company**

Ulandi does not have a lower level of taxation than the UK, since the Ulandian tax of $18\% \times £87,000 = £15,660$ is not less than three quarters of the tax that would be paid in the UK ($\frac{3}{4} \times £90,000 \times 20\% = £13,500$). The subsidiary should not therefore be classified as a controlled foreign company. *(2½m)*

**Capital allowances**

Ukul Ltd plans to replace its computer systems. If these are purchased by a Ulandian branch, capital allowances will be available. They will not be available if they are purchased by a Ulandian subsidiary, since the Ulandian tax system does not give relief for capital expenditure. It might be possible to get round this problem by Ukul Ltd purchasing the computer systems itself, and leasing them to the Ulandian subsidiary, although there are restrictions in respect of international leasing. *(2m)*

**Tax rates**

The Ulandian subsidiary will be an associated company, reducing the UK corporation tax lower limit to £150,000 ($\frac{300,000}{2}$). This would be relevant if profits increase in the future, and would result in a marginal corporation tax rate of 32.5%. *(1½m)*

**Delayed UK tax payments**

UK corporation tax will be paid on dividends declared by the Ulandian subsidiary, rather than profits made. By delaying dividend payments until after the year to which they relate, the UK corporation tax thereon is delayed by one year. *(1m)*

**Capital gains tax**

Provided all the assets of the Ulandian branch (except for cash) are transferred, and the consideration from the Ulandian subsidiary is in the form of shares, any UK chargeable gains arising on the transfer of assets can be heldover against the base cost of the shares. *(1½m)*

(c)    Sasha's period of employment in the UK will span two tax years. She will be treated as UK resident for a tax year in which she spends 183 days (six months) or more in the UK during that year. Whether Sasha will be resident for one tax year or for both tax years depends on the exact timing of her arrival and departure. Sasha will not be treated as ordinarily resident in the UK. *(2½m)*

Regardless of her residence status, Sasha will be assessed under Schedule E Case II in respect of her UK employment. For any tax year in which Sasha is treated as resident in the UK, she will also be assessed under Schedule E Case III, in respect of any amounts remitted to the UK from her employment with the Ulandian branch. As Sasha is not domiciled in the UK, she will only be assessed on any rental income arising from her main residence if it is remitted to the UK, and she is also treated as resident in the UK for the tax year of basis. *(2½m)*

---

**Did you answer the question?**

You were not asked to cover PAs, expense claims for renting UK property or relief for overseas taxes against UK taxes for an individual.

---

---

| 33 | **(Answer 3 of examination)** |
|----|---|

---

**( Examiner's comments )**

Part (a) tested candidates' ability to calculate the income tax and potential IHT liabilities of a pensioner who has recently been widowed. Part (b) tested candidates' knowledge of the tax implications of making a gift of shares either as a lifetime gift or by way of varying the terms of a will. Part (c) tested candidates' ability to advise a client on the suitability of a portfolio of investments given stated investment criteria.

This was the most popular question on the paper, and was well answered by the majority of candidates. Part (a) was very well answered, although a number of candidates were unable to calculate an income tax liability involving savings income. In part (b), many candidates did not appreciate that there were considerable benefits in making the gift by way of varying the terms of the deceased husband's will. In part (c), the stated investment criteria were often ignored. Candidates therefore stated that a unit trust aimed at capital growth was a suitable investment for an investor wishing to maximise income. A number of candidates suggested that an investment under the enterprise investment scheme was a suitable investment for a risk adverse investor.

**( Step by step answer plan )**

**Overview**

This is a personal tax question concerning an elderly lady recently widowed. As well as income tax and CGT considerations there are IHT planning points to consider both on her estate and on her recently deceased husband's and some general financial planning on investments. A good answer would be difficult to produce in the time.

**Step 1**  Read part (a) of the requirements visualising the shape of your answer and then read through the question looking for the relevant information - eg, the IT and IHT details are not shown separately.

**Step 2**  Glance at the requirements for parts (b) and (c) to have them at the back of your mind when answering part (a).

**Step 3**  Answer part (a) (i) filling in a standard Taxable Income/IT layout not forgetting the WBA and the anomalous entitlement to the age related MCA. Add brief comments but only where necessary and high light the figure for tax refund.

**Step 4**  Answer part (a) (ii) by first working out the used part of her nil band and then scheduling out the chargeable estate. Note that annotations on the valuation rules on shares etc are not needed as long as your figures show you understand the principles.

**Step 5**  Explain why 100% BPR is due. This shows you were aware of the ownership period issue and didn't simply apply the relief without thinking.

**Step 6**  As is common in paper 11, you are asked to state who is liable for any IHT and the due dates. Calculating the estate rate is therefore useful and you must not overlook the instalment option.

**Step 7**  For part (b) there are clearly three alternative proposals to comment on and you must give the layout of your answer some thought.

**Step 8**  On the lifetime gift proposal

  - Compute the capital gain
  - Comment on the holdover option
  - Discuss the IHT implications - PET, BPR etc

**Step 9**  On the variation proposal you must mention the IHT rules for variation and the IHT effect. There is also a CGT and IT aspect to cover.

---

**Step 10** Discuss the IHT and IT implications of generation skipping.

**Step 11** For your answer to part (c), use a separate heading for each of her investments commenting as appropriate.

## The examiner's answer and marking guide

(a)     (i)                      **Income tax liability 1999/00**

|  |  | £ | £ | Tax suffered £ |
|---|---|---|---|---|
| Pensions | – State | 3,471 | | |
| | – Private | 1,200 | | |
| | | | 4,671 | |
| Dividends | – Sparks & Mincer plc | | | |
| | $(20,000 \times 12p \times {}^{100}\!/_{80})$ | 2,667 | | 267 |
| | – Bit-Part Ltd $(45,000 \times 9p \times {}^{100}\!/_{90})$ | 4,500 | | 450 |
| | – Global Trust $(450 \times {}^{100}\!/_{90})$ | 500 | | 50 |
| | | | 7,667 | |
| Interest on government stocks $(100,000 \times 4\%)$ | | 4,000 | | 800 |
| Building society interest $(96,000 \times 6.45\% \times {}^{100}\!/_{80})$ | | 7,740 | | 1,548 |
| Interest on National Savings Bond $(10,000 \times 7\%)$ | | 700 | | |
| Trust income $(2,560 \times {}^{100}\!/_{80})$ | | 3,200 | | 640 |
| | | | 15,640 | |
| Statutory total income | | | 27,978 | |
| Personal allowance | | | (4,335) | |
| Taxable income | | | 23,643 | 3,755 |

*(3½m)*

Analysed for tax rates:

| | Non-savings £ | Savings £ | Dividends £ |
|---|---|---|---|
| STI | 4,671 | 15,640 | 7,667 |
| Less: PA | 3,171 | 1,164 | - |
| Taxable income | 1,500 | 14,476 | 7,667 |

| | £ |
|---|---|
| Income tax: | |
| 1,500 at 10% | 150 |
| 14,476 at 20% | 2,895 |
| 7,667 at 10% | 767 |
| | 3,812 |
| Married couple's allowance $(5,195 \times 10\%)$ | (519) |
| Widow's bereavement allowance $(1,970 \times 10\%)$ | (197) |
| | 3,096 |

| | |
|---|---|
| Tax suffered | (3,755) |
| Tax refund due* | 659 |

*(1½m)*

\* There are sufficient non-dividend tax credits for this amount to be repayable.

Maud's level of income results in her losing her entitlement to age allowance. The married couple's allowance for persons aged 75 or over can be transferred to Maud provided a claim is made by 31 January 2006. The full allowance is available, as the restriction is based on the husband's income, which in this case is nil. *(1½m)*

(ii)     Maud's previous lifetime gift of £108,000 is within seven years of the date of her death. *(½m)*

| | | £ | £ |
|---|---|---|---|
| Value transferred | | | 116,000 |
| Annual exemptions | 1993/94 | 3,000 | |
| | 1992/93 | 3,000 | |
| | | | 6,000 |
| Chargeable transfer | | | 110,000 |
| IHT liability 110,000 at nil % | | | Nil |

*(1m)*

### Inheritance tax computation April 2000

**Free estate**

| | £ | £ |
|---|---|---|
| *Personalty* | | |
| Ordinary shares in Sparks & Mincer plc | | |
| 20,000 at 414p [410 + ¼ (426 – 410)] | | 82,800 |
| Ordinary shares in Bit-Part Ltd | 205,000 | |
| Business property relief – 100% | 205,000 | |
| | | – |
| UK government stocks 100,000 at 91p [90 + ¼ (94 – 90)] | | 91,000 |
| Units in Global Trust 25,000 at 210p | | 52,500 |
| Building society deposits | | 96,000 |
| National Savings Bond | | 10,000 |
| | | 332,300 |
| *Realty* | | |
| Main residence | | 130,000 |
| Net free estate | | 462,300 |
| **Settled property** | | |
| Interest in possession | | 65,200 |
| Chargeable estate | | 527,500 |

*(3m)*

£

IHT liability    231,000 – 110,000 = 121,000 at 0%    –
527,500 – 121,000 = 406,500 at 40%    162,600

162,600

*(½m)*

$$\text{Rate of IHT on estate} = 30.825\% \left( \frac{162,600}{527,500} \times 100 \right)$$ *(½m)*

Business property relief at the rate of 100% is available in respect of the 45,000 ordinary shares in Bit-Part Ltd, as they are a holding in an unquoted company. Although Maud has owned the shares for less than two years, they were acquired upon her husband's death, and would have qualified for business property relief at that date. *(2m)*

IHT of £20,097 (65,200 at 30.825% will be due from the trust. IHT of £142,503 (462,300 at 30.825%) will be due from the estate, of which £40,071 (130,000 at 30.825%) can be paid by instalments. The IHT not payable by instalments will be due on the earlier of 31 October 2000 or the delivery of the account by the personal representatives. The IHT payable by instalments will be due in 10 equal annual amounts commencing on 31 October 2000. *(3m)*

(b)    (i)    **Lifetime gift during April 2000**

A lifetime gift during April 2000 would result in a chargeable gain of £45,000 as follows:

£

Deemed consideration    205,000
Cost    160,000

45,000

*(1m)*

Provided that Maud and the children jointly elect, the gain can be heldover as a gift of business assets (Bit-Part Ltd being an unquoted company). If no election is made, CGT of 15,160 (45,000 – 7,100 at 40%) will be payable, assuming that Maud is a 40% taxpayer for 2000/01. *(2m)*

For IHT purposes, the gift will be a PET during April 2000, with no IHT being due at that date. If the PET becomes chargeable as a result of Maud dying within seven years of the date of the gift, business property relief at the rate of 100% will be available provided the children still own the shares at that date, and the shares are still unquoted. If the children had sold the shares the value of the PET would be £205,000 less annual exemptions of £3,000 each for 1999/00 and 2000/01 = £199,000. *(4m)*

(ii)    **Variation of the terms of the will of Maud's husband**

The will of Maud's husband can be varied by a deed of variation executed within two years of his death. The deed must be in writing, and must be signed by Maud. A written election must then be made to the Inland Revenue within six months of the deed of variation, so that the will is treated as being re-written for IHT purposes. *(2m)*

The 45,000 ordinary shares in Bit-Part Ltd will then pass to Maud's children or grandchildren under the terms of her husband's will. The gift will not result in any liability to IHT, being valued at nil (160,000 less 100% BPR). Maud might consider making further gifts of up to £231,000 by deed of variation, so as to utilise the full nil rate band and thus reduce the potential IHT liability that would arise on her death. *(3m)*

No liability to CGT will arise, as the gift is made on death (provided the corresponding CGT election on the deed of variation is made). However, the gross dividends of £4,500 received by Maud from Bit-Part Ltd during 1999/00 will still be included in her taxable income. *(1½m)*

### Gift to children or to grandchildren?

As a general rule, for IHT purposes it is usually beneficial to miss out a generation when making gifts of assets. This means that assets are only taxed once, rather than twice, before being inherited by the third generation of a family. However as the shares qualify for business property relief at the rate of 100%, for IHT purposes, there is probably no benefit in Maud making the gift to her grandchildren. *(2½m)*

The only benefit in making the gift to the grandchildren is likely to be for income tax purposes, since the dividends received would allow the grandchildren to utilise part of their basic rate bands. This is beneficial if their parents are paying tax at the higher rate. *(1½m)*

---

**Did you answer the question?**

You were not required to consider putting any gift to the grandchildren into a discretionary or accumulation and maintenance trust.

---

(c)     **Ordinary shares in Sparks & Mincer plc**

Although these shares would probably be a suitable holding as a part of a portfolio, they represent an unacceptably high level of risk as a single holding. Maud could reduce this risk by instead investing in a portfolio of six or seven diverse holdings in large blue chip quoted companies, or by investing in a unit or investment trust aimed at producing income. Investment of up to £5,000 pa in the equity element of an Individual Savings Account (ISA) – £7,000 in 1998/99 and £5,000 pa thereafter – may be a viable tax exempt alternative especially if her marginal tax rate continues at 40%. *(4m)*

**Ordinary shares in Bit-Part Ltd**

The shares in a small unquoted company such as Bit-Part Ltd represent an unacceptable level of risk for Maud even if they were to form part of a portfolio. This should not be a problem if they are to be gifted to her children or grandchildren. *(1½m)*

**UK government stocks**

This is a suitable investment for Maud as the early redemption date makes them relatively risk free. *(1m)*

**Units in Global Trust**

As mentioned above, a unit trust is a suitable investment for Maud, but not one which is aimed at capital growth rather than income. *(1m)*

**Deposits with the Sprat & Minnow Building Society**

A deposit with a building society (or a bank) represents a suitable investment for some of Maud's funds, but a small building society probably represents too high a risk for deposits of £96,000. She would be advised to either transfer the deposits to a larger institution, or spread her deposits across a number of smaller ones. Using an ISA for cash deposits would reduce Maud's maximum investment entitlement for equities in an ISA and is therefore not advisable. *(4m)*

**National Savings Pensioners Guaranteed bond**

This represents a suitable risk-free investment for Maud, and she would probably be advised to invest a further £10,000 (up to the maximum limit of £20,000). *(1m)*

## 34      (Answer 4 of examination)

### Examiner's comments

This question tested candidates' ability to explain the tax implications arising from the disposal of shares in two subsidiary companies, and from the disposal of the assets of a subsidiary company. The tax implications were to be considered for (a) the holding company making the disposals, (b) the subsidiary companies concerned, and (c) the holding company making the acquisitions.

This was a reasonably popular question, but was answered quite badly. Too many candidates did not plan their answers, with the result that they repeated the same points two or three times. A considerable number of candidates did not appreciate that the tax implications arising on the disposal of the assets of a subsidiary are completely different from those arising on the disposal of shares in a subsidiary. The group relationships were often confused, especially in respect of Loch Ltd which remained as a 51% subsidiary of the original holding company. It could not therefore be an associate of another company. Very few candidates considered the implications for the year of disposal in respect of the company making the disposals, or for the year of acquisition in respect of the company making the acquisitions. Those candidates who do not know the difference between a 51% subsidiary and a 75% subsidiary cannot expect to pass this examination.

### Step by step answer plan

#### Overview

This is a group question requiring a fairly lengthy essay type answer. Each of the three disposals is structured differently to draw out various tax points. Fortunately the structure of your answer lies in the question. There are three main headings (a), (b) and (c) - one for the vendor parent, one for the 'goods' and one for the purchaser. For each main heading the three proposed disposals become three sub-heading. Even under each sub-heading you are told in the question the points such as 'group status' which may be appropriate. Approached in this way your answer becomes a series of pre-determined 'sections'. Without this structure the examiner will find it very difficult to award you all the marks you deserve so it is important that you keep to this framework.

**Step 1**   For part (a) (impact on the vendor parent) deal first with the disposal of Tarn (which is reducing to a 20% holding). The vendor is clearly concerned with CGT, group status and VAT group registration. It is also concerned with its access to Tarn's trading losses but this should be covered under 'group status'.

**Step 2**   Next go through the same steps with the disposal of Loch. This company remains a 51% sub and an associate so 'group status' comments will obviously differ from those for Tarn. Where comments can be repeated, however, - eg, the CGT treatment - simply indicate which earlier comments are applicable and do not waste time writing them out again.

**Step 3**   Finally under part (a), deal with the disposal of Pool's net assets but only to the extent that it impacts on the parent. The effect on Pool - eg, capital allowances - has to be explained instead in part (b). It is very important to keep to these 'compartments' or you risk putting the right information in the wrong place or wasting time in repetition.

**Step 4**   For part (b) use the same step by step approach, except this time you have to look at the implications for each subsidiary.

**Step 5**   Finally, for part (c) deal with each disposal from the viewpoint of the purchasing company, Sea plc.

---

( **The examiner's answer and marking guide** )

(a) **Tax implications for Ocean plc**

    (i) **Tarn Ltd**

*Capital gains tax*

A chargeable gain will arise in respect of the 80% of Tarn Ltd's ordinary share capital that is disposed of. The chargeable gain will be based on the consideration received from Sea plc, and calculated according to the normal CGT rules. Since the shares are not eligible assets, rollover relief is not available. The gain will result in an increased corporation tax liability for the year of disposal, which will presumably be at the rate of 30% as Ocean plc has a number of associated companies. *(2½m)*

*Group status*

After the disposal, Ocean plc will hold 20% of Tarn Ltd's ordinary share capital. Tarn Ltd will therefore cease to be either a 75% subsidiary, a 51% subsidiary, or an associated company. However, it will still be an associated company for the year of disposal. Since Tarn Ltd will become a 75% subsidiary of Sea plc, it cannot also be a consortium company. Ocean plc and its 75% subsidiaries will be able to claim group relief for trading losses made by Tarn Ltd up to the date of the disposal. For this purpose, Tarn Ltd's trading loss, and the profits of any claimant company, for the year of disposal, will normally be split on a time basis. However, group relief will be denied for any period during which arrangements exist for Tarn Ltd to leave the group. Thus if the arrangements are made substantially in advance of the actual disposal it will significantly affect the amount of any group relief claim. *(5m)*

*VAT*

Tarn Ltd will have to be removed from a group VAT registration if it is included in one. *(½m)*

*(Tutorial note:* two or more companies are eligible to be treated as members of a group if:

- one of them controls each of the others; or
- one person controls all of them.*)*

    (ii) **Loch Ltd**

*Capital gains tax*

A chargeable gain will arise in respect of the 40% of Loch Ltd's ordinary share capital that is disposed of. This will be calculated in the same way as for the disposal of 80% of the ordinary share capital of Tarn Ltd. *(1m)*

*Group status*

After the disposal, Ocean plc will hold 60% of Loch Ltd's ordinary share capital. Loch Ltd will therefore cease to be a 75% subsidiary, but will remain a 51% subsidiary and an associated company. Group relief will be available for any losses made by Loch Ltd up to the date of the disposal. The anti avoidance provisions relating to arrangements being in existence will not apply in this case, as Ocean plc is not transferring control of Loch Ltd. Consortium relief will be available in respect of any losses made by Loch Ltd from the date of the disposal, since 75% or more of its ordinary share capital will be owned by Ocean plc and Sea plc, and it will not be a 75% subsidiary of either company. The loss of the 75% group relationship means that it will no longer be possible to transfer chargeable assets between Loch Ltd and Ocean plc (and other group companies) without a chargeable gain or an allowable loss arising. *(7½m)*

*VAT*

Loch Ltd will be able to remain in a group VAT registration if it is included in one. *(½m)*

(iii)    **Pool Ltd**

*Capital gains tax*

As the net assets of Pool Ltd are to be disposed of, rather than its ordinary share capital, no chargeable gain will arise on Ocean plc. *(½m)*

*Group status*

Pool Ltd will remain a 100% subsidiary of Ocean plc.  However, if Pool Ltd ceases to carry on a trade or a business activity it will not be treated as an associated company.  Ocean plc will have to take care in extracting the sale proceeds from Pool Ltd, so as to avoid a double charge to tax. *(1½m)*

(b)    **Tax implications for the subsidiaries**

(i)    **Tarn Ltd**

*Trading losses*

Tarn Ltd currently has unutilised trading losses.  Since there has been a change in the company's ownership, the carry forward of these losses will be disallowed under S768 ICTA 1988 if there is a major change in the nature or conduct of its trade within three years of (before or after) its acquisition by Sea plc.  By itself, the application of Sea plc's marketing expertise is unlikely to constitute such a change. *(2m)*

*Capital gains tax*

Freehold shops have been transferred from Ocean plc to Tarn Ltd.  As Tarn Ltd is a 75% subsidiary of Ocean plc, these would have been transferred as an intra-group transfer of assets, and would have therefore been at no gain/no loss.  A chargeable gain or allowable loss will now arise in respect of any of the freehold shops that were transferred within six years of the date that Tarn Ltd is to leave the group.  The calculation of this gain or loss will be based on the market value of the shops at the date that they were originally transferred to Tarn Ltd, with indexation allowance being given up to that date.  The chargeable gains or allowable losses will form part of Tarn Ltd's profits chargeable to corporation tax for the period in which it leaves the group.  If the company has a trading loss for that period, it will be able to utilise this against chargeable gains (after deducting allowable losses) under S393A(1)(a) ICTA 1988. *(4½m)*

(ii)    **Loch Ltd**

S391
*Trading losses*

Loch Ltd currently has unutilised trading losses.  The company will be able to carry these forward for set-off against future trading profits without restriction.  Section 768 ICTA 1988 will not apply as there is no change in the control of the company. *(1½m)*

(iii)    **Pool Ltd**

*Capital gains tax*

The disposal of Pool Ltd's freehold shops will result in chargeable gains.  It will be possible to claim rollover relief if qualifying assets (most likely land and buildings) are purchased by Ocean plc or its 75% subsidiaries.  Such assets must be acquired within the period beginning one year before and ending three years after the date that the shops are disposed of.  Only the consideration not reinvested will result in an immediate chargeable gain. *(3m)*

There will also be CGT implications in respect of the disposal of any other chargeable assets owned by Pool Ltd. Should a value be attached to goodwill, then any resultant chargeable gain can also be rolled over. *(1m)*

*Capital allowances*

A balancing adjustment will arise in respect of any assets on which capital allowances have been claimed, such as fixtures and fittings. *(½m)*

*Trading losses*

Pool Ltd will be able to utilise any current year trading losses against its chargeable gains under S393A(1)(a) ICTA 1988. *(1m)*

Since Pool Ltd will presumably cease trading, it will not be possible to carry forward any unutilised trading losses. It is not possible to transfer these losses to Sea plc, despite the fact that this company has taken over the trade of Pool Ltd. If the unutilised trading losses brought forward are substantial, it would appear beneficial to restructure the disposal of Pool Ltd so that the ordinary share capital is disposed of, rather than its assets. This is subject to the proviso that the carry forward of losses is not then denied under S768 ICTA 1988. *(3m)*

*VAT*

VAT will not be charged on the assets disposed of, provided that the business is transferred as a going concern. Pool Ltd will have to deregister if it ceases to make taxable supplies. *(1½m)*

(c)   **Tax implications for Sea plc**

(i)   **Tarn Ltd**

*Capital gains tax*

The base cost of the shares acquired will be the price paid for them. *(½m)*

*Group status*

Tarn Ltd will become a 75% subsidiary, and an associated company of Sea plc. It will therefore be possible for Sea plc (and its 75% subsidiaries) to claim group relief in respect of any trading losses made by Tarn Ltd from the date of its acquisition. For this purpose, Tarn Ltd's trading loss, and the profits of any claimant company, will normally be split on a time basis for the year of acquisition. *(2½m)*

The 75% group relationship also means that chargeable assets can be transferred between Tarn Ltd and Sea plc (and other group companies) without a chargeable gain or an allowable loss arising. *(2m)*

*VAT*

Consideration will have to be given to the inclusion of Tarn Ltd in a group VAT registration. *(½m)*

(ii)   **Loch Ltd**

*Capital gains tax*

The base cost of the shares acquired is as for Tarn Ltd. *(½m)*

*Group status*

Sea plc will hold 40% of Loch Ltd's ordinary share capital. Loch Ltd will therefore not be a 75% subsidiary, a 51% subsidiary or an associated company. Consortium relief will be available in respect of any future losses made by Loch Ltd. *(1½m)*

(iii)    **Pool Ltd**

*Capital gains tax*

The base cost of the freehold shops acquired by Sea plc will be the price paid for them. The freehold shops will qualify as replacement assets for the purposes of rollover relief. Other chargeable assets will also be acquired at the price paid for them. *(1½m)*

*Capital allowances*

Capital allowances will be available in respect of any qualifying assets acquired such as fixtures and fittings. These will be added to Sea plc's existing pool of expenditure, and allowance will be given at the rate of 25% on a reducing balance basis. *(1½m)*

The trade of Pool Ltd will presumably be absorbed into Sea plc's existing business. This is unlikely to have any tax implications. *(½m)*

---

## 35    (Answer 5 of examination)

### Examiner's comments

Part (a) tested candidates' knowledge of the tax implications of a company providing either a company car or a cash alternative to a director and an employee from the company's point of view. Part (b) tested candidates' knowledge of the tax implications of a company providing either a company car or a cash alternative to a director and an employee from the point of view of the director and the employee.

This was another popular question. Many candidates would have benefited by spending more time planning their answers, since although they were able to calculate the individual component parts of the answer, such as the benefits in kind, they were not then able to put these parts into a coherent whole. A common mistake was to combine the calculations for the director and employee, and it was not then possible to appreciate that a different alternative was beneficial in each case. The VAT and NIC aspects of the question were generally answered very badly, or ignored altogether. It was not always appreciated that payments under the fixed profit car scheme are tax-free.

### Step by step answer plan

**Overview**

This is a practical exercise in evaluating the after tax costs of alternative ways of providing the use of a car to an employee either directly or through a cash alternative. This involved computing the income tax, NIC and corporation tax effects. It also required adjustments for VAT.

**Step 1**    Read the question carefully and be clear in your mind exactly what alternatives have to be considered.

**Step 2**    Concentrate on part (a) - ie, the effect on the employer.

**Step 3**    Answer part (a) first evaluating the annual after tax cost (capital and revenue) of providing cars for the two different classes of individual.

**Step 4**    Next evaluate the annual cost of providing a cash alternative.

**Step 5**    Finally for part (a), compare the two alternative methods for each of the categories of individual.

**Step 6**    Answer part (b) noting that the individuals require advice also on the most tax-efficient claims for tax relief.

**Step 7**    Prepare computations for each type of individual showing the annual tax cost of accepting a company car and fuel.

---

Step 8   Compute the cash flow effect of the cash alternative for the different types of individuals.

Step 9   Summarise the tax efficiencies of the two alternatives for each type of individual and mention any other factors relevant to the choice.

## The examiner's answer and marking guide

(a)      **The provision of company motor cars**

The net cost of the motor cars, taking into account their resale value, is as follows:

|  | Director's car £ | Salesman's car £ |
|---|---|---|
| List price | 30,000 | 11,000 |
| Discount (5%) | 1,500 | 550 |
| Purchase price | 28,500 | 10,450 |
| Selling price | 19,000 | 6,000 |
| Net cost | 9,500 | 4,450 |

*(1m)*

This equates to an annual cost of £4,750 $\left(9,500\big/2\right)$ for the director's motor car, and £1,483 $\left(4,450\big/3\right)$ for the salesman's motor car. The VAT element of the cost of the motor cars is not reclaimable. However, Venus plc will be able to claim capital allowances on the net costs of the motor cars, inclusive of the VAT element. Venus plc will have to pay employers Class 1A National Insurance contribution in respect of the car benefits arising on both the director and the salesman, and the fuel benefit arising on the director. No fuel benefit arises on the salesman, as all private fuel is to be reimbursed. Input VAT can be reclaimed in respect of the cost of petrol and diesel, and the cost of servicing and repairs. Because fuel is being provided for private use to the director, Venus plc will have to account for output VAT based on the VAT scale rates. Output VAT will also be due on the reimbursement of private fuel by the salesman. The overall annual cost of providing company motor cars is therefore as follows: *(5½m)*

|  | Director's car £ | Salesman's car £ |
|---|---|---|
| Net cost | 4,750 | 1,483 |
| Employers Class 1A NIC (car benefit) |  |  |
| £10,500 [see(b)] at 12.2% | 1,281 |  |
| £1,650 [see (b)] at 12.2% |  | 201 |
| Employers Class 1A NIC (fuel benefit) |  |  |
| £2,270 [see (b)] at 12.2% | 277 | – |
| Petrol/diesel (net of VAT) |  |  |
| £1,645 × $^{40}\!/_{47}$ | 1,400 |  |
| £2,115 × $^{40}\!/_{47}$ |  | 1,800 |
| Private diesel reimbursed |  |  |
| £2,115 × $^{10,000}\!/_{30,000}$ |  | (705) |
| VAT output tax |  |  |
| £1,585 × $^{7}\!/_{47}$ | 236 |  |
| £705 × $^{7}\!/_{47}$ |  | 105 |
| Servicing/repairs (net of VAT) |  |  |
| £705 × $^{40}\!/_{47}$ | 600 |  |
| £470 × $^{40}\!/_{47}$ |  | 400 |
| Insurance/road tax | 1,000 | 450 |
|  | 9,544 | 3,734 |

|  | | |
|---|---|---|
| Corporation tax relief at 30% | 2,863 | 1,120 |
| | 6,681 | 2,614 |

*(5m)*

The total cost over the life of the motor cars is £13,362 (6,681 × 2) in respect of the director's motor car, and £7,842 (2,614 × 3) in respect of the salesman's motor car. *(1m)*

The VAT output tax charge in respect of the director's motor car could be avoided by not reclaiming any input VAT in respect of petrol. However, this is not beneficial in this case as the input VAT recovery of £245 $(1,645 \times \frac{7}{47})$ exceeds the VAT output charge. *(1½m)*

**Payment of cash alternative**

Venus plc will have to pay employers Class 1 National Insurance contribution in respect of the cash alternative, but not in respect of the mileage allowances. Input VAT can be reclaimed on the business proportion of the cost of petrol and diesel included in the mileage allowance, but not the input VAT on the cost of servicing and repairs. The overall cost of the cash alternative, taken over the same period as the life of the motor cars, is therefore as follows: *(4m)*

| | | Director's car £ | Salesman's car £ |
|---|---|---|---|
| Cash payment | | 13,500 | 5,250 |
| Employers Class 1 NIC at 12.2% | | 1,647 | 640 |
| Mileage allowance | 2,000 at 55 pence for two years | 2,200 | |
| | 20,000 at 10 pence for three years | | 6,000 |
| Input VAT | $£1,645 \times \dfrac{2,000}{18,000} \times \frac{7}{47}$ for two years | (54) | |
| | $£2,115 \times \dfrac{20,000}{30,000} \times \frac{7}{47}$ for three years | | (630) |
| | | 17,293 | 11,260 |
| Corporation tax relief at 30% | | 5,188 | 3,378 |
| | | 12,105 | 7,882 |

*(4m)*

It will be beneficial for Venus plc to pay the cash alternative rather than to provide a company motor car to the director, as this will save £1,257 (13,362 – 12,105) over two years. In the case of the salesman, the situation is virtually neutral, as the provision of a company motor car only saves £40 (7,882 – 7,842) over three years. *(2m)*

(b)    **Accepting company motor cars**

Both the director and the salesman earn over £8,500 pa, and they will therefore be assessed under Schedule E on the benefit of the motor cars and, in the case of the director, on a fuel benefit in respect of the provision of private petrol. The car benefit is based on the list price of the car, with no account taken of the discount available. The salesman's car benefit is calculated at 15%, as he drives over 18,000 business miles pa. The director's benefits will be subject to income tax at the rate of 40%, whilst the salesman's benefit will be subject to income tax at 23% as he has at least £14,335 (28,000 + 4,335 – 18,000) of his 23% tax band remaining. *(3½m)*

| | | Director £ | Salesman £ |
|---|---|---|---|
| Car benefit | £30,000 × 35% | 10,500 | |
| | £11,000 × 15% | | 1,650 |

| | | | |
|---|---|---:|---:|
| Fuel benefit | | 2,270 | |
| | | 12,770 | 1,650 |
| Income tax | at 40% | 5,108 | |
| | at 23% | | 380 |
| Private diesel reimbursed (as above) | | | 705 |
| | | 5,108 | 1,085 |

*(2½m)*

The total cost over the life of the motor cars is £10,216 (5,108 × 2) for the director, and £3,255 (1,085 × 3) for the salesman. *(1m)*

### Accepting the cash alternative

If they accept the cash alternative, the director and the salesman will have to purchase their own motor cars, and pay for the running costs. It is assumed that the 5% discount on list price is not available to an individual purchaser. The total costs incurred will be as follows: *(1m)*

| | | Director £ | Salesman £ |
|---|---|---:|---:|
| List price | | 30,000 | 11,000 |
| Selling price | | 19,000 | 6,000 |
| Net cost | | 11,000 | 5,000 |
| Running costs | £1,645 + £705 + £1,000 for two years | 6,700 | |
| | £2,115 + £470 + £450 for three years | | 9,105 |
| | | 17,700 | 14,105 |

*(1½m)*

The director and the salesman will receive a one-off cash payment, and a mileage allowance in respect of business mileage. The cash payment will be assessed as earnings under Schedule E. Income tax at the rate of 40% will be payable by the director, and at the rate of 23% by the salesman. The director will not be liable to additional employees Class 1 National Insurance contribution, as he already earns in excess of the upper earnings limit of £26,000. The salesman will be liable to additional employees Class 1 National Insurance contribution based on the upper limit for (presumably) one month of £2,167 $\left(\frac{26,000}{12}\right)$. The salesman's monthly salary is £1,500 $\left(\frac{18,000}{12}\right)$, so the additional National Insurance contribution will amount to £67 (2,167 − 1,500 at 10%). The director and the salesman will receive the following: *(4m)*

| | | Director £ | Salesman £ |
|---|---|---:|---:|
| Cash payment | | 13,500 | 5,250 |
| Income tax | at 40% | (5,400) | |
| | at 23% | | (1,208) |
| Class 1 NIC | | | (67) |
| | | 8,100 | 3,975 |
| Mileage allowances | 2,000 miles at 55p for two years | 2,200 | |
| | 20,000 miles at 10p for three years | | 6,000 |
| | | 10,300 | 9,975 |

*(1½m)*

The mileage allowance will be tax-free if it is paid under the fixed profit car scheme. If the mileage allowance paid is less than the Revenue maximum under the fixed profit car scheme, the difference may be claimed by the director and salesman as a business expenses deductible from salary for tax purposes. The figures are not available to quantify the deduction. *(½m)*

Alternatively, the director and the salesman could be assessed on the mileage allowance as a benefit, and then claim for the business proportion of running their motor cars. Capital allowances could also be claimed. In the case of the director, this is not beneficial as the director's potential expense and capital allowance claim only amounts to £1,967 $\left(17,700 \times {}^{2,000}\!/_{18,000}\right)$, which is less than the mileage allowance. However, for the salesman, the claim amounts to £9,403 $\left(14,105 \times {}^{20,000}\!/_{30,000}\right)$, which is greater than the mileage allowance. The alternative will therefore result in tax relief of £783 (9,403 – 6,000 at 23%). *(4m)*

It will be beneficial for the director to opt for the cash alternative as this results in a saving of £2,816, whilst for the salesman it appears to be marginally beneficial to opt for the company motor car as this results in a saving of £92, as follows: *(1½m)*

**Cost of cash alternative**

|  | Director £ | Salesman £ |
|---|---|---|
| Purchasing own motor cars | 17,700 | 14,105 |
| Cash payment/mileage allowances | (10,300) | (9,975) |
| Tax relief re-business mileage | – | (783) |
|  | 7,400 | 3,347 |
| Cost of company motor cars | 10,216 | 3,255 |
| Differential | (2,816) | 92 |

*(2m)*

**Summary**

It will be beneficial for Venus plc to pay the director the cash alternative, as this results in an overall saving of £4,073 (£1,257 for Venus plc and £2,816 for the director) over two years when compared with the provision of a company motor car. In the case of the salesman, providing a company motor car results in a small overall saving of £132 (£40 for Venus plc and £92 for the salesman) over three years. This by itself is not decisive, and other factors will have to be considered. For example, if the salesman were to choose a lower priced private motor car, the cash alternative would become beneficial. *(3m)*

---

**Did you answer the question?**

You were not required to make any adjustments for the time value of money.

---

**36    (Answer 6 of examination)**

---

**Examiner's comments**

Part (a) tested candidates' ability to advise on the tax implications arising from the purchase of a new factory or the rent of a factory, together with the tax implications arising from the issue of debentures and the disposal of a warehouse used for industrial purposes. Part (b) tested candidates' knowledge of the enterprise investment scheme reliefs.

This was not a popular question, although part (a) was generally well answered. In part (a), a number of candidates had problems with the calculation of the deductible element of the lease premium, which is a basic paper 7 calculation. Several candidates did not appreciate that the capitalisation of the debenture interest was irrelevant for tax purposes. Very few candidates could correctly calculate the balancing charge in respect of industrial buildings allowance. In part (b), too many candidates were not aware of the existence of relief under the enterprise investment scheme, despite this being covered in the *Students' Newsletter* articles on the Finance Act 1995, and the same topic being examined at the December 1995 diet. Instead, candidates wrote at length about retirement relief, without appreciating that the proposed stock exchange listing would only affect the entitlement of one of the four shareholders. The reinvestment relief aspects of the question were well answered.

## Step by step answer plan

### Overview

The first part of this question concerns the tax implications of two alternatives for a company needing more factory space and the tax effect of the steps intended to raise the required finance. Once you have spotted what issues need discussing the question is fairly easy to answer well. The second part concerns the same company but looks at the quite separate matter of issuing EIS shares. In effect you have to consider whether certain investors meet the qualifying conditions and then discuss the impact of a subsequent Stock Exchange listing - ie, the effect of losing unquoted status.

**Step 1**     Read part (a) of the question and decide on the shape of your answer. Clearly you will need a separate heading for:

- Construction of new factory
- Acquiring the lease of a factory
- Issuing debentures
- Selling the warehouse.

**Step 2**     Ensure you identify all the issues under each heading and cover them in sufficient depth. Unfortunately there is no indication on the question as to how the 13 marks for part (a) are allocated.

**Step 3**     Under the 'construction' heading the three obvious issues are the IBAs, the CAs on the plant element and the VAT recovery.

**Step 4**     When discussing the lease you will need a paragraph each for:

- VAT recovery
- Trading expense element in the premium
- CT and VAT treatment of the annual rent.

**Step 5**     On the debenture, explain briefly the expense deduction and the requirement to account for tax deducted quarterly.

**Step 6**     The following matters arise from the proposed sale of the warehouse:

- The capital gain
- The rollover/holdover opportunity
- The balancing charge under the IBA rules.

**Step 7**     Re-read part (a) to ensure that all relevant points have been covered.

**Step 8**     Now read part (b). It should be obvious that for part (b) (i) you have to:

- Discuss briefly what is an EIS qualifying company and give the outline of EIS income tax relief
- Cover separately for each shareholder whether EIS income tax relief is available
- Cover the deferral opportunity for Carol.

**Step 9**  For part (b) (ii) you have to remember what share-related tax reliefs for individuals are dependent on a company retaining unquoted status. Apart from EIS income tax relief - fairly obvious in the circumstances - you should have headings for:

- EIS deferral relief
- BPR
- Retirement relief

**Step 10**  Finally re-read part (b) to check that your answer has not overlooked any relevant detail.

## The examiner's answer and marking guide

(a)      **Construction of new factory**

The new factory will qualify for Industrial Buildings Allowance on £301,100 of the cost as follows:

|  | £ |
|---|---:|
| Levelling the land | 10,300 |
| Architects and legal fees | 24,300 |
| Strengthened concrete floor | 16,500 |
| Factory | 187,500 |
| General offices | 62,500 |
|  | ——— |
|  | 301,100 |
|  | ——— |

*(1½m)*

Industrial Buildings Allowance of £12,044 (301,100 × 4%) will be given, commencing in the accounting period that the factory is brought into use. This allowance will be given for the next 25 years, provided that for any accounting period the factory is not used for non-industrial purposes at the end of that period. *(2m)*

The cost of the land does not qualify. The general offices qualify as they cost less than 25% of the total qualifying cost (301,100 × 25% = £75,275). *(1m)*

The input VAT of £70,000 will be reclaimed in full, assuming that Garden Ltd is making standard rated supplies. *(½m)*

The cost of the ventilation and heating systems (£12,500) and the fire alarm and sprinkler system (£6,400) will qualify as plant and machinery. The cost of the strengthened floor, despite being to support machinery, is part of the factory structure. This would only qualify as plant and machinery if it consisted of expenditure on the alteration of an existing building. For allowances to be available, the expenditure must be notified to the Inland Revenue within two years of the end of the accounting period to which it relates. A writing-down allowance of 25% pa on a reducing balance basis will be given, commencing in the accounting period that title to the factory passes to Garden Ltd. For the first year, allowances of £4,725 (12,500 + 6,400 at 25%) will be given. For expenditure incurred on plant before 2 July 2000 a first year allowance of 40% is given instead with 25% WDA applying on a reducing balance basis for subsequent accounting periods. *(4½m)*

---

**Tutorial notes**

1      The comment on availability of FYA assumes that Garden Ltd is not a 'large' company - ie, it satisfies at least two of the following conditions in the current or the previous accounting period:

- Turnover not in excess of £11.2 million
- Assets not valued above £5.6 million
- No more than 250 employees

---

**Lease of factory**

As the owners of the factory have exercised their option to tax the grant of the lease, Garden Ltd will be able to reclaim input tax of £70,000 $(470,000 \times \frac{7}{47})$. This again assumes that Garden Ltd is making standard rated supplies. *(1m)*

The proportion of the premium assessed on the owners as a capital gain will be deductible for corporation tax purposes over the period of the lease, as follows:

|  | £ |
|---|---|
| Premium paid | 400,000 |
| Less: $400,000 \times 2\% \times (40 - 1)$ | 312,000 |
|  | 88,000 |

$$\frac{88,000}{40} = 2,200 \text{ pa}$$                                                       *(2m)*

The deduction is £2,200 will be restricted for the accounting period in which it is paid according to the length of the period from the date of payment to the end of that accounting period. *(1m)*

Garden Ltd will be able to reclaim input tax of £5,250 $(35,250 \times \frac{7}{47})$ in respect of each annual payment of rent. The rent paid of £30,000 (35,250 − 5,250) will be deductible for corporation tax purposes. *(1m)*

**Debenture loan**

Debenture interest is deducted from trading profits on the accruals basis. Whether or not it is capitalised is irrelevant. The annual deduction will therefore amount to £24,000 (200,000 at 12%). Garden Ltd must deduct lower rate tax from the debenture interest paid, and account for it to the Revenue quarterly. *(2½m)*

**Sale of warehouse**

The sale of the warehouse will result in a capital gain of £106,800 as follows:

|  | £ |
|---|---|
| Sale proceeds | 270,000 |
| Cost | 120,000 |
|  | 150,000 |
| Indexation $120,000 \times 0.360$ | 43,200 |
|  | 106,800 |

*(1m)*

**Replacement of business asset**

If the new factory is constructed, the gain can be rolled over against the base cost of the factory. There is no restriction on the amount of the gain that can be rolled over, as the full proceeds of £270,000 will be reinvested. This assumes that the reinvestment of the proceeds will take place in the period beginning one year before and ending three years after the date of disposal. *(1½m)*

If the factory is leased, the gain can only be heldover for a maximum of 10 years. This is because the replacement asset will be a depreciating asset with a life of less than 50 years. *(1m)*

The sale of the warehouse will also result in a balancing adjustment in respect of Industrial Buildings Allowance. The allowances will have been based on the original cost of the warehouse (excluding land) and the remaining life of 25 years due to Garden Ltd, as follows:

| | |
|---|---|
| Qualifying cost (102,000 – 42,000) | £60,000 |
| Remaining life [25 – (10 – 7)] | 22 years |
| Written-down allowance per annum $\left(^{60,000}\!/_{22}\right)$ | £2,727 |
| Total allowances given (2,727 × 7) | £19,089 |

Since the sale proceeds exceed the original cost, the balancing charge will be for the total allowances given of £19,089. *(3m)*

*(Tutorial note:* note that IBAs are calculated on the cost of the warehouse, excluding the cost of the land. However, when the warehouse is sold, the warehouse and the land is treated as a single asset, when calculating the capital gain on disposal.)

(b)     **Subscription for new ordinary share capital**

**Income tax relief under the Enterprise Investment Scheme (EIS)**

Income tax relief under the EIS is available for subscriptions of new ordinary share capital. A qualifying company is one that is unquoted, trading in the UK, and carrying on a qualifying trade. Assuming that all of these conditions are met, the shareholders of Garden Ltd will be entitled to relief as follows: *(2m)*

*Alex Bush* will not be entitled to relief under the EIS as he is connected with Garden Ltd due to his:

(i)     holding more than 30% of the company's share capital; and
(ii)    being a paid director of the company. *(1½m)*

*Carol Daisy* will be entitled to relief under the EIS as she holds less than 30% of Garden Ltd's share capital $\left(^{200,000}\!/_{1,000,000} \times 100 = 20\%\right)$, and has not been a paid director of the company prior to the share issue. In addition, she can claim deferral relief for the re-investment of the sale proceeds of her property in EIS shares (see below). She will only qualify for income tax relief on £150,000 of her investment, being the maximum relief available per tax year (in the same way as Edward - see below). *(2½m)*

*Edward Fern* will be entitled to relief under the EIS as he holds less than 30% of Garden Ltd's share capital $\left(^{200,000}\!/_{1,000,000} \times 100 = 20\%\right)$, and has not been a paid director of the company prior to the share issue. Entitlement to relief under the EIS is not affected by Edward subsequently becoming a paid director of Garden Ltd. He will only qualify for relief on £150,000 of his investment, being the maximum relief available per tax year. The tax relief will be £30,000 (150,000 at 20%), and this will be given as a credit against his tax liability for 1999/00. However, should his tax liability for 1999/00 be less than £20,000, the relief will be restricted to that figure. As the investment has been made between 6 April and 5 October Edward can carry back £5,000 (25,000 at 20%) of the relief to 1998/99 should this be beneficial. *(5m)*

*Gary Hedge* will not be entitled to relief since he was a paid director of Garden Ltd prior to the share issue. *(1m)*

**Deferral relief on re-investment**

Carol should be entitled to deferral relief on the re-investment of her proceeds from the sale of her property, as Garden Ltd is an EIS company. This is provided that the share issue was within the period beginning one year before and ending three years after the date that the property was sold. The relief will be limited to the amount of the share issue of £200,000, as this is less than her chargeable gain of £225,000. £80,000 (200,000 at 40%) of her CGT liability of £90,000 (225,000 at 40%) is therefore postponed. *(3½m)*

*(Tutorial note:* Taper relief will be available when the £80,000 deferred gain becomes chargeable but only at the rate that would have been available had the gain remained chargeable in 1999/00).

---

**Proposed Stock Exchange listing**

*Enterprise investment scheme*

Tax relief given under the EIS will be withdrawn if Garden Ltd ceases to be a qualifying company within three years of the shares being issued. This will be the case if it obtains a Stock Exchange listing before August 2002. *(2m)*

*Deferral relief on re-investment*

The deferral relief given on re-investment will not be withdrawn as a result of Garden Ltd obtaining a Stock Exchange listing. *(½m)*

*Business property relief (BPR)*

At present, all shareholders would be entitled to BPR at the rate of 100% on a chargeable transfer of shares in Garden Ltd as they have shareholdings in an unquoted company. *(1m)*

If Garden Ltd obtains a Stock Exchange listing by issuing 500,000 new shares, the present shareholders' holdings will be diluted by one-third. All four shareholders will therefore lose their entitlement to BPR, since Garden Ltd (or plc) will be quoted, and no shareholder will have control of the company. Alex will have a 36.6% $\left(55 \times \frac{2}{3}\right)$ shareholding. Even if the share issue was restructured so that Alex retained control of Garden Ltd, relief would only be available at the rate of 50%. *(2½m)*

*Retirement relief*

Only Gary's entitlement to retirement relief will be affected by Garden Ltd issuing 500,000 new shares on the Stock Exchange. His shareholding will fall from 5% to 3.3% $\left(5 \times \frac{2}{3}\right)$, and retirement relief will therefore no longer be available upon his retirement. The other three shareholders will still each have a holding of not less than 5%. This is a relevant consideration for Gary, as he is presently 51 years old. However, retirement relief is being phased out and will not be available for disposals after 5 April 2003. *(2m)*

## DECEMBER 1995 QUESTIONS

## 37 (Question 1 of examination)

(a) Highrise Ltd is an unquoted trading company. Highrise Ltd has always had an accounting date of 30 June, with its most recent accounts being prepared to 30 June 1998. However, the company now plans to change its accounting date to 31 December 1999. Highrise Ltd has forecast that its results for the 18 month period to 31 December 1999 will be as follows:

(1) Tax adjusted Schedule D Case I trading profits, before capital allowances, per six monthly period will be:

|  | £ |
|---|---|
| Six months to 31 December 1998 | 141,000 |
| Six months to 30 June 1999 | 126,000 |
| Six months to 31 December 1999 | 165,000 |

(2) The tax written-down value of plant and machinery at 1 July 1998 is £20,000. On 31 May 1999 Highrise Ltd will purchase plant costing £120,000.

(3) Highrise Ltd owns two freehold office buildings which have always been rented out unfurnished. These are both to be sold. The first building at Ampton will be sold on 31 December 1998 resulting in a chargeable gain of £42,000, whilst the second building at Bodford will be sold on 31 May 1999 resulting in an allowable capital loss of £25,000.

(4) The building at Ampton is currently let at £48,000 pa, rent being due quarterly in advance on 1 January, 1 April etc. The building at Bodford was let until 31 March 1998, but has been empty since then. It will be decorated at a cost of £9,000 during May 1999 prior to its disposal. Both lettings are at a full rent and Highrise Ltd is responsible for all repairs.

(5) A dividend of £50,000 (net) will be paid on 10 October 1998.

(6) Highrise Ltd has a 20% shareholding in Shortie Ltd, an unquoted trading company. A dividend of £11,250 (net) will be received from Shortie Ltd on 15 June 1999.

**Required:**

Advise Highrise Ltd of whether it would be beneficial to:

(i) prepare one set of accounts for the 18 month period to 31 December 1999; or

(ii) prepare separate accounts for the six month period to 31 December 1998 and for the year ended 31 December 1999.

Your answer should include a calculation of Highrise Ltd's total corporation tax liability for the 18 month period to 31 December 1999 under each alternative. **(17 marks)**

(b) On 1 January 2000, Highrise Ltd is to purchase the 80% of Shortie Ltd's ordinary share capital that it does not already own. Shortie Ltd's results for the year ended 31 March 2000 are forecast to be:

|  | £ |
|---|---|
| Schedule D Case I trading loss | 155,000 |
| Capital loss on sale of property - 1 September 1999 | 37,000 |
| Dividend paid (net) | 50,000 |

Shortie Ltd has a 10% shareholding in Minute Ltd. This investment is currently standing at a substantial capital loss.

Highrise Ltd has a 5% shareholding in Tiny Ltd. This investment is currently standing at a substantial capital gain.

**Required:**

Briefly discuss how Highrise Ltd's acquisition of Shortie Ltd will affect the utilisation of Shortie Ltd's trading loss and capital loss that are forecast to arise in respect of the year ended 31 March 2000, and its unrealised capital loss in respect of its investment in Minute Ltd.

You should assume that it is not possible for Shortie Ltd to carry back its trading loss to previous accounting periods.

**(8 marks)**

**(Total 25 marks)**

---

## 38    (Question 2 of examination)

---

Sonya Rich is the managing director of Wealthy Ltd, an unquoted trading company. She owns all of the shares in the company. Sonya has asked for your advice regarding tax planning measures that both she and Wealthy Ltd should take during the next six months. You should assume that today's date is 1 January 2000.

Sonya is a 47 year old widow, her husband having died several years ago. She has one daughter, Kate, aged 23. You have the following information:

(1)    Wealthy Ltd is forecast to have Schedule D Case I trading profits of £285,000 for the year ended 30 April 2000. This is after taking into account Sonya's directors' remuneration of £95,000 pa. Wealthy Ltd has not paid any dividends during the year ended 30 April 2000.

At some time during the next six months, Sonya would like to draw an additional amount from Wealthy Ltd, either by way of directors' remuneration or as a dividend, sufficient to leave her with additional post tax income of £60,000.

(2)    During the next six months, Wealthy Ltd will need to purchase new computer equipment costing £80,000, and a new freehold office building costing £95,000. In the case of the office building, Sonya might acquire this herself and rent it to Wealthy Ltd at a market rent of £7,500 pa should this be beneficial.

(3)    Sonya's investments include the following:

(a)    £11,800 in a TESSA account with her local building society. This account was opened on 5 January 1995

(b)    Ordinary shares in quoted companies worth £162,400. Included in this figure are a number of shareholdings which are currently standing at a substantial capital gain.

(c)    £14,500 in two personal equity plans that were opened on 15 March 1996 and 2 April 1997.

(d)    £10,000 in National Savings Certificates which were acquired on 1 February 1995

Sonya does not wish to increase her overall exposure to equity investments. She has not disposed of any assets during 1999/00.

(4)    Kate is to get married on 30 April 2000, and Sonya would like to make a gift worth £20,000 to her on or before the date of the wedding. Sonya has already made substantial lifetime transfers of value to Kate, the last of which was four years ago. Kate is the sole beneficiary under the terms of Sonya's will.

**Required:**

(a)    Advise both Sonya and Wealthy Ltd of tax planning measures that they should take during the period 1 January 2000 to 30 June 2000.

---

Your answer should be confined to the information given in the question, and you should pay particular attention to the timing of any tax planning measures that you have recommended. Where possible, a calculation of the tax saving that will result from each aspect of your advice should be included.    **(18 marks)**

(b)    (i)    State whether or not a certified accountant providing the advice given to Sonya in part (a) above, would need to be authorised to conduct investment business under the Financial Services Act 1986.

**(5 marks)**

(ii)    Briefly state the implications arising from the carrying on of investment business by a person who is not authorised to do so under the Financial Services Act 1986.

**(2 marks)**
**(Total 25 marks)**

---

## 39    (Question 3 of examination)

---

Fred Barley is a 68 year old farmer who has been in business as a sole trader since January 1976. Due to ill health (you should assume that Fred will not live for more than five years), Fred plans to retire on 31 December 1999, and at that date he will sell the farm to his son, Simon, aged 37. The following information is available:

(1)    Simon forecasts that he will make a tax adjusted Schedule D Case I loss of £12,000 for his first year of trading to 31 December 2000 before taking capital allowances into account, but thereafter expects the business to be profitable.

(2)    The tax written-down value of plant and machinery at 31 December 1999 will be £24,000.

(3)    The market value of the business at 31 December 1999 is forecast to be £1,000,000, made up as follows:

|  | £ |
|---|---|
| Farm land and farm buildings | 600,000 |
| Investments | 250,000 |
| Plant and machinery | 35,000 |
| Net current assets | 115,000 |
|  | 1,000,000 |

The farm land and farm buildings were purchased in January 1976 for £55,000, and were valued at £115,000 at 31 March 1982. The agricultural value of the farm land and farm buildings at 31 December 1999 will be £475,000. The investments consist of shares in quoted companies, and were purchased in June 1987 for £35,000. No item of plant and machinery cost in excess of £6,000 or is currently valued in excess of £6,000.

(4)    Simon is to take over all of the assets of the business. He will purchase the farm land and farm buildings at their agricultural value of £475,000, but no consideration is to be paid in respect of the other assets.

(5)    Fred is a widower, he has investment income of £4,000 pa (gross) and has not made any lifetime gifts of assets within the previous seven years. The value of his estate (excluding the business and the consideration to be paid by Simon) is £350,000. His taxable farming profits for 1999/00 will be £10,000.

Simon is married, and is presently employed by Fred as the farm manager of the business at a salary of £42,500 pa.

**Required:**

(a)    Advise Simon of the income tax implications arising from the sale of the business to him on 31 December 1999. You should ignore National Insurance contributions, Agricultural Buildings Allowances, farmers averaging of profits, and the possibility of any repayment supplement being due;

**(5 marks)**

---

(b)      Advise Fred and Simon of the capital gains tax implications arising from the sale of the business to Simon on 31 December 1999;                                                                                   **(7 marks)**

(c)      Advise Fred and Simon of the inheritance tax implications arising from the sale of the business to Simon on 31 December 1999.                                                                                     **(6 marks)**

Your answer should include any tax planning points that you consider relevant.  You should assume that the tax rates and allowances for 1999/00 apply throughout.                                                      **(Total 18 marks)**

Question 3 originally covered the cessation of Fred's business, but as the cessation of a pre 6 April 1994 business before 6 April 2000 is not examinable, this part of the question has been removed.

---

## 40      (Question 4 of examination)

You work in the taxation department of a firm of Certified Accountants, dealing mainly with overseas taxation matters. You are to advise the following clients:

(a)      Angus Ash, a wealthy investor, is to purchase a 15% shareholding in Cedar Inc, a company resident in the country of Yenka.  Angus expects to receive a dividend of £60,000 pa (gross) from his shareholding, which will be subject to withholding tax at the rate of 10%.  The rate of corporation tax in Yenka is 40%, and there is no double taxation treaty between the UK and Yenka.  Angus is unsure whether to:

    (i)      make the investment personally; or

    (ii)     make the investment via a UK resident limited company that would be formed especially for this purpose.  Such a company would be a close investment holding company.  If this option is chosen, Angus would withdraw all surplus funds from the company at the earliest possible opportunity.

Angus earns £250,000 pa from his employment as a director with a UK resident company.

**Required:**

Advise Angus of whether it would be beneficial to make the investment in Cedar Inc personally, or whether it should be made via a UK resident limited company.  Your answer should include a brief discussion (detailed calculations are not required) as to the most beneficial way of Angus extracting surplus funds from such a company.                                                                                                                  **(6 marks)**

(b)      Elm plc, a UK resident holding company, has a number of 100% owned subsidiary companies which are resident overseas.  Elm plc has recently received an enquiry from the Inland Revenue for more information in respect of four of these overseas subsidiary companies.  The aim of the Inland Revenue enquiry is to determine whether or not any of the overseas subsidiaries should be classified as controlled foreign companies.

**Required:**

Advise Elm plc of the tax implications if the Inland Revenue determine that any of its overseas subsidiary companies should be classified as controlled foreign companies.  Briefly state the basis upon which the Inland Revenue will make such a determination.                                                                                         **(6 marks)**

(c)      Francis and Gayle Holm have been married for a number of years, and are both resident, ordinarily resident and domiciled in the UK.  Gayle has recently been offered a 15 month contract of employment in the country of Yenka, with a company that is resident in that country.  During the period that Gayle is employed overseas, Francis plans to travel around the world on holiday.  Gayle will be entitled to a ten week holiday in the middle of her 15 month contract, and she will either spend this in the UK, or will join Francis travelling.

Francis and Gayle will let out their jointly owned main residence in the UK for £1,500 per month during their 15 month period of absence.  They are currently paying mortgage interest of £180 (net) per month within the MIRAS arrangements, in respect of a £28,000 mortgage.

---

**Required:**

Advise both Francis and Gayle of the income tax implications of their leaving the UK for a period of 15 months, and of renting out their main residence in the UK whilst they are away.    **(7 marks)**
**(Total 19 marks)**
**(as amended)**

---

## 41    (Question 5 of examination)

---

Michael Earl, aged 48, died on 30 June 1999. At the time of his death, Michael owned the following assets:

(1)    50,000 £1 ordinary shares in Compact Ltd, an unquoted UK resident trading company with an issued share capital of 1,000,000 shares. Michael originally acquired 100,000 shares at par upon the company's incorporation in April 1991. He made a gift of 50,000 shares to his daughter, Jade, on 10 July 1998. Michael's wife Naomi also owns 50,000 shares in Compact Ltd, which she acquired in April 1991. The relevant values of Compact Ltd's shares, as agreed by the Inland Revenue, are as follows:

|  |  | Value per share at | |
|---|---|---|---|
|  |  | 10 July 1998 | 30 June 1999 |
|  |  | £ | £ |
| Shareholding | 5% | 5.00 | 6.00 |
|  | 10% | 7.00 | 8.40 |
|  | 15% | 10.00 | 12.00 |

(2)    50,000 £1 ordinary shares in Diverse Inc, a quoted trading company with an issued share capital of 10,000,000 shares. The company is resident in the country of Gobolia. Michael originally bought 150,000 shares in March 1988. He made a gift of 100,000 shares into a discretionary trust for the benefit of his grandchildren on 19 August 1998. Michael paid the IHT arising as a result of the gift. Diverse Inc's shares were quoted on the Gobolian Stock Exchange at 308–316 on 19 August 1998, with recorded bargains of 296, 320 and 328 for that day. On 30 June 1999 they were quoted at 279–287, with recorded bargains of 275 and 285. All of the above figures are in pounds sterling.

(3)    Other assets valued for IHT purposes at £850,000. This figure is after providing for any tax liabilities outstanding at 30 June 1999.

Under the terms of his will, Michael left £200,000 in cash to his wife Naomi, and the residue of his estate to his daughter Jade. Michael and Jade are domiciled in the UK, but Naomi is domiciled in Gobolia.

Following Michael's death, the following occurred:

(1)    On 5 September 1999 the executors of Michael's estate sold the 50,000 shares in Compact Ltd for £260,000, and the 50,000 shares in Diverse Inc for £120,000.

(2)    On 10 December 1999 Jade sold her 50,000 shares in Compact Ltd for £285,000.

Up to the date of his death Michael was a 40% taxpayer, Jade is also a 40% taxpayer. Neither Michael nor Jade has ever been a director or employee of either Compact Ltd or Diverse Inc.

Gobolian death duty of £35,000 was paid as a result of Michael's death. There is no double taxation treaty between the United Kingdom and Gobolia.

**Required:**

(a)    (i)    Calculate the IHT liabilities arising as a result of Michael's death on 30 June 1999. Your answer should state who is liable for the payment of each liability, and should show the due date of payment. You should ignore the IHT annual exemption in your answer and use £231,000 as the nil band wherever appropriate.

---

(ii)     State what IHT reliefs will be available as a result of the disposals by the executors of Michael's estate on 5 September 1999, and advise them of whether or not a claim would be beneficial in each case.                                                                                                                       **(16 marks)**

(b)     (i)     Assuming that holdover relief was *not claimed* in respect of the gift made by Michael to Jade on 10 July 1998, calculate Jade's CGT liability for 1999/00.

(ii)     Advise Jade and the executors of Michael's estate as to the tax implications arising from making a claim for holdover relief in respect of the gift on 10 July 1998. You should assume that if a holdover relief claim is made, then the value of Michael's estate will increase by the amount of the CGT no longer payable.

You should *ignore* the CGT annual exemption in your answer.                                                        **(9 marks)**
                                                                                                                                                **(Total 25 marks)**

---

## 42     (Question 6 of examination)

Basil Nadir is a computer programmer. Until 5 April 1999, Basil was employed by Ace Computers Ltd, but since then has worked independently from home. Basil's income for his first 12 months of trading to 5 April 2000 is forecast to be £60,000, of which 50% will be in respect of work done for Ace Computers Ltd. His expenditure for the year will be as follows:

(1)     Computer equipment costing £4,700 (inclusive of VAT) was purchased on 6 April 1999.

(2)     Basil uses two rooms of his eight room private residence exclusively for business purposes. The cost of light, heat and insurance of the house for the year will amount to £1,800 (inclusive of VAT of £100).

(3)     Basil's telephone bills currently amount to £250 per quarter. They were £100 per quarter up to 5 April 1999. Both figures are inclusive of VAT.

(4)     Basil owns a two year old motor car which originally cost £15,000. It was worth £10,000 on 6 April 1999. His motor expenses for the year will amount to £3,500 (inclusive of VAT of £400). Although Basil works from home, he has to visit his clients on a regular basis. His mileage for the year ended 5 April 2000 will be as follows:

| | |
|---|---|
| Visiting Ace Computers Ltd | 10,000 miles |
| Visiting other clients | 10,000 miles |
| Private use | 5,000 miles |

Basil spends 50% of his time working for Ace Computers Ltd, and since 6 April 1999 has been working for them on a 12 month contract to develop a taxation program for accountants. He visits the company's offices twice a week in respect of this contract. Apart from Ace Computers Ltd, Basil presently has five other clients.

On 8 August 1999, Ace Computers Ltd was the subject of an Inland Revenue PAYE compliance visit, and Basil's self-employed status in respect of his contract with the company was queried. The Inland Revenue have stated that they consider Basil to be an employee of Ace Computers Ltd for the purposes of both income tax and National Insurance contribution. Basil has agreed to refund Ace Computers Ltd for any tax liability that the company suffers if the Inland Revenue's view is upheld.

Basil has not yet registered for VAT. He is single, and has no other income or outgoing. You should assume that today's date is 15 August 1999.

**Required:**

(a)     Briefly discuss the criteria that will be used in deciding whether Basil will be classified as employed or self-employed in respect of his contract with Ace Computers Ltd. Your answer should include:

(i)     an explanation as to the likely reasons why the Inland Revenue have queried Basil's self-employed status; and

(ii)    advice to Basil and Ace Computers Ltd as to the criteria that they could put forward in order to justify Basil's self-employed status;    **(9 marks)**

(b)    Calculate Basil's liability to income tax and National Insurance for 1999/00 if he is treated as self-employed in respect of his contract with Ace Computers Ltd, and advise him of by how much this liability will increase if he is instead treated as employed.

You should ignore the implications of VAT, and should note that Basil's self-employed status in respect of his contracts with his other five clients is not in dispute.    **(10 marks)**

(c)    Assuming that Basil is classified as self-employed in respect of his contract with Ace Computers Ltd, state when he will have to compulsorily register for VAT, explain the implications of being so registered, and advise him of whether or not it would be beneficial to voluntarily register before that date. You should assume that Basil's income accrues evenly throughout the year.    **(6 marks)**

**(Total 25 marks)**

# ANSWERS TO DECEMBER 1995 EXAMINATION

## 37 (Answer 1 of examination)

### Examiner's comments and marking guide

Part (a) tested candidates' ability to calculate the corporation tax liability of a company with a long period of account. Part (b) tested candidates' knowledge of the implications of acquiring a subsidiary company, and in particular the related anti-avoidance provisions.

This was a popular question, being attempted by the majority of candidates. There were some very good answers to this question, but a surprising number of candidates were not aware that an 18 month period of account must be split into two accounting periods. Instead, corporation tax was calculated for one 18 month accounting period. This is a matter of some concern considering that candidates will have encountered this topic at paper 7 - Tax Framework. Part (a), apart from the point already mentioned, was generally well answered. Many candidates gave away easy marks by not mentioning the due dates of the different corporation tax liabilities. The treatment of the Schedule A loss and the capital loss also caused a certain amount of confusion. Part (b) was generally answered quite badly. Little knowledge was demonstrated of pre-entry losses, although it is appreciated that this is a fringe area of the syllabus. However, there is no such excuse for the carry forward of trading losses. This aspect was often completely ignored.

| | | Marks |
|---|---|---|
| (a) | *Preparing one set of accounts* | |
| | D1 profits/Capital allowances | 3 |
| | Schedule A | 2 |
| | Capital gain | 1 |
| | Corporation tax | 1 |
| | Summary | 1 |
| | *Preparing separate accounts for the two periods* | |
| | D1 profits/Capital allowances | 3 |
| | Schedule A | 1 |
| | Capital gain | 1 |
| | Corporation tax | 2 |
| | Summary | 1 |
| | Items carried forward | 1 |
| | Overall conclusion | 1 |
| | | — |
| | Available | 18 |
| | | — |
| | Maximum | 17 |
| | | — |
| (b) | Group relief | 2 |
| | Carry forward of trading loss | 3 |
| | Capital losses | 3 |
| | | — |
| | Available | 8 |
| | | — |
| | Maximum | 8 |
| | | — |
| | Available | 26 |
| | | — |
| | Maximum | 25 |
| | | — |

(Certain minor aspects of the original questions and answer have been edited out as being currently outside the syllabus).

( **Step by step answer plan** )

**Overview**

Part (a) is a fairly conventional exercise in CT computations. It hinges around choosing between taxing an 18 month period of profit either as 12 and then 6 month APs or as 6 then 12 month APs. In the first instance a single set of accounts are drawn up for 18 months and these are automatically taxed by apportioning results into the first 12 months and last 6 months. The alternative situation is achieved by preparing accounts for the first 6 months then annually.

Part (b) requires a discussion of group taxation relevant to a proposed acquisition. The points to discuss are carefully spelt out.

**[Step 1]**  Read the question carefully to ensure you understand the main requirement of part (a).

**[Step 2]**  Head up your answer to part (a) (i) with a column for each AP.

**[Step 3]**  You need a working note to:

- Apportion trading profits prior to CAs
- Compute CAs on plant for each AP
- Compute net rental income and give reason for loss set-off

**[Step 4]**  Fill in a standard PCTCT layout and compute CT for each AP cross referencing to working notes as appropriate.

**[Step 5]**  Whether one course of action is 'beneficial' depends partly on when tax is due as well as on the amount of tax payable so include pay days with your summary of tax due under part (a) (i).

**[Step 6]**  Repeat the general approach for part (a) (ii) - note profits are not time apportioned.

**[Step 7]**  Summarise the tax due and the pay days.

**[Step 8]**  High light any other differences such as the unrelieved capital losses c/f under option (ii).

**[Step 9]**  State clearly which option is preferable and give reasons.

**[Step 10]**  For part (b) list out the effect of the proposed acquisition using a separate paragraph heading for each of:

- Trading losses - para each for surrender and for own use
- Capital losses.

**[Step 11]**  Reread the question to ensure you have dealt with all relevant matters.

( **The examiner's answer** )

(a)    (i)    **Preparing one set of accounts for the 18 month period to 31 December 1999**

Highrise Ltd's 18 month period of account will be split into two accounting periods. The company's corporation tax liability for each accounting period will be as follows:

|  | *Year ended*<br>*30 June 1999*<br>*£* | *Period ended*<br>*31 December 1999*<br>*£* |
|---|---|---|
| Schedule D Case I profits (W1) | 288,000 | 144,000 |
| Capital allowances (W2) | 53,000 | 10,875 |
|  | 235,000 | 133,125 |

---

| | | |
|---|---|---|
| Schedule A (W3) | 15,000 | – |
| Capital gain (42,000 – 25,000) | 17,000 | – |
| PCTCT | 267,000 | 133,125 |
| FII $\left(11,250 \times {}^{100}\!/_{90}\right)$ | 12,500 | – |
| Profit | 279,500 | 133,125 |
| Corporation tax at 20.75%/20% | 55,402 | 26,625 |

**Summary**

| | | £ |
|---|---|---|
| MCT | due 1 April 2000 | 55,402 |
| | due 1 October 2000 | 26,625 |
| | | 82,027 |

WORKINGS

(W1)  Schedule D Case I profits

Total Schedule D Case I profits 141,000 + 126,000 + 165,000 = £432,000

| | |
|---|---|
| Year ended 30 June 1999 | $432,000 \times {}^{12}\!/_{18} = 288,000$ |
| Period ended 31 December 1999 | $432,000 \times {}^{6}\!/_{18} = 144,000$ |

(W2)  Capital allowances

| | £ |
|---|---|
| Year ended 30 June 1999 | |
| WDV b/f | 20,000 |
| Addition 31 May 1999 | 120,000 |
| | 140,000 |
| WDA – 25% on £20,000 | (5,000) |
| FYA – 40% on £120,000 | (48,000) |
| | 87,000 |
| Period ended 31 December 1999 | |
| WDA - 25% $\times {}^{6}\!/_{12}$ | 10,875 |
| WDV c/f | 76,125 |

(W3)  Schedule A

| | £ |
|---|---|
| Ampton - rental income 48,000 $\times {}^{6}\!/_{12}$ | 24,000 |
| Bodford - allowable loss | 9,000 |
| Schedule A assessment | 15,000 |

The cost of decorating the Bodford building is allowable on 'business' expense principles. The allowable loss is automatically set off against the rental income from the Ampton building as all lettings are treated as a single business.

(ii)  **Preparing separate accounts for the six month period to 31 December 1998 and for the year ended 31 December 1999**

Highrise Ltd's corporation tax liability for the two accounting periods will be as follows:

|  | *Period ended*<br>*31 December 1998*<br>£ | *Year ended*<br>*31 December 1999*<br>£ |
|---|---|---|
| Schedule D Case I profits (W1) | 141,000 | 291,000 |
| Capital allowances (W2) | 2,500 | 52,375 |
|  | 138,500 | 238,625 |
| Schedule A profit/(loss) (W3) | 24,000 | (9,000) |
| Capital gain | 42,000 | – |
| PCTCT | 204,500 | 229,625 |
| FII $\left(11,250 \times {}^{100}/_{90}\right)$ | – | 12,500 |
| Profit | 204,500 | 242,125 |
| Corporation tax at 31% | 63,395 |  |
| Tapering relief $^1/40$ (750,000 – 204,500) | 13,637 |  |
|  | 49,758 |  |
| Corporation tax at 20.25% |  | 46,499 |
| CT liability | 49,758 | 46,499 |

**Summary**

|  |  | £ |
|---|---|---|
| MCT | due 1 October 1999 | 49,758 |
|  | due 1 October 2000 | 46,499 |
|  |  | 96,257 |

WORKINGS

(W1)    Schedule D Case I profits

Period ended 31 December 1998 = £141,000
Year ended 31 December 1999 126,000 + 165,000 = £291,000

(W2)    Capital allowances

|  | £ |
|---|---|
| Period ended 31 December 1998 |  |
| WDV b/f | 20,000 |
| WDA - 25% × $^6/_{12}$ | (2,500) |
|  | 17,500 |
| Year ended 31 December 1999 |  |
| Addition 31 May 1999 | 120,000 |
|  | 137,500 |
| WDA - 25% on £17,500 | (4,375) |
| FYA – 40% on £120,000 | (48,000) |
| WDV c/f | 85,125 |

(W3)    Schedule A loss

The cost of decorating the Bodford building is allowable on 'business' expense principles. The allowable loss is automatically set off against Highrise Ltd's other income for the year ended 31 December 1999.

The following will be carried forward:

-       capital loss of £25,000.

Preparing one set of accounts for the 18 month period to 31 December 1999 appears to be beneficial, as it results in an overall tax saving of £14,230 (96,257 − 82,027), and also a later due date for some of the corporation tax liability (1 April 2000 compared to 1 October 1999). (However, under the lower tax option the capital loss of £25,000 is extinguished and the unrelieved balance on the capital allowance pool to carry forward is £9,000 (£85,125 − £76,125) lower.)

(b)     **Group relief**

Shortie Ltd will be able to group relieve its trading loss to Highrise Ltd under S402 ICTA 1988. Group relief will be limited to the lower of £38,750 $(155,000 \times \frac{3}{12})$ and $\frac{3}{12}$ of Highrise Ltd's PCTCT for the year ended 31 December 2000.

**Carry forward of trading loss**

After claiming group relief, the balance of Shortie Ltd's trading loss can be carried forward under S393(1) ICTA 1988 against future trading profits. However, as there has been a change in the company's ownership, the carry forward will be disallowed under S768 ICTA 1988 if there is major change in the nature or conduct of Shortie Ltd's trade within three years of 1 January 2000.

**Capital losses**

Shortie Ltd's capital loss of £37,000 is a pre-entry loss. It will also be necessary to ascertain the amount of pre-entry capital loss in respect of the 10% shareholding in Minute Ltd. This can either be done on a time basis when the shareholding is disposed of, or based on the market value of the shareholding as at 1 January 2000. It will not be possible for Highrise Ltd to utilise these pre-entry capital losses against any gain arising on the disposal of its 5% shareholding in Tiny Ltd, by transferring the shareholding to Shortie Ltd (at no gain no loss) prior to disposal outside of the group.

---

**Did you answer the question?**

You were not required to comment on the effect that the acquisition has on the small company band limits.

---

| **38** | **(Answer 2 of examination)** |
| --- | --- |

---

**( Examiner's comments and marking guide )**

**Part (a) tested candidates' knowledge of year end tax planning measures both for an individual and for a company. Part (b) tested candidates' knowledge of the need for authorisation under the Financial Services Act 1986, and the implications of carrying on investment business without being authorised.**

This was another popular question, although the answers of many candidates lacked sufficient depth to score good marks. In part (a), the timing aspect of the tax planning measures was generally ignored. This was particularly the case as regards the drawing of a year end bonus either by way of additional remuneration or as a dividend. The advice given by many candidates in respect of the investments held was very weak, and simply consisted of a discussion of the rules applicable to the various investments without any consideration of maturity dates or tax planning measures that could be taken. Those candidates who wrote at length about the enterprise investment scheme and venture capital trusts cannot expect to score good marks on a question of this nature. The answers to Part (b) were generally quite poor, with a large percentage of candidates believing that membership of the ACCA itself is sufficient in order to conduct investment business.

---

| | | | Marks |
|---|---|---|---|
| (a) | (1) | *Additional drawings* | |
| | | Cost of directors' remuneration | 2 |
| | | Timing | 1 |
| | | Cost of dividend | 2 |
| | | Timing | 2 |
| | | Conclusion | 1 |
| | (2) | *Fixed asset additions* | |
| | | New computer equipment | 1 |
| | | New office building | 2 |
| | (3) | *Investments* | |
| | | Ordinary shares | 2 |
| | | National Savings Certificates | 2 |
| | (4) | *Kate's marriage* | |
| | | Annual exemption/marriage exemption | 2 |
| | | PET/tax saving | 2 |
| | | | — |
| | | Available | 19 |
| | | | — |
| | | Maximum | 18 |
| | | | — |

| | | | Marks |
|---|---|---|---|
| (b) | *Authorisation under FSA 1986* | | |
| | Investments | | 1 |
| | Investment activities | | 2 |
| | Excluded activities | | 1 |
| | Carrying on of a business | | 1 |
| | Conclusion | | 1 |
| | | | — |
| | Available | | 6 |
| | | | — |
| | Maximum | | 5 |
| | | | — |
| | *Implications of non-authorisation* | | |
| | Criminal offence | | 1 |
| | Agreements | | 1 |
| | | | — |
| | Maximum/Available | | 2 |
| | | | — |
| | Available | | 33 |
| | | | — |
| | Maximum | | 25 |
| | | | — |

## ( Step by step answer plan )

**Overview**

The first part of this question required a blend of computation and comment on a number of broadly separate proposals. For the second part you have to know the basic FSA 1986 rules on conducting investment business. The structure of the required answer is fairly clear from the layout of the question.

**Step 1**   Read part (a) of the question and the requirements carefully. In particular note that 'you should pay particular attention to timing'. Also, tax calculations are clearly expected wherever appropriate.

**Step 2**   Note the first two 'scene setting' paragraphs. In particular, Sonya has full control over the company and has one close relative, an adult daughter.

**Step 3**   Work through the 4 main information paragraphs making the appropriate planning points backed up with computations and pay days as necessary.

**Step 4** Answer part (b). Part (b) (i) will require an edited version of your study text tailored to the specific situations in part (a).

**Step 5** Part (b) (ii) is easy to overlook but offers 2 marks for little effort.

## The examiner's answer

(a) **Additional drawings from Wealthy Ltd**

If the additional drawings are taken as directors' remuneration, the total cost will be £89,760 as follows:

|  | £ |
|---|---|
| Gross remuneration = $60,000 \times \frac{100}{60}$ | 100,000 |
| Employers Class 1 NIC at 12.2% | 12,200 |
|  | 112,200 |
| Corporation tax relief at 20% | 22,440 |
|  | 89,760 |

For Sonya, the timing of the payment is not critical as her tax liability of £40,000 (100,000 – 60,000) will be due under PAYE 14 days after the tax month in which the payment is made. There is no additional employees Class 1 National Insurance contribution liability as Sonya has already exceeded the upper limit of £26,000. As regards Wealthy Ltd, the payment should be made by 31 January 2001 (ie, within 9 months of its year end on 30 April 2000). Relief is obtained against its corporation tax liability for that year if it is either paid by the year end or provided for in the accounts and paid within 9 months of the year end.

If the additional drawings are taken as a dividend, the gross dividend will be £88,889 being the cash required grossed up for both higher rate tax and the tax credit $\left(60,000 \times \frac{100}{67.5}\right)$. The total cost will be £80,000 as follows:

|  | £ |
|---|---|
| Cash required | 60,000 |
| Higher rate liability [88,889 at (32½ – 10%)] | 20,000 |
|  | 80,000 |

The dividend should be paid after 5 April 2000. For Sonya, the dividend will then fall into the tax year 2000/01 rather than 1999/00, and her higher rate tax liability of £20,000 will be deferred for one year.

Since the payment of a dividend results in an overall tax saving of £9,760 (89,760 – 80,000), and also a later payment date for Sonya's higher rate tax liability, this is the preferred alternative.

**New computer equipment**

The new computer equipment should be purchased before 30 April 2000. Wealthy Ltd will then benefit from the capital allowances for that year, which will reduce its corporation tax liability by £6,400 (80,000 × 40% = £32,000 at 20%).

**New office building**

Capital allowances will not be available in respect of the new freehold office building, and so the timing of its purchase is not important. It would probably not be beneficial for Sonya to purchase the office building and then to rent it to Wealthy Ltd. The rent paid by Wealthy Ltd would only attract corporation tax relief at the rate of 20%, whilst the rent received by Sonya would be assessed to income tax under Schedule A at the rate of 40%.

---

**Did you answer the question?**

You were not required to comment on the longer term capital gains or IHT aspects of keeping the office building outside the company nor on the Schedule A interest relief for related borrowings nor NIC advantages of taking out rent from the company.

---

### Ordinary shares

Sonya has not yet utilised her CGT annual exemption of £7,100 for 1999/00. She should therefore consider reviewing her portfolio, and selling sufficient shares to realise gains of £7,100, and reinvesting the proceeds. She must not reinvest in the same shares within 30 days, but can, of course, reinvest in other companies in the same industry sectors. The transactions should be carried out by 5 April 2000. This will not result in any immediate tax saving, but should save tax of up to £2,840 (7,100 at 40%) at some future date.

### National Savings Certificates

Sonya's National Savings Certificates will come to the end of their five year investment period on 31 January 2000. After this date, the investment will continue to earn interest, but this will be at the general extension rate which is uncompetitive. Sonya should therefore either encash the National Savings Certificates or reinvest into a current issue. As Sonya is a 40% taxpayer, she would probably be advised to reinvest in a current issue. As this is a reinvestment, Sonya could also invest a further £10,000.

---

**Did you answer the question?**

You were specifically only required to cover the information in the question and should therefore not have mentioned other forms of investment such as Unit or Investment Trusts or VCTs or unquoted shares qualifying for EIS relief.

---

### Kate's marriage

Sonya has not utilised her IHT annual exemption of £3,000 for either 1998/99 or 1999/00. She should therefore make a gift of at least £6,000 to Kate by 5 April 2000 to do so. The balance of the £20,000 can be gifted on 30 April 2000. This will utilise Sonya's £3,000 annual exemption for 2000/01, and a further £5,000 will be exempt as a gift in consideration of marriage. Therefore, only £6,000 (20,000 − 6,000 − 3,000 − 5,000) of the gift will be a PET, and this will also be exempt provided Sonya lives until 30 April 2007 being seven years after the date of the gift. The potential saving of IHT if Sonya were to die within three years of making the gift is £5,600 (20,000 − 6,000 at 40%).

---

**Did you answer the question?**

You are not required to consider how Sonya might fund the gift nor whether the gift should be other than cash.

---

(b)     (i)     There are four basic questions that must be considered in deciding if authorisation is necessary:

(1)     Do the activities involve investments as defined by the Financial Services Act 1986? Since the definition of investments includes shares (National Savings Certificates are not included), the answer to this is yes.

(2)     Are the activities investment activities? The definition of investment activities is extremely wide, and any specific advice in respect of particular investments would probably be included. However, advising on the tax implications of buying and selling an investment would not normally be investment advice.

(3)     Are the activities excluded? Advising on the transfer of an investment by way of a gift would be excluded, but the other activities would not be.

(4)     Do the activities constitute the carrying on of a business? Provided that Sonya is not a friend or relative who is not otherwise a client, and who will not be charged a fee, the answer is yes.

---

Unless the advice given is restricted merely to the tax implications, it would appear that a certified accountant would have to be authorised to conduct investment business under the Financial Services Act 1986 in order to give the advice to Sonya.

(ii)     Anybody who carries on investment business without being authorised to do so under the Financial Services Act 1986 commits a criminal offence, with a maximum penalty of two years imprisonment and/or an unlimited fine.

Any agreement entered into by an unauthorised person is unenforceable by that person. The client or customer may take civil action in the courts to recover any money that they have paid, and to seek compensation for any losses that they have suffered.

---

## 39     (Answer 3 of examination)

### ( Examiner's comments and marking guide )

Part (a) tested candidates' knowledge of the commencement of a business under the CYB rules, including the utilisation of losses. Part (b) tested candidates' knowledge of the CGT implications arising on the gift of a business, including retirement relief. Part (c) tested candidates' knowledge of the IHT implications arising on the gift of a business, including business property relief. Given that this question mainly consisted of topics covered at paper 7, it was surprising that it was not more popular.

Answers to the question were quite variable, reflecting the fact that it was often the third of fourth choice question. There were a number of very good answers to part (a), although the different loss relief claims were generally not dealt with in sufficient depth. Part (b) was generally well answered. The most common mistake was to apply retirement relief as if the business was a company (by calculating the proportion of the gain relating to chargeable business assets). Most candidates mentioned gift relief, but could not calculate the proportion of the gain that could be held over. Answers to part (c) were often disappointing , with far too many candidates not appreciating that the transfer was a PET. The purchase of the farm land and buildings at agricultural value, and the consequent implications for APR and BPR, confused most candidates. As in previous papers, there are still candidates who are confusing the different reliefs available (such as retirement relief and BPR), and therefore cannot expect to pass this paper.

|  |  | *Marks* |
|---|---|---|
| (a) | *Income tax - Simon* | |
| | Assessments | 1 |
| | Capital allowances | 1 |
| | Trading loss - s385 claim | 1 |
| | Trading loss - s381 claim | 2 |
| | | — |
| | Available | 5 |
| | | — |
| | Maximum | 5 |
| | | — |
| (b) | Connected persons | 1 |
| | Farm land/buildings - capital gain | 1 |
| | Retirement relief | 2 |
| | Gift of business assets | 2 |
| | Investments - capital gain | 1 |
| | CGT liability | 1 |
| | Tax planning | 1 |
| | Base cost | 1 |
| | | — |
| | Available | 10 |
| | | — |
| | Maximum | 7 |
| | | — |
| (c) | PET | 1 |
| | Business property relief | 2 |
| | Agricultural property relief | 1 |

| | |
|---|---:|
| IHT liability | 2 |
| Due date | 1 |
| Tax planning | 2 |
| | —— |
| Available | 9 |
| | —— |
| Maximum | 6 |
| | —— |
| Available | 24 |
| | —— |
| Maximum | 18 |
| | —— |

## ( Step by step answer plan )

### Overview

This question tests your knowledge of how income tax, CGT and IHT impact on the disposal of a business to a relative but each tax is dealt with in a separate part.

**Step 1** Read the question carefully to understand the main points of the proposed business succession and note in particular that you are asked for any tax planning points you consider relevant.

**Step 2** For part (a) compute the capital allowances and losses relevant to Simon's commencement to trade.

**Step 3** Consider the best use of the losses and advise accordingly, showing the refunds of tax that will be generated.

**Step 4** Ensure your answer to part (a) carries any necessary explanations such as a brief comment on why Simon has used his trading loss in a particular way.

**Step 5** For part (b), compute the chargeable gains on the farm buildings after retirement relief, gift relief and taper relief. Then compute the gain on the investments.

**Step 6** Compute the CGT liability for Fred.

**Step 7** Comment on the possibility of increasing gift relief by re-allocating the consideration paid by Simon.

**Step 8** State the base costs of the assets acquired by Simon.

**Step 9** Answer part (c). In particular, compute the IHT likely if Fred does die within 5 years.

**Step 10** Again, ensure that the necessary extras such as pay days, reliefs comment on steps taken (or not taken) and tax planning opportunities are adequately covered.

## ( The examiner's answer )

(a)     **Income tax implications - Simon**

*Schedule D Case I assessable amounts*

Simon's assessable amounts for 1999/00 and 2000/01 will both be nil, as he will have a loss for the first 12 months of trading.

*Capital allowances*

**Year ended 31 December 2000**

|  | £ |
|---|---|
| WDV b/f | 24,000 |
| WDA - 25% | 6,000 |
| WDV c/f | 18,000 |

Since Fred and Simon are connected persons an election to transfer the plant and machinery at written down value should be made so as to avoid a balancing charge for Fred. The election must be made jointly by 31 December 2001. First year allowances are not available on plant acquired from a connected person.

*Trading loss*

Simon has a loss of £18,000 (12,000 plus capital allowances of 6,000) for the year ended 31 December 2000. Since a claim under S385 ICTA 1988 to carry this forward against future trading profits would not obtain relief until 2001/02 at the earliest, he should claim under S381 ICTA 1988 as follows:

1999/00  18,000 × $\frac{3}{12}$ = £4,500 set off against income 1996/97
2000/01  18,000 − 4,500 = £13,500 set off against income of 1997/98

This should result in an immediate tax refund of £7,200 (18,000 at 40%).

---

**Did you answer the question?**

You are not required to consider repayment supplement payable on the refund of tax paid in earlier years.

---

(b)     **Capital gains tax - Fred**

Since Fred and Simon are connected persons, the market value of the assets transferred will be used, rather than the sale proceeds.

*Farm land and farm buildings*

Fred is over 50 years old and has owned the business for more than 10 years. He will therefore qualify for maximum retirement relief. Provided that Fred and Simon jointly elect, gift relief will also be available.

|  |  | £ | £ |
|---|---|---|---|
| Deemed proceeds |  |  | 600,000 |
| Market value 31 March 1982 |  |  | 115,000 |
|  |  |  | 485,000 |
| Indexation 115,000 × $\dfrac{162.6 - 79.44}{79.44}$ (1.047) |  |  | 120,405 |
|  |  |  | 364,595 |
| Retirement relief | 200,000 × 100% | 200,000 |  |
|  | 364,595 − 200,000 = 164,595 × 50% | 82,297 |  |
|  |  |  | 282,297 |
|  |  |  | 82,298 |
| Gain held over (note) |  |  | 4,595 |
| Chargeable gain |  |  | 77,703 |
| Tapered to 85% |  |  | 66,048 |

---

The consideration paid by Simon exceeds the market value at 31 March 1982 and the retirement relief available by £77,703 (475,000 − 115,000 − 282,297). Therefore, only £4,595 (82,298 − 77,703) of the gain qualifies to be held over as a gift of business assets.

*Investments*

|  | £ |
|---|---:|
| Deemed proceeds | 250,000 |
| Cost | 35,000 |
|  | 215,000 |
| Indexation $35,000 \times \dfrac{162.6 - 101.9}{101.9}$ | 20,849 |
|  | 194,151 |

*CGT liability*

|  | £ |
|---|---:|
| Chargeable gains 66,048 + 194,151 | 260,199 |
| Annual exemption | 7,100 |
|  | 253,099 |

|  | £ |
|---|---:|
| Capital gains tax: | |
| 19,720 [28,000 - (10,000 + 4,000 − 5,720)] at 20% | 3,944 |
| 233,379 (253,099 − 19,720) at 40% | 93,352 |
|  | 97,296 |

The CGT payable will be £97,296. It would be beneficial if at least £77,703 of the consideration paid by Simon was allocated to other assets. The hold over of the gain on the farm land and farm buildings would then not be restricted, and the CGT payable would be reduced by £66,048 × 40% = £26,419.

**Capital gains tax - Simon**

Simon will take over the farm land and farm buildings at a base cost of £595,405 (600,000 − 4,595), and the investments at base cost of £250,000.

(c)    **Inheritance tax**

The transfer of the business to Simon will be a PET. It will become chargeable as a result of Fred dying within seven years of 31 December 1999. Business property relief at the rate of 100% will be available in respect of all of the assets transferred, except for the investments. This is provided that the business is still owned by Simon at the date of Fred's death, and is still a qualifying business at that date. Agricultural property relief is not relevant, because Simon has purchased the farm land and farm buildings at their agricultural value. Assuming that Fred dies during 2004 (ie, between four and five years after 31 December 1999), the IHT liability arising on the PET as a result of his death will be £5,040 as follows:

|  |  | £ | £ |
|---|---|---:|---:|
| Value transferred | (1,000,000 − 475,000) |  | 525,000 |
| Business property relief | (525,000 − 250,000) |  | 275,000 |
|  |  |  | 250,000 |
| Annual exemptions | 1998/99 | 3,000 | |
|  | 1999/00 | 3,000 | |
|  |  |  | 6,000 |
| Chargeable transfer |  |  | 244,000 |

|  | | £ |
|---|---|---|
| IHT liability | 231,000 at nil | **Nil** |
| | 13,000 at 40% | 5,200 |
| Tapering relief at 40% | | 2,080 |
| | | 3,120 |

The IHT liability will be payable by Simon, and will be due six months after the end of the month in which Fred dies.

It would be beneficial if £244,000 of the consideration paid by Simon was allocated to the investments. This is because all of the business assets qualify for either business property relief or agricultural property relief at the rate of 100%. The IHT liability would then be nil and the £231,000 nil band would be available to set against the death estate.

---

## 40   (Answer 4 of examination)

### Examiner's comments and marking guide

Part (a) tested candidates' ability to calculate double taxation relief for both an individual and for a company. Part (b) tested candidates' knowledge of the controlled foreign company legislation. Part (c) tested candidates' ability to advise individuals on their income tax position during a period of absence from the UK.

This was the least popular question on the paper, and was generally answered quite badly. Part (a) produced some extremely poor answers, with many candidates not appreciating that relief for underlying tax is only applicable to companies. The extraction of funds from the company was virtually ignored. Answers to part (b) were generally better, although a common mistake was to discuss how a company's residence is established, rather than how classification of controlled foreign company status is established. In part (c), there was lot of confusion between being treated as non resident in the UK, and the 100% deduction for a 365 day qualifying period (a relief no longer available). Very few candidates appreciated that it was possible to elect to have mortgage interest allowed as a deductible expense.

| | | *Marks* |
|---|---|---|
| (a) | *Investment made personally* | |
| | Calculation of post-tax income | 1 |
| | *Investment made by limited company* | |
| | Relief for underlying tax | 1 |
| | Corporation tax rate | 1 |
| | Calculation of post-tax income | 2 |
| | *Extraction of income* | |
| | Directors remuneration | 1 |
| | Normal dividend | 1 |
| | Conclusion | 1 |
| | | — |
| | Available | 8 |
| | | — |
| | Maximum | 6 |
| | | — |
| (b) | *Implications* | |
| | Definition of low tax country | 1 |
| | Implications of classification as a CFC | 2 |
| | | |
| | *Exclusion tests* | |
| | Quotation/profit level | 1 |
| | Distribution policy | 2 |

|  |  |
|---|---|
| Exempt activities | 2 |
| Motive test | 1 |
|  | — |
| Available | 9 |
|  | — |
| Maximum | 6 |
|  | — |

(c)    *Francis Holm*

|  |  |
|---|---|
| Residence status | 1 |
| *Gaye Holm* |  |
| Abroad for a complete tax year | 2 |
| *Letting of main residence* |  |
| Liability to income tax | 1 |
| Deduction of tax | 1 |
| Personal allowances | 1 |
| *Mortgage interest* |  |
| Position under MIRAS | 1 |
| Schedule A election | 2 |
| Schedule A profit | 1 |
|  | — |
| Available | 10 |
|  | — |
| Maximum | 7 |
|  | — |
| Available | 27 |
|  | — |
| Maximum | 19 |
|  | — |

## Step by step answer plan

**Overview**

This is effectively three separate questions each requiring advice on overseas taxation. For part (a) the taxpayer is considering whether to invest directly in an overseas company or to invest through a UK company and extract the income from the UK company. Part (b) clearly requires a knowledge of CFCs and part (b) requires a discussion of the income tax implications for a couple planning a short period of absence abroad.

**Step 1**    For part (a) read the question carefully to visualise exactly what is proposed and the alternative steps for Angus to receive the net income from the overseas investment.

**Step 2**    Calculate the net income under option (i).

**Step 3**    Calculate the net income received by the company under option (ii) not forgetting the role of the underlying tax.

**Step 4**    Consider how Angus can extract this income from the company. The two obvious choices are by remuneration or by dividend. Note that the question discounts the need for detailed calculations.

**Step 5**    Comment on the advantage of using the investment company but also highlight the practical expense of this route.

**Step 6**    For part (b) produce the CFC points from your study notes relevant to this question. Essentially, describe the implications of CFC status and list the exclusion tests.

**Step 7**    Part (c) is the largest part of the question and you should take care to identify the questions it poses. A paragraph is clearly needed on each taxpayer and on the taxation of the letting income and on the treatment of the mortgage interest.

---

### The examiner's answer

(a)  **Investment made personally**

Angus' annual income tax liability will be as follows:

|  | £ |
| --- | --- |
| Schedule D Case V | 60,000 |
| Income tax at 32½% | 19,500 |
| Less: Double taxation relief (60,000 at 10%) | 6,000 |
| Income tax liability | 13,500 |

He will therefore have post-tax income of £40,500 pa (54,000 – 13,500).

**Investment made via a UK resident limited company**

The company would own over 10% of the share capital of Cedar Inc, so relief for underlying tax paid in Yenka will be available. The company would be subject to corporation tax at the rate of 30%, as it will be a close investment holding company. The company's UK corporation tax liability will be as follows:

|  | £ |
| --- | --- |
| Schedule D Case V $\left(60,000 \times {}^{100}\!/_{60}\right)$ | 100,000 |
| Corporation tax at 30% | 30,000 |
| Less: Double taxation relief |  |
| (6,000 + 40,000 = 46,000) restricted to: | 30,000 |
| Corporation tax liability | Nil |

The company will therefore have post-tax income of £54,000 pa. As regards this income being extracted by Angus, there are two main alternatives:

(i)  Draw director's remuneration. This will attract employers' Class 1 National Insurance contribution at the rate of 12.2% and excessive director's remuneration is not deductible for an investment company.

(ii)  Pay a normal dividend. This is preferable as NIC liability is avoided.

(b)  The aim of the controlled foreign company legislation is to prevent UK companies diverting income, which would otherwise be taxed in the UK, to a low tax country. A low tax country is one where the rate of tax is less than three-quarters of that which would have been payable on the equivalent profits in the UK.

In respect of any overseas subsidiary that is classified as a controlled foreign company, Elm plc has to assess itself to UK corporation tax on the profits of that subsidiary, rather than on the dividends remitted to the UK. However, relief would be given for any overseas tax paid.

An overseas subsidiary will avoid classification as a controlled foreign company if it can meet any one of five exclusion tests, which are:

(i)  It is quoted on a recognised stock exchange (this is unlikely to be relevant in this case).

(ii)  Its profits are less than £50,000 pa.

(iii)  It has an acceptable distribution policy, which means that 90% of their taxable profits less capital gains and foreign tax must be distributed.

---

(iv)     It is engaged in exempt activities.  This means having a business establishment in the relevant country, effectively managing its business affairs there, and not being engaged in a non-qualifying business.

(v)     It satisfies a motive test, whereby any reduction in UK taxation is minimal, or was not the main purpose of setting up the subsidiary.

(c)     **Francis Holm**

Francis will presumably have no emoluments whilst on holiday, and his residence status is therefore of minor importance.  However, he will probably remain resident in the UK if his 15 month period of absence does not span a complete tax year.  If his absence does span a complete tax year, then Francis will be not resident in the UK for that year: **Reed v Clark** (1985).

**Gayle Holm**

Gayle is going abroad to take up full-time employment.  If her 15 month period of absence spans a complete tax year, she will therefore (by extra-statutory concession) be regarded as not resident and not ordinarily resident in the UK from the date of her departure to the date of her return.  Non-residence status would remove Gayle's overseas emoluments from the scope of UK taxation.

If Gayle's 15 month period of absence does not span a complete tax year, then she will remain resident and ordinarily resident in the UK throughout the whole 15 month period.  Her emoluments will be assessed under Schedule E Case I.

**Letting of main residence**

Regardless of their residence status during the 15 month period of absence, both Francis and Gayle will be liable to UK income tax in respect of the Schedule A profits from letting their main residence.  This is because the income arises in the UK.  Rent paid to a non-UK resident is subject to deduction of tax at the basic rate, unless the Revenue approve a claim to have the rent paid gross.  Both Francis and Gayle will be entitled to personal allowances if they remain resident in the UK.  If they become non-UK resident, then they will still be able to claim for personal allowances if they are citizens of a state in the European Economic Area.

**Mortgage interest**

The position under the MIRAS arrangements is quite complicated, since Francis will be absent for a period of more than one year, and so his share of the property will no longer qualify as being used as a main residence.  In Gayle's case, her period of absence arises from employment, and the permitted period of absence is extended to four years.

However, relief under MIRAS is only at the rate of 10%, and Francis and Gayle would be advised to elect to have the mortgage interest allowed instead as a deductible expense in calculating their Schedule A profits.  Tax relief at a minimum rate of 23% will then be available.  The Schedule A profit for the 15 month period will be as follows:

|  | £ |
|---|---|
| Rental income (15 × 1,500) | 22,500 |
| Interest paid $\left(15 \times 180 \times \frac{100}{90}\right)$ | 3,000 |
| Profit | 19,500 |

| 41 | (Answer 5 of examination) |
|----|---------------------------|

Examiner's comments and marking guide

Part (a) tested candidates' ability to calculate the IHT liabilities arising on lifetime transfers and on death, and their knowledge of post mortem reliefs. Part (b) tested candidates' ability to calculate the CGT liability arising on a gift, and the implications of making a claim for holdover relief.

This was another popular question, and produced a number of good answers. A few candidates even scored maximum marks for this question. In part (a), the calculation of the related property valuation of the unquoted shares caused problems, and business property relief was often overlooked. A number of candidates did not separate lifetime gifts from the estate at death, and lost marks accordingly. Very few candidates were aware of the relief available for the disposal of property valued using the related property rules within three years of death. In part (b), there were again a few very good answers, but the claim for holdover relief confused many candidates.

|  |  | *Marks* |
|--|--|---------|
| (a) | *IHT liability - PET* | |
|  | Value of transfer | 1 |
|  | Business property relief | 1 |
|  | IHT liability | 1 |
|  | Liability/due date | 1 |
|  | *IHT liability - chargeable lifetime transfer* | |
|  | IHT due on lifetime transfer | 2 |
|  | Relief for fall in value | 2 |
|  | Additional IHT due at date of death | 1 |
|  | Liability/due date | 1 |
|  | *IHT liability - estate* | |
|  | Chargeable estate | 2 |
|  | Exempt legacy | 1 |
|  | Double taxation relief | 1 |
|  | Liability/due date | 1 |
|  | *Related property sold within three years of death* | |
|  | Description of relief | 1 |
|  | Calculation of relief | 2 |
|  | *Quoted investments sold within 12 months of death* | |
|  | Description of relief | 1 |
|  | Calculation of relief | 1 |
|  | | ___ |
|  | Available | 20 |
|  | | ___ |
|  | Maximum | 16 |
|  | | ___ |
| (b) | *Jades's CGT liability* | |
|  | Calculation of CGT liability | 2 |
|  | *Claim for holdover relief* | |
|  | Deduction of IHT liability | 1 |
|  | Calculation of heldover gain | 1 |
|  | Calculation of CGT liability | 2 |
|  | Additional IHT liability | 1 |
|  | Conclusion | 2 |
|  | | ___ |
|  | Maximum/Available | 9 |
|  | | ___ |
|  | Available | 29 |
|  | | ___ |
|  | Maximum | 25 |
|  | | ___ |

## Step by step answer plan

**Overview**

This is a fairly typical capital taxes question with an IHT death tax calculation, consideration of post-death reliefs, and a pre-death gift with a decision needed on whether to claim holdover relief.

**Step 1** The requirements are quite detailed so read these carefully to visualise the shape your answer will take.

**Step 2** Next read through the question to understand how the various details relate to the requirements. For example, the information on the lifetime gifts is clearly relevant to part (a) (i) and will have to be dealt with before calculating IHT on the death estate. One of the lifetime gifts is also relevant to part (b).

**Step 3** For your answer to part (a) (i), prepare your calculations on the lifetime gifts taking them in chronological order. Provide brief explanations where you think appropriate - eg, where claiming relief for pre-death fall in value. Don't overlook the instruction to ignore annual exemptions and to assume the current nil band applies. This last point is a common convention for paper 11.

**Step 4** Compute the IHT on the death estate and provide a brief explanation of your use of the foreign tax credit and the spouse exemption restricted for foreign domiciled wife.

**Step 5** Ensure you have said who is liable for any payments of IHT and when the amounts are payable.

**Step 6** IHT is a progressive tax with earlier events impacting on later transfers so, if you have time, re-read the question and the part (a) (i) requirements to ensure you have covered everything.

**Step 7** For part (a) (ii) state the two post-death reliefs relevant to this situation and advise on whether relief should be claimed.

**Step 8** For part (b) (i) calculate the CGT due on the gift to Jade not forgetting the instruction to ignore the CGT annual exemption.

**Step 9** For part (b) (ii) calculate the total of IHT and CGT payable with and without a claim for holdover relief on the gift to Jade providing brief explanations as appropriate.

**Step 10** Comment on whether or not a claim would be beneficial.

## The examiner's answer

(a)     (i)     The gift to Jade on 10 July 1998 will be a PET. No IHT liability will arise until Michael's death on 30 June 1999. Business property relief will be available, as the shares are still held by Jade at that date. The IHT position will be:

|  | £ |
|---|---|
| Value of shares held before the transfer (based on a 15% holding) 100,000 × £10.00 | 1,000,000 |
| Value of shares held after the transfer (based on a 10% holding) 50,000 × £7.00 | 350,000 |
| Value transferred | 650,000 |
| Business property relief - 100% | 650,000 |
| Chargeable transfer | Nil |

The gift to the discretionary trust on 19 August 1998 will be a chargeable lifetime transfer. Since Michael paid the IHT liability, the gift is grossed up as follows:

|  | | £ | £ |
|---|---|---|---|
| Net chargeable transfer | 100,000 × £3.10 | | 310,000 |
| IHT liability | 231,000 at nil | Nil | |
| | 79,000 × $^{20}/_{80}$ | 19,750 | |
| | | | 19,750 |
| Gross chargeable transfer | | | 329,750 |

The IHT liability of £19,750 would have been due on 30 April 1999.

At the date of Michael's death, the value of the shares in Diverse Inc has fallen to £2.80. The discretionary trust can therefore claim to have the additional IHT liability arising on 30 June 1999 to be based on this valuation. The additional IHT liability will be:

|  | £ |
|---|---|
| Gross chargeable transfer (as previous) | 329,750 |
| Less: Relief for fall in value | |
| 100,000 × £0.30 (3.10 – 2.80) | 30,000 |
| | 299,750 |

|  | £ |
|---|---|
| IHT liability 231,000 at nil | Nil |
| IHT liability 68,750 at 40% | 27,500 |
| IHT already paid | 19,750 |
| Additional liability | 7,750 |

The additional IHT liability will be payable by the discretionary trust on 31 December 1999.

The IHT liability due on Michael's estate will be as follows:

|  | £ | £ |
|---|---|---|
| Shares in Compact Ltd | | |
| (based on a 10% holding) 50,000 × £8.40 | | 420,000 |
| Business property relief - 100% | | 420,000 |
| | | – |
| Shares in Diverse Inc 50,000 × £2.80 | | 140,000 |
| Other assets | 850,000 | |
| Exempt legacy - Naomi | 55,000 | |
| | | 795,000 |
| Chargeable estate | | 935,000 |

|  | £ |
|---|---|
| IHT liability 935,000 at 40% | 374,000 |
| Double taxation relief (note) | (35,000) |
| | 339,000 |

The double taxation relief is the lower of the Gobolian tax paid of £35,000 and the UK IHT paid on the shares in Diverse Inc of £56,000 (140,000 at 40%). Only £55,000 of the legacy to Naomi is exempt, as she is not domiciled in the UK. The IHT liability of £339,000 will be payable by the executors of Michael's estate on the earlier of 31 December 1999 or the delivery of their account.

(ii) **Shares in Compact Ltd**

The shares in Compact Ltd were valued as related property in Michael's estate. Since they have been sold within three years of 30 June 1999 at less than their valuation using the related property rules, the executors of Michael's estate can claim for relief based on the unrelated value as at 30 June 1999, ie, 50,000 × £6.00 = £300,000. However, as 100% business property relief already applies, no further benefit arises.

**Shares in Diverse Inc**

The shares in Diverse Inc are quoted investments, and have been sold within 12 months of 30 June 1999 for less than their value at 30 June 1999. The executors of Michael's estate can claim for relief of £20,000 (140,000 − 120,000), which will result in a £8,000 (20,000 at 40%) reduction in the IHT liability of the estate.

(b) (i) **Jade - CGT liability 1999/00**

| | £ |
|---|---|
| Sale proceeds | 285,000 |
| Deemed cost | 250,000 |
| | 35,000 |
| Indexation | - |
| Chargeable gain | 35,000 |
| Capital gains tax at 40% | 14,000 |

(ii) If Jade and the executors of Michael's estate made a claim for holdover relief in respect of the gift on 10 July 1998, then Jade would be able to deduct the IHT payable as a result of the PET becoming chargeable, when calculating her CGT liability. However, as 100% business property relief is available, no IHT is payable in this case. Her CGT liability would be as follows:

| | £ | £ |
|---|---|---|
| Sale proceeds | | 285,000 |
| Deemed cost | 250,000 | |
| Gain held over (working) | 188,918 | |
| | | 61,082 |
| | | 223,918 |
| Indexation | | - |
| Chargeable gain | | 223,918 |
| Capital gains tax at 40% | | 89,567 |

The 1998/99 CGT liability of £75,567 (188,918 at 40%) due out of Michael's estate will no longer be payable. This will increase Michael's estate by £75,567, and additional IHT of £30,227 (75,567 at 40%) will be due. Claiming holdover relief would therefore result in an overall tax increase of £30,227 (89,567 − 119,794) as follows:

| | | | *No claim* | *Holdover relief claim* |
|---|---|---|---|---|
| | | | £ | £ |
| CGT liability | - | Jade | 14,000 | 89,567 |
| | - | Michael's estate | 75,567 | − |

| | | |
|---|---:|---:|
| Additional IHT liability | – | 30,227 |
| | 89,567 | 119,794 |

WORKING

| | £ |
|---|---:|
| Heldover gain | |
| Deemed consideration | |
| (based on a 5% holding) 50,000 × £5.00 | 250,000 |
| Cost | 50,000 |
| | 200,000 |
| Indexation 50,000 × $\dfrac{162.6 - 133.1}{133.1}$ | 11,082 |
| Chargeable gain held over | 188,918 |

---

## 42   (Answer 6 of examination)

**Examiner's comments and marking guide**

**Part (a) tested candidates' knowledge of the criteria used in deciding whether a person is employed or self-employed. Part (b) tested candidates' ability to calculate the income tax and NIC liabilities if a person is classed as self-employed, and the increase in those liabilities if that person is instead treated as employed. Part (c) tested candidates' knowledge of the VAT registration requirements, and to advise on whether or not voluntary registration would be beneficial.**

This was the most popular question on the paper, and was quite well answered by the majority of candidates attempting it. In part (a), a number of candidates wasted time by repeating the same point several times. The candidates who discussed the badges of trade did not score well on this part of the question. Part (b) was generally answered very well. However, NIC calculations continue to be a problem for some candidates, and the interaction of NIC classes 1, 2 and 4 caused a certain amount of confusion. In part (c), a number of candidates discussed aspects of VAT registration (such as the issue of VAT invoices) which were irrelevant to the question. A number of candidates were unable to advise on the date of compulsory VAT registration and the related notification requirements, which, being such an important aspect of VAT, is a matter of some concern.

| | | *Marks* |
|---|---|---:|
| (a) | Contract of service or contract for services | 1 |
| | The control test | 2 |
| | The mutual obligations test | 2 |
| | The economic reality test | 2 |
| | The integration test | 2 |
| | The Inland Revenue viewpoint | 1 |
| | Justifying self-employed status | 2 |
| | | — |
| | Available | 12 |
| | | — |
| | Maximum | 9 |
| | | — |
| (b) | *Treated as self-employed* | |
| | Deductible expenses | 2 |
| | Capital allowances | 2 |
| | Class 4 NIC | 1 |
| | Income tax liability | 1 |
| | Class 2 NIC | 1 |
| | *Treated as employed* | |
| | Travelling costs | 1 |
| | Capital allowances | 1 |

| | |
|---|---:|
| Additional NIC liability | 3 |
| Calculation of additional tax liabilities | 2 |
| | — |
| Available | 14 |
| | — |
| Maximum | 10 |
| | — |

(c)  VAT registration — 3

| | |
|---|---:|
| VAT registration | 3 |
| Implications of VAT registration | 4 |
| Voluntary registration | 3 |
| | — |
| Available | 10 |
| | — |
| Maximum | 6 |
| | — |
| Available | 36 |
| | — |
| Maximum | 25 |
| | — |

## ( Step by step answer plan )

### Overview

This question tests your knowledge of business taxation covering income tax, National Insurance and VAT. Part (a) is concerned with the topical problem of categorisation - ie, does employed or self-employed status apply? Part (b) requires a computation of an individual's tax burden assuming self-employed status applies with comment on the amount by which this would increase if he was re-categorised as an employee. Part (c) tests your understanding of VAT registration and its relevance to this situation.

**Step 1**   Read through the question and note carefully the precise requirements. They are detailed and it would be too easy to misinterpret the examiner's instructions.

**Step 2**   Answer part (a) noting that you have to discuss the categorisation criteria with reference to (i) why the Revenue have raised the point and (ii) the factors in Basil's favour.

**Step 3**   Produce your Taxable Income/IT & NIC computations assuming full self-employed status and assuming he is not registered for VAT. You might find it easier to produce the adjusted profit figure in a separate working but this is not necessary as long as the steps you take are clear.

**Step 4**   Discuss how your figures in step 3 would alter if his relationship with Ace Computers was categorised as employment.

**Step 5**   Summarise the tax/NIC effect of these changes.

**Step 6**   Answer part (c). Note that this is conveniently reduced to three matters:

- When must he register
- Implications of registering
- Should he register voluntarily before he has to.

## ( The examiner's answer )

(a)   When considering Basil's contract with Ace Computers Ltd, the essential distinction is whether it is a contract of service assessable under Schedule E, or a contract for services assessable under Schedule D. In making the distinction, there are a number of tests which must be considered. In the case of **Hall v Lorimer** (1995) it was stated that no single test will be conclusive, and a multiple test approach must be used.

### The control test

Does Ace Computers Ltd have control over Basil as to how his work is performed? Although important, this test is not decisive, since Basil would presumably have had a degree of independence as a computer programmer even when he was an employee. An important consideration in this case is the time that Basil spends at Ace Computers Ltd's offices. If his contract requires him to be there a specific two days each week, then this indicates a contract of service. If, however, he visits as necessary in order to complete the contract, then this indicates a contract for services.

### The mutual obligations test

Does Ace Computers Ltd have an obligation to provide work, and does Basil have an obligation to do the work provided? A yes answer will be an indication of a contract of service. Basil has only one contract with Ace Computers Ltd, which is for a period of 12 months. This is an indication of a contract of service. However the fact that he has five other clients indicates a contract for services. The situation contrasts with that in the case of **Fall v Hitchen** (1973), where a ballet dancer was held to be employed, as his contract provided for a first call on his time.

### The economic reality test

Do the activities of Basil form a profession in their own right? The case of **Market Investigations Ltd v Minister of Social Security** (1969) identified a number of factors that must be considered, although in **Hall v Lorimer** (1995) it was stated that this test may be of little relevance when considering someone involved in a profession. Basil has purchased computer equipment, and has the use of his own office. This indicates self-employment.

### The integration test

Is Basil an integral part of Ace Computers Ltd's business? A yes answer indicates a contract of service. It will be necessary to look at how Basil's position has changed from when he was an employee of Ace Computers Ltd. For example, if he is no longer entitled to sick pay or holiday pay, then this will indicate a contract for services.

### The Inland Revenue viewpoint

The Inland Revenue have presumably queried Basil's self-employed status because of his previous employment with Ace Computers Ltd, and the fact that 50% of his income is from his contract with them.

### Justifying Basil's self-employed status

In justifying his self-employed status, Basil and Ace Computers Ltd can point to the fact that he has five other clients, has purchased his own equipment, and has his own office. He also does not appear to be an integral part of Ace Computers Ltd's business.

However, there is no reason why a person cannot be classified as both employed and self-employed at the same time, and the deciding factor may be the terms of the actual contract between Basil and Ace Computers Ltd. For example, will Basil be paid the same fee if the new tax program is completed early?

---

**Did you answer the question?**

You are not required to list out the categorisation tests in general terms. They must only be discussed in the context of the question.

---

**Did you answer the question?**

You are not required to discuss the tax advantages of self-employed status.

---

(b)    If Basil is classified as self-employed, all of his income will be assessed under Schedule D Case II. The costs of running an office from home, and the costs of travelling between there and the offices of Ace Computers Ltd should be deductible. Basil's liability to income tax and National Insurance contributions for 1999/00 will therefore be as follows:

---

|  | £ | £ |
|---|---|---|
| Income |  | 60,000 |
| **Expenses** |  |  |
| Use of office $\left(1,800 \times \tfrac{2}{8}\right)$ | 450 |  |
| Telephone $((250 - 100) \times 4)$ | 600 |  |
| Motor expenses $\left(3,500 \times \dfrac{20,000}{25,000}\right)$ | 2,800 |  |
| **Capital allowances** |  |  |
| Computer equipment $(4,700 \times 40\%)$ | 1,880 |  |
| Motor car $\left(10,000 \times 25\% \times \dfrac{20,000}{25,000}\right)$ | 2,000 |  |
|  |  | 7,730 |
| Schedule D Case II |  | 52,270 |
| Personal allowance |  | 4,335 |
| Taxable income |  | 47,935 |

|  |  | £ |
|---|---|---|
| Income tax: | 1,500 at 10% | 150 |
|  | 26,500 at 23% | 6,095 |
|  | 19,935 at 40% | 7,974 |
|  |  | 14,219 |
| Class 2 NIC 52 at £6.55 |  | 341 |
| Class 4 NIC 26,000 – 7,530 at 6% |  | 1,108 |
| Total liability to income tax and NIC |  | 15,668 |

If Basil is classified as employed in respect of his contract with Ace Computers Ltd, then his tax liabilities will increase as a result of the following:

(i)    It is likely that Basil's travelling costs between home and the offices of Ace Computers Ltd will not be deductible. This amounts to £1,400 (3,500 × 10,000/25,000). The capital allowances in respect of Basil's motor car will correspondingly be reduced by £1,000 (10,000 × 25% × 10,000/25,000).

(ii)   Basil will be liable to the maximum employee's Class 1 National Insurance contribution in respect of his £30,000 Schedule E earnings from Ace Computers Ltd. This amounts to £2,256 [(52 × £434 × 10%)]. Since Class 2 National Insurance contribution and Class 4 National Insurance contribution are not payable if the maximum Class 1 NIC is paid, this results in an increased NIC liability of £807 (2,256 – 341 – 1,108).

The increase in Basil's total tax liability for 1999/00 is therefore £1,767 as follows:

|  | £ |
|---|---|
| Motor expenses disallowed (1,400 at 40%) | 560 |
| Reduction in capital allowances claim (1,000 at 40%) | 400 |
| Increase in National Insurance contribution | 807 |
|  | 1,767 |

**Did you answer the question?**

You could completely rework the Taxable Income/IT & NIC computations but this would be time consuming and is not required. Also, the question implies that you explain how any differences arise - which would add to the work needed if you followed this approach.

**Did you answer the question?**

You are not required to comment on the paydays for IT or NIC or the changes to the paydays if employment status applied.

**Did you answer the question?**

Any impact of VAT has been carefully excluded for part (b) and should be ignored until it is required in part (c).

(c) **VAT registration**

Basil will become liable to compulsory registration to VAT when his taxable supplies during any 12 month period exceed £51,000. This will happen on 29 February 2000 when his taxable supplies will amount to £55,000 $(60,000 \times 11/12)$. He will have to notify HM Customs & Excise by 30 March 2000, being 30 days after the end of the period, and will be registered from 1 April 2000.

**Implications of VAT registration**

From the date of registration, Basil will have to account for output tax on his income. Since Ace Computers Ltd and his other clients are presumably VAT registered, Basil will be able to charge VAT on top of his fees charged. His output tax for a full year would amount to £10,500 pa (60,000 × 17.5%). Basil will be able to recover the input tax on the business use of light and heat of £25 pa $(100 \times 2/8)$, the business use of his telephone of £89 pa $(250 - 100 = 150 \times 7/47 \times 4)$, and motor expenses of £400. He will have to account for output tax based on the scale charge, since fuel is being provided for private use. This can be avoided by not reclaiming any input tax in respect of fuel, although due to Basil's high business mileage this is unlikely to be beneficial.

**Voluntary registration**

Upon registering for VAT, Basil will also be able to recover pre-registration input tax of £700 $(4,700 \times 7/47)$ in respect of his computer equipment, provided that it is still owned at the date of VAT registration. He will only be able to recover input tax on the business use of light and heat, the business use of his telephone, and motor expenses, incurred within the six months prior to VAT registration. Basil would therefore be advised to voluntarily register for VAT on or before 5 October 1999, in order to maximise the recovery of input tax.

**Did you answer the question?**

While cash accounting or annual accounting might be relevant to Basil in practice, they are not required as part of your answer.

## JUNE 1996 QUESTIONS

## 43    (Question 1 of examination)

You are the tax adviser to the partnership of Smart and Sharp, a firm of management consultants. The partnership consists of four partners who share profits equally. You should assume that today's date is 15 November 1999.

(a)    The firm started trading on 1 May 1996 and there have been no changes to the constitution of the partnership since formation, but on 31 December 1999 a new partner is to be admitted. The tax adjusted Schedule D case II trading profits have been as follows:

|  | £ |
|---|---|
| Period ended 31 December 1996 8 mths . | 560,000 |
| Year ended 31 December 1997 | 710,000 |
| Year ended 31 December 1998 | 640,000 |

The partners are planning to incorporate the partnership's business on 31 December 2003. Forecast profits to this date are as follows:

|  | £ |
|---|---|
| Year ended 31 December 1999 | 750,000 |
| Year ended 31 December 2000 | 800,000 |
| Year ended 31 December 2001 | 860,000 |
| Year ended 31 December 2002 | 930,000 |
| Year ended 31 December 2003 | 1,000,000 |

**Required:**

Advise the partners of the partnership profits that will be assessable on each of them for the years 1996-97 to 2003-04 inclusive. You should assume that the partnership's business is incorporated on 31 December 2003. Your calculations should be made on a monthly basis.    **(10 marks)**

(b)    The partners would like advice as to whether or not it would be beneficial to incorporate the partnership's business when the new partner is admitted on 31 December 1999, rather than on 31 December 2003. They are concerned that the current level of profits of £750,000 may not be high enough for incorporation to be beneficial.

Following the admission of the new partner, the partnership will consist of five partners who will share profits equally. Upon incorporation, the partnership's business will be transferred to a new company, Smash Ltd. The five partners will all become directors of Smash Ltd, and would each receive directors remuneration of £125,000 pa. Each of the five partners has sufficient investment income to utilise their personal allowances and basic rate income tax bands.

**Required:**

Advise the partners as to whether or not it would be beneficial for the partnership's business to be incorporated on 31 December 1999 rather than on 31 December 2003. Your advice should be based upon the following calculations:

(i)    Assuming that the partnership's business is incorporated on 31 December 1999, calculate the Schedule D case II assessable amounts for the partners for 1996-97 to 1999-00, and the profits chargeable to corporation tax of Smash Ltd for the years ended 31 December 2000 to 2003. **(3 marks)**

---

(ii) Basing your answer solely on the current level of profits of £750,000, calculate (1) the annual tax liability of the five partners if the partnership **is not** incorporated, and (2) the annual tax liability of Smash Ltd and its directors if the partnership **is** incorporated.

Your answer should **take into account** the implications of NIC, and should use the tax rates for 1999-00. The figure for profits of £750,000 is **before** the deduction of directors remuneration.

**(8 marks)**

(c) The partners have asked for your advice regarding the CGT and IHT implications of incorporating the partnership's business.

**Required:**

Draft a reply to the partners. **(4 marks)**

**(Total: 25 marks)**

---

## 44 (Question 2 of examination)

---

Albert Bone, a widower aged 64, died on 31 March 2000. The main beneficiary under the terms of Albert's will is his son Harold, aged 37. At the date of his death Albert owned the following assets:

(1) 76,000 £1 ordinary shares in Hercules plc. On 31 March 2000 the shares were quoted at 139 - 147, with bargains on that day of 137, 141 and 143.

(2) Building society deposits of £115,900.

(3) A life assurance policy on his own life. Immediately prior to the date of Alberts' death, the policy had an open market value of £42,000. Proceeds of £55,000 were received following his death.

Albert was a beneficiary of two trusts:

(1) Under the terms of the first trust, Albert was entitled to receive all of the trust income. The trust owned 50,000 units in the Eureka unit trust, which was quoted at 90 - 94 on 31 March 2000. Accrued distributable income at 31 March 2000 was £900 (net).

(2) Under the terms of the second trust, Albert was entitled to receive the income at the discretion of the trustees. The trust's assets were valued at £95,000 on 31 March 2000.

Until 15 March 1991, Albert owned his main residence. On that date, he had made a gift of the property to Harold. Albert continued to live in the house with Harold, rent free, until the date of his death. On 15 March 1991 the property was valued at £65,000, and on 31 March 2000 it was valued at £180,000.

Albert has also made the following gifts during his lifetime:

(1) On 3 December 1992, he made a gift of £169,000 into a discretionary trust.

(2) On 18 October 1995, he made a gift of £24,500 to a granddaughter as a wedding gift.

(3) On 20 April 1996, he made a gift of ordinary shares (a 12% holding) in an unquoted trading company, into a discretionary trust. The shareholding was valued at £190,000, and had been owned for 10 years. At 20 April 1996 one half of the value of the assets in the company consisted of investments. The trust still owned the shares at 31 March 2000.

Any inheritance tax arising from the above gifts was paid by Albert, except for the gift in 1992 when the trustees paid the tax.

At the date of his death, Albert owed £900 in respect of credit card debts, and he had also verbally promised to pay the £750 hospital bill of a neighbour. Albert's funeral expenses came to £1,200.

---

Under the terms of his will, Albert left specific gifts to his grandchildren totalling £40,000. The residue of his estate was left to Harold.

**Required:**

(a)    Calculate the IHT that will be payable as a result of Albert's death. Your answer should show who is liable for the tax, and by what date. You should also include an explanation as to your treatment of Albert's main residence, and a calculation of the amount of the inheritance that Harold will receive.

You should ignore Albert's income tax liability for 1999-00, and should assume that the tax rates and allowances for 1999-00 apply throughout.    **(17 marks)**

(b)    Harold is to make a gift of some of his inheritance to his son, aged 8, so as to utilise his son's personal allowance. Advise Harold of whether or not such a gift would be effective for income tax purposes. Your answer should include any tax planning advice that you consider to be appropriate.    **(4 marks)**

(c)    Harold plans to invest the balance of his inheritance so as to achieve capital growth, since he already has sufficient income. He will require the capital in five years time when he is to purchase a new house. Briefly advise Harold of investments that would be appropriate for such an investment strategy.    **(4 marks)**

**(Total: 25 marks)**

---

## 45    (Question 3 of examination)

Techno plc is a rapidly expanding quoted company involved in management consultancy. The company is looking at ways of both motivating and retaining its 10 directors and 70 key personnel, of which several have recently been lost to competitors. The company has 400 other full-time employees, of whom 120 have joined the company during the past two years. One of the directors, Martin Thatch, owns 35% of the ordinary share capital of Techno plc. The other nine directors are 1% shareholders. None of the directors are connected to each other. The average remuneration of the directors and the key personnel is £100,000 pa and £40,000 pa respectively.

The proposals under consideration are as follows:

(1)    Setting up a profit sharing scheme whereby directors and key personnel would receive fully paid up ordinary shares in Techno plc free of charge each year. Techno plc would set up a trust to run the scheme, with the trust purchasing the shares required through the Stock Exchange, using funds provided by Techno plc.

(2)    Providing each of the directors and key personnel with a new 2400cc petrol powered company motor car. The list price of each motor car is £27,500. In addition, each motor car will be fitted with a mobile telephone costing £180, and other optional accessories costing £2,000. Techno plc will also pay for private petrol, private telephone calls, and will provide free car parking spaces near its offices. The car parking spaces will be rented by Techno plc at a cost of £350 pa each. The motor cars will be driven between 5,000 and 10,000 miles on business each year.

(3)    Providing each of the directors and key personnel with an interest free loan of £25,000. This loan will be written off in two years time, provided that the director or the key person is still employed by Techno plc at that date. The loan will be immediately repayable should a director or key person resign from Techno plc's employ.

(4)    Setting up a share option scheme whereby directors and key personnel would receive options to purchase fully paid up ordinary shares in Techno plc at their present value. The options would be provided free, and would be exercisable in five years time.

Techno plc's ordinary shares are presently quoted at £1.00 each, and are likely to be worth £4.00 each in five years time. Techno plc is a close company.

**Required:**

(a)     Explain the income tax, CGT and NIC implications for the directors and key personnel in respect of each of the four proposals.  You should ignore the implications of VAT, and should assume that Inland Revenue approval, where applicable, **is not obtained** in respect of any of the proposals.

**(11 marks)**

(b)     (i)     **Briefly** state the conditions that must be met in order for the profit sharing scheme to obtain Inland Revenue approval.  Your answer should indicate whether or not the proposed scheme will qualify for approval.

You are not expected to discuss share option schemes or employee share ownership plans (ESOPs).

**(4 marks)**

(ii)    Advise the directors and key personnel of the potential tax saving if Inland Revenue approval **is obtained** for the profit sharing scheme.

**(3 marks)**
**(Total:  18 marks)**
**(as amended)**

---

## 46     (Question 4 of examination)

Hydra Ltd has owned 90% of the ordinary share capital of Boa Ltd and 80% of the ordinary share capital of Cobra Ltd since 1985.  Cobra Ltd acquired 80% of the ordinary share capital of Mamba Ltd on 1 April 1999, the date of that company's incorporation.  All of the companies are involved in the construction industry.  The results of each company for the year ended 31 March 2000 are as follows:

|  | *Tax adjusted Schedule D1 Profit/loss* | *Capital gain/(loss)* | *Patent royalties paid* |
|---|---|---|---|
| Hydra Ltd | (45,000) | 130,000 | (20,000) |
| Boa Ltd | 120,000 | (15,000) | - |
| Cobra Ltd | 85,000 | - | - |
| Mamba Ltd | (12,000) | 8,000 | - |

Hydra Ltd's  capital gain arose from the sale of a factory for £350,000.  As at 31 March 1999 the company had unused trading losses of £15,000.  Boa Ltd purchased a new office building on 1 May 2000 for £280,000.  Mamba Ltd's capital gain arose from the disposal of an investment.

**Required:**

(a)      Calculate the corporation tax liability for each of the four companies in the Hydra Ltd group for the year ended 31 March 2000.  Your answer should include an explanation of your treatment of the trading losses of Hydra Ltd and Mamba Ltd.  You should assume that reliefs are claimed in the most favourable  manner.**(10 marks)**

(b)     (i)     Explain why it would probably be beneficial to transfer the 80% shareholding in Mamba Ltd from Cobra Ltd to Hydra Ltd.

**(3 marks)**

(ii)    Hydra Ltd, Boa Ltd and Cobra Ltd all make standard rated sales, and are registered as a group for VAT purposes.  The sales of Mamba Ltd are exempt.  Briefly discuss the factors that would have to be considered when deciding if Mamba Ltd should be included in the group VAT registration.**(4 marks)**
**(Total:  17 marks)**
**(as amended)**

---

## 47     (Question 5 of examination)

You are the tax adviser to Harry Chan, aged 43.  Harry resigned from his position of sales manager with UTC Ltd, an unquoted trading company, on 31 March 1999.  He had been employed at a salary of £45,000 pa.  On 15 April 1999

Harry sold 80,000 of the 100,000 £1 ordinary shares (a 1% holding) that he held in UTC Ltd for £3.35 per share. Harry originally acquired 25,000 shares at par on 15 June 1981, the date of UTC Ltd's incorporation. On 26 January 1986 UTC Ltd made a 3 for 1 rights issue at £5.00 per share, which Harry took up in full. The market value of UTC Ltd's shares at 31 March 1982 was £1.25 per share. The shares in UTC Ltd were the only chargeable asset that Harry held on 31 March 1982.

Harry used the proceeds from the disposal of his shareholding to purchase an existing business on 1 June 1999. The business is that of selling musical instruments, and Harry has run this as a sole trader. Accounts have been prepared for the 10 month period to 5 April 2000, and the results showed a marked decline compared to the results of the previous owner for the year ended 31 May 1999. The results are as follows:

|  | *Previous owner*<br>*Year ended*<br>*31 May 1999* | *Harry Chan*<br>*Period ended*<br>*5 April 2000* |
|---|---|---|
| Sales  - Cash | 300,000 | 200,000 |
|       - Credit | 60,000 | 50,000 |
| Gross profit | 150,000 | 75,000 |
| Net profit | 108,000 | 40,000 |

Harry's self assessment tax return for 1999-00 was submitted to the Inland Revenue on 31 January 2001. His tax adjusted Schedule D case I profit was the same as the net profit of £40,000. The Inland Revenue proceeded to make an enquiry into Harry's accounts, and gave a written notice stating that they consider the sales shown in the accounts to be understated by £50,000. The Inland Revenue gave written notice that the enquiry was complete and, since Harry did not amend his self-assessment, the Inland Revenue made an amendment on 31 July 2001. Harry immediately raised an appeal but paid the additional tax due on 31 August 2001 to stop interest running should he lose the appeal.

Harry is single, and has no other income or outgoings.

**Required:**

(a)    (i)    State the likely reasons why the Inland Revenue have investigated Harry's 1999-00 return.

**(3 marks)**

(ii)    State possible criteria that Harry could put forward in order to justify the fall in profits from those of the previous owner.    **(2 marks)**

(b)    Assuming that Harry loses his appeal:

(i)    Calculate the interest on overdue tax that Harry will be charged in respect of his 1999-00 income tax liability.

You should ignore the implications of NIC and VAT.    **(2 marks)**

(ii)    State the maximum amount of penalty that the Inland Revenue can charge Harry, and briefly advise him of the factors that will be taken into account in deciding if this maximum amount should be mitigated.    **(2 marks)**

(c)    (i)    Calculate the capital loss that will arise from Harry's disposal of his 80,000 shares in UTC Ltd.

**(4 marks)**

(ii)    Advise Harry as to the most beneficial way of utilising his capital loss. Your answer should cover the possibility of Harry either winning or losing his appeal against the assessment for 1999-00.

**(7 marks)**
**(Total: 20 marks)**

*(Tutorial note:* This question was set before self-assessment was examinable. It has been rewritten to incorporate the self-assessment rules. The marking structure has had to be adjusted and now only totals 20 marks.)*

---

| **48** | **(Question 6 of examination)** |
|---|---|

---

On 31 December 1999 Muriel Grand, aged 52, made a gift of a house in London to her brother Bertie, aged 53. Muriel had bought the house on 1 April 1985 for £60,000. Surplus land adjoining the house was sold for £24,000 to a neighbour in June 1986, at which date the market value of the property retained was £72,000. The market value at 31 December 1999 has been agreed by the Inland Revenue as £320,000. Muriel occupied the house as her main residence until 30 September 1992, and then moved in to another house that she owned in Glasgow. Muriel elected for the house in Glasgow to be treated as her main residence from 1 January 1995 onwards. From 1 January 1987 to 30 September 1992 Muriel used 20% of the house exclusively for business purposes.

Bertie is to rent out the house in London, either unfurnished or as furnished holiday accommodation. In either case, the roof of the house must be repaired at a cost of £24,000 before it will be possible to let the house. The roof was badly damaged by a gale on 5 December 1999. If the house is let unfurnished, then Bertie will have to decorate it at a cost of £3,500. The forecast rental income is £28,000 pa. If the house is let as furnished holiday accommodation, then the house will be converted into two separate units at a cost of £41,000. The total cost of furnishing the two units will be £9,000. This expenditure will be financed by a £50,000 bank loan at an interest rate of 12% pa. The total forecast rental income is £45,000 pa, although 22.5% of this will be deducted by the letting agency. Other running costs, such as cleaning, will amount to £3,500 pa in total.

Bertie plans to sell the house when he retires aged 60, and anticipates making a substantial capital gain. Both Muriel and Bertie are 40% taxpayers. Muriel has a portfolio of investments valued in excess of £1 million, and has already utilised her CGT annual exemption for 1999-00.

**Required:**

(a)     Calculate the CGT liability that will arise from Muriel's gift of the house in London to Bertie.

**(4 marks)**

(b)     Advise Muriel as to how it would be possible to defer the gain on the house in London by making an investment in unquoted trading companies.

Your answer should cover the enterprise investment scheme and venture capital trusts, and you should describe the other tax implications of making such investments.     **(8 marks)**

(c)     Advise Bertie of the tax implications of letting out the house in London either (i) unfurnished, or (ii) as furnished holiday accommodation. Your answer should include details of the tax advantages of letting the house as furnished holiday accommodation.     **(13 marks)**

**(Total: 25 marks)**

## ANSWERS TO JUNE 1996 EXAMINATION

## 43   (Answer 1 of examination)

### Examiner's comments and marking guide

Part (a) tested candidates' ability to calculate the partnership assessments on the change in the constitution of the partnership.  Part (b) tested candidates' ability to advise on the date that a partnership should incorporate, taking into account the profits that will be assessed, and the overall tax liabilities.  Part (c) tested candidates' knowledge of the CGT and IHT implications of incorporating a partnership.

This was a popular question, being attempted by the majority of candidates.  There were some extremely good answers to this question, with many of the candidates attempting it scoring high marks.  (The comments on part (a) refer to the version originally set.  As this has been rewritten for syllabus changes, the comments are redundant and have been omitted.)  Part (b) was also generally answered quite well.  The NIC implications caused problems for some candidates, and there is little excuse for not knowing the correct NIC calculations when the rates are given on the examination paper.  The CGT aspects of part (c) were generally well answered, although many candidates were unsure as to exactly why there would be no CGT liability, very few candidates appreciated the impact (when the question was originally set) that incorporation would have on business property relief.

|  |  | *Marks* |
|---|---|---|
| (a) | **Partner's shares** | |
| | 1996-97 | 2 |
| | 1997-98 and 1998-99 | 1 |
| | 1999-00 | 2 |
| | 2000-01 to 2002-2003 | 2 |
| | 2003-2004 | 1 |
| | Overlap relief | 2 |
| | | — |
| | Maximum/Available | 10 |
| | | — |

*(Tutorial note:*  This part of the question was re written to reflect changes in the syllabus.  The marking guide has also been changed.*)*

| (b) | **Assessable profits** | |
|---|---|---|
| | Profits that will be assessed | 1 |
| | Calculation | 1 |
| | Conclusion | 1 |
| | **Tax liability of partners** | |
| | Income tax | 1 |
| | NIC | 1 |
| | Total liability | 1 |
| | **Tax liability of Smash Ltd** | |
| | Corporation tax | 2 |
| | NIC | 1 |
| | **Tax liability of directors** | |
| | Income tax/NIC | 1 |
| | Total liability | 1 |
| | Overall conclusion | 1 |
| | | — |
| | Available | 12 |
| | | — |
| | Maximum | 11 |
| | | — |

|  | | Marks |
|---|---|---|
| (c) | CGT implications | 2 |
|  | IHT implications | 2 |
|  |  | — |
|  | Maximum/Available | 4 |
|  |  | — |
|  | Available | 26 |
|  |  | — |
|  | Maximum | 25 |
|  |  | — |

## Step by step answer plan

### Overview

This question is clearly testing your knowledge of partnership income tax and NIC treatment and the corporation tax/capital taxes implications of incorporating the business.

**Step 1** Part (a) is a straightforward number crunching exercise. You need a tabular layout and should work through the assessable amounts year by year. Remember, under CYB, profits are allocated to each partner on an accounts basis and each partner is then treated as if he were a sole trader making his share of profit year by year.

**Step 2** Ensure overlap profits are correctly calculated and deducted against the final year's assessment.

**Step 3** For part (b) (i) recalculate the total assessable profits over all the years concerned on the basis of the earlier incorporation date and demonstrate that, thanks to CYB, this makes no difference to the total of profits assessed.

**Step 4** For part (b) (ii) follow the requirements for calculating tax on the £750,000 level of profits under the two alternative situations - ie, before and after incorporation. Do not overlook the instructions to include the NIC effect etc.

**Step 5** Part (b) concerns whether early incorporation is beneficial so ensure that your answer compares the tax and NIC total under the two alternatives and states a conclusion.

**Step 6** For part (c), note only 4 marks are on offer. Obviously it is important not to overlook part (c) but as only 4 marks are given you are clearly not expected to write at length.

**Step 7** Describe the CGT relief for incorporating.

**Step 8** Describe the IHT changes resulting from incorporation. In fact currently there is no effective change - 100% BPR available pre and post incorporation. This was not always the case. However, the point is that it is just as important to state the implications whether or not there is an effective change.

## The examiner's answer

(a) Partners' assessable amounts

|  | Total | 1 | 2 | 3 | 4 | 5 |
|---|---|---|---|---|---|---|
|  | £ | £ | £ | £ | £ | £ |
| 1996/97 | | | | | | |
| (1.5.96 - 5.4.97) | | | | | | |
| $560,000 + \frac{3}{12} \times 710,000$ | 737,500 | 184,375 | 184,375 | 184,375 | 184,375 | |
| 1997/98 | | | | | | |
| (y/e 31.12.97) | 710,000 | 177,500 | 177,500 | 177,500 | 177,500 | |

| | | | | | |
|---|---|---|---|---|---|
| **1998/99** (y/e 31.12.99) | 640,000 | 160,000 | 160,000 | 160,000 | 160,000 | |
| **1999/00** (y/e 31.12.99) | 750,000 | 187,500 | 187,500 | 187,500 | 187,500 | |
| (800,000 × 20% × 3/12) | 40,000 | | | | | 40,000 |
| **2000/01** (y/e 31.12.00) | 800,000 | 160,000 | 160,000 | 160,000 | 160,000 | 160,000 |
| **2001/02** (y/e 31.12.01) | 860,000 | 172,000 | 172,000 | 172,000 | 172,000 | 172,000 |
| **2002/03** (y/e 31.12.02) | 930,000 | 186,000 | 186,000 | 186,000 | 186,000 | 186,000 |
| **2003/04** (1.1.03 - 31.12.03) | 1,000,000 | 200,000 | 200,000 | 200,000 | 200,000 | 200,000 |
| less overlap relief | | | | | | |
| 1.1.97 - 5.4.97 | (177,500) | (44,375) | (44,375) | (44,375) | (44,375) | |
| 1.1.00 - 5.4.00 | (40,000) | | | | | (40,000) |
| | 782,500 | 155,625 | 155,625 | 155,625 | 155,625 | 160,000 |
| | 6,250,000 | | | | | |

---

## Did you answer the question?

You were not required to calculate any tax or NIC on the shares of profit.

(b)    (i)    If the partnership's business is incorporated on 31 December 1999, the assessable profits of the partners and Smash Ltd will be as follows:

|  | £ |
|---|---|
| **Partnership** | |
| 1996-97 (As previous) | 737,500 |
| 1997-98 (As previous) | 710,000 |
| 1998-99 (As previous) | 640,000 |
| 1999-00 (750,000 − 177,500) | 572,500 |
| | |
| **Smash Ltd** | |
| Year ended 31.12.00 | 800,000 |
| Year ended 31.12.01 | 860,000 |
| Year ended 31.12.02 | 930,000 |
| Year ended 31.12.03 | 1,000,000 |
| Total assessments | 6,250,000 |

Total assessable profits therefore remain the same.

(ii)    **Tax liability of partners**

The annual tax liability of each of the five partners will be as follows:

|  | £ |
|---|---|
| Schedule D Case II (750,000/5) | 150,000 |
| Taxable income | 150,000 |
| Income tax at 40% | 60,000 |

---

|  |  |
|---|---|
| Class 2 NIC (6.55 × 52) | 341 |
| Class 4 NIC ((26,0000 − 7,530) at 6%) | 1,108 |
|  | 61,449 |

The total annual tax liability of the five partners will be £307,245 (61,449 × 5).

**Tax liability of Smash Ltd**

The annual tax liability of Smash Ltd will be as follows:

|  | £ | £ |
|---|---|---|
| Trading profit |  | 750,000 |
| Directors remuneration (125,000 × 5) | 625,000 |  |
| Employers Class 1 NIC (625,000 at 12.2%) | 76,250 |  |
|  |  | 701,250 |
| **PCTCT** |  | 48,750 |
| Corporation tax at 20% |  | 9,750 |
| Employers Class 1 NIC |  | 76,250 |
|  |  | 86,000 |

**Tax liability of directors**

The annual tax liability of each director will be as follows:

|  | £ | £ |
|---|---|---|
| Taxable income - Schedule E |  | 125,000 |
| Income tax at 40% |  | 50,000 |
| Employees Class 1 NIC |  | 2,256 |
| 434 ×52 at 10% |  |  |
|  |  | 52,256 |

The total annual tax liability of Smash Ltd and the five directors will be £347,280 (86,000 + (52,256 × 5)). This is an increase of £40,035 (347,280 − 307,245) compared to the total annual tax liability of the five partners.

**Conclusion**

Since incorporating the partnership's business on 31 December 1999 rather than on 31 December 2003 will result in an increase in the overall annual tax liability (based on the current level of profits), incorporation on this date does not appear to be beneficial.

---

**Did you answer the question?**

You were not required to comment on other differences such as paydays for tax and NIC.

---

(c) **CGT implications**

The incorporation of the partnership's business will be a disposal for CGT purposes. Provided that the disposal is in return for shares in Smash Ltd, any gains arising from the disposal of chargeable business assets can be held over against the base cost of the shares received. For this relief to apply, the partnership's business must be transferred as a going concern, and all the assets of the partnership's business (excluding cash) must be transferred. Taper relief entitlement up to the date of incorporation will be lost.

### IHT implications

At present, were they to die, the four existing partners would be entitled to BPR at the rate of 100% in respect of their partnership share. The new partner will not be entitled to BPR until he or she has been a partner for two years. Following the incorporation of the partnership's business, the five partners will become shareholders in Smash Ltd, which will presumably be an unquoted company. The rate of BPR will therefore continue at 100%.

---

**Tutorial notes**

1    Part (a) of this question was originally concerned with the transitional rules; as these are no longer examinable, this question has been updated to the current year basis.

2    The incoming partner participates in profits from 1 January 2000 receiving a £160,000 share in his first year. He is assessable as if he had commenced as a sole trader earning £160,000 of adjusted profit in his first year of 12 months to 31 December 2000.

---

## 44    (Answer 2 of examination)

### Examiner's comments and marking guide

Part (a) tested candidates' ability to calculate the IHT liabilities arising on lifetime transfers and on death, including a gift with reservation. Part (b) tested candidates' knowledge of the income tax implications of a parental gift, and their ability to provide appropriate tax planning advice. Part (c) tested candidates' ability to advise on appropriate investments, given the taxpayer's stated investment strategy.

This was another popular question, being the first choice question for many candidates, and a number of candidates again scored high marks. In part (a), some candidates did not appreciate that two distinct calculations were required in respect of the chargeable lifetime transfer, and the grossing up aspect of the calculation often caused problems. There was also confusion as to the seven year cumulation period, with some candidates ignoring the chargeable lifetime transfer made more than seven years before death altogether, despite this having an impact on subsequent transfers. A disappointing number of candidates included the discretionary trust in the estate at death. Those candidates who combined the lifetime transfers and the estate at death into one confused calculation did not achieve high marks. Part (b) was generally answered quite well, and a number of candidates gave appropriate tax planning advice. Part (c), was again generally well answered, but many candidates wrote in depth on just two or three investments, rather than "briefly" advising on the range of appropriate investments.

|  |  | *Marks* |
|---|---|---|
| (a) | **Lifetime transfers** | |
| | Gift with reservation | 1 |
| | Chargeable transfer 3.12.92 | 1 |
| | PET 18.10.95 | 1 |
| | Chargeable transfer 20.4.96 | 2 |
| | Additional IHT | 2 |
| | Due date/instalment option | 1 |
| | | |
| | **Estate at death** | |
| | Cumulative total | 1 |
| | Ordinary shares | 1 |
| | Other assets/debts and funeral expenses | 2 |
| | Settled property | 1 |
| | Gift with reservation | 1 |
| | IHT liability | 1 |
| | Rate of IHT on estate | 1 |
| | IHT due by estate/due date | 1 |
| | Harold's inheritance | 1 |

---

|  | Other IHT liabilities/due dates | 2 |
|---|---|---|
|  | Available | 20 |
|  | Maximum | 17 |
| (b) | Income tax treatment | 2 |
|  | Variation of terms of will | 2 |
|  | Maximum/Available | 4 |
| (c) | Banks/building societies/National Savings | 2 |
|  | Unit trusts/investment trusts/OEICs/equity shares/ISAs | 3 |
|  | Available | 5 |
|  | Maximum | 4 |
|  | Available | 29 |
|  | Maximum | 25 |

### ( Step by step answer plan )

**Overview**

This is mainly a capital taxes question with the bulk of the marks given in part (a) for calculating IHT on death - lifetime gifts and death estate - and identifying those persons liable for any IHT charge and the pay days for the tax. Parts (b) and (c) concern an anti-avoidance rule and basic investment planning respectively. You might be put off this question by the reference to trusts but this would be unwarranted.

**Step 1**   Read through the question carefully and note the requirements of part (a). You will probably have noticed that parts (b) and (c) require general comments which largely stand alone from the question's details so whatever appears in the detail of the question will almost certainly have a bearing on part (a) alone.

**Step 2**   Deal with the lifetime taxation of the inter vivos (ie, during lifetime) transfers and comment on the treatment of the GWR - ie, it will be included as part of the estate on death.

**Step 3**   Deal with any tax adjustments needed on gifts within 7 years of death. Note that the PET which now becomes chargeable is taken into account in calculating the death tax on the subsequent lifetime chargeable transfer – (a 'biting' PET!)

**Step 4**   List out the death estate following the layout convention of showing life interests separate form the free estate.

**Step 5**   Comment on why the debt of the hospital bill has been left out.

**Step 6**   Compute the IHT on the death estate and note who pays and when payment is due. The question does not specifically mention the instalment option but this is clearly implied and should be commented on.

**Step 7**   Don't forget to claim the 4 easy marks for part (b).

**Step 8**   Finally, answer part (c). Although only 4 marks are on offer, there are several points to make and a rough answer plan would be useful.

( **The examiner's answer** )

(a) **Lifetime transfers of value**

15 March 1991 - The gift of the main residence is a PET. As this is more than seven years before the date of death, no IHT will be due. However, Albert has continued to live rent free in the property until the date of his death. The gift will therefore be classified as a gift with reservation, and the main residence will be included in Albert's estate at its value on 31 March 2000. There is no double charge to tax, as the PET does not become chargeable.

|  | £ | £ |
|---|---|---|
| **3 December 1992** |  |  |
| Value transferred |  | 169,000 |
| Annual exemptions   1992-93 | 3,000 |  |
| 1991-92 | 3,000 |  |
|  |  | 6,000 |
| Gross chargeable transfer |  | 163,000 |

|  | £ | £ |
|---|---|---|
| **18 October 1995** |  |  |
| Value transferred |  | 24,500 |
| Marriage exemption | 2,500 |  |
| Annual exemptions   1995-96 | 3,000 |  |
| 1994-95 | 3,000 |  |
|  |  | 8,500 |
| Potentially exempt transfer |  | 16,000 |

|  | £ |
|---|---|
| **20 April 1996** |  |
| Value transferred | 190,000 |
| Business property relief - ½* × 100% | 95,000 |
|  | 95,000 |
| Annual exemption 1996-97 | 3,000 |
| Chargeable transfer | 92,000 |

| | £ |
|---|---|
| IHT liability 231,000 – 163,000 = 68,000 at nil% | Nil |
| 92,000 – 68,000 = 24,000 × 20/80 | 6,000 |
|  | 6,000 |

\* Excluding excepted assets.

---

**Did you answer the question?**

You were not asked to state who was liable for any lifetime tax nor the due date for such tax. This requirement only applied to the tax due as a result of the death.

---

As a result of Albert's death on 31 March 2000, additional IHT may be due. The revised cumulative total as a result of the PET on 18 October 1995 becoming chargeable is £179,000 (163,000 + 16,000).

The death tax on the transfer of the shares to the trust is

| | | | £ |
|---|---|---|---|
| 231,000 – 179,000 | = | 52,000 at nil% | Nil |
| 98,000 – 52,000 | = | 46,000 at 40% | 18,400 |
|  |  |  | 18,400 |

---

| | | |
|---|---:|---:|
| Less: Taper relief 20% | | (3,680) |
| | | 14,720 |
| Less: Tax paid | | (6,000) |
| Additional tax payable by the discretionary trust | | 8,720 |

**Estate at death - 31 March 2000**

The chargeable transfer on 3 December 1992 is more than seven years before the date of death, and will therefore drop out of the cumulative total. The revised cumulative total is £114,000 (16,000 + 98,000).

| | £ | £ |
|---|---:|---:|
| **Free estate** | | |
| **Personalty** | | |
| Ordinary shares in Hercules plc 76,000 at 140p ((137 + 143)/2) | | 106,400 |
| Building society deposits | | 115,900 |
| Life assurance policy | | 55,000 |
| Accrued trust income | | 900 |
| | | 278,200 |
| Credit card debts | 900 | |
| Funeral expenses | 1,200 | |
| | | (2,100) |
| Net free estate | | 276,100 |
| **Settled property** | | |
| Interest in possession 50,000 at 90p | 45,000 | |
| Accrued income (900 × 100/90) | 1,000 | |
| | | 44,000 |
| Gift with reservation | | 180,000 |
| Chargeable estate | | 500,100 |
| IHT liability    231,000 – 114,000 = 117,000 at nil % | | Nil |
| 500,100 – 117,000 = 383,100 at 40% | | 153,240 |
| | | 153,240 |

The verbal promise by Albert to pay his neighbour's hospital bill is unlikely to be deductible; as it has not been incurred for full consideration.

---

**Did you answer the question?**

It is not always clear whether to comment on an item which is excluded. The rule seems to be that a comment is not necessary unless some assumption is made. For example, discretionary trust property never has a place in a beneficiary's death estate so no comment is required. The neighbour's hospital bill might or might not be included depending on whether valuable consideration was given (to Albert) so a comment is in order.

---

Rate of IHT on estate = 30.642% (153,240/500,100 × 100)

IHT of £84,602 (276,100 at 30.642%) will be due from the estate. This will be payable by the executors of Albert's estate on the earlier of 30 September 2000 or the delivery of their account. Harold will inherit £151,498 (276,100 – 40,000 – 84,602), since specific gifts of UK property do not normally carry their own tax.

IHT of £13,482 (44,000 at 30.642%) will be due from the interest in possession trust, and IHT of £55,156 (180,000 at 30.642%) will be due from Harold in respect of the gift with reservation. It will be possible for him to pay this IHT liability in 10 equal instalments commencing on 30 September 2000.

(b)    Where a parent transfers capital to an unmarried child who is under 18, then the income therefrom continues to be treated as that of the parent. There is a *de minimus* limit where the annual income does not exceed £100. The rule also applies if a parent makes a settlement in favour of the child.

Even if Harold arranges for the terms of Albert's will to be varied so that the capital passes direct to his son, the income arising therefrom would still be taxed as Harold's income.

---

**Did you answer the question?**

It would be inappropriate to mention that the will should have been drafted to include Harold's son as a beneficiary. This would hardly amount to 'tax planning advice' as Albert is already dead!

---

(c)    Harold would be advised to keep some of his funds in high interest accounts with banks or building societies, or in a money market fund, with interest being reinvested. National Savings Certificates would be suitable as interest accumulates over the maximum five year period and the interest is tax-free. The cash element of an ISA would also be suitable and has the advantage of penalty fee withdrawals (at least for tax purposes as the interest is tax-free).

Unit trusts, investment trusts and OEICs offer a number of options for capital growth. Alternatively, Harold could invest directly in equity shares, although such a strategy would carry more risk. These investments could probably be made by way of an ISA, but this would probably only be beneficial if Harold was otherwise utilising his CGT annual exemption and the maximum would be restricted by the amount invested in the cash element of an ISA. Short-dated low-coupon gilts and single premium bonds are other possible investments.

Since Harold requires the capital in five years time, most pension and life assurance based investments are unlikely to be suitable. Harold might consider investing some of his capital in unquoted companies by way of, for example, a venture capital trust, but such an investment may well carry too much risk for him.

---

## 45    (Answer 3 of examination)

---

**Examiner's comments and marking guide**

**Part (a) tested candidates' knowledge of the income tax, CGT and NIC implications of a number of employee incentives (profit sharing, company motor cars, beneficial loans, and share options) assuming that no Inland Revenue approval was obtained. Part (b) tested candidate's knowledge of the conditions that must be met in order for profit sharing schemes to obtain Inland Revenue approval, and the benefit of being so approved.**

Answers to this question were often badly laid out, with parts (a), (b)(i) and (b)(ii) not being separated. A number of candidates scored high marks, but far too many candidates lacked sufficient knowledge of profit sharing schemes. This is disappointing, given the increased popularity of employee incentive schemes in practice, and the fact that this question consisted entirely of paper 7 material. (Share schemes have since been removed from the Paper 7 Syllabus). In part (a), very few candidates appreciated that the provision of free parking did not give rise to a benefit. The CGT aspects of the profit sharing scheme and the share option scheme were generally not answered particularly well, with a number of candidates stating that there would be a CGT liability upon the exercise of the share options. Answers to part (b)(i) lacked depth and part (b)(ii) was generally badly answered, with very few candidates actually calculating the tax saving, even though they had given all the relevant information to do so, elsewhere in their answers.

|       |                       | *Marks* |
|-------|-----------------------|---------|
| (a)   | Profit sharing scheme | 2       |
|       | Company motor cars    | 4       |
|       | Beneficial loans      | 3       |
|       | Share option scheme   | 3       |
|       |                       | —       |
|       | Available             | 12      |

---

|  |  |  |  |
|---|---|---|---|
|  | Maximum |  | 11 |

(b)　(i)　**Profit sharing scheme**

|  |  |
|---|---|
| Shares/trust fund | 1 |
| Retention of shares | 1 |
| Right to participate | 1 |
| Employees with a material interest | 1 |
| Participating employees | 1 |
| Available | 5 |
| Maximum | 4 |

(ii)

|  |  |  |
|---|---|---|
| Profit sharing scheme | - income tax | 3 |
|  | - CGT | 1 |
| Available |  | 4 |
| Maximum |  | 3 |
| Available |  | 21 |
| Maximum |  | 18 |

(The original question, comments and marking guide also referred to the profit related pay scheme but this has been edited out as the topic is no longer in the syllabus).

## Step by step answer plan

**Overview**

This is a question on some of the main elements of remuneration packages for key employees. Your answer is already planned out by the requirements of the question.

**Step 1**　Answer part (a) with a separate main heading for each of the 4 proposals noting carefully that under proposals 1 and 4 you must assume that Revenue approval has not been given.

**Step 2**　Ensure you cover the IT, NIC and CGT implications of each proposal even where there are no implications - eg, no NIC implications for the employee using a company car. Note however that the examiner's answer does not mention that there are no CGT implications for the use of the car or the loan - probably on the grounds that no-one would imagine otherwise!

**Step 3**　Next answer part (b) (i) but restrict yourself to stating the conditions for the profit sharing scheme to obtain Revenue approval and comment on whether the proposed scheme would qualify. Note you are asked to be brief.

**Step 4**　Answer part (b) (ii) and keep to the point - ie, simply give the potential tax savings.

## The examiner's answer

(a)　The directors and key personnel earn over £8,500 pa, and are therefore P11D employees.

**Profit sharing scheme**

The directors and key personnel will be assessed under Schedule E on the difference between the market value of the shares issued to them, and the amount paid for them (which in this case is nil). The assessment will therefore be £1.00 for each share allocated. There are no NIC implications as the upper limit has already been exceeded. A CGT liability will arise when the shares are subsequently sold, with the shares having a base cost of £1.00 each.

## Company motor cars

The directors and key personnel will be assessed under Schedule E on the benefit of the motor cars. In each case, the benefit will be £7,375 (27,500 + 2,000 = 29,500 × 25%). The value of any optional accessory costing less than £100 would be excluded from the price of the motor car if it was fitted after the date of provision. The provision of mobile telephones will not give rise to a separate benefit regardless of whether there is private use. The provision of private petrol will give rise to a fuel benefit of £2,270. The provision of a free parking space near the place of work does not give rise to a benefit. There are no NIC implications.

## Beneficial loans

Each director and key person will be assessed under Schedule E on the difference between the interest paid on the loan and the official rate of interest. The annual benefit will therefore be £2,500 (25,000 × (10% − 0%)). The benefit will cease upon repayment of the loan. Should the loan be used for a qualifying purpose then the deemed interest may qualify for a deduction. For example, if the loan is used for the purchase of a main residence, then a tax credit of £250 (2,500 × 10%) would probably be available, but only up to 5 April 2000. A loan written off after two years will be treated as additional emoluments of £25,000 at the time of write off. There will be no class 1 NIC liability as per above.

## Share option scheme

The options cannot be exercised more than ten years after their grant. There will therefore be no Schedule E charge at the time that they are granted. When the options are exercised in five years time, there will be an assessment based on the market value of the shares at that date, less the amount paid for them. The assessment will therefore be £3.00 (4.00 − 1.00) for each share option exercised. There are no NIC implications as the upper earnings level has been exceeded. A CGT liability will arise when the shares are subsequently sold, with the shares having a base cost of £4.00 each.

---

**Did you answer the question?**

You are not asked for the implications for the employer - eg, the Class 1A NIC liability for providing a company car.

---

(b)     (i)     **Profit sharing scheme**

-       The shares must generally be ordinary, fully paid up, and must be quoted on a recognised Stock Exchange or be shares in a company not controlled by another.

-       The scheme must be run via a trust fund set up by Techno plc, which will be administered by trustees who will use funds provided by Techno plc to purchase the shares.

-       The shares appropriated to employees must be retained by the trustees for at least two years.

-       All employees must be given the right to participate in the scheme, although employees with less than five years service may be excluded. The proposed scheme will therefore not qualify unless it is extended to other employees.

-       Employees with a material interest (25% or more of the ordinary share capital) must be excluded. This will apply to Martin Thatch.

-       All participating employees must do so on equal terms, although variations are allowed according to length of service and level of remuneration.

(ii)    **Profit sharing scheme**

The maximum market value of shares that can be allocated to a director or a key person each year of assessment is the greater of £3,000 or 10% of remuneration, subject to an overall maximum of

£8,000. Provided that the shares are held by the trust for at least three years, there will be no liability to income tax.

Directors will therefore be entitled to shares worth £8,000 each year (100,000 × 10% = £10,000), which is a tax saving of £3,200pa (8,000 at 40%). Key personnel will be entitled to shares worth £4,000 (40,000 × 10%) each year, which is a tax saving of £1,600 pa (4,000 at 40%). There will, however, be a liability to CGT. If the shares are sold after five years, the directors would have a capital gain of £24,000 (8,000 × (4 − 1)), and the key personnel a capital gain of £12,000 (4,000 × (4 − 1)).

---

**Did you answer the question?**

You are not required to comment on the two other share based approved schemes - eg, SAYE schemes and company share option plans (the old 'executive' share option schemes).

---

## 46　(Answer 4 of examination)

### Examiner's comments and marking guide

**Part (a) tested candidates' ability to calculate the corporation tax liabilities for a group of companies, taking into account group relief and rollover relief. Part (b)(i) tested candidates' ability to advise on the implications of restructuring the group. Part (b)(ii) tested candidates' knowledge of group VAT registration.**

This was another popular question, and there were some very good answers to part (a). In part (a), many candidates produced the correct calculations, but then did not explain their treatment of the trading losses as required by the question. The trading loss brought forward and the capital loss caused problems for a number of candidates, with both being subject to group relief claims. These are both basic calculations from paper 7. The rollover claim was often missed. In part (b)(i), hardly any candidates appreciated that the only benefit of transferring the shareholding was that group relief for trading losses would then become available. The company concerned was already a 75% subsidiary as regards the intra-company transfer of assets. Part (b)(ii) was badly answered, with few candidates being aware that the inclusion of an exempt company in the group VAT registration would result in the group becoming partially exempt for VAT purposes.

|     |                                    | *Marks* |
| --- | ---------------------------------- | ------- |
| (a) | Schedule DI profit                 | 1       |
|     | Capital gains/roll-over relief     | 2       |
|     | Trade charge                       | 1       |
|     | Group relief                       | 4       |
|     | Corporation tax                    | 1       |
|     | Amounts carried forward            | 2       |
|     |                                    | ———     |
|     | Available                          | 11      |
|     |                                    | ———     |
|     | Maximum                            | 10      |
|     |                                    | ———     |
| (b) | **Transfer of shareholding**       |         |
|     | Present position                   | 1       |
|     | Surrender of trading losses        | 1       |
|     | Conclusion                         | 1       |
|     | Intra-group transfer               | 1       |
|     | **Group VAT registration**         |         |
|     | VAT recovery if partially exempt   | 2       |
|     | Intra-group supplies               | 1       |
|     | Conclusion                         | 1       |
|     | *De minimis* limit                 | 2       |
|     |                                    | ———     |
|     | Available                          | 10      |
|     |                                    | ———     |
|     | Maximum                            | 7       |
|     |                                    | ———     |

|  | | Available | 21 |
|---|---|---|---|
|  | | Maximum | 17 |

(As ACT is now excluded from the syllabus, references to the topic have been edited out of the question, comments and examiner's answer).

## ( Step by step answer plan )

### Overview

This is a relatively straightforward question on groups with CT computations requiring group relief given for optimum effect and group rollover relief. A minor part of the question concerns group VAT registration to include an exempt company.

**Step 1**   Read the question and part (a) of the requirements carefully noting the items expected in your answer. It might help to sketch out the group structure so you can see clearly which companies are in a group for, say, group relief purposes.

**Step 2**   Prepare a tabular PCTCT layout covering each of the 4 companies side by side.

**Step 3**   Deal with the items which will appear in the layout. This means spotting that £70,000 of Hydra's gain remains chargeable after rollover relief on a group-wide basis and only Cobra can benefit from Mamba's trading loss. Hydra's loss will have best effect in Boa (although it could instead be group relieved to Cobra). All these points should be documented in your answer as explanations are expected.

**Step 4**   Fill in the layout as planned above.

**Step 5**   Compute CT for each company.

**Step 6**   List out any unrelieved amounts to carry forward. It is not specifically asked for but it is good practice and, more to the point, marks are allocated for this task in the marking guide.

**Step 7**   Answer part (b) (i). It might help you to redraft your sketch of the group structure to high light the change proposed and the fact that Mamba now becomes a 75% group company for group relief with Hydra and Boa - not just Cobra.

**Step 8**   Answer part (b) (ii) under the following topic paragraphs:

- Effect of inclusion of an exempt supplier company on group input VAT recovery
- The treatment of inter-company supplies
- Whether inclusion would be beneficial with specific mention of the de minimis limits.

## ( The examiner's answer )

(a)    The corporation tax liability for each of companies in the Hydra Ltd group for the year ended 31 March 2000 is as follows:

|  | Hydra Ltd £ | Boa Ltd £ | Cobra Ltd £ | Mamba Ltd £ |
|---|---|---|---|---|
| Schedule D1 profit |  | 120,000 | 85,000 |  |
| Capital gain | 70,000 |  |  | 8,000 |
|  | 70,000 | 120,000 | 85,000 | 8,000 |
| Trade charge | (20,000) |  |  |  |
|  | 50,000 | 120,000 | 85,000 | 8,000 |

| | | | | |
|---|---|---|---|---|
| Group relief | | | | |
| Hydra Ltd | | (45,000) | | |
| Mamba Ltd | | | (12,000) | |
| PCTCT | 50,000 | 75,000 | 73,000 | 8,000 |
| CT at 20% | 10,000 | 15,000 | 14,600 | 1,600 |
| Trading loss c/f | 15,000 | | | |
| Capital loss c/f | | 15,000 | | |

There are four associated companies in the group, so the lower limit for corporation tax purposes is £75,000 (300,000/4). Mamba Ltd is a 75% subsidiary of Cobra Ltd, but is not a 75% subsidiary of Hydra Ltd (80% × 80% = 64%). Its trading loss can therefore only be surrendered to Cobra Ltd. Hydra Ltd's trading loss of £45,000 has been surrendered to Boa Ltd in order to bring its profits down to the lower limit.

Roll-over relief has been claimed in respect of Hydra Ltd's capital gain, based on the replacement asset purchased by Boa Ltd. Since the proceeds from the disposal of Hydra Ltd's factory were £350,000, and the new office building purchased by Boa Ltd only cost £280,000, £70,000 of Hydra Ltd's capital gain cannot be rolled over.

(b)  (i)  Mamba Ltd is a 75% subsidiary of Hydra Ltd as regards the intra-group transfer of assets. This position would not alter if the 80% shareholding in Mamba Ltd was transferred from Cobra Ltd to Hydra Ltd.

However, Mamba Ltd is not a 75% subsidiary of Hydra Ltd as regards the surrender of trading losses. Mamba Ltd can therefore only surrender trading losses to (or claim trading losses from) Cobra Ltd. For the year ended 31 March 2000 this has not affected the group's overall corporation tax liability, but it could restrict the group's flexibility in utilising trading losses in future years. Unless there are non-tax reasons for not doing so, it would be beneficial for the group to transfer the 80% shareholding in Mamba Ltd from Cobra Ltd to Hydra Ltd. This would be an intra-group transfer of assets, and so would not result in a chargeable gain or an allowable loss. It might be necessary to compensate the minority shareholders of Cobra Ltd.

(ii)  The inclusion of Mamba Ltd in the group VAT registration will result in the group being partially exempt for VAT purposes. The group's recovery of input VAT would then be calculated as follows:

-  That input tax which relates to supplies that are wholly used in making taxable supplies will be fully recoverable.

-  That input tax which relates to supplies that are wholly used in making exempt supplies will not be recoverable.

-  The deductible proportion of the remaining input tax is normally found using the ratio of taxable supplies to total supplies.

The inclusion of Mamba Ltd in the group VAT registration would also mean that supplies of goods and services between Mamba Ltd and the other group companies would be disregarded for VAT purposes. This will be beneficial where supplies are made to Mamba Ltd, as at present the input tax on these is not recoverable.

In order to decide if Mamba Ltd's inclusion in the group VAT registration will be beneficial, it will be necessary for the group to compare the present recovery of input tax to the prospective recovery of input tax under the above rules. It would definitely be beneficial to include Mamba Ltd in the group VAT registration if the total exempt input tax calculated under the above rules amounted to less than the *de minimis* limit of £625 per month on average, and was no more than 50% of the total input VAT. In this case, 100% of the group's input VAT would be recoverable.

However, Customs can exclude a company from group registration 'for the protection of the revenue', although this is likely only to be used in cases of blatant VAT avoidance and it is probable that this would not apply in this case.

## 47    (Answer 5 of examination)

### Examiner's comments and marking guide

Part (a) tested candidates' knowledge of Inland Revenue investigations. Part (b), tested candidates' ability to calculate the interest on overdue income tax and to state the penalties that can be imposed. Part (c) tested candidates' ability to calculate the capital loss on the disposal of shares and their ability to advise on the utilisation of the resultant capital loss.

This was the least popular question on the paper, and was generally answered quite badly. In part (a), many candidates did not appreciate that the main reason for the Inland Revenue investigation was the shortfall in cash sales. The reasons given ranged from the fall in the net profit percentage (despite this being entirely due to the fall in the gross profit percentage) to the fact that the accounting profit was the same figure as the tax adjusted profit. Very few candidates gave valid criteria that the taxpayer could put forward to justify the profit figure, even where they had correctly identified the fall in the gross profit percentage as the reason for the Inland Revenue investigation. Part (b) was also badly answered, with few candidates attempting to calculate the amount of tax not postponed (this point is no longer in the syllabus). In part (c), a disappointing number of candidates included indexation in their calculation for the capital loss, and very few candidates were aware of relief for shares in an unquoted trading company under Section 574 ICTA 1988.

|  |  | *Marks* |
|---|---|---|
| (a) | **Reason for investigation** | |
| | Discussion of GP% | 2 |
| | Shortfall in cash sales | 2 |
| | Impact of adjustment | 1 |
| | **Justification of profits** | |
| | Lower margin/different mix | 1 |
| | Increase in cost price/theft | 1 |
| | Evidence | 1 |
| | | — |
| | Available | 8 |
| | | — |
| | Maximum | 5 |
| | | — |
| (b) | **Interest on overdue tax** | |
| | Period interest runs for | 1 |
| | Amount of interest | 1 |
| | **Penalty** | |
| | Maximum penalty | 1 |
| | Mitigation | 1 |
| | | — |
| | Maximum/Available | 4 |
| | | — |
| (c) | **Capital loss** | |
| | 1982 pool | 2 |
| | Calculation of capital loss | 2 |
| | 31 March 1982 election | 1 |
| | **Utilisation of loss** | |
| | Chargeable gains/carry forward | 1 |
| | Claim under s574 ICTA 1988 | 2 |
| | **If the appeal is won** | |
| | Income tax refund | 1 |
| | Factors to consider | 2 |
| | **If the appeal is lost** | |

| | |
|---|---:|
| Claim against total income of 1999-00 | 1 |
| Tax relief | 1 |
| Impact on interest and penalty | 1 |
| | — |
| Available | 14 |
| | — |
| Maximum | 11 |
| | — |
| Available | 26 |
| | — |
| Maximum | 20 |
| | — |

*(Tutorial note:* Part (b) of this question has been rewritten due to syllabus changes. Originally 9 marks were available - this has been reduced to 4 marks.*)*

## Step by step answer plan

**Overview**

This is a question on a mixture of personal tax topics with the largest single part placed at the end and being clearly dependent on the correct treatment of earlier parts of the question.

**Step 1**   Read the question and the requirements carefully and be sure you understand how they inter-relate. For example, the first paragraph will not be relevant until answering part (c). Unfortunately this is at odds with the normal expectation that information is presented in the order needed in the answer.

**Step 2**   Answer part (a) (i). Notice that part (a) (ii) of the requirements virtually provides the main gist of the answer to part (i).

**Step 3**   Answer part (a) (ii). Most of the points you would make are actually based on a common-sense understanding of how cash businesses work.

**Step 4**   Deal briefly with the interest and penalty matters in part (b). You either know the answers or you don't. Marks are not given for peripheral points.

**Step 5**   For part (c) (i), calculate the loss on the disposal of the 1982 holding. Check your workings as the loss impacts on the next requirement and reread the first paragraph of the question. As these are the only chargeable assets he held in March 1982 a global rebasing election is still possible. You should spot therefore that the allowable loss can be increased if the election is made.

**Step 6**   Part (c) (ii) needs some care. Remember that losses on unquoted trading company subscriber shares attract s574 relief whereby the capital loss can relieve income in a way akin to s380 relief. Your answer therefore divides neatly into discussions on:

- The general choices for relieving the capital loss
- The use of the loss if the appeal is won
- The use if the appeal is lost - ie, use to reduce the profits originally understated.

## The examiner's answer

(a)   (i)   The main reason why the Inland Revenue will have investigated Harry's accounts for the period ended 5 April 2000 is because of the fall in the GP% compared to the accounts of the previous owner. Harry's GP% is 30% (75,000/(200,000 + 50,000) × 100), compared to 41.7% (150,000/(300,000 + 60,000) × 100) for the previous owner. An analysis of the two sets of accounts shows that Harry's credit sales, cost of sales and expenses are all in line with those of the previous owner. However, Harry's cash sales were £200,000 compared to an expected £250,000 (300,000 × 10/12), which is a shortfall of £50,000. The Inland Revenue will therefore contend that cash sales of

£50,000 have not been recorded.  The adjustment will increase Harry's GP% to 41.7% (75,000 + 50,000/(200,000 + 50,000 + 50,000) × 100).

---

**Did you answer the question?**

There are cases where it is not initially obvious why the Revenue open an enquiry.  However, the reason is clear in this case so you are not required to discuss the question in more general terms - eg, enquiries commenced because of observations of a luxurious life style at odds with the level of disclosed income or prompted by letters of denunciation from disgruntled former employees or mistresses!

---

(ii)    Harry could put forward the following criteria to justify the fall in GP% from 41.7% to 30%:

-        He may have been selling goods at a lower margin than the previous owner.

-        He may have been selling a different mix of goods to the previous owner (assuming that different goods have different margins).

-        There may have been an increase in the cost price of goods which could not be passed on (or not fully passed on) to customers.

-        He may have suffered increased theft or wastage of goods.

It will be necessary to provide evidence for any of the above criteria put forward (for example details of cost prices and selling prices), although this would be very difficult in the case of proving theft.

(b)    (i)    Interest will run from 1 February 2001 to 30 August 2001 and will be as follows:

£50,000 at 40% = £20,000 × 10% × 7/12 = £1,167

(ii)    Harry is liable under s95 TMA 1970 for negligently or fraudulently submitting an incorrect return.  The maximum penalty is the amount of income tax underpaid by reason of the incorrectness.  This is £20,000.

The Inland Revenue will mitigate this maximum penalty depending on Harry's co-operation in the enquiry, whether information was disclosed voluntarily, and to what degree his actions are considered to be fraudulent.

(c)    (i)    1982 Pool

|  | Number | Cost £ | 31.3.82 value £ |
|---|---|---|---|
| 15.6.81 | 25,000 | 25,000 | 31,250 |
| Rights issue 26.1.86 | 75,000 | 375,000 | 375,000 |
|  | 100,000 | 400,000 | 406,250 |
| Proceeds (80,000 at 3.35) |  | 268,000 | 268,000 |
| Cost (400,000 × 80,000/100,000) |  | 320,000 |  |
| 31.3.82 value (406,250 × 80,000/100,000) |  |  | 325,000 |
| Capital loss |  | (52,000) | (57,000) |

The indexation allowance cannot increase a loss.  Harry's capital loss for 1999-00 is the lower loss of £52,000.  However, since Harry's shareholding in UTC Ltd is the only chargeable asset that he held at 31 March 1982, it would be beneficial for him to elect by 31 January 2002 to have all of his gains or losses arising from assets held at 31 March 1982 to be computed by reference to their 31 March 1982 value.  This would increase Harry's capital loss to £57,000.

---

(ii)     Harry's capital loss of £57,000 can be utilised as follows:

-        It can be set against chargeable gains if any, for 1999-00.

-        It can be carried forward for relief against chargeable gains (in excess of the annual exemption) of future years.

-        As the loss is in respect of shares in an unquoted trading company, a claim can be made under s574 ICTA 1988 by 31 January 2002 to have the capital loss set against Harry's total income of 1999-00 and/or income of 1998-99.

Unless Harry has substantial chargeable gains in 1999-00 or is anticipating them in 2000-01, it would be beneficial for Harry to claim under s574 ICTA 1988.

### If Harry wins the appeal

If the appeal is won, then Harry's total income for 1999-00 will be £40,000, compared to total income of £45,000 for 1998-99. The income tax refund will be the same whether a claim is made first against total income of 1999-00 and then against 1998-99 or vice versa. The following factors will have to be taken into account when deciding as to the order of the claims:

-        An initial claim against total income of 1999-00 will eliminate Harry's class 4 NIC liability for that year.

-        Whether tax is repaid for 1998/99 or 1999/00 the Revenue will only pay interest from 31 January 2001.

-        A carry back claim to 1998/99 will not reduce payments on account for 1999/00. However, using the loss in 1999/00 reduces payments on account for 2000/01.

-        An initial claim against total income of 1998-99 will preserve the maximum amount of total income for 1999-00 should a subsequent loss claim be made.

### If Harry loses the appeal

If the appeal is lost, then Harry's total income for 1999-00 will be £90,000. The claim should therefore be made against total income of 1999-00. This would obtain tax relief at 40% for the capital loss, reducing Harry's 1999-00 income tax liability by £22,800 (57,000 at 40%). As this would eliminate the additional income tax liability for 1999-00 of £20,000, it would also eliminate the related interest charges (and possible penalties).

## 48     (Answer 6 of examination)

**( Examiner's comments and marking guide )**

**Part (a) tested candidates' ability to calculate the CGT liability on the disposal of a principal private residence that is only partially exempt. Part (b) tested candidates' knowledge of the enterprise investment scheme, and venture capital trusts. Part (c) tested candidates' knowledge of the Schedule A provisions as applied to an unfurnished letting and a furnished holiday letting.**

This question was reasonably popular. Although there were some very good answers, the majority of candidates only scored average marks for this question due to a lack of knowledge as regards the enterprise investment scheme and venture capital trusts, and because they were unaware of the new Schedule A rules. In part (a), although most candidates correctly calculated the capital gain, few could then correctly calculate the chargeable element of the gain. Part (b) was either answered quite well, or quite badly, depending on a candidate's knowledge of the enterprise investment scheme and venture capital trusts. Some candidates did not pick up all the marks available, as they combined the two schemes into one answer. In part (c), it was very disappointing to see that a considerable number of candidates were unaware of the new Schedule A rules, despite this topic being included in the Examiner's article on the Finance Act 1996. Candidates were also often confused as to the distinction between revenue and capital expenditure.

| | | Marks |
|---|---|---|
| (a) | Calculation of capital gain | 2 |
| | CGT liability | 2 |
| | | — |
| | Maximum/Available | 4 |
| | | — |
| | | |
| (b) | Qualifying investments | 1 |
| | Amount to be invested/deferral | 1 |
| | **Enterprise investment scheme** | |
| | Period of investment/qualifying shares | 1 |
| | Other reliefs available | 2 |
| | **Venture capital trusts** | |
| | Period of investment | 1 |
| | Description of VCT | 2 |
| | Other reliefs available | 1 |
| | | — |
| | Available | 9 |
| | | — |
| | Maximum | 8 |
| | | — |
| (c) | Basis of assessment | 1 |
| | **Repairs to roof** | |
| | Classification as capital expenditure | 1 |
| | **Let as unfurnished accommodation** | |
| | Decoration costs | 2 |
| | Capital gain | 1 |
| | **Let as furnished holiday accommodation** | |
| | Conversion costs | 1 |
| | Furnishings | 1 |
| | Deductions | 2 |
| | Furnished holiday letting - reliefs | 2 |
| | Capital gain/enhanced taper relief | 2 |
| | VAT | 1 |
| | Conclusion | 1 |
| | | — |
| | Available | 15 |
| | | — |
| | Maximum | 13 |
| | | — |
| | Available | 29 |
| | | — |
| | Maximum | 25 |
| | | — |

## Step by step answer plan

### Overview

This is a fairly straightforward personal tax question in three parts. Although the house in London is common to all parts, each part can be answered independently so the risk of mistakes impacting more than once is avoided.

**Step 1** Compute the gain on the gift net of PPR relief and compute the CGT payable.

**Step 2** For part (b), start by explaining in general terms how deferral relief would work on the gain where Muriel makes a qualifying reinvestment. Then explain the particular rules applying for each of the two types of reinvestment and give a conclusion.

Step 3     For part (c), first cover any points which do not depend on whether the house is let unfurnished or as a FHL. For example, the cost of roof repairs will be treated as capital regardless of the subsequent type of letting.

Step 4     Your part (b) answer then covers separately the relevant points for the two different forms of letting, in particular mentioning the tax advantages of FHL and concluding with your advice on the preferable form of letting.

## The examiner's answer

(a)

|  | £ |
|---|---:|
| Deemed proceeds | 320,000 |
| Cost (60,000 × 72,000/(72,000 + 24,000)) | 45,000 |
|  | 275,000 |
| Indexation $45,000 \times \dfrac{162.6 - 94.78}{94.78}(0.716)$ | 32,220 |
|  | 242,780 |
| Fully chargeable 242,780 × (87 – 36)/177 (TN 1) | 69,954 |
| Partially chargeable 242,780 × 69/177 × 20% | 18,929 |
|  | 88,883 |
| CGT liability 88,883 at 40% | 35,553 |

**Did you answer the question?**

You are not required to state the pay day for the CGT.

(b)     Muriel will be entitled to deferral relief if the 'proceeds' from the disposal of the house are 're-invested' in the ordinary share capital of an unquoted trading company. For this purpose, companies quoted on the Unlisted Securities Market do not qualify, but those quoted on the Alternative Investment Market do.

Muriel will only need to invest £88,883 in order for the entire gain to be deferred. The gain would normally be deferred until the shares are disposed of, although further re-investment could be made at that time. There are two ways of obtaining deferral relief:

**Enterprise investment scheme (EIS)**

The investment must be made in the period beginning on 1 January 1999 and ending on 31 December 2002, and the investment must be in newly issued shares. In addition to CGT deferral relief, Muriel will be entitled to income tax relief of £17,777 (88,883 at 20%) in respect of an investment under the EIS. Provided the shares are held for five years, their disposal will be exempt from CGT although the deferred gain then becomes chargeable. If a loss is made on the disposal of shares, then relief will be available against either capital gains or income. The calculation of the loss is based on the cost of the shares less any EIS income tax relief obtained and not withdrawn.

**Venture capital trusts (VCTs)**

The investment must be made in the period beginning on 1 January 1999 and ending on 31 December 2000. A VCT must have at least 70% of its investments in unquoted trading companies, and 30% of this investment must be in the form of new ordinary shares. The companies invested in must have gross assets of not more than £15 million before not more than £16 million after the investment. The reliefs available are similar to those under the EIS, with the addition that dividend income from a VCT is exempt from income tax. There is no requirement for the shares in a VCT to be held for five years in order for their disposal to be exempt from CGT. However, there is no relief if a loss is made on the disposal of shares in a VCT.

### Conclusion

Unless Muriel wants to invest in particular unquoted companies, investment in a VCT would appear to be the most beneficial option. This is also the least riskiest method of investing in unquoted companies.

(c)    In either case, Bertie will be assessed on the profits of a business of letting property under Schedule A. The assessment will be on a strict actual basis from 6 April to 5 April, and will be calculated in accordance with most of the rules used in calculating trading profits assessable under Schedule D case I. Rents will be assessable on an accruals basis.

### Repairs to roof

The roof was damaged before Muriel transferred the house to Bertie. Since the roof must be repaired before the house can be let, the house would not appear to be usable at the time of the transfer. The cost of repair of £24,000 is therefore likely to be classed as capital expenditure following **Law Shipping Co Ltd v CIR (1923)**. This will increase Bertie's base cost for CGT purposes.

### Let as unfurnished accommodation

The cost of decoration would normally be a revenue expense. However, the house has been unoccupied since 1 October 1992, and some of the expenditure may be classed as capital if the house was in a bad state of repair on 31 December 1999. The decoration will presumably be carried out before letting commences, and so will be pre-trading expenditure. This will be allowed as an expense on the first day of business. Any capital gain arising on the disposal of the house when Bertie retires at 60, will be fully chargeable with only the non-business rate of taper relief available.

### Let as furnished holiday accommodation

The cost of converting the house into two separate units will be mainly capital expenditure, and this will increase Bertie's base cost for CGT purposes. The figure of £41,000 may include some revenue expenditure, such as decorating costs, and this will be treated as above. The £9,000 cost of furnishing the two units will be capital expenditure. Bertie will be able to claim the following deductions from his annual gross rents of £45,000:

(i)     The loan interest of £6,000 (50,000 at 12%)

(ii)    A wear and tear deduction in respect of the furniture. This will be based on either 10% of the net rent (which is likely to be 45,000 × 10% = £4,500) or on a renewals basis.

(iii)   The letting agency fees of £10,125 (45,000 at 22.5%).

(iv)    The other running costs of £3,500.

Expenses will be restricted if Bertie occupies the house for his own use. Given Bertie's level of rental income the letting is likely to qualify for the special rules applicable to furnished holiday lettings. This will mean that:

(i)     Capital allowances will be available on plant and machinery, such as furniture and kitchen equipment. This will almost certainly be more beneficial than the wear and tear allowance.

(ii)    The Schedule A profit will qualify as net relevant earnings for personal pension purposes.

(iii)   Loss relief will be available against total income.

Qualification as furnished holiday accommodation will also mean that Bertie will be entitled to the business rate of taper relief when the house is disposed of. Retirement relief will not be available for disposals after 5 April 2003.

The letting of holiday accommodation is standard rated for VAT purposes. The forecast rental income of £45,000 is below the VAT registration limit of £51,000, but the impact of VAT will have to be considered if Bertie is already registered for VAT, or if there is an increase in rental income.

---

**Did you answer the question?**

You were not asked to state the minimum qualifying conditions for FHLs and it was clear from the question that this term was understood by Bertie.

---

### Conclusion

Letting the house as a furnished holiday letting will produce annual income of approximately £25,375 (45,000 − 6,000 − 10,125 − 3,500), compared to £28,000 if the house is let unfurnished. It will also be necessary to incur additional expenditure of £46,500 (41,000 + 9,000 − 3,500). This must be compared against the potential CGT saving upon the disposal of the house arising from the business rate of taper relief..

---

**Tutorial notes**

1       PPR periods of London house:

Total ownership period - 1 April 1985 to 31 December 1999 = 177 months

Period of non-occupation (excluding final 36 months):
1 October 1992 to 31 December 1996 = 51 months

Period of partial use as main residence:
1 January 1987 to 30 September 1992 = 69 months

Note that provided the property has been the owner's main residence at some time, the last 36 months of ownership are treated as 'occupation' regardless of whether an election has already been made for some other property to be the main residence.

---

## DECEMBER 1996 QUESTIONS

## 49 (Question 1 of examination)

ABC Ltd is an unquoted trading company that is under the control of three sisters, Agnes, Betty and Chloe, and is a close company. The share capital of ABC Ltd consists of 100,000 £1 ordinary shares, of which Agnes owns 20,000, Betty 40,000 and Chloe 40,000. Agnes and Betty are full-time working directors of the company, but Chloe is neither a director nor an employee.

Agnes is 57 years old, and is to retire on 31 December 1999. She will sell her 20,000 shares in ABC Ltd to Betty and Chloe for £20 per share. ABC Ltd's shares are currently worth £30 each for a minority shareholding. Agnes acquired her shares at their par value on 1 July 1992, the date of ABC Ltd's incorporation. She became a full-time working director of ABC Ltd on 1 July 1993. The market value of ABC Ltd's assets at 31 December 1999 is forecast to be as follows:

|  | £ |
| --- | --- |
| Goodwill | 500,000 |
| Freehold property - factory and warehouse | 1,050,000 |
| Plant and machinery (costing more than £6,000 per item) | 400,000 |
| Investments in quoted companies | 700,000 |
| Motor cars | 100,000 |
| Current assets | 750,000 |
|  | 3,500,000 |

Agnes personally owns a freehold office building that is used rent free by ABC Ltd. This cost £78,000 on 1 January 1996, and is to be sold to Betty and Chloe for its current market value of £125,000 on 31 December 1999.

ABC Ltd will make an interest free loan of £200,000 to Chloe in order to help her finance the acquisitions from Agnes. This loan will be repaid over the next four years. ABC Ltd has an accounting date of 30 September, and is expected to have profits chargeable to corporation tax of £800,000 for the year ended 30 September 2000. No dividends will be paid during the year.

Agnes, Betty and Chloe are all 40% taxpayers. Agnes has not made any lifetime gifts of assets, and has an estate (excluding the above assets and the consideration to be paid by Betty and Chloe) valued at £400,000 which she has left to her children.

**Required:**

(a)     Calculate Agnes' CGT liability for 1999-00. Your answer should include an explanation of the amount of retirement relief that will be available to Agnes. You should assume that holdover relief is **not claimed** in respect of the gift of business assets.     **(12 marks)**

(b)     Calculate the IHT liabilities that would arise if Agnes were to die on 30 June 2002. You should assume that the shareholding in ABC Ltd is still owned by Betty and Chloe at that date, and that the tax rates for 1999-00 apply throughout.     **(7 marks)**

(c)     Briefly advise both ABC Ltd and Chloe of the tax implications arising from the provision of the interest free loan of £200,000.     **(4 marks)**

(d)     As an alternative to Agnes selling her shareholding in ABC Ltd to Betty and Chloe, it has been suggested that the shareholding should instead by purchased by ABC Ltd for £20 per share. The purchase will not qualify for the special treatment applying to a company's purchase of its own shares, and will therefore be treated as a distribution.

Advise Agnes of the tax implications arising from the company making a distribution. You are **not expected** to calculate ABC Ltd's corporation tax liability.     **(2 marks)**

**(Total: 25 marks)**

## 50    (Question 2 of examination)

(a)    "Every man is entitled if he can to order his affairs so that the tax attaching . . . is less than it otherwise would be".

*Duke of Westminster v CIR (1935).*

**Required:**

Briefly explain the difference between tax avoidance and tax evasion.    **(2 marks)**

(b)    You are the tax adviser to Lucy Lee, who has been a self-employed architect for the previous 20 years.  You should assume that today's date is 20 April 2000.  Lucy has asked for your advice on the following matters:

(1)    From 1 April 2000 Lucy has employed her husband, who was previously unemployed, as a personal assistant at a salary of £28,000 pa.  This is more than Lucy's previous personal assistant was paid, but she considers this to be good tax planning.  Lucy estimates that her Schedule D case II profit for the year ended 31 March 2001 will be £180,000.  Her husband has no other income.

Lucy wants to know if employing her husband at a salary of £28,000 will result in an overall tax saving, and how such an arrangement will be viewed by the Inland Revenue.

(2)    On 1 April 2000 Lucy set up a new business venture in partnership with her brother.  The partnership designs building extensions for the general public at a fixed fee of £1,000 (including VAT).  The forecast fee income is £35,000 pa.  A deposit of £500 is paid upon the commencement of each contract, which takes one month to complete.  An invoice is then issued 21 days after the completion of the contract, with the balance of the contract price being due within a further 14 days.  The partnership uses the office premises, equipment and employees of Lucy's architectural business.

(i)    Lucy wants to know if the partnership will automatically have to account for VAT on its income as a result of her architectural business being registered for VAT.

(ii)    Assuming that the new partnership **does** automatically have to account for VAT on its income, Lucy wants advice as to the basis that output VAT will have to be accounted for.

(3)    Lucy's daughter is to get married on 25 May 2000, and Lucy is to make her a wedding gift of £12,500.  Lucy's husband does not have any capital of his own, so Lucy is to make a gift of £12,500 to him on 24 May 2000 in order that he can make a similar wedding gift to the daughter.  Neither Lucy nor her husband have made any lifetime transfers of value within the previous three years.  Lucy wants to know the tax implications of such an arrangement.

**Required:**

Advise Lucy in respect of the matters that she has raised.  You should assume that the tax rates and allowances for 1999-00 apply throughout.

You should note that marks for this part of the question will be allocated on the basis of:

7 marks to (1)
6 marks to (2)
4 marks to (3)
    **(17 marks)**
    **(Total: 19 marks)**

*(Tutorial note:  Part of (b), worth 6 marks, related to the transitional rules for Schedule D Cases I & II which are no longer examinable and has been deleted.)*

## 51 (Question 3 of examination)

(a) Walter Smith, aged 59, retired from his employment on 6 April 1999. He receives pensions of £21,690 pa commencing on 6 April 1999. Walter has re-invested all of his savings overseas, and will receive the following income for 1999-00:

    (1) Rental income of £8,500 (gross) from property situated in Arcadia. The rental income will be subject to Arcadian tax at the rate of 40%.

    (2) Interest of £4,200 (gross) from Arcadia government stocks. The interest will be subject to Arcadian tax at the rate of 15%.

**Required:**

Calculate Walter's UK income tax liability for 1999-00. **(6 marks)**.

(b) In two years time, Walter and his wife are to leave the UK and are going to live in Arcadia. After leaving the UK, Walter will have the following chargeable assets:

|  | £ |
|---|---|
| Assets situated in the UK | 310,000 |
| Assets situated in Arcadia | 190,000 |
| Total assets | 500,000 |

If Walter were to die after moving to Arcadia, Arcadian death duty of £125,000 (500,000 at 25%) would be payable on his worldwide assets. There is no double taxation treaty between the UK and Arcadia. Walter has not made any lifetime transfers of value.

**Required:**

(i) Advise Walter of when he will cease to be treated as domiciled in the UK for the purposes of IHT.

**(3 marks)**

(ii) Calculate Walter's liability to UK IHT if he were to die after leaving the UK and (1) be treated as domiciled in the UK , or (2) be treated as not domiciled in the UK. You should use the IHT rates for 1999-00. **(4 marks)**

**(Total: 13 marks)**

**(as amended)**

(A further part of the question has been excluded as it concerns a topic no longer examinable.)

## 52 (Question 4 of examination)

Jock and Maggie McHaggis are a married couple aged 36 and 38 respectively. Jock is a self-employed computer programmer, with annual tax adjusted Schedule D case II trading profits of £40,000. Of this figure, £34,000 relates to writing business software, whilst £6,000 relates to writing games software. The profits of £34,000 for writing business software are after taking into account capital allowances on Jock's private motor car, which currently has a tax written down value of £14,500. Jock drives 20,000 miles per year, of which 16,000 are for business purposes. None of the mileage is in respect of writing games software.

Jock owns 15,000 £1 ordinary shares in Lowloch plc. He inherited the shares on the death of his uncle, at which time they were worth £1.20 each. The shares are now worth £2.50 each. Lowloch plc pays annual dividends of 22.5 pence per share. Jock has deposits of £55,000 with the Ben & Burn Building Society, on which he receives interest at the rate of 7% pa (gross).

His only outgoing is interest at the rate of 10% pa (gross) on a mortgage of £40,000. The mortgage is not within the MIRAS arrangements.

Maggie is employed as a saleswoman at an annual salary of £18,500. She has the use of a new 1600cc company motor car with a list price of £11,500, and drives 20,000 business miles per year. No private fuel is provided.

A financial plan has been prepared for the couple that would reorganise their financial affairs as follows:

(1)    A new limited company, McHaggis Ltd, will be formed, which will be wholly owned by Jock. The writing of business software will be undertaken by Jock for the company. Jock will still write games software on a self-employed basis. Jock will not receive any directors remuneration from the company, but will instead draw dividends of £2,000 per month.

       Jock will continue to use his private motor car for business mileage. McHaggis Ltd will reimburse him for business mileage at the rate of 40 pence per mile for the first 4,000 miles, and 20 pence per mile thereafter. It should be assumed that these rates are the maximum allowed under the fixed profit car scheme.

(2)    The maximum amount possible of the shares in Lowloch plc are to be held in an individual savings account. The remainder of the shares will be sold with the proceeds being invested in an income producing investment trust. The investment trust will produce a similar return to that from the shares in Lowloch plc. The relevant RPI factor in respect of the disposal is 0.390.

(3)    Of the building society deposits £20,000 will be used to repay a proportion of the mortgage. This is the maximum amount that Jock is prepared to repay off the mortgage at the present time.

**Required:**

(a)    Advise Jock and Maggie of the income tax, CGT, corporation tax and NIC implications of the proposed financial plan. You should **ignore** the implications of VAT. Your answer should include:

       (i)     a calculation of the couple's taxable income before the financial plan is implemented,

       (ii)    a calculation of the tax saving that will result from each aspect of the financial plan. Your answer should be confined to the tax saving in the first year following the implementation of the financial plan,

       (iii)   advice as to any further tax planning measures that the couple should take, together with a calculation of the resulting tax saving. Your advice should be confined to the information given in the question,

                                                                                                          **(20 marks)**

(b)    (i)     advise Jock and Maggie as to where they could obtain independent financial advice,    **(2 marks)**

       (ii)    briefly state whether or not you, as a qualified Certified Accountant, would need to be authorised to conduct investment business under the Financial Services Act 1986 in order to provide the financial advice given to Jock and Maggie.                                                       **(3 marks)**

                                                                                                   **(Total: 25 marks)**

---

## 53    (Question 5 of examination)

(a)    You are the tax adviser to Alphabet Engineering, a three person partnership running an engineering business that commenced trading on 1 January 1998. Until 30 June 1999 the partnership consisted of Alfred, Bertie and Claude, with profits being shared in the ratio 5:3:2. On 30 June 1999 Claude resigned as a partner, and was replaced on 1 July 1999 by Daniel. The basis of profit sharing remained unchanged, with Daniel taking over Claude's profit share.

       The partnership's tax adjusted Schedule D case I trading profit for the year ended 31 December 1998 was £122,000 (after capital allowances). The partnership's profit and loss account for the year ended 31 December 1999 is forecast to be as follows:

|  | £ | £ |
|---|---|---|
| Gross profit |  | 420,000 |
| Less:  Administration expenses (all allowable) | 253,600 |  |
| Depreciation | 5,400 |  |
| Amortisation of lease | 2,500 |  |
|  |  | 261,500 |
| Net profit for the year |  | 158,500 |

The partnership paid a premium of £25,000 for the grant of a 10 year lease on a workshop on 1 January 1998. The tax written-down value of plant and machinery at 31 December 1998 was as follows:

|  | £ |
|---|---|
| Pooled assets | 22,000 |
| Partners' motor cars (owned by the partnership): |  |
| Alfred - 40% private use | 14,500 |
| Bertie - 80% private use | 8,000 |
| Claude - 80% private use | 15,000 |

Claude retained his motor car when he resigned from the partnership on 30 June 1999, at which date it was valued at £13,500. On 1 July 1999 Daniel introduced his private motor car into the partnership at a value of £10,000. The private use of this motor car is 70%.

The partnership's estimated tax adjusted Schedule D case I trading profit for the year ended 31 December 2000 is £190,000 (after capital allowances).

**Required:**

Advise the partners of the partnership profits that will be assessed on each of them for 1999-00. Your calculations should be made on a monthly basis. **(12 marks)**

(b)    Alfred Letter, the senior partner of Alphabet Engineering, would like to start saving for his retirement. Alfred was born on 10 December 1961, and has not made any previous payments in respect of an entitlement to a pension. From 6 April 1992 to 31 December 1997 he was in employment at an annual salary of £36,000: but **was not** a member of an occupational pension scheme. Alfred is single, and has no other income or outgoings.

**Required:**

(i)    Calculate the maximum tax deductible contribution that Alfred could make into a personal pension scheme for 1999-00 **(5 marks).**

(ii)   Briefly advise Alfred of whether or not it would be beneficial for him to actually contribute this maximum amount for 1999-00. **(4 marks)**

(c)    On 31 December 2000 Alphabet Engineering is to sell the lease on its leasehold workshop (see part (a)) for £45,000, and will purchase the freehold of a new workshop for £65,000.

**Required:**

Advise the partners of Alphabet Engineering of the tax implications arising from the disposal of the leasehold workshop and the acquisition of the freehold workshop. **(4 marks)**

**(Total:  25 marks)**

## 54 (Question 6 of examination)

Ongoing Ltd holds 80% of the ordinary share capital of Goodbye Ltd. Goodbye Ltd has faced deteriorating results in recent years, and therefore ceased trading on 31 December 1999. The company's recent results up to the date of its cessation are as follows:

|  | Adjusted DI profit/(loss) | Schedule A | Capital gain/ (loss) | Patent royalty paid (gross) | Deed of covenant paid to charity (gross) |
|---|---|---|---|---|---|
|  | £ | £ | £ | £ | £ |
| 12 months to 30.9.95 | 88,500 | 6,000 | (24,000) | (12,000) | - |
| 12 months to 30.9.96 | 59,000 | (1,100) | - | (12,000) | - |
| 6 months to 31.3.97 | 62,500 | 2,600 | - | (6,000) | (1,000) |
| 12 months to 31.3.98 | 47,000 | - | 10,800 | (12,000) | (1,000) |
| 12 months to 31.3.99 | 5,000 | - | - | (15,000) | (1,000) |
| 9 months to 31.12.00 | (248,000) | - | 72,000 | (11,250) | (1,000) |

The rental income relates to one floor of Goodbye Ltd's office building that was let out until 31 March 1997.

The forecast results of Ongoing Ltd for the year ended 31 March 2000 are as follows:

|  | £ |
|---|---|
| Adjusted Schedule D1 profit (before interest payable) | 93,000 |
| Bank interest receivable | 3,500 |
| Debenture interest payable | (12,000) |
| Franked investment income – (non-group) | 3,500 |

As at 31 March 1999 Ongoing Ltd had unused trading losses of £14,500

**Required:**

(a)     Assuming that reliefs for trading losses are claimed in the most favourable manner:

(i)      Calculate Goodbye Ltd's corporation tax liabilities for all of the accounting periods from 1 October 1994 to 31 December 1999          **(8 marks)**.

(ii)     Calculate the tax refunds that will be due to Goodbye Ltd as a result of the loss relief claims in respect of its trading loss for the period ended 31 December 1999. You should ignore the possibility of any repayment supplement being due.          **(3 marks)**

(b)     Calculate Ongoing Ltd's profits chargeable to corporation tax for the year ended 31 March 2000. You should assume that the maximum amount of group relief is claimed from Goodbye Ltd.          **(8 marks)**

**(Total: 14 marks)**
**(as amended)**

# ANSWERS TO DECEMBER 1996 EXAMINATION

## 49 (Answer 1 of examination)

### Examiner's comments and marking guide

Part (a) tested candidates' ability to calculate the capital gain arising on the disposal of shares, including a detailed retirement relief calculation. Part (b) tested candidates' ability to calculate the IHT arising from a partial gift of shares, including business property relief. Part (c) tested candidates' knowledge of a close company making a loan to a participator. Part (d) tested candidates' knowledge of a company purchasing its own shares.

This was a popular question, being attempted by the majority of candidates, and there were a number of very good answers. The question examined several changes made by the Finance Act 1997, and there is little excuse for those candidates who did not read the relevant articles covering these changes. Part (a) was generally well answered, although the calculation of the retirement relief often caused problems. Few candidates were aware that retirement relief was available in respect of the office building sold as an associated disposal. Although there were many very good answers to part (b) (and a few perfect answers), a number of candidates were not aware that a disposal at an undervalue is a PET. Other candidates treated the disposal of the office building as a PET, despite this being sold for full consideration. There were also some very good answers to part (c), although a number of candidates were unaware of the change made to the due dates applicable for a loan to a participator by a close company. Part (d) was not answered by some candidates, and those that did were not generally able to calculate the amount of the distribution, otherwise this part of the question was reasonably well answered.

|  |  | *Marks* |
|---|---|---|
| (a) | **Retirement relief** | |
| | Qualifying conditions | 1 |
| | Restriction to 65% | 1 |
| | Restriction to chargeable business assets | 1 |
| | Associated disposal | 2 |
| | **Calculation of CGT liability** | |
| | Capital gain | 1 |
| | Proportion relating to chargeable business assets | 1 |
| | Retirement relief | 1 |
| | Taper relief | 1 |
| | Gain on freehold office building | 1 |
| | Retirement relief on associated disposal | 1 |
| | Annual exemption/CGT | 1 |
| | Maximum/Available | 12 |
| (b) | **Potentially exempt transfer** | |
| | Value transferred | 1 |
| | Business property relief | 2 |
| | Annual exemptions/IHT liability | 1 |
| | **Estate at death** | |
| | Capital gains tax deduction | 1 |
| | Calculation of IHT liability | 2 |
| | Maximum/Available | 7 |
| (c) | Loan to participator | 1 |
| | Payment to the Inland Revenue | 1 |
| | Treatment of tax/Repayment of loan | 1 |
| | Tax position of participator | 1 |

|  | | *Marks* |
|---|---|---:|
| | Maximum/Available | 4 |
| (d) | Assessment on shareholder | 2 |
| | Maximum/Available | 2 |
| | Maximum/Available | 25 |

### ( Step by step answer plan )

**Overview**

This is primarily a capital taxes question with a business flavour although there are also 6 marks for CT/IT matters.

**Step 1**    Read through the question carefully before attempting part (a). The requirements make it clear that retirement relief, but not hold over relief, will apply and any steps in calculating retirement relief should be explained.

**Step 2**    Produce a working of the gain on the sale of the 20,000 shares remembering the rule where sales are to connected persons - ie, use market value instead of actual sale proceeds.

**Step 3**    Calculate the portion of this gain qualifying for retirement relief. It would help if you produced a separate working analysing the assets of the company between chargeable business assets and total chargeable assets although the examiner's answer shows this less formally.

**Step 4**    Produce a working of the gain on the freehold factory.

**Step 5**    Discuss clearly why retirement relief is available and show the reasons for any restrictions.

**Step 6**    Schedule out the gains with the appropriate reductions for retirement, relief taper relief and the annual exemption and compute the CGT thereon.

**Step 7**    Review the question and part (a) of the requirements to ensure you have covered all the relevant points. All the calculations and principles underlying them are based on straightforward mainstream parts of the syllabus and you cannot afford to perform badly on such a large part of the question. Pity to overlook the requirement for explanations when you could do it.

**Step 8**    Read part (b) and review the question for the relevant information. You should spot that the share sale at undervalue produces a PET and although BPR at 100% should apply, there is a restriction for 'excepted' assets. Death within 7 years makes the PET chargeable and absorbs part of the nil band thereby reducing it for the death estate.

**Step 9**    Produce your answer to part (b).

**Step 10**    Produce your answer to part (c). Although you are asked for the tax implications of the provision of the loan, as the question also mentions the repayment arrangements, their tax implications should also be covered.

**Step 11**    As part (c) is not restricted, except to 'tax implications', the effect for the company should also be covered.

**Step 12**    For part (d) the requirement is carefully spelt out and concerns only Agnes.

**Step 13**    Finally re-read the question to ensure all relevant points appear appropriately in your answer.

## The examiner's answer

(a) Agnes is over 50 years old, is a full-time working director of ABC Ltd, which is a trading company, and owns 5% or more of its ordinary share capital. She will therefore be entitled to retirement relief. The relief will be restricted:

(i) To a factor of 65% since Agnes has only been a full-time working director for six years and six months.

(ii) To the proportion of the gain represented by the ratio of ABC Ltd's chargeable business assets (500,000 + 1,050,000 + 400,000 = £1,950,000) to its total chargeable assets (1,950,000 + 700,000 = £2,650,000).

Retirement relief will also be available in respect of Agnes' disposal of the freehold office building since it is an associated disposal. The building has been let rent free to ABC Ltd, and is sold at the same time as her shareholding. The qualifying period will again be six years and six months.

Agnes' CGT liability for 1999-00 will be as follows:

|  | £ | £ |
|---|---|---|
| **Capital gains arising on business assets** | | |
| Shareholding in ABC Ltd (W1) | | 424,269 |
| Retirement relief | | |
| 200,000 × 65% | 130,000 | |
| 424,269 – 130,000 = 294,269 × 50% | 147,134 | |
| | | 277,134 |
| | | 147,135 |
| Freehold office building (W2) | 40,526 | |
| Retirement relief | | |
| 800,000 × 65% = 520,000 | | |
| Less utilised 424,269 | | |
| 95,731 | | |
| Use actual gain 40,526 × 50% | 20,263 | |
| | | 20,263 |
| | | 167,398 |
| **Capital gain arising on non-business assets** | | |
| Shareholding in ABC Ltd (W1) | | 152,302 |
| | | 319,700 |
| Tapered to 85% | | 271,745 |
| Annual exemption | | 7,100 |
| | | 264,645 |
| Capital gains tax at 40% | | 105,858 |

*(Tutorial note:* Taper relief is also available on the residual gains at the business rate as ABC Ltd is a qualifying company in relation to Agnes. This assumes that the investments do not have a substantial effect on the trading activities of the company. The shares themselves therefore qualify and the office building also qualifies as being used in the trade of a qualifying company.*)*

---

**Did you answer the question?**

You are not required to say when the CGT is payable.

---

### Working 1 - Shareholding in ABC Ltd

Since Agnes, Betty and Chloe are connected persons, the market value of the shareholding in ABC Ltd will be used, rather than the sale proceeds.

|  | £ |
|---|---|
| Deemed proceeds (20,000 × £30) | 600,000 |
| Cost | 20,000 |
|  | 580,000 |
| Indexation $20,000 \times \dfrac{162.6 - 138.8}{138.8}$ | 3,429 |
| Capital gain | 576,571 |

Proportion relating to chargeable business assets
$$576,571 \times \frac{1,950,000}{2,650,000} \qquad 424,269$$

Proportion relating to chargeable non-business assets
576,571 – 424,269     152,302

### Working 2 - Freehold office building

|  | £ |
|---|---|
| Sale proceeds | 125,000 |
| Cost | 78,000 |
|  | 47,000 |
| Indexation $78,000 \times \dfrac{162.6 - 150.2}{150.2} = 0.083$ | 6,474 |
| Capital gain | 40,526 |

(b) **Potentially exempt transfer - 31 December 1999**

|  |  | £ | £ |
|---|---|---|---|
| Value transferred (600,000 – 400,000) |  |  | 200,000 |
| Business property relief: |  |  |  |
| $200,000 \times \dfrac{2,800,000}{3,500,000} (3,500,000 - 700,000) \times 100\%$ |  |  | 160,000 |
|  |  |  | 40,000 |
| Annual exemptions | 1999-00 | 3,000 |  |
|  | 1998-99 | 3,000 |  |
|  |  |  | 6,000 |
| Chargeable transfer |  |  | 34,000 |
| IHT liability 34,000 at nil% |  |  | Nil |

**Estate at death - 30 June 2002**

|  | £ | £ |
|---|---|---|
| Present value of estate |  | 400,000 |
| Consideration received (400,000 + 125,000) | 525,000 |  |
| Less capital gains tax | 105,858 |  |
|  |  | 419,142 |
| Chargeable estate |  | 819,142 |

| IHT liability | 231,000 – 34,000 = 197,000 at nil % | Nil |
|---|---|---|
|  | 819,142 – 197,000 = 622,142 at 40% | 248,857 |
|  |  | 248,857 |

---

**Did you answer the question?**

You are not required to say when the IHT is payable.

---

(c)    The loan of £200,000 is a loan to a participator since Chloe is neither a director nor an employee of ABC Ltd. The company must make a tax payment of £50,000 (200,000 × 25%) to the Inland Revenue being equal to 25% of the loan. This will be due on 30 June 2001, being nine months after the end of the accounting period in which the loan is to be made. Tax will not be due on any part of the loan repaid before 30 June 2001. When the loan is repaid, the tax will be refunded, with the tax repayment being made nine months after the end of the accounting period in which the loan repayment occurs. There are no tax implications for Chloe unless part of the loan is written off.

(d)    Agnes will be assessed on the grossed up distribution of £422,222 (380,000 × 100/90), and this will result in an additional income tax liability of £95,000 (422,222 × 32½% = 137,222 – 42,222) for 1999-00.

---

**Did you answer the question?**

As this part only carries 2 marks you were clearly not required to contrast the result with the alternative capital gains treatment as performed in part (a).

---

## 50    (Answer 2 of examination)

( **Examiner's comments and marking guide** )

**Part (a) tested candidates' ability to explain the distinction between tax avoidance and tax evasion. Part (b) tested candidates' ability to advise on (1) employment of a spouse, (2) the VAT disaggregation rules, and the time of supply for services, and (3) the transfer of assets to a spouse so as to utilise IHT exemptions.**

This was another popular question, although answers generally lacked the depth or thought needed to score high marks. Part (a) was well answered by virtually all candidates, with the majority scoring maximum marks. The mistake made by some candidates was to waste time by writing at length on tax avoidance and the related decided cases, despite there only being two marks available. The marks given on the examination paper are a clear indication of how much time to spend on a particular part of a question. Part (b) was generally well answered, although very few candidates mentioned the possibility of the arrangement being classed as an associated operation. (The comments on the part of the question now outside the syllabus have been similarly deleted.)

|  |  | *Marks* |
|---|---|---|
| (a) | Tax avoidance | 1 |
|  | Tax evasion | 1 |
|  | Maximum/Available | 2 |

---

(b)     **Employment of husband**

| | |
|---|---|
| Income tax saving - wife | 2 |
| Additional income tax - husband | 1 |
| Class 1 NIC | 1 |
| Overall tax saving | 1 |
| Deductibility of salary | 1 |
| Disallowance of salary | 1 |
| Justification of salary | 1 |

**New business venture**

| | |
|---|---|
| Separate taxable person | 1 |
| VAT registration | 1 |
| Aggregation rules | 1 |
| Application of rules | 1 |

**Accounting for output VAT**

| | |
|---|---|
| Tax point | 1 |
| Output VAT on the deposit | 1 |
| Output VAT on the balance | 1 |

**Wedding gifts**

| | |
|---|---|
| Exemptions available | 1 |
| Potentially exempt transfer | 1 |
| Inter-spouse transfer | 1 |
| Associated operation | 2 |

| | |
|---|---|
| Available | 20 |
| Maximum | 17 |
| Available | 22 |
| Maximum | 19 |

*(Tutorial note:* Part of (b), worth 6 marks, related to the transitional rules which are no longer examinable and has been deleted.*)*

## Step by step answer plan

**Overview**

Part (a), though brief, sets the scene. This question concerns the more robust side of tax planning. Part (b) of this question tests your knowledge of some of the simpler tax avoidance schemes which are available.

**Step 1**   Write out your answer to part (a) keeping it brief.

**Step 2**   Each of the 4 questions (2 in point (2)) of part (b) stand alone so will be dealt with under 4 quite separate headings.

**Step 3**   For part (b) (1) compute the tax and NIC net savings of shifting £28,000 of income to the husband.

**Step 4**   Do not overlook the comment required on the Revenue's attitude to this form of tax saving.

**Step 5**   For part (b) (2) there are effectively two questions to answer for a total of 6 marks. Therefore neither question warrants a lengthy answer. Start by reading the details thoroughly and thinking about what is at issue. Don't just mention aggregation without explaining the registration advantage of being a 'separate' person when supplying to non-registered persons.

**Step 6**   For the output tax accounting question (b) (2) (ii)) state clearly the rules for identifying the tax point and apply them to the current situation. After all this, don't fail to mention the obvious point that VAT is due one month after the period end.

Step 7    Part (b) (3) covers a common IHT planning device - the 'spouse conduit'. However, read the question carefully and ensure your answer deals with all three gifts and comments on the associated operation point.

## The examiner's answer

(a)    Tax avoidance involves the reduction of tax liabilities by the use of lawful means. The ambit within which tax avoidance can be applied is limited both by specific anti-avoidance legislation, and by the courts in relation to artificial arrangements to avoid tax.

Tax evasion involves the reduction of tax liabilities by illegal means.

(b)    **Employment of Husband**

Lucy's employment of her husband on a salary of £28,000 pa will reduce her income tax liability by £12,320 as follows:

|  | £ |
|---|---|
| Salary paid | 28,000 |
| Employers class 1 NIC (28,000 – 4,335 = 23,665 at 12.2%) | 2,887 |
|  | 30,887 |
| Income tax at 40% | 12,355 |

There is no NIC saving as Lucy's Schedule D case II profits will still be in excess of the upper limit of £26,000.

Additional income tax and NIC of £10,392 will be due on the husband's salary as follows:

|  | £ |
|---|---|
| Taxable income - Schedule E | 28,000 |
| Personal allowance | 4,335 |
| Taxable income | 23,665 |

|  | £ | £ |
|---|---|---|
| Income tax: 1,500 at 10% |  | 150 |
| 22,165 at 23% |  | 5,098 |
|  |  | 5,248 |
| Employees Class 1 NIC |  |  |
| 434 × 52 at 10% |  | 2,257 |
| Employers Class 1 NIC |  | 2,887 |
|  |  | 10,392 |

Lucy's employment of her husband therefore results in an overall tax saving of £1,963 (12,355 – 10,392).

The salary paid to Lucy's husband will not be a deductible expense for Lucy unless it is incurred wholly and exclusively for business purposes. The salary will therefore have to be reasonable in relation to the duties performed by the husband. Since Lucy's husband is paid more than the previous personal assistant, the additional salary is likely to be disallowed unless it can be justified on the grounds that the husband has more duties than the previous assistant.

---

**Did you answer the question?**

You are not required to mention other tax saving opportunities such as making contributions to pension funds.

---

### New business venture

For VAT purposes, the partnership is a separate taxable person from Lucy's architectural business which she runs as an individual. On this basis, the partnership would not be liable to register for VAT as its taxable supplies are below the VAT registration threshold of £51,000.

However, HM Customs and Excise can apply aggregation rules where a business is operated as separate entities. The partnership will then be classed as the same taxable person as Lucy, and would have to account for VAT on its income. The aggregation provisions may be applied whatever the reason for the separate operation.

### Accounting for output VAT

The tax point for a supply of services is the earliest of (i) the date that the service is completed, or (ii) the date that an invoice is issued or payment is received. If an invoice is issued within 14 days of the service being completed, then this date replaces that in (i).

Output VAT of £74.47 (500 × 7/47) will be included on the VAT return for the period in which the deposit of £500 is received. The output VAT of £74.47 on the balance of the fee will be included on the VAT return for the period in which the contract is completed, since an invoice is not raised within 14 days. The VAT will be due within one month from the end of the relevant period.

---

**Did you answer the question?**

No mention of cash accounting is expected. This can be deduced from the fact that there are insufficient marks. Also, payment is expected half before work commences and the other half fairly soon after completion so cash accounting will make little difference. Finally, the overall business probably has a turnover over £350,000 - Lucy's profit alone is £180,000 – which excludes it from cash accounting.

---

### Wedding gifts

Lucy's wedding gift of £12,500 will utilise her IHT annual exemptions of £3,000 for 1999-00 and 2000-01, and a further £5,000 will be exempt as a gift in consideration of marriage. The balance of £1,500 (12,500 – 6,000 – 5,000) will be a PET, and this will also be exempt if Lucy survives for seven years after the date of the gift.

Lucy's gift of £12,500 to her husband will be exempt from IHT as an inter-spouse transfer of assets, and the same reliefs will then be available in respect of his wedding gift. Such an arrangement could be classed as an associated operation, although the rules are unlikely to be applied in this situation. This assumes that the first gift is not conditional upon the second gift being made.

---

## 51    (Answer 3 of examination)

---

### ( Examiner's comments and marking guide )

**Part (b) tested candidates' ability to advise on domicile for IHT purposes, and to calculate the IHT liability if the taxpayer was (i) domiciled in the UK, and (ii) not domiciled in the UK. This was a popular question, and many candidates scored very high marks.**

There were also some very good answers to part (a), with a number of candidates scoring maximum marks. Both the application of the 20% tax rate on savings income, and the calculation of the double taxation relief presented problems for a number of candidates. Some candidates incorrectly gave the married couple's allowance as a deduction in calculating taxable income. Part (b) was again well answered, although a number of candidates incorrectly gave double taxation relief when the taxpayer was not domiciled in the UK.

| | | | *Marks* |
|---|---|---|---|
| (a) | | Taxable income | 1 |
| | | Income tax liability/MCA | 2 |
| | | DTR on government stocks | 1 |
| | | DTR on rental income | 2 |
| | | | — |
| | | Maximum/Available | 6 |
| | | | — |
| (c) | (i) | Domicile of choice | 1 |
| | | Requirements | 1 |
| | | IHT position | 1 |
| | | | — |
| | | Maximum/Available | 3 |
| | | | — |
| | (ii) | **Domiciled in UK** | |
| | | Principle | 1 |
| | | Calculation of IHT liability | 1 |
| | | DTR on assets situated in Arcadia | 1 |
| | | **Not domiciled in UK** | |
| | | Principle | 1 |
| | | Calculation of IHT liability | 1 |
| | | | — |
| | | Available | 5 |
| | | | — |
| | | Maximum | 4 |
| | | | — |
| | | Available | 14 |
| | | | — |
| | | Maximum | 13 |
| | | | — |

*(Note*: A major part of the original question has been deleted along with the relevant parts of the comments and the marking guide – as it concerns a topic no longer examinable).

## Step by step answer plan

### Overview

This is a question covering a variety of overseas tax matters for an individual. Most of your answer would clearly be in the form of computations. While most candidates tend to prefer computations to essay type answers be warned that foreign element can throw up some quite difficult number crunching. In the exam you should only choose this question if you could deal successfully with all the main points:

- Applying the foreign tax credit restriction where there is foreign savings and foreign non-savings income (part (a))

- Applying foreign tax IHT credit and understanding the effect of domicile status on IHT liability.

**Step 1** Each of parts (a) and (b) effectively stand alone so aim to answer each part as if a separate question.

**Step 2** For part (a) construct the taxable income figure and the tax liability before DTR. It is relatively easy up to that point and important that you avoid any careless mistakes such as omitting relief for MCA or taxing the interest as if it were non-savings income.

**Step 3**  Consider the essence of part (a) - ie, the relief for the foreign tax credit - and deal with it in a clearly labelled working.

**Step 4**  Complete your answer to part (a) and re-read the question checking that you have covered everything.

**Step 5**  Answer part (c) (i) using a carefully tailored extract from what you can remember of your study notes on general domicile and its IHT extension.

**Step 6**  For part (c) (ii), produce the computations based on the two alternative assumptions. Again, as the use of the foreign tax credit is clearly at the heart of the question make sure you explain its treatment - preferably in a working.

## The examiner's answer

(a)  Walter Smith - Income tax liability 1999-00

|  | £ | £ |
|---|---|---|
| Schedule E - Pensions | | 21,690 |
| Schedule D case V - Rental income | | 8,500 |
| Schedule D case IV - Interest on government stocks | | 4,200 |
| | | 34,390 |
| Personal allowance | | 4,335 |
| Taxable income | | 30,055 |
| **Income tax:** | | |
| 1,500 at 10% | | 150 |
| 24,355 (30,055 – 4,200 – 1,500) at 23% | | 5,602 |
| 2,145 (28,000 – 1,500 – 24,355) at 20% | | 429 |
| 2,055 (4,200 – 2,145) at 40% | | 822 |
| | | 7,003 |
| Married couple's allowance (1,970 at 10%) | | 197 |
| | | 6,806 |
| Double taxation relief | | |
| Interest on government stocks (4,200 × 15%) | 630 | |
| Rental income (working) | 2,304 | |
| | | 2,934 |
| Tax payable | | 3,872 |

Working - Double taxation relief

The DTR on the rental income is the lower of :

| | | |
|---|---|---|
| (i)  The overseas tax paid – 8,500 × 40% = | | 3,400 |
| (ii) The UK tax on the overseas income. | | |
| 6,445 at 23% = | 1,482 | |
| 2,055 at 40% = | 822 | |
| | | 2,304 |

*Note:* The above calculation of DTR on the rental income of £2,304 is that expected from candidates. The strict statutory basis of comparing the income tax charged on total income, and income tax on that income excluding the rental income, results in DTR of £2,366.

(*Tutorial note:* The UK tax on overseas income is the difference between the tax payable including the overseas income and that payable excluding the overseas income.

UK tax on overseas rental income.

|  | £ | £ |
|---|---|---|
| Tax payable including overseas rental income | | 7,003 |

Tax payable excluding overseas rental income.

| | £ | £ |
|---|---|---|
| Schedule E - Pensions | 21,690 | |
| Schedule D Case IV - Interest on government stocks | 4,200 | |
| | 25,890 | |
| Personal allowance | 4,335 | |
| Taxable income | 21,555 | |

| Income tax: | | |
|---|---|---|
| 1,500 at 10% | 150 | |
| 15,855 (21,555 – 4,200 – 1,500) at 23% | 3,647 | |
| 4,200 at 20% | 840 | |
| | | 4,637 |
| UK tax on overseas rental income | | 2,366 |

The difference of £62 (2,366 – 2,304) results from the 'knock-on' effect of bringing the interest of £2,055 into the basic rate band saving an extra 3% (23-20)% tax.)

(b)    (i)    Domicile is a concept of general law and is not solely a taxation matter. Under general law, Walter will cease to be domiciled in the UK when he acquires another domicile of choice. This will require severing all ties with the UK, and settling in another country (Arcadia) with the intention of staying there indefinitely. Walter will have to demonstrate this intention by positive actions such as selling his home in the UK, and purchasing property in Arcadia. However, for IHT purposes Walter will be treated as domiciled in the UK for three years after ceasing to be domiciled in the UK under general law.

---

**Did you answer the question?**

As there are only 3 marks available, there is no need to discuss in great detail the concept of domicile other than is relevant to the situation.

---

(ii)    If Walter were to die and be treated as domiciled in the UK, he would be charged to IHT on his world-wide assets as follows:

| | £ |
|---|---|
| Chargeable estate | 500,000 |
| IHT liability    231,000 at nil % | Nil |
| 269,000 at 40% | 107,600 |
| | 107,600 |
| Double taxation relief (working) | 40,888 |
| | 66,712 |

If Walter were to die and be treated as not domiciled in the UK, only his assets situated in the UK would be charged to IHT as follows:

|  |  | £ |
|---|---|---|
| Chargeable estate | | 310,000 |
| IHT liability | 231,000 at nil % | Nil |
| | 79,000 at 40% | 31,600 |
| | | 31,600 |

Working - Double taxation relief

The rate of IHT on Walter's estate is 21.52 (107,600/500,000 × 100).

On the assets situated in Arcadia, the DTR is the lower of the Arcadian tax paid of £47,500 (190,000 at 25%) and the UK IHT paid on those assets of £40,888 (190,000 at 21.52%). No DTR is given in respect of Walter's UK assets of £310,000. Relief may be given in Arcadia.

---

## 52    (Answer 4 of examination)

( **Examiner's comments and marking guide** )

**Part (a) tested candidates' ability to advise on the tax implications resulting from a proposed financial plan, together with further tax planning measures that could be taken. Part (b) tested candidates' ability to advise on authorisation under the Financial Services Act 1986.**

Many answers to this question were badly presented, and lacked sufficient depth to score high marks. In part (a), most candidates correctly calculated the couple's taxable income, but then wasted time by also calculating their income tax liability. (Thanks to the complications in the dividend tax regime applying since 6 April 1999 this is now not such a bad idea.) This calculation only scored marks if it was related to similar calculation showing the income tax liability after the implementation of the financial plan, and hence the tax saving. Most candidates seemed unaware of the NIC saving by extracting profits from the company by way of a dividend. As already stated, many candidates mentioned relevant points in their answers, but simply did not go into sufficient depth. For example, candidates correctly stated the wife's 23% tax band was not being fully utilised, but then did not show the possible tax saving, or indicate how the wife's income could be increased. A number of candidates mentioned the enterprise investment scheme or venture capital trusts as part of the further tax planning measures that should be taken, despite the requirements of the question stating that answers should be confined to the information given. In part (b), very few candidates stated that there are both tied advisers and independent advisers, and were unsure of where independent advice could be obtained. Many candidates did not appreciate that authorisation under the Financial Services Act 1986 was required, despite a similar question being set at the December 1996 diet.

|  |  | *Marks* |
|---|---|---|
| (a) | Calculation of taxable income | 2 |
| | **Formation of McHaggis Ltd** | |
| | Class 4 NIC | 1 |
| | Tax saving | 1 |
| | Capital allowances adjustment | 1 |
| | Mileage allowances | 1 |
| | Tax credit on dividends | 1 |
| | **Dividends/Mileage allowance** | |
| | Calculation of income | 1 |
| | Mileage allowance | 1 |
| | Class 1 NIC | 3 |
| | Tax saving | 1 |
| | **Disposal of shares in Lowloch plc** | |
| | Transfer to an ISA | 1 |
| | Calculation of capital gain | 1 |
| | Tax planning | 1 |

---

| | |
|---|---:|
| **Individual savings accounts** | |
| Maximum investment | 1 |
| Qualifying investment | 1 |
| Dividend yield | 1 |
| Tax saving | 1 |
| **Investment trust** | |
| Tax position/Level of risk | 1 |
| Advice | 1 |
| **Repayment of mortgage** | |
| Tax saving on BSI | 1 |
| Tax relief on mortgage interest | 1 |
| **Utilisation of 23% tax band** | |
| Amount not utilised | 1 |
| Tax saving/Advice | 1 |
| | — |
| Available | 26 |
| | — |
| Maximum | 20 |
| | — |

| | | | |
|---|---|---|---:|
| (b) | (i) | Tied advisers | 1 |
| | | Independent advisers | 1 |
| | | | — |
| | | Maximum/Available | 2 |
| | | | — |
| | (ii) | Carrying on of a business | 1 |
| | | Authorisation | 1 |
| | | Investments/Investment activities | 1 |
| | | | — |
| | | Maximum/Available | 3 |
| | | | — |
| | | Available | 31 |
| | | | — |
| | | Maximum | 25 |
| | | | — |

## Step by step answer plan

**Overview**

This is primarily a planning question involving all the taxes except VAT and IHT with a brief section needed on the FSA 1986 requirements.

**Step 1**    It is a fairly lengthy and detailed question so read it through carefully - especially the contents of the financial plan.

**Step 2**    Part (a) requires you to work through the financial plan and tells you what calculations and advice to include. This does not necessarily mean that no other calculations and advice may be needed but is a fair indication.

**Step 3**    Prepare the Taxable Income computations prior to implementing any part of the plan as the first step in your answer to part (a).

**Step 4**    Next calculate the annual CT and the annual income tax and NIC saving for Jock resulting from the first step in the financial plan.

**Step 5**    Brief explanations of any tax treatments applied in step 4 above should be recorded.

**Step 6**    Explain how the Lowloch shares could effectively be transferred to an ISA. This will involve a separate heading for

-         Disposal of shares - so the proceeds can be transferred to an ISA
-         ISAs - explaining the limit on investments and the likely net yield.

**Step 7**    Note the amount that will be placed in an investment trust and discuss the tax and commercial effects.

**Step 8**    Calculate the tax saving from repaying the mortgage.

**Step 9**    Consider any other tax saving the couple could make. A discussion centred on using Maggie's basic rate band to the full is clearly expected.

**Step 10**    Summarise the tax savings calculated above.

**Step 11**    Answer part (b) bearing in mind that you are told to be brief and there are only 5 marks for the 2 questions.

## The examiner's answer

(a)      Taxable income

The couple's present taxable income is as follows:

|  | Jock £ | Maggie £ |
|---|---|---|
| Schedule D case II | 40,000 | |
| Schedule E | | 18,500 |
| Car benefit (11,500 × 15%) | | 1,725 |
| Dividends - Lowloch plc (15,000 × 22.5p × 100/90) | 3,750 | |
| BSI (55,000 at 7%) | 3,850 | |
| | 47,600 | 20,225 |
| Personal allowances | 4,335 | 4,335 |
| Taxable income | 43,265 | 15,890 |

---

**Did you answer the question?**

You were not expected to calculate income tax liability. When the question was first set it was perfectly easy to calculate tax savings below by considering their marginal effect on taxable income as appropriate. With the introduction of the special regime for dividend income it is simpler to work through the tax liabilities and take the difference!

---

### Formation of McHaggis Ltd

By transferring the writing of business software to McHaggis Ltd, class 4 NIC will no longer be payable. The profits of £6,000 relating to the writing of games software are below the class 4 NIC lower limit of £7,530. This is a tax saving of £1,108 ((26,000 – 7,530) at 6%). Class 2 NIC of £341 (6.55 × 52) will still be payable.

McHaggis Ltd's corporation tax liability will be £6,480 calculated as follows:

|  | £ | £ |
|---|---|---|
| Tax adjusted Schedule D case II profit per sole tradership | | 34,000 |
| Add:   Capital allowances no longer available | | |
|      3,000 (maximum WDA) × 16,000/20,000 | | 2,400 |
| | | 36,400 |

| Less: | Mileage allowance | 4,000 at 40 pence | 1,600 | |
|---|---|---|---|---|
| | | 12,000 at 20 pence | 2,400 | |
| | | | | 4,000 |
| **PCTCT** | | | | 32,400 |
| Corporation tax at 20% | | | | 6,480 |

However, the dividends will carry a tax credit of £2,667 (2,000 × 12 × 10/90) so the net tax cost will be £3,813 (6,480 − 2,667).

### Dividends/Mileage allowance

Following the implementation of the financial plan, Jock's software writing related income will become £36,667 consisting of the following:

| | £ |
|---|---|
| Schedule D case II | 6,000 |
| Dividends from McHaggis Ltd (2,000 × 12 × 100/90) | 26,667 |
| Mileage allowance | 4,000 |
| | 36,667 |

The mileage allowance will be tax-free as the rates are within the limits set by the fixed rate profit car scheme.

### Tax saving

Jock's income with the company formation:

| | Non-savings £ | Savings £ | Dividends £ |
|---|---|---|---|
| Schedule D Case II | 6,000 | | |
| BSI | | 3,850 | |
| Dividends  -  McHaggis | | | 26,667 |
|     -  Lowloch | | | 3,750 |
| Personal allowance | (4,335) | - | - |
| (Total £35,932) | 1,665 | 3,850 | 30,417 |

Tax liability:

| | £ |
|---|---|
| 1,500 × 10% | 150 |
| 165 × 23% | 38 |
| 3,850 × 20% | 770 |
| 22,485 × 10% | 2,248 |
| 28,000 | |
| 7,932 × 32½% | 2,578 |
| 35,932 | 5,784 |

Jock's tax liability without company formation (see taxable income above).

| | |
|---|---|
| 1,500 × 10% | 150 |
| 26,500 × 23% | 6,095 |
| 28,000 | |

|  |  |
|---|---|
| 11,515 × 40% | 4,606 |
| 3,750 × 32½% | 1,219 |
| 43,265 | 12,070 |

Tax saving: 12,070 – 5,784 – 3,813 (CT)                    £2,473

NIC saving:                    £1,108

The extraction of profits by way of dividends will mean that neither employers nor employees class 1 NIC will be payable.

**Disposal of shares in Lowloch plc**

It is not normally possible to transfer shares directly into an ISA.  Therefore, Jock will have to dispose of all 15,000 shares in Lowloch plc.  This will result in a chargeable gain of £5,380 as follows:

|  | £ |
|---|---|
| Sale proceeds (15,000 × 2.50) | 37,500 |
| Cost (15,000 × 1.20) | 18,000 |
|  | 19,500 |
| Indexation 18,000 × 0.390 | 7,020 |
|  | 12,480 |
| Annual exemption | 7,100 |
|  | 5,380 |

Prior to the disposal, Jock should transfer 6,466 (15,000 × 5,380/12,480) of the shares in Lowloch plc to Maggie.  The transfer will be at no gain/no loss, and will enable her annual exemption to be utilised.  No CGT will then be payable.

**Individual savings accounts**

The maximum investment in an ISA is £5,000 pa.  It will therefore be possible for Jock and Maggie to invest a total of £10,000 pa in ISAs holding the ordinary shares of Lowloch plc.  This assumes that Lowloch plc is incorporated in, and listed on a Stock Exchange and is thus a qualifying investment.  The dividend yield on the ordinary shares of Lowloch plc is 10% as follows:

$$\frac{22.5 \, \text{pence}}{250 \, \text{pence}} \times \frac{100}{1} \times \frac{100}{90} = 10\%$$

The dividend income from the ISAs of £1,000 (10,000 at 10%) will be tax-free, which is an income tax saving of £325 (1,000 at 32½%).  Note, the ISAs can recover the dividend tax credit on dividends received up to 5 April 2004.

**Investment trust**

The investment in the income producing investment trust of £27,500 (37,500 – 10,000) will not result in any tax saving.  It will, however, carry a lower level of risk compared to an investment in the shares of only one company such as Lowloch plc.

---

**Did you answer the question?**

You were not required to comment on other tax efficient forms of investment such as National Savings, single premium bonds, VCTs or EIS investments.

---

### Repayment of mortgage

The £20,000 repayment of Jock's mortgage will result in an income tax saving of £410 as follows:

|  |  | £ | £ |
|---|---|---|---|
| Building society interest foregone (20,000 at 7%) |  |  | 1,400 |
| Tax saving 1,400 at 42½%* |  |  | 595 |
| Less: Tax relief on mortgage interest |  |  |  |
| no longer available | 10,000 at nil% | Nil |  |
|  | 10,000 at 10% | 100 |  |
|  |  |  | 100 |
|  |  |  | 495 |

* 1,400 at 32½% and 1,400 at (20 − 10)%

### Utilisation of Maggie's 23% tax band

Maggie is not utilising £12,110 (28,000 − 15,890) of her 23% tax band. Since Jock pays 32½% tax on £5,532 of income after taking account of the above steps (7,932 − 1,000 − 1,400), the potential annual income tax savings is £1,245 (5,532 × (32½ − 10)%). The transfer of income from Jock to Maggie could be achieved by making Maggie a 20.75% (100% × 5,532/26,667) shareholder of McHaggis Ltd.

### Overall tax saving

The overall annual tax saving from the implementation of the financial plan together with the further tax planning measures is £5,646 (1,108 + 2,473 + 325 + 495 + 1,245).

(b)    (i)    Financial advisers are classified into tied advisers and independent advisers. Tied advisers only recommend the investment products of one financial institution, and do not therefore provide independent financial advice. Generally, accountants, solicitors and stockbrokers are independent advisers, along with some banks and building societies. Independent advisers can recommend investment products from any source.

(ii)    Unless the activities do not constitute the **carrying on of a business** (such as providing financial advice to a friend or relative who is not otherwise a client, and who will not be charged a fee), a qualified Certified Accountant would have to be authorised to conduct investment business under the Financial Services Act 1986 in order to give the advice to Jock and Maggie. This is because the definition of **investments** includes shares, ISA equity investments and investment trusts (but not mortgages), and the definition of **investment activities** includes specific advice regarding the purchase or sale of investments.

---

## 53    (Answer 5 of examination)

---

**( Examiner's comments and marking guide )**

**Part (a) tested candidates' ability to calculate the assessable profits for a partnership where there is a change in the constitution of the partnership. Part (b) tested candidates' ability to calculate the maximum tax deductible personal pension contribution that can be paid, and to advise whether or not the maximum should be paid. Part (c) tested candidates' ability to advise on the implications of the disposal of a short lease.**

This was another reasonably popular question, and there were a number of good answers, especially to part (a). A common mistake in part (a) was to not appreciate that capital allowances are deducted as an expense. Candidates therefore prepared two separate capital allowance computations to take account of the partnership change, when only one was needed. Other mistakes included missing out the overlap relief for the partner leaving, the assessment of the partners on a 6 April to 5 April basis, or simply not being aware of how a partnership change is dealt with under the current year basis rules. In part (b), the calculation of the maximum tax deductible pension contribution was generally

---

well done, with some candidates scoring full marks, but the advice as to whether the maximum amount should actually be contributed caused problems. There was little discussion as to how tax relief at the rate of 40% could be obtained on the whole contribution. Part (c) was reasonably well answered, although very few candidates divided the capital gain between the partners, thus losing a very easy mark.

|  |  |  | *Marks* |
|---|---|---|---|
| (a) | **Adjusted Schedule D1 profit** | | |
| | Depreciation/Amortisation | | 1 |
| | Balancing allowance | | 1 |
| | Capital allowances | | 2 |
| | Lease deduction | | 2 |
| | Division of profits | | 1 |
| | **Partners' 1999-00 Schedule D1 assessments** | | |
| | Alfred and Bertie | | 1 |
| | Claude | | 2 |
| | Daniel | | 2 |
| | | | — |
| | Maximum/Available | | 12 |
| | | | — |
| (b) | (i) | Schedule E 1993-94 to 1997-98 | 2 |
| | | Schedule D 1997-98 | 1 |
| | | Schedule D 1998-99 | 1 |
| | | Schedule D 1999-00 | 1 |
| | | | — |
| | | Maximum/Available | 5 |
| | | | — |
| | (ii) | Limitation to 40% | 1 |
| | | Calculation of income taxable at 40% | 1 |
| | | Premium for 1999-00 | 1 |
| | | Premium for 1998-99 | 1 |
| | | Carry forward of unused relief | 1 |
| | | | — |
| | | Available | 5 |
| | | | — |
| | | Maximum | 4 |
| | | | — |
| (c) | **Sale of leasehold workshop** | | |
| | Overall calculation of capital gain | | 1 |
| | Lease percentage | | 1 |
| | Lease deductions (bonus) | | 1 |
| | Division of gain | | 1 |
| | Rollover relief | | 1 |
| | **Purchase of freehold workshop** | | |
| | Industrial buildings allowance | | 1 |
| | | | — |
| | Available | | 6 |
| | | | — |
| | Maximum | | 4 |
| | | | — |
| | Available | | 28 |
| | | | — |
| | Maximum | | 25 |
| | | | — |

## ( Step by step answer plan )

**Overview**

This question tests various mainstream tax topics in the context of partnerships.

[Step 1]  Read part (a) of the question carefully and try to visualise the workings you will need.

**Step 2**  Prepare a plant capital allowance computation for the year to 31 December 1999 in a separate working.

**Step 3**  Use a working note to calculate the annual income allowance on the lease premium.

**Step 4**  Calculate the adjusted trading profits for the year to 31 December 1999 and allocate this between the partners in accordance with their profit sharing arrangements not forgetting that two of the partners were only there for part of the year.

**Step 5**  One of the partners is retiring so calculate his overlap relief brought forward using a separate working.

**Step 6**  Show the assessments on the partners for 1999/00 remembering that the closing year rules will apply to one and the opening year rules will apply to another.

**Step 7**  Re-read part (a) of the question to ensure all the relevant points have been properly dealt with and review your answer for such matters as cross-referencing working notes.

**Step 8**  Read part (b) of the question.

**Step 9**  Prepare your answer to part (i) using a tabular layout showing NRE, the relevant age related percentage, and the maximum relief for the year in question, 1999/00, and the 6 previous years.

**Step 10**  For part (ii) produce computations to show the tax effect of paying the maximum pension contribution for 1999/00 and discuss the best way of maximising tax relief.

**Step 11**  Read part (c) of the question.

**Step 12**  Compute the gain on the sale of the lease and show its division between the partners commenting on taper relief.

**Step 13**  Comment on the possibility of rollover relief.

**Step 14**  Explain the IBA implications of acquiring the new workshop.

### The examiner's answer

(a)    Alphabet Engineering - Adjusted Schedule D case 1 profit for the year ended 31 December 1999

|  | £ | £ |
|---|---|---|
| Net profit per accounts |  | 158,500 |
| Add:  Depreciation |  | 5,400 |
| Amortisation of lease |  | 2,500 |
|  |  | 166,400 |
| Less:  Capital allowances (W1) | 8,750 |  |
| Lease deduction (W2) | 2,050 |  |
|  |  | 10,800 |
| Schedule D case 1 profit |  | 155,600 |
| Divisible    Alfred - 50% |  | 77,800 |
| Bertie - 30% |  | 46,680 |
| Claude - 20% × 6/12 |  | 15,560 |
| Daniel - 20% × 6/12 |  | 15,560 |

**Partners' 1999-00 Schedule D case 1 assessments**

|  |  |  |
|---|---|---|
| Alfred (year ended 31.12.99) |  | 77,800 |
| Bertie (year ended 31.12.99) |  | 46,680 |
| Claude(1.1.99 to 30.6.99) | 15,560 |  |

|  |  |  |
|---|---|---|
| Less:  Overlap relief (W3) | 6,100 | |
|  | | 9,460 |
| Daniel (Actual 1.7.99 to 5.4.00) | | |
| 1.7.99 to 31.12.99 | 15,560 | |
| 1.1.00 to 5.4.00 190,000 × 20% × 3/12 | 9,500 | |
|  | | 25,060 |

The cessation rules apply to Claude who resigned as a partner on 30 June 1999, and the commencement rules apply to Daniel who joined the partnership on 1 July 1999.

### Working 1 - Capital allowances

|  | Pool | | Motor cars | | | Allowances |
|---|---|---|---|---|---|---|
|  | | *Alfred* | *Bertie* | *Claude* | *Daniel* | |
|  | £ | £ | £ | £ | £ | £ |
| WDV b/f | 22,000 | 14,500 | 8,000 | 15,000 | | |
| Addition | | | | | 10,000 | |
| Deemed proceeds | | | | 13,500 | | |
| Balancing allowance | | | | 1,500 × 20% | | 300 |
| WDA - 25% | 5,500 | | | | | 5,500 |
| WDA - Restricted | | 3,000 × 60% | | | | 1,800 |
| WDA - 25% | | | 2,000 × 20% | | | 400 |
| WDA - 25% | | | | | 2,500 × 30% | 750 |
| WDV c/f | 16,500 | 11,500 | 6,000 | | 7,500 | 8,750 |

### Working 2 - Lease deduction

The income proportion of the premium assessed on the owners will be deductible against the partnership's Schedule D1 assessment over the period of the lease.

|  | £ |
|---|---|
| Premium paid | 25,000 |
| Less:  25,000 × 2% × (10 − 1) | 4,500 |
|  | 20,500 |
| 20,500/10 = | 2,050 pa |

### Working 3 - Overlap relief

Claude will have overlap profits for the period 1 January 1998 to 5 April 1998 as follows:

122,000 × 20% × 3/12 =   £6,100

---

**Did you answer the question?**

There is no need to calculate the amounts of overlap relief that the other partners are carrying forward.

---

*(**Tutorial note:** Apportionment should strictly be made using days, but the nearest month has been used in the answer due to the inclusion of estimated figures in the question.)*

(b)    (i)      Alfred's maximum tax deductible personal pension contribution is £60,354 calculated as follows:

| | | Net relevant earnings £ | Relevant percentage | Maximum premium £ |
|---|---|---|---|---|
| 1993-94 | Schedule E | 36,000 | 17.5 | 6,300 |
| 1994-95 | Schedule E | 36,000 | 17.5 | 6,300 |
| 1995-96 | Schedule E | 36,000 | 17.5 | 6,300 |
| 1996-97 | Schedule E | 36,000 | 17.5 | 6,300 |
| 1997-98 | Schedule E | | | |
| | 36,000 × 9/12 | 27,000 | | |
| | Schedule D (working) | 15,250 | | |
| | | 42,250 | 17.5 | 7,394 |
| 1998-99 | Schedule D (working) | 61,000 | 20 | 12,200 |
| 1999-00 | Schedule D | 77,800 | 20 | 15,560 |
| | | | | 60,354 |

Unused relief is carried forward for six years, and utilised on a FIFO basis.

**Working - Schedule D assessments**

| | £ |
|---|---|
| 1997-98 (Actual 1.1.98 to 5.4.98) 122,000 × 50% × 3/12 = | 15,250 |
| 1998-99 (Year ended 31.12.98) 122,000 × 50% | 61,000 |

(ii)      Alfred has sufficient Schedule D profits for 1999-00 to utilise a personal pension premium of £60,354, but it would be beneficial to limit the premium to the earnings that are taxable at the rate of 40%. A premium of £45,465 should therefore be paid for 1999-00, calculated as follows:

| | £ |
|---|---|
| Schedule D | 77,800 |
| Personal allowance | 4,335 |
| Taxable income | 73,465 |
| 10/23% tax band | 28,000 |
| Taxable at 40% | 45,465 |

The premium can either be paid during 1999-00 or, alternatively, could be paid by 5 April 2001 with an election being made by Alfred to relate the premium back to 1999-00. The unused relief of £14,889 (60,354 – 45,465) can be utilised by:

(1)      Paying a premium before 5 April 2000, and electing to relate it back to 1998-99.
(2)      Carrying it forward and paying a premium in respect of 2000-01.

In either case tax relief at the rate of 40% will be obtained.

---

**Did you answer the question?**

There is no point in calculating the tax payable with and without the premium deduction as the marginal effect can be determined by inspection.

---

(c)     **Sale of leasehold workshop**

The disposal of the leasehold property will result in a capital gain as follows:

|  | £ | £ |
|---|---|---|
| Proceeds |  | 45,000 |
| Cost    $25,000 \times \dfrac{35.414}{46.695}$ | 18,960 |  |
| Less:    Lease deductions $2,050 \times 3$ | 6,150 |  |
|  |  | 12,810 |
|  |  | 32,190 |
| Indexation $12,810 \times \dfrac{162.6 - 159.5}{159.5}(0.019)$ |  | 243 |
| Capital gain |  | 31,947 |
| Divisible:    Alfred - 50% |  | 15,973 |
|                      Bertie - 30% |  | 9,584 |
|                      Daniel - 20% |  | 6,390 |

Each partner will be assessed to his share of the capital gain for 2000-01. Alternatively, it will be possible for a partner to rollover his share of the gain against his share of the cost of the freehold workshop, since all of the proceeds from the disposal of the leasehold workshop have been re-invested. Any gain which remains chargeable (before annual exemption) will be reduced to 77.5% by taper relief for Alfred and Bertie and to 92.5% for Daniel.

**Note:** The lease deduction is a specialised point, and is therefore treated as a bonus mark in the marking scheme.

**Purchase of freehold workshop.**

Industrial buildings allowance of £2,600 pa (65,000 at 4%) will be available, commencing in the period of account during which the workshop is brought into use.

---

## 54     (Answer 6 of examination)

---

( **Examiner's comments and marking guide** )

**Part (a) tested candidates' ability to calculate a company's corporation tax liabilities for a number of periods after claiming relief for both trading and non-trading losses, and to calculate the tax refunds due.  Part (b) tested candidates' ability to calculate profits after taking into account a group relief claim.**

This was the least popular question on the paper, often being the fourth choice question, and was generally answered quite badly, especially part (a). The Schedule A loss and the capital loss caused problems. Candidates performed better in part (b), although answers were often badly laid out, and the group relief claim caused problems.

Some of the more difficult parts of the original question have had to be deleted as they depend on legislation modified or deleted and the examiner has confirmed that such points are no longer examinable. The examiner's comments above have been edited to make them relevant to the current version of the question.

|  |  |  | *Marks* |
|---|---|---|---|
| (a) | (i) | Schedule A/Schedule A loss | 1 |
|  |  | Capital gain/Capital loss | 1 |
|  |  | Utilisation of loss of period ended 31.12.99 | 2 |
|  |  | Patent royalties/Deed of covenant | 1 |

---

|  |  |  |
|---|---|---|
| | Corporation tax | 1 |
| | | — |
| | Maximum/Available | 6 |
| | | — |

(ii) **Corporation tax refunds**

|  |  |
|---|---|
| Year ended 30.9.96 | 1 |
| Period ended 31.3.97 | 1 |
| Year ended 31.3.98 | 1 |
| | — |
| Maximum Available | 3 |
| | — |

(b) **Calculation of chargeable profits**

|  |  |
|---|---|
| Schedule DI profit/Debenture interest | 1 |
| Loss relief/Schedule DIII | 1 |
| **Claim under s402** | |
| Corresponding period | 1 |
| Calculation of claim | 2 |
| | — |
| Maximum/Available | 5 |
| | — |
| Maximum/Available | 14 |
| | — |

---

( **Step by step answer plan** )

**Overview**

The first half of the question concerns a company ceasing to trade and making a 'terminal' loss. A number of the more complex points have been deleted from the original version being no longer in the syllabus. The second half of the question involves group corporation tax matters – but has also been substantially simplified to remove items no longer examinable.

[Step 1]  Read the requirements of part (a). It should be fairly clear that it concerns only Goodbye Ltd so you only need to concentrate on the first part of the question down to but not including Ongoing's forecast results. Potentially Goodbye's loss will be group relieved but as Ongoing's marginal tax rate appears to be only the small company rate this loss option will not command priority over S393A(1) relief in Goodbye.

[Step 2]  Construct a standard tabular layout of PCTCT for Goodbye for all the years concerned and slot in the figures including the loss.

[Step 3]  Calculate CT for any PCTCT remaining.

[Step 4]  For part (a) (ii) calculate any tax refunds by considering the marginal effect of loss relief. It is an unnecessary use of time to recompute CT on PCTCT prior to loss relief.

[Step 5]  Read part (b) of the requirements and the second half of the question.

[Step 6]  In a separate working calculate how much of Goodbye Ltd's loss remains and add in any excess charges available for group relief.

[Step 7]  Calculate Ongoing's PCTCT set-off for the year to 31 March 2000 with the appropriate deduction for group relief. Include a note of explanation on the 'corresponding period' restriction.

[Step 8]  Re-read the whole question and ensure that all points have been included at the relevant place in your answer.

## The examiner's answer

(a)  (i)

| Period ended | 30.9.95 £ | 30.9.96 £ | 31.3.97 £ | 31.3.98 £ | 31.3.99 £ | 31.12.99 £ |
|---|---|---|---|---|---|---|
| D1 Profits | 88,500 | 59,000 | 62,500 | 47,000 | 5,000 | |
| Schedule A | 6,000 | | 2,600 | | | |
| Schedule A loss b/f | | | (1,100) | | | |
| Capital gain | | | | 10,800 | | 72,000 |
| Capital loss b/f | | | | (10,800) | | (13,200) |
| | 94,500 | 59,000 | 64,000 | 47,000 | 5,000 | 58,800 |
| Less s393A(1) | | | | | | |
| P/E 31.12.99 (W1) | | 23,500 | 58,000 | 35,000 | 5,000 | 58,800 |
| | 94,500 | 35,500 | 6,000 | 12,000 | - | - |
| Patent royalty | 12,000 | 12,000 | 6,000 | 12,000 | - | - |
| | 82,500 | 23,500 | - | - | - | - |
| Deed of covenant | | | - | - | - | - |
| PCTCT | 82,500 | 23,500 | - | - | - | - |

---

### Did you answer the question?

You were not required to list out the unrelieved and thereby wasted deed of covenant payments.

---

CT at 25%/24.5%    20,625    5,757

### Working 1 - s393A(1) loss relief

The claim under s393A(1) ICTA 1988 for the year ended 30 September 1996 is £47,000 (59,000 − 12,000) × 6/12 = £23,500. Alternative calculations of the claim would be acceptable.

(ii)   As a result of the claims under s393A(1) ICTA 1988 the following corporation tax refunds will be due:

Year ended 30.9.96    £5,757 due to loss relief (23,500 at 24.5% = £5,757)

Period ended 31.3.97    £13,680 due to loss relief (58,000 − 1,000 = 57,000 × 24%. Profits 57,000 lower limit 300,000 × $\frac{9}{12}$ × $\frac{1}{2}$ = 75,000).

Year ended 31.3.98    £7,140 due to loss relief (35,000 − 1,000 = 34,000 at 21% = £7,140)

(b)   Ongoing Ltd's profits chargeable to corporation tax for the year ended 31 March 2000 will be as follows:

| | £ |
|---|---|
| Schedule D1 Profit (93,000 − 12,000) | 81,000 |
| Less s393(1) | 14,500 |
| | 66,500 |
| Schedule DIII | 3,500 |
| | 70,000 |
| Less s402 (W1) | 52,500 |
| PCTCT | 17,500 |

---

---

**Did you answer the question?**

You were not required to calculate Ongoing's GCT.

---

**Working 1 - Claim under s402 ICTA 1988**

Losses under s402 ICTA 1988 can only be offset against profits of the corresponding period. Goodbye Ltd ceased trading on 31 December 1999 so the corresponding period is 1 April 1999 to 31 December 1999. The group relief claim is therefore limited to £52,500 (70,000 × 9/12). This is less than Goodbye Ltd's unrelieved losses available for group relief for the period ended 31 December 1999 of £79,950, calculated as follows:

|  | £ |
|---|---|
| Schedule D1 trading loss | 248,000 |
| Utilised under s393A(1) (58,800 + 5,000 + 35,000 + 58,000 + 23,500) | (180,300) |
|  | 67,700 |
| Excess charges (11,250 + 1,000) | 12,250 |
|  | 79,950 |

---

**Did you answer the question?**

You were not required to highlight the amount of Goodbye's loss that remained finally unrelieved.

*(**Tutorial note:** The deed of covenant to charity of £1,000 is included in the unrelieved losses of £79,950 since excess non-trade charges can be group relieved.)*

---

**Tutorial notes**

1   Trading losses and trading charges arising in the final 12 months of trade can be carried back for 36 months from the start of the period of account in which the loss arises - ie, for 36 months prior to 1.4.99.

---

## JUNE 1997 QUESTIONS

## 55     (Question 1 of examination)

Charles Choice, aged 47, is an assistant manager with the Northwest Bank plc on a gross annual salary of £23,500.

You should assume that today's date is 2 April 2000, and that the tax rates and allowances for 1999-00 apply throughout. You are *not expected* to take the time value of money into account in any of your answers.

(a)     As from 6 April 2000, Charles will be required to drive 8,000 miles each year for business purposes. The Northwest Bank plc have offered him a choice of either a company car or a cash alternative, as follows:

1.     A new 1398cc diesel powered motor car with a list price of £14,400. All running costs, including private fuel, will be paid for by the Northwest Bank plc. Charles will be required to contribute £50 per month towards the private use of the motor car, of which £15 will be partial reimbursement of private fuel. Under this alternative, Charles would not run a private motor car.

2.     Additional salary of £2,800 pa. Charles would then use his private motor car for business mileage. The private motor car is leased at a cost of £285 per month, and has a list price of £11,500. The annual running costs, including fuel, are £1,650. He will drive a total of 12,000 miles per year. The Northwest Bank plc pays a business mileage allowance of 24 pence per mile. The relevant rates allowed under the fixed profit car scheme are 35 pence per mile for the first 4,000 miles, and 20 pence per mile thereafter.

**Required:**

Advise Charles as to which of the two alternatives will be the most beneficial from his point of view. Your answer should include:

-     Calculations of the additional annual tax liabilities that will arise under each alternative, and

-     a comparison of a claim for business expenditure and a claim based on the fixed profit car scheme.

**(13 marks)**

(b)     Charles joined the Northwest Bank plc four years ago, but has not joined the company's Inland Revenue approved occupational pension scheme. He has been offered the chance to join on 6 April 2000.

Before joining the Northwest Bank plc, Charles regularly changed employers. He has therefore saved for a pension by contributing into a personal pension plan. For 1999-00 he made the maximum amount of tax deductible contributions, based on his salary of £23,500.

Under the Northwest Bank plc's occupational pension scheme, Charles would contribute 6% of his salary (you should assume that this is £23,500), and the company would contribute a further 6%. The benefits payable on retirement would be based on final salary.

**Required:**

(i)     Advise Charles of the factors that he will have to take into account when deciding whether or not to join the Northwest Bank plc's occupational pension scheme.     **(5 marks)**

(ii)     Charles is concerned that if he joins the Northwest Bank plc's occupational pension scheme, his tax deductible contributions will be less than under a personal pension scheme.

Advise Charles of how he could make additional voluntary contributions in order to increase his entitlement to a pension.     **(2 marks)**

**(Total: 20 marks)**
**(as amended)**

---

| 56 | **(Question 2 of examination)** |
|---|---|

(a) William Wiles acquired three houses on 6 April 1999. Houses 1 and 2 were acquired freehold, and are let as furnished holiday accommodation. House 3 was acquired on a 25 year lease, and is let furnished. During 1999-00 the houses were let as follows:

**House 1** was available for letting for 42 weeks during 1999-00, and was actually let for 14 weeks at £375 per week. During the 10 weeks that the house was not available for letting, it was occupied rent free by William's sister. Running costs for 1999-00 consisted of business rates £730, insurance £310, and advertising £545.

**House 2** was available for letting for 32 weeks during 1999-00, and was actually let for eight weeks at £340 per week. The house was not available for letting for 20 weeks due to a serious flood. As a result of the flood, £6,250 was spent on repairs. The damage was not covered by insurance. The other running costs for 1999-00 consisted of business rates £590, insurance £330, and advertising £225.

**House 3** was unoccupied from 6 April 1999 until 31 December 1999. On 1 January 2000 the house was sub-let on a four year lease for a premium of £8,000, and a rent of £8,600 pa payable annually in advance. William had paid a premium of £85,000 for the 25-year lease. During 1999-00 he paid the rent of £6,200 due annually in advance on 6 April 1999, and spent £710 on redecorating the property during June 1999.

Immediately after their purchase, William furnished the three houses at a cost of £5,200 per house. With the exception of the 10 week rent-free letting of house 1, all the lettings are at a full rent.

During 1999-00 William also rented out one furnished room of his main residence. He received rent of £4,600, and incurred allowable expenditure of £825.

**Required:**

(i) Briefly explain why both house 1 and house 2 qualify to be treated as a trade under the furnished holiday letting rules. State the tax advantages of the houses being so treated.

**(5 marks)**

(ii) Calculate William's allowable Schedule A loss for 1999-00, and advise him as to the possible ways of relieving the loss. **(14 marks)**

(b) On 30 June 1999 William permanently separated from his wife. William and his wife are both aged 39, and they have a son, aged 15, who is in full-time education. The son spends an average of two days each week living with William. Since 1 July 1999 William has been paying his wife maintenance of £475 per month. He has also been paying his son's school fees of £1,800 per term, and the mortgage interest of £550 (gross) per month on a mortgage of £80,000 that was used to purchase a new property for his wife. Until 31 December 1999, these payments were made voluntarily, but on 1 January 2000 they were confirmed by a written agreement as part of the divorce settlement. Under the agreement, William made a lump sum payment of £25,000 to his wife, and will continue the regular payments until the son completes his full-time education in three years time.

**Required:**

(i) Explain the tax implications arising from the payments made by William to support his wife and son (1) voluntarily between 1 July 1999 and 31 December 1999, and (2) under the divorce settlement from 1 January 2000 onwards, **(4 marks)**

(ii) State what personal allowances William will be entitled to for both 1999-00 and 2000-01.

**(2 marks)**
**(Total: 25 marks)**

---

---

| 57 | (Question 3 of examination) |
|----|------------------------------|

You are the tax adviser to Expansion Ltd, a company involved in the computer business. Expansion Ltd wishes to acquire Target Ltd, and has made an offer to the shareholders of that company which it would like to finalise on 1 July 1999. At present, the ordinary share capital of Target Ltd is owned equally by Arc Ltd, Bend Ltd and Curve Ltd, and it is not known whether one, two or all three of these companies will accept the offer. You should assume that today's date is 15 May 1999. The forecast results of Expansion Ltd and Target Ltd for the year ended 31 December 1999 are as follows:

|  | Expansion Ltd £ | Target Ltd £ |
|---|---|---|
| Adjusted Schedule D1 profit/(loss) | 214,000 | (137,700) |
| Trading losses brought forward | - | (9,200) |
| Capital gain | - | 51,300 |
| Capital losses brought forward | (9,600) | - |
| Interest received on Government Stocks (gross) | 4,800 | - |

Expansion Ltd purchased £120,000 of 8% Government Stock on 1 May 1999. On 31 January 2000 the company is to purchase a new freehold factory for £118,000.

Target Ltd's capital gain is in respect of the proposed sale of a freehold office building for £140,000 on 15 October 1999. One of the building's four floors has never been used for the purposes of Target Ltd's trade.

Expansion Ltd has sufficient internal funds in order to finance the acquisition of either one third or two thirds of Target Ltd's share capital. However, if it acquires all of Target Ltd's share capital it will have to issue £250,000 of 10% debentures on 1 July 1999. The debentures will be issued at a 3% discount to their nominal value, and will be redeemable in five years time. Debenture interest will be paid on 1 July and 1 January, and professional fees of £15,250 will be incurred in respect of the issue. Expansion Ltd's adjusted Schedule D1 profit for the year ended 31 December 1999 has been calculated *before* taking into account the issue of debentures. The company's accounting policy is to write off the cost of finance on a straight-line basis over the period of the loan.

Neither Expansion Ltd nor Target Ltd has any subsidiary companies. Arc Ltd, Bend Ltd and Curve Ltd are all profitable companies, and they are not connected to each other or to Expansion Ltd. All the companies are resident in the UK.

**Required:**

Calculate the corporation tax liability for both Expansion Ltd and Target Ltd for the year ended 31 December 1999 if:

(i)     Expansion Ltd acquires one third of Target Ltd's ordinary share capital from Arc Ltd on 1 July 1999.

**(6 marks)**

(ii)    Expansion Ltd acquires two thirds of Target Ltd's ordinary share capital from Arc Ltd and Bend Ltd on 1 July 1999.     **(3 marks)**

(iii)   Expansion Ltd acquires all of Target Ltd's ordinary share capital from Arc Ltd, Bend Ltd and Curve Ltd on 1 July 1999.     **(8 marks)**

Your answer should include an explanation of your treatment of Target Ltd's losses, Target Ltd's capital gain, and Expansion Ltd's issue of debentures. You should assume that reliefs are claimed in the most favourable manner.

**(Total: 17 marks)**
**(as amended)**

---

| 58 | (Question 4 of examination) |
|---|---|

You are the tax adviser to Dorothy Lake, aged 75. Under the terms of her will, Dorothy has left her entire estate to her daughter Alice, since Dorothy's husband is wealthy in his own right. Dorothy does not expect to live past her eightieth birthday which is on 31 December 2004, and she therefore wants to know whether or not it would be beneficial for tax purposes to make a lifetime gift of assets to Alice. The gift will be made on 30 June 2000, and will consist of the following assets:

(1)    50,000 £1 ordinary shares in Windermere Ltd, an unquoted trading company. Dorothy owns a total of 100,000 shares in Windermere Ltd, and her husband also owns 100,000 shares in the company. Windermere Ltd has an issued share capital of 400,000 £1 ordinary shares. At present, the relevant values of Windermere Ltd's shares are as follows:

| Shareholding | Value per share £ |
|:---:|:---:|
| 50% | 4.50 |
| 37.5% | 3.55 |
| 25% | 2.95 |
| 12.5% | 2.50 |

By 31 December 2004, these values are likely to have increased by 40%. Windermere Ltd owns investments in quoted shares that represent 12% of the value of its total assets.

Dorothy originally acquired 50,000 £1 ordinary shares in Coniston Ltd in March 1988 for £96,000. Coniston Ltd was taken over by Windermere Ltd on 15 October 1997, at which time Dorothy received two £1 ordinary shares in Windermere Ltd and £0.80 in cash for each share held in Coniston Ltd. On 15 October 1997 a 25% holding of Windermere Ltd's ordinary shares was worth £1.20 per share. Dorothy has never been a director of either Coniston Ltd or Windermere Ltd.

Alice is a risk averse investor, and would therefore sell the shares in Windermere Ltd soon after receiving them.

(2)    An antique painting worth £8,500. This was acquired in June 1988 for £1,400. The painting is not likely to change in value before 31 December 2004.

(3)    A holiday cottage worth £165,000. Dorothy inherited the cottage on the death of her sister in May 1995 when it was worth £188,000. Because the cottage is situated on cliffs that are being eroded, it is only likely to be worth £105,000 on 31 December 2004. The cottage does not qualify to be treated as a furnished holiday letting.

Dorothy has other assets worth £350,000 has not made any previous lifetime transfers of assets, has not disposed of any assets during 2000-01, and is a 40% taxpayer. Apart from the shares in Windermere Ltd, it is likely that the assets gifted to Alice will still be owned by her at the date of Dorothy's death. Alice is also a 40% taxpayer.

**Required:**

Advise Dorothy of whether or not it would be beneficial for tax purposes to make the gift of assets to Alice on 30 June 2000. Your answer should include a calculation of the inheritance tax and capital gains tax liabilities that would arise if Dorothy:

(i)     *Makes* the gift to Alice on 30 June 2000.
(ii)    Does *not make* the gift to Alice on 30 June 2000.

You should assume that Dorothy dies on 31 December 2004, that wherever possible, elections or claims are made to postpone tax liabilities, and that the tax rates and allowances for 1999-00 apply throughout.

Your answer should show the due date of any IHT liabilities, and the amount of IHT that can be paid under the instalment option. You should include tax planning advice that you consider to be relevant.

**(Total: 25 marks)**

| 59 | **(Question 5 of examination)** |

(a)     Ming Khan and Nina Lee are in partnership running a music recording studio. The partnership commenced trading on 1 May 1999, and their first accounts for the 15 month period to 31 July 2000 show a tax adjusted Schedule D case 1 trading loss (*before* capital allowances) of £61,800. On 1 May 1999 the partnership purchased a freehold building and converted it into a recording studio at a cost of £211,500, made up as follows:

|  | £ |
|---|---|
| Land and building | 69,500 |
| Recording equipment | 70,300 |
| Installation of electrical system for the recording equipment | 19,400 |
| Sound insulation | 13,200 |
| Replacement doors and windows | 2,500 |
| Heating system | 5,100 |
| VAT | 31,500 |
|  | 211,500 |

Profits and losses are shared 60% to Ming and 40% to Nina. The partnership is registered for VAT, and all of its supplies are standard rated.

**Required:**

(i)     Show how the partnership's Schedule D 1 trading loss for the 15 month period to 31 July 2000 will be allocated between Ming and Nina for 1999-00 and 2000-01. Your calculations should be made on a monthly basis.     **(4 marks)**

(ii)     State the possible ways of relieving the Schedule D 1 trading loss.     **(3 marks)**

(b)     Ming was previously employed by a music company at an annual salary of £42,000. She was made redundant on 28 February 1999, and received an *ex gratia* redundancy payment of £60,000.

Nina was previously a student. She had inherited investments on the death of her parents, and sold these for £125,000 on 31 March 1999 in order to finance her partnership capital. The disposal resulted in a chargeable gain of £39,200. Until 31 March 1999 Nina received dividend income of £6,250 (gross) pa.

Both Ming and Nina are single, and have no other income or outgoings. They forecast that the partnership will make a Schedule D Case 1 profit (*after* capital allowances) of approximately £40,000 for the year ended 31 July 2001.

**Required:**

(i)     Advise Ming and Nina as to which loss relief claims would be the most beneficial for them.

**(4 marks)**

(ii)     Calculate the tax refunds that will be due to Ming and Nina. You should ignore the possibility of any repayment supplement being due.

You should use the tax rates and allowances for 1999-00 throughout.     **(7 marks)**

(c)     Ming and Nina are concerned about the partnership's financial position. They have asked for your advice on the following matters:

(1)     One of the partnership's clients owes the partnership £23,500, and this amount is now four months overdue. Ming and Nina want to know how relief for bad debts can be obtained.

(2)     The partnership needs to purchase computer equipment costing £61,100, but does not have sufficient funds to do so outright. The computer equipment can either be leased for three years at a cost of £28,200 pa or can be bought on hire-purchase for an initial payment of £11,100 (including VAT of £9,100), followed by 35 monthly payments of £2,000.

The computer equipment will be replaced after three years use, at which time it will be worthless. Ming and Nina want to know the tax implications of each alternative method of financing the computer equipment.

All figures are inclusive of VAT where appropriate.

**Required:**

Advise Ming and Nina in respect of the matters that they have raised. Your answer should cover both the income tax and the VAT implications. You should ignore the implications of SSAP 21: Accounting for Leases and Hire-Purchase Contracts.                                                         **(7 marks)**

**(Total: 25 marks)**

---

## 60     (Question 6 of examination)

You are the tax adviser to Eyetaki Inc, a company resident in the country of Eyeland. Eyetaki Inc manufactures cameras in Eyeland, and has been selling these in the UK since 1 January 2000. Initially, Eyetaki Inc employed a UK based agent to sell their cameras, and rented a warehouse in London in order to maintain a stock of goods. On 1 March 2000 Eyetaki Inc sent an office manager and two sales managers to the UK from their head office in Eyeland, and rented an office building and showroom in London.

As the sale of cameras in the UK has been profitable, on 1 July 2000 Eyetaki Inc is to form a 100% subsidiary, Uktaki Ltd, which will be incorporated in the UK. The subsidiary will commence trading on 1 August 2000, and will make up its first accounts for the 18 month period to 31 December 2001. Uktaki Ltd is to initially sell cameras on a wholesale basis, but is to commence retail sales during 2001.

Uktaki Ltd is to purchase a new freehold building. The building will be used to:

-       assemble cameras from components imported from Eyeland, and

-       to store components prior to their assembly, and assembled cameras prior to sale.

The building will also contain a showroom and general offices. It is possible that the building will be situated in a designated enterprise zone.

Eyetaki Inc is to export the camera components to the UK at their normal trade selling price plus a markup of 25%. This is because the company wishes to maximise its own profits which are only subject to corporation tax at the rate of 15% in Eyeland.

Eyetaki Inc is to assign a director to the UK for a period of between two and three years in order to manage Uktaki Ltd. The director, who is currently resident and domiciled in Eyeland, will continue to be employed by Eyetaki Inc, and will perform duties both in the UK and in Eyeland. The director has income from investments situated in Eyeland.

There is no double taxation treaty between the UK and Eyeland. Eyeland is not currently a member of the European Union, but is expected to become a member in the near future.

**Required:**

(a)     (i)     Advise Eyetaki Inc of whether or not it will be liable to UK corporation tax during the period from 1 January 2000 to 31 December 2001, and, if so, how the corporation tax liability will be calculated.

(ii)     Set out Uktaki Ltd's accounting periods for the period up to, and including, 31 December 2001.

**(7 marks)**

---

(b)       Explain as to what extent the new freehold building to be purchased by Uktaki Ltd will qualify for Industrial Buildings Allowance, and state the Industrial Buildings Allowance that will be available.     **(6 marks)**

(c)       Briefly advise Uktaki Ltd of the basis on which it will have to account for VAT on the components imported from Eyeland.  Explain how this basis will alter if Eyeland becomes a member of the European Union.

                                                       **(4 marks)**

(d)       Advise Eyetaki Inc and Uktaki Ltd of the tax implications arising from the invoicing of camera components at their normal trade selling price plus a markup of 25%.     **(3 marks)**

(e)       Briefly state the circumstances in which the director of Eyetaki Inc will be liable to UK income tax in respect of:

        (i)       Emoluments for duties performed in the UK.

        (ii)      Emoluments for duties performed in Eyeland.

        (iii)     Investment income arising in Eyeland.                **(5 marks)**

                                                           **(Total: 25 marks)**

## ANSWERS TO JUNE 1997 EXAMINATION

## 55    (Answer 1 of examination)

### Examiner's comments and marking guide

**Part (a) tested candidates' ability to advise on two alternative remuneration packages. The first option consisting of a company car, and the second option consisting of additional salary and the payment of a mileage allowance. Part (b) tested candidates' knowledge of personal pension schemes and occupational pension schemes.**

This was a reasonably popular question, but was not answered as well as would be expected given that all the topics covered are examinable at paper 7. In part (a), most candidates got the basic points correct, but the comparison of a claim for business expenditure and a claim based on the fixed profit car scheme caused problems. In part (b), many candidates wrote at length on personal pension plans and occupational pension schemes without relating their answer to the requirements of the question. This involved a comparison of the two schemes, and therefore no marks were available for factors which applied equally to both schemes. Few candidates had any knowledge of how additional voluntary contributions could be made.

|  |  | *Marks* |
|---|---|---|
| (a) | Accepting the company motor car | |
| | Car benefit | 1 |
| | Contributions | 1 |
| | Fuel benefit | 1 |
| | Total annual cost | 1 |
| | Accepting the cash alternative | |
| | Income tax liability | 1 |
| | Class 1 NIC | 1 |
| | Mileage allowance | 1 |
| | Running and leasing costs | 1 |
| | Expense claim | |
| | Based on business expenditure | 2 |
| | Based on fixed profit car scheme | 2 |
| | Conclusion | 1 |
| | | — |
| | Maximum/Available | 13 |
| | | — |
| (b) | Factors | |
| | Contributions | 2 |
| | Company contributions | 1 |
| | Flexibility of personal pension scheme | 1 |
| | Pension payable | 1 |
| | Retirement age | 1 |
| | Income tax implications | 1 |
| | Additional voluntary contributions | |
| | Additional contributions | 1 |
| | Schemes available | 1 |
| | Tax relief | 1 |
| | | — |
| | Available | 10 |
| | | — |
| | Maximum | 7 |
| | | — |
| | Available | 23 |
| | | — |
| | Maximum | 20 |
| | | — |

*(**Tutorial note**: a further part of the original question has been deleted as it concerns a topic no longer examinable. The comments etc, have been edited accordingly).*

## Step by step answer plan

**Overview**

This is a fairly straightforward question on employee taxation in two separate parts. In part (a) you have to evaluate two ways of funding the use of a car building in the tax and NIC effects of the alternatives. Part (b) tests a knowledge of the contrasts between a personal pension scheme and an occupational pension scheme.

**Step 1**   Read part (a) carefully and decide how to evaluate the choices. Clearly you have to find the after tax (and NIC) costs to the employee. The requirements even spell out the key workings needed.

**Step 2**   Calculate the net cost under option 1.

**Step 3**   For option 2, calculate first the relief for running expenses under the 'actual' and under the FPCS bases and choose the better method.

**Step 4**   Identify the income under option 2 - ie, the extra salary and the mileage allowance; identify the non-tax outgoings - ie, the leasing and running costs; and identify the tax implications - ie, extra tax and NIC on the extra salary but tax relief as the mileage allowance is less than the FPCS rates.

**Step 5**   Compare the net effect of the two options and state which is preferable.

**Step 6**   For part (b) (i) list out the factors in choosing between the two pension provision options. Note that you are not restricted to just the tax factors but are expected to comment on the commercial aspects.

**Step 7**   For part (b) (ii) explain the treatment of AVCs and calculate the maximum amount payable.

## The examiner's answer

(a)     **Accepting the company motor car**

|  | £ | £ |
|---|---|---|
| Car benefit £14,400 × 25% |  | 3,600 |
| Less: contributions 12 × £35 (50 - 15) |  | 420 |
|  |  | 3,180 |
| Fuel benefit |  | 1,540 |
|  |  | 4,720 |
| Additional income tax liability at 23% |  | 1,086 |
| Contributions 12 × £50 |  | 600 |
| Total annual cost to employee |  | 1,686 |

**Accepting the cash alternative**

|  | £ | £ |
|---|---|---|
| Salary |  | 2,800 |
| Less:   income tax at 23% | 644 |  |
| Class 1 NIC |  |  |
| 2,500 (52 × 500 = 26,0000 – 23,500) at 10% | 250 |  |
|  |  | 894 |
|  |  | 1,906 |
| Mileage allowance 8,000 at 24p |  | 1,920 |
| Tax relief on expense claim (working) |  | 336 |
|  |  | 4,162 |

| | | |
|---|---|---|
| Running costs | 1,650 | |
| Leasing cost 12 × £285 | 3,420 | |
| | | 5,070 |

Total annual cost to employee                                                            908

Based on purely financial criteria, the cash alternative appears to be the most beneficial as it results in a saving of £778 (1,686 – 908).

*Working - expense claim*

### Based on business expenditure

The mileage allowance will be assessed as a benefit.

| | £ |
|---|---|
| Running and leasing costs | |
| 5,070 × 8,000/12,000 | 3,380 |
| Less: mileage allowance | 1,920 |
| | 1,460 |
| Income tax relief at 23% | 336 |

### Based on fixed profit car scheme

The mileage allowance will be tax free, and Charles will be able to make the following expense claim:

| | £ |
|---|---|
| 4,000 miles at 35p | 1,400 |
| 4,000 miles at 20p | 800 |
| | 2,200 |
| Mileage allowance | 1,920 |
| | 280 |
| Income tax relief at 23% | 64 |

The claim based on business expenditure results in greater income tax relief.

(b)     (i)     Charles will have to take the following factors into account when deciding whether or not to join the Northwest Bank plc's occupational pension scheme:

  (1)     Charles' contributions to his personal pension scheme for 1999-00 were £5,875 (23,500 at 25%). Under the company's occupational pension scheme, Charles' contributions for 2000-01 will be £1,410 (23,500 at 6%). The saving net of tax is £3,438 (5,875 – 1,410 = 4,465 less 23%). Any unused personal pension relief brought forward from years prior to 1999-00 will be lost.

  (2)     With the occupational pension scheme, the Northwest Bank plc will also contribute £1,410 each year on Charles' behalf.

  (3)     A personal pension scheme is generally more flexible than an occupational pension scheme, and this will be an important factor if Charles plans to leave the Northwest Bank plc in the foreseeable future.

  (4)     The ultimate pension payable under a personal pension scheme depends upon the performance of the underlying investment fund. The ultimate pension payable under an occupational pension scheme is based upon final salary and number of years' service.

(5) Under a personal pension scheme, benefits can be taken from the age of 50. The normal earliest retirement age under an occupational pension scheme is 60.

(6) The income tax implications are similar for both schemes.

---

**Did you answer the question?**

As only 5 marks are on offer for part (b) (i) you were only required to mention the main differences between the two choices.

---

(ii) The maximum tax deductible contributions that Charles could make into the Northwest Bank plc's occupational pension scheme are £3,525 pa (23,500 at 15%). He could therefore make additional contributions of £2,115 pa (3,525 – 1,410).

Additional voluntary contributions of this amount could either be paid into the Northwest Bank plc's occupational pension scheme, or into a separate free-standing scheme. If Charles contributes into the company scheme then tax relief will be given as a deduction against Charles' Schedule E income. If he contributes into a free-standing scheme then tax relief will be given by making the payments net of basic rate tax.

---

## 56 (Answer 2 of examination)

### Examiner's comments and marking guide

Part (a) tested candidates knowledge of Schedule A, and in particular the furnished holiday letting rules and Schedule A loss relief. Part (b) tested candidates ability to advise on the tax implications of divorce, including tax relief for maintenance payments.

This was not as popular as some of the other questions, although those candidates who attempted it often scored high marks. In part (a), many candidates did not appreciate that the furnished holiday let properties had to be dealt with separately from the other properties. Very few candidates gave the correct capital allowances for properties one and two, or the wear and tear allowance for property three, and the calculation of the taxable element of the premium received caused problems. Part (b) was poorly answered, with hardly any candidates appreciating that the only tax relief available was for the maintenance payments made under a written agreement. Surprisingly, few candidates correctly stated which personal allowances were available, with the most common mistake being the time apportionment of the married couple's allowance for the year of separation.

|  |  |  | *Marks* |
|---|---|---|---|
| (a) | (i) | Qualification as furnished holiday letting |  |
|  |  | Commercial basis | 1 |
|  |  | 140 day rule | 1 |
|  |  | 70 day rule | 1 |
|  |  | 31 day test | 1 |
|  |  | Tax advantages |  |
|  |  | Capital allowances/Net relevant earnings | 1 |
|  |  | Loss relief/Retirement relief/Taper relief | 1 |
|  |  | Available | 6 |
|  |  | Maximum | 5 |
|  | (ii) | Furnished holiday accommodation |  |
|  |  | Separate identification | 1 |
|  |  | Rental income | 1 |
|  |  | Expenses | 2 |
|  |  | Capital allowance claim | 1 |
|  |  | Non-business use adjustment | 2 |

---

| | |
|---|---:|
| Other lettings | |
| Rental income/Premium received - house 3 | 3 |
| Furnished room | 1 |
| Expenses | 2 |
| Relief for losses | |
| Furnished holiday lettings | 1 |
| Schedule A loss | 1 |
| | |
| Available | 15 |
| | |
| Maximum | 14 |

(b)    (i)    Voluntary payments

| | |
|---|---:|
| No tax relief | 1 |
| Mortgage interest | 1 |
| Divorce settlement | |
| Maintenance payments | 2 |
| Other payments | 1 |
| | |
| Available | 5 |
| | |
| Maximum | 4 |

(ii)

| | |
|---|---:|
| Married couple's allowance | 1 |
| Additional personal allowance | 1 |
| | |
| Available | 2 |
| | |
| Maximum | 2 |
| | |
| Available | 28 |
| | |
| Maximum | 25 |

## Step by step answer plan

**Overview**

In part (a) you have to spot that all the furnished holiday lettings (houses 1 & 2) constitute a single business and the rest of the letting constitutes another single business. In effect there are two separate Schedule A losses although the question implies there is only one loss so as not to give you too much help. For part (b) you have to know the basics of taxation on separation.

**Step 1**    Explain clearly why houses 1 & 2 qualify as FHLs. This is best done by stating the conditions and showing that they are satisfied particularly regarding an averaging of actual letting to meet the 70 day test.

**Step 2**    Don't overlook the requirement of part (a) (i) to state the tax advantages of FHL status.

**Step 3**    Compute the loss on the composite 'business' of houses 1 and 2 not forgetting capital allowances and the need for private use adjustment on house 2.

**Step 4**    Compute the loss on the other lettings treated again as a single business. Here capital allowances on plant (ie, furnishings) used in a dwelling are not allowed but, a 10% wear and tear allowance can be claimed. A separate working for the income tax treatment of the premium is desirable.

**Step 5**    Explain why rent-a-room relief is preferable.

Step 6    Highlight the two Schedule A losses and explain how relief can be taken.

Step 7    Read part (b) of the question carefully.

Step 8    Answer part (b) (i) distinguishing clearly between the situation up to 31 December 1999 and the situation thereafter.

Step 9    Don't waste the two easy marks on offer by overlooking the requirements of part (b) (ii).

## The examiner's answer

(a)    (i)    The houses qualify as a trade under the furnished holiday letting rules, because the following conditions appear to be met:

        (1)    The houses are let on a commercial basis with a view to the realisation of profits.

        (2)    The houses are available as holiday accommodation for at least 140 days during 1999-00 (294 days and 224 days respectively).

        (3)    The houses are so let for at least 70 days. House 2 satisfies this test since the average for the two houses is 77 days (14 + 8 = 22 × 7 = 154/2 = 77).

        (4)    For at least seven months during 1999-00, the houses are not in same occupation for more than 31 days.

       The tax advantages of the houses being treated as a trade under the furnished holiday letting rules are that:

        (1)    Capital allowances will be available on plant and machinery.

        (2)    Loss relief will be available against total income.

        (3)    The Schedule A profit will qualify as net relevant earnings for personal pension purposes.

        (4)    Retirement relief may be available when the properties are disposed of.

        (5)    Business rates of taper relief for CGT apply.

     (ii)    It is necessary to separately identify the profits from the trade of letting furnished holiday accommodation (houses 1 and 2) as follows:

| **Rental income** | | £ | £ |
|---|---|---:|---:|
| House 1 | 14 at £375 | | 5,250 |
| House 2 | 8 at £340 | | 2,720 |
| | | | 7,970 |
| **Expenses** | | | |
| Business rates (730 + 590) | | 1,320 | |
| Insurance (310 + 330) | | 640 | |
| Advertising (545 + 225) | | 770 | |
| Repairs | | 6,250 | |
| Capital allowances | | | |
|    House 1 (5,200 × 25%) | | 1,300 | |
|    House 2 (5,200 × 25%) | | 1,300 | |
| | | | 11,580 |
| | | | 3,610 |

Non-business use (re house 1).

(730 + 310 + 1,300 = 2,340 × 10/52)      450

Schedule A loss      3,160

William's Schedule A loss in respect of his other lettings (house 3 and furnished room) is as follows:

| **Rental income** | £ | £ |
|---|---|---|
| House 3 (8,600 × 3/12) | | 2,150 |
| Premium received (working) | | 448 |
| Furnished room (4,600 − 4,250) | | 350 |
| | | 2,948 |
| **Expenses** | | |
| Rent | 6,200 | |
| Repairs | 710 | |
| Wear and tear allowance (2,150 × 10%) | 215 | |
| | | 7,125 |
| Schedule A loss | | 4,177 |

William should claim 'rent a room' relief in respect of the letting of the furnished room in his main residence, since this is more beneficial than the normal basis of assessment (4,600 − 825 = 3,775).

**WORKING**

| | £ | £ |
|---|---|---|
| Premium received | | 8,000 |
| Less: 8,000 × 2% × (4 − 1) | | 480 |
| | | 7,520 |
| Less allowance for premium paid | | |
| Premium paid | 85,000 | |
| Less: 85,000 × 2% × (25 − 1) | 40,800 | |
| | 44,200 | |
| Relief available 44,200 × 4/25 | | 7,072 |
| | | 448 |

William can claim under s380 ICTA 1988 to have the Schedule A loss of £3,160 arising in respect of furnished holiday lettings to be set off against his total income for 1999-00, and/or his total income for 1998-99.

The Schedule A loss of £4,177 will be carried forward and set against the first available Schedule A profits.

---

**Did you answer the question?**

Except where you were making a choice on rent-a-room relief, you were not required to annotate your answer with explanations of the steps in the above computations.

---

(b)     (i)     **Voluntary payments made between 1 July 1999 and 31 December 1999**

No tax relief will be due in respect of voluntary maintenance payments, school fees paid, or mortgage interest paid. The mortgage interest has not been paid for a qualifying purpose, as the property is not William's main residence.

**Payments made under the divorce settlement from 1 January 2000 onwards**

The lump sum payment of £25,000 will not attract any tax relief.

The maintenance payments made under written agreement will attract tax relief of £142 (475 × 3 = 1,425 at 10%) for 1999-00, and nil for 2000/01. The tax relief will cease from 6 April 2000, or on the earlier of the cessation of maintenance payments, or the remarriage of William's wife.

As per above, no tax relief will be due in respect of school fees paid or mortgage interest paid.

---

**Did you answer the question?**

You were not required to mention the tax treatment of the payments in the hands of the recipients even though all you could say was that in both situations they were exempt.

---

(ii)     In addition to his personal allowance, William will be entitled to:

(a)     The married couple's allowance of £1,970 for 1999-00, unless a claim to transfer all or half of it to his wife has been made.

(b)     No allowance in 2000-01. The additional personal allowance is abolished from 6 April 2000.

---

## 57 ✕ (Answer 3 of examination)

---

**Examiner's comments and marking guide**

This question tested candidates' ability to calculate the corporation tax liability for a company with (i) a consortium company, (ii) a 51% subsidiary, and (iii) a 75% subsidiary. It covered group relief, intra-group transfer of assets, rollover relief and the loan relationship resulting from an issue of debentures.

This also was not a popular question, and resulted in some varied answers. Those candidates who appreciated the implications of the three different shareholdings, and that consortium relief was available in the first two instances, scored high marks. Those candidates who stated that there were four associated companies under option (i) (when there were none), or who set off the capital losses against trading profits will find it difficult to pass this examination. The loan relationship aspects were generally not well answered, which is disappointing since this topic was dealt with in the Finance Act article published in the *Students' Newsletter* written specifically for this paper.

|  | *Marks* |
|---|---|
| **One third of ordinary share capital acquired** |  |
| Target Ltd | 1 |
| Schedule DI/Schedule DIII | 2 |
| Section 402 ICTA 1988 | 3 |
|     Corporation tax |  |
|  | 1 |
| **Two thirds of ordinary share capital acquired** |  |
| Schedule DI/Schedule DIII | 1 |
| Section 402 ICTA 1988 | 1 |
| Corporation tax |  |
|  | 2 |

**All of ordinary share capital acquired**

| | |
|---|---:|
| Transfer of office building | 1 |
| Rollover relief | 1 |
| Calculation of gain | 2 |
| Issue of debentures | 2 |
| Schedule DI profit | 2 |
| Section 402 ICTA 1988 | 1 |
| Corporation tax | 1 |
| | — |
| Available | 21 |
| | — |
| Maximum | 17 |
| | — |

(The question has been amended to exclude reference to topics no longer examinable. The examiner's comments have been edited to reflect this.)

## ( Step by step answer plan )

### Overview

This is a corporation tax 'groups' question with three alternative plans - a company either acquires one-third, two-thirds, or the entire issued share capital of 'Target'. In each case the CT of both companies is required. With this clearly in mind, as you read through the question you will notice certain items whose tax treatment may depend on which proportion of share capital is acquired. For example, Target's loss can only be group relieved under the third option. However, consortium relief might be available under the other two options.

The question is presented in three parts. Clearly, some information generated in one part may be required again for a later part. Be on the look out for this as you do not want to waste time 'reinventing the wheel'. The marks given for each part provide a clue to the amount of work required.

**Step 1** Start by reading the question carefully. It might help to make notes. In particular, a rough diagram of the relationships of all the companies mentioned should make it obvious that a consortium will arise in parts (i) and (ii). It might also help to jot down points which could arise. For example, in part (iii), group relief and relief for inter-company asset transfers could be relevant (75% group) in addition to the 51% group points identified for part (ii).

**Step 2** Answer part (i). Start with Target Ltd as this will be a source of figures - portion of its current year loss - for Expansion Ltd's PCTCT.

**Step 3** Comment on your treatment of consortium relief.

**Step 4** As a matter of course, highlight any unrelieved balances with an indication of their fate. For example, 'capital loss c/f'.

**Step 5** Re read the question to ensure nothing relevant has been over looked.

**Step 6** Move on to part (ii). There is no need to repeat computations etc, which don't differ from part (i) - eg, Target Ltd's PCTCT - but make sure short cuts are clear in your answer.

**Step 7** Apart from being entitled to twice as much loss, Expansion Ltd's tax comp in part (ii) will differ from that of part (i) because it now has an associate and the small company limits are therefore reduced.

**Step 8** Move on to part (iii) once you have checked that all the points in the question relevant for part (ii) have been included.

**Step 9**    Deal with the effect of issuing the debenture necessitated by acquiring all the share capital of Target. The examiner gives a detailed discussion of whether the non-trading or trading treatment should be used with the conclusion that ultimately it makes no difference. Interestingly, this is only given 2 marks in the marking scheme so we can assume far less detail would be required for the full 2 marks.

**Step 10**    Consider the changes which result from a 75% + holding. Target can route the proposed gain now tax free through Expansion Ltd. It can be reduced through rollover relief and the capital loss brought forward. Rollover is allowed on a group-wide basis so the disposal outside the group could just as effectively have been made by Target. The purpose of the transfer was, however, to utilise the capital loss against the part of the gain not attracting rollover.

**Step 11**    Compute the CT for Expansion Ltd in part (iii) taking account of the full available group relief.

**Step 12**    Ensure any necessary comments have been made. For example, explain why full rollover of the business portion is possible even when there is only partial reinvestment.

<hr>

**The examiner's answer**

**One third of Target Ltd's ordinary share capital acquired**

| **Target Ltd** | **£** |
|---|---:|
| Capital gain | 51,300 |
| Less s393A(1) | 51,300 |
| | ———— |
| PCTCT | - |
| | ———— |

Target Ltd is a consortium company, and will therefore be able to surrender one third of its trading loss to Expansion Ltd. Target Ltd must take into account its own current year profits when calculating the surrender. Only the current year loss can be surrendered, and this is restricted to the corresponding period of 1 July 1999 to 31 December 1999. Assuming that all of Target Ltd's current year loss is surrendered to the members of the consortium, trading losses of £9,200 will be carried forward.

| **Expansion Ltd** | **£** |
|---|---:|
| Schedule DI profit | 214,000 |
| Schedule DIII (120,000 at 8% × 8/12) | 6,400 |
| | ———— |
| | 220,400 |
| Less s402 (137,700 − 51,300 = 86,400 × 1/3 × 6/12) | 14,400 |
| | ———— |
| PCTCT | 206,000 |
| | ———— |
| Corporation tax:    206,000 × 20.25% | 41,715 |
| | ———— |
| Capital loss c/f | 9,600 |
| | ———— |

*(handwritten note: CONSORTIUM NO REDUCTION FOR RELIEF. LIMITS All @ Small Co Rate)*

*(**Tutorial note:** Government stocks acquired after 5 April 1998 pay interest gross so there is no income tax to recover against Corporation Tax.)*

**Two thirds of Target Ltd's ordinary share capital acquired**

Target Ltd's corporation tax position will be the same as for a one third acquisition of its ordinary share capital.

Target Ltd is a 51% subsidiary and an associated company. The lower limit for corporation tax purposes is therefore reduced to £150,000 (300,000/2).

| **Expansion Ltd** | £ |
|---|---|
| Schedule DI profit | 214,000 |
| Schedule DIII | 6,400 |
| | 220,400 |
| Less s402 | |
| $(137,700 - 51,300 = 86,400 \times 2/3 \times 6/12)$ | 28,800 |
| PCTCT | 191,600 |
| Corporation tax | |
| $191,600 \times 30.25\%$ | 57,959 |
| Tapering relief $\frac{1}{40}$ $(750,000 - 191,600)$ | (13,960) |
| | 43,999 |
| Capital loss c/f | 9,600 |

### All of Target Ltd's ordinary share capital acquired

Target Ltd is a 51% subsidiary, a 75% subsidiary and an associated company.

Target Ltd should transfer the freehold office building to Expansion Ltd prior to its disposal. This will be an intra-group transfer of an asset, and will not result in a chargeable gain. Expansion Ltd's capital losses brought forward can then be utilised. Rollover relief can be claimed based on the freehold factory to be purchased by Expansion Ltd. Expansion Ltd's chargeable gain arising from the disposal of the freehold office building will be as follows:

| | £ |
|---|---|
| Capital gain | 51,300 |
| Less rolled over - 75% business use | (38,475) |
| | 12,825 |
| Capital losses b/f | (9,600) |
| | 3,225 |

The cost of the new freehold factory (£118,000) exceeds the business proportion of the proceeds from the disposal of the freehold office building (140,000 × 75% = £105,000), and so there is no further restriction on the gain to be rolled over.

| **Expansion Ltd** | £ |
|---|---|
| Schedule DI profit (working) | 199,225 |
| Schedule DIII | 6,400 |
| Capital gain | 3,225 |
| | 208,850 |
| Less s402 (137,700 × 6/12) | 68,850 |
| PCTCT | 140,000 |

| | | £ |
|---|---|---|
| Corporation tax: | 140,000 at 20.25% | 28,350 |

WORKING - Schedule DI profit

The loan relationship legislation introduced by the Finance Act 1996 does not define 'trading purposes'. If the issue of debentures is for trading purposes, then the debenture interest, the cost of the 3% discount on the issue of the debentures and the incidental costs of obtaining the finance will be deductible as a Schedule D1 expense. Expansion Ltd's Schedule DI profit for the year ended 31 December 1999 is as follows:

|  | £ |
|---|---|
| Previous Schedule DI profit | 214,000 |
| Debenture interest (250,000 at 10% × 6/12) | (12,500) |
| Discount (250,000 × 3% = 7,500 × 6/60) | (750) |
| Incidental costs (15,250 × 6/60) | (1,525) |
| Revised Schedule DI profit | 199,225 |

If the issue of debentures is not for trading purposes, then there will be a net loss on loan relationships of £8,375 (6,400 – 12,500 – 750 – 1,525). The calculation of Expansion Ltd's PCTCT would be as follows:

|  | £ |
|---|---|
| Schedule D1 profit | 214,000 |
| Capital gain | 3,225 |
|  | 217,225 |
| Less loss on loan relationships | 8,375 |
|  | 208,850 |
| Less s402 (137,700 × 6/12) | 68,850 |
| PCTCT | 140,000 |

Either of these approaches would be acceptable.

Note that under FRS 4: Capital Instruments, the debenture interest, discount, and incidental costs should have been written off so as to achieve a constant rate on the outstanding balance in each period. However, the above calculations are those expected from candidates.

---

**Did you answer the question?**

You are not required to comment on the tax treatment of the other three companies mentioned in the question.

---

**Did you answer the question?**

You are not required to comment on any alternative acquisition structures. For example, in practice the trade of Target might be hived down to a new 'clean' company prior to sale.

---

## 58   (Answer 4 of examination)

**Examiner's comments and marking guide**

**This question tested candidates' knowledge of the IHT (Inheritance Tax) and CGT (Capital Gains Tax) consequences of making either a lifetime gift or a gift at death. It included the related property rules, business property relief, and relief for the fall in value of a lifetime gift.**

This was a popular question, and was well answered by a number of candidates. The answers of some candidates, however were badly presented, and it was often difficult to know which part of the question was being answered. The use of headings is recommended for a question of this nature. For the lifetime gift, many candidates did not keep the PET (Potentially Exempt Transfer) and the estate at death separate, and therefore incorrectly applied tapering relief to the value of the estate. The calculation of the capital gain on the shares (following a part disposal) caused problems for a number of candidates, with several wasting time by calculating the capital gain in respect of the previous part disposal.

|  | *Marks* |
|---|---|
| **Gift made on 30 June 2000** | |
| Inheritance tax - PET | |
| Shares in Windermere Ltd | 2 |
| Business property relief/advice | 2 |
| Antique painting/Holiday cottage | 1 |
| Annual exemptions | 1 |
| Fall in value of lifetime gift | 1 |
| IHT liability | 1 |
| Due date/Instalment option | 2 |
| Inheritance tax - estate | |
| Shares in Windermere Ltd | 1 |
| Business property relief | 1 |
| IHT liability/Due date | 1 |
| Capital gains tax | |
| Shares in Windermere Ltd | 2 |
| Antique painting | 1 |
| Holiday cottage | 1 |
| Taper relief | 1 |
| CGT liability | 1 |
| Holdover relief | 1 |
| Tax planning | 1 |
| **Gift not made on 30 June 2000** | |
| Shares in Windermere Ltd | 1 |
| Business property relief | 1 |
| Other assets | 1 |
| IHT liability/Estate rate | 1 |
| Instalment option | 2 |
| CGT implications | 1 |
| **Conclusion** | 2 |
| | |
| Available | 30 |
| | |
| Maximum | 25 |

## ( Step by step answer plan )

**Overview**

This is a CGT/IHT planning question in three parts. The first considers one route - ie, gift assets during lifetime - the second considers allowing the assets instead to pass on death, but the third part requires your conclusion. The question is fairly straightforward provided you work through it logically and follow all the requirements such as stating pay days and discussing tax planning within the framework of the question. You are not required to uncover some other means of mitigating the tax liabilities except based on the information given.

**Step 1**    Calculate the IHT on the lifetime gift showing first the PET and then the adjusted PET value when it becomes chargeable on death.

**Step 2**    Calculate the IHT on assets remaining in Dorothy's estate on death.

Step 3    State the pay days for these two amounts and discuss the instalment option.

Step 4    Calculate the capital gains and losses arising on the proposed gifts and calculate the CGT not forgetting taper relief.

Step 5    Discuss any obvious CGT planning points and explain why gift relief is inappropriate.

Step 6    Calculate the IHT on the death estate assuming Dorothy does not make the gifts, again giving the pay day and explaining how much can be paid by instalments.

Step 7    Explain the CGT implications of not making the gifts but allowing the property to pass on death.

Step 8    Contrast the total tax payable under the two alternatives and state your preference. This is the point at which any conditions or modifications could be mentioned.

## The examiner's answer

**Gift made to Alice on 30 June 2000**

*Inheritance tax implications*

The gift on 30 June 2000 will be a PET as follows:

|  | £ | £ |
|---|---|---|
| Shares in Windermere Ltd |  |  |
| Value of shares held before the transfer |  |  |
| (based on a 50% holding) 100,000 at £4.50 |  | 450,000 |
| Value of shares held after the transfer |  |  |
| (based on a 37.5% holding) 50,000 at £3.55 |  | 177,500 |
| Diminution in value |  | 272,500 |
| Business property relief |  |  |
| $272,500 \times \dfrac{88(100-12)}{100} \times 100\%$ |  | 239,800 |
|  |  | 32,700 |
| Antique painting |  | 8,500 |
| Holiday cottage |  | 165,000 |
|  |  | 206,200 |
| Annual exemptions         2000-01 | 3,000 |  |
|                                  1999-00 | 3,000 |  |
|  |  | 6,000 |
| Potentially exempt transfer |  | 200,200 |

No IHT liability will arise at that time. As a result of Dorothy's death within seven years, the PET will become chargeable. The following must be taken into account:

(i)     Business property relief will not be available in respect of the shares in Windermere Ltd if Alice disposes of the holding before 31 December 2004.

Alice should therefore consider retaining the shares until 31 December 2004, since there is no more risk in her retaining the shares than if they remain part of Dorothy's estate until that date.

(ii)    At the date of Dorothy's death, the value of the holiday cottage will have fallen to £105,000, and Alice can claim to have the IHT liability calculated on this valuation.
       IHT will be due as follows:                                                                £

|                                                    |                   |         |
| -------------------------------------------------- | ----------------- | ------- |
| PET (as originally calculated)                     |                   | 200,200 |
| BPR no longer available                            |                   | 239,800 |
|                                                    |                   | 440,000 |
| Less relief for fall in value (165,000 – 105,000)  |                   | 60,000  |
|                                                    |                   | 380,000 |
| IHT liability                                      | 231,000 at nil %  | Nil     |
|                                                    | 149,000 at 40%    | 59,600  |
|                                                    |                   | 59,600  |
| Tapering relief at 40%                             |                   | 23,840  |
|                                                    |                   | 35,760  |

The IHT liability will be payable by Alice on 30 June 2005. It will be possible to pay IHT of £9,727 (35,760 × 105,000/386,000 (380,000 + 6,000) in respect of the holiday cottage in ten equal instalments commencing on 30 June 2005. The IHT payable by instalments could be increased if the gift of the holiday cottage was made subsequent to the other gifts, since the nil rate band of £231,000 would be allocated to the earlier gifts.

The IHT liability due on Dorothy's estate will be as follows:

|                                                                      | £       |
| -------------------------------------------------------------------- | ------- |
| Shares in Windermere Ltd (based on a 37.5% holding)                  |         |
| 50,000 at £4.97 (3.55 plus 40%)                                       | 248,500 |
| Business property relief                                             |         |
| $248,500 \times \dfrac{88(100-12)}{100} \times 100\%$                | 218,680 |
|                                                                      | 29,820  |
| Other assets                                                         | 350,000 |
| Chargeable estate                                                    | 379,820 |
| IHT liability 379,820 at 40%                                         | 151,928 |

The IHT liability will be payable by the executors of Dorothy's estate on the earlier of 30 June 2005 or the delivery of their account.

*Capital gains tax implications*

Shares in Windermere Ltd

|                                                                      | £       |
| -------------------------------------------------------------------- | ------- |
| Deemed consideration (based on a 12.5% holding)                      |         |
| 50,000 at £2.50                                                       | 125,000 |
| Cost                                                                 |         |
| $96,000 \times \dfrac{2.40(2 \text{ at } £1.20)}{2.40+0.80} \times \dfrac{50,000}{100,000}$ | 36,000  |
|                                                                      | 89,000  |
| Indexation $36,000 \times \dfrac{162.6-104.1}{104.1}$                | 20,230  |
| Capital gain                                                         | 68,770  |

*(Tutorial note:* This qualifies for taper relief as a business asset since Dorothy holds 25% of the shares, thereby making Windermere Ltd a qualifying company. However, the 77.5% taper can only be applied after loss relief (see below)).

---

**Did you answer the question?**

You were not required to calculate the gain on the previous disposal involving the cash received on the takeover.

---

|  | £ |
|---|---|
| Antique painting |  |
| Deemed consideration | 8,500 |
| Cost | 1,400 |
|  | 7,100 |
| Indexation $1,400 \times \dfrac{162.6 - 106.6}{106.6} (= 0.525)$ | 735 |
| Capital gain | 6,365 |
| Limited to: $(8,500 - 6,000) \times 5/3 =$ | 4,167 |
| Holiday cottage |  |
| Deemed consideration | 165,000 |
| Cost | 188,000 |
| Capital loss | (23,000) |

Dorothy's CGT liability will be £12,640 (68,770 + 4,167 − 23,000 = 49,937 × 77.5% = 38,701 − 7,100 = 31,601 at 40%). The gain of £68,770 in respect of the shares in Windermere Ltd can be held over if Dorothy and Alice make a joint election. However, a claim does not appear to be beneficial since Alice is to sell the shares soon after receiving them (thus crystallising the gain), and Dorothy's taper relief and capital loss would then be wasted. Dorothy would be advised to postpone the gift of the painting until 2001-02 so as to partly utilise that year's annual exemption.

**Gift not made to Alice on 30 June 2000**

*Inheritance tax implications*

An IHT liability will arise in respect of Dorothy's estate, as follows:

| *Personalty* | £ |
|---|---|
| Shares in Windermere Ltd (based on a 50% holding) 100,000 at £6.30 (4.50 plus 40%) | 630,000 |
| Business property relief $630,000 \times \dfrac{88(100 - 12)}{100} \times 100\%$ | 554,400 |
|  | 75,600 |
| Antique painting | 8,500 |
| Other assets | 350,000 |
|  | 434,100 |
| *Realty* |  |
| Holiday cottage | 105,000 |
|  | 539,100 |
| IHT liability    231,000 at nil % | Nil |

308,100 at 40%                                              123,240
                                                           ─────────
                                                            123,240
                                                           ─────────

Rate of IHT on estate = 22.860% (123,240/539,100)

The IHT liability will be payable as previously. It will be possible to pay the IHT of £24,003 (105,000 at 22.860%) in respect of the holiday cottage in 10 equal instalments commencing on 30 June 2005. It will not be possible to pay the IHT in respect of the shares in Windermere Ltd by instalments if they are immediately sold by Alice.

*Capital gains tax implications*

No CGT liability arises in respect of transfers on death, and Alice will take over the assets with a base cost based on their market values at 31 December 2004.

**Conclusion**

The total tax liability if the gift of assets is made to Alice on 30 June 2000 is £200,328 (35,760 + 151,928 + 12,640), compared to a total tax liability of £123,240 if the gift of assets is not made. Although it therefore appears to be beneficial for Dorothy to not make the gift to Alice, the figure of £200,328 would be substantially reduced if the tax planning advice was followed, and there is always the possibility that Dorothy may live beyond 31 December 2004.

---

**Did you answer the question?**

You were not required to suggest other ways of mitigating IHT based on such strategies as gifting property via the husband - assuming his life expectancy was higher.

---

**Tutorial notes**

1    The adding back of BPR on the PET where the shares gifted are no longer held by the donee at death is accumulated for the purpose of calculating IHT on subsequent transfers.

2    The fall in value of the lifetime gift can only reduce the IHT calculation on that gift. The chargeable value carried forward for calculating IHT on subsequent transfers is not reduced by the fall in value.

3    Strictly you could have ignored the BPR on the gifted shares as it is clear the shares are likely to be sold before the donor dies. However, it does initially reduce the value of the PET so it should be shown.

---

## 59    (Answer 5 of examination)

( **Examiner's comments and marking guide** )

**Part (a) tested candidates' knowledge of the treatment of a partnership trading loss in the first period of trading, including the calculation of capital allowances. Part (b) tested candidates' ability to advise on the most beneficial loss relief claims, and to calculate the tax refunds due. Part (c) tested candidates' knowledge of the income tax and VAT implications of (i) bad debts and (ii) leasing and hire purchase agreements.**

This was another popular question and again there were a number of good answers. A common mistake in part (a) was to not restrict the loss relief for the second year of assessment to the balance remaining, but to instead calculate an 'overlap loss'. A number of candidates incorrectly gave an industrial buildings allowance on the recording studio. In part (b), most candidates claimed relief against the correct income, but many incorrectly did so by applying loss relief under s381 - ICTA 1988 rather than under s380. It was disappointing that for Nina, the majority of candidates combined the loss claim against income and the loss claim against capital gains into one calculation. This then resulted in the personal allowance being set off against capital gains. Part (c) was generally well answered although as already mentioned a number of candidates missed marks by not showing the appropriate figures.

*Marks*

| | | |
|---|---|---:|
| (a) | Capital allowances | 2 |
| | Allocation of loss | 2 |
| | Section 385 ICTA 1988 | 1 |
| | Section 380 ICTA 1988/Section 72 FA 1991 | 2 |
| | Section 381 ICTA 1988 | 1 |
| | | |
| | Available | 8 |
| | | |
| | Maximum | 7 |

| | | |
|---|---|---:|
| (b) | Ming Khan | |
| | Loss relief claims | 2 |
| | Refund 1998-99 | 3 |
| | Refund 1997-98 | 2 |
| | Nina Lee | |
| | Loss relief claims | 2 |
| | Refund 1998-99 | 3 |
| | | |
| | Available | 12 |
| | | |
| | Maximum | 11 |

| | | |
|---|---|---:|
| (c) | Bad debts | |
| | Income tax | 1 |
| | VAT | 2 |
| | Computer equipment - Hire purchase | |
| | Capital allowances | 1 |
| | Short-life asset | 1 |
| | Finance charge | 1 |
| | VAT | 1 |
| | Computer equipment - Leasing | |
| | Lease rental payments | 1 |
| | VAT | 1 |
| | | |
| | Available | 9 |
| | | |
| | Maximum | 7 |
| | | |
| | Available | 29 |
| | | |
| | Maximum | 25 |

## ( Step by step answer plan )

**Overview**

This is an attractive question as it breaks down into a number of fairly separate parts and concerns mainstream areas of the syllabus. The key is not to muddle your answer. Wherever possible break your answer down into separate well labelled sections. For example, in part (c), bad debts have a VAT and an income tax implication which are subject to quite separate tax rules. This separation should be reflected in your answer.

**Step 1**   Start with your answer to part (a);

- Calculate the capital allowances for the 15 month period not forgetting to use the VAT exclusive amounts
- Add the CAs to the loss
- Allocate the loss to the two fiscal years and to the two partners
- State the fact that assessments for the two years are therefore nil
- State in general terms the forms of loss relief available.

**Step 2**   As the loss amounts calculated in part (a) are used in part (b) quickly check that you have not made some error. Forcing yourself to do this will not be easy as you are under time pressure but it is important that you have not slipped in the arithmetic - eg, miscounting the number of months for apportionment.

**Step 3**   In part (b) treat each partner and each loss quite separately. Think carefully about where to achieve relief at the highest marginal tax rate and how to avoid wasting personal allowances.

**Step 4**   For Ming, 1998/99 is clearly a particularly high income tax year while the higher rate is also payable in 1997/98. It is therefore fairly obvious how to maximise use of her two loss amounts.

**Step 5**   For Nina, the substantial gain in 1998/99 is the obvious target.

**Step 6**   Your answer for part (b) should therefore state the best use of each of the four loss amounts and calculate as appropriate the tax refunds generated.

**Step 7**   Answer part (c) covering separately the income tax and VAT implications for each of the three points - ie, the bad debt, the HP option and the leasing option.

## The examiner's answer

(a)   The partnership's capital allowances for the 15 month period to 31 July 2000 are £43,200 as follows:

|  | Pool £ |
|---|---|
| Additions |  |
| Recording equipment | 70,300 |
| Electrical system | 19,400 |
| Sound insulation | 13,200 |
| Heating system | 5,100 |
|  | 108,000 |
| FYA – 40% | 43,200 |
| WDV carried forward | 64,800 |

The Schedule DI tax adjusted loss is therefore £105,000 (61,800 + 43,200), and this is allocated between Ming and Nina as follows:

|  | Total £ | Ming (60%) £ | Nina (40%) £ |
|---|---|---|---|
| 1999-00 (1.5.99 to 5.4.00) |  |  |  |
| 105,000 × 11/15 | 77,000 | 46,200 | 30,800 |
| 2000-01 (Balance of loss) | 28,000 | 16,800 | 11,200 |

The assessments for 1999-00 and 2000-01 will be nil.

The trading loss can be relieved in the following ways:

(1)     Carrying the full amount of the loss forward under s385 ICTA 1988 against future trading profits.

(2)     Claiming relief against total income under s380 ICTA 1988. The loss for 1999-00 can be set against total income for 1999-00 and/or 1998-99, and the loss for 2000-01 can be set against total income for 2000-01 and/or 1999-00. A claim could then be made under s72 FA 1991 to extend the set off to chargeable gains of the same year.

(3)     Since the loss is incurred in the first four years of trading, Ming and Nina can claim loss relief under s381 ICTA 1988 against their total income of the three years preceding the year of the loss, earliest year first.

(b)     **Ming Khan**

Ming should claim under s380 ICTA 1988 to set the loss of £46,200 for 1999-00 against her total income for 1998-99. The tax refund will be £16,774 as follows:

|  |  |  | £ | £ |
|---|---|---|--:|--:|
| Schedule E | - | Salary 42,000 × 11/12 |  | 38,500 |
|  |  | Compensation | 60,000 |  |
|  |  | Exemption | 30,000 |  |
|  |  |  |  | 30,000 |
|  |  |  |  | 68,500 |
| Loss claim s380 ICTA 1988 |  |  |  | 46,200 |
|  |  |  |  | 22,300 |
| Personal allowance |  |  |  | 4,335 |
|  |  |  |  | 17,965 |
| Tax refund | 10,035 (28,000 – 17,965) at 23% |  |  | 2,308 |
|  | 36,165 (46,200 – 10,035) at 40% |  |  | 14,466 |
|  |  |  |  | 16,774 |

Ming does not have any income for 1999-00 or 2000-01, and so a claim under s380 ICTA 1988 in respect of her loss for 2000-01 is not available. She should therefore make a claim under s381 ICTA 1988 against her total income for 1997-98. The tax refund will be £5,507 as follows:

|  |  | £ |
|---|---|--:|
| Schedule E - salary |  | 42,000 |
| Loss claim s381 ICTA 1988 |  | 16,800 |
|  |  | 25,200 |
| Personal allowance |  | 4,335 |
|  |  | 20,865 |
| Tax refund: | 7,135 (28,000 – 20,865) at 23% | 1,641 |
|  | 9,665 (16,800 – 7,135) at 40% | 3,866 |
|  |  | 5,507 |

Neither claim will waste personal allowances, and Ming's 40% tax liability will be eliminated for 1997-98 and 1998-99.

**Nina Lee**

Nina's taxable income for 1996-97 and 1997-98 is only £1,915 (6,250 – 4,335), and so a claim under s381 ICTA 1988 does not appear to be beneficial. She should therefore utilise her loss of £30,800 for 1999-00 by claiming under s380 ICTA 1988 against her total income for 1998-99, and then under s72 FA 1991 against her chargeable gain for the same year. The total tax refund will be £6,669 as follows:

|  |  | £ |
|---|---|---|
| Dividends |  | 6,250 |
| Loss claim s380 ICTA 1988 |  | 6,250 |
|  |  | Nil |
| Tax refund: (Dividend tax credits are not recoverable) |  | Nil |
| Chargeable gain |  | 39,200 |
| Loss claim s72 FA 1991 (30,800 – 6,250) |  | 24,550 |
|  |  | 14,650 |
| Annual exemption |  | 7,100 |
|  |  | 7,550 |
| Tax refund: | 18,535 (28,000 + 4,335 – 6,250 – 7,550) at 23% | 4,263 |
|  | 6,015 (24,550 – 18,535) at 40% | 2,406 |
|  |  | 6,669 |

Nina's loss of £11,200 for 2000-01 should be carried forward under s385 ICTA 1988 against her Schedule D1 trading profits for 2000-01 (year ended 31 July 2001).

---

**Did you answer the question?**

As stated in the question there was no need to comment on the possibility of repayment supplement.

---

**Did you answer the question?**

Note that although more than one tax year is involved you not required to use rates or allowances other than those applying for 1999/00. For example, you were not supposed to know that Nina's 1998-99 dividend credits of £383 ((6,250 – 4,335) = 1,915 at 20%) would have been recoverable.

---

(c)     **Bad debts**

For income tax purposes, relief will be given in the period of account when the bad debt is either written off or provided for by specific provision. No relief is available for a general provision. The relief will be for £20,000 (23,500 × 100/117.5) less any amount that is recoverable.

For VAT purposes, relief will be given on the appropriate VAT return when the date on which payment of the debt was due is over six months old, and the debt has been written off. The relief will be for £3,500 (23,500 × 17.5/117.5). However, if the partnership operates the cash accounting scheme, then relief is automatic, since output VAT would not have been paid in respect of the original invoice.

**Computer equipment - Hire purchase**

The partnership will be able to claim capital allowances on the cost of the computer equipment of £52,000 (61,100 × 100/117.5). Since the computer equipment is to be replaced in three years time, it will be beneficial to make a claim for treatment as a short-life asset. Capital allowances of £52,000 will then be given over the three years.

The finance charge of £20,000 (36 at £2,000 = 72,000 − 52,000) will be a deductible expense for the partnership, and will be allocated to periods of account using normal accounting principles.

The input VAT of £9,100 will be reclaimed on the VAT return for the period in which the computer equipment is purchased.

### Computer equipment - Leasing

The lease rental payments of £24,000pa (28,200 × 100/117.5) will be a deductible expense for the partnership, and will be allocated to periods of account in accordance with the accruals concept.

The input VAT of £4,200 (28,200 × 17.5/117.5) included in each lease rental payment will be reclaimed on the tax return for the period during which the appropriate tax point occurs.

---

**Did you answer the question?**

You were not required to consider how the partnership would record the transactions (HP/Leasing) in their accounts.

---

## 60    (Answer 6 of examination)

---

### Examiner's comments and marking guide

**This question tested candidates' knowledge of the tax implications of a non-UK resident company trading in the UK. Part (a) dealt with the liability to corporation tax, part (b) dealt with industrial buildings allowance, part (c) dealt with VAT on imports, part (d) dealt with transfer pricing, and part (e) dealt with the income tax implications of an individual coming to work in the UK.**

This was the least popular question on the paper and was generally answered quite badly. In part (a) many candidates incorrectly stated that a non-UK company can only be liable to UK corporation tax if its central management and control is situated in the UK. Far too many candidates applied the opening year rules for an unincorporated business, rather than the rules applicable to a company. Part (b) was reasonably well answered although very few candidates answered in sufficient depth as to why the respective parts of the building qualified for industrial buildings allowance. In part (c), many candidates were not aware of the basis of accounting for VAT on imports, and hardly any candidates were aware of the implications of acquiring goods from a member state of the European Union. Part (d) was well answered, but answers to part (e) were quite varied. Too many candidates wrote at length on residence, without applying this to the facts of the question.

| | | |
|---|---|---|
| (a) | Liability to corporation tax | |
| | Trading within the UK/Trading with the UK | 1 |
| | 1 January 2000 to 28 February 2000 | 2 |
| | 1 March 2000 to 31 July 2000 | 2 |
| | Rate of corporation tax/Uktaki Ltd | 1 |
| | Accounting periods | |
| | First accounting period | 1 |
| | Second accounting period | 1 |
| | | — |
| | Available | 8 |
| | | — |
| | Maximum | 7 |
| | | — |
| (b) | Qualification as an industrial building | |
| | Camera assembly | 1 |
| | Storage of goods | 2 |
| | Showroom and general offices | 1 |

|  |  |  |
|---|---|---:|
| | Designated enterprise zone | |
| |   Qualifying costs | 1 |
| | Allowances | |
| |   Writing-down allowance | 1 |
| |   Designated enterprise zone | 1 |
| | Available | 7 |
| | Maximum | 6 |
| (c) | Accounting for VAT/Value | 1 |
| | Input tax | 1 |
| | Deferred payment | 1 |
| | Member of European Union | 2 |
| | Available | 5 |
| | Maximum | 4 |
| (d) | Reduction of UK corporation tax | 1 |
| | Substitution of market price | 1 |
| | Market price | 1 |
| | Maximum/Available | 3 |
| (e) | Emoluments for duties performed in the UK | |
| |   Assessment under Schedule E | 1 |
| | Emoluments for duties performed in Eyeland | |
| |   Resident and ordinarily resident in the UK | 1 |
| |   Resident in the UK | 1 |
| |   Resident status of director | 2 |
| | Investment income arising in Eyeland | |
| |   Basis of assessment | 1 |
| | Available | 6 |
| | Maximum | 5 |
| | Available | 29 |
| | Maximum | 25 |

## Step by step answer plan

**Overview**

This question is conveniently divided into 5 separate parts. Before choosing such a question in the exam you should consider how well you could do on each part. For example, part (d) clearly concerns the fairly straightforward 'arms length' principle for transfer pricing and part (e) requires knowledge of the exposure of non-domiciliaries to UK income tax - again, not difficult. However, do you know the treatment of overseas companies trading in/with the UK or through a UK subsidiary for part (a) or all the IBA points needed for the 6 marks in part (b)? Before answering this question consider carefully which parts of the text are relevant to each of the 5 requirements.

**Step 1**  Answer part (a) (i) covering clearly the situation pre and post forming a 'permanent establishment' and the change when a UK subsidiary is used.

**Step 2** Don't overlook the two easy marks for part (a) (ii).

**Step 3** Consider carefully the requirements of part (b) - ie, what attracts IBA and what rates will apply. The question throws up a number of points - 'process' use and 'storage' use, possible location in EZ and non-qualifying use with the 25% de minimis position left open. The examiner will expect your answer to contain some sensible remark about all of them.

**Step 4** Your answer to part (c) must deal with the two situations separately.

**Step 5** For part (d), cover transfer pricing as it applies to the proposed invoicing arrangements.

**Step 6** Deal separately with each of the 3 requirements of part (e) explaining R, OR and D as the points arise. For example, residence status is irrelevant for part (i) but should be discussed by the time you are covering part (ii). It would be acceptable in such a question to commence with a discussion of status but only to the extent it is relevant to the situation given.

## The examiner's answer

(a)  (i)  **Liability to UK corporation tax**

Eyetaki Inc will be liable to UK corporation tax if it is trading through a branch or agency in the UK (trading within the UK). The company will not be liable to UK corporation tax if it is merely trading with the UK. From 1 January 2000 to 28 February 2000, Eyetaki Inc employed a UK agent, and maintained a stock of cameras in the UK. Provided that contracts for the sale of cameras are concluded in Eyeland, Eyetaki Inc will probably not be liable to UK corporation tax on profits made during this period.

On 1 March 2000, Eyetaki Inc would appear to have opened a permanent establishment in the UK by renting an office and showroom, and it is likely that the sales managers will be empowered to conclude contracts in the UK. Eyetaki Inc will therefore be liable to UK tax on the profits made in the UK during the period from 1 March 2000 to the date that the trade is transferred to Uktaki Ltd (presumably 31 July 2000). Corporation tax will be at the full rate regardless of the level of profits made in the UK, or by Eyetaki Inc, since there is no double taxation treaty between the UK and Eyeland.

Uktaki Ltd is incorporated in the UK, and will therefore be liable to UK corporation tax on its world-wide income.

---

**Did you answer the question?**

A discussion of residence being determined by the place of 'central management and control' is clearly not relevant.

---

(ii)  **Uktaki Ltd's accounting periods**

Uktaki Ltd's first accounting period will run from when the company commences trading on 1 August 2000, and will end on 31 July 2001, being 12 months after its start. The next accounting period will run from 1 August 2001 to 31 December 2001, the end of Uktaki Ltd's period of account.

(b)  **Qualification as an industrial building**

Each part of the building must be considered separately:

(i)  Part of the building is to be used to assemble cameras from components imported from Eyeland. This part will qualify for Industrial Buildings Allowance since it is to be used in a trade consisting of the subjection of goods to a process.

(ii)  Part of the building is to be used in a trade consisting in the storage of goods which are to be subjected to a process, and to store manufactured goods not yet delivered. Whether the cameras are sold wholesale or retail should not affect the building's classification as an industrial building *Saxone Lilley & Skinner (Holdings) Ltd v CIR (1967)*.

The proportion of the building attributable to the showroom and general offices will also qualify if they represent 25% or less of the total cost of the building. Otherwise, the Industrial Buildings Allowance will be restricted to the qualifying proportion of the building. The cost of the land is disallowed.

*Designated enterprise zone*

If the building is situated in a designated enterprise zone, then the full cost of the building (excluding the land) would qualify for Industrial Buildings Allowance, regardless of the proportion of the cost represented by the showroom and general offices.

*Allowances*

A writing-down allowance at the rate of 4% on a straight-line basis will be given, commencing with the accounting period that the building is brought into use. If the building is situated in a designated enterprise zone, then an initial allowance of 100% will be available at the time that the building is built. If the initial allowance is not taken in full, then a writing-down allowance at the rate of 25% on a straight-line basis will be given.

(c)     **Eyeland is not a member of the European Union**

Uktaki Ltd will have to account for VAT on the value of the components imported from Eyeland at the time of their importation. The value of the components will include carriage costs, and all taxes, dues and other charges levied on importation. An input VAT deduction will then be given on the company's next VAT return.

If Uktaki Ltd arranges for an appropriate guarantee to be given, then the VAT payable on importation can be deferred, and instead be accounted for on a monthly basis.

**Eyeland becomes a member of the European Union**

The essential difference if components are acquired from a member of the European Union is that Uktaki Ltd will not have to account for VAT at the time of importation. Instead, output VAT will be accounted for on the relevant VAT return form according to the date that they are acquired. The date of acquisition is the earlier of the date of issue of a VAT invoice or the 15th of the month following the removal of the goods.

(d)     The invoicing of camera components by Eyetaki Inc at the normal trade selling price plus 25% will have the effect of reducing Uktaki Ltd's trading profits, and hence UK corporation tax. The purchases are at an overvaluation from a non-resident holding company, and so Uktaki Ltd should substitute a market price for the transfer price when calculating its profits chargeable to UK corporation tax. The market price will be an 'arm's-length' one that would be charged if the parties to the transaction were independent of each other.

(e)     (i)     **Emoluments for duties performed in the UK**

The director will be assessed under Schedule E on emoluments for duties performed in the UK regardless of his or her residence status.

(ii)    **Emoluments for duties performed in Eyeland**

The director will be assessed under Schedule E on emoluments for duties performed in Eyeland if he or she is both resident and ordinarily resident in the UK. If the director is resident in the UK, but not ordinarily resident, then an assessment under Schedule E will only arise in respect of those emoluments remitted to the UK.

The director is to come to the UK in order to take up employment for a period in excess of two years, and so will be treated as UK resident for the entire period. The director will only be treated as ordinarily resident in the UK if there is the intention to stay in the UK for three years or more, or if he or she actually remains for three years.

(iii)    **Investment income arising in Eyeland**

The director is domiciled in Eyeland, and so will only be assessed to UK income tax on investment income arising in Eyeland if he or she is resident in the UK, and the income is remitted to the UK.

---

**Did you answer the question?**

A general discussion of status is not required. For example, you do not need to mention how domicile status is determined or altered.

---

## DECEMBER 1997 QUESTIONS

### 61    (Question 1 of examination)

(a)    Cecile Grand has been a self employed antiques dealer since 1987.  Her income for 1998/99 was as follows:

|  | £ |
|---|---|
| Adjusted Schedule D1 profit | 38,400 |
| Dividends (net) | 4,860 |
| Schedule A profit | 800 |
| Capital gain | 7,800 |

The capital gain was in respect of a let property that was sold on 30 June 1998.  The Schedule A profit is for the period 6 April 1998 to 30 June 1998.  During 1998/99 Cecile paid a personal pension contribution of £3,500.  Cecile's husband died on 15 June 1997, and she has not remarried.

Her forecast income for 1999/00 is as follows:

|  | £ |
|---|---|
| Adjusted Schedule D1 profit | 21,750 |
| Dividends (net) | 4,320 |
| Capital gain | 13,300 |

The capital gain is in respect of quoted shares sold on 30 July 1999.  Due to the fall in profits, Cecile will not pay a personal pension contribution during 1999/00.

**You are required to:**

(i)    Calculate Cecile's payments on account and balancing payment or repayment for 1999/00.  You should assume that Cecile *does not* make a claim to reduce her payments on accounts, and that the rates and allowances for 1999/00 (including treatment of dividends) apply throughout.    **(10 marks)**

(ii)    Based on the above figures, advise Cecile of the amount of the maximum claim that she could make to reduce her payments on account for 1999/00.    **(2 marks)**

(b)    Cecile's adjusted Schedule D1 profit for 1999/00 is an estimated figure based on her provisional accounts for the year ended 31 March 2000.  The actual figures will not be available until 31 August 2000, because of the difficulty that Cecile has in separating antiques acquired for business purposes, from those acquired for private purposes.

**You are required:**

(i)    Assuming that Cecile makes the maximum claim to reduce the payments on account for 1999/00, explain the tax implications if her actual taxable income for 1999/00 is higher than the estimated figure.    **(2 marks)**

(ii)    Advise Cecile of the powers that the Inland Revenue have with regard to enquiring into her tax return for 1999/00.    **(2 marks)**

(iii)    Briefly advise Cecile of the tax implications if the Inland Revenue enquire into her tax return for 1999/00, and decide that the Schedule D1 profits for the year ended 31 March 2000 are understated.    **(2 marks)**

(c)    Cecile is planning to change her accounting date from 31 March to 30 September by preparing her next accounts for the six month period to 30 September 2000.  The forecast profit for this period is £18,000.

**You are required to:**

(i)     State the qualifying conditions that must be met for Cecile's change of accounting date to be valid.

**(2 marks)**

(ii)    Explain the tax implications of Cecile changing her accounting date from 31 March to 30 September. Your answer should include a calculation of the Schedule DI profits that Cecile will be assessed to for 2000/01.     **(2 marks)**

(iii)   Briefly advise Cecile of the advantages and the disadvantages for tax purposes, of changing her accounting date from 31 March to 30 September.     **(3 marks)**

**(Total: 25 marks)**

---

## 62     (Question 2 of examination)

---

Monty Noble, aged 72, died on 15 July 1999. You should assume that today's date is 31 October 1999. At the date of his death Monty owned the following assets:

1.      His main residence valued at £255,000.

2.      Three holiday cottages valued at £55,000 each.

3.      Building society deposits of £295,000.

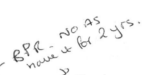

4.      20,000 50p ordinary shares in Congo Ltd, an unquoted trading company. The shares were acquired by Monty on 1 May 1999 and on 15 July 1999 were valued at £3.50. Congo Ltd has 20% of the value of its total assets invested in property which is let out.

5.      Agricultural land and buildings valued at £225,000, but with an agricultural value of £180,000. Monty purchased the land on 1 January 1992, and it has always been let out to tenant farmers. The most recent tenancy commenced on 1 January 1999.

Monty was survived by his wife, Olive, and their two children Peter and Penny. Penny has three children aged 6, 15 and 17. Under the terms of his will, Monty left all of his estate to Olive. She is aged 70 and does not own any assets. Olive is not in good health, and does not expect to live past 31 December 2002. Under the terms of her will, Olive has left all of her estate to Peter and Penny. The Noble family appreciate that Monty's estate has not been distributed in a tax efficient manner, and have therefore agreed the following plan:

1.      The three holiday cottages are to be sold on 10 December 1999. The expected selling prices are £47,500, £58,100 and £54,400. Professional fees of £500 will be incurred in respect of each sale.

2.      A field adjoining the existing farm land and buildings is to be purchased for £27,000 on 18 December 1999. Professional fees of £600 are included in the purchase price.

3.      The terms of Monty's will are to be varied so that Olive is left the main residence and £270,000 in cash. The agricultural land and buildings, together with the field purchased on 18 December 1999, will be put into a trust for the benefit of Penny's children. Under the terms of the trust, the income will be used to pay the children's school fees, with the balance being accumulated until the youngest child reaches the age of 18. The assets of the trust will then be distributed as the trustees so decide at that date. The remaining assets will be left to Peter and Penny.

4.      On 25 December 1999, Olive will make a gift of the main residence to Peter. She will continue to live in two rooms of the house, but will pay Peter a commercial rent.

With the exception of the holiday cottages, the only asset which is likely to change in value before 31 December 2002 is the main residence which will then be worth £330,000. Neither Monty nor Olive have made any lifetime transfers of value prior to 15 July 1999.

**You are required to:**

(a)    Advise the Noble family of the inheritance tax implications of the proposed plan.  Your answer should consist of:

    (i)    A calculation of the inheritance tax that will be saved as a result of implementing the plan.

        **(16 marks)**

    (ii)    An explanation of the conditions that must be met for the plan to be valid for inheritance tax purposes.    **(2 marks)**

    (iii)    Advice as to any improvements that could be made to the plan.    **(3 marks)**

You should assume that Olive dies on 31 December 2002, and that the tax rates and allowances for 1999/00 apply throughout.  You should ignore the instalment option.

(b)    Explain whether or not the proposed trust for the benefit of Penny's children will qualify to be treated as an accumulation and maintenance trust.  Briefly state the tax advantages of the trust being treated as an accumulation and maintenance trust rather than a discretionary trust.    **(4 marks)**

        **(Total:  25 marks)**

---

## 63    (Question 3 of examination)

(a)    Alex Zong, aged 38, commenced self-employment as a builder on 1 October 1996.  The business has been quite successful, and Alex is therefore going to incorporate his trade into a new limited company, Lexon Ltd, on 31 December 1999.  The following information is available:

    1.    Tax adjusted Schedule D1 profits are as follows:

|  | £ |
|---|---|
| Period ended 30.6.97 | 28,000 |
| Year ended 30.6.98 | 44,000 |
| Year ended 30.6.99 | 53,000 |
| Period ended 31.12.99 (estimated) | 29,000 |

    The above figures are before capital allowances.

    2.    Alex has purchased the following assets:

|  |  | £ |
|---|---|---|
| 1.10.96 | Freehold premises | 32,000 |
| 1.10.96 | Lorry | 8,800 |
| 15.6.97 | Plant | 6,400 |
| 30.11.98 | Motor car | 13,500 |
| 10.7.99 | Plant | 1,050 |

    On 1 October 1996 Alex introduced his private motor car into the business at its market value of £4,000. This was sold on 30 November 1998 for £2,800, and replaced by the motor car bought on that date.  Alex drives 12,000 miles per year, of which 4,800 are for private purposes.

    On 10 December 1997 Alex extended the freehold premises using his own materials and labour at a cost of £6,700.  The extension would have cost £10,000 if the work had been carried out externally.

    3.    The estimated market value of the business assets at 31 December 1999 is as follows:

|  | £ |
|---|---|
| Goodwill | 40,000 |
| Freehold premises | 75,000 |

---

| | |
|---|---:|
| Lorry | 4,300 |
| Plant | 5,200 |
| Motor car | 11,500 |
| Net current assets | 24,000 |
| | 160,000 |

4.   All of the business assets are to be transferred to Lexon Ltd.  The consideration will consist of 1,000 £1 ordinary shares in Lexon Ltd, and a loan account balance of £10,000.

5.   Alex has capital losses of £12,500 resulting from the sale of investments.

6.   Alex is registered for VAT.

7.   Assume the current date is 5 December 1999.

**You are required to:**

(i)   Calculate Alex's Schedule D case I assessment for 1999/00.  You should ignore NIC.   **(11 marks)**

(ii)   Advise Alex of the capital gains tax implications of incorporating his business on 31 December 1999.
**(7 marks)**

(iii)   Advise Alex of the VAT implications of incorporating his business on 31 December 1999.
**(2 marks)**

You should include any tax planning points that you consider relevant.

*31/12/99 Due·*

(b)   Alex is in the process of completing his VAT return for the quarter ended 30 November 1999, and wants advice on how to deal with the following:

*8000 net·*

1.   On 20 May 1999 Alex completed a contract for a customer, and an invoice was raised for £9,400 (inclusive of VAT) on 15 June 1999.  The customer paid £2,350 on 31 July 1999, but the balance of the amount owing is now considered to be a bad debt.

2.   Alex has mistakenly not been claiming for the input VAT on plant which is leased for £475 (inclusive of VAT) per month.  The same amount has been paid since the commencement of business on 1 October 1996.

3.   A customer was invoiced for £3,400 (excluding VAT) on 30 September 1999.  The customer was offered a 5% discount for payment within 30 days, but this was not taken and the customer paid the amount due on 28 November 1999.

Alex does not operate the cash accounting scheme.

**You are required to:**

Advise Alex in respect of the points raised.                                       **(5 marks)**

*Divide Limits*
*Possible 75% group·*
*for loss relief*                                       **(Total: 25 marks)**

---

**64     (Question 4 of examination)**

---

Paddington Ltd, a UK resident company, has two 80% owned subsidiaries, Victoria Ltd and Waterloo Ltd.  Victoria Ltd is a UK resident company, but Waterloo Ltd is resident in the country of Westoria.  Paddington Ltd manufactures specialised medical equipment, and the equipment is then sold by its two subsidiaries.  The forecast results of Paddington Ltd and Victoria Ltd for the year ended 31 March 2000 are as follows:

|  | Paddington Ltd £ | Victoria Ltd £ |
|---|---|---|
| Adjusted Schedule D1 profit | 79,000 | 245,000 |
| Capital gain | 6,000 | – |
| Patent royalty paid (Gross) | (12,000) | – |

As at 1 April 1999 Paddington Ltd had unused trading losses of £7,000.

The forecast results of Waterloo Ltd for the year ended 31 March 2000 are as follows:

|  | £ | £ |
|---|---|---|
| Trading profit |  | 420,000 |
| Taxation: |  |  |
| Corporation tax | 117,600 |  |
| Deferred tax | 8,400 |  |
|  |  | 126,000 |
| Distributable profits |  | 294,000 |
| Dividends paid: |  |  |
| Net | 217,800 |  |
| Withholding tax at 1% | 2,200 |  |
|  |  | 220,000 |
| Retained profits |  | 74,000 |

Waterloo Ltd's dividends will all be paid during, and are in respect of, the year ended 31 March 2000. The figures are in pounds sterling. Waterloo Ltd is controlled from Westoria, and is not classified as a controlled foreign company. The double taxation treaty between the UK and Westoria provides that taxes suffered in Westoria are relieved as a tax credit against UK corporation tax.

In order to encourage inward investment, the country of Westoria is to reduce its rate of corporation tax on 1 April 2000, from the present rate of 30% to 10%.

**You are required to:**

(a)    Calculate Paddington Ltd's corporation tax liability for the year ended 31 March 2000.

**(8 marks)**

(b)    Advise Paddington Ltd as to whether or not the reduction of the corporation tax rate in Westoria will result in Waterloo Ltd being classified as a controlled foreign company. Briefly explain the tax implications of Waterloo Ltd being so classified.

**(6 marks)**
**(Total: 14 marks)**
*(as amended)*

---

## 65    (Question 5 of examination)

(a)    On 1 May 1999 Chow Tong, aged 35, bought a derelict property at an auction for £132,000. She paid cash of £42,000, and borrowed the remaining £90,000 from her bank at an interest rate of 8% p.a. On 15 July 1999 Chow obtained planning permission to convert the property into six holiday apartments, and entered into a contract with a builder to carry out the conversion. The work was completed on 30 September 1999 at a cost of £63,000, and Chow immediately put the six holiday apartments up for sale. Five of the holiday apartments were sold during November 1999 for £75,000 each. On 30 November 1999 Chow paid her builder and repaid the bank loan. She decided to keep the remaining holiday apartment, valued at £75,000, for her own use. Legal fees of £750 were paid in respect of each of the five holiday apartments sold, and advertising costs amounted to £1,200.

---

Since the sale of the holiday apartments is an isolated transaction Chow believes that it should be treated as a capital gain rather than as an adventure in the nature of a trade. Chow is the director of an engineering company on an annual salary of £90,000, and has not disposed of any other assets during 1999/00.

**You are required to:**

(i)      Calculate Chow's tax liability arising from her property activities during 1999/00 if she is treated as (1) trading, and (2) not trading. You should ignore the implications of NIC and VAT.      **(9 marks)**

(ii)     Advise Chow of whether or not you would agree with her belief that the property activities should be treated as a capital gain rather than an adventure in the nature of a trade.

Your answer should include a brief explanation of the criteria that would be used by the courts in determining whether or not an isolated sale transaction will be treated as an adventure in the nature of a trade. You are not expected to quote from decided cases.

**(8 marks)**

(b)      On 15 March 2000 Chow is to invest £180,000 of the proceeds from the sale of the holiday apartments by subscribing for 50,000 £1 ordinary shares in an unquoted trading company, Knife-Edge Ltd. The company, which is involved in computer technology, has an issued share capital of 1,000,000 £1 ordinary shares. Chow considers the investment in Knife-Edge Ltd to be quite risky, since the company's future is dependent upon a new computer microchip which is currently being developed. It will be at least two years before the outcome of the development is known. Chow is aware that tax relief under the enterprise investment scheme may be available as a result of making the investment, but wants advice on the following:

1.       The amount of tax relief that she will be entitled to as a result of making the investment, and whether this will be affected by the treatment of her property activities (as per (a) above) as either trading or non-trading. Chow also wants to know whether part of the investment should be postponed until 2000/01.

2.       If the new microchip is successful, then Chow will become a director of Knife-Edge Ltd, and the company will obtain a listing on either the Alternative Investment Market or the Stock Exchange. Chow would probably take this opportunity to sell some of her shareholding at a substantial profit. She wants to know whether or not these events would lead to the withdrawal of any tax relief previously given.

3.       If the new microchip is not successful, then Knife-Edge Ltd will go into liquidation. Chow's investment will become worthless, and she wants to know if any tax relief can be claimed as a result of this.

**You are required to:**

Advise Chow in respect of the queries she has raised.      **(8 marks)**

**(Total:  25 marks)**

---

**66      (Question 6 of examination)**

---

Benny Fitt is the managing director of Usine Ltd, an unquoted trading company. Benny, aged 39, is paid a salary of £45,000 p.a. You should assume that today's date is 20 December 1999. Benny has asked for your advice on the following matters:

(a)      On 6 October 1999 Usine Ltd provided Benny with a new 2600cc petrol powered motor car with a list price of £28,400. The motor car was subsequently fitted with a sun-roof costing £700 and a mobile telephone costing £180. Benny made a capital contribution of £2,500 towards the cost of the motor car. During 1999/00 Benny will drive 1,100 business miles. He has a business meeting planned for 8 April 2000, which is a round trip of 190 miles from his home. The round trip from work to the meeting would be 180 miles, and Benny drives a total of 45 miles each day to work and back. It may be possible to bring this meeting forward to 4 April 2000. Benny has the use of a company credit card. During 1999/00 this will be used to pay for motor repairs of

£460, business accommodation of £380, entertaining of customers £720 and petrol of £425. Included in the figure for petrol is £180 in respect of private mileage which is not reimbursed to Usine Ltd.

**You are required to:**

Advise both Benny and Usine Ltd of the tax implications arising from the provision of the company motor car and the company credit card. Your answer should include an explanation of why it would be beneficial if Benny (i) brought his business meeting forward to 4 April 2000, and (ii) paid Usine Ltd £180 for his private petrol. You should ignore VAT, and confine your answer to the implications for 1999/00.    **(11 marks)**

(b)      On 10 December 1999 Usine Ltd dismissed their sales director, and paid him a lump sum redundancy payment of £45,000. This consisted of the following:

|  | £ |
|---|---|
| Statutory redundancy pay | 2,100 |
| Payment in lieu of notice | 3,100 |
| Holiday pay | 2,800 |
| *Ex gratia* compensation for loss of office | 34,000 |
| Agreement not to work for a rival company | 3,000 |
|  | 45,000 |

A new sales director is to commence employment on 1 January 2000. She is to be paid a lump sum payment of £10,000 upon commencement of employment. The new director currently lives 120 miles from Usine Ltd's head office, so the company has offered her two alternative arrangements:

(i)      Usine Ltd will pay £9,500 towards the cost of the director's relocation, and will also provide an interest free loan of £50,000 in order for the director to purchase a property.

(ii)     Usine Ltd will provide accommodation for the director. The company owns a house which it purchased in 1990 for £86,000, and improved at a cost of £8,000 during 1998. The house has a rateable value of £4,400, is currently valued at £105,000 and has recently been furnished at a cost of £10,400. Usine Ltd will pay for the annual running costs of £3,200.

**You are required to:**

Explain the income tax implications of the lump sum payments of £45,000 and £10,000, and the two alternative arrangements offered to the new sales director. You are not expected to consider the tax implications for Usine Ltd, and you should confine your answer to the implications for 1999/00.

**(9 marks)**

(c)      Usine Ltd runs an occupational pension scheme for its employees. Employees contribute 4% of their salary, and the company contributes a further 8%. The benefits on retirement are based upon final salary. At present the scheme is not approved by the Inland Revenue, but Usine Ltd is planning to amend the conditions of the scheme so that Inland Revenue approval can be obtained.

**You are required to:**

Advise Usine Ltd of the tax advantages for both itself and for its employees if Inland Revenue approval is obtained for the occupational pension scheme.    **(5 marks)**
**(Total: 25 marks)**

# ANSWERS TO DECEMBER 1997 EXAMINATION

## 61    (Answer 1 of examination)

### Examiner's comments and marking guide

Part (a) tested candidates' ability to calculate payments on account and the subsequent balancing repayment under self-assessment. Part (b) tested candidates' knowledge of self-assessment, including a claim to reduce payments on account, interest and penalties, and Inland Revenue enquiry. Part (c) tested candidates' knowledge of change of accounting date. This was the most popular question on the paper, and many candidates produced very good answers.

In part (a), a disappointing number of candidates continue to combine their income tax and capital gains tax computation, and lost marks accordingly. The class 4 NIC calculations were often omitted, and the treatment of the personal pension and widow's bereavement allowance caused problems for some candidates. Part (b) was not generally as well answered as the other parts of the question, with a number of candidates not appreciating the full extent of the self-assessment rules. Many candidates stated that the Inland Revenue would raise an assessment following the conclusion of an enquiry, when under self-assessment it is the responsibility of the tax-payer to amend his or her own return. The failure to give due dates lost several easy marks. Part (c) was well answered by the vast majority of candidates.

|  |  | Marks |
|---|---|---|
| (a) | *Payment on account* | |
| | Taxable income | 2 |
| | Income tax liability | 1 |
| | Class 4 NIC | 1 |
| | Payments on account | 1 |
| | *Balancing refund* | |
| | Taxable income | 1 |
| | Income tax liability/Class 4 NIC | 2 |
| | Capital gains tax | 2 |
| | Refund due | 1 |
| | *Claim to reduce payments on account* | |
| | Amount of reduction | 1 |
| | Revised tax liabilities | 1 |
| | | — |
| | Available | 13 |
| | | — |
| | Maximum | 12 |
| | | — |
| (b) | *Incorrect payments on account* | |
| | Interest | 1 |
| | Penalty | 1 |
| | *Inland Revenue enquiries* | |
| | Right of enquiry | 1 |
| | Time limit | 1 |
| | Fraud or negligence | 1 |
| | *Understatement of profits* | |
| | Amendment of return/Due date | 1 |
| | Interest | 1 |
| | Surcharge/Penalty | 1 |
| | | — |
| | Available | 8 |
| | | — |
| | Maximum | 6 |
| | | — |

(c)    *Qualifying conditions*
       Notification
       Change within five years                                                          1
       18 month limit                                                                     1
       *Tax implications*                                                                 1
       2000/01 assessment                                                                 1
       Overlap profits                                                                    1
       *Advantages and disadvantages*
       Payment on account                                                                 1
       Payment of related tax liability                                                   1
       Disadvantages                                                                      1

                                                                                    ____

                                                       Available       8
                                                                                    ____

                                                       Maximum         7
                                                                                    ____

                                                       Available      29
                                                                                    ____

                                                       Maximum        25
                                                                                    ____

## Step by step answer plan

**Overview**

This is a fairly straightforward exercise on the self-assessment rules and a proposed change of accounting date for business profits with the question broken down into three reasonably separate parts.

**Step 1**    To calculate the payments on account needed for 1999/00 you have to calculate the tax payable for 1998/99 not forgetting the Class 4 NIC due.

**Step 2**    Don't overlook Part (ii) of (a) concerning the reduction to claim in the 1999/00 payments on account.

**Step 3**    Part (b) is really three separate questions. As there is only 2 marks for each part you should be fairly brief in your answers

**Step 4**    Again in part (c) there are three separate questions each with only sufficient marks to warrant only the bare facts.

**Step 5**    Finally read through the question to ensure you have answered all the parts.

## The examiner's answer

(a)    (i)    Cecile's payments on account will be based on her income tax and Class 4 NIC liability for 1998/99 as follows:

|                                  | £       |
|----------------------------------|--------:|
| Schedule D case I                | 38,400  |
| Pension contribution             | 3,500   |
|                                  | 34,900  |
| Schedule A                       | 800     |
| Dividends (4,860 × 100/90)       | 5,400   |
|                                  | 41,100  |
| Personal allowance               | 4,335   |
| Taxable income                   | 36,765  |

Income Tax:

| | |
|---|---:|
| 1,500 at 10% | 150 |
| 26,500 at 23% | 6,095 |
| 3,365 at 40% | 1,346 |
| 5,400 at 32½% | 1,755 |
| | 9,346 |
| Widow's bereavement allowance (1,970 at 10%) | 197 |
| | 9,149 |
| Tax suffered at source – Dividends (5,400 at 10%) | 540 |
| | 8,609 |
| Class 4 NIC 26,000 – 7,530 at 6% | 1,108 |
| | 9,717 |
| Payment on account due 31.1.00 – 50% | 4,858 |
| Payment on account due 31.7.00 – 50% | 4,859 |

Cecile's actual tax liability for 1999/00 is as follows:

| | £ |
|---|---:|
| Schedule D case I | 21,750 |
| Dividends (4,320 × 100/90) | 4,800 |
| | 26,550 |
| Personal allowance | 4,335 |
| Taxable income | 22,215 |

| | £ | £ |
|---|---:|---:|
| Income tax: | | |
| 1,500 at 10% | | 150 |
| 15,915 (22,215 – 4,800 – 1,500) at 23% | | 3,660 |
| 4,800 at 10% | | 480 |
| | | 4,290 |
| Tax suffered at source – Dividends (4,800 at 10%) | | 480 |
| | | 3,810 |
| Class 4 NIC 21,750 – 7,530 at 6% | | 853 |
| | | 4,663 |
| Capital gain | 13,300 | |
| Annual exemption | 7,100 | |
| Chargeable gain | 6,200 | |
| Capital gains tax: | | |
| 5,785 (28,000 – 22,215) at 20% | 1,157 | |
| 415 (6,200 – 5,785) at 40% | 166 | |
| | | 1,323 |
| | | 5,986 |
| Paid on account | | 9,717 |
| Balancing refund due 31.1.01 | | 3,731 |

(ii)     Cecile can ignore the CGT liability when claiming to reduce her payments on account. She should therefore claim to reduce her payments on account by £5,054 (9,717 – 4,663) so that £2,331 (4,663/2) will be due on 31 January 2000, £2,332 will be due on 31 July 2000, and the CGT liability of £1,323 will be due on 31 January 2001.

---

**Did you answer the question?**

You were not required to use the 1998/99 tax rates and allowances in calculating the 1998/99 liability nor comment on the possibility of paying a personal pension contribution for 1999/00.

---

(b)     (i)     If Cecile's payments on account are too low, then she will be charged interest. This will run from the due dates of 31 January 2000 and 31 July 2000, up to the date of payment, which will presumably be 31 January 2001. A penalty will be charged if a claim to reduce payments on account is made fraudulently or negligently.

(ii)     The Inland Revenue have the right to enquire into any tax return, provided they give written notice. Enquiries may be made by reference to information in the tax return, but they may also be made on a random basis. The time limit for giving notice of an enquiry for 1999/00 tax returns is 31 January 2002. An enquiry after that date can normally only be made where the taxpayer has been fraudulent or negligent.

(iii)    Following the completion of an enquiry, the tax return would normally be amended by the taxpayer. The additional tax liability will be due 30 days from the date of the notice of amendment. Interest will be charged on the additional tax liability from 31 January 2001 (the due date for the tax return) up to the date of payment. No surcharge will be due provided that the additional tax liability is paid within 28 days of the due date. A penalty will only be charged where a tax return is filed incorrectly due to fraud or negligence.

(c)     (i)     For Cecile's change of accounting date to be valid.

1.      The change must be notified to the Inland Revenue by 31 January 2002.

2.      There must not have been a change of accounting date within the previous five tax years prior to 2000/01. This condition will not apply if the present change is to be made for genuine commercial reasons.

3.      The first accounts to the new accounting date must not exceed 18 months in length.

(ii)    For 2000/01 Cecile will be assessed to Schedule D1 profits for the year ended 30 September 2000 of £28,875, calculated as follows:

|  | £ |
|---|---|
| Year ended 31.3.00 21,750 × 6/12 | 10,875 |
| Period ended 30.9.00 | 18,000 |
|  | 28,875 |

The profits of £10,875 for the period 1 October 1999 to 31 March 2000 are overlap profits, having already been assessed in 1999/00, and these will normally be relieved when Cecile ceases trading.

(iii)   The main advantage of Cecile changing her accounting date from 31 March to 30 September is that she should have actual Schedule D1 profits available before the first payment on account is due on 31 January in the tax year. Also, the time between earning profits and paying the related tax liability will be six months later. The disadvantages are that the final assessment upon cessation may be for a longer period with a 30 September year end, and the fact that there is a double assessment of profits upon the actual change of accounting date.

---

## 62     (Answer 2 of examination)

Part (a) tested candidates' ability to calculate the inheritance tax savings from a proposed plan based upon a change to the deceased's will using a deed of variation. Included in the question were IHT valuation rules, business and agricultural property relief, a lifetime gift and exempt transfers to a spouse. Part (b) tested candidates' knowledge of accumulation and maintenance trusts.

This was another popular question, although the majority of candidates answered it quite badly. The main mistake was to not realise that the original transfer on death was exempt since it was to the deceased's spouse. Also, many candidates did not appreciate that the proposed plan was tax effective without any major alternation, since it utilised the spouse's nil rate band, and established a low transfer value for the only appreciating asset by the use of a lifetime transfer. The transfer to the trust caused problems, since many candidates treated this as a PET despite the transfer being made on death. In questions of this nature it is essential that candidates clearly indicate (ie, by the use of headings) which aspect of the questions is being answered. Answers to part (b) were also poor since most candidates simply did not know the qualifying conditions that must be met for a trust to be treated as an accumulation and maintenance trust.

|  |  | Marks |
|---|---|---|
| (a) | *IHT position prior to implementing the plan* | |
|  | Building society deposits/Ordinary shares | 1 |
|  | Business property relief | 1 |
|  | Agricultural property | 1 |
|  | Realty | 1 |
|  | LHT liability/Due date | 1 |
|  | *IHT position after implementing the plan* | |
|  | Building society deposits/Ordinary shares | 1 |
|  | Agricultural property | 1 |
|  | Realty | 1 |
|  | Land and buildings sold without four years of death | 2 |
|  | Exempt legacy | 1 |
|  | IHT liability/Due date | 1 |
|  | Gift with reservation | 1 |
|  | Value of PET | 1 |
|  | IHT liability/Due date | 2 |
|  | HIT liability on estate | 1 |
|  | Calculation of IHT saving | 1 |
|  | *Variation of terms of will* | |
|  | Deed of variation | 1 |
|  | Written election | 1 |
|  | *IHT planning* | |
|  | Shares in Congo Ltd | 2 |
|  | Fall in value | 2 |
|  |  | |
|  | Available | 24 |
|  |  | |
|  | Maximum | 21 |
|  |  | |
| (b) | Non-qualification | 2 |
|  | Advantages | 2 |
|  |  | |
|  | Maximum/Available | 4 |
|  |  | |
|  | Available | 28 |
|  |  | |
|  | Maximum | 25 |

## Step by step answer plan

**Overview**

This question clearly concerns only inheritance tax and covers a number of fairly simple tax planning moves.

**Step 1**    Before starting your answer to part (a) become familiar with the situation presented in the question and the planning steps the family intend to take. Note that the planning concerns using the nil band on the first death as the surviving spouse is not expected to live long.

**Step 2**    For part (a) (i) first calculate the IHT that would be due without any planning and then calculate the IHT if the planning steps are taken and the relevant reliefs claimed and make a comparison of the results. If reliefs such as APR or BPR are claimed a brief explanation may be expected.

**Step 3**    For part (a)(ii)  and (iii) there are additional marks for giving explanations and offering advice on improving the plan

**Step 4**    Finally in part (b) you have to comment briefly on whether the proposed trust will have A & M status. You have to apply the definition to the situation and not just state the definition in isolation. You also have to explain the "tax" advantages which, in this context, means the IHT advantages.

## The examiner's answer

(a)    *IHT position prior to the implementation of the plan*
No IHT liability will arise at the date of Monty's death since his entire estate is left to his wife.  Upon Olive's death on 31 December 2002, the IHT liability will be as follows:

|  | £ | £ |
|---|---|---|
| *Personalty* | | |
| Building society deposits | | 295,000 |
| Ordinary shares in Congo Ltd | | |
| 20,000 at £3.50 | 70,000 | |
| Business property relief | | |
| $70,000 \times \dfrac{80\ (100-20)}{100} \times 100\%$ | 56,000 | |
| | ——— | 14,000 |
| Agricultural land and buildings | 225,000 | |
| Agricultural property relief | 180,000 | |
| | ——— | 45,000 |
| | | 354,000 |
| *Realty* | | |
| Main residence | | 330,000 |
| Holiday cottages (47,500 + 58,100 + 54,400) | | 160,000 |
| | | ——— |
| Chargeable estate | | 844,000 |
| | | ——— |
| IHT liability   231,000 at nil% | | Nil |
| 613,000 at 40% | | 245,200 |
| | | ——— |
| | | 245,200 |

The IHT liability of £245,200 will be payable by the executors of Olive's estate on the earlier of 30 June 2003 or the delivery of their account.  BPR is only given in respect of assets used wholly or mainly for the purposes of the business, and this is unlikely to include property that is let out.  APR is available since the property is let out for the purposes of agriculture, and has been owned for at least seven years. Olive is deemed to own the property for the period that Monty owned it.

*IHT position following the implementation of the plan*
If the plan is implemented, then the IHT liability upon Monty's death on 15 July 1999 will be as follows:

|  | £ | £ |
|---|---|---|
| *Personalty* | | |
| Building society deposits | | 295,000 |
| Ordinary shares in Congo Ltd | | 70,000 |
| Agricultural land and buildings | 225,000 | |
| Agricultural property relief | 180,000 | |
| | | 45,000 |
| | | 410,000 |
| *Realty* | | |
| Main residence | | 255,000 |
| Holiday cottages (3 × £55,000) | 165,000 | |
| Relief for reduction in value (note) | 3,300 | |
| | | 161,700 |
| | | 826,700 |
| Exempt legacy – Olive (255,000 + 270,000) | | 525,000 |
| Chargeable estate | | 301,700 |
| IHT liability 231,000 at nil% | | Nil |
| 70,700 at 40% | | 28,280 |
| | | 28,280 |

The IHT liability of £28,280 will be payable by the executors of Monty's estate on the earlier of 31 January 2000 or the delivery of their account. BPR is not available since Monty has not owned the shares in Congo Ltd for at least two years.

**Note: land and buildings sold within four years after death.**

A claim can be made to reduce the value of the holiday cottages to the gross sale proceeds. The relief is restricted because of the reinvestment in farm land.

|  | £ |
|---|---|
| Cottage 1 55,000 – 47,500 = | 7,500 |
| Cottage 2 55,000 – 58,100 = | (3,100) |
| | 4,400 |
| Restriction $4,400 \times \dfrac{27,000 - 600}{47,500 + 58,100}$ | (1,100) |
| | 3,300 |

The loss on cottage 3 of £600 (55,000 – 54,400) is ignored as it is less than £1,000.

The gift of the main residence by Olive on 25 December 1999 will be a PET. The transfer is unlikely to be treated as a gift with reservation since Olive is paying a commercial rent for the use of the two rooms. As a result of Olive's death within seven years, the PET will become chargeable on 31 December 2002 as follows:

|  | £ | £ |
|---|---|---|
| Main residence |  | 255,000 |
| Annual exemptions   1999/00 | 3,000 |  |
|                              1998/99 | 3,000 |  |
|  |  | 6,000 |
|  |  | 249,000 |
|  |  |  |
| IHT liability 231,000 at nil % |  | Nil |
|                    18,000 at 40% |  | 7,200 |
|  |  | 7,200 |
| Tapering relief at 20% |  | 1,440 |
|  |  | 5,760 |

The IHT liability will be payable by Peter on 30 June 2003. The IHT liability on Olive's estate will be as follows:

|  | £ |
|---|---|
| Cash | 270,000 |
|  |  |
| IHT liability 270,000 at 40% | 108,000 |

The IHT liability will be payable as previously. The IHT liability if the plan is implemented is £142,040 (28,280 + 5,760 + 108,000) compared to £245,200 if the plan is not implemented. This is an IHT saving of £103,160. Most of the IHT liability is delayed until Olive's death.

---

**Did you answer the question?**

You were not required to comment on the instalment option.

---

*Variation of the terms of Monty's will*
Monty's will can be varied by a deed of variation within two years of his death. The deed must be in writing, and must be signed by Olive. A written election must then be made to the Inland Revenue within six months, so that the will is treated as re-written for IHT purposes. As the IHT election results in an IHT liability on Monty's estate, the personal representative must join in the election.

*IHT planning*
The plan could be improved as follows:

1.      The shares in Congo Ltd should be left to Olive. BPR will then be available, resulting in an IHT saving of £22,400 (56,000 at 40%). IHT of £5,600 (14,000 at 40%) will be postponed until Olive's death.

2.      The full £7,500 fall in value of cottage 1 would be available if (i) cottage 2 is left to Peter or Penny (who could subsequently sell it), and (ii) the trust purchased the field itself by being left additional cash. This would save IHT of £1,680 (7,500 – 3,300 = 4,200 at 40%).

(b)      The trust will only qualify as an accumulation and maintenance trust if the beneficiaries become beneficially entitled to the trust assets on or before the age of 25. This condition is not met because the two oldest children will be over the age of 25 by the time that the youngest child becomes 18.

The advantages of an accumulation and maintenance trust are in relation to IHT. An accumulation and maintenance trust is not subject to the 10 yearly principal charge, or to an exit charge when a distribution is made to a beneficiary or when a beneficiary becomes absolutely entitled to the trust property.

---

---

**63**     **(Answer 3 of examination)**

---

**Examiner's comments and marking guide**

Part (a) tested candidates' ability to calculate the Schedule D case I assessments on a cessation of a business, and to advise on the capital gains tax and VAT implications on incorporation. Part (b) tested candidates' knowledge of various aspects of VAT, including recent changes to bad debt relief and the refund of VAT.

This was another popular question that was answered quite well by a number of candidates. In part (a), too many candidates were unable to produce a relatively straight-forward capital allowances computation, often because they did not know that capital allowances are calculated in accordance with periods of account rather than basis periods or tax years. Poorly laid out answers and a failure to show workings (such as the private use adjustment) will lead to a loss of marks. A number of candidates incorrectly calculated industrial buildings allowance on the freehold premises, or included this asset in the general pool for plant and machinery. Several easy marks were lost by candidates who did not calculate the capital gains arising on the deemed disposal, and few candidates appreciated that appropriate tax planning could utilise the taxpayer's annual exemption and capital losses. Part (b) was generally well answered, although few candidates were aware of the three-year restriction on the refund of VAT, despite this being covered in my *Students' Newsletter* article.

|  |  | Marks |
|---|---|---:|
| (a) | *Capital allowances* | |
| | Period ended 30.6.97 | 2 |
| | Year ended 30.6.98 | 1 |
| | Year ended 30.6.99 | 2 |
| | Period ended 31.12.99 | 1 |
| | Election for WDV | 2 |
| | *Schedule DI assessment* | |
| | Revised DI profits | 1 |
| | 1999/00 profits | 1 |
| | Overlap relief | 2 |
| | *Capital gains tax* | |
| | Goodwill | 1 |
| | Freehold premises | 2 |
| | Rollover relief | 1 |
| | Immediate capital gain | 1 |
| | Increase in loan account | 2 |
| | Amount rolled over/Base cost of shares | 1 |
| | *Value added tax* | |
| | Transfer as going concern | 1 |
| | Transfer of VAT registration | 1 |
| | | — |
| | Available | 22 |
| | | — |
| | Maximum | 20 |
| | | — |
| (b) | Bad debt | 2 |
| | Refund of VAT | 2 |
| | Discount | 1 |
| | | — |
| | Maximum/Available | 5 |
| | | — |
| | Available | 27 |
| | | — |
| | Maximum | 25 |
| | | — |

---

## Step by step answer plan

### Overview

The question is effectively broken down into 6 parts - 3 in part (a) and 3 in part (b) and concerns a self-employed builder on the brink of incorporating his business. This brings into play the usual income tax, CGT and VAT issues in part (a) and requires some fairly easy calculations. Part (b) requires knowledge of three mainstream VAT points - treatment of bad debts, back claims for input tax and whether to charge VAT on the pre or post discount price.

**Step 1**    With the requirements of part (a) (i) in mind read through the question deciding what workings will be needed. It is fairly clear that the life of the business has to be covered as the plant tax WDV is not given and overlap relief must be calculated.

**Step 2**    Construct a plant capital allowances working for the life of the business assuming that an election to carry over the tax WDV is most likely. This means that capital allowances in the final period will be as normal except for time apportioning the WDA. You have to assume that the cost figures only include VAT if it is irrecoverable (ie, on the car)

**Step 3**    Next compute the assessable amount for 1999/00. This is quite involved as two periods of account contribute to the final assessment and two years of assessment contain overlap profits.

**Step 4**    Decide what is needed to answer part (a) (ii) - the CGT implications of incorporating. Two assets result in capital gains - the goodwill and the freehold. Incorporation relief will apply automatically but with an annual exemption and capital losses available there is a clear invitation to take advantage of the proposed loan account.

**Step 5**    Don't overlook part (a) (iii) as it offers 2 easy marks for covering the VAT aspects.

**Step 6**    Answer each section of part (b) in separate paragraphs. With only 5 marks in total you are not required to provide detailed reasons for your advice.

## The examiner's answer

(a)    *Capital allowances*
Capital allowance claims over the life of the business will be as follows:

| | £ | Pool £ | Motor car £ | | Allowances £ |
|---|---|---|---|---|---|
| *Period ended 30.6.97* | | | | | |
| Additions | | 15,200 | 4,000 | | |
| WDA – 25% × 9/12 | | 2,850 | | | 2,850 |
| WDA – 25% × 9/12 | | | | 750 × 60% | 450 |
| WDV carried forward | | 12,350 | 3,250 | | 3,300 |
| | | | | | |
| *Year ended 30.6.98* | | | | | |
| WDA – 25% | | 3,088 | | | 3,088 |
| WDA – 25% | | | | 813 × 60% | 488 |
| WDV carried forward | | 9,262 | 2,437 | | 3,576 |
| | | | | | |
| *Year ended 30.6.99* | | | | | |
| Disposal | | | 2,800 | | |
| Balancing charge | | | | 363 × 60% | (218) |
| Addition | | | 13,500 | | |

| | | | | | |
|---|---|---|---|---|---|
| WDA – 25% | | 2,316 | | | 2,316 |
| WDA – Restricted | | | 3,000 × 60% | | 1,800 |
| WDV carried forward | | 6,946 | 10,500 | | 3,898 |

*Period ended 31.12.99*

| | | | | | |
|---|---|---|---|---|---|
| WDA – 25% × 6/12 | | 868 | | | 868 |
| WDA – 25% × 6/12 | | | 1,313 × 60% | | 788 |
| Addition | 1,050 | | | | |
| FYA – 40% | 420 | | | | 420 |
| | | 630 | | | |
| WDV carried forward | | 6,708 | 9,187 | | 2,076 |

Alex should elect to transfer the plant to Lexon Ltd at its written-down value. This avoids the balancing charges that would otherwise arise. The market values of the lorry and plant (4,300 + 5,200 = £9,500) and the motor car (£11,500) both exceed their respective written-down values of £7,996 (6,946 + 1,050) and £10,500.

*Schedule D1 assessments*
The revised Schedule D1 profits are as follows:

| | | £ |
|---|---|---|
| | | |
| P/E 30.6.97 | 28,000 – 3,300 = | 24,700 |
| Y/E 30.6.98 | 44,000 – 3,576 = | 40,424 |
| Y/E 30.6.99 | 53,000 – 3,898 = | 49,102 |
| P/E 31.12.99 | 29,000 – 2,076 = | 26,924 |

Alex's Schedule D1 assessment for 1999/00 will be:

| | £ |
|---|---|
| | |
| Y/E 30.6.99 | 49,102 |
| P/E 31.12.99 | 26,924 |
| | 76,026 |
| Relief for overlap profits | 26,573 |
| | 49,453 |

Overlap profits are calculated as follows

| | £ |
|---|---|
| | |
| 1996/97 (1.10.96 to 5.4.97) 24,700 × 6/9 | 16,467 |
| 1997/98 (1.7.97 to 30.9.97) 40,424 × 3/12 | 10,106 |
| | 26,573 |

*Capital gains tax*
Since Alex and Lexon Ltd are connected persons, assets will be transferred at market value.

| | £ | £ |
|---|---|---|
| *Goodwill* | | |
| Proceeds | | 40,000 |
| Cost | | Nil |
| Capital gain | | 40,000 |

*Freehold premises*

|  |  |  |
|---|---:|---:|
| Proceeds |  | 75,000 |
| Cost | 32,000 |  |
| Enhancement expenditure | 6,700 |  |
|  | ——— | 38,700 |
|  |  | 36,300 |

$$\text{Indexation} \quad 32,000 \times \frac{162.6 - 153.8}{153.8} \; (0.057) \qquad 1,824$$

$$6,700 \times \frac{162.6 - 160.0}{160.0} \; (0.016) \qquad 107$$

|  |  |
|---|---:|
|  | ——— |
|  | 1,931 |
|  | 34,369 |

The total gains of £74,369 (40,000 + 34,369) will be automatically rolled over against the base cost of the shares in Lexon Ltd, since the business is transferred as a going concern, and all of the business assets are being transferred. Alex will have an immediate capital gain of £4,648 (74,369 × 10,000/160,000). Since he has unused capital losses of £12,500, an annual exemption of £7,100 for 1999/00 and gains prior to the annual exemption are tapered to 85% it would be beneficial to increase the amount of the loan account to:

$$160,000 \times \frac{12,500 + 8,353^*}{74,369} = 44,864$$

$$* \quad \frac{7,100 \times 100}{85} = £8,353$$

The immediate chargeable gain would then be £20,853 (74,369 × 44,864/160,000), with £53,516 (74,369 – 20,853) of the gain being rolled over. The base cost of the shares will be £61,620 (160,000 – 44,864 – 53,516).

*Note:    the answer only covers one possible approach to incorporating a business, and alternative approaches would be acceptable.*

*Value added tax*
Output VAT will not have to be charged on the value of stocks and other assets on which VAT has been claimed, since the business is transferred as a going concern. This assumes that Lexon Ltd immediately registers for VAT.

Lexon Ltd will be able to take over Alex's VAT registration number provided that the company assumes his VAT liabilities.

---

**Did you answer the question?**

As there were only 2 marks for the VAT aspects of incorporation you were not expected to comment on the situation where a building transferred as a going concern is under an option to tax.

---

(b)    *Bad debt*
Relief for bad debts is given six months after the time that payment was due, provided that the debt has been written off. Since an invoice was not raised until 15 June 1999, bad debt relief cannot be claimed in the VAT return for the quarter ended 30 November 1999. The amount of the relief to be claimed in the following VAT return will be £1,050 (9,400 – 2,350 = 7,050 × 17.5/117.5).

---

**Tutorial note**

The answer assumes that payment must have been due for the full amount at some time between 15 June and 31 July 1999.

---

*Refund of VAT*
A claim must be made for the repayment of the VAT underclaimed, since the error exceeds £2,000. Claims for the refund of VAT are subject to a three year time limit, and so the claim will cover the period 1 December 1996 to 30 November 1999. The repayment will be for £2,547 (475 × 36 × 17.5/117.5).

*Discount*
Where a discount is offered for prompt payment, VAT is due on the net amount even if the discount is not taken. The output VAT due is therefore £565 (3,400 less 5% = 3,230 × 17.5%).

---

## 64 (Answer 4 of examination)

### Examiner's comments and marking guide

Part (a) tested candidates' ability to calculate the corporation tax liability of a company with both a UK resident subsidiary and a subsidiary resident overseas and part (b) tested candidates' knowledge of the controlled foreign company legislation.

This question was also quite popular, and there were again some good answers by a number of candidates. In part (a) the inclusion of information for the UK resident subsidiary confused many candidates. They either calculated the corporation tax liability of the subsidiary (when there was no requirement to do so), or, far worse amalgamated these figures with those of the parent company. The controlled company legislation in part (b) was well understood.

|  |  | Marks |
|---|---|---|
| (a) | *Corporation tax liability* |  |
|  | Schedule D case 1/Trading loss | 1 |
|  | Capital gain | 1 |
|  | 10% shareholding | 1 |
|  | chedule D case V | 2 |
|  | Charge on income | 1 |
|  | Corporation tax | 2 |
|  | Double taxation relief | 1 |
|  | Available | 9 |
|  | Maximum | 8 |
| (b) | Low tax country | 1 |
|  | Quoted/Profits less than £50,000 | 1 |
|  | Acceptable distribution policy | 1 |
|  | Exempt activities test | 2 |
|  | Motive test | 1 |
|  | Classification as CEC | 1 |
|  | Available | 7 |
|  | Maximum | 6 |
|  | Available | 16 |
|  | Maximum | 14 |

## Step by step answer plan

**Overview**

This question has been substantially simplified to remove corporation tax topics no longer examinable. The examiner's comments and the marking guide have been edited appropriately. It now contains a straightforward exercise in calculating corporation tax with relief for foreign taxation in part (a). It is hardly an exam standard question anymore but it remains a useful exercise in the application of double tax relief. Part (b) concerns controlled foreign companies. Under self assessment for corporation tax - for periods ending on or after 1 July 1999 - CFCs will have a higher profile in practice because companies will have to self-assess whether a shareholding in a foreign company requires a CFC apportionment. It will no longer be necessary for the Revenue to issue a direction for the CFC rules to bite.

**Step 1**     Read the question in relation to part (a) of the requirements and decide the form of workings needed.

**Step 2**     Produce a layout of PCTCT analysed between UK and foreign profits using a separate working to calculate the Schedule DV figure.

**Step 3**     Compute the corporation tax on the total PCTCT and apportion it between UK and foreign profits. It is conventional to use a separate working to calculate the corporation tax but for paper 11 the emphasis is more on producing a clear answer than following the preferred layouts etc. of the examiner.

**Step 4**     Answer part (b) by fitting your knowledge on CFCs to the particular points at issue.

## The examiner's answer

(a)  Paddington Ltd – corporation tax liability for the year ended 31 March 2000.

|  | Total £ | UK £ | Overseas £ |
|---|---:|---:|---:|
| Schedule D case I | 79,000 | 79,000 | |
| Trading loss brought forward | 7,000 | 7,000 | |
|  | 72,000 | 72,000 | |
| Capital gain | 6,000 | 6,000 | |
| Schedule D case V (W1) | 246,400 | | 246,400 |
|  | 324,400 | 78,000 | 246,400 |
| Charge on income | 12,000 | 12,000 | |
| PCTCT | 312,400 | 66,000 | 246,400 |
| Corporation tax (W2) | 89,030 | 18,809 | 70,221 |
| Double taxation relief (W3) | 70,221 | - | 70,221 |
| Corporation tax liability | 18,809 | 18,809 | - |

**Working 1 – Dividend from Waterloo Ltd**

Paddington Ltd owns 10% or more of the share capital of Waterloo Ltd, so relief for the underlying tax paid in Westoria is available.

| | £ |
|---|---:|
| Dividend received     217,800 × 80% | 174,240 |
| Withholding tax at 1% | 1,760 |
| | 176,000 |

$$\text{Underlying tax} \qquad 176{,}000 \times \frac{117{,}600}{294{,}000} \qquad\qquad 70{,}400$$

Schedule D case V income $\qquad\qquad\qquad\qquad\qquad$ 246,400

### Working 2 – Corporation tax

The upper limit of £1,500,000 is divided by three, since both Victoria Ltd and Waterloo Ltd are associated companies.

|  |  | £ |
|---|---|---|
| Corporation tax | 312,400 at 30% | 93,720 |
| Tapering relief | 1/40 × (500,000 – 312,400) | 4,690 |
|  |  | 89,030 |
|  |  |  |
| UK income | 89,030 × 66,000/312,400 | 18,809 |
| Overseas income | 89,030 × 246,400/312,400 | 70,221 |

### Working 3 – Double taxation relief

Double taxation relief is restricted to the lower of:

|  | £ |
|---|---|
| Overseas tax (1,760 + 70,400) | 72,160 |
| UK corporation tax on overseas income | 70,221 |

(b) As a result of its reduction in corporation tax rates from 30% to 10%, Westoria will become a 'low tax country', since its rate of tax will be less than three quarters of that payable on the equivalent profits in the UK. Waterloo Ltd does not meet the following exclusion tests:

1.   It is not quoted on a recognised Stock Exchange.

2.   Its profits are not less than £50,000.

3.   It does not have an acceptable distribution policy, since less than 90% of taxable profits are distributed. Since Westoria Ltd's corporation tax liability is £117,600, 90% of its taxable profits (less Westoria tax) is presumably £246,960 (117,600 × 7/3 × 90%).

Waterloo Ltd may satisfy.

4.   The exempt activities test. This assumes that Waterloo Ltd has a business establishment in Westoria, and effectively manages its business affairs there. However, it is possible that Waterloo Ltd is engaged in a non–qualifying business, since it is dealing in goods for delivery from a connected person (Paddington Ltd).

5.   The motive test. Paddington Ltd can contend that Waterloo Ltd does not exist for the main purpose of avoiding UK tax. The fact that Waterloo Ltd was set up prior to the reduction in the rate of Westoria's corporation tax, supports this argument.

If Waterloo Ltd is classified as a controlled foreign company, then Paddington Ltd will be assessable to UK corporation tax on its share (80%) of the profits of Waterloo Ltd, rather than on the dividends remitted to the UK. Relief would be given for tax paid in Westoria.

## 65     (Answer 5 of examination)

### Examiner's comments and marking guide

Part (a) tested candidates' knowledge of the badges of trade, and required a calculation of the tax liability if property activities were (i) treated as trading, and (ii) if they were treated as not trading. Part (b) tested candidates' knowledge of tax relief under the enterprise investment scheme. This was the least popular question on the paper, although there some high scoring answers by many of those candidates that attempted it. Part (a) was generally well answered, although many candidates wasted time by calculating the taxpayer's total tax liability for the year, when only the tax liability (which was at 40%) on the property activities was required. The retention of one of the six properties by the taxpayer caused problems, with many candidates restricting the expenditure under Schedule D case 1, rather than including the property at market value. There were a number of good answers dealing with badges of trade, and most candidates reached the correct conclusion that the taxpayer would most likely be treated as trading. Part (b) was badly answered, since the relief was not well understood. Few candidates supported their answers by calculating the tax relief available.

|  |  | Marks |
|---|---|---|
| (a) | *Treated as trading* | |
| | Sale proceeds | 1 |
| | Cost of property/Cost of conversion | 1 |
| | Loan interest | 1 |
| | Legal fees/Advertising/Income tax | 1 |
| | *Treated as not trading* | |
| | Proceeds/Incidental costs | 2 |
| | Cost of property/Cost of conversion | 2 |
| | Annual exemption/CGT | 1 |
| | *Badges of trade* | |
| | The subject matter of the transaction | 2 |
| | The length of ownership | 1 |
| | Frequency of similar transactions | 1 |
| | Work done on the property | 1 |
| | Circumstances responsible for the realisation | 1 |
| | Motive | 2 |
| | Other factors | 1 |
| | Conclusion | 1 |
| | | — |
| | Available | 19 |
| | | — |
| | Maximum | 17 |
| | | — |
| (b) | *Tax relief* | |
| | Income tax relief | 1 |
| | CGT exemption | 1 |
| | Deferral relief | 2 |
| | *Withdrawal of relief* | |
| | Director/listing on the AIM | 1 |
| | Stock Exchange listing | 1 |
| | Sale of shares | 1 |
| | Gain deferred | 1 |
| | *Loss on disposal* | |
| | Relief available | 1 |
| | | — |
| | Available | 9 |
| | | — |
| | Maximum | 8 |
| | | — |
| | Available | 28 |

Maximum 25

---

## Step by step answer plan

**Overview**

In part (a) there is a property transaction which could either be taxed as a trading activity or as a capital gain. The requirement is then to calculate the tax liability on the two alternative treatments and then to discuss which would be likely to apply in this case in practice. The calculations are very straightforward particularly now as indexation allowance cannot apply in the updated version (acquisition post April 1998). In part (b) knowledge of the Enterprise Investment Scheme is required. In its original form you also had to know about a further relief called Reinvestment Relief but the FA 1998 combined the two reliefs into a single scheme - (new form) EIS.

**Step 1** Read the question carefully to identify the points relevant to the two alternative tax treatments in part (a).

**Step 2** Prepare computations of the two different tax treatments explaining in each case how the apartment kept for the taxpayer is treated.

**Step 3** For part (a) (ii) discuss the situation with reference to the badges of trade

**Step 4** In part (b) there are three main question paragraphs but some contain more than one question. Ensure each of the questions is answered clearly but briefly using the three paragraph headings suggested in the question.

---

## The examiner's answer

(a)  (i)  *Treated as trading*

If Chow is treated as trading she will be liable under Schedule D case 1. The holiday apartment retained by her will be included at its market value of £75,000 (as per *Sharkey v Wernher* (1956)). Chow's income tax liability will be:

| | £ | £ |
|---|---:|---:|
| Sale proceeds (6 × 75,000) | | 450,000 |
| Cost of property | 132,000 | |
| Cost of conversion | 63,000 | |
| Loan interest (90,000 × 8% × 7/12) | 4,200 | |
| Legal fees (5 × 750) | 3,750 | |
| Advertising | 1,200 | |
| | | 204,150 |
| Taxable profit | | 245,850 |
| Income tax at 40% | | 98,340 |

*Treated as not trading*

If Chow is treated as not trading, she will be subject to capital gains tax. The holiday apartment retained by her will not be charged to tax. Chow's CGT liability will be:

| | £ | £ |
|---|---:|---:|
| Proceeds (5 × 75,000) | | 375,000 |
| Incidental costs of disposal (3,750 + 1,200) | | 4,950 |
| | | 370,050 |

|  |  |  |
|---|---|---|
| Cost of property (132,000 × 5/6) | 110,000 | |
| Cost of conversion (63,000 × 5/6) | 52,500 | |
| | | 162,500 |
| | | 207,550 |
| Annual exemption | | 7,100 |
| | | 200,450 |
| Capital gains tax at 40% | | 80,180 |

(ii)     There is no single test as to what constitutes trading, but certain tests, *the badges of trade*, will be used to determine whether or not the purchase and resale of property is a trading transaction. The tests are:

*The subject matter of the transaction:* Property which does not yield an income nor gives personal enjoyment to its owner is likely to form the subject matter of a trading transaction. Chow has not received any income from the property, and there is no indication that she purchased the property with a view to residing in it. This is a strong indication of trading.

*The length of ownership:* The sale of property within a short time of its acquisition is an indication of trading. Chow immediately put the holiday apartments up for sale following the completion of the conversion.

*Frequency of similar transactions:* Repeated transactions in the same subject matter will be an indication of trading. Although Chow's sale of the holiday apartments is an isolated transaction, this does not prevent the property activities being treated as an adventure in the nature of a trade.

*Work done on the property:* Carrying out work to the property in order to make it more marketable, or taking steps to find purchasers, will indicate a trading motive. The conversion of the property into six separate holiday apartments at a cost of £63,000 is a clear indication of trading.

*Circumstances responsible for the realisation:* A forced sale to raise cash for an emergency will by presumption indicate that the transaction is not an adventure in the nature of a trade. There is no indication that Chow's sale of the holiday apartments was a forced sale.

*Motive:* If a transaction is undertaken with the motive of realising a profit, this will be a strong indication of trading. There is no clear indication of Chow's motive, although such factors as obtaining planning permission lead to the conclusion that she undertook the property transaction with a view to a profit. However, the absence of a profit motive does not prevent a person from being treated as trading.

*Other factors*
The property was acquired deliberately, rather than unintentionally such as by gift or inheritance, with the purchase being financed by a loan of £90,000. Both factors are an indication of trading.

*Conclusion*
Despite being an isolated transaction, Chow's sale of the holiday apartments is likely to be treated as an adventure in the nature of a trade.

---

**Did you answer the question?**

The badges of trade were distilled from case law decisions available in 1955 and you were only required to explain the principles, not the underlying case law background.

---

(b)     *Tax relief*
Under the enterprise investment scheme (EIS), Chow will be entitled to income tax relief of £30,000 (150,000 at 20%) in 1999/00. She will be entitled to tax relief of £6,000 (£30,000 at 20%) for 2000/01 if £30,000 of the investment is delayed until that year. There will be no CGT on the disposal of the shares provided they are held for five years.

If Chow's property activities are treated as a capital gain, then she will be entitled to EIS deferral relief of £180,000. This would reduce her CGT liability to £8,180 (200,450 – 180,000 = 20,450 at 40%) by deferring the capital gain. Deferral relief will be available provided the investment is made before November 2002.

### Withdrawal of relief

Tax relief given under the EIS will not be withdrawn as a result of Chow becoming a director of Knife-Edge Ltd, or as a result of the company obtaining a listing on the AIM. Tax relief will be withdrawn if Knife-Edge Ltd obtains a listing on the Stock Exchange before 15 March 2003 (three years from the date of subscription), or Chow sells shares before 15 March 2004 (five years from the date of subscription). Where shares are sold, the relief withdrawn will be limited to that given on those shares. The capital gain deferred will become chargeable when the shares are sold, or if Knife-Edge Ltd obtains a listing on the Stock Exchange before 15 March 2003.

### Loss on disposal

If a loss is made on the disposal of shares, then relief will be available against either capital gains or income. The calculation of the loss will be based on the cost of the shares less any EIS relief obtained and not withdrawn.

---

**Did you answer the question?**

You were not required to discuss whether Knife-Edge Ltd qualified under the EIS rules. There could be a problem if the company never actually traded but this point was not specifically mentioned for your comment.

---

## 66    (Answer 6 of examination)

---

### ( Examiner's comments and marking guide )

Part (a) tested candidates' knowledge regarding the provision of various benefits in kind to an employee, including a company motor car, mobile telephone and company credit card. Part (b) tested candidates' knowledge of the taxation of lump sum payments on redundancy and taking up employment, relocation costs and living accommodation provided by an employee. Part (c) tested candidates' knowledge of occupational pension schemes.

This was a popular question although answers were somewhat disappointing given that most of the material being examined was of a paper 7 level. Candidates are advised to read the requirements carefully, since in this question the tax implications for the company were only required in part (a). Many candidates wasted time by also giving them for part (b). Part (a) was generally answered satisfactorily, although the failure to time-apportion the value of the car and fuel benefits was a common mistake. This then lead to problems when dealing with the tax planning aspects of the question. In part (b) many candidates were unsure of the benefits arising on the provision of living accommodation, and although most candidates were aware of the relief for the costs of relocation, little detail was given in their answers. Marks were lost when dealing with the lump sum paid on redundancy because each aspect of the payment was not dealt with separately. Part (c) was generally well answered, although candidates will miss out on marks if they give vague answers such as 'the contributions are tax-free'.

|  |  | *Marks* |
|---|---|---:|
| (a) | *Benny* |  |
|  | Car benefit | 2 |
|  | Other benefits | 1 |
|  | Expense claim | 1 |
|  | Income tax liability | 1 |
|  | *Usine Ltd* |  |
|  | Capital allowances | 2 |
|  | Deductible expenses | 1 |
|  | Class lA NIC | 1 |
|  | *Business meeting* |  |
|  | Business mileage | 2 |
|  | Tax saving | 1 |
|  | *Private petrol* |  |
|  | Tax saving | 1 |

---

|  |  | Available | 13 |
|---|---|---|---|
|  |  | Maximum | 11 |

| (b) | *Lump sum payments* |  |  |
|---|---|---|---|
|  | Wages in lieu of notice |  | 1 |
|  | Taxable amount |  | 2 |
|  | Lump sum on taking up employment |  | 1 |
|  | *Beneficial loan* |  |  |
|  | Taxable benefit |  | 1 |
|  | *Relocation costs* |  |  |
|  | Exempt amount |  | 1 |
|  | Expenses covered |  | 1 |
|  | *Accommodation* |  |  |
|  | Additional benefit |  | 2 |
|  | Furniture/Running costs |  | 1 |
|  |  | Available | 10 |
|  |  | Maximum | 9 |

| (c) | Deduction of contributions |  | 1 |
|---|---|---|---|
|  | Non-taxable benefits |  | 1 |
|  | Schedule E deduction |  | 1 |
|  | Investment fund |  | 1 |
|  | Tax-free lump sums |  | 1 |
|  |  | Maximum/Available | 5 |
|  |  | Available | 28 |
|  |  | Maximum | 25 |

## ( Step by step answer plan )

### Overview

This is clearly a Schedule E question on car benefits, redundancy, relocation costs and occupational pensions with some fairly straightforward advice and simple planning points required. It contrasts very favourably with a Schedule E question set at a previous sitting requiring detailed calculations to decide on whether a car or a cash alternative was more tax efficient. The examiner has clearly seen from marking this previous question that a less complicated question is needed even though this is a mainstream area of the syllabus. An attractive feature of this question is the way it is separated into three quite independent parts.

**Step 1**  Read part (a) carefully and identify in principle the disproportionate advantages of the employee crossing the 2,500 business miles threshold and paying in full for the private use petrol. Although VAT is to be ignored, the Schedule E and NIC effects are clearly required.

**Step 2**  Show the tax effect for Benny of the benefits as they stand including the scope for a s.198 claim and a comment on how the extra liability will be paid. The examiner's answer omits any comment on the NIC implications as his earnings are clearly above the upper limit. It would be good practice to mention the point.

**Step 3**  Show how the information impacts on Usine Ltd in terms of reducing chargeable profits. The examiner expected the reporting requirements to be covered. This includes the quarterly return system updating the Revenue on the changes to company car provision for employees in the fiscal quarter just ended.

**Step 4**  Describe the changes if the business mileage is increased for 1999/00.

**Step 5**  Calculate the tax and Class 1A saving if the employee pays for the private petrol.

**Step 6**  Answer part (b) with a separate heading for each of the topics mentioned - viz, redundancy payment, lump sum on commencement, beneficial loan (not forgetting the tax reducer effect for loans outside MIRAS), relocation costs and the provision of accommodation.

**Step 7**  List out the tax advantages of obtaining approval for an occupational pension scheme with particular reference to the actual scheme in place - eg, it is contributory so cover that point.

### The examiner's answer

(a)  Benny

Benny will be assessed under Schedule E on benefits-on-kind totalling £6,890 as follows:

|  | £ |
|---|---|
| *Car benefit* | |
| $28,400 + 700 – 2,500 = 26,600 \times 35\% \times 6/12$ | 4,655 |
| Fuel benefit $2,270 \times 6/12$ | 1,135 |
| Expense payments $380 + 720$ | 1,100 |
| | 6,890 |

Benny will be able to claim a deduction under s.198 ICTA 1988 for the expense payments of £1,100, so his additional income tax liability for 1999/00 will be £2,316 (6,890 – 1,100 = 5,790 at 40%). The tax on the car and fuel benefits will be collected under PAYE, with the remaining liability being due on 31 January 2001.

*Usine Ltd*
Usine Ltd will claim capital allowances on the cost of the motor car £26,600, with the writing-down allowance initially restricted to £3,000. Capital allowances of £72 (180 at 40% FYA) will be available in respect of the mobile telephone. Credit card expenses of £1,265 (460 + 380 + 425) will be deducted in calculating Schedule D Case I profits. The cost of entertaining is disallowed.

Class 1A NIC of £706 (4,655 + 1,135 = 5,790 at 12.2%) will be due on 19 July 2000. Usine Ltd will have to provide details of Benny's company car to the Inland Revenue within 28 days of 5 January 2000.

*Business meeting*
For 1999/00 the 2,500 business mileage limit is reduced to 1,250 (2,500 × 6/12). The business mileage for the meeting on 8 April 2000 will be 190 miles, being the distance from home to the meeting. If the meeting is brought forward to 4 April 2000, then Benny's business mileage for 1999/00 will be 1,290 (1,100 + 190). His income tax liability for 1999/00 will be reduced by £532 (4,655 × $^{10}\!/_{35}$ = 1,330 at 40%). Usine Ltd's Class 1A NIC liability will be reduced by £162 (1,330 at 12.2%).

---

**Did you answer the question?**

You are not told the employer's marginal tax rate, so you were not required to compute the effect for Usine Ltd net of corporation tax.

---

*Private petrol*

The payment by Benny of £180 for his private petrol would eliminate his fuel benefit of £1,135, and therefore reduce his income tax liability by £454 (1,135 at 40%). The net saving for Benny is £274 (454 – 180). Usine Ltd's Class 1A NIC liability will be reduced by £138 (1,135 at 12.2%).

(b)     *Redundancy payment*

Wages in lieu of notice are exempt from income tax provided there is no contractual entitlement. Although exempt, the statutory redundancy payment reduces the exempt amount of £30,000. The redundancy payment of £45,000 is therefore taxable as follows:

|  | £ | £ |
|---|---|---|
| Holiday pay | | 2,800 |
| Restrictive covenant | | 3,000 |
| *Ex-gratia* payment | 34,000 | |
| *Less*: Exempt amount (30,000 – 2,100) | 27,900 | |
| | | 6,100 |
| Taxable | | 11,900 |

*Lump sum payment on taking up employment*

The lump sum payment of £10,000 to the new sales director will be taxable, unless the payment represents compensation for a right or asset given up on taking up employment with Usine Ltd.

*Beneficial loan*

The new sales director will be assessed under Schedule E on a taxable benefit of £1,250 (50,000 at 10% - 5,000 × 3/12). She will be able to claim tax relief of £75 (1,250 × 30,000/50,000 at 10%).

*Relocation costs*

There will be no taxable benefit in respect of eligible removal expenses up to £8,000 paid for by Usine Ltd since the new sales director does not live within a reasonable daily travelling distance from the company's head office. The expenses must be incurred by 5 April 2001. The exemption covers such items as legal and estate agents' fees, stamp duty, removal costs, and the cost of new domestic goods where existing goods are not suitable for the new residence.

*Accommodation*

The new sales director will be assessed under Schedule E on the benefit of the living accommodation provided to her. The additional benefit will be based on the market value of £105,000 since the house was purchased more than six years before being provided to the director. The benefit assessed in 1999/00 will be:

|  | £ |
|---|---|
| Rateable value 4,400 × 3/12 | 1,100 |
| Additional benefit | |
| 105,000 – 75,000 = 30,000 at 10% × 3/12 | 750 |
| Furniture 10,400 at 20% × 3/12 | 520 |
| Running costs 3,200 × 3/12 | 800 |
| | 3,170 |

(c)     The following tax advantages will result from Usine Ltd's occupational pension scheme obtaining Inland Revenue approval:

(i)     Usine Ltd's contributions will be deductible in calculating Schedule D profits. Contributions will be deductible in the accounting period in which they are paid.

(ii)     Usine Ltd's contributions will not be treated as taxable benefits in the hands of the employees. There will be no liability to NIC.

(iii)     The contributions made by the employees will be deductible against their Schedule E income. The deduction will be restricted to 15% of remuneration, subject to an earnings cap of £90,600.

(iv)     The pension scheme investment fund will not be subject to tax on either income or capital gains although it will not be able to recover tax credits on UK dividend income.

(v)     A tax-free lump sum may be taken by an employee upon retirement.

(vi)     Subject to certain limits, provision can be made for a tax-free lump sum to be paid upon an employee's death in service.

## JUNE 1998 QUESTIONS

## 67    (Question 1 of examination)

(a)    Velo Ltd manufactures bicycles, making up its accounts to 31 March. The company is planning to move into new business premises during March 2000 (you should assume that today's date is 15 February 2000). The company's plans are as follows:

(1)    On 25 March 2000 Velo Ltd is to sell its existing freehold factory for £920,000. The factory was purchased from a builder on 1 April 1989 for £326,000, and was immediately brought into use. The cost and selling price are made up as follows:

|  | Cost £ | Selling price £ |
|---|---|---|
| Land | 95,000 | 180,000 |
| Factory | 160,000 | 575,000 |
| General office | 71,000 | 165,000 |
|  | 326,000 | 920,000 |

(2)    On 1 March 2000 Velo Ltd is to purchase a freehold factory at a cost of £725,000, and this will be brought into use immediately. The factory was originally constructed between 1 January and 31 March 1991 at a cost of £640,000, and was brought into use on 1 July 1991. The original cost and purchase price are made up as follows:

|  | Original Cost £ | Purchase price £ |
|---|---|---|
| Land | 132,000 | 154,000 |
| Factory | 478,000 | 531,000 |
| General office | 30,000 | 40,000 |
|  | 640,000 | 725,000 |

Velo Ltd will immediately install a new overhead crane in the factory at a cost of £53,000. The crane is a long-life asset.

(3)    On 1 March 2000 Velo Ltd is to pay a premium of £80,000 for the grant of a 15 year lease on an office building. An annual rental of £16,200 will be payable quarterly in advance. The company will immediately install new computer equipment in the office building at a cost of £14,000. The computer equipment will probably be replaced in three years time.

The tax written-down value of Velo Ltd's plant and machinery at 1 April 1999 is £38,000. The company is registered for VAT, and all of the above figures are net of VAT. Velo Ltd is a medium-sized company as defined by the Companies Acts.

**You are required to:**

Advise Velo Ltd of the tax implications arising from each aspect of its proposed plan. Your answer should be supported by appropriate calculations.                                                     **(17 marks)**

(b)    Following further enquiries regarding Velo Ltd's proposed plan, the following additional information is now available in respect of the factory that is to be sold on 25 March 2000:

(1)    On 10 March 1997 Velo Ltd installed heating and ventilation systems in the factory at a cost of £54,000. All of the expenditure qualified as plant and machinery.

(2)    On 31 January 2000 Velo Ltd installed an overhead crane in the factory at a cost of £64,000. The crane is a long-life asset, and has a current market value equivalent to its cost.

The market value of each of these assets is included in the value of the factory of £575,000.

**You are required to:**

Advise Velo Ltd of the tax implications arising from this additional information, and how it affects your answer to part (a) above. You should include tax planning advice in your answer as appropriate.    **(8 marks)**
**(Total: 25 marks)**

---

## 68    (Question 2 of examination)

Barney Hall is employed by Sutol (UK) Ltd as a motor car designer, and he is currently resident, ordinarily resident and domiciled in the UK. You should assume that today's date is 15 October 1999. On 1 November 1999 Barney is to be sent to the country of Yalam, where he will work on assignment for the parent company of Sutol (UK) Ltd. The assignment will be for a period of either six months or eighteen months.

The company will pay for his travel expenses of £2,400, and subsistence expenses of £850 per month whilst working in Yalam. Barney's wife will visit him during January 2000, and he will pay for her travel expenses of £700. This amount will be reimbursed by Sutol (UK) Ltd if the overseas assignment exceeds twelve months. Barney is paid a salary of £33,600 p.a. by Sutol (UK) Ltd, and he will continue to be paid at the same rate whilst working overseas. Barney will not be subject to Yalamese tax in respect of his salary. He has the following other income:

(1)    Schedule A profits of £2,600 p.a. from the rental of a property situated in the UK.

(2)    Interest of £5,460 (net) pa, from a bank deposit account in Yalam. The interest is subject to Yalamese tax at the rate of 30%.

Barney is to dispose of the following assets during 1999-00:

(1)    On 15 December 1999 Barney is to sell a plot of land situated in Yalam for 180,000 Yalamese dollars. The exchange rate is currently $8 to £1. The plot of land was acquired on 1 January 1996 for 84,000 Yalamese dollars, when the exchange rate was $6 to £1. The disposal will not be subject to Yalamese tax.

(2)    On 20 December 1999 Barney is to make a gift of 8,000 ordinary shares in ZYX plc to his daughter. The shares are currently quoted on the UK Stock Exchange at 210 — 218, and were acquired on 31 January 1996 for £9,450.

There is no double taxation agreement between the UK and Yalam. All of the above figures are in Pounds sterling unless indicated otherwise.

**You are required to:**

(a)    Briefly explain the rules which determine whether a person is resident in the UK during a tax year. Your answer should include details of people leaving the UK and people coming to the UK.    **(5 marks)**

(b)    Advise Barney of the income tax and capital gains tax implications for 1999-00 if he works overseas for:
   (i)     A period of six months, returning to the UK on 30 April 2000.
   (ii)    A period of eighteen months, returning to the UK on 30 April 2001.

Your answer should include a calculation of Barney's statutory total income and capital gains for 1999-00 in each case. You are not expected to calculate the tax liabilities.    **(12 marks)**

(c)    Explain why Barney should carefully plan both the timing and length of any return visits to the UK if his overseas assignment is for a period of eighteen months.    **(2 marks)**
**(Total: 19 marks)**
*(as amended)*

---

## 69    (Question 3 of examination)

Moon Ltd is the holding company for a group of companies.  The group structure is as follows:

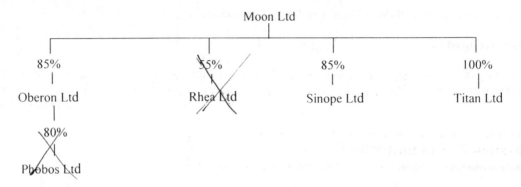

Each percentage holding represents a holding of ordinary share capital.  The shareholdings were all held throughout the year ended 31 March 2000 except for Moon Ltd's 100% shareholding in Titan Ltd that was acquired on 1 October 1999.  All of the companies have an accounting date of 31 March.  The results of each company (except Titan Ltd) for the year ended 31 March 2000 are as follows:

|  | *Tax adjusted Schedule Dl profit £* |
|---|---|
| Moon Ltd | 278,000 |
| Oberon Ltd | 57,000 |
| Rhea Ltd | 124,000 |
| Sinope Ltd | 72,000 |
| Phobos Ltd | 4,000 |

Sinope Ltd's tax adjusted profit of £72,000 is entirely in respect of an overseas branch.  Overseas taxation of £25,920 has been paid on the branch profits.

Titan Ltd previously had an accounting date of 30 September, but has produced accounts for the six month period to 31 March 2000 to make its accounting date coterminous with the other group companies.  Due to a reorganisation following its takeover by Moon Ltd, Titan Ltd made a tax adjusted Schedule Dl loss of £95,000 for the six month period to 31 March 2000.  On 31 December 1999 the company received bank interest of £1,500, and on 15 February 2000 it paid a patent royalty of £4,000 (gross).  For the year ended 30 September 1999 Titan Ltd had profits chargeable to corporation tax of £18,000.

**You are required to:**

(a)    Explain the possible ways that Titan Ltd can relieve its Schedule Dl trading loss for the six month period to 31 March 2000.    **(5 marks)**

(b)    State, giving appropriate reasons, the companies to which Titan Ltd can surrender its Schedule Dl trading loss.    **(3 marks)**

(c)    Advise the Moon Ltd group as to which loss relief claims as specified in (I) and (ii) above would be the most beneficial.  Your answer should be supported by appropriate calculations.    **(7 marks)**

You are not expected to calculate the corporation tax liabilities for any of the companies.

**(Total:  15 marks)**
*(as amended)*

---

## 70    (Question 4 of examination)

---

Yaz Pica commenced trading as a self-employed printer on 1 January 2000. He is to make up his accounts to 31 December 2000, and has produced the following quarterly profit forecast:

|  | Q/E 31.3.00 £ | Q/E 30.6.00 £ | Q/E 30.9.00 £ | Q/E 31.12.00 £ | Total for year £ |
|---|---|---|---|---|---|
| Sales |  |  |  |  |  |
| Standard rated | 19,400 | 28,600 | 40,200 | 51,200 | 139,400 |
| Zero rated | 5,100 | 7,500 | 9,700 | 12,500 | 34,800 |
|  | 24,500 | 36,100 | 49,900 | 63,700 | 174,200 |
| Purchases | (14,900) | (16,700) | (18,400) | (20,600) | (70,600) |
| Opening stock | (3,600) | (3,800) | (4,400) | (5,700) | (3,600) |
| Closing stock | 3,800 | 4,400 | 5,700 | 7,200 | 7,200 |
| Subcontractor costs | - | (3,100) | (8,800) | (12,400) | (24,300) |
| Expenses |  |  |  |  |  |
| Standard rated | (9,900) | (5,200) | (5,600) | (6,100) | (26,800) |
| Exempt | (1,100) | (1,300) | (1,600) | (1,800) | (5,800) |
| Profit/(Loss) | (1,200) | 10,400 | 16,800 | 24,300 | 50,300 |

Yaz registered for VAT on 1 January 2000, even though the VAT registration turnover limit was not exceeded until May 2000. All of Yaz's sales are to members of the general public. The purchases are all standard rated. Because of the pressure of work, Yaz was late submitting his first VAT return due on 30 April 2000.

The opening stock of £3,600 represents purchases made during December 1999. On 10 December 1999 Yaz purchased printing equipment for £18,000, and spent £1,400 on an advertising campaign that ran throughout December. All the expenses are allowable for tax purposes, but do not include capital allowances or the cost of the advertising campaign.

The above figures are all net of VAT.

On 1 May 2000 Yaz started sub-contracting some of his work to another printer, Albert Elite. As a result of the continued expansion of the business it is likely that as from 1 October 2000 Albert will work for Yaz on a full-time basis. Yaz considers Albert to be self-employed because he issues invoice for the work done. Albert is not registered for VAT.

Until 30 November 1999 Yaz was employed on a salary of £42,000 p.a., and PAYE of £7,080 has been deducted during 1999-00. He is single and has no other income or outgoings.

**You are required to:**

(a)    (i)    Calculate the amount of income tax that Yaz will have to pay on 31 January 2001 if he makes up his accounts for the year ended 31 December 2000.                              **(6 marks)**

(ii)    Advise Yaz of whether it will be beneficial to make up his accounts for the three month period to 31 March 2000, rather than for the year ended 31 December 2000.                  **(4 marks)**

You are only expected to calculate Yaz's Income tax liability for 1999-00. NIC should be ignored.

(b)    (i)    With hindsight, it is evident that Yaz should not have registered for VAT until 1 July 2000. Explain why this is the case, and calculate the additional profit that Yaz would have made if he had registered for VAT as from 1 July 2000 rather than from 1 January 2000.                  **(5 marks)**

(ii)    State the implications of Yaz being late in submitting any further VAT returns during 2000.
                                                                                          **(2 marks)**

(iii)    Advise Yaz of the advantages of using the annual accounting scheme, and explain when he will be permitted to join.                                                                      **(3 marks)**

---

(c) Briefly explain the criteria that will be used in deciding whether Albert should be treated as employed or self-employed. State the implications for Yaz if Albert is incorrectly treated as self-employed rather than employed. **(5 marks)**

**(Total: 25 marks)**

---

**71 (Question 5 of examination)**

---

You are a Chartered Certified Accountant who is authorised to conduct investment business under the Financial Services Act 1986. Mary Mole, a client, inherited £25,000 on 15 December 1999, and has asked for your advice regarding a number of recommendations that she has received as to how this sum should be invested. The recommendations are as follows:

(1) Mary's bank manager has suggested that she invest the maximum amount possible in an 'equity' ISA, with the balance invested in a unit trust aimed at capital growth. The bank offers each of these investments.

(2) An insurance salesperson has suggested that Mary contribute the maximum tax deductible amount into a personal pension scheme. Mary was born on 1 December 1960, and has not previously made any provision for retirement. She is a partner in a business that writes computer software, and her recent Schedule Dl assessable amounts are as follows:

|  | £ |
|---|---|
| 1992-93 | 4,600 |
| 1993-94 | 46,200 |
| 1994-95 | 12,600 |
| 1995-96 and 1996-97 | Nil (studying at university) |
| 1997-98 | 8,100 |
| 1998-99 | 18,300 |
| 1999-00 | 58,400 |

(3) One of Mary's business partners has suggested that she make an investment in a venture capital trust. He believes that unquoted companies will offer an attractive investment return over the next five years, and that using a venture capital trust will diversify the risk of holding unquoted shares.

(4) Mary's post office manager has given her a leaflet on government stocks. She understands that these offer a competitive return, and has read that it is possible to purchase government stocks ex div and then to sell them cum div so that interest is effectively turned into a capital gain.

Mary's investment criteria are as follows:

(1) She would like to reduce her income tax and class 4 NIC liability of £17,412 that you have advised her will be payable in respect of the 1999-00 partnership profits.

(2) Capital growth is more important than additional income.

(3) She is prepared to take a moderate amount of risk.

(4) Some or all of the capital may be needed in four years time when her daughter is expected to go to university.

**You are required:**

(a) In respect of each of the four recommendations:

(i) Explain the potential income tax and CGT implications. Your answer should include details of the maximum amount that can be invested in each case.

(ii) Advise Mary as to the suitability of each recommendation in relation to her investment criteria.

**(21 marks)**

(b) (i) Explain the difference between a tied adviser and an independent adviser.

(ii) The ACCA has issued Statements of Principle which cover the standards expected of an authorised person. State briefly what these principles are. **(4 marks)**

**(25 marks)**

---

## 72  (Question 6 of examination)

Bluetone Ltd is an unquoted trading company that manufactures compact discs. The company has four full-time working directors, each of whom owns 25% of its share capital of 200,000 £1 ordinary shares. These are currently valued as follows:

| Shareholding | Value per share £ |
|---|---|
| 15% | 9.00 |
| 25% | 11.00 |
| 35% | 12.50 |
| 50% | 15.00 |

Melody Brown

Melody has recently been appointed a director after inheriting her father's 50,000 shares in Bluetone Ltd. Melody's father purchased the shareholding on 12 November 1999, but died on 15 February 2000. At the date of his death he also owned the following assets:

(1)     42,000 50p ordinary shares in Expanse plc quoted at 312 — 320, with bargains of 282, 288, 306 and 324.

(2)     26,000 units in World-Growth, a unit trust. The bid price was 80 and the offer price was 84.

(3)     Building society deposits of £32,000 of which £11,000 were in a TESSA.

(4)     His main residence valued at £125,000 with an outstanding repayment mortgage of £42,000.

(5)     A life insurance policy on his own life with an open market value of £53,000. Proceeds of £61,000 were received on 4 March 2000.

On 15 February 2000, Melody's father had an income tax liability of £6,600 and gambling debts of £1,200. Funeral expenses came to £3,460. Under the terms of his will, Melody was left the shares in Bluetone Ltd. The shares are to bear their own IHT. Melody wants to retain the full 25% holding, so she is to personally account for the IHT liability. The residue of the estate was left to Melody's brother. Melody's father made the following lifetime gifts:

(1)     On 10 February 1996 he made a wedding gift of £30,000 to Melody.

(2)     On 4 June 1996 he made a gift of £153,000 into a discretionary trust.

Liam and Opal White

Liam and Opal, a married couple aged 37 and 32 respectively, have been directors and shareholders of Bluetone Ltd since its incorporation on 1 October 1992 when they acquired their shares at par. On 20 March 2000 Liam is to sell 30,000 of his shares in Bluetone Ltd to their son for £75,000. Liam is a 40% taxpayer, and has not previously made any lifetime gifts of assets.

Noel Green

Noel is aged 52 and has been a director and shareholder of Bluetone Ltd since its incorporation on 1 October 1992. For the past two years he has disagreed with the other directors of Bluetone Ltd over the company's business policies. He is therefore to resign as a director on 31 March 2000, and it has been agreed that Bluetone Ltd will purchase his shareholding for £550,000. The Inland Revenue has given advance clearance that the purchase qualifies for the special treatment applying to a company's purchase of its own shares, and can therefore be treated as a capital gain.

Noel acquired the shares at par, and is a 40% taxpayer.

For the year ended 31 March 2000 Bluetone Ltd is forecast to have profits chargeable to corporation tax of £1,100,000 and to pay dividends of £250,000 during the year. The company has no chargeable non-business assets.

**You are required to:**

(a)     Calculate Melody's IHT liability and state when this will be due.     **(10 marks)**

(b)     Advise Liam of the CGT and IHT implications of selling the 30,000 shares in Bluetone Ltd to his son.  You should assume that reliefs are claimed in the most favourable manner.     **(8 marks)**

(c)     Advise Noel of whether it will be beneficial to have the purchase of 25% shareholding treated as a capital gain under the special treatment, rather than as a distribution by Bluetone Ltd.     **(7 marks)**

**(Total:  25 marks)**

The rates and allowances for 1999-00 should be used throughout.     *(as amended)*

---

## ANSWERS TO JUNE 1998 EXAMINATION

---

## 67     (Answer 1 of examination)

---

### Examiner's comments and marking guide

This question tested candidates' ability to advise on the capital allowance and capital gains tax implications arising from a number of transactions: the sale of an industrial building (including fixtures), the purchase of a second-hand industrial building, a long-life asset and a short-life asset, and the payment of a premium for a short lease. This was the least popular question on the paper, and produced very few good answers. The sale of the industrial building was generally dealt with well, and most candidates correctly advised that a claim for rollover relief could be made. However, few candidates were aware that a joint election was possible to determine how much of the sale price related to fixtures. The calculation of the industrial buildings allowance on the second hand industrial building caused problems for many candidates, and few appreciated the implications of the £100,000 limit applicable to long-life assets. The short-life asset and the payment of a premium for a short lease were well answered.

|  |  | Marks |
|---|---|---:|
| (a) | *Sale of factory* | |
|  | Capital gain | 1 |
|  | Rollover relief/Amount reinvested | 1 |
|  | Immediate gain/Amount rolled over | 1 |
|  | Depreciating assets | 1 |
|  | Allocation of gain | 1 |
|  | Balancing charge | 2 |
|  | | |
|  | *New factory* | |
|  | Base cost for IBA | 1 |
|  | 25 year life | 1 |
|  | Writing-down allowance | 1 |
|  | | |
|  | *New overhead crane* | |
|  | Limit of £100,000 | 1 |
|  | First-year allowance | 1 |
|  | Subsequent periods | 1 |
|  | | |
|  | *Leasehold office building* | |
|  | Premium paid/Amortisation | 2 |
|  | Rent paid | 1 |
|  | | |
|  | *Computer equipment* | |
|  | Short-life asset | 1 |
|  | Balancing allowance | 1 |
|  | First-year allowance | 1 |
|  | | |
|  | | Available   19 |
|  | | |
|  | | Maximum   17 |
|  | | |
| (b) | *Heating and ventilation systems* | |
|  | Joint election | 1 |
|  | Lower and upper limits | 1 |
|  | Balancing charge | 1 |
|  | Writing-down allowance | 1 |
|  | | |
|  | *Overhead crane* | |
|  | Limit of £100,000 | 1 |
|  | Long-life asset pool | 1 |
|  | First-year allowance | 1 |

---

Tax planning                                                                    1

*Rollover relief*
Reduction in capital gain                                                       1
                                                                         _____
                                                        Available        9
                                                                         _____
                                                        Maximum          8
                                                                         _____
                                                        Available        28
                                                                         _____
                                                        Maximum          25
                                                                         _____

## ( Step by step answer plan )

### Overview

Although some computations are required, this question requires a mainly written answer on a number of straightforward capital gains and capital allowance transactions. The question is clearly split into a number of separate parts. Part (b), in fact, must not be considered while answering part (a) as it is prefaced with "Following further enquiries". However, the selling and buying of capital assets inevitably conjures up roll-over relief so care is needed in organising your answer. For example, the roll-over opportunities in steps (2) and (3) in part (a) should be dealt with alongside the capital gain you will calculate in part (1). Essentially the basic material in this question could be expected in a paper 7 (Tax Framework) exam. But for paper 11 you have to consider how the transactions may interact.

**Step 1** Read part (a) carefully and plan out your answer under the natural headings suggested by the transactions - viz, sale of existing factory (CG and IBA implications), purchase of new factory (IBAs), new crane (CAs), acquisition of lease (expense deductions) and purchase of computer (CAs). Recognise that it is "neater" to cover the roll over point when dealing with the sale of the factory.

**Step 2** Answer part (a) using the headings decided upon in step 1 and leave space in case something further occurs to you later. It is important that you mention any point that is relevant. For example, why have you given FYA on a long-life asset?

**Step 3** Part (b) is a "what if" section so read it careful and plan out the implication of each item and the knock-on effect it may have on the part (a) transactions. It is easier to spot the long-life effect of the second crane while you are planning rather than when you are writing your answer. Your planning should include advice on mitigating tax "as appropriate".

**Step 4** Answer part (b) keeping to the two headings suggested by the question with an extra heading for roll over relief.

**Step 5** Read the question again and consider whether there are any points which you may have missed in your answer. For example, perhaps you claimed FYA without making clear that you appreciated the significance of company size - only available to small or medium sized companies as defined under the Company Act.

## ( The examiner's answer )

(a)     *Sale of factory*

The disposal of the factory will result in a capital gain of £446,322 calculated as follows:

|                 |   £       |
|-----------------|-----------|
| Proceeds        | 920,000   |
| Cost            | 326,000   |
|                 | _____   |
|                 | 594,000   |

$$\text{Indexation } 326{,}000 \times \frac{166.1 - 114.3}{114.3} = (0.453) \qquad\qquad 147{,}678$$

$$\overline{\phantom{xxxx}}$$

$$446{,}322$$

$$\overline{\phantom{xxxx}}$$

Velo Ltd can claim rollover relief against the replacement cost of the freehold factory, the leasehold office building and the overhead crane to be purchased on 1 March 2000. The overhead crane should qualify as fixed plant and machinery. The amount reinvested is £858,000 (725,000 + 80,000 + 53,000), and so £62,000 (920,000 – 858,000) of the capital gain is chargeable in the year ended 31 March 2000, with £384,322 (446,322 – 62,000) being rolled over.

The leasehold office building and the overhead crane are both depreciating assets, and so any proportion of the gain rolled over against them will only be held over until the earlier of their disposal or ten years from the date of acquisition. However, in this situation the legislation would appear to allow the claim to be effectively made wholly against the value of the freehold factory. The base cost of the freehold factory will be £340,678 (725,000 – 384,322).

**Note:** Alternative allocations of the gain between the respective base costs of the replacement assets would be acceptable.

The disposal of the factory, which is an industrial building, will also result in a balancing charge of £64,000 as follows:

|  | £ |
|---|---|
| Original cost | 160,000 |
| WDA – 4% × 10 (years ended 31.3.90 to 31.3.99) | 64,000 |
|  | |
| Residue before sale | 96,000 |
| Disposal proceeds (restricted to cost) | 160,000 |
|  | |
| Balancing charge | 64,000 |

IBAs are not available in respect of the land, or the general office since it is more than 25% of the building cost (160,000 + 71,000 = 231,000 × 25% = £57,750).

*New factory*
Velo Ltd will be able to claim IBA on £508,000 (478,000 +30,000) being the lower of the price paid and the original cost of the building. The drawing office is eligible expenditure. The allowance will be based on the remaining 196 months of the 25 year life of the factory (this runs from the date that the building was first brought into use). For the year ended 31 March 2000 and subsequent years, a WDA of £31,102 (508,000 × 12/196) can therefore be claimed.

*New overhead crane*
Although the new overhead crane is a long-life asset, it will not be treated as such because Velo Ltd has not exceeded the annual *de minimis* limit of expenditure on long-life assets of £100,000. The crane is plant and machinery, and will qualify for a first year allowance of £21,200 (53,000 at 40%) in the year ended 31 March 2000 as Velo Ltd is a medium-sized company. In subsequent periods, the balance of expenditure remaining after the FYA claim will qualify for WDA at the rate of 25%.

*Leasehold office building*
Velo Ltd can deduct £1,670 in calculating its Schedule Dl profits for the year ended 31 March 2000, as follows:

|  | £ |
|---|---|
| Premium paid | 80,000 |
| Less: 80,000 × 2% × (15 — 1) | 22,400 |
|  | |
|  | 57,600 |

Relief available 57,600/15 × 1/12 =          320
Rent paid 16,200/12 =                      1,350
                                            _____
                                            1,670
                                            _____

The amortisation of the lease will have to be added back when calculating the Schedule DI profits.

*Computer equipment*
Velo Ltd should make a short-life asset claim to de-pool the computer equipment. The claim, which should be made by 31 March 2002, will be beneficial provided the computer equipment is disposed of before 31 March 2004 at less than its written-down value. Provided this is the case, then a balancing allowance will be given in the year of disposal.

For the year ended 31 March 2000 the computer equipment will qualify for a first year allowance of £5,600 (14,000 at 40%) as per the new crane.

(b)     *Heating and ventilation systems*
Velo Ltd and the purchaser of the building can make a joint election before 25 March 2002 in order to determine how much of the sale price of the factory of £575,000 relates to the fixtures (the heating and ventilation systems). This figure cannot be below £28,000 or the anti-avoidance provisions that prevent the acceleration of capital allowances may apply, and it cannot exceed the original cost of £54,000. It would be beneficial for Velo Ltd to keep the figure used below £38,000 so as to avoid a balancing charge. Assuming that an election to use the minimum figure of £28,000 is made, Velo Ltd will have a WDA of £2,500 (38,000 − 28,000 = 10,000 at 25%) for the year ended 31 March 2000.

---

**Tutorial note**

It is not clear why the examiner used the figure of £28,000 as the minimum disposal value. S.59A CAA 1990 requires the minimum to be the notional written down amount on the assumption that the original cost of £54,000 had been separately written down. After three years worth of WDA, this becomes £22,781, not £28,000.

---

*Overhead crane*
The overhead crane is a long-life asset costing £64,000, and its acquisition during the year ended 31 March 2000 will mean that Velo Ltd would exceed the *de minimis* limit of £100,000 should it also purchase the new overhead crane on 1 March 2000 (64,000 + 53,000 = £117,000). The crane is purchased and disposed of for the same value, and therefore does not impact upon the calculation of the long-life asset pool. No first-year allowances will be given for the new overhead crane, but WDAs will be given at the rate of 6%. Velo Ltd would be advised to postpone the purchase of the new overhead crane until 1 April 2000 or later, so as to avoid exceeding the £100,000 limit during the year ended 31 March 2000.

*Rollover relief*
The capital gain on the disposal of the factory will be reduced by £92,000 (28,000 + 64,000) to £354,322 (446,322 — 92,000). It will be possible to rollover the full gain against the cost of the replacement assets as the full sale proceeds of £828,000 (920,000 — 92,000) will now have been reinvested.

---

## 68     (Answer 2 of examination)

Part (a) tested candidates' knowledge of the rules determining residence in the UK, including people leaving the UK and coming to the UK. Parts (b) and (c) tested candidates' ability to advise on the income tax and capital gains tax implications for a person leaving the UK for:

(i)      a period of six months (remaining resident in the UK; and

(ii)     a period of eighteen months (becoming non-resident in the UK).

This was a popular question that was reasonably well answered.

In part (b), it was often not apparent which aspect of the question was being answered. When answering a question of this nature with two distinct sections (ie, the 6 and 18 month overseas periods), it is essential that each section is clearly labelled with a heading. The six month period was well answered, particularly the capital gains tax aspects. Whilst few candidates were aware that if the person was outside the UK for an eighteen month period then no capital gains tax liability would arise (note this no longer applies).

|  |  | Marks |
|---|---|---|
| (a) | 183 day rule | 1 |
| | 91 day rule | 1 |
| | Leaving the UK permanently | 1 |
| | Leaving the UK to work abroad | 1 |
| | Coming to the UK permanently/Three years | 1 |
| | Coming to the UK to take up employment | 1 |
| | | ___ |
| | Available | 6 |
| | | ___ |
| | Maximum | 5 |
| | | ___ |
| (b) | *Working overseas for six months* | |
| | Assessed on world-wide income | 1 |
| | Calculation of statutory income | 2 |
| | Wife's travel expenses | 1 |
| | Double taxation relief | 1 |
| | Plot of land | 2 |
| | Ordinary shares | 2 |
| | | |
| | *Working overseas for 18 months* | |
| | Not resident or ordinarily resident | 1 |
| | Liability to UK income tax | 1 |
| | Statutory total income/Double taxation relief | 2 |
| | CGT | 1 |
| | | ___ |
| | Available | 14 |
| | | ___ |
| | Maximum | 12 |
| | | ___ |
| (c) | *Working overseas for 18 months* | |
| | 91 day rule | 2 |
| | | ___ |
| | Available | 2 |
| | | ___ |
| | Maximum | 2 |
| | | ___ |
| | Available | 22 |
| | | ___ |
| | Maximum | 19 |
| | | ___ |

## Step by step answer plan

**Overview**

The theme of this question is clearly the tax implications of going to work abroad. (Overseas students doing the UK Tax option paper will hopefully forgive us for using examination terminology such as "abroad" or "foreign" when we really mean "outside the UK" or "non-UK".) The question has been simplified in the updating to remove a topic that no longer applies - the 100% exemption for overseas earnings where a 365 day period abroad is established. This was abolished in the FA 1998 and thereby gives the concession on non-residence much more importance. At the same time the trick of escaping CGT by using the concession was made much more difficult so personal "foreign element" questions are still highly likely. Note that the examiner's comments and marking guide have been edited to bring them into line with the updated version of the Q and A.

**Step 1**    For part (a) construct an answer dealing with the three questions - viz, general rules, departures and arrivals. There are only 5 marks so keep to the main points.

Step 2    For each of the two scenarios in part (b) describe the taxpayers residence status and effect this has on his IT and CGT liability and calculate the STI and CG amounts. There is no need to repeat the CG calculations in part (b)(ii) - a statement that the same result applies is sufficient. Note you are specifically told not to calculate the tax itself.

Step 3    Don't overlook the 2 easy marks in part (c).

## The examiner's answer

(a)    A person will be resident in the UK during a tax year if they are present in the UK for 183 days or more (the days of arrival and departure are ignored), or they visit the UK regularly, with visits averaging 91 days or more a tax year over a period of four or more consecutive tax years (days spent in the UK due to exceptional circumstances are ignored).

A person leaving the UK will be treated as not resident in the UK from the date of departure if they are to live permanently abroad. A person who leaves to work full-time abroad under a contract of employment will be treated as not resident in the UK during the term of the contract provided the period includes a complete tax year abroad.

A person coming to the UK to take up permanent residence or to stay for at least three years is treated as resident in the UK from the date of arrival. A person who comes to the UK to take up employment for at least two years is treated as resident in the UK from the date of arrival to the date of departure.

---

**Tutorial note**

From 17 March 1998 this split year treatment only applies for CGT if, for arrivals, the person was neither resident nor ordinarily resident in the UK in each of the 5 preceding years, or, for departures, if the person has been non resident and not ordinarily resident in the UK for at least 4 of the 7 previous years.

---

**Did you answer the question?**

You were not required to deal with the rules regarding ordinary residence (or domicile for that matter).

---

(b)    (i)    *Working overseas for a period of six months*

Barney will remain resident and ordinarily resident in the UK since the period abroad is less than a complete tax year. He will therefore be assessed on his world-wide income which will consist of the following:

|  | £ |
|---|---|
| Schedule E — Salary | 33,600 |
| Benefits ((2,400/2) + (850 × 5)) | 5,450 |
|  | 39,050 |
| Allowable deductions | 5,450 |
|  | 33,600 |
| Schedule A | 2,600 |
| Schedule D case V (5,460 × 100/70) | 7,800 |
| Statutory total income | 44,000 |

A deduction can be claimed for the travel and subsistence expenses paid by Sutol (UK) Ltd, but no deduction is available in respect of the £700 paid by Barney personally in respect of his wife's travel expenses. Double taxation relief will fully relieve the Yalamese tax of £2,340 (7,800 — 5,460) paid on the bank interest, since this is less than the UK tax on that income (savings income forms the top slice of income, and so the relevant tax rate is 40%).

---

Barney will be liable to CGT on the disposal of assets situated anywhere in the world. His chargeable gains are therefore as follows:

| *Plot of land in Yalam* | £ |
|---|---|
| Proceeds (180,000/8) | 22,500 |
| Cost (84,000/6) | 14,000 |
| | 8,500 |
| Indexation $14,000 \times \dfrac{162.6 - 150.2}{150.2}$ $(= 0.083)$ | 1,162 |
| | 7,338 |

| *Ordinary shares in ZYX plc* | |
|---|---|
| Deemed proceeds (8,000 at 212p) | 16,960 |
| Cost | 9,450 |
| | 7,510 |
| Indexation $9,450 \times \dfrac{162.6 - 150.2}{150.2}$ | 780 |
| | 6,730 |

(ii)    *Working overseas for a period of 18 months*

Barney will be treated as not resident or ordinarily resident in the UK from 1 November 1999 to 30 April 2001, since he is working full-time abroad and the term of the contract includes a complete tax year. He will therefore only be liable to UK income tax in respect of income arising in the UK during this period, but will be liable on his world-wide income up to the date of leaving the UK. His statutory total income for 1999-00 will be as follows:

| | £ |
|---|---|
| Schedule E —Salary (33,600 × 7/12) | 19,600 |
| Schedule A | 2,600 |
| Schedule D case V (7,800 × 7/12) | 4,550 |
| Statutory total income | 26,750 |

The bank interest will now be taxable at the rate of 20% in the UK, and double taxation relief will be restricted to this figure. Barney would only not be liable to CGT from the date of his departure if he remained abroad as non-resident for at least 5 years. Otherwise, disposals in the year of departure remain chargeable in that year. Thus both of his disposals are chargeable to UK tax as per (i) above.

(c)    *Working overseas for a period of 18 months*

Although Barney is abroad for a complete tax year, he will remain resident in the UK if return visits to the UK are 91 days or more a tax year on average (the 183 day rule is unlikely to be relevant to Barney). The income tax cost is considerable if this test is broken.

## 69    (Answer 3 of examination)

## Examiner's comments and marking guide

Part (a) tested candidates' ability to advise on the ways in which a company can relieve a trading loss; the ways in which a company can relieve a trading loss; (b) the companies to which the loss could be group relieved; and (c) the most beneficial loss relief claims.

This was a very popular question, with a number of very good answers. Most candidates had few problems with part (a) and (b), although some confused the income tax and corporation tax loss reliefs. When considering the most beneficial loss relief claims, it was not always appreciated that only one group relief claim could result in double taxation relief being wasted.

|     |                                           | Marks |
| --- | ----------------------------------------- | ----- |
| (a) | *Relieving the trading loss*              |       |
|     | 393(1) ICTA 1988                          | 1     |
|     | 393A(1) ICTA 1988 - current year          | 1     |
|     | 393A(1) ICTA 1988 - previous 12 months    | 1     |
|     | Restriction on carry back                 | 1     |
|     |                                           |       |
|     | Group relief                              | 1     |
|     | Restriction                               | 1     |
|     |                                           |       |
| (b) | *75% subsidiaries*                        |       |
|     | Qualification                             | 1     |
|     | Companies qualifying                      | 1     |
|     | Companies not qualifying                  | 1     |
|     |                                           |       |
| (c) | *Loss relief claims*                      |       |
|     | 393A(1) ICTA 1988                         | 1     |
|     | Amount of group relief                    | 1     |
|     | Marginal rate                             | 1     |
|     | Sinope Ltd                                | 1     |
|     | Oberon Ltd                                | 2     |
|     | Moon Ltd                                  | 1     |
|     | Rate of tax relief                        | 1     |

|           |    |
| --------- | -- |
| Available | 17 |
| Maximum   | 15 |

## Step by step answer plan

### Overview

This is a corporation tax "groups" question which has had to be simplified to remove topics no longer examinable. The examiner's comments and marking guide have been edited accordingly. Nevertheless, it remains a useful if uncomplicated exercise in making best use of a group loss. Note that you are not required to calculate corporation tax liabilities and any figure work will be fairly subsidiary to the written text required.

**Step 1**   Familiarise yourself with the group structure perhaps annotating the structure conveniently provided in the question to show acquisition dates and "looping" companies in a group relief relationship. A modified "loop" for consortium relationships would also be advisable if the situation arose as it is easy to overlook consortium relief. Rhea might be a consortium company but no detail is provided on the holders of its other 45% of shares so we cannot tell.

**Step 2** Answer part (a) in general terms and include a remark on the anti-avoidance restriction on carrying back losses where there has been a change of ownership etc. The question does not ask for the treatment of excess charges but the examiner's answer covers the point and it would be sensible to make a brief mention of group relieving excess charges.

**Step 3** Answer part (b) remembering that as only 3 marks are available excess detail is not required. Just state the conditions for group relief and whether those conditions are met for the companies concerned.

**Step 4** For part (c) you have to decide the optimum use of the loss. This usually requires identifying the marginal tax rates of potential claimants. Here there is an additional problem of interaction with double tax relief.

## The examiner's answer

(a)     Titan Ltd can relieve its Schedule DI trading loss as follows:

   (1)     Carrying the loss forward against future trading profits under s.393(1) ICTA 1988. No specific claim is required.

   (2)     Against the total profits of the six month period ended 31 March 2000 under s.393A(1) ICTA 1988. Relief is given before the set off of annual charges and is therefore not by itself beneficial, since the bank interest of £1,500 is fully covered by the royalty paid of £4,000.

   (3)     Provided a claim has been made under (2) above, a claim can then be made under s.393A(1) ICTA 1988 against the total profits of the 12 months preceding the loss making period. This claim is after the set off of trade charges. On 1 October 1999 there was a change in the ownership of Titan Ltd, so the carry back of losses will be disallowed under s.768 ICTA 1988 if there is a major change in the nature or conduct of the company's trade within three years of that date. The reorganisation may be treated as a major change. The claims under s.393A(1) ICTA 1988 must be made by 31 March 2002.

   (4)     Losses and excess charges can be surrendered to group companies under s.402 ICTA 1988. The claim must be made by the claimant company by 31 March 2002, and will require the consent of Titan Ltd. Group relief will be limited to the lower of Titan Ltd's trading losses and excess charges for the six months to 31 March 2000, and 6/12ths of the claimant company's PCTCT.

(b)     Titan Ltd will be able to group relieve its trading loss and excess charges to Moon Ltd and its 75% subsidiaries. To qualify as a 75% subsidiary, Moon Ltd must hold 75% or more of the subsidiary's ordinary share capital, and have the right to receive 75% or more of its distributable profits and net assets (were it to be wound up). Group relief can therefore be claimed by Moon Ltd, Oberon Ltd (85% holding) and Sinope Ltd (85% holding). Moon Ltd does not have the requisite 75% shareholding in Phobos Ltd (85% $\times$ 80% = 68%) or Rhea Ltd (55%).

(c)     The most important factor in deciding between the respective loss relief claims is the rate of corporation tax relief that will be obtained. A claim under s.393A(1) ICTA 1988 against the total profits of the year ended 30 September 1999 does not appear to be beneficial, since relief will only be obtained at the rate of 20.5%.

The amount available for group relief is therefore £97,500 (95,000 + (4,000 - 1,500)). Surrender should be made initially to companies subject to corporation tax at the marginal rate of 32.5%. For the Moon Ltd group of companies, the relevant lower and upper limits are £50,000 (300,000/6) and £250,000 (1,500,000/6) respectively, since there are five companies associated with Moon Ltd.

Sinope Ltd has paid overseas taxation at the rate of 36% (25,920/72,000 $\times$ 100) on its branch profits, and any surrender of group relief would result in DTR being wasted. Oberon Ltd's marginal tax rate is only 20%. The full group relief claim should therefore be made by Moon Ltd (£97,500 is less than £139,000 (278,000 $\times$ 6/12)). The first £28,000 (278,000 — 250,000) of the loss will be relieved at the rate of 30%, with the remainder relieved at 32.5%.

---

**Did you answer the question?**

Note that calculating the actual amounts of tax saved is not required.

---

| 70 | **(Answer 4 of examination)** |
|---|---|

**Examiner's comments and marking guide**

Part (a) tested candidates' ability to calculate a person's income tax liability for the first year of trading if (i) accounts are made up for a twelve month period, and (ii) if accounts are made up for a three month period (resulting in a trading loss). Part (b) tested candidates' ability to (i) calculate the additional profit arising from the delay of VAT registration, (ii) explain the advantages of the VAT annual accounting scheme. Part (c) tested candidates' knowledge of the criteria that are used in deciding whether a person is treated as employed or self-employed, and the implications of being incorrectly treated as self-employed. This was the least popular question after question 1, although it was reasonably well answered by many candidates. The calculations in part (a) caused few problems, although a number of candidates did not appreciate that the most beneficial loss relief claim was against income of the preceding three years under s.381 ICTA 1988. In part (b), few candidates were able to correctly calculate the additional profit arising from the delay of VAT registration, whilst the annual accounting scheme was often confused with the cash accounting scheme. Part (c) was generally well answered.

|   |   | Marks |
|---|---|---|
| (a) | *Year ended 31 December 2000* | |
|   | Schedule E | 1 |
|   | Schedule D | 2 |
|   | 1999-00 assessment | 1 |
|   | Personal allowance/Tax liability | 1 |
|   | Collected under PAYE/Payment on account | 1 |
|   | | |
|   | *Period ended 31 March 2000* | |
|   | Trading loss | 1 |
|   | S.381 ICTA 1988 claim | 1 |
|   | Income tax refund | 1 |
|   | Tax liability/Payments on account | 1 |
|   | Conclusion | 1 |
|   | | |
|   | Available | 11 |
|   | | |
|   | Maximum | 10 |
|   | | |
| (b) | *Additional profit* | 2 |
|   | Income | |
|   | Cost of goods sold | 2 |
|   | Pre-trading expenditure | 2 |
|   | | |
|   | *Late submission of VAT returns* | |
|   | Surcharge liability notice | 1 |
|   | Late payment | 1 |
|   | | |
|   | *Annual accounting scheme* | |
|   | VAT return | 1 |
|   | Payments on account | 1 |
|   | Advantages | 1 |
|   | Use of scheme | 1 |
|   | | |
|   | Available | 12 |
|   | | |
|   | Maximum | 10 |
|   | | |
| (c) | Contract of service/Contract for services | 1 |
|   | Control test | 1 |
|   | Mutual obligations test | 1 |
|   | The economic reality test | 1 |
|   | The integration test | 1 |
|   | Incorrect treatment | 1 |

|  | |
|---|---:|
| Available | 6 |
| Maximum | 5 |
| Available | 29 |
| Maximum | 25 |

## ( Step by step answer plan )

### Overview

This is a question showing an array of figures which is far less daunting than appears at first sight. It is otherwise a clearly attractive question because it is made up of three quite independent parts albeit related to the one basic situation. Some candidates are put off by VAT in a question. This is a pity because the VAT requirements invariably require only basic knowledge of VAT rules and some common-sense application.

**Step 1**    As all the requirements are linked to the same information it would be helpful to decide which bits of information can be related solely to part (a), (b) or (c). For example, the paragraph on the sub-contractor will only be relevant in part (c) whereas the final paragraph is only relevant to part (a).

**Step 2**    Answer part (a) (i) concentrating on how pay days arise under self-assessment. For example, you are expected to comment on why payments on account for 1999/00 will not be due. Whether the Sch D amount is calculated in a working note or on the face of your answer is at your discretion. Don't overlook the 2000/01 payment on account for 31 January 2000 which runs off the 1999/00 liability.

**Step 3**    Consider the relevance in part (ii) of closing off the first accounts within the first fiscal year. This produces an allowable loss and the cash flow advantage of a s381 claim. You are asked to "advise". Therefore the figures you calculate are secondary to the your decisions for best use and the description of the knock-on effects.

**Step 4**    For part (b) (i) you have to calculate the net VAT effect of being registered for the first six months when it could have been avoided. Again the calculation merely supports the explanation. This reflects practical situations where clients usually have to be advised in words rather than bare calculations.

**Step 5**    For part (ii) there is only 2 marks so just give a brief summary of the default surcharge rules relevant to the client's position of having missed one recent return deadline.

**Step 6**    Part (iii) requires a brief explanation of annual accounting noting that there are only 3 marks available.

**Step 7**    Finally don't overlook part (c). There are two matters to concentrate on. Firstly "categorisation" ie, how to decide on employed or self-employed "status". The discussion should cover the main principles tailored where appropriate to the particular situation. Secondly you have to explain Yaz's problems if he should have treated Albert as an employee.

**Step 8**    If time permits skim through the question to check you have not missed out any of the requirements.

## ( The examiner's answer )

(a)    (i)    Payments on account are not due for 1999-00 since Yaz's income tax liability for 1998-99 would have been met under PAYE. The total income tax liability for 1999-00 will therefore be due on 31 January 2001. This is as follows:

|  | £ | £ |
|---|---:|---:|
| Schedule E (42,000 × 8/12) | | 28,000 |
| Schedule D Case I | | |
| Profit per accounts | 50,300 | |
| Pre-trading expenditure | (1,400) | |

|  |  |  |
|---|---|---|
| First-year allowance (18,000 at 40%) | (7,200) |  |
|  | 41,700 |  |
| 1999-00 assessment (41,700 × 3/12) |  | 10,425 |
|  |  | 38,425 |
| Personal allowance |  | 4,335 |
| Taxable income |  | 34,090 |
| Income tax: 1,500 at 10% |  | 150 |
| 26,500 at 23% |  | 6,095 |
| 6,090 at 40% |  | 2,436 |
|  |  | 8,681 |
| Tax collected under PAYE |  | 7,080 |
|  |  | 1,601 |
| Payment on account due for 2000-01 — 50% |  | 800 |
| Due 31 January 2001 |  | 2,401 |

---

### Did you answer the question?

You were not required to account for the Class 4 NIC which would have been due on 31 January 2001. This is fortunate as it would have required consideration of the annual NIC maximum - Class 1 having been paid up to November 1999 with Class 2 thereafter.

---

(ii)    If Yaz makes up his accounts for the three months to 31 March 2000 he will have a trading loss for 1999-00 of £9,800 calculated as follows:

|  | £ |
|---|---|
| Loss per accounts | 1,200 |
| Pre-trading expenditure | 1,400 |
| First-year allowance | 7,200 |
|  | 9,800 |

The most beneficial claim would appear to be under s.381 ICTA 1988 against the Schedule E income for 1996-97. This could result in an income tax refund of £3,920 (9,800 at 40%) if Yaz's income for 1996-97 was sufficiently high. No tax liability will arise until 31 January 2002, since payments on account will not be due for 2000-01 (the income tax liability for 1999-00 is met under PAYE), and a refund of PAYE will be due for 1999-00. In addition, no overlap profits will arise. There is therefore a short-term cash flow advantage in making up accounts to 31 March 2000 (and subsequently 31 March 2001), although the tax liability for 2000-01 is likely to be considerably higher than if accounts are made up to 31 December 2000.

(b)    (i)    If Yaz had delayed his VAT registration until 1 July 2000, then the output VAT charged during the period 1 January to 30 June 2000 would have been additional income. This is because sales are to the general public, and so Yaz could have still charged the same selling price. Input VAT could have still been recovered on the standard rated expenses (incurred within 6 months of registration), stock held at 1 July 2000 and the printing equipment. Input VAT would not be recovered in respect of the advertising as this is incurred outside the 6 month time limit. The additional profit made from delaying VAT registration until 1 July 2000 is as follows:

|  | £ | £ |
|---|---|---|
| Additional income (output VAT) |  |  |
| 19,400 + 28,600 = 48,000 at 17.5% |  | 8,400 |
| Additional expenditure (input VAT) |  |  |

---

Cost of goods sold
      14,900 + 16,700 + 3,600—4,400 = 30,800 at 17.5%       5,390
      Pre-trading expenditure 1,400 at 17.5%       245
                                                                                          5,635

      Additional profit                                                      2,765

(ii)    Although the first VAT return due on 30 April 2000 is in respect of a VAT repayment, its late submission will result in HM Customs & Excise issuing a surcharge liability notice specifying a surcharge period running to 31 March 2001. A late payment of VAT during the surcharge period will result in a surcharge plus an extension of the surcharge period. The surcharge is initially 2% of the VAT due, but can rise to a maximum of 15% if four or more payments are late.

(iii)   Under the annual accounting scheme only one VAT return is submitted each year, and this is due two months after the year end. Nine monthly payments on account must be made, based on the previous year's VAT liability. Any balance is due when the VAT return is submitted. The late payment of a payment on account does not lead to a surcharge liability notice (although it is then necessary to leave the scheme). The use of the annual accounting scheme will therefore be beneficial to Yaz as the reduced administration required should mean that default surcharges are avoided. However, Yaz cannot apply to use the scheme until he has been registered for 12 months, and at that date he must be up to date with his VAT returns and the expected taxable turnover for the next 12 months must not exceed £300,000.

---

### Did you answer the question?

As Yaz's turnover is clearly above £100,000 you were not required to explain the modifications to the annual accounting scheme where turnover is below that level.

---

(c)    When considering Yaz's contract with Albert the essential distinction is between a contract of service (employed) and a contract for services (self-employed). There are a number of tests that have to be considered, and no single test will be conclusive:

*The control test:*  If Yaz has control over Albert as to how his work is performed, then this indicates a contract of service.

*The mutual obligations test:*  If Yaz has an obligation to provide work, and Albert has an obligation to do the work provided, then this indicates a contract of service.

*The economic reality test:*  If the activities of Albert form a profession in their own right, then this indicates a contract for services. For example, does he have his own premises and printing equipment, can he profit from sound management, and does he take a degree of financial risk?

*The integration test:*  If Albert is an integral part of Yaz's business, then this indicates a contract of service. For example, is he entitled to holiday pay?

If Albert uses his own premises and printing equipment, he is likely to be treated as self-employed even if he works full-time for Yaz.

*Incorrect treatment*
As an employer, Yaz would be responsible for applying PAYE, deducting employee's class 1 NIC and accounting for employer's class 1 NIC. If Albert is incorrectly treated as self-employed, then Yaz will be liable for any loss of tax or NIC, and may be liable to penalties and interest.

| 71 | **(Answer 5 of examination)** |
|---|---|

**Examiner's comments and marking guide**

Part (a) tested candidates' knowledge of (i) PEPs, TESSAs and unit trusts, (ii) personal pension schemes, (iii) venture capital trusts and (iv) government stocks. Part (b) tested candidates' knowledge of (i) the difference between a tied adviser and an independent adviser, and (ii) the Statements of Principle issued by the ACCA. This was another reasonably popular question, although answers were not as good as expected for what is an important topic that is regularly examined. The main problem was a lack of depth in the answers given, with many candidates showing poor examination technique by repeating the same points several times. PEPs and TESSAs were dealt with well, although the tax implications of unit trusts were often incorrectly stated or ignored altogether. A disappointing number of candidates could not calculate the maximum tax deductible personal pension premium, and there was little discussion as to when this should be paid. The income tax and capital gains tax implications of investing in venture capital trusts and government stocks were often not understood, and there was little knowledge of the accrued income scheme. The first requirement of part (b) was well answered, but few candidates were aware of the Statements of Principle issued by the ACCA.

The question has been updated to exclude PEPs and TESSAs – no longer available – but to replace them with ISAs being the practical successor to these tax favoured 'vehicles'. The marking guide is amended accordingly.

|  |  |  | *Marks* |
|---|---|---|---:|
| (a) | *Option 1* | | |
| | ISAs | — Exemption | 1 |
| | | — Tax credits/withdrawals | 1 |
| | | — Investment limits | 1 |
| | Unit trust | | 1 |
| | Tax saving | | 1 |
| | Capital growth | | 1 |
| | Risk/Liquidity | | 1 |
| | | | |
| | *Option 2* | | |
| | Tax deductible amount | | 2 |
| | Income tax saving | | 1 |
| | Payment during 1999-00 | | 1 |
| | Payment during 2000-01 | | 1 |
| | Benefits on retirement | | 1 |
| | Suitability | | 1 |
| | | | |
| | *Option 3* | | |
| | Tax relief/Five year period | | 1 |
| | Dividends/Disposal | | 1 |
| | Re-investment relief | | 1 |
| | Suitability | | 1 |
| | | | |
| | *Option 4* | | |
| | Paid gross | | 1 |
| | Disposals/No maximum limit | | 1 |
| | Accrued income scheme | | 1 |
| | Suitability | | 1 |
| | | | |
| | | Available | 22 |
| | | | |
| | | Maximum | 21 |
| | | | |
| (b) | *Advisers* | | |
| | Tied advisers/independent advisers | | 1 |
| | | | |
| | *Statements of principle* | | |
| | Integrity/Skill, care and diligence | | 1 |
| | Information | | 1 |

Conflict of interests/safeguard assets                                                              1
Financial resources/regulator                                                                       1
                                                                                                  ___

                                                                                Available            5
                                                                                                  ___

                                                                                Maximum              4
                                                                                                  ___

                                                                                Available           27
                                                                                                  ___

                                                                                Maximum             25
                                                                                                  ___

## Step by step answer plan

**Overview**

The theme of this question is personal financial planning with a consideration of the FSA requirements for being a financial adviser. You have to take careful note of the client's investment criteria.

**Step 1**    For part (a) there are 4 separate investment options to consider and within each you must explain the personal tax implications and discuss their suitability for the client's investment criteria. Thus the structure of your answer is pre-determined.

**Step 2**    Part (b) requires a copy out of material in your study text. There is only 4 marks available so be brief.

## The examiner's answer

(a)    *Option 1*

Income and gains realised on investments held within an ISA are exempt from income tax and CGT. The tax credits on dividends and interest received are reclaimed by the account manager (although for dividends this is only possible until 5 April 2004). Withdrawals from an ISA can be made at any time and are free of CGT. The annual equity investment limit is £5,000 although for 1999/00 – the first year ISAs are available – the limit is £7,000.

The balance of £18,000 (25,000 — 7,000) invested in a unit trust will not attract any tax relief. Distributions from unit trusts are received net of 10% tax, taxed as dividend income, and disposals are subject to CGT.

This option will not reduce Mary's 1999-00 tax liability (it may increase it), although the exemption from income tax for ISAs will save tax at the rate of 32.5%. Funds invested in an equity ISA can be applied in acquiring a wide range of investments, including ordinary shares, investment trusts and unit trusts, so it is possible to invest for capital growth. Neither the ISA nor the unit trust investments would normally be considered as high risk, and can all be easily liquidated in four years time if necessary without any tax exemption being forfeited. Mary would be advised to look at a wide range of ISAs and unit trusts, rather than just those offered by the bank.

*Option 2*

Mary's maximum tax deductible personal pension premium is £27,250 calculated as follows:

|         | Net relevant earnings £ | Relevant percentage | Maximum premium £ |
|---------|------------------------:|--------------------:|------------------:|
| 1993-94 | 46,200                  | 17.5                | 8,085             |
| 1994-95 | 12,600                  | 17.5                | 2,205             |
| 1997-98 | 8,100                   | 20                  | 1,620             |
| 1998-99 | 18,300                  | 20                  | 3,660             |
| 1999-00 | 58,400                  | 20                  | 11,680            |
|         |                         |                     | _____           |
|         |                         |                     | 27,250            |

Mary can therefore contribute the full £25,000 into a personal pension scheme, and this will reduce her 1999-00 income tax liability by £10,000 (25,000 at 40%). Only £1,065 (58,400 - 4,335 – 28,000 - 25,000) of the partnership profits will then be taxable at 40%. If the premium is paid during 1999-00 then this will also reduce the 2000-01 payments on account. Alternatively, the premium can be paid during 2000-01 with Mary electing to relate it back to 1999-00, but this will not reduce payments on account. 1999-00 is the final year in which the unused relief of £8,085 from 1993-94 can be utilised. Benefits under a personal pension can be taken when Mary reaches 50, and at that date she can withdraw 25% of the accumulated fund as a tax-free lump sum. The pension will be taxable.

This option will reduce Mary's tax liability for 1999-00, should result in capital growth, and should not be high risk. However, the capital will not be available in four years time.

*Option 3*

Provided Mary subscribes for new ordinary shares in a venture capital trust (VCT), then she will obtain tax relief of £5,000 (25,000 at 20%) in respect of the investment (it is below the annual limit of £100,000). The shares must be held for five years or the tax relief will be withdrawn. Dividends received are exempt from income tax, and any disposal should be exempt from CGT. Mary will also be entitled to deferral relief if she has a chargeable gain during the period beginning one year before and ending one year after the date of subscription.

This option will reduce Mary's 1999-00 income tax liability, and may result in capital growth. However, VCT's must be considered as high risk, and a disposal in four years time will result in a withdrawal of the tax relief.

*Option 4*

Interest on government stocks is paid gross but Mary will be liable to income tax on the interest received. Disposals of government stocks are exempt from CGT. Purchasing stock ex div and selling it cum div is known as bondwashing, and is caught by the accrued income scheme. This applies if an individual holds stock with a total nominal value in excess of £5,000, and will result in the interest included in the selling price being effectively treated as taxable income. There is generally no maximum limit as to the amount that can be invested.

This option will not reduce Mary's 1999-00 income tax liability (it may increase it). Mary could buy short dated stocks due for redemption in four years time. She will then be certain of maintaining her capital intact, and be able to achieve capital growth. Government stocks are not high risk, and can be easily liquidated in four years time.

(b)    *Advisers*

Tied advisers only recommend the investment products of the one financial institution to which they are tied, whilst independent advisers (who are not tied to any financial institution) can recommend investment products from any source. The insurance salesperson will be a tied adviser, and the bank manager appears to be as well. The partner and post office manager are not financial advisers.

*Statements of principle*
An authorised person should:
(1)    Act with high standards of integrity and fair conduct.
(2)    Act with due skill, care and diligence.
(3)    Obtain relevant information about, and provide appropriate information to, clients.
(4)    Avoid conflicts of interest.
(5)    Safeguard assets held on behalf of clients.
(6)    Maintain adequate financial resources and internal organisation.
(7)    Deal with the regulator (ACCA) in an open and co-operative manner.

## 72    (Answer 6 of examination)

### Examiner's comments and marking guide

Part (a) tested candidates' ability to calculate the inheritance tax liability arising on a person's death, including the impact of lifetime transfers. Part (b) tested candidates' ability to advise on the capital gains tax and inheritance tax implications of a disposal of shares in an unquoted trading company at an under valuation. Part (c) tested candidates' ability to advise on the tax implications of a company purchasing its own shares. This was the most popular question on the paper, and was very well answered by many candidates. The calculations in part (a) caused few problems, although some candidates incorrectly treated the shares as a separate lifetime gift, despite the gift being clearly made on death. In part (b) the different share valuation rules for capital gains tax and inheritance tax purposes were not appreciated by a number of candidates. Part (c) was well answered, although some candidates wasted time by explaining the conditions to be met for the purchase to be treated as a capital gain when this was clearly not a requirement of the question.

|  |  |  | Marks |
|---|---|---|---|
| (a) | Lifetime transfer 10 February 1996 |  | 1 |
|  | Lifetime transfer 4 June 1996 |  | 1 |
|  | Shares in Expanse plc |  | 1 |
|  | Shares in Bluetone Ltd/Units in World-Growth |  | 1 |
|  | Business property relief not available |  | 1 |
|  | Building society deposits/Life assurance policy |  | 1 |
|  | Income tax/funeral expenses |  | 1 |
|  | Realty |  | 1 |
|  | IHT liability/IHT due by Melody |  | 2 |
|  | Due date |  | 1 |
|  |  | Available | 11 |
|  |  | Maximum | 10 |
| (b) | *Capital gains tax* |  |  |
|  | Gift relief |  | 2 |
|  | Deemed consideration |  | 1 |
|  | Cost/Indexation |  | 1 |
|  | Taper relief |  | 1 |
|  | Annual exemption/CGT |  | 1 |
|  | *Inheritance tax* |  |  |
|  | Value transferred |  | 2 |
|  | Business property relief |  | 1 |
|  |  | Available | 9 |
|  |  | Maximum | 8 |
| (c) | *Capital gain* |  |  |
|  | Entitlement to retirement relief |  | 1 |
|  | Capital gain |  | 1 |
|  | Retirement relief |  | 1 |
|  | Taper relief |  | 1 |
|  | CGT |  | 1 |
|  | *Distribution* |  |  |
|  | Additional income tax liability |  | 1 |
|  | Conclusion |  | 1 |
|  |  | Available | 7 |
|  |  | Maximum | 7 |
|  |  | Available | 27 |
|  |  | Maximum | 25 |

## Step by step answer plan

### Overview

This is the capital taxes question and it comes in three relatively independent sections. It isn't even necessary to split up the information in the question between the three parts. In the first part you have to list out an estate on death, identify the unused part of the nil band following lifetime transfers, calculate the IHT on a specific legacy out of the death estate and state when the tax is payable. All the knowledge was mainstream. For part (b) you have to calculate the CGT and potential IHT position resulting from a sale of shares at undervalue. Finally you have to advise on whether a purchase of own shares by a company is more efficient as a capital disposal or as a distribution.

**Step 1**    Read through the part of the question involving Melody and decide the steps to take for your answer.

**Step 2**    Show how much of Melody's father's IHT nil band remains at his death. Whether you follow the examiner's approach or lay out your workings in computational format is at your discretion though you are less likely to make a mistake with the latter method.

**Step 3**    Schedule out the estate at death showing the prices taken for valuing such assets as quoted shares. It is always difficult to know the level of explanation to provide. Here the examiner explains why BPR is not available but avoids mentioning why gambling debts are ignored. Arguably both points should be mentioned. Obviously if you have, say, valued the life policy correctly from a choice of two values you probably appreciate the correct approach and further comment is unnecessary.

**Step 4**    Finally for part (a) calculate the estate rate of tax and hence the tax due by Melody, and refer to the pay day and instalment option.

**Step 5**    For part (b) first calculate the CGT effect of the sale of shares at undervalue, apply gift relief, then taper relief, then the AE and then compute the CGT.

**Step 6**    Next show the value transferred for IHT purposes not forgetting that there are different valuation rules for CGT and IHT. Comment on the BPR position.

**Step 7**    Finally prepare the computations for part (c), including sufficient explanation of the treatment applied and stating clearly the preferred treatment

## The examiner's answer

(a)    Both the lifetime transfers are within seven years of the death of Melody's father. The wedding gift on 10 February 1996 is valued at £19,000 (£30,000 less marriage exemption (£5,000) and annual exemptions for 1995-96 and 1994-95 2 × £3,000)). The gift into a discretionary trust on 4 June 1996 is valued at £150,000 (£153,000 less annual exemption 1996-97 (£3,000)). The proportion of the nil rate band not utilised is £62,000 (231,000 - 19,000 - 150,000).

|  | £ | £ |
|---|---|---|
| Estate at death — 15 February 2000 |  |  |
| Personalty |  |  |
| Ordinary shares in Bluetone Ltd |  |  |
| (50,000 at £11.00) |  | 550,000 |
| Ordinary shares in Expanse plc |  |  |
| (42,000 at 303p ((282 + 324)/2)) |  | 127,260 |
| Units in World-Growth (26,000 80p) |  | 20,800 |
| Building society deposits |  | 32,000 |
| Life assurance policy |  | 61,000 |
|  |  | ——— |
|  |  | 791,060 |
| Income tax | 6,600 |  |
| Funeral expenses | 3,460 |  |
|  | ——— |  |
|  |  | 10,060 |
|  |  | ——— |
|  |  | 781,000 |

| | | |
|---|---:|---:|
| Realty | | |
| Main residence | 125,000 | |
| Repayment mortgage | 42,000 | |
| | ——— | 83,000 |
| | | ——— |
| Chargeable estate | | 864,000 |
| | | ——— |
| IHT liability | | |
| 62,000 at nil% | | Nil |
| 864,000 — 62,000 = 802,000 at 40% | | 320,800 |
| | | ——— |
| | | 320,800 |
| | | ——— |

Business property relief is not available in respect of the shares in Bluetone Ltd because Melody's father did not own them for two years. The rate of IHT on the estate is 37.13% (320,800/864,000 × 100), so Melody will have to pay IHT of £204,215 (550,000 at 37.13%). This will be due on the earlier of 31 August 2000 or the delivery of the executor's account, or alternatively it can be paid in 10 equal annual installments commencing on 31 August 2000.

---

**Tutorial notes**

1. The gambling debts are not an allowable deduction because they are not legally enforceable (even if there may be other reasons why they are likely to be honoured by the beneficiaries!)

2. Specific legacies are free of IHT unless the will specifies to the contrary.

---

(b)     *Capital gains tax*

The consideration paid by Liam's son exceeds the allowable cost by £45,000 (75,000 — 30,000), and this amount is immediately chargeable to CGT. Provided that Liam and his son jointly elect, the balance of the gain can be held over as a gift of business assets since Bluetone Ltd is an unquoted trading company. A CGT liability of £12,460 will be due on 31 January 2001 as follows:

| | £ |
|---|---:|
| Deemed consideration (30,000 at £9.00) | 270,000 |
| Cost | 30,000 |
| | ——— |
| | 240,000 |
| Indexation $30,000 \times \dfrac{162.6 - 139.9}{139.9}$ | 4,868 |
| | ——— |
| | 235,132 |
| Gift relief (235,132 — 45,000) | 190,132 |
| | ——— |
| | 45,000 |
| Tapered to 85% | 38,250 |
| Annual exemption | 7,100 |
| | ——— |
| Chargeable gain | 31,150 |
| | ——— |
| Capital gains tax at 40% | 12,460 |

---

**Tutorial note**

It seems odd that a 32 year old woman would have a son old enough to pay £75,000 for shares in his own right and to legally join in an election to hold over a gain but there is no need to read too much into the question! The ages were probably chosen to avoid any thoughts of retirement relief and the examiner overlooked the practical impact. In any case if the son was still a minor the same effect is achievable if funds from, say, a grandparent are held in trust for him and the trustees effect the transactions.

---

*Inheritance tax*

Liam's disposal of 30,000 shares in Bluetone Ltd at an under valuation will be a PET for £425,000 as follows:

|  |  | £ |
|---|---|---:|
| Value of shares held before the transfer | | |
| 50,000 × £15.00 | | 750,000 |
| Value of shares held after the transfer | | |
| 20,000 × £12.50 | | 250,000 |
| | | 500,000 |
| Consideration paid | | 75,000 |
| Value transferred | | 425,000 |

Business property relief at the rate of 100% will be available, so an IHT liability will only arise if Liam dies before 20 March 2007 and his son has disposed of the shares before that date (subject to the replacement property rules).

(c)    *Treated as a capital gain*

Noel will be entitled to retirement relief because he is over 50 years old, is a full-time working director of Bluetone Ltd, which is a trading company, and owns not less than 5% of its ordinary share capital. Retirement relief will be restricted by a factor of 75% since Noel will have been a director and shareholder for seven years six months. His CGT liability for 1999-00 due on 31 January 2001 is as follows:

|  | £ | £ |
|---|---:|---:|
| Sales proceeds | | 550,000 |
| Cost | | 50,000 |
| | | 500,000 |
| Indexation 50,000 × $\dfrac{162.6 - 139.9}{139.9}$ | | 8,113 |
| | | 491,887 |
| Retirement relief | | |
| 200,000 × 75% | 150,000 | |
| 491,887 − 150,000 = 341,887 × 50% | 170,943 | |
| | | 320,943 |
| | | 170,944 |
| Tapered to 85% | | 145,302 |
| Annual exemption | | 7,100 |
| Chargeable gain | | 138,202 |
| Capital gains tax at 40% | | 55,281 |

*Treated as a distribution*

Noel will be assessed on a grossed up distribution of £555,556 (500,000 × 100/90). This will result in an additional income tax liability of £125,000 (555,556 at 32.5% = 180,556 − 55,556) for 1999-00, which will be due on 31 January 2001.

*Conclusion*

The special treatment results in a tax saving of £69,719 (125,000 − 55,281). It is therefore beneficial, and is in any case compulsory if the relevant conditions are met.

**Did you answer the question?**

You were not required to state the conditions necessary for capital gains treatment to apply. The original question also required a comment on the effect on the company of making a distribution -ie, the requirement to account for advance corporation tax but ACT is abolished from 6 April 1999.

## DECEMBER 1998 QUESTIONS

## 73 (Question 1 of examination)

Ming Wong, aged 63, was born in the country of Yanga, but has lived in the UK since 6 April 1985. Ming is resident and ordinarily resident in the UK, but is not domiciled in the UK. Following her marriage to a UK citizen, Ming is planning to become UK domiciled.

Ming is employed by the Yangan National Bank in London, and was paid a salary of £31,040 during 1999-00. At 5 April 2000 Ming owned the following assets:

(1) A main residence valued at £245,000. This is situated in the UK, and has an outstanding endowment mortgage of £80,000.

(2) A house in Yanga worth £60,000, from which rental income of £7,500 (gross) was received during 1999-00. Yangan tax at the rate of 35% was paid on the rental income.

(3) 40,000 shares in Ganyan Inc., a company quoted on the Yangan Stock Exchange at 308 – 316. Dividends of £5,950 (net) were received during 1999-00, after the deduction of Yangan tax at the rate of 15%.

(4) Antiques worth £35,000. These were bought in Yanga, but are now situated in Ming's UK residence.

(5) Bank deposits of £50,000 with the Yangan National Bank, of which £30,000 is held at the London branch and £20,000 at the main branch in Yanga. During 1999-00 interest of £1,680 (net) was credited to the account in London, and £1,530 (net of Yangan tax at the rate of 15%) was credited to the account in Yanga.

(6) An interest-free loan of £15,000 to Ming's brother who is resident in Yanga. The loan was used to purchase property situated in the UK.

(7) Ming has recently become the beneficiary of a trust set up by her father. Under the terms of the trust, she is entitled to receive all of the trust income, although no income was actually received during 1999-00. The trust owns UK government stocks with a nominal value of £20,000, quoted at 92 – 94. Ming's father was domiciled in Yanga at the time of setting up the trust.

None of the income arising in Yanga has been remitted to the UK.

Under the terms of her will, Ming has left all of her assets to her three children. If she were to die, Yangan death duty of £48,000 would be payable in respect of the house situated in Yanga and the 40,000 shares in Ganyan Inc., irrespective of her domicile.

There is no double taxation agreement between the UK and Yanga. All of the above figures are in Pounds sterling.

**You are required to:**

(a) Advise Ming of (i) when she will be treated as domiciled in the UK for the purposes of IHT, and (ii) how she could acquire domicile in the UK under general law. **(4 marks)**

(b) Advise Ming as to the potential increase in her liability to UK IHT if she were to become domiciled in the UK. Your answer should include an explanation of why Ming's assets are or are not subject to UK IHT. **(12 marks)**

(c) (i) Calculate the UK income tax payable by Ming for 1999-00.

(ii) Calculate the additional UK income tax that would have been payable by Ming for 1999-00 if she had been domiciled in the UK as from 6 April 1999. **(9 marks)**

**(Total: 25 marks)**

## 74 (Question 2 of examination)

(a) Tony Tort commenced <u>self-employment as a solicitor on 6 April 1998</u>. His tax adjusted <u>Schedule DII profit</u> for the first year of trading to 5 April 1999 was <u>£58,500</u>, and the income tax and <u>class 4 NIC liability</u> for 1998-99 based on this figure was £18,000. The Inland Revenue issued a tax return for 1998-99 on 31 May 1999, but Tony did not submit this until 15 April 2000. He has made the following payments of income tax and class 4 NIC during 2000:

1998-99 Balancing payment *Sur charge.* £18,000 paid 10 May 2000
1999-00 First payment on account *No surcharge* £2,500 paid 15 June 2000
1999-00 Second payment on account £2,500 paid 31 July 2000

*Due dates*
*31\1\00* } *interest*
*31/1/00* *&*
*31/7/00* } *surcharges.*

Because of <u>cash flow problems,</u> Tony claimed to reduce each of his payments on account for 1999-00 from £9,000 to £2,500.

Tony's tax adjusted Schedule DII profit for the year ended 5 April 2000 (before capital allowances) is £52,100. He purchased a new computer on 15 May 1999 for £2,600 and a new photocopier on 20 January 2000 for £5,500. The tax written-down values of plant and machinery and Tony's motor car at 6 April 1999 were £13,600 and £17,800 respectively. The private use of the motor car is 10%.

Prior to 6 April 1998 Tony was employed by a firm of solicitors. He is single, and has no other income or outgoings.

**You are required to:**

(i) Calculate the interest on overdue tax that Tony will be charged in respect of the late payments of income tax and class 4 NIC made during 2000. You should assume that the balancing payment for 1999-00 is made on the due date (use an interest rate of 10%).

(ii) Explain what surcharges and penalties Tony may be liable to. **(12 marks)**

(b) On 10 September 2000 Tony received written notice from the Inland Revenue that they were to enquire into his tax return for 1998-99. The Inland Revenue gave written notice of the completion of the enquiry on 5 December 2000, stating that he had incorrectly claimed for entertaining expenditure of £4,500 in calculating his tax adjusted Schedule DII profit for the year ended 5 April 1999.

No adjustment is required to Tony's tax adjusted Schedule DII profit for the year ended 5 April 2000.

**You are required to:**

(i) State the possible reasons why the Inland Revenue has enquired into Tony's tax return for 1998-99.

(ii) Explain the options open to Tony following the completion of the Inland Revenue enquiry.

(iii) Advise Tony of the interest on overdue tax, surcharges and penalties that he may be liable to as a result of the Inland Revenue enquiry into his 1998-99 tax return. **(7 marks)**

(c) Tony is planning to make a contribution of £20,000 into a personal pension scheme on 15 February 2001. A claim will then be made to relate the contribution back so that it is treated as paid during 1999-00.

Tony is aged 43, and prior to 6 April 1998 was a member of the occupational pension scheme run by his employer.

**You are required to:**

Advise Tony of the tax implications of making the contribution into a personal pension scheme and claiming to relate it back to 1999-00. Your answer should include a calculation of the maximum tax deductible contribution that Tony could make into a personal pension scheme for 1999-00.

**(6 marks)**
**(Total: 25 marks)**

---

## 75    (Question 3 of examination)

(a)    Star Ltd has two 100% subsidiaries, Zodiac Ltd and Exotic Ltd. All three companies are involved in the construction industry.  The results of each company for the year ended 31 March 2000 are as follows:

|  | Star Ltd £ | Zodiac Ltd £ | Exotic Ltd £ |
|---|---|---|---|
| Tax adjusted Schedule DI profit/(loss) | (125,000) | 650,000 | 130,000 |
| Capital gain/(loss) | 130,000 | (8,000) | – |
| Royalty paid (gross) | (10,000) | – | – |
| Franked investment income | – | – | 15,000 |

Star Ltd's capital gain arose from the sale of a warehouse on 15 April 1999 for £380,000. As at 31 March 1999 Star Ltd had unused trading losses of £7,500.

**You are required to:**

Calculate the corporation tax liability for each of the group companies for the year ended 31 March 2000. You should assume that reliefs are claimed in the most favourable manner.                    **(8 marks)**

(b)    Star Ltd is considering the following alternative ways of reinvesting the proceeds of £380,000 from the sale of its warehouse on 15 April 1999:

(1)    A freehold office building can be purchased for £290,000.

(2)    A leasehold office building on a 45-year lease can be purchased for a premium of £400,000.

(3)    A loan could be made to Zodiac Ltd so that it can purchase a freehold warehouse for £425,000.

Regardless of which alternative is chosen, the reinvestment will take place during February 2001.

**You are required to:**

(i)    Advise Star Ltd as to the 'rollover relief' that will be available in respect of each of the three alternative reinvestments.

(ii)    Briefly explain how the claims for rollover relief will affect the way in which Star Ltd's Schedule DI loss for the year ended 31 March 2000 is relieved (as per (a)).                    **(9 marks)**
                                                                                    **(Total: 17 marks)**
                                                                                    *(as amended)*

---

## 76    (Question 4 of examination)

Sally and Trevor Acre, a married couple aged 53 and 48 respectively, have been in partnership as estate agents since 1 October 1996. Due to Sally's ill health, they are to sell the business on 31 March 2000 to an unrelated third party. You should assume that today's date is 15 March 2000. The following information is available:

(1)    Tax adjusted Schedule DII profits/(losses) are as follows:

|  | £ |
|---|---|
| Period ended 31 March 1997 | 48,000 |
| Year ended 31 March 1998 | 74,000 |
| Year ended 31 March 1999 | 52,000 |
| Year ended 31 March 2000 (estimated) | (68,000) |

These figures are all net of capital allowances.

(2)    Profits and losses, whether revenue or capital in nature, have always been shared 70% to Sally and 30% to Trevor.

---

(3)     The market values of the partnership assets at 31 March 2000 are forecast to be as follows:

|  | £ |
|---|---|
| Goodwill | 110,000 |
| Freehold property | 230,000 |
| Fixtures and fittings | 140,000 |
| Net current assets | 70,000 |
|  | 550,000 |

The freehold property was purchased on 1 October 1996 for £187,850 (indexed to April 1998). The fixtures and fittings qualify as plant and machinery for capital allowances purposes. The partnership assets will all be sold on 31 March 2000 for their market value.

(4)     Sally personally owns a leasehold office building that is used rent-free by the partnership. She was granted a 25-year lease on 1 July 1997 for £91,500 (indexed to April 1998). This property is to be sold on 31 March 2000 for £90,000.

(5)     Sally has Schedule A profits of £6,000 p.a., and Trevor receives building society interest of £1,600 (net) p.a. Neither of them plans to reinvest the proceeds from the sale of the business.

**You are required to:**

(a)     Advise Sally and Trevor of the chargeable gains that will be assessed on them for 1999-00 (before taking account of taper relief). Your answer should include an explanation as to the amount of retirement relief that will be available.                                                                                                           **(8 marks)**

(b)     (i)     State the possible ways of relieving the partnership's Schedule DII trading loss of £68,000 for the year ended 31 March 2000.

        (ii)    Advise Sally and Trevor as to which loss relief claims would be the most beneficial for them.

        (iii)   After taking into account your advice in (ii), calculate Sally and Trevor's taxable income for the tax years 1996-97 to 1999-00, and their net chargeable gains for 1999-00 (after taking account of taper relief).

You should assume that the tax rates and allowances for 1999-00 apply throughout.             **(17 marks)**
                                                                                                              **(Total:  25 marks)**

---

## 77     (Question 5 of examination)

Schooner Ltd is an unquoted company that constructs yachts. The company has recently accepted a large contract to supply yachts to Highseas plc. The new contract will commence on 1 January 2000, and will have the following implications for Schooner Ltd:

(a)     Each yacht will take three months to construct, and will be sold for £350,000. Highseas plc will pay a deposit of £50,000 at the beginning of the three-month period, and a further payment on account of £100,000 two months later. An invoice for the total price of £350,000 plus VAT will be raised ten days after completion of each yacht, and the balance due will be paid within 60 days. The three-monthly construction periods will be coterminous with Schooner Ltd's quarterly VAT periods.

(b)     Schooner Ltd will acquire new equipment costing £800,000 on 1 January 2000.

        (1)     The company has sufficient funds to purchase £250,000 of the equipment outright, and all of this is to be imported into the UK. Equipment costing £160,000 will be imported from countries that are members of the European Union, with the remainder imported from countries that are outside the European Union.

(2)    Equipment costing £200,000 will be bought on hire purchase, with the company making 16 quarterly payments of £17,250 commencing on 1 January 2000. VAT will be paid with the first quarterly payment.

(3)    Equipment costing £350,000 will be leased at a cost of £145,000 p.a. The lease will be treated as a finance lease, and the equipment will accordingly be capitalised as a fixed asset by Schooner Ltd.

All figures are exclusive of VAT where appropriate.

(c)    Schooner Ltd will raise additional finance of £650,000 on 1 January 2000 in order to provide working capital.

(1)    The managing director of Schooner Ltd, Alex Barnacle, will borrow £100,000 at an interest rate of 8% using his main residence as security. This amount will be lent interest free to Schooner Ltd. At present, the main residence is not mortgaged. Alex owns 35% of Schooner Ltd's ordinary share capital.

(2)    An issue of 10% debentures will raise a loan of £300,000. The debentures will be issued at a 5% discount to their nominal value, and will be redeemable in five years time. Professional fees of £8,000 will be incurred in respect of the issue.

(3)    An issue of new ordinary £1.00 shares at £1.60 per share will raise £250,000. Chloe Dhow is to subscribe for 100,000 of the new shares. She presently has no connection with Schooner Ltd, but will be appointed a director following the share issue. Professional fees of £12,500 will be incurred in respect of the issue.

Schooner Ltd makes up its accounts to 31 December. It is a close company, currently has an issued share capital of 1,000,000 £1 ordinary shares, and is a small company as defined by the Companies Acts. The company's sales are all standard rated.

**You are required to:**

(a)    Advise Schooner Ltd of the VAT rules relating to the time of supply for goods, and explain the output tax entries that will be made in respect of the new contract on its quarterly VAT returns.

**(5 marks)**

(b)    (i)    Advise Schooner Ltd of the effect that the acquisition of the new equipment will have on its tax adjusted Schedule DI profits for the year ended 31 December 2000.

(ii)    Advise Schooner Ltd of the VAT implications of acquiring the new equipment.

**(9 marks)**

(c)    (i)    Advise Schooner Ltd of the effect that raising the additional finance will have on its tax adjusted Schedule DI profits for the year ended 31 December 2000.

(ii)    Advise Alex and Chloe of the tax relief that will be available to them in respect of their investment in Schooner Ltd.
**(11 marks)**
**(Total: 25 marks)**

## 78    (Question 6 of examination)

Duncan McByte is a computer programmer currently living in Scotland. He has recently accepted the offer of a contract of employment with Mainframe plc for a period of three years commencing on 1 July 1999 and ceasing on 30 June 2002. Duncan will be based in London during the period of the contract. The remuneration package comprises:

(1)    A salary of £65,000 p.a., together with a termination bonus of £40,000 upon satisfactory completion of the three year contract.

(2)    Mainframe plc is providing accommodation for Duncan in London. This is in an apartment that was purchased in 1987 for £94,000, and was improved at a cost of £35,000 during 1996. The apartment has a rateable value of £6,700 and is currently valued at £170,000. The furniture in the apartment cost £21,000 and Mainframe plc is paying for the annual running costs of £6,200.

(3)    Duncan is using his private motor car for business mileage. The motor car is leased at a cost of £380 per month, and the annual running costs, including fuel, are £1,800. He drives a total of 1,200 miles per month, of which 1,000 miles are for business purposes. Mainframe plc pays a mileage allowance of 40 pence per mile for business mileage. The relevant rates allowed under the Fixed Profit Car Scheme are 63 pence per mile for the first 4,000 miles, and 36 pence per mile thereafter.

(4)    On 1 July 1999 Mainframe plc provided Duncan with a loan of £60,000 that he has used to purchase a holiday cottage in France. The loan has an interest rate of 4% p.a., and will be repaid by six half-yearly instalments of £10,000 commencing on 31 December 1999.

(5)    Mainframe plc will pay for Duncan's annual subscription of £125 p.a. to the Institute of Chartered Computer Consultants, a sports club membership of £800 p.a., an annual premium of £650 for liability insurance, and £1,200 p.a. for computer training courses that will keep him up to date with the latest software developments. These amounts will all be paid during January of each year.

(6)    On 1 July 1999 Duncan was granted options to purchase 15,000 £1 ordinary shares in Mainframe plc at their value on that date. The options were provided free, and will be exercised by Duncan upon the termination of his contract on 30 June 2002. Mainframe plc's shares were valued at £1.75 on 1 July 1999, and are forecast to be worth £5.00 by 30 June 2002.

Duncan's options have been granted under the Inland Revenue approved company share option scheme that is operated by Mainframe plc.

From 1 July 1999, Duncan has rented out his main residence in Scotland as furnished holiday accommodation. The forecast rental income for 1999-00, based on 22 weeks letting, is £18,000, of which 22.5% will be paid to a letting agency. Running costs will amount to £900. The house was furnished at a cost of £14,000 during October 1998. Duncan has a mortgage of £60,000 on which interest of £5,400 (gross) will be paid during 1999-00. The mortgage is under MIRAS.

**You are required to:**

(a)    Explain the income tax and NIC implications arising from the remuneration package that Mainframe plc has given to Duncan.

Your answer should include calculations of the amounts assessable under Schedule E for 1999-00.

**(17 marks)**

(b)    Explain why it was beneficial for Duncan's share options (see note (6)) to be granted under an Inland Revenue approved company share option scheme.    **(3 marks)**

(c)    Advise Duncan of the Schedule A profit that he will be assessed on for 1999-00.    **(5 marks)**
**(Total: 25 marks)**

# ANSWERS TO DECEMBER 1998 EXAMINATION

## 73    (Answer 1 of examination)

### Examiner's comments and marking guide

Part (a) tested candidates knowledge of the law of domicile.  Part (b) tested candidates' ability to calculate the potential increase in inheritance tax liability for a person becoming domiciled in the UK.  Candidates were also required to explain the rules that apply in determining the location of assets.  Part (c) tested candidates ability to calculate the additional UK income tax liability for a person becoming domiciled in the UK.

This was the most popular question on the paper, and was the first choice for many candidates.  The majority of candidates answered the question very well, and there were a number of near perfect answers.  Part (a) was well answered, although some candidates wasted time discussing domicile of origin and domicile of dependency.  A few candidates confused the domicile rules with those of residence.  Both parts (b) and (c) were also well answered by the majority of candidates.  Some candidates failed to score easy marks in part (b) by not explaining the rules applicable to the location of assets (despite this being a requirement of the question), and the double taxation relief calculation often caused problems.  Those candidates who included income as part of their inheritance tax computation cannot expect to pass this examination.  In part (c) a number of candidates lost marks by trying to take a shortcut in calculating the additional income tax liability.  Simply taking 40% of the Schedule D Case V income produced the incorrect answer, because of the effect of the rate of income tax on savings income.

|  |  |  | *Marks* |
|---|---|---|---|
| (a) | *Domicile for IHT purposes* | | |
| | 17 out of 20 years of assessment | | 1 |
| | Application to Ming | | 1 |
| | | | |
| | *Domicile under general law* | | |
| | Domicile of choice | | 1 |
| | Procedure involved | | 1 |
| | | | — |
| | | Maximum/Available | 4 |
| | | | — |
| (b) | *Location of assets* | | |
| | Land and buildings | | 1 |
| | Registered shares and securities | | 1 |
| | Bank accounts | | 1 |
| | Chattels/Debtor | | 1 |
| | Property held in trust | | 1 |
| | | | |
| | *IHT liabilities* | | |
| | Chargeable estate | - Not domiciled in UK | 2 |
| | | - Domiciled in UK | 2 |
| | IHT liability | | 1 |
| | Estate rate | | 1 |
| | Double taxation relief | | 1 |
| | Endowment mortgage | | 1 |
| | Additional IHT liability | | 1 |
| | | | — |
| | | Available | 14 |
| | | | — |
| | | Maximum | 12 |
| | | | — |
| (c) | *Income tax liability – Not domiciled in the UK* | | |
| | Taxable income | | 1 |
| | Income tax | | 2 |
| | Remittance basis | | 1 |

| *Income tax liability – Domiciled in the UK* | | |
|---|---|---|
| Taxable income | | 2 |
| Income tax | | 1 |
| Double taxation relief | | 2 |
| Additional income tax liability | | 1 |
| | Available | 10 |
| | Maximum | 9 |
| | Available | 28 |
| | Maximum | 25 |

## Step by step answer plan

### Overview

This is an IHT/income tax question involving a non-domicilary who has been UK R and OR for many years. Two basic principles are involved - (1) Non-domiciled individuals are only liable to UK IHT on UK situs assets and, (2) Non-domiciled individuals are only liable to UK IT on their foreign income if it is remitted to the UK. Although there is clearly some time pressure, this is essentially a very straightforward question.

**Step 1** Read the question carefully noting that the subject is a non-domicilary contemplating acquiring UK domicile.

**Step 2** Answer part (a) using the two headings specified. There is so little to include that neither paragraph should need to be formally planned. As there are only 4 marks there is no point in making a long list of the steps to demonstrate domicile of choice.

**Step 3** Note that part (b) carries 12 marks and there are three sections to it - viz, exposure to UK IHT asset by asset, IHT if dom and IHT if non-dom.

**Step 4** Produce a Taxable income/ Income tax payable computation for Part (c) (i) noting that no foreign income is taxable as none remitted.

**Step 5** Repeat the exercise for the second section of part (c) but this time including the foreign income as an arising basis applies and highlight the additional IT payable.

**Step 6** Re-read the question ensuring that you have not overlooked anything.

## The examiner's answer

(a)     *Domicile for IHT purposes*

Ming will be deemed domiciled in the UK for the purposes of IHT if she is resident in the UK for 17 out of the 20 years of assessment ending with the year of assessment in which a chargeable transfer is made. Ming has been resident in the UK since 1985-86, and will therefore be subject to UK IHT in respect of her overseas assets as well as her UK assets if she dies or makes a chargeable transfer during 2001-02 or a subsequent year.

*Domicile under general law*

Ming can only have one place of domicile at any given time denoting the country considered her permanent home. She can become domiciled in the UK by acquiring a domicile of choice. This will require the severing of all ties with Yanga, and settling in the UK with the intention of staying there indefinitely. The intention will have to be demonstrated by positive actions, such as making a will under UK law and obtaining British citizenship.

(b)     If Ming is not domiciled in the UK she will only be charged to UK IHT in respect of her UK assets. The following rules apply in determining the location of assets:

(i)    Land and buildings are situated where they are physically located, so the property in the UK is chargeable, whilst the property in Yanga is not.

(ii)    Registered shares and securities are situated where they are registered, or where they would normally be dealt with in the ordinary course of business, so the shares in Ganyan Inc. are not chargeable.

(iii)    Chattels are situated where they are physically located at the relevant time, so the antiques are chargeable.

(iv)    Bank accounts are situated at the branch that maintains the account, so the deposit at the London branch is chargeable, whilst the deposit at the Yangan branch is not.

(v)    A debt is situated where the debtor resides, so the loan is not chargeable.

(vi)    Government stocks are situated at the place of registration. Property held in trust follows the normal rules, so the UK government stocks are chargeable.

Ming will be charged to UK IHT on her world-wide assets if she becomes domiciled in the UK (whether this is under general law or is deemed for IHT purposes).

|  | Not-domiciled in UK £ | Domiciled in UK £ |
|---|---|---|
| *Free estate* | | |
| *Personalty* | | |
| Shares in Ganyan Inc. (40,000 at 310p) | | 124,000 |
| Antiques | 35,000 | 35,000 |
| Bank accounts | 30,000 | 50,000 |
| Debtor | | 15,000 |
| | | |
| *Realty* | | |
| Main residence | 245,000 | 245,000 |
| House in Yanga | | 60,000 |
| | | |
| *Settled property* | | |
| Interest in possession (20,000 at 92.5p) | 18,500 | 18,500 |
| | | |
| Chargeable estate | 328,500 | 547,500 |
| | | |
| IHT liability 231,000 at nil% | Nil | Nil |
| 97,500/316,500 at 40% | 39,000 | 126,600 |
| | 39,000 | 126,600 |

Estate rate 23.123% (126,600/547,500 × 100)
Double taxation relief being the lower of:
(i)    £48,000
(ii)    £184,000 (124,000 + 60,000) × 23.123%                                                    42,546

                                                                                                84,054

An endowment mortgage is repaid upon death by the related life assurance contract, and is not therefore deductible as a debt. The potential increase in Ming's liability to UK IHT if she were to become domiciled in the UK is £45,054 (84,054 − 39,000).

(c)    *Ming Wong – Income tax liability 1999-00 (not domiciled in the UK)*

|  | £ |
|---|---|
| Schedule E | 31,040 |
| Bank interest (1,680 × 100/80) | 2,100 |
| | 33,140 |

|  |  |
|---|---|
| Personal allowance | 4,335 |
| Taxable income | 28,805 |

| Income tax: | 1,500 at 10% | 150 |
|---|---|---|
|  | 25,205 (28,805 – 2,100 – 1,500) at 23% | 5,797 |
|  | 1,295  (28,000 – 1,500 – 25,205) at 20% | 259 |
|  | 805  (2,100 – 1,295) at 40% | 322 |
|  |  | 6,528 |
| Tax suffered at source: Bank interest (2,100 x 20%) |  | 420 |
| Tax payable |  | 6,108 |

Ming is not domiciled in the UK, and is therefore not assessed on her overseas income since it is not remitted to the UK.

*Ming Wong – Income tax liability 1999-00 (domiciled in the UK)*

|  | £ | £ |
|---|---|---|
| Taxable income (as above) |  | 28,805 |
| Schedule D case V |  |  |
| Rental income |  | 7,500 |
| Dividends (5,950 × 100/85) |  | 7,000 |
| Bank interest (1,530 × 100/85) |  | 1,800 |
| Taxable income |  | 45,105 |

| Income tax: | 1,500 at 10% | 150 |
|---|---|---|
|  | 26,500 at 23% | 6,095 |
|  | 10,105 at 40% | 4,042 |
|  | 7,000 at 32½% | 2,275 |
|  |  | 12,562 |

| Double taxation relief |  |  |
|---|---|---|
| Rental income (7,500 × 35%) | 2,625 |  |
| Dividends (7,000 × 15%) | 1,050 |  |
| Bank interest (1,800 × 15%) | 270 |  |
|  |  | 3,945 |
|  |  | 8,617 |
| Tax suffered at source: Bank interest |  | 420 |
| Tax payable |  | 8,197 |

Ming's additional UK income tax liability if she had been domiciled in the UK during 1999-00 is £2,089 (8,197 – 6,108).

---

**Did you answer the question?**

You were not required to suggest tax planning measures suitable for a non-domiciled individual prior to becoming UK domiciled. For example, transferring overseas assets into a trust. Such assets are thereby sheltered from IHT being settled by a settlor who was non-domiciled when they were put into trust.

---

**Tutorial note**

Double tax relief in the second section of part (c) was not restricted because each category of foreign income was clearly subject to a higher rate of UK tax. Where there is more than one source of foreign income the UK tax is found by taking away the sources in whichever order is most beneficial. Thus with foreign non-savings income (eg rents), interest and dividends the UK tax on the rents could be determined by first excluding the rents and the tax on the foreign dividends can next be found by excluding the rents and the dividends. However, whatever remains in the computation is still subject to the basic rule of dividends as top slice, with interest next and non-savings income as the lowest part.

---

## 74    (Answer 2 of examination)

---

Part (a) tested candidates' knowledge of interest on overdue tax, surcharges and penalties under self-assessment. Part (b) tested candidates' knowledge of the Inland Revenue enquiry procedures under self-assessment, including the potential liability to interest, surcharges and penalties. Part (c) tested candidates ability to advise on the tax implications of making a contribution into a personal pension scheme.

This was the least popular question on the paper, and was answered quite badly by the majority of candidates attempting it. This was disappointing given that self-assessment has been covered in my articles in the *Students' Newsletter*. In part (a), the majority of candidates did not appreciate that they had to calculate the income tax and Class 4 NIC liability for 1999-00, and there was little knowledge of the implications of incorrectly claiming to reduce payments on account. Answers to parts (b) and (c) were somewhat better, although few candidates appreciated the correct procedure following the completion of the enquiry. The 1999-00 income tax calculation was often prepared for part (c) and it was disappointing that a fairly straight-forward capital allowance computation was beyond the ability of many candidates.

|  |  | *Marks* |
|---|---|---:|
| (a) | *Tax return for 1998-99* | |
| | Fixed penalty | 1 |
| | Daily penalty | 1 |
| | | |
| | *Balancing payment 1998-99* | |
| | Interest | 1 |
| | Surcharge | 1 |
| | Mitigation | 1 |
| | | |
| | *Payments on account 1999-00* | |
| | Calculation of taxable income | 2 |
| | Income tax | 1 |
| | Class 4 NIC | 1 |
| | Underpayment of payments on account | 1 |
| | Calculation of interest | 2 |
| | Penalty | 2 |
| | | |
| | Available | 14 |
| | | |
| | Maximum | 12 |
| | | |
| (b) | *Reasons for enquiry* | |
| | Inland Revenue suspicions | 1 |
| | Random enquiry | 1 |
| | | |
| | *Completion of the enquiry* | |
| | Amendment of self assessment | 1 |
| | Inland Revenue amendment/Right of appeal | 1 |
| | | |
| | *Interest, surcharges and penalties* | |
| | Income tax liability | 1 |
| | Interest | 1 |
| | Surcharge | 1 |
| | Penalty | 1 |
| | | |
| | Available | 8 |
| | | |
| | Maximum | 7 |
| | | |
| (c) | Calculation of maximum tax deductible premium | 2 |
| | Conclusion | 1 |

---

| | | |
|---|---|---|
| Income tax reduction | | 2 |
| Set off in 2000-01/Claim for refund | | 1 |
| Interest/Payments on account | | 1 |
| | | — |
| | Available | 7 |
| | | — |
| | Maximum | 6 |
| | | — |
| | Available | 29 |
| | | — |
| | Maximum | 25 |
| | | — |

## Step by step answer plan

### Overview

This question favours candidates who work in personal tax departments as it deals with practical aspects of self-assessment (SA). The main point in part (a) is that last years income tax (other than deducted at source) and Class 4 determine the following years payments on account (POA) although with, for example, declining income, a claim can be made to reduce the POAs. Part (b) concerns Revenue enquiries. Under SA the Revenue are no longer able to raise informal queries. Even the smallest "aspect" requires the issue of a notice of enquiry. Part (c) highlights the cash flow disadvantage of paying PPS contributions after the relevant year has ended rather than making an in-year payment.

**Step 1** Before choosing this question read each part quickly but carefully to ensure you can make a reasonable stab at all of it. Then read part (a). Parts (b) and (c) can be ignored at this stage.

**Step 2** The examiner has answered the two sections of part (a) together - ie, surcharges and penalties have been mentioned alongside each calculation of interest or other event if appropriate. You might prefer to keep the two sections separate in your answer.

**Step 3** Using the examiner's approach - ie, integrated - and keeping to a chronological order break part (a) into the following headings - Late Tax Return; Late paid balancing payment for 1998-99; Liability for 1999-00 (to test whether POAs have been reduced too far); and Late paid POAs.

**Step 4** Cover the points and make the calculations needed under each heading.

**Step 5** Read part (b) and answer each of the three sections separately.

**Step 6** Read part (c) and identify the information given or calculated earlier in the question needed at this point. Clearly he has no relevant earnings prior to 1998-99 so you need just the NRE for 1998-99 and 1999-00. Calculate the marginal effect of making the maximum PPS contribution and comment on how the relief is given.

**Step 7** Re-read the entire question and your answer to check you have dealt with all the points. The "requirement" text is quite detailed and it would be easy to miss something.

## The examiner's answer

*(a)*     *Tax return for 1998-99*

Tony's tax return for 1998-99 should have been submitted on 31 January 2000. The late submission on 15 April 2000 will result in a penalty of £100, unless there is a reasonable excuse (this must apply for the whole period of default) for the late filing. In addition, a daily penalty of up to £60 may have been imposed (provided leave was given by the Commissioners) since the tax at risk was substantial.

*Balancing payment 1998-99*

Interest on the balancing payment for 1998-99 will run from 31 January 2000 (the due date) to 10 May 2000 (the date of payment), and therefore amounts to £488.22 ($18,000 \times 10\% \times 99/365$).

Since the balancing payment was not made by 28 February 2000 (within **28** days of the due date), a surcharge of £900.00 (18,000 × 5%) will be imposed. A surcharge is imposed by formal notice, and interest is charged if it is not paid within 30 days. The Inland Revenue will mitigate the surcharge if there is a reasonable excuse for the non-payment of tax.

*Payments on account 1999-00*

Tony's income tax and class 4 NIC liability for 1999-00 is as follows:

|  | £ | £ |
|---|---|---|
| Schedule D case II | | 52,100 |
| Capital allowances: | | |
| Pool (13,600 at 25%) | 3,400 | |
| First year allowance (2,600 at 40%) | 1,040 | |
| First year allowance (5,500 at 40%) | 2,200 | |
| Motor car (maximum WDA = 3,000 × 90%) | 2,700 | |
| | | 9,340 |
| | | 42,760 |
| Personal allowance | | 4,335 |
| Taxable income | | 38,425 |
| Income tax:    1,500 at 10% | | 150 |
|       26,500 at 23% | | 6,095 |
|       10,425 at 40% | | 4,170 |
| | | 10,415 |
| Class 4 NIC (26,000 – 7,530 at 6%) | | 1,108 |
| | | 11,523 |

Tony should have reduced his payments on account for 1999-00 to £5,761 (11,523/2) rather than £2,500. He has underpaid on his payments on account by £3,261 (5,761 – 2,500), and in addition the first payment on account was made after the due date. Interest will be charged as follows:

*First payment on account* from 31 January 2000 to 15 June 2000 £213.08 (5,761 × 10% × 135/365).

*First payment on account* from 15 June 2000 to 31 January 2001 £205.49 (3,261 × 10% × 230/365).

*Second payment on account* from 31 July 2000 to 31 January 2001 £164.39 (3,261 × 10% × 184/365).

In addition, a taxpayer will be charged a penalty if a claim to reduce payments on account is made fraudulently or negligently. Since Tony reduced his payments on account for cash flow purposes, a penalty of up to £6,522 (3,261 × 2) could be charged, although the Inland Revenue may mitigate this amount.

(b)    *Reasons for enquiry*

The Inland Revenue has the right to enquire into the completeness and accuracy of any tax return. The enquiry into Tony's tax return for 1998-99 may have been made because they suspected that he had not declared all of his income, or had incorrectly claimed a deduction. Alternatively, the enquiry could have been made on a completely random basis. No reason has to be given by the Inland Revenue for making an enquiry.

*Completion of the enquiry*

Following the completion of the enquiry on 5 December 2000, Tony has 30 days in which to amend his self-assessment for 1998-99 to reflect the additional tax liability. If the self-assessment is not amended within the 30-day period, the Inland Revenue can make their own amendment during the next 30 days, and Tony would then have the right of appeal to the Commissioners.

*Interest, surcharges and penalties*

The additional income tax liability for 1998-99 is £1,800 (4,500 at 40%), since the maximum class 4 NIC has already been paid. Interest on this amount will be charged from 31 January 2000 to the date of payment (the due date is 30 days from the date of the amendment). A surcharge will only arise if Tony does not pay the additional liability within 28 days of the due date. A penalty of up to £1,800 can be imposed under s.95 TMA 1970 for negligently or fraudulently submitting a tax return, but this amount will be mitigated according to, for example, Tony's co-operation in the enquiry.

(c)    Tony's maximum tax deductible personal pension premium is £21,100 calculated as follows:

|  | *Net relevant earnings* | *Relevant percentage* | *Maximum premium* £ |
|---|---|---|---|
| 1998-99 | 63,000 (58,500 + 4,500) | 20 | 12,600 |
| 1999-00 | 42,760 | 20 | 8,552 |
|  |  |  | 21,152 |

Tony can therefore contribute the full £20,000 into a personal pension scheme and relate it back to 1999-00. The payment of the personal pension premium will result in an income tax reduction of £6,372 as follows:

|  | £ |
|---|---|
| 10,425 at 40% | 4,170 |
| 9,575 (20,000 – 10,425) at 23% | 2,202 |
|  | 6,372 |

Although the tax reduction is calculated by reference to 1999-00, Tony's tax liability for that year is not adjusted. The tax reduction will either be set off against his tax liability for 2000-01, or a refund can be claimed.

The payment of the personal pension premium will not affect either the calculation of the interest due in respect of the 1999-00 payments on account, or the payments on account for 2000-01.

---

**Did you answer the question?**

You were not required to calculate the actual balancing payment for 1999-00 or POAs for 2000-00 or comment on their due dates.

---

**Tutorial note**

Part (c) highlights the advantage of making a PPS contribution before the end of the year it is to relieve. With a 5 April year end this is not easy. It would be good planning however to make a conservative estimate of taxable profits around mid-March so that most of the PPS can be paid in-year where the taxpayer regularly uses the maximum entitlement. The small amount of unused relief can always be mopped up by a payment in the following year and related back although it will not reduce POAs for the following year.

---

## 75    (Answer 3 of examination)

**Examiner's comments and marking guide**

Part (a) tested candidates' ability to calculate the mainstream corporation tax liability for each of a group of companies, after taking account of group relief.  Part (b) tested candidates knowledge of rollover relief, including holdover relief for a depreciating asset and rollover relief within a 75% group of companies.

---

This was a popular question, and most candidates had few problems with either parts. In part (a), some candidates continue to incorrectly claim group relief for brought forward losses and capital losses. Several candidates, despite appreciating that the lower and upper limits were reduced to £100,000 and £500,000 respectively, could not then identify the most beneficial basis of claiming group relief, or apply the correct rate of corporation tax. Although answers to part (b) were generally correct, many candidates failed to score full marks by, for example, giving insufficient detail as to when heldover gain will crystallise. Many candidates were unaware that rollover relief is available where reinvestment is made by a 75% subsidiary.

The examiner's comments and marking guide have been edited to exclude topics no longer examinable.

|  |  | *Marks* |
|---|---|---|
| (a) | Schedule D1 profit | 1 |
|  | Capital gain/Charge on income | 1 |
|  | Lower and upper limits | 1 |
|  | Loss relief | 1 |
|  | Group relief | 2 |
|  | FII/Profit | 1 |
|  | Corporation tax | 1 |
|  | Losses carried forward | 1 |
|  | Available | 9 |
|  | Maximum | 8 |
| (b) | Reinvestment within three years/Provisional claim | 1 |
|  | *Freehold office building* |  |
|  | Immediate gain | 1 |
|  | Base cost | 1 |
|  | *Leasehold office building* |  |
|  | Whole gain rolled over | 1 |
|  | Depreciating asset | 1 |
|  | Date of sale/Ten years | 1 |
|  | *Freehold warehouse* |  |
|  | 75% subsidiary | 1 |
|  | Whole gain rolled over/Base cost | 1 |
|  | *Loss relief* |  |
|  | Profits less than £100,000 | 1 |
|  | Additional surrender | 1 |
|  | Charge on income | 1 |
|  | Available | 11 |
|  | Maximum | 9 |
|  | Available | 20 |
|  | Maximum | 17 |

> ### Step by step answer plan

**Overview**

Originally parts (a) and (b) included consideration of advance corporation tax which is now outside the syllabus. There was also a part (c) concerning certain group aspects of VAT. This has been excluded because of uncertainty over how Customs intend to use newly acquired anti-avoidance powers on group VAT registration. What remains is still a useful exercise on group taxation. Part (a) covers the standard planning point of giving priority in group relief claims to companies with the highest marginal tax rate. Part (b) looks at rollover relief and its interaction with the earlier decisions on maximising group relief.

**Step 1** For part (a) use a tabular layout to show PCTCT for each of the three group companies using a combination of s.393A(1) and group relief to relieve tax first at 32.5% then at 30%. Then calculate the CT on the PCTCT.

**Step 2** Give a brief explanation of why you have chosen the loss claims used.

**Step 3** Explain what happens to any unused losses. The question does not ask for this but there is a mark for it in the marking scheme. It seems to be good practice to comment on unrelieved items even when not specifically required.

**Step 4** Read part (b) carefully noting that the three investments are "alternatives". Deal with the rollover effect of each one. However, in your answer you should not overlook the obvious point that the rollover three year time limit is satisfied whichever investment is made.

**Step 5** Then comment on the interaction with part (a) .

**Step 6** Finally, re-read the question to ensure you have answered all the points.

## The examiner's answer

(a)    The mainstream corporation tax liability of each of the group companies for the year ended 31 March 2000 is as follows:

|  | Star Ltd £ | Zodiac Ltd £ | Exotic Ltd £ |
|---|---|---|---|
| Schedule DI profit |  | 650,000 | 130,000 |
| Capital gain | 130,000 |  |  |
|  | 130,000 | 650,000 | 130,000 |
| Charge on income | (10,000) |  |  |
|  | 120,000 | 650,000 | 130,000 |
| Loss relief s.393A(1) | (20,000) |  |  |
| Group relief s.402 |  | (60,000) | (45,000) |
| PCTCT | 100,000 | 590,000 | 85,000 |
| FII |  |  | 15,000 |
| Profit | 100,000 | 590,000 | 100,000 |
| Corporation tax at 20% | 20,000 |  | 17,000 |
| Corporation tax at 30% |  | 177,000 |  |
|  | 20,000 | 177,000 | 17,000 |

Star Ltd's brought forward trading losses of £7,500 and Zodiac Ltd's capital loss of £8,000 are carried forward.

*Working – Loss and group relief*
Star Ltd has two associated companies, so the lower and upper limits for corporation tax purposes are £100,000 (300,000/3) and £500,000 (1,500,000/3) respectively. Star Ltd's trading loss has been relieved so as to reduce both its own and Exotic Ltd's profits down to the lower limit.

(b)    A claim for rollover relief is possible because the reinvestment is to take place within three years of the sale of the warehouse on 15 April 1999. A provisional claim for relief can be made in Star Ltd's CT600 for the year ended 31 March 2000.

*Freehold office building*

If the freehold office building is purchased for £290,000, then £90,000 (380,000 − 290,000) of the sale proceeds will not be reinvested. Therefore £90,000 of the capital gain will remain chargeable in the year ended 31 March 2000. The base cost of the office building will be reduced to £250,000 (290,000 − (130,000 − 90,000)).

*Leasehold office building*

If the leasehold office building is purchased for £400,000, then the whole of the gain can be rolled over. However, the office building is a depreciating asset (the lease is for less than 60 years), so the gain will only be held over (deferred) until the earlier of (i) the date the office building is sold, (ii) ten years from the date of acquisition or (iii) the date the office building ceases to be used in Star Ltd's trade. The base cost of the office building is not adjusted.

*Freehold warehouse*

Zodiac Ltd is a 75% subsidiary, and so it and Star Ltd are treated as the same person for the purposes of rollover relief. Provided a joint claim is made, the whole gain of £130,000 can be rolled over since the full sale proceeds are reinvested. The base cost of the warehouse will be reduced to £295,000 (425,000 − 130,000).

*Loss relief*

Under each alternative, the claim for rollover relief will reduce Star Ltd's profits to less than £100,000. A loss relief claim under s.393A(1) ICTA 1988 is therefore not beneficial, so an additional £20,000 of the trading loss can be surrendered to Zodiac Ltd. Under the second and third options, Star Ltd's charge on income of £10,000 will be unrelieved and can also be surrendered to Zodiac Ltd.

---

**Did you answer the question?**

You were not required to comment on how the loss claims should be presented. For example, The group relief claims should first be made in the amounts required - ie, £60,000 and £45,000 - thereby leaving £20,000 for the s.393A (1) claim. If s.393A (1) was claimed first it would have to use up all Star's available profits as partial claims are not allowed.

---

## 76     (Answer 4 of examination)

**Examiner's comments and marking guide**

Part (a) tested candidates' ability to calculate the chargeable gains arising on the sale of a business run by a partnership, including the calculation of retirement relief. Part (b) tested candidates' ability to (i) explain the possible ways of relieving a loss arising in the final period of trading, (ii) advise on the most beneficial loss relief claim, and (iii) calculate the taxable income and chargeable gains given the advice on loss relief.

This was another popular question, and there were a number of very good answers. However, the fact that the question was based on a partnership caused problems for some candidates. Typical mistakes included giving retirement relief to the husband because his spouse was retiring due to ill health, and treating the partnership as a separate entity (rather than as two individuals) when dealing with the claim for loss relief. Candidates are advised to read a question carefully, since a significant number confused the ages of the two partners, with serious implications for the ability of retirement relief. Subject to these comments, part (a) was well answered although few candidates appreciated that there were no capital gains tax implications for the fixtures and fittings that qualified as plant and machinery for capital allowances purposes. Part (b) was reasonably well answered, although many candidates did not provide adequate justification for their choice of loss relief. A number of candidates wasted time calculating capital allowance claims (despite the question clearly stating that the Schedule DII profits were net of capital allowances) and giving details of loss relief under s.385 ICTA 1988, when the carry forward of the loss was clearly impossible due to the cessation of trading. Marks are not awarded unless information is relevant to the question.

| | | *Marks* |
|---|---|---|
| (a) | *Capital gains* | |
| | Goodwill | 1 |
| | Freehold property | 1 |

| | | |
|---|---|---:|
| | Leasehold property | 2 |
| | *Trevor Acre* | |
| | Share of chargeable gains | 1 |
| | Retirement relief not available | 1 |
| | *Sally Acre* | |
| | Retirement relief | 1 |
| | Associated disposal | 2 |
| | Share of chargeable gains | 1 |
| | Calculation of retirement relief | 1 |
| | Available | 11 |
| | Maximum | 9 |

| | | | |
|---|---|---|---:|
| (b) | *Partnership trading loss* | | |
| | S.380 ICTA 1988 | | 1 |
| | S.72 FA 1991 | | 1 |
| | s.388 ICTA 1988 | | 1 |
| | *Partnership assessments* | | |
| | 1996-97 to 1998-99 | | 2 |
| | Division of loss | | 1 |
| | *Sally Acre* | | |
| | Marginal rates of income tax | | 1 |
| | Claim under s.388 ICTA 1988 | | 1 |
| | *Trevor Acre* | | |
| | Marginal rates of income tax | | 1 |
| | Claim under S.380 ICTA 1988 | | 1 |
| | Claim under s.72 FA 1991 | | 1 |
| | *Sally Acre – Taxable income and chargeable gains* | | |
| | Schedule DII/Terminal loss | | 1 |
| | Schedule A/personal allowance | | 1 |
| | Chargeable gain | | 1 |
| | *Trevor Acre – Taxable income and chargeable gains* | | |
| | Schedule DII/BSI | | 1 |
| | S.380 ICTA 1988 | | 1 |
| | Personal allowance | | 1 |
| | Chargeable gains/S.72 FA 1991 | | 1 |
| | Available | | 18 |
| | Maximum | | 16 |
| | Available | | 29 |
| | Maximum | | 25 |

## ( Step by step answer plan )

**Overview**

This a fairly straightforward question on the income tax and CGT treatment of a partnership ceasing with a terminal loss. As one partner is over 50 retirement relief will almost certainly apply and as profits etc. are unevenly split (70:30) the partners are likely to have different marginal tax rates and therefore make different choices for relieving losses .

**Step 1**  Read through the question taking note of the computations you are likely to have to prepare.

**Step 2**  For part (a), calculate the partnership capital gains and split them between the partners on a 70:30 basis.

**Step 3**  Calculate the gain on the leasehold property held by Sally personally.

**Step 4**  Explain why retirement relief is available (for Sally but not for Trevor) and summarise the resulting gains for the two partners.

**Step 5**  Now read the requirements of part (b) and plan out your answer to cover each of the three sections.

**Step 6**  For the first section simply state the options for the use of the loss stressing that each partner can choose independently of the other for his/her share of the loss.

**Step 7**  The second section requires some thought. In these circumstances a rough working of the pre-loss relief income and gains year by year should help to decide where the loss can have best effect. It is time well spent as you then have the figures for showing the effect of the loss when you answer the third section.

**Step 8**  Having decided the best use of the loss answer section two giving reasons for the choices.

**Step 9**  Next schedule out the income tax and CGT calculations for the 4 years showing clearly how the losses have been used.

**Step 10**  As usual re-read the question and check that your answer is complete as possible. For example, have you mentioned that the MCA in 1999-00 could still be used by transferring it to Sally?

## The examiner's answer

(a)  The disposal of the business and leasehold office building will result in the following capital gains:

|  | Goodwill £ | Freehold Property £ | Leasehold property £ |
|---|---|---|---|
| Proceeds | 110,000 | 230,000 | 90,000 |
| Indexed cost | – | 187,850 | |
| $91,500 \times \dfrac{76.813}{81.100}$ (working) | | | 86,663 |
| Capital gain | 110,000 | 42,150 | 3,337 |

The capital gains on the goodwill and freehold property will be split between the partners in their profit sharing ratio. Trevor will therefore have chargeable gains of £45,645 (110,000 + 42,150 = 152,150 × 30%) for 1999-00. Trevor does not qualify for retirement relief since he is not 50 years old. Sally's ill health is irrelevant.

Sally is over 50 years old. She will therefore be entitled to retirement relief, with the relevant qualifying period being three years and six months (1 October 1996 to 31 March 2000). Retirement relief will also be available in respect of Sally's disposal of the leasehold office building since it is an associated disposal. The building has been let rent free to the partnership, and is sold at the same time as the business. The qualifying period will also be three years and six months (the period of actual ownership is irrelevant). Sally's chargeable gains for 1999-00 are as follows:

|  | £ | £ |
|---|---|---|
| Partnership assets (152,150 × 70%) | | 106,505 |
| Leasehold office building | | 3,337 |
| | | 109,842 |
| Retirement relief | | |
| 200,000 × 35% | 70,000 | |

$$109{,}842 - 70{,}000 = 39{,}842 \times 50\% \qquad\qquad 19{,}921$$

|  |  |
|---|---|
|  | 89,921 |
|  | 19,921 |

### Working

The lease has 22 years 3 months left to run at 31 March 2000. The appropriate lease percentage is therefore 76.813 (76.399 + 3/12 (78.055 − 76.399)).

(b) *Partnership trading loss*

There are two possible ways in which the partnership trading loss can be relieved.

(1) A claim can be made under s.380 ICTA 1988 against a partner's total income for 1999-00 and/or 1998-99. A claim could then be made under s.72 FA 1991 to extend the set off to chargeable gains of the same year.

(2) Terminal loss relief could be claimed under s.388 ICTA 1988 against a partner's Schedule DII profits for 1999-00 and the three preceding years of assessment.

Each partner can claim whichever loss relief is the most beneficial to his or her circumstances.

*Partnership assessments*

The partnership Schedule DII profits will be assessed on Sally and Trevor as follows:

|  | Total | Sally (70%) | Trevor (30%) |
|---|---|---|---|
|  | £ | £ | £ |
| 1996-97 P/E 31 March 1997 | 48,000 | 33,600 | 14,400 |
| 1997-98 Y/E 31 March 1998 | 74,000 | 51,800 | 22,200 |
| 1998-99 Y/E 31 March 1999 | 52,000 | 36,400 | 15,600 |

The trading loss of £68,000 for the year ended 31 March 2000 is divided between Sally £47,600 (70%) and Trevor £20,400 (30%).

*Sally Acre*

Sally's marginal rate of tax is 40% for the years 1996-97 to 1998-99, but only 23% for 1999-00. She should therefore make a claim to relieve her share of the partnership loss under s.388 ICTA 1988. Since the relief is only against Schedule DII profits, Sally's personal allowance can be utilised against her Schedule A profits of £6,000 p.a.

*Trevor Acre*

Trevor's marginal rate of tax is 40% for 1999-00, but only 23% for the years 1996-97 to 1998-99. He should therefore make a claim to relieve his share of the partnership loss under s.380 ICTA 1988 against his total income of £2,000 (1,600 × 100/80) for 1999-00, and then claim under s.72 FA 1991 against his chargeable gains of £45,645 for the same year. This only wastes his personal allowance for 1999-00 (there is insufficient income to fully utilise this in any case), and the married couple's allowance for that year can be transferred to Sally.

*Sally acre - Taxable income and chargeable gains*

|  | 1996-97 | 1997-98 | 1998-99 | 1999-00 |
|---|---|---|---|---|
|  | £ | £ | £ | £ |
| Schedule DII | 33,600 | 51,800 | 36,400 | – |
| Terminal loss |  | (11,200) | (36,400) |  |
|  | 33,600 | 40,600 | – | – |

| Schedule A | 6,000 | 6,000 | 6,000 | 6,000 |
|---|---|---|---|---|
| | 39,600 | 46,600 | 6,000 | 6,000 |
| Personal allowance | (4,335) | (4,335) | (4,335) | (4,335) |
| Taxable income | 35,265 | 42,265 | 1,665 | 1,665 |

| | | | | |
|---|---|---|---|---|
| Chargeable gain | | | | 19,921 |
| Taper relief (19,921 × 15% (100% - 85%)) | | | | 2,988 |
| | | | | 16,933 |
| Annual exemption | | | | 7,100 |
| | | | | 9,833 |

*Trevor Acre - Taxable income and chargeable gains*

| | 1996-97 £ | 1997-98 £ | 1998-99 £ | 1999-00 £ |
|---|---|---|---|---|
| Schedule DII | 14,400 | 22,200 | 15,600 | – |
| BSI | 2,000 | 2,000 | 2,000 | 2,000 |
| | 16,400 | 24,200 | 17,600 | 2,000 |
| Loss claim s.380 ICTA 1988 | | | | (2,000) |
| Personal allowance | (4,335) | (4,335) | (4,335) | |
| Taxable income | 12,065 | 19,865 | 13,265 | – |

| | | | | |
|---|---|---|---|---|
| Chargeable gain | | | | 45,645 |
| Loss claim s.72 FA 1991 (20,400 – 2,000) | | | | 18,400 |
| | | | | 27,245 |
| Taper relief (27,245 × 15%) | | | | 4,087 |
| | | | | 23,158 |
| Annual exemption | | | | 7,100 |
| | | | | 16,058 |

All the assets are business assets acquired before 17 March 1998. They therefore qualify for taper relief based on two complete years.

*Note*: Loss relief under s.381 ICTA 1988 is also available, but a claim is not beneficial for either partner.

---

**Did you answer the question?**

You were not required to calculate the income tax or the CGT - just the taxable income and the net chargeable gains. Also note rollover or reinvestment relief is ruled out as "neither plans to reinvest".

---

**Tutorial notes**

Retirement relief claims on grounds of ill-health are always carefully scrutinised by the Revenue Temporary medical conditions are ruled out. For example, becoming an alcoholic is not adequate grounds as alcoholism is held to be curable. The trader may never recover - it is merely sufficient that he might recover. In any case, the ill-health must be that of the trader - his or her spouse's incapacity does not count although this is not an uncommon cause for a trader retiring.

---

| 77 | **(Answer 5 of examination)** |
|----|-------------------------------|

## Examiner's comments and marking guide

Part (a) tested candidates' knowledge of the VAT rules relating to the time of supply. Part (b) tested candidates knowledge of the corporation tax and VAT implications of acquiring new equipment by (i) outright purchase (to be imported from countries that are member of the European Union and from countries that are outside the European Union), (ii) hire purchase, and (iii) leasing. Part (c) tested candidates knowledge of the corporation tax implications of raising new finance as (i) an interest free loan, (ii) a new issue of debentures, and (iii) a new issue of ordinary share capital, and also the income tax implications of making a loan to a close company and relief under the enterprise investment scheme.

This was not a popular question, and it was not particularly well answered by those attempting it. Along with question 2, this question was often the fourth choice of many candidates. Most of the topics dealt with by the question have appeared in recent examination papers, and candidates are advised to practice as many past questions as possible as part of their revisions for this paper. In part (a), the VAT rules regarding time of supply were fairly well understood, although most candidates then had problems relating the rules to the information given in the question. Many candidates failed to score high marks in part (b) because they did not deal with each aspect of the question separately. Answers that gave general details about capital allowances and the recovery of VAT scored just two or three marks. Only a few candidates appreciated the difference for VAT purposes between importing goods from countries that are members of the European Union and from countries that are outside the European Union. Many candidates did not know the difference in corporation tax treatment between acquiring equipment under hire purchase and leasing. Part (c) produced somewhat better answers, although insufficient detail was generally given on the enterprise investment scheme even where a candidate appreciated that relief was available.

|    |                                              |                      | *Marks* |
|----|----------------------------------------------|----------------------|---------|
| (a) | *Tax point*                                 |                      |         |
|    | Goods removed or made available              |                      | 1       |
|    | Invoice issued or payment received           |                      | 1       |
|    | Issue of invoice within 14 days              |                      | 1       |
|    |                                              |                      |         |
|    | *Output VAT*                                 |                      |         |
|    | Payments on account                          |                      | 1       |
|    | Balance of output tax                        |                      | 1       |
|    |                                              | Maximum/Available    | 5       |
|    |                                              |                      |         |
| (b) | *Outright purchase*                         |                      |         |
|    | First year allowance                         |                      | 1       |
|    | cquisition from the European Union           |                      | 1       |
|    | Date of acquisition                          |                      | 1       |
|    | Importation from outside the European Union  |                      | 1       |
|    | Input tax                                    |                      | 1       |
|    |                                              |                      |         |
|    | *Hire purchase*                              |                      |         |
|    | First year allowance                         |                      | 1       |
|    | Finance charge                               |                      | 1       |
|    | Input tax                                    |                      | 1       |
|    |                                              |                      |         |
|    | *Leasing*                                    |                      |         |
|    | Lease rental payment                         |                      | 1       |
|    | Capitalisation                               |                      | 1       |
|    | Input tax                                    |                      | 1       |
|    |                                              | Available            | 11      |
|    |                                              | Maximum              | 9       |
|    |                                              |                      |         |
| (c) | *Personal loan*                             |                      |         |
|    | Schooner Ltd                                 |                      | 1       |

| | |
|---|---|
| Charge on income | 1 |
| Deduction for 1999-00 | 1 |
| | |
| *10% Debentures* | |
| Schedule DI expense | 1 |
| Debenture interest | 1 |
| Discount | 1 |
| Incidental costs | 1 |
| | |
| *Ordinary share capital* | |
| Incidental expenses | 1 |
| Relief under the EIS | 1 |
| Qualification | 1 |
| Becoming paid director | 1 |
| Tax relief | 1 |
| Restriction | 1 |

|  | |
|---|---|
| Available | 13 |
| Maximum | 11 |
| Available | 29 |
| Maximum | 25 |

## Step by step answer plan

### Overview

This is effectively three fairly separate questions albeit concerning the same company. Part (a) concerns the tax point where goods are paid for in stages. Part (b) involves the tax and VAT implications of acquiring plant either by outright purchase from suppliers inside or outside the EU, or on HP or by leasing. Finally part (c) looks at three different ways of raising finance including the effect on an investor using the EIS provisions. There is a lot of ground to cover but there is nothing particularly difficult. As long as the answer keeps to clearly labelled parts it should be possible to earn most of the marks on offer.

**Step 1** Invest a little time in deciding whether this question is a wise choice for you. If so, then note that (a) in the text corresponds to (a) in the requirements and so on. (In fact the question would look less daunting if it had been presented like that!)

**Step 2** Concentrate on part (a). Firstly describe the "rules". Next apply them to the three events in relation to each sale.

**Step 3** Answer part (b) with a separate heading for each of the three means of acquisition giving a separate paragraph for the tax effect and for the VAT implications. Don't worry if you are unsure of the VAT treatment on overseas acquisitions as these relate to only a small portion of the overall marks and have no "knock-on" effect.

**Step 4** Read part (c) and structure your answer under the five obvious paragraphs required.

**Step 5** Go back over each part of the question to ensure you have given complete answers. Although the question is well-structured, the requirement to "advise" is somewhat open ended and it is easy to overlook a vital point.

## The examiner's answer

(a) The time of supply is known as the tax point. For the supply of goods the tax point is the earliest of (i) the date goods are removed or made available to the customer, or (ii) the date an invoice is issued or payment received.

If an invoice is issued within 14 days of the goods being removed or made available, this date will replace that in (i). The tax point then becomes the earliest of payment being received and an invoice being issued.

The payments on account of £50,000 and £100,000 must be included as supplies on the VAT return for the quarter in which they are received. Output tax will be £22,340 ($50,000 + 100,000 = 150,000 \times 17.5/117.5$). The balance of the output tax of £38,910 ($350,000$ at $17.5\% = 61,250 - 22,340$) will be included on the VAT return for the following quarter when the invoice is issued.

(b)    *Outright purchase*

Schooner Ltd will be able to claim a first year allowance of £100,000 ($250,000 \times 40\%$) as a Schedule DI expense for the year ended 31 December 2000.

As regards the equipment acquired from countries that are members of the European Union, VAT of £28,000 ($160,000$ at $17.5\%$) will be accounted for according to the date of acquisition. This is the earliest of (i) the date an invoice is issued, or (ii) the 15$^{th}$ of the month following the removal of the goods. As regards the equipment imported from countries that are not members of the European Union, VAT of £15,750 ($250,000 - 160,000 = 90,000$ at $17.5\%$) will be accounted for at the time of importation.

In both cases, a corresponding input tax deduction will be given. However, with an acquisition there is no 'VAT cost' as the input tax and VAT charge will effectively contra out on the VAT return. With an import, VAT must actually be paid subsequent to its recovery as input tax.

*Hire purchase*

Schooner Ltd will be able to claim a first year allowance of £80,000 ($200,000 \times 40\%$) on the cost of the equipment as per outright purchase. The finance charge of £76,000 ($16$ at $17,250 = 276,000 - 200,000$) will be deductible as a Schedule DI expense. The proportion relating to the year ended 31 December 2000 will be calculated using normal accounting principles.

Input tax of £35,000 ($200,000$ at $17.5\%$) will be reclaimed on the VAT return for the period in which the equipment is purchased.

*Leasing*

The lease rental payment of £145,000 for the year ended 31 December 2000 will be deductible as a Schedule DI expense. The fact that the equipment is capitalised is in theory irrelevant, although the Inland Revenue may allow the deductions (depreciation and finance charge) calculated on this basis. Capital allowances are not available.

Input tax of £25,375 ($145,000$ at $17.5\%$) included in each lease rental payment will be reclaimed on the VAT return for the period during which the appropriate tax point occurs.

(c)    *Personal loan*

There are no tax implications for Schooner Ltd since the loan is interest free.

The interest paid by Alex will be a charge on income as it is a qualifying loan to a close company. Alex's taxable income will effectively be reduced by the amount of interest paid each tax year, thus obtaining tax relief at his marginal rate. The deduction for 1999-00 will be £2,000 ($100,000$ at $8\% \times 3/12$).

*10% Debentures*

The issue of debentures is for trading purposes, so the interest, the cost of the 5% discount and the incidental expenses will be deductible as a Schedule DI expense. The deduction for the year ended 31 December 2000 using the accruals basis will be £34,600 as follows (note that strictly the write off should be so as to achieve a constant rate of return):

|  | £ |
|---|---|
| Debenture interest ($300,000$ at $10\%$) | 30,000 |
| Discount ($300,000 \times 5\% = 15,000/5$) | 3,000 |

*Official* **ACCA** *Revision Series, published by AT Foulks Lynch*

|  |  |
|---|---|
| Incidental costs (8,000/5) | 1,600 |
|  | 34,600 |

*Ordinary share capital*

The incidental expenses of raising share capital are not deductible as a Schedule DI expense.

The conditions for relief under the enterprise investment scheme (EIS) appear to be met since Schooner Ltd is unquoted and is carrying on a qualifying trade. The company's gross assets must be less than £15 million prior to the share issue.

Chloe Dhow will be entitled to relief under the EIS as she currently has no connection with Schooner Ltd, and will hold less than 30% of the company's share capital (100,000/[1,000,000 + (250,000/1.60)] = 8.6%). Entitlement to relief under the EIS will not be affected by Chloe subsequently becoming a paid director of Schooner Ltd. Chloe will be entitled to a tax credit of £30,000 (150,000 at 20%) for 1999-00.

The remaining £10,000 of her investment (100,000 × 1.60 = 160,000 – 150,000) will not qualify for relief. Relief will be restricted if Chloe's income tax liability for 1999-00 is less than £30,000.

---

**Did you answer the question?**

You were not required to discuss in detail the company's suitability as an EIS investment nor the EIS deferral relief available to Chloe.

---

**Tutorial note**

Under the loan relationship rules applying to companies since 1996 the cost of borrowing for trade purposes is allowed as a trading expense and calculated on an accruals basis. In effect the costs of borrowing should be matched to the period of the loan so the answer spreads the incidental borrowing costs and the cost of the discount evenly over the 5 years concerned.

---

## 78    (Answer 6 of examination)

**Examiner's comments and marking guide**

Part (a) tested candidates' ability to explain the income tax and NIC implications arising from a remuneration package including a termination bonus, the benefit of living accommodation, a mileage allowance, a beneficial loan and share options. Part (b) tested candidates ability to explain the benefit of share options being granted under an Inland Revenue approved compare share option scheme. Part (c) tested candidates ability to calculate a Schedule A profit after giving appropriate advice regarding mortgage interest.

Although not as popular as questions, 1, 3 and 4, this was a reasonably popular question that was generally well answered. However it was often a third or fourth choice question, and many answers showed signs of being rushed. it is important that candidates allocate their time so as to be able to fully attempt four questions. As a result, many candidates failed to score fairly straightforward marks by not showing, for example, full workings in respect of the mileage allowance or the beneficial loan. Subject to this comment, part (a) was quite well answered. However several candidates wasted time by not carefully reading the requirements of the question, since there was no need to calculate the income tax liability or to give details of the deductions available to the employer. Part (b) was badly answered, with few candidates being aware of the advantages of an Inland Revenue approved company share option scheme. Many candidates incorrectly stated that such a scheme gives exemption from capital gains tax. Part (c) was very well answered, although most candidates failed to score fully marks by not explaining their treatment of the mortgage interest or why the house qualified to be treated as a furnished holiday letting.

---

Marks

(a)  *Salary and termination bonus*
    Salary    1
    Termination bonus    1
    Employees class 1 NIC    2

    *Living accommodation*
    Basic benefit    1
    Additional benefit    2
    Furniture/Running costs    1

    *Mileage allowance*
    Fixed profit car scheme    2
    Expense claim based on business expenditure    2

    *Beneficial loan*
    Basis of charge    1
    Average method    2
    Actual basis    1

    *Other payments*
    Sports club membership    1
    Other payments    1

    *Share options*
    No Schedule E charge    1
    £30,000 limit/Three year limit    1

        Available    20

        Maximum    17

(b)  Schedule E charge    1
    Postponement of tax liability    1
    Lower tax charge    1

        Maximum/Available    3

(c)  Qualification as furnished holiday letting    2
    Mortgage interest    1
    Rental income/Letting agency    1
    Running costs/Interest    1
    Capital allowances    1

        Available    6

        Maximum    5

        Available    29

        Maximum    25

## Step by step answer plan

**Overview**

Most of the marks are given for the IT/NIC implications of a remuneration package with a minor part added on for Schedule A FHL. There is nothing technically difficult about this question. It offers a lot of marks to candidates who have learnt the detailed rules on benefits in kind.

**Step 1**   Before you choose this question read through the details of Duncan's package to ensure that you know how to tackle most if not all of the points.

**Step 2**   For part (a) deal with each of the 6 elements using a separate heading for each item. In each case you have to explain IT and NIC implications and calculate the Schedule E effect for 1999-00. Note that there are only 9 months of employment in that year. In the examiner's answer the NIC implications are calculated for item 1 but, as NIC has no impact on the other items, a statement is made to that effect and no further mention is made.

**Step 3**   Read and answer part (b) noting that there are only 3 marks so a lengthy explanation is not expected.

**Step 4**   For part (c) it is necessary to explain why FHL treatment applies. If it was just a Schedule A business there would be no capital allowances on the furniture. Instead a 10% wear and tear allowance would be likely.

**Step 5**   Re-read the question to ensure none of the information has been overlooked and if you have time check that you have not made a slip in your calculations

## The examiner's answer

(a)   Duncan earns over £8,500 p.a., and is therefore a P11D employee.

*Salary and termination bonus*

The salary will be assessed under Schedule E on the receipts basis. The termination bonus of £40,000 will be taxable in full since Duncan is contractually entitled to it. Duncan's salary exceeds the employees class 1 NIC upper limit of £26,000 (52 × £500), so the NIC liability for 1999-00 will be:

|  | £ |
|---|---|
| 22,568 (26,000 – 52 × 66) at 10% × 9/12 | 1,693 |

There are no NIC implications as regards any other aspect of the remuneration package.

*Living accommodation*

Duncan will be assessed under Schedule E on the benefit of the living accommodation provided to him. There will be an additional benefit based on the market value of £170,000, since the apartment cost in excess of £75,000 and was purchased more than six years before first being provided. The benefit assessed in 1999-00 will be:

|  | £ |
|---|---|
| Rateable value 6,700 × 9/12 | 5,025 |
| Additional benefit 170,000 – 75,000 = 95,000 at 10% × 9/12 | 7,125 |
| Furniture 21,000 at 20% × 9/12 | 3,150 |
| Running costs 6,200 × 9/12 | 4,650 |
|  | 19,950 |

*Mileage allowance*

Under the fixed profit car scheme the mileage allowance received will be tax-free. Duncan can make the following expense claim for 1999-00:

|  | £ |
|---|---|
| 4,000 miles at 63p | 2,520 |
| 5,000 miles (9 × 1,000 = 9,000 – 4,000) at 36p | 1,800 |
|  | 4,320 |
| Mileage allowance  9,000 at 40p | 3,600 |
|  | 720 |

The alternative of making an expense claim based on actual business expenditure is not beneficial, since the deduction would only be £3,975 as follows:

|  | £ |
|---|---|
| Leasing costs  380 × 9 × 1,000/1,200 | 2,850 |
| Running costs  1,800 × 9/12 × 1,000/1,200 | 1,125 |
|  | 3,975 |

*Beneficial loan*

Duncan will be assessed under Schedule E on the difference between the interest paid on the loan and the official rate of interest. Based on the 'average' method, the taxable benefit for 1999-00 is as follows:

|  | £ | £ |
|---|---|---|
| Interest at official rate: | | |
| $\dfrac{60,000 + 50,000}{2}$ at 10% × 9/12 | | 4,125 |
| Interest paid:  60,000 × 6/12 at 4% | 1,200 | |
| 50,000 × 3/12 at 4% | 500 | |
|  | | 1,700 |
|  | | 2,425 |

Calculating the interest at the official rate on the actual basis is not beneficial ((60,000 × 6/12) + (50,000 × 3/12) at 10% = £4,250).

*Other payments*

Only the cost of the sports club membership of £800 will be assessed as a taxable benefit on Duncan for 1999-00. The subscription of £125 will be assessed, but a corresponding expense deduction can then be claimed since it is a professional subscription. No taxable benefit arises in respect of the payment of liability insurance or the cost of work-related training.

*Share options*

No Schedule E charge will arise either at the time of grant or upon the exercise of the options. The exemption is available since the total market value of Duncan's options at the time of grant (15,000 × 1.75 = £26,250) does not exceed £30,000, and the options will not be exercised less than three years from the time of grant.

(b)    If the share options had not been granted under the company share option scheme, then a Schedule E charge would have arisen at the time that they are exercised. This charge on 30 June 2002 would be based on the market value at that date less the amount paid for the shares. The total assessment would therefore have been £48,750 (15,000 × 3.25 (5.00 – 1.75)).

Granting the options under the company share option scheme is therefore beneficial since (i) the tax liability is postponed until such time as the shares are actually disposed of, and (ii) the resulting CGT liability on the disposal will be lower than the income tax liability based on the above Schedule E assessment.

(c)     Duncan's letting of his main residence should qualify to be treated as a trade under the furnished holiday letting rules. It is to be let for 154 days (22 × 7) so that it is both available for letting for at least 140 days and so let for at least 70 days. Capital allowances on plant and machinery will therefore be available. Duncan can make a claim to have the mortgage taken out of MIRAS, so that interest is instead deductible in calculating the Schedule A profit. This will result in tax relief at 40% rather than at 10%. His Schedule A profit for 1999-00 will be as follows:

|  | £ | £ |
|---|---|---|
| Rental income | | 18,000 |
| Expenses | | |
| Letting agency (18,000 at 22.5%) | 4,050 | |
| Running costs | 900 | |
| Interest (5,400 × 9/12) | 4,050 | |
| Capital allowances (14,000 at 40%) | 5,600 | |
| | | 14,600 |
| Schedule A profit | | 3,400 |

---

**Did you answer the question?**

You were not required to explain the tax and NIC effect of the package from the viewpoint of Mainframe plc. That conclusion is not entirely obvious except that the whole tenor of the question is to consider the effects from Duncan's perspective.

---

## JUNE 1999 QUESTIONS

### 79 (Question 1 of examination)

**FOUR questions ONLY to be attempted**

*Full Rate Company).*

Global plc is a UK resident manufacturing company whose Schedule D case I profits for the year ended 30 September 2000 are forecast to be £2,250,000. The company has asked for your advice regarding transactions taking place during the year ended 30 September 2000. You should assume that today's date is 15 March 2000.

(1) On 1 November 1999 Global plc purchased a 90% shareholding in Nouveau Inc., a manufacturing company resident in and controlled from the country of Northia. Its forecast profits for the year ended 31 March 2000 are £700,000, and these will be subject to corporation tax at the rate of 25% in Northia. On 15 April 2000 Nouveau Inc. is planning to pay a dividend of £300,000, and this will be subject to withholding tax at the rate of 5%.

(2) During May 2000 Global plc is planning to sell 10,000 units of a product to Nouveau Inc. at a price of £12·75 per unit. This is 25% less than the trade-selling price given to other customers.

(3) On 1 November 1999 Global plc set up a branch in the country of Eastina. The branch is controlled from Eastina, and its forecast profits for the period to 30 September 2000 are £175,000. These are subject to tax at the rate of 40% in Eastina. 50% of the net of tax profits will be remitted to the UK.

(4) On 1 December 1999 Global plc set up a 100% subsidiary, Middleman Inc., a company resident in and controlled from the country of Westonia. The subsidiary only sells products manufactured by Global plc, and its forecast profits for the period to 30 September 2000 are £450,000. These will be subject to Westonian corporation tax at the rate of 10%. On 15 October 2000 Middleman Inc. will pay a dividend of £85,000.

(5) On 31 March 2000 Global plc is planning to sell its 80% shareholding in Surplus Ltd, a company resident in the UK, for £1,750,000. The disposal will result in a chargeable gain (after indexation allowance) of £840,000. However, the sale agreement states that the sale proceeds will be reduced by any corporation tax liability that Surplus Ltd has in respect of intra-group capital transactions taking place prior to the date of sale.

Global plc transferred a factory to Surplus Ltd on 20 June 1995, when the factory was valued at £630,000. The factory originally cost Global plc £260,000 on 17 May 1990. It is still owned by Surplus Ltd, and is currently valued at £720,000. The indexation allowance from May 1990 to June 1995 is £67,200, and from May 1990 to March 2000 it is £113,700. Surplus Ltd makes up its accounts to 30 September and pays corporation tax at the full rate.

(6) On 1 February 2000 Global plc purchased an 85% shareholding in Wanted Ltd, a UK resident company. The company is forecast to make a Schedule D case I trading loss of £240,000 for the year ended 30 September 2000. On 20 December 1999 Wanted Ltd sold investments for £425,000, resulting in a capital loss of £170,000.

In all cases, the overseas forecast profits are the same for accounting and taxation purposes. The double taxation treaties between the UK and Northia, Eastina and Westonia provide that overseas taxes are relieved as a tax credit against UK corporation tax.

**Required:**

(a)    Advise Global plc of the corporation tax implications of each of the transactions during the year ended 30 September 2000. Your answer should explain whether or not the overseas subsidiaries will be classified as controlled foreign companies, and should be supported by appropriate calculations.

**(21 marks)**

(b)    Explain how Global plc will be affected by the requirement to make quarterly instalment payments in respect of its corporation tax liability for the year ended 30 September 2000.    **(4 marks)**

You are *not expected* to calculate Global plc's corporation tax liability for the year ended 30 September 2000.

## 80    (Question 2 of examination)

Delia Jones, aged 42, has been running a successful restaurant business as a sole trader since 1 September 1995. She has recently accepted an offer from Fastfood Ltd, an unconnected company quoted on the Alternative Investment Market, to purchase her business. Fastfood Ltd would like to complete the purchase on 31 March 2000, but are prepared to delay until 30 April 2000 should this be beneficial for Delia. The purchase consideration will consist of either cash or ordinary shares in Fastfood Ltd. The following information is available:

(1)    Delia's Schedule D case I profits are as follows:

|  | £ |
| --- | --- |
| Year ended 31 August 1998 | 65,400 |
| Year ended 31 August 1999 | 77,200 |
| Period ended 31 March 2000 (forecast) | 58,500 |
| April 2000 (forecast) | 9,000 |

The figures for the years ended 31 August 1998 and 1999 are adjusted for capital allowances, whilst those for the period ended 31 March 2000 and for April 2000 are before taking account of capital allowances. Delia has overlap profits brought forward of £24,200.

(2)    The forecast market values of Delia's business assets at both 31 March 2000 and 30 April 2000 are as follows:

|  | £ |
| --- | --- |
| Goodwill | 125,000 |
| Freehold property (1) | 462,000 |
| Freehold property (2) | 118,000 |
| Fixtures and fittings | 240,000 |
| Net current liabilities | (95,000) |
|  | 850,000 |

Freehold property (1) cost £230,000 in 1995 (indexed to April 1998). Freehold property (2) was purchased during June 1999 for £94,000. The goodwill has a nil cost.

(3)    The tax written down value of the fixtures and fittings at 31 August 1999 was £114,000. Fixtures and fittings costing £31,000 were purchased on 15 December 1999. All of Delia's fixtures and fittings qualify as plant and machinery for capital allowances purposes, and are being sold for less than original cost.

(4)     Delia has unused capital losses of £12,400 brought forward from 1998-99.

(5)     Delia currently has no other income or outgoings. Her investment income will exceed £40,000 p.a. for 2000-01 onwards, regardless of whether the consideration is taken as cash or shares.

(6)     Delia will not become an employee or director of Fastfood Ltd. If the consideration is in the form of shares in Fastfood Ltd, then Delia's holding will represent 7.5% of the company's share capital. Delia will sell the shares at regular intervals over the next ten years.

(7)     Both Delia and Fastfood Ltd are registered for VAT.

**Required:**

(a)     Assuming that the business is sold on 31 March 2000 with the consideration being wholly in the form of cash:

(i)     Calculate Delia's Schedule D case I assessment for 1990-00.          **(5 marks)**

(ii)    Calculate Delia's CGT liability for 1999-00.          **(6 marks)**

(iii)   Advise Delia of the VAT implications arising from the sale.          **(2 marks)**

(b)     Advise Delia as to the income tax, CGT and NIC implications of:

(i)     Delaying the sale of the business until 30 April 2000.          **(7 marks)**

(ii)    Taking the consideration wholly in the form of ordinary shares in Fastfood Ltd, rather than as cash.          **(5 marks)**

You should assume that the tax rates and allowances for 1999-00 apply throughout.

**(Total:  25 marks)**

---

| **81** | **(Question 3 of examination)** |
|---|---|

Arthur Rich, aged 62, has asked for your advice regarding the following gifts that he has made during 1999-00:

(1)     On 20 May 1999 Arthur gave 100,000 of his 200,000 ordinary shares in Legacy Ltd, an unquoted trading company, to his son. Legacy Ltd has an issued share capital of 500,000 ordinary shares.  His wife also owns 100,000 shares in the company. On 20 May 1999 the relevant values of Legacy Ltd's shares were as follows:

| *Shareholding* | *Value per share* |
|---|---|
| | £ |
| 60% | 5.50 |
| 40% | 3.75 |
| 20% | 3.40 |

Arthur has been a full-time working director of Legacy Ltd for eight years, and has owned his shares for six years.  The cost of his total shareholding of 200,000 shares (indexed to April 1998) prior to the gift was £189,200.

(2)     On 30 June 1999 Arthur made a gift of a freehold property worth £275,000 into a discretionary trust for the benefit of his children. Arthur purchased the property on 1 July 1982 for £47,600, and

occupied the house as his main residence until 31 December 1990. Since then it has been rented out as furnished accommodation.

(3)    On 28 November 1999 Arthur gave 24,000 ordinary shares in Grant plc, a quoted company, to his granddaughter as a wedding gift. On that day the shares were quoted at 304 - 320, with recorded bargains of 288, 310, 315 and 326. Arthur originally purchased 15,000 shares in Grant plc during 1990, and the cost of these shares (indexed to April 1998) prior to the gift was £27,600. Arthur also bought 10,000 shares on 30 June 1999 for £23,700, and has subsequently bought 2,000 shares on 16 December 1999 for £6,500 and 3,000 shares on 5 January 2000 for £10,350. Grant plc has an issued share capital of 1,000,000 ordinary shares.

(4)    On 8 December 1999 Arthur signed a legally binding agreement that transferred the ownership of a vintage Aston Martin motor car worth £125,000 to his son. Arthur purchased the motor car in August 1983 for £26,500. Under the terms of the agreement the motor car is garaged at Arthur's main residence, and may be driven by him when he pleases.

Arthur is a 40% taxpayer, and has not previously made any lifetime transfers of assets. He is to pay any CGT and IHT liabilities arising from the above gifts.

Required:

(a)    Advise Arthur of the CGT and IHT implications arising from the gifts made during 1999-00. Your answer should be supported by appropriate calculations, and should include an explanation of any reliefs that are available. You should ignore the effect of annual exemptions both for CGT and for IHT.

(b)    (i)    The trustees of the discretionary trust set up on 30 June 1999 wish to purchase an insurance policy to cover against any IHT liability that may arise as a result of Arthur's death. Advise the trustees as to the maximum amount of insurance cover that they should obtain. You should ignore tapering relief.    **(3 marks)**

     (ii)    Briefly explain any other circumstances in which the discretionary trust will be liable to IHT.    **(2 marks)**

**(Total: 25 marks)**

---

| **82** | **(Question 4 of examination)** |
|---|---|

Harold and Wilma Chan are a married couple aged 66 and 55 respectively. Following Harold's retirement from full-time employment on 31 March 1999, the couple have become aware that there may be tax planning measures that they could take in order to reduce their combined income tax liability. Harold and Wilma have the following income and outgoings for 1999-00:

(1)    Harold receives an annual pension of £16,600.

(2)    Wilma is employed on a gross annual salary of £45,000. She contributes 6% of her salary into her employer's Inland Revenue approved occupational pension scheme. Wilma is not planning to retire for several years.

(3)    Wilma receives building society interest of £3,600 (net) p.a., interest of £2,400 (gross) p.a. from UK government stocks, and interest of £900 (gross) p.a. from index linked National Savings Certificates.

(4)    Wilma owns a property situated in the UK that is rented out unfurnished. The annual Schedule A profit is £4,800.

(5)    Harold and Wilma jointly own a property situated overseas. The annual profit is £2,300 (gross), and this is subject to overseas tax at the rate of 35%.

**Required:**

(a)     Before taking account of any tax planning measures, calculate the income tax liability of Harold and Wilma for 1999-00. **(8 marks)**

(b)     Advise Harold and Wilma of tax planning measures that they could have taken in order to reduce their overall income tax liability for 1999-00. Your answer should include an explanation of any suggested proposals, and a calculation of the amount of income tax that could have been saved.

**(8 marks)**
**(Total: 16 marks)**
*(as amended)*

---

| 83 | (Question 5 of examination) |
|----|------------------------------|

Gewgaw Ltd commenced trading as a manufacturer of children's toys on 1 April 1999, and will make up its accounts to 31 March 2000.

## VAT return

Gewgaw Ltd is in the process of completing its VAT return for the quarter ended 31 March 2000. The following information is available:

(1)     Standard rated sales amounted to £62,500, with £54,200 being received from customers. Gewgaw Ltd offers its customers a 2·5% discount for payment within 30 days, and this is taken by 70% of them.

(2)     Standard rated purchases amounted to £21,000, with £19,400 being paid to suppliers.

(3)     On 31 March 2000 the company wrote off bad debts of £2,000 and £840 in respect of invoices due for payment on 10 August and 5 November 1999 respectively.

(4)     On 1 January 2000 the company purchased a new 1600 cc motor car costing £17,300 for the use of its managing director. This figure includes a sunroof costing £800 that was fitted prior to the delivery of the motor car. Both these figures are *inclusive* of VAT.

(5)     Standard rated expenses amounted to £14,640. This includes £480 for entertaining suppliers, £1,200 for repairs to the managing director's motor car, and the cost of petrol for this motor car of £900. The figure for petrol includes both business and private mileage. The relevant quarterly scale charge is £396 (*inclusive* of VAT).

Unless stated otherwise all of the above figures are *exclusive* of VAT.

Gewgaw Ltd does not operate the cash accounting scheme. The company's first three VAT returns were submitted on 20 August 1999, 26 October 1999 and 25 January 2000 respectively. The VAT payable in respect of the second and third returns was not paid until 11 November 1999 and 5 March 2000 respectively.

## Managing director's motor car

The managing director drove a total of 11,000 miles during the period 1 January to 31 March 2000 (see (4) and (5) above). His ordinary commuting is a daily total of 85 miles, and this was driven 60 times during the period. In addition, he drove into work on three occasions at the weekend in order to turn off the burglar alarm. For five days the managing director drove directly from home to attend business meetings, with the average daily journey being 120 miles. He also drove 105 miles to attend the annual dinner party of a customer. Private travel amounted to 1,100 miles during the period, with the balance of the mileage being in respect of journeys made in the performance of the managing director's duties.

## Bookkeeping

Gewgaw Ltd's bookkeeping is currently maintained by a bookkeeping agency at a cost of £525 per month net of VAT (this is included within the standard rated expenses of £14,640). An employee of Gewgaw Ltd with the relevant financial experience has offered to do the bookkeeping by working one extra day per week. The employee is currently paid a salary of £15,000 p.a., and wants £100 per week, net of all taxes, for the extra day's work. He has no other income.

**Required:**

(a)  (i)   Calculate the amount of VAT payable by Gewgaw Ltd for the quarter ended 31 March 2000, and explain the implications if this VAT payable is not paid until 20 May 2000.

**(8 marks)**

(ii)  State the conditions that Gewgaw Ltd needs to satisfy before it will be permitted to use the cash accounting and annual accounting schemes, and advise the company of whether it will be beneficial for it to use either scheme. **(6 marks)**

(b)  Advise both the managing director and Gewgaw Ltd of the income tax, corporation tax and NIC implications arising from the provision of the company motor car. **(8 marks)**

(c)  Advise Gewgaw Ltd as to whether it would be beneficial to accept the employee's offer to maintain the company's bookkeeping. **(3 marks)**

**(Total: 25 marks)**

---

## 84     (Question 6 of examination)

Easy-Speak Ltd is an unquoted trading company that manufactures mobile telephones. You should assume that today's date is 15 August 1999.

During 1998 Easy-Speak Ltd purchased a plot of land adjacent to its office building for £224,000, with the intention of having a new factory built on the site. However, the company has now decided to acquire a nearby factory that has recently been built by a building company, and the plot of land is therefore to be sold.

The new factory can be purchased at a cost of £430,000. This includes £80,000 for land, £87,000 for a general office, £44,500 for a drawing office and £28,500 for the heating and ventilation systems. As an alternative to outright purchase, the building company is prepared to grant a 15-year lease on the factory for a premium of £280,000, with an annual rent of £27,600 payable in advance.

Easy-Speak Ltd has two alternatives regarding the plot of land acquired during 1998:

(1)  The land can be sold in its existing state to a property development company for £320,000 on 25 September 1999. Easy-Speak Ltd will then have sufficient funds with which to acquire the leasehold of the new factory. The premium of £280,000 and the annual rent of £27,600 will be paid on 1 October 1999.

(2)  The company can develop the land itself. To finance this development, Easy-Speak Ltd will need to take out a short-term bank loan of £150,000 on 1 September 1999. Interest will be charged on this loan at an annual rate of 12·5%. A building company will then be contracted to construct three industrial units on the site at a cost of £147,500.

All three industrial units will be sold to a property investment company during December 1999 for £550,000. The short-term loan will be repaid on 31 December 1999. Easy-Speak Ltd will then have sufficient funds with which to purchase the new factory outright for £430,000 on 1 January 2000. This will be brought into trade use immediately.

The managing director of Easy-Speak Ltd understands that if the plot of land is sold in its existing state, then the transaction will be treated as a capital gain. However, if the land is developed, then the transaction is likely to be treated as an adventure in the nature of a trade.

Easy-Speak Ltd's Schedule D case I profits for the year ended 31 March 2000 are forecast to be £270,000. This is *before taking account* of any of the above transactions. As at 31 March 1999 Easy-Speak Ltd had unused capital losses of £61,600. The company is a small company as defined by the Companies Acts, and has no associated companies.

**Required:**

(a)     Explain the criteria that are used by the courts in deciding whether or not an isolated sale transaction will be treated as an adventure in the nature of a trade. Your answer should include an explanation as to why the managing director of Easy-Speak Ltd is probably correct in her understanding of the tax implications arising from the two alternatives regarding the plot of land. You are *not expected* to quote from decided cases. **(9 marks)**

(b)     Calculate Easy-Speak Ltd's forecast corporation tax liability for the year ended 31 March 2000 if the company:

   (1)     Sells the plot of land in its existing state and acquires the leasehold of the new factory.

   (2)     Develops the plot of land and purchases the new factory outright.

Your answer should include advice as to whether or not it is beneficial for Easy-Speak Ltd to undertake the development of the plot of land. You should assume that the sale of the land in its existing state is treated as a capital gain, whilst the development of the land is treated as an adventure in the nature of a trade. The indexation allowance and rollover relief should be ignored. **(16 marks)**
**(Total: 25 marks)**

## ANSWERS TO JUNE 1999 EXAMINATION

## 79 (Answer 1 of examination)

### Examiner's comments and marking guide

Part (a) tested candidates' knowledge of the corporation tax implications for six different transactions: (1) the acquisition of an overseas subsidiary, (2) transfer pricing, (3) the setting up of an overseas branch, (4) the setting up of an overseas subsidiary likely to be classed as a controlled foreign company, (5) the sale of a 75% subsidiary that has received a no gain/no loss transfer within the previous six years, and (6) the acquisition of a subsidiary that has both a current year trading loss and a pre-entry capital loss. Part (b) tested candidates' knowledge of the requirement for large companies to make quarterly instalment payments of their corporation tax liability. This was probably the most popular question on the paper, although candidates' answers were somewhat mixed. Many candidates tried to answer the question in general terms, without providing any supporting calculations of, for example, the relevant income and double taxation relief. A number of candidates incorrectly identified the overseas subsidiary in (1) as a controlled foreign company, despite the overseas tax rate clearly ruling out this possibility. The fairly straightforward double taxation relief calculation for this part of the question also caused problems for the majority of candidates. The calculation of the chargeable gain in part (5) was another area that was badly dealt with. Part (b) was generally answered quite well, although the actual due dates given were often incorrect.

|  |  |  | *Marks* |
|---|---|---|---|
| 1 | (a) | Rate of corporation tax | 1 |
|  |  | **Shareholding in Nouveau Inc**. |  |
|  |  | Not classified as a controlled foreign company | 1 |
|  |  | 10% limit | 1 |
|  |  | Calculation | 2 |
|  |  | Double taxation relief | 1 |
|  |  | **Transfer pricing** |  |
|  |  | Reduction in UK corporation tax/Market price | 1 |
|  |  | Adjustment under self assessment | 1 |
|  |  | Calculation | 1 |
|  |  | **Branch in Eastina** |  |
|  |  | UK corporation tax | 1 |
|  |  | Double taxation relief | 1 |
|  |  | **Controlled foreign company** |  |
|  |  | Low tax country | 1 |
|  |  | Quoted on stock exchange/Limit of £50,000 | 1 |
|  |  | Acceptable distribution policy/Exempt activities | 1 |
|  |  | Motive test | 1 |
|  |  | Tax implications | 2 |
|  |  | **Sale of shareholding** |  |
|  |  | Transfer within six years | 1 |
|  |  | Chargeable gain/Corporation tax liability | 2 |
|  |  | Implications for Global plc | 1 |
|  |  | **Trading loss and capital loss** |  |
|  |  | Group relief | 1 |
|  |  | Restriction | 1 |
|  |  | Pre-entry loss | 1 |
|  |  |  | — |
|  |  | Available | 24 |
|  |  |  | — |
|  |  | Maximum | 21 |
|  |  |  | — |

|  | (b) | Large company | 1 |
|---|---|---|---|
|  |  | Implications | 1 |
|  |  | Exception | 1 |
|  |  | Due dates | 1 |
|  |  | Maximum/Available | 4 |
|  |  | Available | 28 |
|  |  | Maximum | 25 |

## Step by step answer plan

### Overview

This is a fairly standard corporation tax question on overseas aspects with minor parts on relief for group losses and the new quarterly instalment rules for corporation tax paydays of large companies.

**Step 1** Read through the question noting that the bulk of the marks (part (a)) are given for dealing with 6 separate points. You are told the trading profit figure for the relevant period but this is just to fix the marginal tax rate at 30%.

**Step 2** Answer each of the 6 sections of part (a) under a separate heading commenting on CFC status wherever a foreign sub is encountered. In particular note that DTTs apply but they have the same effect as if unilateral relief was taken for foreign tax credits.

**Step 3** Ensure you include appropriate calculations especially in regard of the CT implications.

**Step 4** Answer part (b) on quarterly instalments. The question does not actually state that the paydays are required but it is difficult to see how your answer would be complete without them.

**Step 5** Re-read the question and your answer to ensure nothing has been overlooked.

## The examiner's answer

**(a)** **Rate of corporation tax**

The full rate of corporation tax for the year ended 30 September 2000 is 30%.

**Shareholding in Nouveau Inc.**

Northia is not a low tax country since its corporation tax rate of 25% is higher than 22.5% (30% × 75%). Therefore, Nouveau Inc. will not be classed as a controlled foreign company.

The dividend received from Nouveau Inc. will be included as Schedule D Case V income when calculating Global plc's corporation tax liability for the year ended 30 September 2000. Global plc owns 10% or more of the share capital of Nouveau Inc., so relief will be given for the underlying tax paid in Northia:

|  |  | £ |
|---|---|---|
| Dividend received | 300,000 × 90% | 270,000 |
| Underlying tax | 270,000 × 25/(100 − 25) | 90,000 |
| Schedule D case V income |  | 360,000 |

The total tax paid in Northia is £103,500 (90,000 + (270,000 at 5%)), and this is less than the UK corporation tax on the Schedule D case V income (360,000 at 30% = £108,000), and so can be relieved in full as a tax credit.

### Transfer pricing

Sales are going to be made to a non-resident group company at an undervalue. This will reduce UK trading profits and hence UK corporation tax, so a true market price must be substituted for the transfer price. The market price will be an 'arms length' one that would be charged if the parties to the transaction were independent of each other. For the year ended 30 September 2000 Global plc will be subject to self assessment, so the company is required to make the adjustment itself. An adjustment of £42,500 (10,000 × £12.75 × 25/75) will be required, unless the discount is justified by different trading terms.

### Branch in Eastina

The branch in Eastina is controlled from that country, and Global plc will therefore be assessed under Schedule D case V. The branch profits are subject to UK corporation tax in full regardless of the amount remitted to the UK.

The tax paid in Eastina of £70,000 (175,000 at 40%) is more than the UK corporation tax on the Schedule D case V income of £52,500 (175,000 at 30%), and so double taxation relief will be restricted to £52,500.

### Controlled foreign company

Westonia is a low tax country since its corporation tax rate of 10% is less than 75% of the rate that would have been payable in the UK. Middleman Inc. does not meet the following exclusion tests:

(1)    It is not quoted on a recognised stock exchange.

(2)    Its profits are not less than £50,000 p.a.

(3)    It does not have an acceptable distribution policy, since less than 90% of taxable profits are distributed.

(4)    The exempt activities test. Middleman Inc. would appear to be engaged in a non-qualifying business, since it is dealing in goods for delivery from a connected person (Global plc).

Unless the motive test can be satisfied in that Middleman Inc. does not exist for the purpose of avoiding UK tax, it will be classed as a controlled foreign company. Global plc will then be assessed to UK corporation tax on apportioned profits of £450,000 in the year ended 30 September 2000, rather than on the dividend remitted to the UK in the following year. Double taxation relief will be given for the tax paid in Westonia of £45,000 (450,000 at 10%). Global plc must include details of the apportioned profits in its self assessment tax return without any direction from the Inland Revenue.

### Sale of shareholding

The factory was transferred from Global plc to Surplus Ltd, a 75% subsidiary, within six years of the date that Surplus Ltd is to leave the group. The transfer would originally have been at no gain/no loss, but a chargeable gain of £302,800 (630,000 - 260,000 - 67,200) will now be assessed on Surplus Ltd for the year ended 30 September 2000. The related corporation tax liability is £90,840 (302,800 at 30%).

Global plc's chargeable gain on the sale of the shareholding in Surplus Ltd will be reduced to £749,160 (840,000 – 90,840), and so the related corporation tax liability for the year ended 30 September 2000 will be £224,748 (749,160 at 30%).

### Trading loss and capital loss

Wanted Ltd will be able to group relieve its trading loss to Global plc (and 75% subsidiaries) under s.402 ICTA 1988. Relief will be limited to the lower of £160,000 (240,000 × 8/12) and 8/12 of the claimant company's PCTCT (assuming coterminous accounting periods).

The capital loss of £170,000 is a pre-entry loss. It will not be possible for Global plc to utilise this loss against the gain arising on the disposal of the shares in Surplus Ltd, by transferring the shareholding to Wanted Ltd prior to disposal outside of the group.

**(b)**    Global plc is a large company since for the year ended 30 September 2000 it will pay the full rate of corporation tax. Global plc will therefore have to pay 72% of its corporation tax liability by instalments, with the remaining 28% being paid on the normal due date of 1 July 2001. However, an exception will apply if profits do not exceed £10 million (reduced according to the number of associated companies), and Global plc was not a large company for the year ended 30 September 1999.

The four quarterly instalments will be due on 14 April 2000, 14 July 2000, 14 October 2000 and 14 January 2001. Instalments will be based on the expected corporation tax liability for the year ended 30 September 2000, and so Global plc will have to produce an accurate forecast of its corporation tax liability for the year.

---

**Did you answer the question?**

You were not required to calculate the total CT liability for Global plc – just the tax effect of the individual items where appropriate.

---

**Tutorial note**

The change to self-assessment for companies (applying for accounting periods ending on or after 1 July 1999) has an important impact where the CFC or transfer pricing rules are concerned. The onus is now on the company to decide if the provisions apply with penalties if it transpires that they made the wrong decision. For transfer pricing the company has to keep detailed evidence of the reasons for their decisions so that they can show they were not negligent even if with benefit of hindsight, they got it wrong.

---

## 80    (Answer 2 of examination)

( **Examiner's comments and marking guide** )

This question dealt with the disposal of an unincorporated business. Part (a) tested candidates' ability to (1) calculate the Schedule D case I assessment for the year of disposal, (2) calculate the CGT liability, and (3) advise on the VAT implications. Part (b) tested candidates' ability to advise on the income tax, CGT and NIC implications of (1) delaying the disposal until the following tax year, and (2) taking the consideration wholly in the form of shares rather than as cash. This was a reasonably popular question, and there were a number of very good answers. It was disappointing, however, that very few candidates appreciated that the disposal of the business would result in a balancing charge for plant and machinery, and many therefore wasted time in preparing an unnecessarily detailed capital allowances computation. The other aspects of part (a) were generally well answered. In part (b), the implications of delaying the disposal until the following tax year caused a number of problems. In particular, many candidates were unsure as to how this would affect the Schedule D case I assessments, and did not appreciate that additional class 4 NIC would be payable.

|  |  | *Marks* |
|---|---|---:|
| (a) | **Schedule D case I assessment** | |
|  | Balancing charge | 2 |
|  | Year ended 31 August 1999 | 1 |
|  | Period ended 31 March 2000 | 1 |
|  | Relief for overlap profits | 1 |
|  |  | — |
|  | Maximum/Available | 5 |
|  |  | — |
|  | **Capital gains tax liability** | |
|  | Goodwill | 1 |
|  | Freehold properties | 1 |
|  | Capital loss brought forward | 1 |
|  | Taper relief | 2 |
|  | Annual exemption/CGT liability | 1 |
|  |  | — |
|  | Maximum/Available | 6 |
|  |  | — |

**VAT**
Transfer as a going concern                                               1
VAT registration                                                         1
                                                                      ———
                                        Maximum/Available     2
                                                                      ———

(b)     **Disposal on 30 April 2000**
        1999-00 assessment                                               1
        2000-01 assessment                                               2
        Due dates                                                        1
        Class 4 NIC                                                      1
        Taper relief                                                     2
        CGT due date                                                     1
        Conclusion                                                       1
                                                                      ———
                                                Available     9
                                                                      ———
                                                Maximum     7
                                                                      ———

        **Consideration as ordinary shares**
        Gain rolled over                                                 1
        Conditions                                                       1
        Base cost                                                        1
        Taper relief                                                     1
        Non-business asset                                               1
        Conclusion                                                       1
                                                                      ———
                                                Available     6
                                                                      ———
                                                Maximum     5
                                                                      ———
                                                Available     28
                                                                      ———
                                                Maximum     25
                                                                      ———

---

## Step by step answer plan

**Overview**

This is a straightforward exercise on the sale of a business with the requirements conveniently broken down into 5 separate questions. Although there are 4 different taxes to consider – IT, CGT, VAT and NIC – there is nothing unduly difficult.

**Step 1** Read through the question carefully and realise that for part (a) you have to assume the sale occurs on 31 March 2000. There is an alternative cessation date but this can be left until part (b).

**Step 2** Answer the first section of part (a). The main issue is the balancing charge on cessation. Otherwise it should be easy to see that the 1999/00 assessment is made up of the profits of the periods ending in that year less the overlap relief brought forward.

**Step 3** Next calculate the CGT on the disposal making it clear how losses are allocated to maximise the taper relief.

**Step 4** For section 3 of part (a) cover the VAT points. As there are only 2 marks there will not be much to say.

**Step 5** For section 1 of part (b) you should highlight the differences resulting from delaying cessation by a month. This time a comment is needed on the NIC effect.

**Step 6** Your answer for section 2 of part (b) concerns only the CGT differences of being paid in shares rather than in cash and several points can be made. Remember there are 5 marks available.

---

**Step 7** Read through the question and ensure all the information has been used – eg, have the capital losses brought forward been set-off?

## The examiner's answer

**(a)** **Schedule D case I assessment for 1999-00**

The disposal of the fixtures and fittings will result in a balancing charge of £95,000 as follows:

|  | £ |
|---|---|
| WDV brought forward | 114,000 |
| Addition | 31,000 |
|  | 145,000 |
| Disposal proceeds | 240,000 |
| Balancing charge | 95,000 |

Delia and Fastfood Ltd are not connected persons, and so they cannot elect to transfer the fixtures and fittings at their written down value. Delia's 1999-00 Schedule D case I assessment is £206,500 as follows:

|  | £ | £ |
|---|---|---|
| Year ended 31 August 1999 |  | 77,200 |
| Period ended 31 March 2000 | 58,500 |  |
| Balancing charge | 95,000 |  |
|  |  | 153,500 |
|  |  | 230,700 |
| Relief for overlap profits |  | 24,200 |
|  |  | 206,500 |

**Capital gains tax liability 1999-00**

Delia's disposal of her business on 31 March 2000 will result in a CGT liability of £123,180 as follows:

|  | £ | £ |
|---|---|---|
| Goodwill (125,000 - Nil cost) |  | 125,000 |
| Freehold property (1) (462,000 – 230,000) |  | 232,000 |
| Freehold property (2) (118,000 – 94,000) | 24,000 |  |
| Capital loss brought forward | 12,400 |  |
|  |  | 11,600 |
|  |  | 368,600 |
| Taper relief (working) |  | 53,550 |
|  |  | 315,050 |
| Annual exemption |  | 7,200 |
| Chargeable gain |  | 307,950 |
| Capital gains tax at 40% |  | 123,180 |

**Working – Taper relief**

Assets acquired before 17 March 1998 qualify for taper relief based on one additional complete year. Taper relief is maximised by setting the capital loss brought forward of £12,400 against the capital gain of £24,000 arising on freehold property (2). Taper relief is therefore £53,550 (125,000 + 232,000 = 357,000 × 15% (100% – 85%)).

**Value added tax**

Output VAT will not have to be charged on the value of stocks and other assets on which VAT has been claimed, since Delia's business is being transferred as a going concern. Delia will have to inform HM Customs & Excise by 30 April 2000 that she has ceased to make taxable supplies. They will then cancel her VAT registration as from 31 March 2000.

**(b)** **Disposal on 30 April 2000**

There are a number of implications if the disposal is delayed until 30 April 2000:

(1) Delia's Schedule D case I assessments will be as follows:

|  | £ | £ |
|---|---|---|
| 1999-00 Year ended 31 August 1999 |  | 77,200 |
| 2000-01 Period ended 30 April 2000 |  |  |
| (58,500 + 9,000) | 67,500 |  |
| Balancing charge | 95,000 |  |
|  | 162,500 |  |
| Relief for overlap profits | 24,200 |  |
|  |  | 138,300 |

The balancing payment of the related income tax liability will be due on 31 January 2002 rather than on 31 January 2001, although payments on account will be required on 31 January and 31 July 2001 based on the 1999-00 assessment.

(2) Delia will have to pay maximum class 4 NIC contributions for 1999-00 and 2000-01 rather than just for 1999-00. This is an additional cost of £1,108 ((26,000 - 7,530) at 6%).

(3) Taper relief will be based on a holding period of three complete years. This will reduce the CGT liability by £10,710 (357,000 × 7·5% (85% - 77.5%) at 40%).

(4) The CGT liability will be due on 31 January 2002 rather than on 31 January 2001.

A disposal date of 30 April 2000 therefore appears to be beneficial.

**Consideration as ordinary shares in Fastfood Ltd**

If the consideration is in the form of ordinary shares then the capital gain of £381,000 (125,000 + 232,000 + 24,000) will automatically be rolled over against the base cost of the shares in Fastfood Ltd. This is because Delia's business is transferred as a going concern, and all of the business assets are being transferred. The fact that she does not become an employee or director of Fastfood Ltd is irrelevant. The base cost of the shares will be £469,000 (850,000 – 381,000).

On a subsequent disposal of the shares in Fastfood Ltd, only the period of ownership of the shares will count in deciding how much taper relief is due. The shares will be treated as a non-business asset for taper relief purposes, since Delia's holding is not 25% or more. The maximum reduction is therefore 40% (100% – 60%) if the shares are held for ten complete years.

From a tax point of view, taking the consideration in the form of shares appears to be beneficial since the CGT liability is postponed until such time as the shares are sold. This must be balanced against the relatively risky nature of an investment quoted on the AIM.

**Did you answer the question?**

You were not required to make any planning suggestions such as re-allocating the disposal proceeds of £850K between the assets of the business to give a more tax efficient result.

## 81    (Answer 3 of examination)

**Examiner's comments and marking guide**

Part (a) tested candidates' ability to advise on the CGT and IHT implications arising from four gifts: (1) shares in an unquoted company for which retirement relief and business property relief were available, (2) a principal private residence, (3) shares in a quoted company, and (4) a motor car subject to a reservation of benefit. Part (b)(i) tested candidates' ability to calculate the additional IHT that will become payable on death in respect of a chargeable lifetime transfer, and part (b)(ii) required candidates to explain the circumstances in which a discretionary trust will be liable to IHT. This was a popular question, and there were many very good answers. As already mentioned, however, the answers of some candidates to part (a) were badly presented making it difficult to know which aspect of the question was being answered. The shares in the quoted company caused another problem, where many candidates did not know the correct matching rules. A number of candidates wasted time by preparing a CGT computation in respect of the disposal of the motor car, despite this being exempt. Other candidates wasted time by giving unnecessary information regarding the treatment of PETs. Part (b) was not answered so well, with only a few candidates correctly calculating the additional IHT liability.

|  |  | *Marks* |
|---|---|---|
| **(a)** | **Ordinary shares in Legacy Ltd - CGT implications** |  |
|  | Entitlement to retirement relief | 1 |
|  | Gift relief | 1 |
|  | Capital gain | 1 |
|  | Retirement relief | 1 |
|  |  |  |
|  | **Ordinary shares in Legacy Ltd - IHT implications** |  |
|  | Potentially exempt transfer | 1 |
|  | Value transferred | 2 |
|  | Business property relief | 1 |
|  |  |  |
|  | **Gift to discretionary trust - CGT implications** |  |
|  | Capital gain | 1 |
|  | Exemption | 2 |
|  | Letting relief | 1 |
|  | Gift relief | 1 |
|  |  |  |
|  | **Gift to discretionary trust - IHT implications** |  |
|  | Chargeable lifetime transfer | 1 |
|  | IHT liability | 1 |
|  |  |  |
|  | **Ordinary shares in Grant plc - CGT implications** |  |
|  | Value per share | 1 |
|  | Acquisition on 16 December 1999 | 1 |
|  | Acquisition on 30 June 1999 | 1 |
|  | 1985 pool | 1 |
|  | CGT liability | 1 |
|  |  |  |
|  | **Ordinary shares in Grant plc - IHT implications** |  |
|  | Wedding exemption/Potentially exempt transfer | 1 |
|  |  |  |
|  | **Motor car** |  |
|  | CGT exemption | 1 |
|  | Gift with reservation | 1 |
|  | Potentially exempt transfer | 1 |
|  | Included in estate/Relief for double charge | 1 |

|  | Available | 25 |
|---|---|---|
|  | Maximum | 20 |

| **(b)** | Additional IHT liability | 1 |
|---|---|---|
|  | Business property relief not available | 1 |
|  | Conclusion | 1 |
|  | Principal charge | 1 |
|  | Exit charges | 1 |

|  | Maximum/Available | 5 |
|---|---|---|
|  | Available | 30 |
|  | Maximum | 25 |

---

### Step by step answer plan

**Overview**

The main part of the question concerns the IHT and CGT implications of a number of lifetime gifts. Part (b) – for only 5 marks – concerns IHT and a discretionary trust. Only 2 of the marks relate to the special rules for applying IHT to such trusts so this should not discourage you from choosing the question. A number of minor items such as IHT tapering relief, IHT annual exemptions and the CGT annual exemption are excluded so that you can concentrate on the more important features of the question.

**Step 1**    As usual read the question noting carefully the general points such as the fact that the donor will pay any CGT or IHT due and annual exemptions can be ignored.

**Step 2**    Answer part (a) keeping separate headings for each of the 4 gifts and separate sub-headings for the two taxes concerned with the necessary calculations and explanations where reliefs have been applied. Leave some space here and there in case you have time to review your answer and decide to add something further.

**Step 3**    For part (b) consider how the settlor's death could result in an IHT charge for the trustees. You should spot the risk of BPR being lost on the earlier PET and hence a 'biting' PET scenario.

**Step 4**    Don't forget the second section of part (b). Note that you only have to say when the trust will be liable to IHT. Thankfully you do not have to explain how the tax charge is calculated.

**Step 5**    Check through your answer and the corresponding parts of the question to ensure no slips in your calculations. You might want to use some of the space you left earlier to enlarge on explanations.

---

### The examiner's answer

**(a)    Ordinary shares in Legacy Ltd – CGT implications**

|  | £ | £ |
|---|---|---|
| Deemed consideration (100,000 at £3.40) |  | 340,000 |
| Indexed cost (189,200 × 100,000/200,000) |  | 94,600 |
|  |  | 245,400 |
| Retirement relief |  |  |
| 200,000 × 60% | 120,000 |  |
| 245,400 − 120,000 = 125,400 × 50% | 62,700 |  |
|  |  | 182,700 |
| Chargeable gain |  | 62,700 |

---

Arthur is entitled to retirement relief because he is over 50 years old, is a full-time working director of Legacy Ltd, which is a trading company, and owns not less than 5% of its ordinary share capital. Retirement relief is restricted by a factor of 60%, since this is the period that Arthur has been a shareholder. Provided Arthur and his son jointly elect, the balance of the gain can be heldover as a gift of business assets, since Legacy Ltd is an unquoted trading company.

**Ordinary shares in Legacy Ltd - IHT implications**

Arthur's gift of shares in Legacy Ltd will be a PET for £725,000 as follows:

| | £ |
|---|---|
| Value of shares held before the transfer | |
| 200,000 × £5.50 (part of a 60% holding) | 1,100,000 |
| Value of shares held after the transfer | |
| 100,000 × £3.75 (part of a 40% holding) | 375,000 |
| | |
| Value transferred | 725,000 |

Business property relief at the rate of 100% will be available, so an IHT liability will only arise if Arthur dies before 20 May 2006 and his son has disposed of the shares before that date.

**Gift to discretionary trust - CGT implications**

| | £ | £ |
|---|---|---|
| Deemed consideration | | 275,000 |
| Cost | | 47,600 |
| | | |
| | | 227,400 |
| Indexation to April 1998 $47,600 \times \dfrac{162.6-81.88}{81.88}$ (0.986) | | 46,934 |
| | | |
| | | 180,466 |
| Exemption (180,466 × 11·5/17) | 122,080 | |
| Letting relief | 40,000 | |
| | | 162,080 |
| | | |
| Chargeable gain | | 18,386 |

The period from 1 July 1982 to 31 December 1990 (8.5 years) and the last three years of ownership are exempt. Letting relief is available for the period from 1 January 1991 to 30 June 1996 (180,466 × 5.5/17 = £58,386) but is restricted to £40,000. Arthur can elect to have the balance of the gain heldover because there is an immediate charge to IHT.

**Gift to discretionary trust - IHT implications**

The gift of the freehold property will be a chargeable lifetime transfer. The gift of £275,000 must be grossed up, so IHT of £11,000 (275,000 − 231,000 = 44,000 × 20/80) will be due by 30 April 2000. The gross value of the transfer is £286,000 (275,000 + 11,000).

**Ordinary shares in Grant plc - CGT implications**

The shares are valued at 307p ((288 + 326)/2) per share.

| Acquisition | Proceeds £ | Cost £ | Gain £ |
|---|---|---|---|
| 16 December 1999 | 6,140 (2,000 at 307p) | 6,500 | (360) |
| 30 June 1999 | 30,700 (10,000 at 307p) | 23,700 | 7,000 |
| 1985 Pool | 36,840 (12,000 at 307p) | 22,080 | 14,760 |
| | | | |
| Chargeable gain | | | 21,400 |

The disposal must initially be matched with the acquisition on 16 December 1999, since this is within the following 30 days. The indexed cost of the 1985 pool is calculated as £27,600 × 12,000/15,000 = £22,080. Taper relief is nil as the shares are not business assets, so CGT of £8,560 (21,400 at 40%) will be due on 31 January 2001.

**Ordinary shares in Grant plc - IHT implications**

The gift of the shares is in consideration of marriage, and will therefore qualify for an exemption of £2,500. The balance of the gift of £71,180 (24,000 at 307p = 73,680 - 2,500) will be a PET made on 28 November 1999.

**Motor car - CGT and IHT implications**

Motor cars are exempt assets for CGT purposes, and so there are no CGT implications in making the gift.

Although Arthur has made a gift of the motor car, he has reserved a benefit for himself in that the agreement allows him unrestricted use of the motor car. It will therefore be a gift with reservation. The gift will be a PET for £125,000 as normal on 8 December 1999, but Arthur will still be treated as beneficially entitled to the motor car. It will therefore be included in his estate when he dies at its market value at that date, although relief will be given should there be a double charge to IHT. Arthur could avoid these provisions by paying full consideration for the use of the motor car.

**(b)** If Arthur dies before 30 June 2006, then an additional IHT liability of £11,000 ((286,000 - 231,000) at 40% = 22,000 - 11,000) will arise. However, should business property relief not be available in respect of the gift made on 20 May 1999, and Arthur dies before 20 May 2006, the additional IHT liability becomes £103,400 (286,000 at 40% = 114,400 − 11,000). The trustees should therefore take out insurance cover for £103,400.

The discretionary trust will be subject to a principal charge at each tenth anniversary after 30 June 1999. The charge will be based on the value of the trust property at that time. An exit charge will arise if property leaves the trust, either before or after the ten-year anniversary.

---

**Did you answer the question?**

You were not required to explain how the tax charge is calculated when property leaves a discretionary trust or when a principal charge arises.

---

**Tutorial note**

In this exam sitting the examiner has occasionally provided the figure for cost as indexed to April 1998 to make capital gains calculations easier.

---

## 82 (Answer 4 of examination)

**Examiner's comments and marking guide**

This question required candidates to calculate the income tax liability for a husband and wife, and then to advise on tax planning measures that could be taken in order to reduce their overall liability. This was another popular question, and there were a number of very good answers. As regards the calculation of the tax liabilities, the only aspects to cause problems were that very few candidates appreciated that interest from National Savings Certificate is exempt from tax, and the inability to correctly calculate the age related personal allowances. Many candidates also able to give appropriate advice as regards tax planning measures, although far too many candidates incorrectly discussed transferring the married couples allowance.

*Marks*

**Income tax liability 1999-00**

| | |
|---|---|
| Pension/Schedule E | 1 |
| Pension Contribution | 1 |

---

| | |
|---|---|
| BSI/Gilt interest | 1 |
| Schedule A/Schedule D case V | 1 |
| Personal allowances | 1 |
| Income tax | 1 |
| MCA | 1 |
| Double taxation relief | 1 |
| Maximum/Available | 8 |

**Income tax saving**

| | |
|---|---|
| Utilisation of basic rate band | 1 |
| BSI/Gilt interest/UK property | 2 |
| Overseas property | 1 |
| Age related allowances | 1 |
| Effectiveness for future years | 1 |
| Calculation: Interest/Schedule A | 1 |
| Calculation: Schedule D case V | 1 |
| Calculation: Personal allowance/MCA | 1 |
| Available | 9 |
| Maximum | 8 |
| Available | 17 |
| Maximum | 16 |

### ( Step by step answer plan )

#### Overview

This is a personal tax question which hinges on one of the few opportunities left for husband and wife to save income tax. For the first part, the couples' tax liability has to be calculated with the minor complexities of age relief and double tax relief to consider. For the second part the tax saving from shifting income is required. The tax effect of each step is shown by using the marginal effect eg, the extra tax payable when the age relief is lost, instead of recalculating the tax liability form scratch. There was an extra part concerning the transition from PEPs and TESSAs to the ISA regime for tax efficient saving but we have removed it as PEPs and TESSAs are now outside the syllabus. The examiner's comments and marking guide have been edited accordingly.

**Step 1**  Read the question and answer part (a) with the appropriate layouts of Taxable Income/Income tax liability.

**Step 2**  Consider including any necessary notes in support of your calculations. For example, the examiner comments that NSC interest is exempt and shows the age relief adjustment but he does not say why the age related MCA is given in full ie, that wife's income is irrelevant. You have to judge for yourself how much to say although the marking guide does not offer any credit for specific comments at this point.

**Step 3**  For part (b), think carefully about the possible tax planning steps. Your answer should start by setting the scene – ie, the differences in marginal tax rates. Each step should be explained and the tax saving evaluated in terms of the change in tax rate applying.

**Step 4**  Review your answer and the detail of the question. Have you thought through all the tax planning steps? For example, the advantage of transferring Wilma's share of the overseas profit.

**The examiner's answer**

(a)    **Income tax liability 1999-00**

| | Harold £ | Wilma £ |
|---|---|---|
| Pension | 16,600 | |
| Schedule E | | 45,000 |
| Pension contribution (45,000 at 6%) | | 2,700 |
| | | 42,300 |
| BSI (3,600 × 100/80) | | 4,500 |
| Gilt interest | | 2,400 |
| Schedule A | | 4,800 |
| Schedule D case V (2,300/2) | 1,150 | 1,150 |
| Statutory total income | 17,750 | 55,150 |
| Personal allowance (working) | 5,245 | 4,335 |
| Taxable income | 12,505 | 50,815 |
| Income tax:  1,500 at 10% | 150 | 150 |
|    11,005/26,500 at 23% | 2,531 | 6,095 |
|    22,815 at 40% | | 9,126 |
| | 2,681 | 15,371 |
| Married couple's allowance (5,125 at 10%) | (512) | |
| Double taxation relief | | |
| Harold (1,150 × 23%) | (265) | |
| Wilma (1,150 × 35%) | | (403) |
| Income tax liability | 1,904 | 14,968 |

The interest from National Savings Certificates is exempt from income tax.

**Working - Personal allowance**

Harold's personal allowance of £5,720 is reduced by £475 as the income limit is exceeded by £950 (17,750 − 16,800).

(b)    **Income tax saving**

Wilma falls into the 40% tax bracket, whilst Harold's basic rate tax band is not fully utilised. The couple's overall income tax liability for 1999-00 could therefore have been reduced by transferring taxable income from Wilma to Harold, as follows:

(1)    Wilma's building society deposits, UK government stocks and UK property should be transferred unconditionally to Harold. The tax saving will be 20% (40% − 20%) in respect of the interest, and 17% (40% − 23%) in respect of the Schedule A profit.

(2)    Although Harold receives less DTR than Wilma, it is also beneficial to transfer the overseas property entirely into Harold's name. At present, Wilma has an additional 5% (40% − DTR of 35%) UK tax liability on this income.

The transfer of income to Harold will mean that he loses any entitlement to either the age related personal allowance or the age related married couple's allowance, since his statutory total income will exceed the income limit by £13,800 (16,600 + 4,500 + 2,400 + 4,800 + 2,300 - 16,800). Although the tax planning measures cannot be implemented for 1999-00, they should be effective for future years (at least until Wilma retires). The tax saving for 1999-00 would have been £1,729 as follows:

|  | £ |
|---|---|
| BSI/Gilt interest (4,500 + 2,400 = 6,900 at 20%) | 1,380 |
| Schedule A (4,800 at 17%) | 816 |
| Schedule D case V (1,150 at 5%) | 57 |
| Personal allowance (5,245 − 4,335 = 910 at 23%) | (209) |
| Married couple's allowance (5,125 − 1,970 = 3,155 at 10%) | (315) |
|  | 1,729 |

---

**Tutorial note**

As explained above there was a further part on the tax favoured investments of PEPs and TESSAs which are no longer available. For the future this type of question would be likely to require a knowledge of ISAs. In particular taxpayers with a marginal tax rate of 40% and who regularly use their CGT annual exemption would find tax savings from holding equities in an ISA. They would have the bonus of recovering the 10% dividend tax credit but this might be dissipated by management charges and is not due to continue beyond 5 April 2004.

---

## 83    (Answer 5 of examination)

### Examiner's comments and marking guide

Part (a)(i) required candidates to calculate the amount of VAT payable for a number of transactions and to explain the implications of late payment. Part (a)(ii) tested candidates' knowledge of the cash accounting and annual accounting schemes. Part (b) tested candidates' ability to advise on the income tax, corporation tax and NIC implications arising from the provision of a company motor car. Part (c) tested candidates' ability to calculate the cost of using a self-employed person as compared to the cost of using an employee. This was a reasonably popular question, and parts (a) and (b) were generally well answered. In Part (a)(i), many candidates failed to appreciate the default surcharge implications of making a late payment of VAT, despite the question clearly indicating that previous VAT returns and payments had been made late. Part (a)(ii) was well answered, and it was pleasing to see that only a few candidates were confused between the two different schemes. In part (b) the main problem was that many candidates either ignored or incorrectly identified the amount of business mileage driven. Part (c) was very badly answered, with hardly a single candidate being able to calculate the correct cost for the employee. This required the grossing up of net pay for income tax and employees class 1 NIC.

|  |  | *Marks* |
|---|---|---|
| **(a)** | **VAT return** | |
| | Output VAT on sales | 1 |
| | Scale charge | 1 |
| | Purchases | 1 |
| | Bad debts | 1 |
| | Motor car/Sunroof | 1 |
| | Expenses | 1 |
| | **The default surcharge** | |
| | Surcharge liability notice | 1 |
| | Surcharges | 1 |
| | Implications for VAT return to 31 March 2000 | 1 |
| | **Cash accounting scheme** | |
| | Use of scheme | 1 |
| | Tax point | 1 |
| | Bad debt relief | 1 |
| | Quarter ended 31 March 2000 | 1 |
| | **Annual accounting scheme** | |
| | Use of scheme | 1 |
| | VAT return/Payments on account | 1 |
| | Balancing payment/Advantages | 1 |

|  |  | Available | 16 |
|---|---|---|---|
|  |  | Maximum | 14 |

**(b)**  **Managing director**

| | |
|---|---|
| Car benefit | 1 |
| Fuel benefit | 1 |
| Mileage limits/reduction to 25% | 1 |
| Ordinary commuting | 1 |
| Private mileage | 1 |
| NIC implications | 1 |

**Gewgaw Ltd**

| | |
|---|---|
| Capital allowances | 1 |
| Fuel and repairs | 1 |
| Class 1A NIC | 1 |

|  |  | Available | 9 |
|---|---|---|---|
|  |  | Maximum | 8 |

**(c)**

| | |
|---|---|
| Bookkeeping agency | 1 |
| Employee | 2 |
| Conclusion | 1 |

|  |  | Available | 4 |
|---|---|---|---|
|  |  | Maximum | 3 |
|  |  | Available | 29 |
|  |  | Maximum | 25 |

## Step by step answer plan

### Overview

The examiner had warned that VAT would become a more prominent topic and this question bears that out. Part (a) covers VAT items which could easily appear in paper 7. These were discounts, bad debt relief, irrecoverable input tax, default surcharge, and the cash accounting and annual accounting schemes none of which should have been a problem. Part (b) looked at the various tax and NIC effects of a company car. Even here you had to know that VAT on cars was included in the price for benefits and for capital allowances. By contrast to a question on cars – supply a car or offer a cash alternative – set in an earlier paper this was far easier. Part (c) dealt with the relative costs including tax and NIC between using an employee or outsourcing a task. As usual the examiner is testing whether you understand the main points in a common practical situation.

**Step 1**  Read the question and realise that it is basically in three separate parts. It is a good question to choose as it is clearly basic topics of VAT etc – so choose it.

**Step 2**  In section 1 of part (a) note that (1) figures supplied are exclusive, (2) cash accounting n/a, and (3) the company is clearly not partially exempt. The work through the 5 items to calculate VAT payable.

**Step 3**  Return regularly to the requirements. Section 1 is not finished until you explain what happens when the VAT is paid late. Start by working out how far the company has fallen into the default surcharge mire.

**Step 4**  For section 2 of part (a) explain the basics of the two accounting schemes without getting them mixed up and reflect on whether the company could or should join. You will not get all the 6 marks just by trotting out your study notes.

**Step 5** For part (b), read the relevant paragraph in the question and items (4) and (5) under 'VAT return'. Then work out how much of the mileage is 'business'. This is the only difficult point. Otherwise your answer simply works through the tax effects for the employee and then effects for the employer. You do not have to mention VAT separately except to the extent it impacts on the taxes specified.

**Step 6** Part (c) is straightforward in that you have to work out the total cost of each route. There is only 3 marks so it is unlikely to be difficult.

**Step 7** Skim through your answer and the question checking that nothing has been overlooked.

## The examiner's answer

**(a)** **VAT Return – Quarter ended 31 March 2000**

|  | £ | £ |
|---|---|---|
| Output VAT |  |  |
| Sales (62,500 × 97·5% (100 - 2.5) × 17.5%) |  | 10,664 |
| Motor car scale charge (396 × 17·5/117.5) |  | 59 |
|  |  | 10,723 |
| Input VAT |  |  |
| Purchases (21,000 × 17·5%) | 3,675 |  |
| Bad debt (2,000 × 17·5%) | 350 |  |
| Expenses (14,640 – 480 = 14,160 × 17.5%) | 2,478 |  |
|  |  | 6,503 |
| VAT due 30 April 2000 |  | 4,220 |

The calculation of output VAT on sales must take into account the discount for prompt payment, even if customers do not take it. Relief for a bad debt is not given until six months from the time that payment is due. Therefore relief in respect of the invoice raised on 5 November 1999 cannot be claimed until the following VAT return. Input VAT cannot be reclaimed in respect of either the motor car or the sunroof, as this was not fitted subsequent to the original purchase and invoiced for separately. The managing director's private use of the motor car does not affect the recovery of input VAT on the repairs. VAT on business entertaining cannot be reclaimed.

**The default surcharge**

Gewgaw Ltd's first VAT return due on 31 July 1999 was submitted late, so HM Customs & Excise will have issued a surcharge liability notice specifying a surcharge period running to 30 June 2000. Although the second and third returns were submitted by the due dates of 31 October 1999 and 31 January 2000 respectively, the VAT due was paid late in each case. Surcharges of 2% and 5% will therefore have been charged, and a further late payment will result in a surcharge of £422 (4,220 × 10%). In addition, the surcharge period will be extended to 31 March 2001.

**Cash accounting scheme**

Gewgaw Ltd can use the cash accounting scheme if (i) its expected taxable turnover for the next 12 months does not exceed £350,000, and (ii) it is up to date with its VAT returns and VAT payments. The scheme will result in the tax point becoming the date that payment is received from customers. This should be advantageous since it delays the payment of output VAT, and also provides for automatic bad debt relief should a customer not pay. In the quarter ended 31 March 2000 the company would have accounted for output VAT on sales of £9,485 (54,200 × 17.5%) instead of £10,664. However, the recovery of input VAT on purchases would have been reduced from £3,675 to £3,395 (19,400 × 17.5%).

### Annual accounting scheme

Gewgaw Ltd can apply to use the annual accounting scheme if (i) it has been VAT registered for 12 months, (ii) its expected taxable turnover for the next 12 months does not exceed £300,000, and (iii) it is up to date with its VAT returns. Under the scheme only one VAT return is submitted each year, with nine monthly payments being made on account. The balancing payment is due two months after the end of the year. It should be beneficial for Gewgaw Ltd to join the scheme, since the reduced administration required should mean that default surcharges are avoided.

**(b)    Managing director**

For 1999-00, the managing director will be assessed under Schedule E on benefits in kind totalling £1,466 as follows:

|  | £ |
|---|---|
| Car benefit 17,300 × 25% × 3/12 | 1,081 |
| Fuel benefit  1,540 × 3/12 | 385 |
|  | 1,466 |

For 1999-00 the 2,500 and 18,000 business mileage limits are reduced to 625 (2,500 × 3/12) and 4,500 (18,000 × 3/12) respectively. The managing director's ordinary commuting totals 5,355 miles (85 × (60 + 3)), since this includes the weekend journeys to turn off the burglar alarm. Private mileage totals 1,205 miles (1,100 + 105), since the journey to the annual dinner party of a customer is not for the purposes of work. Business mileage therefore totals 4,440 miles (11,000 − 5,355 − 1,205), and so the managing director only qualifies for the reduction to 25% of list price. The tax on the car and fuel benefits will be collected under PAYE. There are no NIC implications for the managing director.

**Gewgaw Ltd**

Gewgaw Ltd can claim capital allowances on the VAT inclusive cost of the motor car of £17,300, with the writing-down allowance for the year ended 31 March 2000 being restricted to £3,000. The company can deduct the cost of fuel and repairs in calculating its Schedule D case I trading profit without any adjustment for private use. Class 1A NIC of £179 (1,466 at 12.2%) will be due on 19 July 2000.

**(c)**    The annual cost of using the bookkeeping agency is £6,300 (525 × 12), since any VAT charged is reclaimed as input VAT.

The employee requires £5,200 p.a. (100 × 52) net of income tax at the rate of 23% and employees class 1 NIC at the rate of 10%, so additional gross salary of £7,761 (5,200 × 100/(100 − 23 − 10)) will have to be paid. Employers class 1 NIC will increase the annual cost to £8,708 (7,761 × 112.2/100).

It is therefore beneficial, all other factors being equal, for Gewgaw Ltd to continue to use the bookkeeping agency, since this results in an overall annual saving of £2,408 (8,708 − 6,300).

---

**Did you answer the question?**

You were not required to discuss whether the employee could claim self-employed status in respect of the extra work.

---

**Tutorial note**

It seems unfair that the mileage to attend the premises when the alarm went off at the weekend counts as ordinary commuting when it seems anything but 'ordinary'. However, the legislation merely defines ordinary commuting as travel between an employee's home and permanent workplace with no exclusion for abnormal circumstances.

---

## 84    (Answer 6 of examination)

### Examiner's comments and marking guide

Part (a) tested candidates' knowledge of the criteria that are used by the courts in deciding whether or not an isolated sale transaction will be treated as an adventure in the nature of a trade. Part (b) required candidates to calculate the corporation tax liability for a company if the disposal of a plot of land is (1) treated as a capital gain, and (2) treated as an adventure in the nature of a trade. In the first instance the company would pay rent and a premium for the leasehold of a new factory, and in the second it would qualify for industrial buildings allowance as a result of purchasing the factory outright. This was not a popular question. However, there were some very high scoring answers from many of the few candidates that attempted it. Part (a) was generally well answered, although the answers of several candidates would have benefited from the use of appropriate headings. Part (b) was well answered, provided that candidates read the question carefully. If not, the deductions for either the rent/premium or the industrial buildings allowance were given in the wrong part of the answer. A number of candidates did not appreciate that treatment as an adventure in the nature of a trade would result in additional Schedule D profits, and therefore incorrectly deducted the brought forward capital loss.

|  | | *Marks* |
|---|---|---|
| (a) | The subject matter of the transaction | 1 |
|  | The length of ownership | 1 |
|  | Frequency of similar transactions | 1 |
|  | Work done on the property | 1 |
|  | Circumstances responsible for the realisation | 1 |
|  | Motive | 1 |
|  | Sale of land in existing state | 1 |
|  | Development of land | 1 |
|  | Isolated transaction | 1 |
|  | Profit motive | 1 |
|  | Available | 10 |
|  | Maximum | 9 |
| **(b)** | **Sale of plot of land in its existing state** | |
|  | Lease premium | 2 |
|  | Rent payable | 1 |
|  | Capital gain | 1 |
|  | Capital loss | 1 |
|  | Corporation tax | 1 |
|  | **Development of the plot of land** | |
|  | Industrial buildings allowance | 2 |
|  | Office building | 1 |
|  | First-year allowance | 1 |
|  | Sale proceeds/Cost of land | 1 |
|  | Construction costs | 1 |
|  | Loan interest | 1 |
|  | Corporation tax | 1 |
|  | **Advice on undertaking the development** | |
|  | Additional profits | 1 |
|  | Corporation tax implications | 1 |
|  | Conclusion | 1 |
|  | Other factors | 1 |
|  | Available | 18 |
|  | Maximum | 16 |

Available   28
―――
Maximum   25
―――

### Step by step answer plan

**Overview**

This is not an easy question to understand under exam conditions as there are two sets of choices although the examiner's requirements try to help you follow just two routes. The first part is a 'badges of trade' question with additional comment needed on how they relate to the proposed alternative transactions. For the second part you have to follow through the tax effects under two separate sets of choices. These are carefully spent out and are not difficult to action.

**Step 1**   Read the question carefully and concentrate on part (a) of the requirements. This concerns mainly the background for the alternative tax treatments of an isolated transaction – capital gain or trading profit. Your answer should list out the badges of trade with brief explanations and then discuss their relevance to the alternative regarding the plot of land.

**Step 2**   Note that part (b) has three sections, the third being advice to the company on developing the land.

**Step 3**   Compute the PCTCT and CT assuming the disposal is a capital gain and the company pays a premium for the leasehold. As the lease is for less than 50 years the parties cannot elect for the lessee to claim IBAs but the lessee can claim relief for the income element of the premium.

**Step 4**   Compute PCTCT and CT assuming the company has a trading profit from developing the site and acquires a new industrial building. Use working notes as appropriate.

**Step 5**   Finally for part (b) compare your figures from steps 3 and 4 and write a paragraph of advice on whether to develop the land.

**Step 6**   Review the question to ensure nothing is missed. For example, did you try to include indexation allowance when the question required it to be ignored?

### The examiner's answer

(a)    There is no single test as to what constitutes trading, but certain tests, the badges of trade, will be used to determine whether or not the purchase and resale of the plot of land is a trading transaction. The tests are:

**The subject matter of the transaction**: Property which does not yield an income nor gives personal enjoyment to its owner is likely to form the subject matter of a trading transaction.

**The length of ownership**: A sale of property within a short time of its acquisition is an indication of trading.

**Frequency of similar transactions**: Repeated transactions in the same subject matter are an indication of trading.

**Work done on the property**: Carrying out work to the property in order to make it more marketable, or taking steps to find purchasers, will indicate a trading motive.

**Circumstances responsible for the realisation**: A forced sale to raise cash for an emergency will by presumption indicate that the transaction is not an adventure in the nature of a trade.

**Motive**: If a transaction is undertaken with the motive of realising a profit, this will be a strong indication of trading.

The sale of the land in its existing state is likely to be treated as a capital gain. Easy-Speak Ltd purchased the land with a view to building a factory on it, and has not carried out any supplementary work. These are both strong indications that the company is not trading.

Conversely, the development of the land would appear to establish an adventure in the nature of a trade. The sale of the industrial units soon after their completion, and the financing of the development by way of a bank loan, support this conclusion. Although the disposal is an isolated transaction, this does not prevent it being treated as an adventure in the nature of a trade. A profit motive is indicated by factors such as developing the land, although the absence of a profit motive will not prevent Easy-Speak Ltd from being treated as trading.

**(b)** **Sale of plot of land in its existing state**

|  | £ | £ |
|---|---|---|
| Schedule D1 profits |  | 270,000 |
| Lease premium (working) |  | (6,720) |
| Rent payable (27,600 × 6/12) |  | (13,800) |
|  |  | 249,480 |
| Capital gain (320,000 − 224,000) | 96,000 |  |
| Capital loss brought forward | 61,600 |  |
|  |  | 34,400 |
| PCTCT |  | 283,880 |
| Corporation tax at 20% |  | 56,776 |

**Working - Lease premium**

|  | £ |
|---|---|
| Premium paid | 280,000 |
| Less 280,000 × 2% × (15 − 1) | 78,400 |
|  | 201,600/15 = £13,440 |

The deduction for the year ended 31 March 2000 is restricted to £6,720 (13,440 × 6/12).

**Development of the plot of land**

|  | £ |
|---|---|
| Schedule D1 profits | 270,000 |
| Industrial buildings allowance (working 1) | (9,380) |
| First-year allowance (working 1) | (11,400) |
| Additional trading profit (working 2) | 172,250 |
| PCTCT | 421,470 |
| Corporation tax at 30% | 126,441 |
| Taper relief 1/40 (1,500,000 − 421,470) | 26,963 |
|  | 99,478 |

**Working 1 - Capital allowances**

The factory will qualify for IBA on £234,500 (430,000 − 80,000 − 87,000 − 28,500). The cost of land does not qualify. The general office also does not qualify since it is more than 25% of the total cost (234,500 + 87,000 = 321,500 × 25% = £80,375). IBA of £9,380 (234,500 × 4%) will be given in the year ended 31 March 2000. The cost of the heating and ventilation systems qualifies as plant and machinery, and a FYA of £11,400 (28,500 at 40%) will be given for the year ended 31 March 2000.

### Working 2 - Additional trading profit

|  | £ | £ |
|---|---:|---:|
| Sale proceeds |  | 550,000 |
| Cost of land | 224,000 |  |
| Construction costs | 147,500 |  |
| Loan interest (150,000 × 12.5% × 4/12) | 6,250 |  |
|  |  | 377,750 |
| Profit |  | 172,250 |

### Advice on undertaking the development

The development of the plot of land by Easy-Speak Ltd will mean that the company makes additional profits of £76,250 (172,250 − 96,000). However, this alternative results in an increased corporation tax liability for the year ended 31 March 2000 of £42,702 (99,478 − 56,776), so the overall benefit is only £33,548 (76,250 − 42,702). Given the high risk of developing the plot of land compared to a sale in its existing state, Easy-Speak Ltd may prefer to forego this potential additional profit. The company's preference between outright purchase of the new factory and the acquisition of a leasehold interest may be the deciding factor.

# DECEMBER 1999 QUESTIONS

## 85 (Question 1 of examination)

Oliver Seas, an engineer, commenced employment with Overseas Aid, a charity involved in helping third world countries, on 1 July 1999. Prior to 30 June 1999 he was unemployed. On 1 December 1999 Oliver was sent to the country of Changa for an eighteen-month assignment to help local farmers. Until 30 November 1999 he has always been resident and ordinarily resident in the UK. Oliver has no intention of changing his UK domicile status.

Oliver is paid a salary of £2,600 per month by Overseas Aid, and Changan tax of £140 per month will be payable in respect of the salary while he is working in Changa. Oliver has the following other income for 1999-00:

(1)     Schedule A profits of £1,050 per month commencing on 1 December 1999 from the rental of his main residence situated in the UK.

(2)     Building society interest of £3,200 (net) and £2,080 (net) that was received on 30 June and 31 December 1999 respectively.

(3)     Schedule D case V profits of £800 (gross) per month from the rental of a holiday apartment situated in the country of Farland. The profits are subject to Farlandian tax at the rate of 35%.

(4)     Interest of £510 (net) per month from a bank deposit account situated in Farland. The interest is subject to Farlandian withholding tax at the rate of 15%. This account was closed on 5 April 2000, and the capital was reinvested in a bank deposit account situated in the UK.

During 1999-00 Oliver undertook the following transactions in the £1 ordinary shares of Medusa plc, a UK company:

| | | |
|---|---|---|
| 12 May 1999 | Bought | 4,500 shares for £27,450 |
| 5 October 1999 | Sold | 6,500 shares for £58,500 |
| 25 October 1999 | Bought | 2,000 shares for £18,400 |
| 3 April 2000 | Sold | 5,000 shares for £54,000 |

He had originally purchased 10,000 £1 ordinary shares in the company during 1994. The cost of these shares (indexed to April 1998) is £46,400. The shares in Medusa plc do not qualify as a business asset for CGT purposes.

There is no double taxation treaty between the UK and Changa. The double taxation treaty between the UK and Farland provides that taxes suffered in Farland are relieved as a tax credit against UK income tax.

All of the above figures are in Pounds sterling.

**Required:**

(a)     Explain why Oliver will be treated as not resident or ordinarily resident in the UK during the eighteen-month period working overseas commencing on 1 December 1999.            **(3 marks)**

(b)     (i)        Calculate the UK income tax payable by Oliver for 1999-00. Your answer should include an explanation of the double taxation relief that is available to Oliver.            **(10 marks)**

          (ii)       Advise Oliver of his UK CGT liability for 1999-00.            **(6 marks)**

(c)    Explain why it would have been beneficial for Oliver to have:

    (i)    Reinvested the capital from the bank deposit account closed on 5 April 2000 in another overseas bank account rather than in an account situated in the UK.    **(2 marks)**

    (ii)    Delayed the disposal of the 5,000 shares in Medusa plc on 3 April 2000 until 6 April 2000.
**(4 marks)**
**(Total: 25 marks)**

---

## 86    (Question 2 of examination)

(a)    Jane Macbeth, aged 61, died on 20 November 1999. At the date of her death Jane owned the following assets:

    (1)    A main residence valued at £235,000. This has an outstanding repayment mortgage of £40,000.

    (2)    Building society deposits of £87,000.

    (3)    10,000 £1 ordinary shares in Banquo plc. On 20 November 1999 the shares were quoted at 945 - 957, with bargains on that day of 937, 961 and 939.

        Jane inherited the shares as a specific gift on the death of her sister on 10 August 1997 when they were valued at £68,000. The sister's executors paid IHT of £54,000 on an estate valued at £360,000.

    (4)    A life assurance policy on her own life. Immediately prior to the date of Jane's death, the policy had an open market value of £86,000. Proceeds of £104,000 were received following her death.

    (5)    Agricultural land valued at £168,000, but with an agricultural value of £110,000. The land was purchased during 1991, and it has always been let to tenant farmers. The most recent tenancy commenced on 1 January 1999.

Jane made the following gifts during her lifetime (any IHT arising was paid by Jane):

    (1)    On 28 November 1991 she made a cash gift of £84,000 into a discretionary trust.

    (2)    On 15 April 1995 she made a gift of 50,000 shares in Shakespeare Ltd, an unquoted trading company, to her son as a wedding gift. The shares were valued at £155,000, and were originally acquired by Jane in 1990. Her son still owned the shares on 20 November 1999. Shakespeare Ltd has 20% of the value of its total assets invested in quoted shares.

    (3)    On 10 March 1996 she made a cash gift of £240,000 into a discretionary trust.

Jane's husband Duncan is wealthy in his own right. Under the terms of her will Jane has therefore left a specific gift of £100,000 to her brother, with the residue of the estate being left to her children.

**Required:**

    (i)    Calculate the IHT that will be payable as a result of Jane's death.    **(15 marks)**

    (ii)    State who is primarily liable for the tax; the due dates of the IHT liabilities; the amount of IHT that can be paid under the instalment option; and the amount of inheritance that will be received by Jane's children.    **(4 marks)**

---

(b)     Jane's husband Duncan is aged 58. He is in good health, and expects to live for at least ten more years.

The Macbeth family appreciate that Jane's estate may not have been distributed in a tax efficient manner. They have therefore agreed that the terms of her will are to be varied so that the entire estate is left to Duncan.

Duncan will then make gifts totalling £500,000 to the children and Jane's brother during 2000 and 2001.

**Required:**

(i)     State the conditions that must be met in order that the variation of the terms of Jane's will is valid for IHT purposes.                                                                                          **(2 marks)**

(ii)    Advise the Macbeth family of the IHT implications of the proposed plan. You are not expected to calculate the revised IHT liability or to consider anti-avoidance legislation.
**(4 marks)**
**(Total: 25 marks)**

---

## 87     (Question 3 of examination)

Basil Perfect commenced self-employment on 1 July 1997, and is involved in the provision of educational services. His wife Sybil commenced self-employment on 1 June 1999, and is also involved in the provision of educational services.

You should assume that today's date is 20 March 2000, and that the tax rates and allowances for 1999-00 apply throughout.

(a)     Basil and Sybil are planning to combine their two businesses into a partnership on 1 April 2000. Basil's tax adjusted Schedule D1 profits are as follows:

|  | £ |
|---|---|
| Year ended 30 June 1998 | 38,640 |
| Year ended 30 June 1999 | 49,920 |
| Period ended 31 March 2000 (forecast) | 47,700 |

Sybil's forecast tax adjusted Schedule D1 profits for the ten-month period to 31 March 2000 are £11,100. The partnership is planning to have an accounting date of 31 March. Its forecast profits for the year ended 31 March 2001 are £80,000, and these are to be shared 75% to Basil and 25% to Sybil.

**Required:**

(i)     Calculate Basil and Sybil's Schedule D1 assessments for 1999-00 and 2000-01.     **(5 marks)**

(ii)    Advise Basil and Sybil of the advantages and disadvantages of having an accounting date of 31 March as compared to an accounting date of 30 June.                                         **(3 marks)**

(b)     Basil is registered for VAT. Sybil is not registered because she is below the VAT registration turnover limit and her supplies are all to the general public in a competitive market. Basil and Sybil are concerned that they will have to pay additional VAT as a result of forming a partnership on 1 April 2000, compared to operating as sole-traders. Their individual sales and expenses for the year ended 31 March 2001 are forecast to be as follows:

|  |  | Basil £ | Sybil £ |
|---|---|---|---|
| Sales: | Standard rated | 170,000 | 47,000 |
|  | Exempt | 115,000 | - |
| Expenses: | Standard rated | 160,000 | 26,000 |

25% of Basil's expenses directly relate to standard rated sales, 30% directly relate to exempt sales, with the balance not directly attributable. Basil's standard rated sales include a supply of £15,000 to Sybil. There are no expenses related to this supply. All of the above figures are *exclusive* of VAT where applicable.

**Required:**

(i)     Advise Basil and Sybil of the additional amount of VAT that will be payable for the year ended 31 March 2001 if they form the partnership on 1 April 2000, as compared to the position if they had remained as sole traders.                                    **(8 marks)**

(ii)    Basil and Sybil understand that even if a partnership is not formed, they could still be required to account for VAT as a single taxable person if HM Customs and Excise make a direction under the disaggregation rules. Explain the circumstances in which such a direction will be made.                                    **(3 marks)**

(c)    Although they are planning to share the forecast partnership profits of £80,000 for the year ended 31 March 2001 on the basis of 75% to Basil and 25% to Sybil, the couple want to know if it would be beneficial to instead share profits 60% to Basil and 40% to Sybil. Basil is aged 54, and always makes the maximum amount of tax deductible contributions into a personal pension scheme. Neither Basil nor Sybil has any other income or outgoings.

**Required:**

Advise Basil and Sybil of the income tax and NIC implications of the two alternative profit sharing arrangements.                                    **(6 marks)**
                                    **(Total: 25 marks)**

---

## 88    (Question 4 of examination)

---

Landscape Ltd is an unquoted trading company that operates a nation-wide chain of retail shops. Landscape Ltd is a close company.

(a)    Landscape Ltd employed Peter Plain as a computer programmer until 31 December 1999. On that date he resigned from the company, and set up as a self-employed computer programmer. Peter has continued to work for Landscape Ltd, and during the period 1 January to 5 April 2000 has invoiced them for work done based on an hourly rate of pay. Peter works five days each week at the offices of Landscape Ltd, uses their computer equipment, and does not have any other clients. The computer function is an integral part of Landscape Ltd's business operations. Peter now considers himself to be self-employed but Landscape Ltd's accountant is not sure if this is the correct interpretation.

(b)    Landscape Ltd operates an Inland Revenue approved company profit sharing scheme whereby employees receive fully paid up ordinary shares in the company free of charge. On 1 January 1997 Richard Rosland, the personnel manager, received the maximum entitlement of shares allowed under the scheme based on his salary of £36,000 p.a. At that date the shares were worth £1.50 each. He sold half of these shares on 30 June 1999 for £2,800, and the other half on 31 January 2000 for £3,200.

---

(c) On 15 March 2000 Landscape Ltd dismissed Simon Savannah, the manager of their shop in Manchester, and gave him a lump sum redundancy payment of £55,000. This amount included statutory redundancy pay of £2,400, holiday pay of £1,500, and £5,000 for agreeing not to work for a rival company. The balance of the payment was compensation for loss of office, and £10,000 of this was not paid until 31 May 2000.

(d) Trevor Tundra is one of Landscape Ltd's shareholders, but is neither a director nor employee of the company. On 6 April 1999 Landscape Ltd provided Trevor with a new motor car with a list price of £13,500. No private petrol was provided, and Trevor did not drive any business mileage during 1999-00. On 1 July 1999 Landscape Ltd made a loan of £40,000 to Trevor. He repaid £26,500 of the loan on 31 August 1999, and the balance of the loan was written off on 31 March 2000.

(e) On 1 October 1999 Landscape Ltd opened a new shop in Cambridge, and assigned three employees from the London shop to work there on a temporary basis.

   (1) Ursula Upland is to work in Cambridge for a period of 18 months. Her ordinary commuting is a daily total of 90 miles, and her daily total from home to Cambridge is 40 miles. She uses her private motor car for business mileage.

   (2) Violet Veld was initially due to work in Cambridge for a period of 30 months, but this was reduced to a period of 20 months on 1 January 2000. In London, Violet walks to work whereas the cost of her train fare from home to Cambridge is £30 per day. This is paid by Landscape Ltd.

   (3) Wilma Wood is to work in Cambridge for a period of six months. Her ordinary commuting is a daily total of 30 miles, and her daily total from home to Cambridge is 150 miles. Wilma passes the London shop on her daily journey to Cambridge. She uses her private motor car for business mileage.

   All three employees worked at Cambridge for 120 days during 1999-00. Landscape Ltd pays a mileage allowance of 36 pence per mile for business use. The relevant rates under the Fixed Profit Car Scheme are 45 pence per mile for the first 4,000 miles, and 25 pence per mile thereafter.

**Required:**

Explain the income tax implications arising from the payments and benefits that have been made or provided by Landscape Ltd to Peter, Richard, Simon, Trevor, Ursula, Violet and Wilma. Your answer should be confined to the implications for 1999-00.

Marks for this question will be allocated on the basis of:

**(6 marks to (a))**
**(4 marks to (b))**
**(4 marks to (c))**
**(4 marks to (d))**
**(7 marks to (e))**
**(Total: 25 marks)**

---

**89    (Question 5 of examination)**

You are the tax adviser to Fiona Fung, aged 59, and have the following information regarding her tax affairs for 1999-00:

(1) On 31 August 1999 Fiona retired as a director of Garments Ltd, an unquoted trading company manufacturing women's clothing. On that date she sold her entire holding of 100,000 £1 ordinary shares in the company for £650,000. Fiona had been a shareholder of Garments Ltd since its incorporation on 1 January 1988, when she subscribed for her shares at par. Fiona did not become a

full-time working director of the company until 1 September 1990. Garments Ltd has a share capital of 400,000 £1 ordinary shares. The market value of its assets at 31 August 1999 was as follows:

|  | £ |
|---|---|
| Goodwill | 400,000 |
| Freehold property (factory and warehouse) | 760,000 |
| Plant and machinery | |
| (costing more than £6,000 per item) | 240,000 |
| Motor cars NOT A CHARGEABLE ASSET | 90,000 |
| Investments in quoted companies | 280,000 |
| Net current assets NOT A CHARGEABLE ASSET. | 730,000 |
| | 2,500,000 |

You should assume that the quoted investments held by Garments Ltd do not preclude it from being treated as a trading company.

(2)    Fiona used the proceeds from the disposal of her shareholding to set up in business on 1 October 1999 as a self-employed manufacturer of women's clothing. Her tax adjusted Schedule D1 profit for the period ended 5 April 2000 is £25,400. This figure is before capital allowances, and before any adjustments that might be necessary as a result of the actions detailed in (4) below.

(3)    On 1 October 1999 Fiona purchased a freehold factory for £338,000 (including land valued at £65,000). This was immediately brought into trade use. The factory was originally constructed at a cost of £229,000 (including land valued at £40,000), and was first brought into use on 1 April 1992. On 1 October 1999 Fiona also purchased plant and equipment for £172,500, and a motor car for £22,000. The motor car has been used 20% for private mileage.

(4)    Because of concern about her high tax liability for 1999-00, Fiona took the following actions during the week ending 5 April 2000:

   (i)    Bonuses totalling £20,000 were given to the employees of the business in respect of the period ended 5 April 2000. The bonuses were not actually paid until June 2000.

   (ii)    A contract for the sale of goods that was due to take place on 5 April 2000 was postponed until the following day. The sale would have resulted in additional gross profit of £9,600. The relevant goods are included in closing stock.

   (iii)    Closing stock that cost £15,400 was written down to its net realisable value of £5,600.

(5)    Fiona received directors remuneration of £17,500 from Garments Ltd during 1999-00. Her remuneration in previous years was £39,000 p.a. Fiona is single, and has no other income or outgoings.

**Required:**

(a)    Calculate the chargeable gain (before taper relief) that Fiona will be assessed on for 1999-00.

**(5 marks)**

(b)    Advise Fiona as to whether the actions that she undertook during the week ending 5 April 2000 are likely to be viewed by the Inland Revenue as tax avoidance or as tax evasion.    **(3 marks)**

(c)    Assuming that the actions during the week ending 5 April 2000 are *not treated* as tax evasion:

   (i)    Calculate Fiona's Schedule D1 trading loss for 1999-00.    **(6 marks)** (ii)　　Explain why Fiona's most beneficial loss relief claim is under s.380 ICTA 1988 against total income for 1999-00, and then under s.72 FA 1991 against the chargeable gain of the same year.　　**(5 marks)**

(iii)　　After taking account of the loss relief claim in (ii), calculate Fiona's income tax and CGT liabilities for 1999-00.　　**(6 marks)**

**(Total: 25 marks)**

---

| **90** | **(Question 6 of examination)** |
|---|---|

You should assume that today's date is 30 November 2000.

Apple Ltd has owned 80% of the ordinary share capital of Bramley Ltd and 85% of the ordinary share capital of Cox Ltd since these two companies were incorporated on 1 April 1998. Cox Ltd acquired 80% of the ordinary share capital of Delicious Ltd on 1 April 1999, the date of its incorporation.

The tax adjusted Schedule D1 profits/(losses) of each company for the years ended 31 March 1999, 2000 and 2001 are as follows:

|  | Year ended 31 March 1999 | Year ended 31 March 2000 | Year ended 31 March 2001 (forecast) |
|---|---|---|---|
|  | £ | £ | £ |
| Apple Ltd | 620,000 | 250,000 | 585,000 |
| Bramley Ltd | (64,000) | 52,000 | 70,000 |
| Cox Ltd | 83,000 | (58,000) | 40,000 |
| Delicious Ltd | n/a | 90,000 | (15,000) |

The following information is also available:

(1)　　Apple Ltd sold a freehold office building on 10 March 2000 for £380,000, and this resulted in a capital gain of £120,000.

(2)　　Apple Ltd sold a freehold warehouse on 5 October 2000 for £365,000, and this resulted in a capital gain of £80,000.

(3)　　Cox Ltd purchased a freehold factory on 20 September 2000 for £360,000.

(4)　　Delicious Ltd is planning to sell a leasehold factory building on 15 February 2001 for £180,000, and this will result in a capital loss of £44,000.

Because each of the subsidiary companies has minority shareholders, the managing director of Apple Ltd has proposed that:

(1)　　Schedule D1 trading losses should initially be carried back and relieved against profits of the loss making company, with any unrelieved amount then being carried forward.

(2)　　Chargeable assets should not be transferred between group companies, and rollover relief should only be claimed where reinvestment is made by the company that incurred the chargeable gain.

**Required:**

(a)　　(i)　　Explain the group relationship that must exist for Schedule D1 trading losses to be surrendered between group companies. Distinguish this from the relationship that must exist for chargeable assets to be transferred between two companies in a group without incurring a chargeable gain or an allowable loss.　　**(4 marks)**

(ii)    Explain the factors that should be taken into account by the Apple Ltd group when deciding which group companies the Schedule D1 trading losses should be surrendered to.

**(3 marks)**

(iii)   Explain why it may be beneficial for all of the eligible subsidiary companies to transfer chargeable assets to Apple Ltd prior to the chargeable assets being disposed of outside of the group.    **(2 marks)**

(b)    (i)    Assuming that the managing director's proposals are followed, calculate the profits chargeable to corporation tax for each of the companies in the Apple Ltd group for the years ended 31 March 1999, 2000 and 2001 respectively.    **(5 marks)**

(ii)    Advise the Apple Ltd group of the amount of corporation tax that could be saved for the years ended 31 March 1999, 2000 and 2001 if reliefs were instead claimed in the most beneficial manner. You should assume that the corporation tax rates for the financial year 1999 will continue to apply.    **(11 marks)**

**(Total:  25 marks)**

# ANSWERS TO DECEMBER 1999 EXAMINATION

## 85    (Answer 1 of examination)

(a)    A person is normally treated as resident in the UK during a tax year if they are present in the UK for 183 days or more. However, Oliver is leaving the UK to work full-time abroad under a contract of employment and the period overseas includes a complete tax year (2000-01). He will therefore be treated as not resident or ordinarily resident in the UK from the date of departure (1 December 1999) to the date of return (31 May 2001). Oliver will remain resident in the UK if return visits to the UK are 91 days or more per tax year on average.

(b)    **Oliver Seas - Income tax liability 1999-00**

Oliver will be liable to UK income tax on his world-wide income up to the date of leaving the UK. However, he will only be liable in respect of income arising in the UK during the period from 1 December 1999 to 5 April 2000. His income tax liability for 1999-00 is as follows:

|  | £ | £ |
|---|---|---|
| Schedule E (2,600 × 5) | | 13,000 |
| Schedule A (1,050 ×4) | | 4,200 |
| Building society interest | | |
| ((3,200 + 2,080) × 100/80) | | 6,600 |
| Schedule D case V | | |
| Rental income (800 × 8) | | 6,400 |
| Bank interest (510 × 100/85 × 8) | | 4,800 |
| | | 35,000 |
| Personal allowance | | 4,335 |
| Taxable income | | 30,665 |
| Income tax | | |
| 1,500 at 10% | | 150 |
| 17,765 (30,665 - 6,600 - 4,800 - 1,500) at 23% | | 4,086 |
| 8,735 (28,000 - 1,500 - 17,765) at 20% | | 1,747 |
| 2,665 (6,600 + 4,800 = 11,400 - 8,735) at 40% | | 1,066 |
| | | 7,049 |
| Double taxation relief (working) | | |
| Rental income | 1,925 | |
| Bank interest | 720 | |
| | | 2,645 |
| | | 4,404 |
| Tax suffered at source | | |
| Building society interest (6,600 × 20%) | | 1,320 |
| Tax payable | | 3,084 |

**Working - Double taxation relief**

The salary from Overseas Aid is not assessable for the period 1 December 1999 to 5 April 2000, and so the Changan tax paid is irrelevant. The rate of foreign tax on Oliver's rental income (35%) is greater than the rate of tax on his bank interest (15%), so the rental income is treated as the top slice of income. The double taxation relief on the bank interest is therefore £720 (4,800 at 15%), whilst on the rental income it is the lower of:

| | | £ | £ |
|---|---|---|---|
| (i) | The overseas tax paid 6,400 at 35% = | | 2,240 |
| (ii) | The UK tax on the overseas income | | |
| | 3,735 at 23% | 859 | |
| | 2,665 at 40% | 1,066 | |
| | | | 1,925 |

Note that this calculation of DTR is that expected from candidates, and that the relief would be different if calculated under the strict statutory basis.

### Oliver Seas - CGT liability 1999-00

The 6,500 shares sold on 5 October 1999 are initially matched with the 2,000 shares acquired on 25 October 1999 (this is within the following 30 days) and then with the 4,500 shares acquired on 12 May 1999, as follows:

| *Acquisition* | *Proceeds*<br>£ | *Cost*<br>£ | *Gain*<br>£ |
|---|---|---|---|
| 25.10.99 | 18,000 (58,500 × 2,000/6,500) | 18,400 | (400) |
| 12.5.99 | 40,500 (58,500 × 4,500/6,500) | 27,450 | 13,050 |
| Chargeable gain | | | 12,650 |

The 5,000 shares sold on 3 April 2000 are chargeable to CGT (in the tax year of departure) because they were acquired before Oliver left the UK, and he is leaving for a period of less than five complete tax years. The shares are matched entirely with the 1985 pool, as follows:

| | £ |
|---|---|
| Proceeds | 54,000 |
| Cost (46,400 × 5,000/10,000) | 23,200 |
| Chargeable gain | 30,800 |

Oliver's CGT liability for 1999-00 is £14,540 (12,650 + 30,800 - 7,100 = 36,350 at 40%). Taper relief is nil as the shares do not qualify as a business asset.

(c)    **Reinvestment of capital from bank deposit account**

Oliver will not be liable to UK income tax in respect of income arising overseas until he returns to the UK on 31 May 2001. No UK income tax liability would have therefore arisen on the interest if the capital had been reinvested in an overseas bank account.

### Delaying the disposal of the shares in Medusa plc

Unless made in the year of departure, gains made by a person who has left the UK for a period of temporary non-residence are not charged until the year that the person resumes residence in the UK. If Oliver had delayed the disposal of the 5,000 shares in Medusa plc until 6 April 2000, then the gain of £30,800 would not have been assessed until 2001-02. In addition to the cash flow advantage, Oliver's annual exemption for that year may also have been available.

| 86 | **(Answer 2 of examination)** |
|---|---|

**(a)**    **Lifetime transfers of value**

|  | £ | £ |
|---|---|---|
| *28 November 1991* |  |  |
| Value transferred |  | 84,000 |
| Annual exemptions 1991-92 | 3,000 |  |
| 1990-91 | 3,000 |  |
|  | —— | 6,000 |
|  |  |  |
| Chargeable transfer |  | 78,000 |
|  |  |  |
| *15 April 1995* |  |  |
| Value transferred |  | 155,000 |
| Business property relief: |  |  |

$$155,000 \times \frac{80}{100} \frac{(100-20)}{} \times 100\% \qquad 124,000$$

|  | £ | £ |
|---|---|---|
|  |  | 31,000 |
| Marriage exemption | 5,000 |  |
| Annual exemptions 1995-96 | 3,000 |  |
| 1994-95 | 3,000 |  |
|  | —— | 11,000 |
|  |  |  |
| Potentially exempt transfer |  | 20,000 |
|  |  |  |
| *10 March 1996* |  |  |
| Net chargeable transfer |  | 240,000 |
| IHT liability |  |  |
| 231,000 - 78,000 = 153,000 at nil% | Nil |  |
| 240,000 - 153,000 = 87,000 × 20/80 | 21,750 |  |
|  | —— | 21,750 |
|  |  |  |
| Gross chargeable transfer |  | 261,750 |

As a result of Jane's death on 20 November 1999, additional IHT will be due. The revised cumulative total as a result of the PET on 15 April 1995 becoming chargeable is £98,000 (78,000 + 20,000).

|  | £ |
|---|---|
| Gross chargeable transfer | 261,750 |
|  |  |
| IHT liability 231,000 − 98,000 = 133,000 at nil% | Nil |
| 261,750 − 133,000 = 128,750 at 40% | 51,500 |
|  |  |
|  | 51,500 |
| Tapering relief 51,500 at 20% | 10,300 |
|  |  |
|  | 41,200 |
| IHT paid | 21,750 |
|  |  |
|  | 19,450 |

**Estate at death - 20 November 1999**

Although the chargeable transfer on 28 November 1991 is more than seven years before the date of death, the revised cumulative total of £281,750 (20,000 + 261,750) still fully utilises the nil rate band of £231,000.

|  | £ | £ |
|---|---|---|
| *Personalty* |  |  |
| Building society deposits |  | 87,000 |
| Ordinary shares in Banquo plc |  |  |
| 10,000 at 948p (945 + ¼ (957 − 945)) |  | 94,800 |
| Life assurance policy |  | 104,000 |
|  |  |  |
| *Realty* |  |  |
| Main residence | 235,000 |  |
| Mortgage | 40,000 |  |
|  | ——— |  |
|  |  | 195,000 |
| Agricultural land | 168,000 |  |
| Agricultural property relief | 110,000 |  |
|  | ——— |  |
|  |  | 58,000 |
|  |  |  |
| Chargeable estate |  | 538,800 |
|  |  |  |
| IHT liability 538,800 at 40% |  | 215,520 |
| Quick succession relief: |  |  |
| $68,000 \times \dfrac{54,000}{360,000} \times 60\%$ |  | 6,120 |
|  |  | ——— |
|  |  | 209,400 |

APR is available since the property is let out for the purposes of agriculture, and has been owned for at least seven years.

**Payment of IHT liability**

The additional IHT of £19,450 in respect of the gift made on 10 March 1996 will be payable by the trustees of the discretionary trust on 31 May 2000.

The IHT liability of £209,400 will (in practice) be payable by the executors of Jane's estate on the earlier of 31 May 2000 or the delivery of their account. It will be possible to pay IHT of £98,326 (209,400 × (195,000 + 58,000)/538,800) in respect of the main residence and agricultural land in ten equal instalments commencing on 31 May 2000.

**Inheritance**

Jane's children will inherit £339,400 (538,800 + 110,000 − 100,000 − 209,400), since specific gifts of UK property do not normally carry their own tax.

(b)    **Variation of the terms of Jane's Will**

Jane's will can be varied by a deed of variation (or deed of family arrangement) within two years of the date of her death. The deed must be in writing, and be signed by Duncan, the children, and Jane's brother. A written election must then be made to the Inland Revenue within six months of the deed of variation, so that the will is treated as being re-written for IHT purposes.

**Proposed plan**

Under the revised terms of Jane's will, the entire estate is left to Duncan. This will be an exempt transfer, and so the IHT liability of £209,400 will no longer be payable.

The gifts from Duncan to the children and Jane's brother will be PETs, and these will be completely exempt if he lives for seven years after making the gifts. Should the PETs become chargeable, tapering relief will be available after three years. His annual exemptions of £3,000 for 1998-99 to 2001-02 may also be available. The IHT liability should not be materially different from £209,400 even if Duncan dies before three years (subject to agricultural property relief being available), and this will be postponed until six months after the end of the month of his death.

| 87 | (Answer 3 of examination) |
|----|---------------------------|

(a)     **Schedule D1 assessments**

Because he is continuing in business, Basil will be treated as changing his accounting date. The change will allow all of the brought forward overlap profits to be offset.

|                                                             | £      |
|-------------------------------------------------------------|--------|
| *1999-00*                                                   |        |
| Year ended 30 June 1999                                     | 49,920 |
| Period ended 31 March 2000                                  | 47,700 |
|                                                             | 97,620 |
| Relief for overlap profits                                  |        |
| 1997-98 (1.7.97 to 5.4.98) 38,640 × 9/12                    | 28,980 |
|                                                             | 68,640 |
| *2000-01*                                                   |        |
| Year ended 31 March 2001 (80,000 × 75%)                     | 60,000 |

Sybil's Schedule D1 assessments are as follows:

|                                                             | £      |
|-------------------------------------------------------------|--------|
| *1999-00*                                                   |        |
| 1.6.99 to 5.4.00                                            | 11,100 |
| *2000-01*                                                   |        |
| Year ended 31 March 2001 (80,000 × 25%)                     | 20,000 |

**Accounting date**

The advantages and disadvantages of an accounting date of 31 March (or 5 April) as compared to 30 June (or any date early in the tax year) are as follows:

(1)     The calculation of assessable profits is simplified with an accounting date of 31 March (there are no overlap profits).

(2)     An assessment of up to 21 months profits may arise in the year of cessation with an accounting date of 30 June. This is not the case with 31 March.

(3)     An accounting date of 30 June will mean that the interval between earning profits and paying the related tax liability is nine months longer than with an accounting date of 31 March. This is advantageous where profits are rising. There is also longer to prepare the related tax return, and to plan for personal pension contributions.

(b)     **Additional VAT**

(1)     As a sole trader, Basil would have to pay output VAT of £2,625 (15,000 × 17.5%) on the supply to Sybil. She could not recover this as input VAT. No such charge will be necessary if a partnership is formed.

(2)     Output VAT will have to be charged on Sybil's income. Since supplies are to the general public in a competitive market, this will have to be absorbed by the partnership. The cost is £7,000 (47,000 × 17.5/117.5), but input VAT of £1,925 (26,000 − 15,000 = 11,000 × 17.5%) can be reclaimed on the related expenses.

(3)     Basil is partially exempt (the de minimis limit of £625 per month on average is exceeded), and the inclusion of Sybil's standard rated sales will improve the recovery of input VAT on expenses that are

not directly attributable. As a sole trader the recovery is restricted to 60% (170,000/(170,000 + 115,000) = 59.6%). This will increase to 63% if a partnership is formed:

$$\frac{195,000}{310,000} \frac{(170,000 - 15,000 + 47,000 - 7,000)}{(195,000 + 115,000)} = 62.9\%$$

The additional recovery is £378 (160,000 × 17.5% × 45% (100 − 25% − 30%) × 3% (63% − 60%)). The recovery relating to directly attributable expenses is not affected.

The additional VAT payable for the year ended 31 March 2001 as a result of forming a partnership is therefore £2,072 (7,000 − 2,625 − 1,925 − 378).

**Direction under the disaggregation rules**

HM Customs and Excise will apply the disaggregation rules where Sybil's business is effectively an extension of Basil's business. The decision will be based on financial links (for example, Sybil may have received financial support from Basil), economic links (for example, both Sybil and Basil may supply the same customers), and organisational links (for example, Sybil and Basil may use the same employees, premises or equipment).

(c)     **Income tax**

Since Basil is 54 years old, he can contribute 30% of his net relevant earnings into a personal pension scheme. His taxable income if profits are shared 75:25 is therefore £37,665 (60,000 less 30% = 42,000 − 4,335), and £29,265 (80,000 × 60% = 48,000 less 30% = 33,600 − 4,335) if profits are shared 60:40. In both cases, relief for the personal pension contributions is at the rate of 40%. However, the reduced pension contributions if profits are shared 60:40 will mean that £1,440 (60,000 − 48,000 = 12,000 × 30% = 3,600 at 40%) less tax relief is available.

If profits are shared 75:25, then Sybil will not be utilising £12,335 (28,000 − (20,000 − 4,335)) of her basic rate tax band. Only £335 (28,000 − (80,000 × 40% = 32,000 − 4,335)) is not utilised if profits are shared 60:40, which is an overall tax saving of £2,040 (12,335 − 335 = 12,000 at 17% (40% − 23%)).

**Class 4 NIC**

With a profit sharing arrangement of 75:25, Basil will pay the maximum Class 4 NIC of £1,108 (26,000 − 7,530 = 18,470 at 6%), whilst Sybil will pay £748 (20,000 − 7,530 = 12,470 at 6%). If profits are shared 60:40, then Sybil will also be liable to the maximum Class 4 NIC, which is an additional cost of £360 (1,108 − 748).

**Conclusion**

A profit sharing basis of 60:40 only results in an overall tax saving of £240 (2,040 − 1,440 − 360), and reduces Basil's level of personal pension contributions (this may be important given his age, but it may be possible for Sybil to make contributions based on her earnings).

---

| 88 | **(Answer 4 of examination)** |

**Peter Plain**

It is necessary to consider the essential distinction between a contract of service (employed) and a contract for services (self-employed). The relevant tests point towards a contract of service:

*The control test:* Peter works at Landscape Ltd's offices for five days each week, so the company appears to have control over the way he performs his work.

*The mutual obligations test:* Peter's only client is Landscape Ltd, so there appears to be an obligation for the company to provide work, and an obligation for him to do the work provided.

---

*The economic reality test:* Peter's activities do not appear to form a profession in their own right, since he uses Landscape Ltd's offices and computer equipment, and is paid an hourly rate. There is no indication that Peter has assumed any financial risk by becoming 'self-employed'.

*The integration test:* The computer function (and hence Peter) is an integral part of Landscape Ltd's business operations.

The Inland Revenue are therefore almost certain to contend that Peter is in fact still 'employed' by Landscape Ltd.

### Richard Rosland

The maximum market value of shares that can be allocated to Richard in any year of assessment is the greater of £3,000 or £3,600 (36,000 x 10%)(since this is less than £8,000). He will therefore have received 2,400 (3,600/1.50) shares during 1996-97.

The 1,200 (2,400/2) shares sold on 30 June 1999 have not been held for the required three years. Richard will therefore be assessed in 1999-00 to a Schedule E charge based on the initial market value of £1,800 (3,600/2), since this is lower than the sale proceeds of £2,800. The shares sold on 31 January 2000 have been held for the required three years, and no charge to income tax therefore arises.

### Simon Savannah

The statutory redundancy payment of £2,400 is exempt. The holiday pay of £1,500 and the restrictive covenant of £5,000 are both taxable under Schedule E in 1999-00.

The treatment of the balance of the lump sum redundancy payment of £46,100 (55,000 - 2,400 - 1,500 - 5,000) is unlikely to be fully taxable provided it is a genuine redundancy payment. Assuming that this is the case Simon will be entitled to the exemption of £30,000, although this is reduced by the statutory redundancy payment. This payment is assessed on a receipts basis, so only £36,100 (46,100 - 10,000) relates to 1999-00. Simon will therefore be assessed to £8,500 (36,100 - (30,000 - 2,400)) in 1999-00.

### Trevor Tundra

Trevor is a participator of Landscape Ltd, since he is neither a director nor an employee of the company. The provision of a company motor car to Trevor is therefore treated as a distribution. The amount of the distribution for 1999-00 is £4,725 (13,500 × 35%), being the benefit that would have been assessed on him had he been a P11D employee. The gross income is £5,250 (4,725 × 100/90), with a related tax credit of £525 (5,250 × 10%).

The loan of £40,000 to Trevor is treated as his income as and when it is written off, so he will be assessed on gross income of £15,000 (40,000 - 26,500 = 13,500 × 100/90) in 1999-00. The related tax credit is £1,500 (15,000 × 10%) *(note that a distribution may also arise under the beneficial loan rules).*

In both instances, Trevor will only have an additional income tax liability if he is a higher rate taxpayer.

### Ursula Upland, Violet Veld and Wilma Wood

All three employees are attending Cambridge in the performance of their duties. Relief will therefore be given for the cost of travel between home and Cambridge, provided this qualifies as a temporary place of work. A place of work is classed as a temporary workplace if an employee does not work there continuously for a period which lasts (or is expected to last) more than 24 months.

*Ursula:* All of her journeys to Cambridge qualify for relief. Under the fixed profit car scheme the mileage allowance received will be tax-free, and she can make the following expense claim for 1999-00:

|  | £ |
|---|---|
| 4,000 miles at 45p | 1,800 |
| 800 miles (120 × 40 = 4,800 – 4,000) at 25p | 200 |
|  | 2,000 |
| Mileage allowance 4,800 at 36p | 1,728 |
|  | 272 |

*Violet:* From 1 October to 31 December 1999, Cambridge will be treated as a permanent workplace since Violet's assignment is expected to exceed the 24-month limit. No relief for travel costs during this period is given, so she will be assessed under Schedule E on a benefit of £1,800 (120 x 3/6 x £30) for 1999-00. However, relief will be given from 1 January 2000 onwards, since she no longer expects to exceed the 24-month limit.

*Wilma:* All of her journeys to Cambridge should qualify for relief. Although Wilma passes her normal permanent workplace on the way to Cambridge, full relief will be available provided she does not stop at the London shop (or any stop is incidental i.e. to pick up some papers).

Wilma will be assessed on a Schedule E benefit for 1999-00 as follows:

|  | £ |
|---|---|
| 4,000 miles at 45p | 1,800 |
| 14,000 miles (120 × 150 = 18,000 – 4,000) at 25p | 3,500 |
|  | 5,300 |
| Mileage allowance 18,000 at 36p | 6,480 |
|  | 1,180 |

## 89    (Answer 5 of examination)

Fiona's chargeable gain for 1999-00 is as follows:

|  | £ | £ |
|---|---|---|
| Proceeds |  | 650,000 |
| Cost |  | 100,000 |
|  |  | 550,000 |
| Indexation $100,000 \times \dfrac{162.6 - 103.3}{103.3}$ |  | 57,406 |
|  |  | 492,594 |
| Retirement relief |  |  |
| 200,000 × 90% | 180,000 |  |
| 410,495 – 180,000 = 230,495 × 50% | 115,248 |  |
|  |  | 295,248 |
| Chargeable gain |  | 197,346 |

Retirement relief is restricted by a factor of 90% since this is the period that Fiona was a full-time working director. The proportion of the gain relating to chargeable business assets is:

$$492,594 \times \frac{1,400,000 \; (400,000 + 760,000 + 240,000)}{1,680,000 \; (1,400,000 + 280,000)} = 410,495$$

The availability of retirement relief is not affected by Fiona's subsequent decision to set up in business as a self-employed person.

(b)    Tax avoidance involves the reduction of tax liabilities by the use of lawful means. By contrast, tax evasion involves the reduction of tax liabilities by illegal means. Fiona's actions during the week ending 5 April 2000 appear to be within the ambit of tax avoidance, since they involve the careful timing of transactions in order to reduce her tax liability. However, if the reality of the situation has been misrepresented (for example, the sale of goods actually took place on 5 April 2000, but the sales invoice was dated 6 April 2000), then this comes within the scope of tax evasion.

(c)    **Schedule D1 trading loss for 1999-00**

Fiona's Schedule D1 trading loss for 1999-00 is as follows:

|  | £ | £ |
|---|---|---|
| Original profit |  | 25,400 |
| Adjustments: |  |  |
| Bonuses | 20,000 |  |
| Stock write-down (15,400 − 5,600) | 9,800 |  |
|  |  | 29,800 |
|  |  | 4,400 |
| Capital allowances: |  |  |
| Industrial buildings allowance (working) | 5,400 |  |
| First year allowance (172,500 at 40%) | 69,000 |  |
| Motor car (3,000 × 6/12 × 80%) | 1,200 |  |
|  |  | 75,600 |
| Tax adjusted Schedule D1 trading loss |  | 80,000 |

The bonuses totalling £20,000 are deductible since they were paid within nine months of the period end. No adjustment is necessary for the postponed contract, since the relevant goods are included in closing stock.

**Working - Industrial buildings allowance**

IBA can be claimed on £189,000 (229,000 − 40,000), being the lower of the price paid and the original cost of the building. The allowance is based on the remaining 210 months of the 25-year life of the factory, so the WDA for the period ended 5 April 2000 is £5,400 (189,000 × 6/210).

**Loss relief claim**

Claiming relief under s.380 ICTA 1988 against total income for 1999-00, and then under s.72 FA 1991 against the chargeable gain of the same year, means that Fiona's loss of £80,000 is fully relieved and mainly at the rate of 40%. The claim wastes her personal allowance for 1999-00. The alternative ways of relieving the loss are as follows:

(1)    The loss could be carried forward under s.385 ICTA 1988 against future trading profits, but relief would be delayed and might not be at the rate of 40%.

(2)    The loss is incurred in the first four years of trading, so relief could be claimed under s.381 ICTA 1988 against total income for 1996-97 to 1998-99. Relief would only partly be at the rate of 40%, and personal allowances for two years will be wasted.

(3)    A claim could be made under S.380 ICTA 1988 against total income for 1998-99, but the same comments as per (2) apply.

**Income tax and CGT liabilities for 1999-00**

Fiona will have a nil income tax liability for 1999-00 as her Schedule E income of £17,500 is fully relieved by the claim under s.380 ICTA 1988. Fiona's CGT liability for 1999-00 is as follows:

|  | £ |
|---|---|
| Chargeable gain | 197,346 |
| Loss claim s.72 FA 1991 (80,000 − 17,500) | 62,500 |
|  | 134,846 |
| Taper relief 134,846 × 15% (100% − 85%) | 20,227 |
|  | 114,619 |

|  |  |
|---|---|
| Annual exemption | 7,100 |
|  | 107,519 |

|  |  |
|---|---|
| Capital gains tax 28,000 at 20% | 5,600 |
| 79,519 at 40% | 31,808 |
|  | 37,408 |

A 25% shareholding qualifies as a business asset for taper relief. The relief is based on two complete years since the shareholding was acquired before 17 March 1998.

---

## 90    (Answer 6 of examination)

### (a)    Group relationships

For group relief purposes, two companies are members of a 75% group where one of them is a 75% subsidiary of the other, or both of them are 75% subsidiaries of the holding company. To qualify as a 75% subsidiary, the holding company must hold 75% or more of the subsidiary's ordinary share capital, and have the right to receive 75% or more of its distributable profits and net assets (were it to be wound up). The 75% holding must be an effective interest that is held directly or indirectly. For the purposes of transferring chargeable assets between two companies without incurring a chargeable gain or an allowable loss, the definition of a 75% subsidiary is 'less rigorous' than for group relief. The 75% holding must only be met at each level in the group structure, subject to the top company having an effective interest of over 50%.

### Surrender of Schedule D1 trading losses

The most important factor that should be taken into account when deciding which group companies the Schedule D1 trading losses should be surrendered to is the rate of corporation tax applicable to those companies. Surrender should be made initially to companies subject to corporation tax at the marginal rate of 32.5% (FY 1998 33.5%). The amount surrendered should be sufficient to bring the claimant company's PCTCT down to the lower limit. Surrender should then be to those companies subject to the full rate of corporation tax of 30% (FY 1998 31%), and lastly to companies subject to corporation tax at the small company rate of 20% (FY 1998 21%). The ability of companies with minority interests to compensate for group relief surrenders will be another factor.

### Chargeable assets

It would probably be beneficial for all of the eligible subsidiary companies to transfer chargeable assets to Apple Ltd prior to their disposal outside of the group, because capital losses cannot be group relieved. Such transfers would therefore allow chargeable gains and allowable losses to arise in the same company. These losses can then either be offset against chargeable gains of the same period, or carried forward against future chargeable gains.

### (b)    Profits chargeable to corporation tax

|  | Apple Ltd £ | Bramley Ltd £ | Cox Ltd £ | Delicious Ltd £ |
|---|---|---|---|---|
| *Year ended 31 March 1999* |  |  |  |  |
| Schedule D1 Profit | 620,000 | - | 83,000 |  |
| Loss relief s.393A(1) |  |  | (58,000) |  |
| PCTCT | 620,000 | - | 25,000 |  |
|  |  |  |  |  |
| *Year ended 31 March 2000* |  |  |  |  |
| Schedule D1 Profit | 250,000 | 52,000 | - | 90,000 |
| Loss relief s.393(1) |  | (52,000) |  |  |

---

| | | | | |
|---|---|---|---|---|
| Capital gain | 120,000 | | | |
| Loss relief s.393A(1) | | | | (15,000) |
| PCTCT | 370,000 | - | - | 75,000 |

| *Year ended 31 March 2001* | | | | |
|---|---|---|---|---|
| Schedule D1 Profit | 585,000 | 70,000 | 40,000 | - |
| Loss relief s.393(1) | | (12,000) | | |
| Capital gain | 80,000 | | | |
| PCTCT | 665,000 | 58,000 | 40,000 | - |

## Corporation tax saving

Until 31 March 1999 Apple Ltd has two associated companies, and three associated companies thereafter. The relevant lower and upper limits for the Apple Ltd group of companies are therefore £100,000 (300,000/3) and £500,000 (1,500,000/3) for the year ended 31 March 1999, and £75,000 (300,000/4) and £375,000 (1,500,000/4) for the years ended 31 March 2000 and 2001. Delicious Ltd is a 75% subsidiary of Apple Ltd for the purposes of transferring chargeable assets, but not for group relief (85% × 80% = 68%). Losses can, however, be surrendered between Delicious Ltd and Cox Ltd. The corporation tax saving if reliefs were claimed in the most beneficial manner is as follows:

(1)     The leasehold factory building to be sold by Delicious Ltd on 15 February 2001, should be transferred to Apple Ltd prior to its disposal outside of the group. The capital loss of £44,000 can then be offset against Apple Ltd's capital gain of £80,000 for the year ended 31 March 2001. The corporation tax saving is £13,200 (44,000 at 30%).

(2)     A claim for rollover relief is possible because the reinvestment by Cox Ltd on 20 September 2000 took place within three years of Apple Ltd selling both of its freehold buildings. It is beneficial (due to marginal tax rates and the capital loss setoff in the year ended 31 March 2001) to make the claim in respect of the freehold office building sold on 10 March 2000. Only £20,000 (380,000 − 360,000) of the sale proceeds are not reinvested, and so £100,000 (120,000 − 20,000) of the gain is rolled over. The corporation tax saving is £32,500 (100,000 at 32.5%).

(3)     Bramley Ltd's loss of £64,000 for the year ended 31 March 1999 should be surrendered to Apple Ltd, rather than being carried forward under s.393(1) ICTA 1988. Relief will then be at the full rate of 31% rather than the small company rate of 20%. The corporation tax saving is £7,040 (64,000 at 11% (31% - 20%)).

(4)     Cox Ltd's loss of £58,000 for the year ended 31 March 2000 should be surrendered to Apple Ltd, rather than being carried back under s.393A(1) ICTA 1988. Relief will then be at the marginal rate of 32.5% rather than at the small company rate of 21%. The corporation tax saving is £6,670 (58,000 at 11.5% (32.5% − 21%).

Delicious Ltd's loss of £15,000 for the year ended 31 March 2001 is relieved at the marginal rate of 32.5%, and so the claim under s.393A(1) ICTA 1988 should not be altered. The total corporation tax saving is £59,410 (13,200 + 32,500 + 7,040 + 6,670). Minority shareholders can be compensated by claimant companies paying for group relief.

**Professional Examination – Paper 11(U)**                                   **Marking Scheme**
**Tax Planning (UK Stream)**

| | | | | *Marks* |
|---|---|---|---|---|
| **1** | **(a)** | Normal treatment | | 1 |
| | | Working full-time abroad | | 1 |
| | | Complete tax year | | 1 |
| | | Return visits | | 1 |
| | | | | — |
| | | | Available | **4** |
| | | | | — |
| | | | Maximum | **3** |
| | | | | — |
| | **(b)** | *Income tax liability* | | |
| | | Schedule E/Schedule A/Dividends | | 2 |
| | | Schedule D case V | | 2 |
| | | Personal allowance/Income tax liability | | 2 |
| | | DTR on bank interest | | 1 |
| | | DTR on rental income | | 2 |
| | | Explanation | | 1 |
| | | Tax suffered on dividends | | 1 |
| | | | | |
| | | *CGT liability* | | |
| | | Matching rules | | 1 |
| | | Disposal on 5 October 1998 | | 2 |
| | | Disposal on 3 April 1999 – Chargeable to CGT | | 1 |
| | | Calculation | | 2 |
| | | Annual exemption/CGT liability | | 1 |
| | | | | — |
| | | | Available | **18** |
| | | | | — |
| | | | Maximum | **16** |
| | | | | — |
| | **(b)** | *Reinvestment of capital from bank deposit account* | | |
| | | Income arising overseas | | 1 |
| | | No UK income tax liability | | 1 |
| | | | | |
| | | *Delaying the disposal of the shares in Medusa plc* | | |
| | | Gains charged in year of return | | 1 |
| | | Assessment in 2000–01 | | 1 |
| | | Cash flow advantage | | 1 |
| | | Annual exemption | | 1 |
| | | | | — |
| | | | Maximum/Available | **6** |
| | | | | — |
| | | | Available | **28** |
| | | | | — |
| | | | Maximum | **25** |
| | | | | — |
| **2** | **(a)** | *Lifetime transfers of value* | | |
| | | Chargeable transfer on 28 November 1990 | | 1 |
| | | PET on 15 April 1994 – BPR | | 1 |
| | | Marriage exemption | | 1 |
| | | Annual exemptions | | 1 |
| | | Chargeable transfer on 10 March 1995 | | 2 |
| | | Revised cumulative total | | 1 |
| | | Additional IHT | | 2 |

| | |
|---|---|
| *Estate at death* | |
| Cumulative total | 1 |
| Building society deposits/Life assurance policy | 1 |
| Ordinary shares in Banquo plc | 1 |
| Main residence | 1 |
| Agricultural land | 1 |
| IHT liability | 1 |
| Quick succession relief | 1 |
| | |
| *Payment of IHT liability* | |
| Additional IHT | 1 |
| Estate | 1 |
| Instalment option | 2 |
| | |
| *Inheritance* | |
| Calculation of inheritance | 1 |
| | |
| **Available** | **21** |
| | |
| **Maximum** | **19** |

**(b)** *Variation of the terms of Jane's will*

| | |
|---|---|
| Conditions | 1 |
| Written election | 1 |
| | |
| *Proposed plan* | |
| Exempt transfer | 1 |
| PETs/Completely exempt after seven years | 1 |
| Tapering relief/Annual exemptions | 1 |
| IHT liability | 1 |
| Due date | 1 |
| | |
| **Available** | **7** |
| | |
| **Maximum** | **6** |
| | |
| **Available** | **28** |
| | |
| **Maximum** | **25** |

**3  (a)** *Schedule DI assessments*

| | |
|---|---|
| Change of accounting date | 1 |
| Basil – 1998–99 | 2 |
| Sybil – 1998–99 | 1 |
| 1999–00 | 1 |
| | |
| *Accounting date* | |
| Calculation of assessable profits | 1 |
| Year of cessation | 1 |
| Tax liability | 1 |
| Tax return/Personal pension contributions | 1 |
| | |
| **Available** | **9** |
| | |
| **Maximum** | **8** |

**(b)**  *Additional VAT*

| | |
|---|---:|
| Supply to Sybil | 1 |
| Output VAT | 2 |
| Input VAT | 1 |
| Partial exemption | 1 |
| Percentage recovered | 2 |
| Additional recovery | 1 |
| Additional VAT payable | 1 |

*Direction under the disaggregation rules*

| | |
|---|---:|
| Extension of Basil's business | 1 |
| Financial links/Economic links | 1 |
| Organisational links | 1 |

| | |
|---|---:|
| **Available** | **12** |
| **Maximum** | **11** |

**(c)**  *Income tax*

| | |
|---|---:|
| Personal pension contributions | 1 |
| Tax relief at 40% | 1 |
| Reduced tax relief | 1 |
| Sybil's basic rate tax band | 1 |
| Tax saving | 1 |

*Class 4 NIC*

| | |
|---|---:|
| Maximum Class 4 NIC | 1 |
| Additional cost | 1 |

| | |
|---|---:|
| Conclusion | 1 |

| | |
|---|---:|
| **Available** | **8** |
| **Maximum** | **6** |
| **Available** | **29** |
| **Maximum** | **25** |

**4**    *Peter Plain*

| | |
|---|---:|
| Contract of service v contract for services | 1 |
| Control  test | 1 |
| Mutual obligations test | 1 |
| The economic reality test | 2 |
| The integration test | 1 |
| Conclusion | 1 |

*Richard Rosland*

| | |
|---|---:|
| Number of shares | 1 |
| Three year time limit | 1 |
| Schedule E charge | 1 |
| Shares sold on 31 January 1999 | 1 |

*Simon Savannah*

| | |
|---|---:|
| Statutory redundancy pay | 1 |
| Holiday pay/Restrictive covenant | 1 |
| Balance of lump sum payment | 1 |
| Receipts basis | 1 |
| Calculation | 1 |

*Trevor Tundra*

| | |
|---|---|
| Participator | 1 |
| Company car | 1 |
| Tax credits | 1 |
| Loan | 1 |
| Additional income tax liability | 1 |

*Ursula Upland, Violet Veld and Wilma Wood*

| | |
|---|---|
| Performance of duties | 1 |
| Temporary workplace | 1 |
| Ursula | 2 |
| Violet | 2 |
| Wilma | 2 |
| | — |
| **Available** | **29** |
| | — |
| **Maximum** | **25** |
| | — |

**5** **(a)**

| | | |
|---|---|---|
| Proceeds/Cost | | 1 |
| Indexation | | 1 |
| Retirement relief – Factor of 90% | | 1 |
|                Chargeable business assets | 1 | |
|                Calculation | | 1 |
| | | — |
| **Maximum/Available** | | **5** |
| | | — |

**(b)**

| | |
|---|---|
| Tax avoidance | 1 |
| Tax evasion | 1 |
| Fiona's actions | 2 |
| | — |
| **Available** | **4** |
| | — |
| **Maximum** | **3** |
| | — |

**(c)** *Schedule D1 trading loss for 1998–99*

| | |
|---|---|
| Bonus | 1 |
| Stock write-down | 1 |
| Industrial buildings allowance | 2 |
| First year allowance | 1 |
| Motor car | 1 |
| Postponed contract | 1 |

*Loss relief claim*

| | |
|---|---|
| S.380 ICTA 1988 and s.72 FA 1991 | 2 |
| S.385 ICTA 1988 | 1 |
| S.381 ICTA 1988 | 2 |
| S.380 ICTA 1988 for 1997–98 | 1 |

*Income tax and CGT liabilities for 1998–99*

| | |
|---|---|
| Nil income tax liability | 1 |
| Loss claim | 1 |
| Taper relief | 2 |
| Annual exemption | 1 |
| Capital gains tax | 1 |
| | — |
| **Available** | **19** |
| | — |

|  | | Maximum | **17** |
|--|--|---------|--------|
|  | | | — |
|  | | Available | **28** |
|  | | | — |
|  | | Maximum | **25** |
|  | | | — |

**6  (a)** *Group relationships*

| | |
|---|---|
| 75% subsidiary | 1 |
| Ordinary share capital | 1 |
| Distributable profits/Net assets | 1 |
| Effective interest | 1 |
| Chargeable gains | 1 |

*Surrender of Schedue D1 trading losses*

| | |
|---|---|
| Rate of corporation tax | 1 |
| Order of setoff | 1 |
| Minority interests | 1 |

*Chargeable assets*

| | |
|---|---|
| Capital losses cannot be group relieved | 1 |
| Optimum use of capital losses | 1 |

| | | |
|--|--|--|
| | Available | **10** |
| | | — |
| | Maximum | **9** |
| | | — |

**(b)** *Profits chargeable to corporation tax*

| | |
|---|---|
| Schedule D1 Profits | 1 |
| Capital gains | 1 |
| Bramley Ltd's loss | 1 |
| Cox Ltd's loss | 1 |
| Delicious Ltd's loss | 1 |

*Corporation tax saving*

| | |
|---|---|
| Associated companies | 1 |
| Lower and upper limits | 1 |
| Delicious Ltd | 1 |
| Capital loss | 2 |
| Rollover relief – Three year limit | 1 |
| Freehold office building | 1 |
| Corporation tax saving | 1 |
| Bramley Ltd's loss | 2 |
| Cox Ltd's loss | 2 |
| Delicious Ltd's loss | 1 |
| Corporation tax saving | 1 |

| | | |
|--|--|--|
| | Available | **19** |
| | | — |
| | Maximum | **16** |
| | | — |
| | Available | **29** |
| | | — |
| | Maximum | **25** |
| | | — |

# RATES AND ALLOWANCES (up to and including Finance Act 1999)

(A)    INCOME TAX

(1)    **Rates**

| | 1998/99 | | | | 1999/00 | |
|---|---|---|---|---|---|---|
| Rate % | Band of income £ | Cumulative tax £ | | Rate % | Band of income £ | Cumulative tax £ |
| 20 | 1 - 4,300 | 860 | | 10 | 1 - 1,500 | 150 |
| 23 | 4,301 - 27,100 | 5,244 | | 23 | 1,500 - 28,000 | 6,095 |
| | | 6,104 | | | | 6,245 |
| 40 | 27,100 - | | | 40 | 28,001 - | |

(2)    **Personal allowances and reliefs**

| | 1998/99 £ | 1999/00 £ |
|---|---|---|
| Personal allowance | 4,195 | 4,335 |
| Married couple's allowance | 1,900* | 1,970* |
| Age allowance (65 - 74) | | |
| personal | 5,410 | 5,720 |
| married couple's | 3,305* | 5,125* |
| income limit | 16,200 | 16,800 |
| Age allowance (75 or over) | | |
| personal | 5,600 | 5,980 |
| married couple's | 3,345* | 5,195* |
| income limit | 16,200 | 16,800 |
| Additional personal allowance | 1,900* | 1,970* |
| Widow's bereavement allowance | 1,900* | 1,970* |
| Blind person's allowance | 1,330 | 1,380 |

\*    Relief restricted to 10% in 1999/00 (15% in 1998/99)

(3)    **Pension contribution limits**

| Age at start of tax year | Personal pension schemes (%) |
|---|---|
| 35 or less | 17½ |
| 36 - 45 | 20 |
| 46 - 50 | 25 |
| 51 - 55 | 30 |
| 56 - 60 | 35 |
| 61 and over | 40 |

Subject to an earnings cap of £90,600

(4)    **Capital Allowances**

| | % |
|---|---|
| Plant and machinery | |
| Writing-down allowance | 25 |
| First-year allowance (2 July 1997 to 1 July 1998) | 50 |
| (2 July 1998 to 1 July 2000) | 40 |

Long-life assets
Writing-down allowance                                              6
First-year allowance (2 July 1997 to 1 July 1998)                 12

Industrial buildings allowance
Writing-down allowance                                             4

Agricultural buildings allowance
Writing-down allowance                                             4

## (B)    CORPORATION TAX

|  | FY 1995 | FY 1996 | FY 1997 | FY 1998 | FY 1999 |
|---|---|---|---|---|---|
| Rate | 33% | 33% | 31% | 31% | 30% |
| Small companies rate (up to £300,000) | 25% | 24% | 21% | 21% | 20% |

Section 13(2) ICTA 1988 relief
$(M-P) \times \frac{1}{P} \times$ fraction

$\left(\text{UPPER LIMIT} - \text{PROFITS}\right) \times \dfrac{\text{~~LOWER~~ } \text{ATCT}}{\text{Profit}} \times \dfrac{1}{40}$

where M is £1,500,000

| Fraction | $\frac{1}{50}$ | $\frac{9}{400}$ | $\frac{1}{40}$ | $\frac{1}{40}$ | $\frac{1}{40}$ |
|---|---|---|---|---|---|
| Dividend tax credit | $\frac{20}{80}$ | $\frac{20}{80}$ | $\frac{20}{80}$ | $\frac{20}{80}$ | $\frac{10}{90}$ |

## (C)    CAPITAL GAINS TAX

### (1)    **Annual exemption**

|  | £ |
|---|---|
| 1995/96 | 6,000 |
| 1996/97 | 6,300 |
| 1997/98 | 6,500 |
| 1998/99 | 6,800 |
| 1999/00 | 7,100 |

### (2)    **Retail price index** (RPI)

|  | 1982 | 1983 | 1984 | 1985 |
|---|---|---|---|---|
| January | - | 82.61 | 86.84 | 91.20 |
| February | - | 82.97 | 87.20 | 91.94 |
| March | 79.44 | 83.12 | 87.48 | 92.80 |
| April | 81.04 | 84.28 | 88.64 | 94.78 |
| May | 81.62 | 84.64 | 88.97 | 95.21 |
| June | 81.85 | 84.84 | 89.20 | 95.41 |
| July | 81.88 | 85.30 | 89.10 | 95.23 |
| August | 81.90 | 85.68 | 89.94 | 95.49 |
| September | 81.85 | 86.06 | 90.11 | 95.44 |
| October | 82.26 | 86.36 | 90.67 | 95.59 |
| November | 82.66 | 86.67 | 90.95 | 95.92 |
| December | 82.51 | 86.89 | 90.87 | 96.05 |

| | 1986 | 1987 | 1988 | 1989 | 1990 | 1991 | 1992 | 1993 |
|---|---|---|---|---|---|---|---|---|
| January | 96.25 | 100.0 | 103.3 | 111.0 | 119.5 | 130.2 | 135.6 | 137.9 |
| February | 96.60 | 100.4 | 103.7 | 111.8 | 120.2 | 130.9 | 136.3 | 138.8 |
| March | 96.73 | 100.6 | 104.1 | 112.3 | 121.4 | 131.4 | 136.7 | 139.3 |
| April | 97.67 | 101.8 | 105.8 | 114.3 | 125.1 | 133.1 | 138.8 | 140.6 |
| May | 97.85 | 101.9 | 106.2 | 115.0 | 126.2 | 133.5 | 139.3 | 141.1 |
| June | 97.79 | 101.9 | 106.6 | 115.4 | 126.7 | 134.1 | 139.3 | 141.0 |
| July | 97.52 | 101.8 | 106.7 | 115.5 | 126.8 | 133.8 | 138.8 | 140.7 |
| August | 97.82 | 102.1 | 107.9 | 115.8 | 128.1 | 134.1 | 138.9 | 141.3 |
| September | 98.30 | 102.4 | 108.4 | 116.6 | 129.3 | 134.6 | 139.4 | 141.9 |
| October | 98.45 | 102.9 | 109.5 | 117.5 | 130.3 | 135.1 | 139.9 | 141.8 |
| November | 99.29 | 103.4 | 110.0 | 118.5 | 130.0 | 135.6 | 139.7 | 141.6 |
| December | 99.62 | 103.3 | 110.3 | 118.8 | 129.9 | 135.7 | 139.2 | 141.9 |

| | 1994 | 1995 | 1996 | 1997 | 1998 | 1999 | 2000 |
|---|---|---|---|---|---|---|---|
| January | 141.3 | 146.0 | 150.2 | 154.4 | 159.5 | 163.4 | e165.9 |
| February | 142.1 | 146.9 | 150.9 | 155.0 | 160.3 | e164.1 | e166.1 |
| March | 142.5 | 147.5 | 151.5 | 155.4 | 160.8 | e164.3 | e166.1 |
| April | 144.2 | 149.0 | 152.6 | 156.3 | 162.6 | e164.7 | e166.3 |
| May | 144.7 | 149.6 | 152.9 | 156.9 | 163.5 | e164.5 | |
| June | 144.7 | 149.8 | 153.0 | 157.5 | 163.4 | e164.8 | |
| July | 144.0 | 149.1 | 152.4 | 157.5 | 163.0 | e165.1 | |
| August | 144.7 | 149.9 | 153.1 | 158.5 | 163.7 | e165.2 | |
| September | 145.0 | 150.6 | 153.8 | 159.3 | 164.4 | e165.0 | |
| October | 145.2 | 149.8 | 153.8 | 159.5 | 164.5 | e165.6 | |
| November | 145.3 | 149.8 | 153.9 | 159.6 | 164.4 | e165.7 | |
| December | 146.0 | 150.7 | 154.4 | 160.0 | 164.4 | e165.6 | |

e - estimated

(3)    **Lease percentages**

| Years | Percentage | Years | Percentage | Years | Percentage |
|---|---|---|---|---|---|
| 50 or more | 100.000 | 33 | 90.280 | 16 | 64.116 |
| 49 | 99.657 | 32 | 89.354 | 15 | 61.617 |
| 48 | 99.289 | 31 | 88.371 | 14 | 58.971 |
| 47 | 98.902 | 30 | 87.330 | 13 | 56.167 |
| 46 | 98.490 | 29 | 86.226 | 12 | 53.191 |
| 45 | 98.059 | 28 | 85.053 | 11 | 50.038 |
| 44 | 97.595 | 27 | 83.816 | 10 | 46.695 |
| 43 | 97.107 | 26 | 82.496 | 9 | 43.154 |
| 42 | 96.593 | 25 | 81.100 | 8 | 39.399 |
| 41 | 96.041 | 24 | 79.622 | 7 | 35.414 |
| 40 | 95.457 | 23 | 78.055 | 6 | 31.195 |
| 39 | 94.842 | 22 | 76.399 | 5 | 26.722 |
| 38 | 94.189 | 21 | 74.635 | 4 | 21.983 |
| 37 | 93.497 | 20 | 72.770 | 3 | 16.959 |
| 36 | 92.761 | 19 | 70.791 | 2 | 11.629 |
| 35 | 91.981 | 18 | 68.697 | 1 | 5.983 |
| 34 | 91.156 | 17 | 66.470 | 0 | 0.000 |

(4)    **Taper Relief**

| Number of complete years after 5/4/98 for which asset held | Percentage of Gain chargeable | |
| :---: | :---: | :---: |
| | *Business Assets* | *Non-business Assets* |
| 0 | 100 | 100 |
| 1 | 92.5 | 100 |
| 2 | 85 | 100 |
| 3 | 77.5 | 95 |
| 4 | 70 | 90 |
| 5 | 62.5 | 85 |
| 6 | 55 | 80 |
| 7 | 47.5 | 75 |
| 8 | 40 | 70 |
| 9 | 32.5 | 65 |
| 10 or more | 25 | 60 |

(D)    CAR AND FUEL BENEFITS

(1)    **Car scale benefit**

Percentage of list price when new including accessories, delivery charges and VAT (subject to £80,000 maximum).

| Business mileage | |
| :--- | :---: |
| Less than 2,500 pa | 35% |
| 2,500 to 17,999 pa | 25% |
| 18,000 or more pa | 15% |
| Second car 18,000 or more pa | 25% |
| Reduction for cars 4 years old and over at end of tax year | ¼ |

Cars over 15 years old at tax year end with an open market value of more than £15,000 (which is also higher than the original list price) taxed by reference to the open market value.

(2)    **Van scale benefit**

| Vans (under 3.5 tonnes) including fuel | Under 4 years | 4 years and over |
| :--- | :---: | :---: |
| | £ | £ |
| 1999/00 | 500 | 350 |
| 1998/99 | 500 | 350 |
| 1997/98 | 500 | 350 |
| 1996/97 | 500 | 350 |

(3)    **Car Fuel Scale Charge**

| Engine size | Petrol £ | Diesel £ |
| :--- | :---: | :---: |
| 1,400cc or less | 1,210 | 1,540 |
| 1,401cc to 2,000cc | 1,540 | 1,540 |
| 2,001cc and over | 2,270 | 2,270 |

**(E)** **INHERITANCE TAX**

    **(1)** **The nil rate band**

        6 April 1999 onwards                £231,000

    **(2)** **Tax rates**

| | Rate on gross transfer | Rate on net transfer |
|---|---|---|
| Transfers on death | 40% | ⅔ |
| Chargeable lifetime transfers | 20% | ¼ |

**(F)** NATIONAL INSURANCE CONTRIBUTIONS 1999/00

    **(1)** **Class 1 employed** From 6 April 1999

        **Employee**

| £ per week earnings | Contracted in | Contracted out |
|---|---|---|
| Up to £65.99 | Nil | Nil |
| Rates for earnings between £66.00 and £500.00 | | |
| (a)    on first £66.00 | Nil | Nil |
| plus | | |
| (b)    £66.01 to £500.00 | 10% | 8.4% |

        **Employer**

        Contracted in:       12.2% on all earnings above £83.00 pw.

        Contracted out:    (a) 9.2% on earnings above £83.00 but below £500; plus
        (salary related)   (b) 12.2% on all earnings above £500; minus
                            (c) 3.0% on earnings between £66 and £83.

        (For contracted out rates using a money purchase scheme the (a) rate is 11.6% and the (c) rate is 0.6%.)

    **(2)** **Class 2 Self-employed**

        Weekly rate £6.55

        Small earnings exemption £3,770 pa

    **(3)** **Class 3 Voluntary**

        Weekly rate £6.45

    **(4)** **Class 4 Self-employed**

        6% on annual profits £7,530 to £26,000

(G)    VALUE ADDED TAX

£

Registration limit                                    51,000
Deregistration limit                                  49,000

(H)    RATES OF INTEREST

'Official rate' of interest:  10% (assumed).

Rate of interest on underpaid/overpaid tax: 10% (assumed).

Accumulation and maintenance settlement    39, 40
Acquisitions from EU member states    274
Additional personal allowance (APA)    107, 257
Additional voluntary contributions    253
Age allowance (AA)    86, 135
Aggregation    225
Agricultural property relief (APR)    36, 38, 55, 170, 287
Annual accounting scheme    322, 383
Arrangements    139
Associated companies    103, 139, 203, 259
Associated operation    225

Bad debts    270
Badges of trade    57, 104, 298
Beneficial loan    48, 200, 358
Benefits-in-kind    303
Business transferred as a going concern    141
Business property relief (BPR)    38, 56, 59, 87, 109, 115, 135, 151, 170, 176, 194, 196, 221, 263, 287,

Capital allowances    25, 28, 43, 51, 72, 77, 106, 128, 132, 160, 165, 169, 182, 236, 255, 313
Capital gains group    46, 49, 54, 103, 106, 139
Car benefits    302
Cash accounting    383
Cessation of a business    291
Cessation of a trade    59, 76, 237
Change in ownership    49
Change of accounting date    283
Chargeable lifetime transfer (CLT)    37, 40, 87, 176, 196
Charity    82
Chattels    39, 55, 265
Class 1 NIC    21, 46, 29, 58, 75, 99, 127, 144, 165, 182, 193, 224
Class 1    127, 144
Class 1A National Insurance contribution    22, 143
Class 2 NIC    182, 193, 231
Class 4 NIC    32, 108, 182, 193, 207, 231
Close company    48
Close investment holding company    173
Commencement of trade    127
Company car    21, 76, 113, 143, 200, 251
Company purchasing its own shares    329
Connected persons    128, 169, 221
Consortium relief    47, 103, 139, 141, 259
Contract for services    404
Contract of service    404
Controlled foreign company    132, 173, 295
Corresponding period    259
Covenants    82

Deed of variation    36, 136, 287, 402
Depreciating asset    54, 149
Disposal of an unincorporated business    373
Domicile    55, 115, 228, 275, 340
Double tax relief (DTR)    24, 55, 80, 114, 131, 177, 227, 295, 399

Earnings cap    74, 100

Employed/self employed    50, 180, 322
Enquiries    205
Enterprise investment scheme (EIS)    113, 150, 209
Enterprise zone    72, 75, 274
Ex gratia payment    45, 77, 269
Excluded property    55

FA 1982 holding    34
FA 1982 Pool    206
FA 1985 pool    33
Fall in value of lifetime gift    263
Fall in value    177
First year allowances (FYA)    27
Fixed profit car scheme    122, 405
Furnished holiday letting    29, 86, 108, 210, 255

Gift aid    83
Gift relief    39, 40, 55, 59, 87, 127, 169, 178, 265
Gift with reservation    29, 37, 60, 196
Goodwill    127
Government stocks    134, 137
Group income election    47
Group relief    102, 139, 163, 203, 242, 320, 347, 408
Group VAT registration    139. 203

Holdover relief    127, 136, 347
Husband and wife    380

IHT account    37
IHT    377, 401
Imports    274
Incorporation relief    76, 193
Industrial building    27, 75, 106, 239, 273, 313
Industrial Buildings Allowance (IBA)    148, 407
Inheritance tax (IHT)    287, 328
Initial allowance (IA)    72
Inland Revenue enquiry    283
Instalments    136
Interest in possession    109, 135, 197
Interest on late paid tax    206
Interest on overdue tax    344
Investment activity    166, 234
ISAs    326

Late notification penalty    107
Lease    70, 149, 236
Living accommodation    83
Loan relationship    261
Loan to a participator    49, 222
Long accounting period    160
Loss on shares in an unquoted trading company    207

Maintenance payments    257
Management charges    81, 84
Management expenses    102
Marriage exemption    35, 79, 166, 196, 225
Married couple's allowance (MCA)    25, 107, 135, 257
Mileage allowance    83, 145, 232, 252, 358

Mortgage interest    30, 74, 107, 114, 174, 234, 257
Motor cars    106

**N**ational Savings Bond    134
Nature of a trade    387
Net relevant earnings (NRE)    74, 100
Non-domiciled spouse    178
Non-resident (NR)    76

**O**rdinarily resident (OR)    55, 113, 132, 174, 274
Overlap profits    31, 127
Overlap relief    59, 237
Overseas assets    114
Overseas subsidiary    370
Own consumption    129
Ownership    140, 163

**P**artially exempt    84, 203, 403
Partnership    32, 59, 108, 127, 192, 236, 350
Partnership's capital allowances    268
Patents    27
Payments on account    283
Penalty tax    49, 222
Penalty    206
Pension scheme    45, 75, 101, 252, 326
Personal equity plans (PEPs)    233
Personal pension    73, 99, 108, 238, 252, 255
PET    37, 40, 59, 87, 128, 136,
    166, 170, 176, 196, 221, 225, 263
Plant and machinery    26, 148
Pre-entry loss    163
Pre-registration input tax    106, 183
Principal private residence (PPR)    41, 115, 209
Profit sharing scheme    199
Purchase of a company's own shares    44, 111
Purchase of own shares by a company    222

**Q**uick succession relief (QSR)    115

**R**ebasing election    54, 206
Redundancy payment    49, 304
Redundancy    302
Registration    106
Re-investment relief    76, 112, 150
Related property    178, 263
Relocation costs    83
Remittance basis    54, 113, 275
Remittance    132
Remuneration package    358
Rent a room relief    256
Rental income    75, 85, 108
Replacement of business asset    43, 71, 140, 149,
    203, 239, 260
Residence in the UK    316
Resident    52, 113, 132, 174, 274, 399
Retirement relief    39, 46, 59, 75, 86, 109, 111,
    151, 169, 220, 255, 406
Revenue enquiry    344
Rollover relief    140, 149, 313, 347

**S**380    26, 28, 32, 78, 269
S381    28, 78, 169, 269
S385    32, 77, 169, 269
S391    140
S393(1)    49, 72, 163
S393A(1)(a)    140
S393A(1)    72, 99, 241, 259
S393A    42, 141
S768    140
Sale of shares within 12 months of death    36, 178
Schedule A    23, 161, 174, 210, 255, 358
Schedule D Case I    26, 28, 32, 168, 236
Schedule D Case II    51, 74, 108, 182, 192, 224
Schedule D Case IV    227
Schedule D Case V    54, 80, 131, 173, 227
Schedule E    21, 45, 48, 52, 76, 86, 113, 302
Second-hand goods scheme    107
Self-assessment    283, 344
Share options    21, 200, 358
Subscription    114

**T**akeover    33
Taper relief    36, 79
Tax avoidance    73, 224, 406
Taxable income    52
Trading stock    46
Transfer of a business as a going concern    59, 76, 141
Transfer pricing    274. 370

**U**K branch or agency    273
Underlying tax    80, 131,173

**V**AT    291, 355, 383
VAT group    49, 81, 84
VAT registration    126, 183, 225
Venture capital trusts (VCT)    209, 326

**W**ear and tear allowance    85
Widow's bereavement allowance (WBA)    134
Withholding tax    80

**Y**ear of marriage    107

## HOTLINES

Telephone: 00 44 (0) 20 8844 0667
Enquiries: 00 44 (0) 20 8831 9990
Fax: 00 44 (0) 20 8831 9991

## AT FOULKS LYNCH LTD

Number 4, The Griffin Centre
Staines Road, Feltham
Middlesex TW14 0HS

| Examination Date: ☐ June 2000 ☐ December 2000 | Publications | | | | Distance Learning | Open Learning |
|---|---|---|---|---|---|---|
| | Textbooks (Pub'd July 99) | Revision Series (Pub'd Feb 2000) | Lynchpins Pub'd Feb 2000 | Tracks (Audio Tapes) | Include helpline & marking (except for overseas Open Learning) | |
| **Module A – Foundation Stage** | | | | | | |
| 1 Accounting Framework | £18.95 [UK] [IAS] | £10.95 [UK] [IAS] | £5.95 [UK] [IAS] | £10.95 ☐ | £85 [UK] [IAS] | £89 ☐ |
| 2 Legal Framework | £18.95 ☐ | £10.95 ☐ | £5.95 ☐ | £10.95 ☐ | £85 ☐ | £89 ☐ |
| **Module B** | | | | | | |
| 3 Management Information | £18.95 ☐ | £10.95 ☐ | £5.95 ☐ | £10.95 ☐ | £85 ☐ | £89 ☐ |
| 4 Organisational Framework | £18.95 ☐ | £10.95 ☐ | £5.95 ☐ | £10.95 ☐ | £85 ☐ | £89 ☐ |
| **Module C – Certificate Stage** | | | | | | |
| 5 Information Analysis | £18.95 ☐ | £10.95 ☐ | £5.95 ☐ | £10.95 ☐ | £85 ☐ | £89 ☐ |
| 6 Audit Framework | £18.95 [UK] [IAS] | £10.95 [UK] [IAS] | £5.95 [UK] [IAS] | £10.95 ☐ | £85 [UK] [IAS] | £89 ☐ |
| **Module D** | | | | | | |
| 7 Tax Framework  FA99 - D/J00 | £18.95 ☐ | £10.95 ☐ | £5.95 ☐ | *£10.95 ☐ | £85 ☐ | £89 ☐ |
| 8 Managerial Finance | £18.95 ☐ | £10.95 ☐ | £5.95 ☐ | £10.95 ☐ | £85 ☐ | £89 ☐ |
| **Module E – Professional Stage** | | | | | | |
| 9 ICDM | £18.95 ☐ | £10.95 ☐ | £5.95 ☐ | £10.95 ☐ | £85 ☐ | £89 ☐ |
| 10 Accounting & Audit Practice | £22.95 [UK] [IAS] (£23.95) | £10.95 [UK] [IAS] | £5.95 [UK] [IAS] | £10.95 ☐ | £85 [UK] [IAS] | £89 ☐ |
| 11 Tax Planning        FA99 - J/D00 | £18.95 ☐ | £10.95 ☐ | £5.95 ☐ | *£10.95 ☐ | £85 ☐ | £89 ☐ |
| **Module F** | | | | | | |
| 12 Management & Strategy | £18.95 ☐ | £10.95 ☐ | £5.95 ☐ | £10.95 ☐ | £85 ☐ | £89 ☐ |
| 13 Financial Rep Environment | £20.95 [UK] [IAS] | £10.95 [UK] [IAS] | £5.95 [UK] [IAS] | £10.95 ☐ | £85 [UK] [IAS] | £89 ☐ |
| 14 Financial Strategy | £19.95 ☐ | £10.95 ☐ | £5.95 ☐ | £10.95 ☐ | £85 ☐ | £89 ☐ |
| | | | P7 & 11 Pub'd 7/99 | *Available Feb 2000 | | |
| **P & P + Delivery**   UK Mainland | £2.00/book | £1.00/book | £1.00/book | £1.00/tape | £5.00/subject | £5.00/subject |
| NI, ROI & EU Countries | £5.00/book | £3.00/book | £3.00/book | £1.00/tape | £15.00/subject | £15.00/subject |
| Rest of world standard air service | £10.00/book | £8.00/book | £8.00/book | £2.00/tape | £25.00/subject | £25.00/subject |
| Rest of world courier service† | £22.00/book | £20.00/book | Not applicable | Not applicable | £47.00/subject | £47.00/subject |

**SINGLE ITEM SUPPLEMENT FOR TEXTBOOKS AND REVISION SERIES:**

If you only order 1 item, INCREASE postage costs by £2.50 for UK, NI & EU Countries or by £15.00 for Rest of World Services

| TOTAL | | | | | | |
|---|---|---|---|---|---|---|
| Sub Total £ | | | | | | |
| Post & Packing £ | | | | | | |
| Total £ | | | | | | |

†*Telephone number essential for this service*   *Payments in Sterling in London*   Order Total   £ _____

---

**DELIVERY DETAILS**

☐ Mr  ☐ Miss  ☐ Mrs  ☐ Ms  Other

Initials                    Surname

Address

Postcode

Telephone                    Deliver to home ☐

Company name

Address

Postcode

Telephone            Fax

Monthly report to go to employer ☐        Deliver to work ☐

**PAYMENT**

1  I enclose Cheque/PO/Bankers Draft for £_____
   Please make cheques payable to AT Foulks Lynch Ltd.

2  Charge Mastercard/Visa/Switch A/C No:

   | | | | | | | | | | | | | | | | | | |

   Valid from: |___|___|___|        Expiry Date: |___|___|___|

   Issue No: (Switch only)        |___|___|

Signature                    Date

**DECLARATION**

I agree to pay as indicated on this form and understand that AT Foulks Lynch Terms and Conditions apply (available on request). I understand that AT Foulks Lynch Ltd are not liable for non-delivery if the rest of world standard air service is used.

Signature                    Date

| **Please Allow:** | UK mainland | - 5-10 w/days |
|---|---|---|
| | NI, ROI & EU Countries | - 1-3 weeks |
| | Rest of world standard air service | - 6 weeks |
| | Rest of world courier service | - 10 w/days |

**Notes:** All delivery times subject to stock availability. Signature required on receipt (except rest of world standard air service). Please give both addresses for Distance Learning students where possible.

*Form effective December 99*        *All details correct at time of printing*        Source:  ACRS00